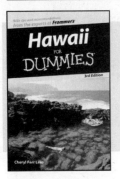
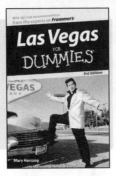

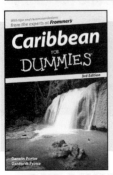
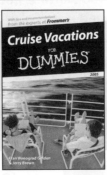

Caribbean

FOR

DUMMIES®

4TH EDITION

by Darwin Porter and
Danforth Prince

BICENTENNIAL
1807
WILEY
2007
BICENTENNIAL

Wiley Publishing, Inc.

Caribbean For Dummies, 4th Edition

Published by
Wiley Publishing, Inc.
111 River St.
Hoboken, NJ 07030-5774
www.wiley.com

For general information on our other products and services, please contact our Customer Care Department within the U.S. at 800-762-2974, outside the U.S. at 317-572-3993, or fax 317-572-4002.

For technical support, please visit www.wiley.com/techsupport.

Wiley also publishes its books in a variety of electronic formats. Some content that appears in print may not be available in electronic books.

Library of Congress Control Number: 2006934810

ISBN-13: 978-0-471-96251-9

ISBN-10: 0-471-96251-1

Manufactured in the United States of America

10 9 8 7 6 5 4 3 2 1

4B/QR/RR/QW/IN

WILEY

About the Authors

A native of North Carolina, **Darwin Porter** was a bureau chief for the *Miami Herald* when he was 21, and later worked in television advertising. A veteran travel writer, he is the author of numerous best-selling Frommer's guides, including those to the Caribbean, Bermuda, and The Bahamas. He is assisted by **Danforth Prince,** formerly of the Paris Bureau of the *New York Times.* They have been frequent travelers to the Caribbean for years.

Publisher's Acknowledgments

We're proud of this book; please send us your comments through our Dummies online registration form located at www.dummies.com/register/.

Some of the people who helped bring this book to market include the following:

Editorial

Editors: M. Faunette Johnston, Tim Ryan

Copy Editor: Annie Owen

Cartographer: Guy Ruggiero

Senior Photo Editor: Richard Fox

Cover Photos:
Front Cover: © Darrell Jones Photography
Back Cover: © Macduff Everton Photography

Cartoons: Rich Tennant (www.the5thwave.com)

Composition Services

Project Coordinator: Patrick Redmond

Layout and Graphics: Lavonne Cook, Joyce Haughey, Heather Ryan, Julie Trippetti

Special Art: Anniversary Logo Design: Richard Pacifico

Proofreaders: David Faust, Jessica Kramer, Techbooks

Indexer: Techbooks

Publishing and Editorial for Consumer Dummies

Diane Graves Steele, Vice President and Publisher, Consumer Dummies

Joyce Pepple, Acquisitions Director, Consumer Dummies

Kristin A. Cocks, Product Development Director, Consumer Dummies

Michael Spring, Vice President and Publisher, Travel

Kelly Regan, Editorial Director, Travel

Publishing for Technology Dummies

Andy Cummings, Vice President and Publisher, Dummies Technology/General User

Composition Services

Gerry Fahey, Vice President of Production Services

Debbie Stailey, Director of Composition Services

Contents at a Glance

Maps at a Glance

Table of Contents

Introduction

○○○

*B*ookshelves groan with guidebooks on the Caribbean, but this one's different. In *Caribbean For Dummies,* 4th Edition, we help you choose the right island for you and yours. We don't try to give you an exhaustive guide to the Caribbean. Lots of other books do that (and often leave you more confused than when you started).

Indeed, we leave out a whole string of islands, sticking to those that are the most popular with sun-seeking visitors. On the islands we cover, we keep information pared to the basics: what you'll encounter when you land, where to stay, where to eat, and where to go to have fun while you're there.

About This Book

You can use this book in three ways:

- ✔ **As a trip planner:** If you're trying to decide between two or more islands, we steer you in the right direction. Then you can skip straight to the chapters on your particular destination to plan every aspect of your trip, from booking your flight to getting the best deal on your resort.

- ✔ **As an island guide:** Bring this book with you to your island destination. We let you know what to expect and tell you our favorite places to go — from the best beaches to the coolest bars to the most romantic restaurants.

- ✔ **As a fun overview:** If you want to get a good feel for the Caribbean as a whole, read this book straight through, because we hit all the high points.

Be advised that travel information is subject to change at any time — and this point is especially true of prices. Therefore, we suggest that you call, fax, or e-mail your hotel for confirmation when making your travel plans. Make sure the hotel sends a confirmation fax or e-mail back to you, and bring a copy of it with you on your trip. The authors, editors, and publisher cannot be held responsible for the experiences of readers while traveling. Your safety is important to us, however, so we encourage you to stay alert and be aware of your surroundings. Keep a close eye on cameras, purses, and wallets, all favorite targets of thieves and pickpockets.

Dummies Post-it® Flags

As you're reading this book, you'll find information that you'll want to reference as you plan or enjoy your trip — whether it's a new hotel, a must-see attraction, or a must-try walking tour. Mark these pages with the handy Post-it® Flags included in this book to help make your trip planning easier!

Conventions Used in This Book

In this book, we list our favorite hotels and restaurants, as well as information about special attractions on each island. As we describe each, we often include abbreviations for commonly accepted credit cards. The following list explains each abbreviation:

AE: American Express

DC: Diners Club

DISC: Discover

MC: MasterCard

V: Visa

We also use a system of dollar signs to show a range of costs for hotels and restaurants. Unless we say otherwise, the lodging rates are for a standard double room during high season (typically mid-Dec to mid-Apr). For restaurants, we give the price range for main courses. Check out the following table to decipher the dollar signs.

Cost	Hotel	Restaurant
$	$100 or less per night	Less than $10 or less
$$	$101–$200	$11–$15
$$$	$201–$300	$16–$20
$$$$	$301–$500	$21–$25
$$$$$	$501 and up	$26 and up

Foolish Assumptions

We make some assumptions about you and what your needs may be as a traveler. Here's what we assume:

✔ You may be an inexperienced traveler looking for guidance about whether to take a trip to the Caribbean and how to plan a trip to specific islands.

✔ You may be an experienced traveler, but you don't have a lot of time to devote to trip planning or to spend in the Caribbean after you get there. You want expert advice on how to maximize your time and enjoy a hassle-free trip.

✔ You're not looking for a book that provides every bit of information available about the Caribbean or that lists every hotel, restaurant, or attraction you could experience. Instead, you're looking for a book that focuses on the places where you'll get the best experience in the Caribbean.

If you fit any of these criteria, then *Caribbean For Dummies,* 4th Edition, provides the information you're looking for.

How This Book Is Organized

Caribbean For Dummies, 4th Edition, is divided into four parts. The chapters within each part cover specific topic areas in detail. Feel free to skip around; you don't have to read this book in order. It's kind of like a cafeteria: You can pick and choose what you like.

Part 1: Introducing the Caribbean

In this part, we tell you about the popular islands that we preview. Each Caribbean island is different from the others, so you need to carefully consider which one sounds right for you. We also explain in detail the various seasons that describe more- and less-popular times of year for people to travel to the Caribbean. We discuss what kind of prices and weather you can expect during each season, as well as the dreaded *h* word *(hurricane)* and how much you should take hurricanes into consideration in your planning — if at all.

Part 11: Planning Your Trip to the Caribbean

Here we wrap up all the critical information you need in order to decide whether to use a travel agent, a packager, or the Internet when planning your trip. We give you details about which airlines will get you where and what connections you can make to reach some of the more-remote areas. You'll also find a chapter that helps you create a trip budget and answers all your questions about money in the Caribbean, from the currency used on each island to what size tips you should give.

Of course, you're going to need a place to stay, so we explain the different accommodations you'll find in the Caribbean, along with all the various meal plans and the scoop on what *all-inclusive* means. And for those of you who have special needs, including families, seniors, travelers with disabilities, and gay and lesbian vacationers, we highlight some resources and tips. We wrap up this part by addressing safety concerns, car rentals (and whether they're necessary for you), travel insurance, and other odds and ends.

Part III: Exploring the Islands

Now we get down to the fun stuff. For each island we cover, we tell you what you can expect when you actually land on the island (from the airport to taxi drivers) and make recommendations on where to stay and dine and what to do.

Part IV: The Part of Tens

Every *For Dummies* book has a Part of Tens. Here we tell you what we consider the best Caribbean souvenirs and where to get them, and we ruminate over the best local meals we've enjoyed in our island travels.

In back of this book we've included an *appendix* — your Quick Concierge — containing lots of handy information you may need when traveling in the Caribbean. Check out this appendix when searching for answers to lots of little questions that may come up as you travel. You can find the Quick Concierge easily because it's printed on yellow paper.

Icons Used in This Book

Throughout this book, you'll find icons in the margins, which draw your attention to particular bits of information you may find especially helpful. Here's an explanation of what each icon means:

 Attention, bargain hunters: This icon highlights money-saving tips and/or great finds.

 This icon highlights the best the destination has to offer in all categories — hotels, restaurants, attractions, activities, shopping, and nightlife.

 Watch for this icon to identify annoying or potentially dangerous situations, such as tourist traps, unsafe neighborhoods, rip-offs, and other things to be aware of.

 This icon highlights attractions, hotels, restaurants, or activities that are particularly hospitable to children or people traveling with kids.

 This icon points out useful advice, things to do, and ways to schedule your time.

This icon directs you to secret little finds or useful resources that are worth the extra bit of effort to get to or search out.

Where to Go from Here

Whether you've been to the Caribbean a dozen times or have never set foot outside your hometown, we know that you'll find what you're looking for in *Caribbean For Dummies,* 4th Edition. So sit back, relax, and enjoy your trip planning. After all, the planning part lasts a lot longer than the trip itself — why not make it part of the fun?

Part I

Introducing the Caribbean

In this part . . .

*P*lanning a trip to a place that you know only as a dot on the map? You need to get a sense of where you're going before you commit to the destination. In Part I, we help you point your compass in the right direction.

First, we detail for you the very best of the Caribbean — from hotels to restaurants, scuba diving to snorkeling — and we even preview the best golf courses, tennis courts, shopping, and nightlife.

Next, the basics: What is each island like, and which one will mesh with your island fantasy? Finally, we give you the info to help you decide when you want to go.

Chapter 1

Discovering the Best of the Caribbean

In This Chapter

▶ Having fun on land and sea
▶ Seeking out honeymoon havens, family resorts, and everything in between
▶ Enjoying sports and outdoor recreation
▶ Going out on the town: dining, shopping, and nightlife

*W*hatever you want to do on a tropical vacation — play on the beach with the kids (or with your mate), enjoy a romantic honeymoon, go scuba diving to meet the denizens of the deep — you'll find it on one of the Caribbean islands. We don't want you to waste precious hours searching for the best beaches or the best experiences, so we've done all the legwork for you. Following are our picks for the finest the Caribbean has to offer.

The Best Beaches

✔ **Palm Beach (Aruba):** Hailed by such magazines as *Condé Nast Traveler* as one of the best beaches in the world, the powder-white sands of Palm Beach put Aruba on the tourist map. On the tranquil leeward side of the island, this beach is set against a backdrop of Aruba's leading resorts. When there weren't enough palm trees for that Caribbean portrait of cliché charm, the government planted more. For beach buffs, Palm Beach is about as good as it gets in the Caribbean. See Chapter 9.

✔ **The Gold Coast (Barbados):** Some aficionados call this strip of white sand on the island's tranquil western coast "the Platinum Coast." Either name will do. This isn't one beach but a string of white-sand beaches that lie along this coast — take your pick. Naturally, all the swanky and fabled Barbados resorts chose this coastline for their tony locations. Expect tropical gardens, miles of palm trees, and secluded little coves with shallow reefs teeming with rainbow-hued fish. The shoreline is overcrowded and overbuilt, but this coast has plenty of sand and water for everyone. See Chapter 10.

✔ **Seven Mile Beach (Grand Cayman):** Beginning north of George Town, the capital, this beautiful beach of white sand stretches for 8.8km (5½ miles). So, technically, it's not 7 miles, but when you're here that hardly seems to matter. With its deluxe resorts and string of small hotels and condos, this rather overbuilt beach evokes Aruba's Palm Beach. But even in winter when the resorts operate at peak capacity, the sands and tranquil waters still have plenty of room for everybody — families, honeymooners, and singles alike. Australian pines form a backdrop, and the beach strip offers an array of water sports. Most people describe its waters as translucent aquamarine. See Chapter 12.

✔ **Seven Mile Beach (Negril, Jamaica):** The Caribbean has another seven mile beach, and this one is actually 11km (7 miles) long, unlike the sandy coast of Grand Cayman. The Jamaican beach at this hedonistic resort is the biggest party beach in the West Indies. Envision an adult summer camp at its raunchiest — plenty of nudity, drinking, and illicit drugs. With all this debauchery, you may forget the sands and sea. That'd be a mistake. They're spectacular. See Chapter 13.

✔ **Luquillo Beach (Puerto Rico):** Lying 48km (30 miles) east of San Juan, this crescent-shaped public beach of golden sand is the best the island has to offer. Set near the tacky town of Luquillo, the beach stretches for 0.8km (½ mile) along a crescent-shaped bay fronting a backdrop of coconut palms. *Sanjuaneros* (you know, natives of San Juan) flock here by the hundreds on weekends for fun in the sun, but weekdays are more tranquil. A festive party atmosphere prevails here, with many water-sports kiosks to hook you up with everything from sailing to windsurfing. Dozens of beach shacks offer tasty island snacks such as cod fritters. See Chapter 14.

The Best Places to Get Away from It All

✔ **Guavaberry Spring Bay Vacation Homes (Virgin Gorda, British Virgin Islands):** On the idyllic island of Virgin Gorda, the second island of the British Virgin chain, stands Guavaberry Spring Bay Vacation Homes at **Spring Bay,** with 18 redwood-built hexagonal houses in a tropical setting of flowers and shrubs. Lodging here is like being in your own private little Caribbean villa. An on-site commissary sells provisions for your home-cooked meals. See Chapter 11.

✔ **Morritt's Tortuga Club and Resort (Grand Cayman):** Tucked away in the eastern sector of this island, 42km (26 miles) from the international airport, stands this plantation-style escapist's retreat. Living is condo-style here on 3.2 beachfront hectares (8 acres). Because the area is known for its excellent diving, many scuba divers check in here — but the resort is suitable for nondivers as well, with its two pools (one with a waterfall) and comfortably furnished one- and two-bedroom town houses, each with a fully equipped kitchen. See Chapter 12.

✔ **Banana Shout Resort (Negril, Jamaica):** If you want your Caribbean life to be laid-back, like it was in the 1950s, you might head to this offbeat resort in fun-loving Negril. Set on 1 hectare (2½ acres) of tropical gardens with waterfalls, it isn't for the faint of heart. You can find the resort in **West End,** where you can still see hippies who arrived in the 1960s and never left — nor changed their flower-child garb. Your host is Detroit-born Mark Conklin, a psychologist who wrote a racy and hilarious novel of local life called *Banana Shout.* See Chapter 13.

✔ **Jake's (Treasure Beach, Jamaica):** On Jamaica's southern shoreline, east of Negril, Jake's is funky and fun. Trouble is, if you check in, you may never leave. The ultimate escapist's retreat, this place is even more laid-back than Negril, which appears almost cosmopolitan from Jake's perspective. Built on a cliff overlooking a panoramic bay, the complex consists of 15 cottages and 4 villas, everything evocative of a casbah in Morocco. See Chapter 13.

✔ **Hacienda Tamarindo (Vieques, Puerto Rico):** Two Vermonters on the island of Vieques, off the coast of Puerto Rico, have created this idyllic 16-room inn that lies 0.6km (1 mile) west of the main settlement of Esperanza, but far removed from any bustling life. Now that the U.S. Navy presence is gone (and they're no longer testing weapons on the island), Vieques has returned to its once-sleepy state. A footpath leads to a pool and the beach. Walking it is about all the strenuous activity you need to perform here. See Chapter 14.

✔ **Pavilions and Pools Hotel (St. Thomas, U.S. Virgin Islands):** To find an escapist's retreat on this overbuilt and overcrowded island is a bit of an achievement, but Pavilions and Pools is such a place. The 25-room resort lies 11km (7 miles) east of the capital of Charlotte Amalie. It stands close to one of the island's best beaches, **Sapphire Bay.** Ensured total privacy, you get your own villa here, with wide doors opening directly onto your own private swimming pool where you can bathe as Adam and Eve did (or Adam/Adam, Eve/Eve, whatever). See Chapter 17.

The Best Honeymoon Resorts

✔ **Sandy Lane Hotel & Golf Club (St. James, Barbados):** The classiest resort in the southern Caribbean, Sandy Lane is a celebrity-haunted retreat of the rich and famous. On the **Gold Coast** of Barbados, this place is clearly the star attraction as resorts go. As soon as a honeymoon couple — or any guest, for that matter — enters this coral-stone Palladian-style mansion, they're pampered and coddled in supreme comfort. Romantic couples generally request one of the sumptuous suites that come with luxurious bathrooms and even their own personal butler. See Chapter 10.

✔ **Sandals Dunn's River Villagio Beach & Spa (Ocho Rios, Jamaica):** An estimated three-fourths of the guests here are young honeymooners (make that male/female romantics only — other couplings are strictly prohibited in the Sandals chain). One of the better members of the Sandals all-inclusive chains taking over Jamaica, this North Coast resort opens onto a wide beach of white sands. Complete honeymoon packages are available, the price fluctuating with the season. See Chapter 13.

✔ **Horned Dorset Primavera (Rincón, Puerto Rico):** The most special and romantic inn on the West Coast of Puerto Rico is both secluded and elegant, a 52-room bastion of luxury, taste, and refinement where two people can be alone and undisturbed until they're ready to emerge again into the real world. A Relais & Châteaux property, this pocket of posh is set in an enchanted garden with a large swimming pool. Bedrooms are custom-designed and fitted with four-poster beds. Opt for one of the delicious suites facing the sea. See Chapter 14.

✔ **Ladera Resort (St. Lucia):** Why not begin your new life together by waking up and taking in the most panoramic and dramatic view in the Caribbean? That view is of Gros Piton and Petit Piton, twin volcanic cones soaring straight up out of the earth from some prehistoric past. Your hilltop aerie here has no west wall, but don't worry that a Peeping Tom will share your honeymoon with you. The Bali Ha'i–like villas were designed so that your privacy won't be violated. Villas have private pools fed by waterfalls. How romantic can you get? See Chapter 15.

✔ **La Samanna (Sint Maarten/St. Martin):** On a totally secluded rooftop sun deck, honeymooners often discover love in the afternoon, with only the wild birds expressing shock. In this Casablanca-like village complex, you live lush and plush at the island's finest luxury nest, either on the Dutch or French side. Everything here is designed to put you in the mood, from a romantic terrace on a bluff overlooking the moonlit bay to even the bar, crowned by a multihued Indian wedding tent. A Caribbean cliché? Perhaps — but lovely just the same. All couplings are welcome here. See Chapter 16.

✔ **The Buccaneer (St. Croix, U.S. Virgin Islands):** Many couples not only prefer a honeymoon here, but they also get married on the premises. The hotel staff can take care of all the arrangements. The lush setting, 3.2km (2 miles) east of the main town of Christiansted, is on a 138-hectare (340-acre) site, a former cattle ranch and sugar plantation. Honeymooners enjoy the property's deluxe facilities, including a first-rate golf course. The cuisine, the accommodations (including a romantic four-poster bed), and the facilities are the best on the island. See Chapter 17.

The Best Family Resorts

- ✓ **Occidental Grand Aruba (Aruba):** Opening right onto Aruba's fabled **Palm Beach,** this handsomely landscaped all-inclusive resort has long been a family favorite. Its children's programs for ages 4 to 12 are among the best on the island and are well supervised and planned. Families frolic daily around the mammoth freeform pool with its cascading waterfalls — a Disney-like setting. Kids delight in the iguanas roaming the property, who are looking for a handout. See Chapter 9.

- ✓ **Turtle Beach (Barbados):** The flagship of a London-based chain, this all-inclusive resort is the most family oriented on this populous island in the southern Caribbean. Many families book package deals here to take advantage of the resort's Kids Club (ages 3–11), which is the best on the island and includes such fun activities as treasure hunts, painting, and safari-style island expeditions. Throughout the year, the resort offers packages for children. In the off season, for example, one child (age 2–12) stays free, and any others pay half the adult rate. See Chapter 10.

- ✓ **Little Dix Bay (Virgin Gorda, British Virgin Islands):** This 98-room posh resort opens onto a half-moon-shaped private bay with a sandy beach, occupying a 200-hectare (500-acre) protected preserve. Some families book a return every year. Not only does it offer the best children's program in the British Virgin Islands, but Little Dix Bay is also a luxuriously comfortable place to stay, filled with many diversions for any age. Families delight in taking up residence in the two-story rondavels designed like Tiki huts on stilts. See Chapter 11.

- ✓ **Westin Casuarina Resort (Grand Cayman):** Occupying some of the best beachfront along palm-lined **Seven Mile Beach,** this top-ranking resort operates the most activity-filled calendar on the island, yet isn't obtrusive for those families seeking some R & R. Its Camp Scallywag features the best children's program on the island for ages 4 to 12. Bedrooms can accommodate even large families comfortably. The resort's pool is one of the largest on the island. See Chapter 12.

- ✓ **Half Moon (Montego Bay, Jamaica):** Kids view this sprawling resort — one of the greatest in Jamaica — as a virtual Shangri-La, with their own special pool, playhouses, donkey rides, and other diversions. The beachfront is one of the best occupied by any Jamaican resort — and, indeed, it's shaped like a half-moon and sheltered by a reef offshore, making it safe for swimming. Special programs occupy teens who are far too mature to settle for "all that under-12 kid stuff." See Chapter 13.

- ✓ **Club St. Lucia by Splash (St. Lucia):** This all-inclusive resort lies at the very northern tip of the lush island and is the best bet for families visiting St. Lucia. It wisely divides its children's clubs into three different age groups, recognizing the varied and different interests each grouping of kids may have. Not only does the resort open onto two white sandy beaches, but it's also close to the **Pigeon Island National Park,** long a family favorite for adventure and a picnic. Families stay in one of five fantasy villages, with such amusing names as "Banana Liming." The spacious family suites are the best on the island. See Chapter 15.

The Best Restaurants

✔ **The Cliff (Barbados):** Paul Owens, who's published his prizewinning recipes in a cookbook, is clearly the master chef of Barbados, where the competition is fierce. His highly creative spin on international and Caribbean cuisine attracts a never-ending stream of some of the most discerning palates in the world. The setting for his sublime cuisine is on open-air terraces spilling down to a coral cliff overlooking the sea. See Chapter 10.

✔ **Norma's on the Terrace (Kingston, Jamaica):** Norma Shirley is *the* most celebrated chef on this island. Her culinary wares are showcased at the landmark Devon House in Jamaica's capital. Her menu changes with the season but reflects the flavors of Jamaica as few competitors do. She serves intensely flavored gutsy fare such as island lobster and conch, and her grilled fish, such as whole red snapper, are flavored with fresh herbs. See Chapter 13.

✔ **Parrot Club (San Juan, Puerto Rico):** The hottest restaurant in Old San Juan operates out of a converted hair-tonic factory. The chefs create the town's most finely honed *Nuevo Latino* cuisine, with intense island flavors and first-rate products, many from Puerto Rico itself. Expect a fresh sea flavor in the fish dishes and a touch of exoticism in many of the dishes, including seared pork medallions with a sweet plantain chorizo. Come here and make an evening of it. See Chapter 14.

✔ **Dasheene Restaurant and Bar (St. Lucia):** Between those two much-photographed volcanic peaks, Gros Piton and Petit Piton, this restaurant at the swank **Ladera Resort** focuses on a zesty international and West Indian cuisine — and does so exceedingly well. A meal at Dasheene will provide your most memorable and romantic dinner on this island. Exceptional products are prepared with a finely honed technique, and dishes such as seafood-studded pasta burst with flavors. See Chapter 15.

✔ **La Vie en Rose (Sint Maarten/St. Martin):** This island, a dual nation (France and the Netherlands), has as its most famous restaurant a French classic. Located in the capital of Marigot on the French side, it's also the island's best and most dependable choice for fine (although pricey) dining. Tables are placed on a second-floor balcony overlooking the harbor, and the cuisine, always based on the best of current market offerings, displays forthright flavors. See Chapter 16.

> ✔ **Hervé Restaurant & Wine Bar (St. Thomas, U.S. Virgin Islands):**
> Nowhere on this U.S. Virgin Island can you find such a harmonious
> blend of the kitchens of France, the West Indies, and the United
> States. Opening onto a panoramic view of the yacht-clogged harbor
> at Charlotte Amalie, the restaurant offers tables on a spacious
> terrace. Each season, the chef adds enticing new dishes to his
> repertoire, and diners take delight in the first-rate products deftly
> handled and beautifully served. It was here that we became addicted
> to mango cheesecake. See Chapter 17.

The Best Active Vacations

Of course, the major sporting activities in the Caribbean revolve around
scuba diving, snorkeling, fishing, sailing, playing tennis, and golfing. For
the best of these activities, see the corresponding sections later in this
chapter. However, here are some other outdoor diversions to consider:

> ✔ **Exploring the cunucu by Jeep (Aruba):** On the rugged, almost
> desertlike island of Aruba, you can travel into the interior — called
> the *cunucu* — with its cactus-studded terrain that evokes the out-
> back in Australia. You'll encounter not only cacti but also birds,
> such as the *shoko* (owl) and the *prikichi* (the Aruban parakeet),
> plus other wildlife. Mammoth boulders, aloe plants, and the famous
> divi-divi trees (their coiffures permanently bent by the harsh
> winds) fill the landscape. To the northeast of the town of Hooiberg
> stand Casa Bari and Ayo, two building-size stacks of diorite boul-
> ders that evoke a lunar landscape. You can rent Jeeps and four-
> wheel-drive vehicles. See Chapter 9 for more on car rentals.

> ✔ **Windsurfing in Barbados:** In the Western Hemisphere, you'd have
> to go all the way to Hawaii to discover winds as good as those in
> the southern Caribbean off the island of Barbados. Windsurfers
> from all over the world flock here between November and April
> when trade winds are the most ideal for this increasingly popular
> sport. The best windsurfing is found at the shallow offshore reef of
> **Silver Sands,** where surfers reach speeds of up to 50 knots. For out-
> fitters, refer to Chapter 10.

> ✔ **Scaling Jamaica's highest peaks:** The Blue Mountains, famed for
> "the java of kings" (their expensive mountain coffee), reach a pinna-
> cle of 2,255m (7,400 ft.). Nowhere in the Caribbean are you treated
> to such dramatic and panoramic mountain scenery as you explore
> almost junglelike forests, cascading waterfalls, and roaring rivers.
> Many hikers arrive early just to watch the sun come up over these
> mountains. For the adventurer, organized hikes through these
> treacherous mountains may be a memory that lasts forever. For
> outfitters, see Chapter 13.

> ✔ **Hiking in a rain forest (Puerto Rico):** Officially called the **Caribbean
> National Forest,** islanders refer to it as *El Yunque.* Designated a forest

reserve by President Theodore Roosevelt, El Yunque is the only tropical rain forest in the U.S. National Park Service. Riddled with 11,331 hectares (27,988 acres) of trails, it lies only a 45-minute drive east of San Juan. One statistic alone suggests its enchantment for hikers: The forest has 240 species of tropical trees. It's also home to the rare Puerto Rican parrot as well as many other nearly extinct wildlife, including the Puerto Rican boa, growing to a length of 2.1m (7 ft.). The highest peak reaches 1,073m (3,519 ft.). Following the trail of the Indians, you can hike deep into this forest. See Chapter 14.

✔ **Galloping across St. Croix:** Our nomination for the Caribbean's finest stables is **Paul and Jill's Equestrian Stables** at Sprat Hall, the island's oldest plantation near Frederiksted on St. Croix, which is the largest of the U.S. Virgin Islands. You're taken on two-hour trail rides through a rain forest and along the beach. For a memorable romantic adventure, ask about moonlight expeditions. See Chapter 17.

The Best Diving

✔ **Aruba:** The neighboring island of Bonaire is known for some of the best scuba diving in the Caribbean, ranking along with Grand Cayman. Scuba divers flock to Aruba, on the other hand, for its wreck diving. Aruba, along with Bermuda, is ranked near the top for wreck diving in the Caribbean and Atlantic. One of the most significant dive sites in the world is the *Antilla,* a German freighter that sank off Malmok Beach in World War II. For more details, see Chapter 9.

✔ **The British Virgin Islands:** This archipelago is better known for its sailing than its diving, but its waters contain the single most celebrated dive site in the Caribbean: the wreck of the **RMS** *Rhone,* the 93m (310-ft.) royal mail steamer that sank in 1867, lying in waters off the coast of Salt Island. *Skin Diver* magazine hailed it as "the world's most fantastic shipwreck dive," and the sunken ruins were featured in the Peter Benchley movie *The Deep.* Many scuba-diving outfitters in the BVIs link you up to this site. See Chapter 11.

✔ **Grand Cayman:** Scuba divers justifiably rate Grand Cayman as one of the world's top dive sites. The island boasts the best full-service dive operators in the Caribbean. They take you to spectacular coral reefs and the famous **Cayman Wall,** which plummets straight down for 150m (500 ft.) before becoming a steep slope. In addition to the reefs, you find old shipwrecks. Visibility of coral formations and exotic marine life can exceed 30m (100 ft.) in some places. See Chapter 12.

✔ **St. Lucia:** Surrounded by coral reefs, St. Lucia offers excellent — not spectacular — diving, but it's some of the best in the southern Caribbean. Its multicolored reefs are beautiful to explore, and at the divers' hangout, **Anse Chastanet,** you can enjoy good diving right off the beach. Visibility of an astonishing 45m (150 ft.) has been reported in some places off the coast. To make St. Lucia more of a temptation for divers, the government in recent years has deliberately sunk old boats off the coast, creating a haven for varied marine life. To hook up, check out Chapter 15.

✔ **Sint Maarten/St. Martin:** Divers report some of the greatest underwater visibility in the Caribbean off the shores of this island with its dual nationality (France and the Netherlands). Visibility extends from 23 to 38m (75–125 ft.). Countless hidden coves beckon adventurous scuba divers. A major site is the **HMS *Proselyte,*** a British man-of-war that went down in 1801. Both the French and Dutch sides of the island have outfitters who link you with this underwater world. See Chapter 16.

✔ **St. Thomas, U.S. Virgin Islands:** With its series of 30 magnificent coral reefs, St. Thomas is rated by *Skin Diver* magazine as one of the best underwater worlds in the West Indies. The best scuba diving takes place at **Cow and Calf Rocks** at the southeastern end of the island. Divers discover a network of coral tunnels riddled with caves. Another popular dive site is ***Cartanser Sr.,*** a sunken World War II cargo lying in water 11m (35 ft.) deep. St. Thomas offers highly respected outfitters. Find out more about St. Thomas in Chapter 17.

The Best Snorkeling

✔ **Aruba:** Snorkeling just offshore is limited on Aruba, but boats sail out for some fascinating trips. The highlight is a stop at *Antilla,* the German freighter sunk off the coast in World War II (see the preceding section). This wreck is one of the few close enough to the surface for snorkelers to enjoy. You can enjoy the best snorkeling trips on the island by sailing aboard *Mi Dushi,* a Swedish vessel built in 1925. Today it specializes in four-hour guided snorkeling trips. See Chapter 9 for details.

✔ **Barbados:** Although it has nothing to compare with Buck Island off St. Croix, snorkelers in Barbados find that it's well worth their time to rent some gear. The **Carlisle Bay Marine Reserve** is shallow enough for snorkeling, and the bay teems with such marine life as hawksbill turtles and sea horses. At the **Folkestone Marine Park,** you can rent snorkeling gear and explore an underwater trail around Dottin's Reef. See Chapter 10 for more information.

✔ **Stingray City (Grand Cayman):** Lying 3.2km (2 miles) off the northwestern tip of Grand Cayman, this unique snorkeling site is called the best 3.6m (12-ft.) dive site in the world. Hordes of graceful stingrays swim by you. Originally, the stingrays were lured to this feeding station when local fishermen began dumping their leftovers overboard — the fish flocked here to feed off the debris. The phenomenon continues, much to the delight of snorkelers. See Chapter 12.

✔ **St. Martin:** The waters off the northwestern coastal shores of French St. Martin have been classified as a regional underwater nature reserve and are government protected. With a fair amount of reef life to explore, the waters off the coast are known for their visibility. Our favorite spot for snorkeling is **Pine Island (Ilet Pinel),** lying just off the northern coast and reached by any number of boats. This uninhabited island also boasts one of the best beaches in the area. Between snorkeling adventures, you can enjoy food and drink at two beach bars. See Chapter 16.

✔ **Buck Island (St. Croix, U.S. Virgin Islands):** Our favorite snorkeling spot in all the Caribbean is the offshore 121-hectare (300-acre) Buck Island Reef, a volcanic islet enveloping 223 hectares (550 acres) of underwater coral gardens. This islet boasts one of the best underwater snorkeling trails in all the West Indies, and the government has protected it ever since President Kennedy declared it a national treasure. Boat departures for this piece of underwater enchantment are from Kings Wharf in Christiansted, St. Croix. See Chapter 17 for boatmen who'll take you here.

✔ **Trunk Bay (St. John, U.S. Virgin Islands):** The biggest attraction on the small island of St. John is the idyllic beach of Trunk Bay. Sure, it's overcrowded, especially when cruise ships are in port, but it's one of the loveliest beaches in the West Indies. You can rent snorkeling gear here and follow an underwater trail of stunning beauty. The self-guided tour stretches 205m (672 ft.), and underwater signs identify species of coral and other items of marine life. See Chapter 17.

The Best Sailing

✔ **British Virgin Islands:** Rivaled only by the Grenadines (part of St. Vincent), this is the greatest sailing mecca in the Caribbean, attracting yachties from around the world. No place in the West Indies has better marina and shore facilities than the two main islands, Tortola and Virgin Gorda. Tortola, incidentally, is the number-one charter-boat headquarters in the Caribbean Basin. The marvelous attraction of the archipelago of the British Virgins is that you can sail from island to island in just a short time, perhaps landing for a picnic on Norman Island, said to be the inspiration for Robert Louis Stevenson's *Treasure Island.* See Chapter 11.

✔ **Grand Cayman:** We'd hardly call it sailing, but Grand Cayman offers a different type of high-seas adventure. The 80-ton *Atlantis XI* is a submersible 20m-long (65-ft.) ship that carries 48 passengers into the murky depths of the ocean. On the vessel, you experience a close encounter with tropical fish and other sea denizens that you miss when sailing the waves. You go to a depth of 30m (100 ft.), exploring a world known only to scuba divers. The *Seaworld Explorer* is also a semisubmarine that plunges into the sea. We explore both of these options in Chapter 12.

✔ **Puerto Rico:** Although this island Commonwealth of the U.S. isn't the sailor's dream that the British Islands are, boaters still consider it a haven. The best port for embarkations is **Fajardo,** along the East Coast, where you have unlimited sailing possibilities. You can sail over to Puerto Rico's two major offshore islands, Vieques and Culebra, or go to more unspoiled cays such as Icacos or Palimino, lying only an hour or two away. See Chapter 14.

✔ **St. Thomas, U.S. Virgin Islands:** St. Thomas is the charter-boat head-quarters of the U.S. Virgin Islands, occupying the same position that Tortola holds for the BVIs. This place is an ideal embarkation point because so many islands lie close to St. Thomas, including the BVIs. You can sail aboard an estimated 100 vessels, which are rented out to qualified sailors — sail on your own or book a crew through a charter outfit. Many boat lovers sign up for a seven-day sail that takes in the highlights of both the British and U.S. Virgin Islands. See Chapter 17.

The Best Golf Courses

✔ **Tierra del Sol (Aruba):** One of the top golf courses in the southern Caribbean, this 18-hole, par-71, 6,198m (6,776-yard) course was designed by Robert Trent Jones, Jr. It combines lush greens with the beauty of the island's indigenous flora, such as the windblown divi-divi tree. The location is near the California Lighthouse, and the Northwest Coast setting is one of natural but rugged beauty, taking in a saltwater marsh inhabited by egrets, odd rock forma-tions, and a bird sanctuary whose inhabitants include the rare bur-rowing owl. See Chapter 9.

✔ **The Royal Westmoreland Golf and Country Club (Barbados):** This $30-million, 18-hole golf course is the premier links of Barbados. Designed by Robert Trent Jones, Jr., the course is spread across 200 landscaped hectares (500 acres), overlooking the **Gold Coast** on the western coastline of the island. To play, you have to be a guest of one of the swanky properties along the coast. Open to all and also a championship golf area is the 18-hole course of the **Sandy Lane Hotel,** also on the West Coast. Golfers can play on "The Old Nine" or on two 18-hole championship courses, each designed by famous golf architect Tom Fazio. See Chapter 10.

✔ **Brittania Golf Club (Grand Cayman):** The course, the first of its kind in the world, was designed by Jack Nicklaus. It incorporates three different courses in one: a 9-hole championship layout, an 18-hole executive setup, and an 18-hole Cayman course. The last was designed for play with the Cayman ball, which goes about half the distance of a regulation ball. The course lies next to the luxurious Hyatt Regency on Seven Mile Beach. See Chapter 12.

✔ **Tryall Golf, Tennis, and Beach Club (Montego Bay, Jamaica):** Lying 24km (15 miles) west of Montego Bay, this 18-hole championship course is laid out on the grounds of a 19th-century sugar plantation. It gained world fame as the site of the annual Johnnie Walker World Championship. The par-71 course exults in its 6,108m (6,678 yards) of hills and dales. The course is known for constantly changing wind directions. See Chapter 13.

✔ **Rose Hall Resort & Country Club (Montego Bay, Jamaica):** Lying 6.4km (4 miles) east of the airport at Montego Bay, Rose Hall has a challenging 18-hole golf course with a backdrop of both the ocean and the mountains. It's a par-71, 6,033m (6,596-yard) course, with an eighth hole that skirts the water. The 15th green is next to a 12m (40-ft.) waterfall once featured in a James Bond movie. See Chapter 13.

✔ **Carambola Golf Course (St. Croix, U.S. Virgin Islands):** On the northeast side of the island, this 6,257m (6,843-yard) 18-hole course was created by Robert Trent Jones, Sr., who called it "the loveliest course I ever designed." The par-three holes here are known to golfers as the best in the tropics, and the course has been compared to a botanical garden. See Chapter 17.

The Best Tennis Facilities

✔ **Half Moon (Rose Hall, Montego Bay, Jamaica):** This sprawling resort boasts Jamaica's most extensive tennis complex, a total of 13 courts, 7 of which are lit for night play. Tennis players from all over the world are attracted to these courts, following a long-standing British-based affinity for the game. See Chapter 13.

✔ **Tryall Golf, Tennis, and Beach Club (Montego Bay, Jamaica):** Four on-site pros welcome you to these nine state-of-the-art, hard-surface courts, three of which are illuminated for night play. Lessons are also available. The deluxe resort lies 19km (12 miles) west of Montego Bay on the site of an 880-hectare (2,200-acre) former sugar plantation and maintains the aura of an elegant country estate. See Chapter 13.

✔ **Westin Rio Mar Beach Golf Resort & Spa (Puerto Rico):** This $180-million resort on 195 landscaped hectares (481 acres), near the most popular beach on Puerto Rico, also boasts some of the northern Caribbean's best tennis facilities. It features a total of 13 championship tennis courts, which can be illuminated for night play. See Chapter 14.

✔ **St. Lucia Racquet Club (St. Lucia):** The island's finest tennis courts, among the best in the Lesser Antilles, lie at the St. Lucia Racquet Club, adjacent to **Club St. Lucia.** Its seven illuminated courts are maintained in state-of-the-art condition; a top pro shop is on the grounds. See Chapter 15.

✔ **The Buccaneer (St. Croix, U.S. Virgin Islands):** This resort is not only the top one on this U.S. Virgin Island, but it also features the best tennis facilities on the island — in fact, the finest in all the U.S. Virgin Islands. The resort hosts several prestigious tournaments every year. Eight all-weather Laykold tennis courts, two of which are illuminated at night, plus a top-notch pro shop are on-site. See Chapter 17.

The Best Fishing

✔ **Barbados:** Deep-sea fishing is the name of the game in Barbados. Sports fishermen set out to hunt for billfish, sailfish, and blue and white marlin, along with barracuda and kingfish. The fishing is first-rate in the waters around Barbados, where catches have also included dolphin fish (mahi-mahi) and such big game fish as wahoo; the occasional cobia may turn up on your line. Some highly skilled charter boat captains set out, usually carrying five to six fishermen. See Chapter 10.

✔ **British Virgin Islands:** This archipelago lies at the center of some of the richest game-fishing channels on earth, notably the 80km (50-mile) **Puerto Rican Trench** near the sparsely inhabited island of Anegada. Fishermen have chalked up record catches in marlin, shark, bluefish, tuna, sailfish, and the big game wahoo. Bonefishing in the saltwater flats of the British Virgin Islands is also a popular sport. You can book excellent boat charters on the island. See Chapter 11.

✔ **Puerto Rico:** Some 30 world records have been racked up in the waters off the coast of Puerto Rico. The big catches here are white and blue marlin, dolphin fish (mahi-mahi), yellow and blackfin tuna, mackerel, tarpon, snook, Allison tuna, and wahoo, plus bonefish in the shallows. Puerto Rico's annual billfish tournament is the largest of its kind in the world. You can book some excellent boat charters. See Chapter 14.

✔ **St. Thomas, U.S. Virgin Islands:** On this island, 19 fishing world records (8 of these for blue marlin) have been set in recent years. Blue marlin weighing 453kg (1,000 lbs.) have been caught in **North Drop** off the North Coast of the island. Big catches in wahoo, tuna, skipjack, sailfish, and dolphin fish (mahi-mahi) have also been chalked up. For charter-boat recommendations, flip to Chapter 17.

The Best Shopping

Because the U.S. government allows its citizens to take (or send) home more duty-free goods from the U.S. Virgins than from other ports of call, those islands remain the shopping bazaar of the Caribbean. U.S. citizens may carry home $1,200 worth of goods untaxed, as opposed to only $400 worth of goods from most other islands in the Caribbean. (The only exception to this rule is Puerto Rico, where you can carry any purchase, regardless of the amount, back to the U.S. mainland tax-free.) Although it isn't a U.S. possession, Sint Maarten/St. Martin, which France and the Netherlands rule jointly, gives the Virgins some serious shopping competition. The island is virtually a shopper's mall, especially on the Dutch side. The U.S. doesn't grant the generous Customs allowances on Sint Maarten/St. Martin that it does to its own islands, but the island doesn't charge duty, so you still can find some lovely bargains.

- ✔ **Aruba:** The wisest shoppers on Aruba are cost-conscious souls who've carefully checked the prices of comparable goods before leaving home. Duty is relatively low (only 3.3 percent). Much of the European china, jewelry, perfumes, watches, and crystal has a disconcerting habit of reappearing in every shopping mall and hotel boutique on the island, so after you determine exactly which brand of watch or china you want, you can comparison shop. See Chapter 9.

- ✔ **Barbados:** Local shops seem to specialize in all things English. Merchandise includes bone china from British and Irish manufacturers, watches, jewelry, and perfumes. **Bridgetown's Broad Street** is the shopping headquarters of the island, although some of the stores here maintain boutiques (with similar prices but a less-extensive range of merchandise) at many of the island's hotels and in malls along the congested Southwestern Coast. Except for cigarettes and tobacco, any buyer can haul off duty-free items as soon as he or she pays for them. Duty-free status is extended to anyone showing a passport or ID and an airline ticket with a date of departure from Barbados. See Chapter 10.

- ✔ **Grand Cayman:** Goods are sold tax-free from a daunting collection of malls and minimalls throughout Grand Cayman. Most of these malls are along the highway that parallels the Seven Mile Beach; you need a car to shop around. You can also find lots of stores in **George Town,** which you can explore on foot, poking in and out of some large emporiums in your search for bargains. See Chapter 12.

- ✔ **Jamaica:** The shopping was better in the good old days, before new taxes added a 10 percent surcharge. Despite that, Jamaica offers a wealth of desirable goods, including flavored rums, Jamaican coffees, handicrafts (such as woodcarvings, woven baskets, and sandals), original paintings and sculptures, cameras, watches, and VCRs. Unless you're a glutton for handmade souvenirs (which are available on virtually every beach and street corner), you'd be wise to limit most of your purchases to bona fide merchants and stores. See Chapter 13.

- ✔ **Puerto Rico:** U.S. citizens don't have to pay duty on anything they buy on Puerto Rico. You're not guaranteed that prices will be particularly low, however. Jewelry and watches abound, often at competitive prices, especially in the island's best-stocked area, **Old San Juan.** Also of great interest are such Puerto Rican handicrafts as charming folkloric papier-mâché carnival masks and *santos,* carved wooden figures depicting saints. See Chapter 14.

✔ **Sint Maarten/St. Martin:** Because of the massive influx of cruise ships, shopping on Dutch Sint Maarten is now about the finest in the Caribbean, though you may have to fight the crowds. Because you don't have to pay duty, prices can be 30 to 50 percent lower than in the U.S. Forget about local crafts and concentrate on leather goods, electronics, cameras, designer fashions, watches, and crystal, along with linens and jewelry. **Philipsburg,** the capital of the island's Dutch side, is the best place to shop. Although it can't compete with Dutch Sint Maarten, French St. Martin is becoming a more popular shopping destination, especially for fashion or perfumes imported from France. See Chapter 16.

✔ **St. Thomas, U.S. Virgin Islands:** Many of its busiest shops are in restored warehouses that were originally built in the 1700s. **Charlotte Amalie,** the capital, is a shopper's town, with a staggering number of stores stocked with more merchandise than elsewhere in the Caribbean. However, despite all the fanfare, real bargains are hard to come by. Look for two local publications, *This Week* and *Best Buys;* either may steer you to the type of merchandise you're seeking. If at all possible, try to avoid shopping when more than one cruise ship is in port — the shopping district is a madhouse on those days. See Chapter 17.

✔ **St. Croix, U.S. Virgin Islands:** This island doesn't have the massive shopping development of St. Thomas, but its merchandise has never been more wide-ranging than it is today. Even though most cruise ships call at Frederiksted, with its urban mall, our favorite shops are in **Christiansted,** which boasts many one-of-a-kind boutiques and many special finds. Prices are about the same here as on St. Thomas. See Chapter 17.

The Best Nightlife

✔ **Aruba:** This island has ten big, splashy casinos, each with its own unique décor and each with a following of devoted gamblers. Some offer their own cabarets and comedy shows, dance floors with live or recorded music, restaurants of all degrees of formality, and bars. See Chapter 9.

✔ **Barbados:** Bridgetown is home to such boats as the *Jolly Roger,* which embarks at sundown for rum-and-reggae cruises, as well as oversize music bars like **M/V Harbour Master.** Otherwise, a host of bars, British-style pubs, dozens of restaurants, and discos (both within and outside large hotels) beckon from **St. Lawrence Gap** or the crowded Southwest Coast. See Chapter 10.

✔ **Jamaica:** Many visitors are drawn here by a love for the island's distinct musical forms. Foremost among these are reggae and soca, both of which you can hear at hotels, resorts, and raffish dives throughout the island. Hotels often stage folkloric shows that include entertainers who sing, dance, swallow torches, and walk on broken glass. You also find plenty of indoor/outdoor bars where you might actually be able to talk to people. Local tourist boards in Negril and Montego Bay sometimes organize weekly beach parties called *boonoonoonoos*. See Chapter 13.

✔ **Puerto Rico:** Puerto Rico contains all the raw ingredients for great nightlife, including casinos, endless rows of bars and *bodegas,* cabaret shows with girls and glitter, and discos that feature everything from New York imports to some of the best salsa and merengue anywhere. The country's gaming headquarters lies along the **Condado** in San Juan, although you can also find casinos in megaresorts scattered throughout the island. The casinos here are the most fun in the Caribbean, and they're also some of the most spectacular. Each contains lots of sideshows (restaurants, merengue bars, art galleries, piano bars, shops) that can distract you from the tables. If you're a really serious partier, you'll have lots of company on Puerto Rico. See Chapter 14.

✔ **Sint Maarten/St. Martin:** This island has a rather cosmopolitan nightlife and contains the densest concentration of restaurants in the Caribbean, each with its own bar. Discos are often indoor/outdoor affairs. Low-key hotel casinos abound on the Dutch side. See Chapter 16.

✔ **St. Thomas, U.S. Virgin Islands:** The most active nightlife in all the Virgin Islands (U.S. or British) takes place on St. Thomas. Don't expect glitzy shows like those in San Juan's Condado area, and don't expect any kind of casino. But you'll find plenty of fun at the bars, restaurants, concerts, clubs, and folklore and reggae shows. See Chapter 17.

Chapter 2

Choosing Where to Go

In This Chapter

▶ Picking the right island for you

▶ Examining the pros and cons of island hopping

*I*f you're not sure which island you want to visit, you're in good company. Even the Caribbean's first tourist was overwhelmed by the choices. "I saw so many islands that I could hardly decide which to visit first," Christopher Columbus wrote to Spain's Queen Isabella. We know just how he felt.

That sweep of aquamarine blue-on-blue sea called the Caribbean stretches nearly 3,218km (1,995 miles) from Cuba to South America and encompasses more than 30 different nations and a mind-boggling 7,000 islands — give or take a few. Technically, The Bahamas and Turks and Caicos aren't even in the Caribbean. As for the islanders themselves, they, too, are a diverse group, representing 100 different cultures. On most Caribbean islands, the majority of the population is descended from African slaves.

That said, read on for a glimpse at each of our favorite Caribbean islands.

Introducing the Islands

Which island is right for you depends, of course, on what you enjoy and what kind of vacation you want. For example, if you love shopping, glittering nightlife, the beach, and golf, we recommend Aruba, Puerto Rico, Jamaica, or St. Thomas. If you're the independent type seeking adventure and discovery, head for Jamaica, as thrilling and mysterious as it often is dangerous. If you prefer to veg out on the beach, a Caribbean island will suit you — notably the manicured and relatively safe Grand Cayman, where your biggest exercise of the day may be walking from your hotel room onto the golden sand of Seven Mile Beach.

In this section, we list the Caribbean's top destinations, with the lowdown on the ins and outs of each.

Arriving in Aruba

Sugar-white beaches. Splashy casinos. A stark, otherworldly, cactus-dotted landscape known as the *cunucu,* where divi-divi (watapana) trees have been bowed to a 45-degree angle by the constantly blowing trade winds. Think Arizona with a beach, and you've got Aruba, an independent country within the Kingdom of the Netherlands.

Located a scant 24km (15 miles) north of Venezuela, this Dutch treat has a diverse heritage. In fact, the lyrical local language, Papiamento, is laced with Spanish, Dutch, and Portuguese, as well as African, French, and Arawak Indian dialects.

Aruba is surprisingly small, but this island — popular with the package-tour crowd and cruise ships, as well as honeymooners and families — welcomed more than 1 million visitors in 2003. It's famed for its wide, 11km (7-mile) stretch of white-sand beach, where most of its 30 or so hotels are tightly packed. Aruba's tiny capital, Oranjestad, with its pastel, stucco walls topped by wedding-cake cupolas and terra-cotta roofs, makes for a scenic afternoon stroll.

If you want a hassle-free, relaxing introduction to the Caribbean, Aruba ranks high on the list. The hotels offer affordable packages, and even though Aruba is one of the more far-flung islands, you can get a direct flight from several major cities in the U.S. and Europe. What we like about this place is that it's easy to navigate and the people are hospitable. Even though the island heavily relies on tourism, the locals exude a small-town friendliness. Plus, thanks to a heavy Latin influence from nearby South America and the plethora of gambling casinos, Aruba's nightlife is the most active in the southern Caribbean.

With more than 40 distinct nationalities represented in a population of 95,000, Aruba has some of the Caribbean's best and most varied dining options. You can look forward to an array of more than 100 restaurant choices. Sophisticated travelers, however, find little island spice on Aruba and may be disappointed by the bland buildup along its stunning beaches. A building moratorium now restricts new construction, but the island long ago reached the saturation point. Aruba is far from our definition of a tropical getaway.

As long as you've come this far, reserve a few days to visit Aruba's next-door neighbors: **Bonaire,** which offers the Caribbean's best diving and snorkeling, and **Curaçao,** which boasts a postcard-perfect Dutch colonial city that looks like a mini-Amsterdam. Each island is just a brief plane or boat ride away.

Top aspects of a vacation on Aruba include

- ✔ **Lots of variety:** From gambling to windsurfing to horseback riding along the beach, Aruba delivers the fun factor.

- ✔ **Lively nightlife:** You won't feel overdressed in your designer duds on Aruba. You can try your luck at a dozen casinos, reserve a stage-side table for the productions at one of the showrooms, or dance the night away at hot spots.

- ✔ **Consistently perfect weather:** Aruba lies outside the hurricane belt. Trade winds and low humidity keep its average year-round temperature of 28°C (82°F) from feeling uncomfortably hot. The island gets only 43cm (17 inches) of rainfall annually.

- ✔ **Good vibes:** Cosmopolitan Arubans are friendly, and just about everyone speaks English.

But also consider the following:

- ✔ **It's built up:** High-rise hotels with little island flair crowd the prime beaches.

- ✔ **Tourism reigns supreme:** Forget your Robinson Crusoe fantasy.

- ✔ **The scenery is desertlike, not lush:** This dry, cactus-dotted countryside may clash with your vision of a tropical paradise.

Basking in the Barbados sun

Steeped in English tradition and more strait-laced than some of its neighbors, pricey Barbados has been giving the wealthy and famous the royal treatment for centuries. The easternmost of the Caribbean's Lesser Antilles chain, Barbados juts out into the Atlantic Ocean and used to serve as a gateway to the West Indies for ships coming to and from Europe and South America. As a result, its islanders got first pick of the bounty flowing into the Caribbean. The island's prosperity remains in evidence today, especially in the bustling shopping district (which we didn't find to be overly impressive or a bargain).

Visiting Aruba, Bonaire, and Curaçao: As easy as ABC

We usually don't recommend trying to visit more than one island during your trip (see the section "Visiting More than One Island," later in this chapter), but the ABC islands — as Aruba, Bonaire, and Curaçao are known — offer a golden opportunity. Both Bonaire and Curaçao rank among our favorites, though for different reasons. If you're a diver or nature lover, include Bonaire (☎ **800-BONAIRE,** or 800-266-2473; www.infobonaire.com) on your itinerary. History buffs gravitate to Curaçao (☎ **800-328-7222;** www.curacao-tourism.com). Thanks to Willemstad, its Dutch colonial capital, Curaçao has joined such sites as the Great Wall of China and the Pyramids as a UNESCO World Heritage Site.

Known for its posh resorts from **Sandy Lane** to **Royal Pavilion** (think *Lifestyles of the Rich and Famous*), Barbados offers a range of accommodations, whether you're seeking idyllic days at an intimate guesthouse or the frenetic activity of a sprawling resort.

Barbados maintains certain traditions that remain from its almost continual rule by the British — beginning some three centuries ago and continuing right up until its independence in 1966. Most resorts, for example, serve afternoon tea, but often around the swimming pool instead of in some staid Victorian parlor.

Another traditional holdover is dressing up for dinner; you must at top restaurants and resorts in Barbados. You quickly see firsthand why Barbados garners international acclaim for its restaurants.

Barbados is also known for its gardens — again, the British influence. Don't come expecting the lush, junglelike beauty of St. Lucia or Barbados's wild cousin, Jamaica. Barbados is green, but years of use by planters have left its countryside restrained and managed.

The mood in Barbados is unmistakably civilized — so much so that you may feel a little stifled and hamstrung by all that tradition. Of course, away from the fancy West Coast resorts, Barbados attracts a younger and more informal crowd, including the surfers who hang out near **Bathsheba.** With their hip attitudes, they definitely clash with the island's character. Barbados residents, called Bajans (pronounced *bay-jahns*), cut loose only when it comes to rum. Bajans are extremely proud of the locally made rums, and several little dives around the island serve the potent brew at all hours.

If your idea of paradise is the feel of an English outpost in the tropics, Barbados will be your cup of tea.

Top aspects of a vacation in Barbados include

- ✔ **The dining scene:** Chefs in Barbados, unlike those on some Caribbean islands, are experimental, sophisticated, and eager to meet the challenges of demanding palates.

- ✔ **The scenery:** In the countryside, you find some panoramic vistas of both sea and land.

- ✔ **Snap-to service:** You don't want for attention; you have help at your beck and call.

But also consider the following:

- ✔ **You'll need to mind your manners:** The "have it your way" philosophy doesn't belong here — it's the queen's rules all the way. Better polish up on which fork to use with which course.

✔ **You'll faint at the prices:** Rates are out-of-sight unless you're willing to look hard. Prices are high on everything from food to hotel rooms to greens fees.

✔ **You'll encounter claustrophobia-inducing roads and traffic jams around Bridgetown and the popular coasts:** Oddly, you're likely to find busy, narrow roads right next to your room at many hotels.

Breezing into the British Virgin Islands

Even if you've never been on a boat in your life, the British Virgin Islands (BVIs) make you want to hoist a sail and swill some grog. Brace yourself for the moment when you finally glimpse Jimmy Buffett's idea of paradise. These sleepy little islands — like a giant's stepping-stones scattered across the sea — are a sailor's and water-lover's delight. You're never out of sight of the next island as you tool around on your choice of watercraft.

Getting here is a royal pain, but the extra effort is worth it. And because getting to the BVIs is neither easy nor cheap, you may feel like you have the islands all to yourself at times. You can fly into Tortola, but you'll probably need to ply the Caribbean waters by water taxi or ferry to reach your hotel, villa, or guesthouse. Thankfully, you don't find any monolithic, high-rise hotels straddling the beaches here. You also don't find any rah-rah all-inclusive resorts.

Still a British colony, the BVIs — actually more than 50 islands are in the chain, though only a handful are inhabited — are remarkably undeveloped and sparsely populated, with only 18,000 inhabitants. Tourism began here in the mid-1960s when Laurance Rockefeller opened **Little Dix Bay** on Virgin Gorda. Like nearby St. John, much of the BVIs' land is preserved in national park areas.

If you must have your MTV, shopping, golf, or casino, skip the BVIs. But if you want to chill out and spend your afternoons doing nothing more stressful than napping in a hammock by the sea, the BVIs are a perfect choice.

Although you'll find a touch of British formality, the vibe here is casual and fun. When you're at the beach bar, you sit alongside captains of industry, rock stars, famous actors, and colorful local characters, all gathered to sip Painkillers — a rum concoction — with their new best friends.

About the only place where you see much evidence of tourism is at the most famous spot on Virgin Gorda, called **The Baths.** Here, grand granite boulders frame the most perfect blue Caribbean you could desire. Cruise ships are allowed to dock on that island, but the number of passengers they can bring each day is tightly controlled.

The BVIs we cover in this book are

- ✔ **Tortola:** The largest of the BVIs, Tortola is only 34km (21 miles) long. Its name means "turtledove" in Spanish. The BVI capital, Road Town, is here, as well as a huge marina filled with hundreds of yachts that account for half of the BVIs' tourist beds.

- ✔ **Virgin Gorda:** Home to some of the most spectacular resorts in the BVIs, Virgin Gorda packs a world of beauty into a mere 14km (8⅔ miles). It has two national parks, both great for hiking. (Gorda Peak reaches 457m/1,500 ft.)

- ✔ **Anegada:** Although this stretch of land is within sight of the other islands, you can easily overlook the flat, sandy island that looks like a giant beach and feels like the ends of the earth.

Picnics on deserted beaches, sunset sails in a tiny boat, and morning walks where you don't run into another soul make the British Virgin Islands one of our favorites.

Top aspects of a vacation in the British Virgin Islands include

- ✔ **Sailing like a Caribbean pirate:** Free spirits love just drifting from one isle to the next through Sir Francis Drake Channel, called the world's loveliest sailing grounds.

- ✔ **A picture-postcard setting:** The Caribbean doesn't get any better than this. You can find that island getaway and snag your own private strand of beach.

- ✔ **Unexpected fun:** When you're at Foxy's or Bomba's beach bar, you may encounter Jimmy Buffett plucking out his latest ode to sailing or the Beach Boys jamming the night away.

But also consider the following:

- ✔ **No posh nightlife:** You need to whip up your own entertainment.

- ✔ **Transportation hassles:** Getting around can be expensive and time-consuming unless you rely on the regularly scheduled ferries.

- ✔ **Limited dining choices:** If you don't happen to like the chef at certain isolated resorts, you're cooked.

Greeting Grand Cayman

We have to be honest upfront: Unless you're a diver or a serious snorkeler, go elsewhere. You can find more island flavor in other places for a much cheaper price. The Cayman Islands, the birthplace of the Caribbean's recreational diving, rely on a good reputation for their relatively healthy reefs and dramatic wall dives with almost 200 dive sites and visibility up to 31m (100 ft.). Of the trio that makes up the Cayman Islands — Grand Cayman, Cayman Brac, and Little Cayman, just south of

Cuba — Grand Cayman is the primary draw with its famed 8.8km (5½-mile) **Seven Mile Beach.**

So why is Grand Cayman one of the top tourist destinations in the Caribbean? Diving aside, Grand Cayman is easy to reach and easy to navigate. It's safe and sanitized in every way — the kind of place where you can go to sleep in your beach chair, wake up, and still have all your stuff intact. Natives speak English, vendors accept U.S. dollars, and, most importantly, they all make you feel welcome.

Grand Cayman's top-drawer restaurants, cool attractions like **Stingray City,** tidy beaches, and a plethora of water sports make it a popular choice with families, honeymooners, and divers who are traveling with nondivers. Grand Cayman is also one of the main stops for the many cruise ships in the Caribbean.

If you crave glittery nightlife, Grand Cayman has gotten a little hipper post-millennium, but we'd still send you to Puerto Rico or Aruba instead. Even though the banking industry has made this island wealthy, gambling it away at casinos isn't the thing here either. Expect to be in the company of the old-money crowd, whose idea of fun is watching the sunset from a lantern-festooned deck while celebrating happy hour at a British-style pub.

You'll find friendly islanders who speak with a lilting brogue echoing their Scotch/Irish/Welsh heritage. They also probably have a bigger bank account than you do. About the only time a party atmosphere sets in is during **Pirates Week;** parades, street dances, and fireworks break out everywhere during this national event in October.

If you're the active type who loves water sports, pricey gourmet food, and a dash of history, Grand Cayman is a winner.

Top aspects of a vacation on Grand Cayman include

- ✔ **Divers' heaven:** The Cayman Islands are renowned for some of the Caribbean's best diving.

- ✔ **Great dining:** Gourmet restaurants offer truly inventive island cuisine.

- ✔ **Classy, but casual:** The Cayman Islands are sophisticated and upscale islands without attitude.

- ✔ **Untrammeled isles:** Peaceful Cayman Brac and Little Cayman lie within easy reach.

But also consider the following:

- ✔ **Your wallet gets hit:** The Cayman Islands are expensive, especially when it comes to food — although the island has taken the bite out of prices with discounts during the off season in recent years.

- **Nightlife? What nightlife?** Diver, tuck in early.

- **Day-trippers are everywhere:** The famed beach and popular dive sites get overrun — especially when cruise ships are in port.

Jamming in Jamaica

Quintessential ladies' man Errol Flynn called Jamaica "more beautiful than any woman I've ever seen." Nobody ever comes back from Jamaica and labels the island just "nice" — it stands out from the other Caribbean islands as an in-your-face kind of place. It's an assault on the senses: the continual throbbing of reggae and rock-steady music that reverberates in taxis and on the streets; lush places with improbable names like **Fern Gully** and **Bamboo Alley;** the fiery taste of jerk chicken; and the plucky salesmanship of self-taught artists eking out a living in the craft markets.

Does your island fantasy include rafting a river and swimming in a blue lagoon? How about racing to the top of a waterfall, or sitting on a veranda sipping your morning coffee while overlooking the bushes from which the coffee beans were plucked? Choose your favorite sunny spot from Jamaica's 322km (200 miles) of beaches. Hike the 2,256m (7,400-ft.) summits of the Blue Mountains. Cuddle under a heated duvet to ward off the cool mountain air at night.

Jamaica owes part of its success to the prevalence of all-inclusive resorts, which were first popularized here and have spread to several other Caribbean islands. However, these compounds have proven both a blessing and a curse. Many visitors like them because they take a lot of the guesswork out of their trip, letting them control the costs upfront. Unfortunately, the self-contained attractions also make it highly unlikely that you'll venture from the cushy confines of your resort and experience the real Jamaica. In turn, the lack of vacationers willing to actually visit the island and not just an all-inclusive resort has hit restaurants and attractions hard, making Jamaicans even more desperate for your business.

We have a love/hate relationship with the island. We adore the less-touristy parts and the way people warm up if you're kind to them and show interest in their country. We abhor the brazen approaches of the shady characters peddling drugs and the prostitutes that you're likely to encounter on the beaches and outside the resorts' gates. Although the government has tried in recent years to educate the local population about how important visitors are to the economy, the message has had little effect on aggressive vendors and sometimes-surly service people. On the other hand, if you're looking for local color in a lush country, you've found your island.

The island has four main resort areas — and some up-and-coming spots — each tempting in a different way, with tennis, golf, horseback riding, and water sports:

✔ **Montego Bay:** Here in Mo Bay (as locals call it), green hills cup the blue harbor of Jamaica's number-one tourist destination (some may say "trap"). One of the livelier Caribbean destinations, it offers everything from duty-free shopping to craft markets to legends of witchcraft at **Rose Hall,** an 18th-century plantation _Great House_ (the plantation houses from the days when sugar cane covered the island) said to be haunted.

On the plus side, you'll find a decent selection of restaurants and nightclubs in Mo Bay, which has brought in the college spring-break crowd. But Mo Bay is big, poor, and crowded, and it lacks the fine architecture that gives St. Thomas's Charlotte Amalie its allure. If you spend your entire vacation here, you're probably going to leave feeling a little let down.

✔ **Negril:** A hedonistic pulse courses through this resort area at Jamaica's western tip. Known as a counterculture escape in the 1970s (when it didn't even have electricity), this sleepy little haven was discovered by hip, young visitors when the 1980s rolled around.

Negril has retained its funky edge and is still celebrated for its sunsets and 11km (7 miles) of beach as soft as talc, but the masses have definitely embraced it, some coming for the clothing-optional sections of beach. The all-inclusive resorts occupy much of the fabulous beach with smaller properties tucked in between. Sun seekers looking for a little less frenzy can find it on Negril's **West End,** where boutique resorts hug the cliffs above a honeycomb network of caves. For a taste of what Negril used to be like, head to the Southwest Coast where trendy, beautiful people have adopted **Treasure Beach,** a tiny fishing village, as a hangout.

✔ **Ocho Rios:** Cruise ships regularly disgorge passengers in Ochi (the local name, pronounced _oh_-chee). The tourists stampede for the shopping and then make the obligatory climb up **Dunn's River Falls,** where a natural stone staircase leads to the top of the 183m (600-ft.) cascading waterfall. After that trek, these tourists then run the gauntlet past vendors hawking "I survived the Falls" T-shirts. Unfortunately, that experience has led many to dismiss Ochi as a kitschy town for tourists. Actually, you don't have to venture far off the well-beaten path here to see Ochi's Eden-like nature — we love the **Coyaba Gardens** tucked away above the city. Ocho Rios boasts some of the country's more exquisite resorts, as well as our absolute favorite all-inclusive resort, **San Souci Resort & Spa.**

✔ **Port Antonio:** Those who know and love Jamaica often pick lush and mountainous Port Antonio as the most romantic region of the country. Indeed, Port Antonio, on the Northeast Coast and in the foothills of the Blue Mountains, fueled Errol Flynn's passion and remains removed from the primary flurry of tourism. Rafting by torchlight on the gentle Rio Grande is the main attraction here. Although Port Antonio doesn't have the high profile of the other resort areas, stars like Johnny Depp, Glenn Close, and Robin Williams have fallen for it.

We're willing to overlook Jamaica's rough edges, because, overall, its rugged beauty delivers the quintessential Caribbean experience.

Top aspects of a vacation in Jamaica include

- **Choice of destinations:** Whether your pace is languid or action-packed, you can easily find a resort to match your vacationing style.

- **Cool digs:** Accommodations range from hyperactive all-inclusive resorts to old-world villas where butlers serve tea on silver trays to funky cottages by the beach.

- **The breadth of natural beauty:** The variations of Jamaica's terrain are unparalleled: expansive beaches; lush jungles punctuated with waterfalls; the cool, misty Blue Mountains; and savannas that echo the African plains.

- **All-inclusive resorts:** You know how much your vacation will cost before you even leave home. And you don't have to think of a thing when you're here.

- **The vibrant culture:** Reggae by the late Bob Marley still rules the airwaves from Houston to Copenhagen. In tiny crafts stores and grand galleries, you find earthy, made-in-Jamaica items, such as woodcarvings and handmade pottery.

But also consider the following:

- **The most aggressive vendors in the Caribbean:** Travelers need to be cautious. Think New York City on a beach. Vendors on the beach and in the markets can be maddeningly persistent.

- **Traffic accidents:** The roadways here are in disrepair, and the island has the dubious ranking as one of the top spots for car wrecks in the world.

- **Grinding poverty:** Next to Haiti, Jamaica has the lowest standard of living in the Caribbean, and some visitors find it hard to enjoy themselves when the islanders are so obviously struggling.

- **Litter:** The natural beauty of the island is marred by trash.

- **Crime:** Unless you're a Bob Marley fanatic and want to make a pilgrimage to his house, now a museum, steer clear of Kingston, where much of Jamaica's crime occurs.

Partying on Puerto Rico

Puerto Rico scores high on our list of favorite Caribbean islands for more reasons than native son Ricky Martin can shake his bon-bon at. This stunner of a destination dishes out everything that your heart could desire in an island vacation — all with a steamy Latin beat. The colonial city of Old San Juan, with its well-preserved forts and narrow stone streets overhung with balconies brimming with flowers, has managed to avoid much of the T-shirt tackiness that mars so many of this hemisphere's port cities. Yet with its chic art galleries and vibrant restaurant scene, it has gracefully bridged the gap between old and new.

Those who want high-rise hotels, a happening beach scene, high-energy discos, and frenetic casinos can find them on Condado and Isla Verde in San Juan. That's our least favorite part of the island, because it's touristy with vendors hawking tacky trinkets and little island charm.

Puerto Rico has enough natural wonders to keep you more than occupied, including one of the world's largest river caves for spelunking, extensive rain forests for hiking, bioluminescent bays and good corals for diving, and 438km (272 miles) of Atlantic and Caribbean coastline for horseback riding, swimming, surfing, and walking hand-in-hand. The island also rates well with people who love golf and deep-sea fishing. Escape artists find a more laid-back scene in Vieques and Rincon. Think of San Juan like Miami. Vieques is considered the Spanish Virgin Island.

As for accommodations, Puerto Rico arguably has the broadest range of choices in the Caribbean, from a hotel converted from a 500-year-old convent to megaresorts with all the bells and whistles. It also yields gems called *paradores* — clean, comfortable, and reasonably priced bed-and-breakfasts that must pass government inspection.

Of course, because Puerto Rico is a U.S. territory, you never have a problem finding English speakers — although Spanish is the dominant language of the people. To make your life as a traveler even easier, you can take the cash you're most accustomed to; the U.S. dollar is the currency on Puerto Rico.

Puerto Rico runs the gamut. It packs sizzle to spare with a sexy nightlife scene, but eco-hounds and sports fans will be in paradise, as will those souls who are content to sit on the beach sipping margaritas.

Top aspects of a vacation on Puerto Rico include

- ✔ **A convenient location:** You won't have a problem getting to Puerto Rico. Almost all the airlines that service the Caribbean fly through this airport.

- ✔ **No passport, no problema:** You get the intoxicating mix of both worlds here: the exotic Latin flavor blended with the comforting familiarity of home. If you're from the United States, you don't have to worry about a passport or changing money.

- ✔ **Living la vida loca:** Put on your designer duds and tango until the sun comes up. Puerto Ricans love the nightlife.

- ✔ **Culture club:** The art scene and intriguing history meld to bring a level of sophistication to Puerto Rico that you don't find on most of the other Caribbean islands.

But also consider the following:

- ✔ **The secret's out:** Puerto Rico is a popular stop for cruise ships, and its more-famous beaches (all are public) get crowded and dirty.

- ✔ **Hurricanes are regular visitors:** During the hurricane season, Puerto Rico regularly goes on alert.

- ✔ **Spring break and holiday crowds abound:** During the time that most people think about coming to the Caribbean, finding room at the inn can be almost impossible. Unlike other places, travel traffic doesn't slow down in April either, thanks to spring break and Easter celebrations.

Sailing into St. Lucia

Lush, avocado-shaped St. Lucia (pronounced *loo*-shah), the second largest of the Windward Islands, is known for its volcanic peaks, splendid sandy beaches, and the finest mountain scenery in the West Indies. It appeals to the adventurer who wants to explore one of the world's most accessible volcanoes, pools of boiling water (not for swimming), and valleys that evoke Tarzan country.

Midway between French Martinique and the old British colony of St. Vincent, St. Lucia was a political bouncing ball for centuries, passed between the two powerful European countries that controlled its neighboring islands. By 1967, St. Lucia was still under British domination until it became a self-governing state, granted full sovereignty in 1979.

St. Lucia, at long last, has awakened to tourism — and with a powerful bang. Today the island is dotted with luxurious all-inclusive resorts, including the lead player in the field, **Sandals** — and that number keeps growing. Although it has yet to overtake Barbados, prices climb skyward every year.

Castries, St. Lucia's capital and a beautiful natural harbor, is one of the dullest such cities in the southern Caribbean, having been razed by fires in 1948 and 1951 and unattractively rebuilt. After you escape Castries, you'll find a land of tropical trees, flowering plants, and mountains — the highest peak being Mount Gimie, at 959m (3,145 ft.).

Although the island is no longer undiscovered, many undisturbed spaces remain open for exploration. St. Lucia's diverse terrain is far more dramatic than its southern Caribbean competitors such as Aruba or Barbados. Much of the scenery, including its tropical abundance and the twin volcanic pyramids of the Pitons, evokes the South Pacific.

More and more, honeymooners are escaping to these shores instead of booking into one of the Sandals resorts on the troubled island of Jamaica. In our view, St. Lucia is arguably more for the single adventurer or the fun-loving couple — not necessarily a kiddies' playground. Families with children will find much more to do on Puerto Rico.

Top aspects of a vacation in St. Lucia include

- ✔ **Terrific walking and hiking:** The island and climate is split by accessible trails that lead to pockets of beauty almost at every curve. Most of St. Lucia's resorts lie north of Castries, leaving much of the rest of the island intact, with its beauty unmarred by development.

- ✔ **A chance to experience the Caribbean that used to be:** Escaping from the Sandals resorts, you can still find tranquil towns and uncrowded beaches in the vast wilds of St. Lucia. Plus, you're treated to one of the most magnificent coastlines in the West Indies.

- ✔ **Luxurious living:** For those who seek the posh, pampered life, where everything is done for you in an elegant setting, St. Lucia offers a series of spectacular resorts, with such amenities as spa treatments, private pools fed by waterfalls, and double hammocks with panoramic views of the Pitons.

 But also consider the following:

- ✔ **The corruption of mass tourism:** At one time, St. Lucians were known as the most hospitable people in the southern Caribbean. The struggle for the Yankee dollar has made many of them belligerent. Sometimes guides denounce you if you refuse their services.

- ✔ **A capital devoid of style:** Forget colonial charm in Castries, which was swept away by two devastasting fires. As rebuilt, the place is bland and utilitarian and doesn't entice with its architecture or shopping like, say, St. Thomas does.

- ✔ **All-inclusive resorts harming local restaurants:** The all-meals-inclusive requirements of the megaresorts are driving island eateries featuring the rich produce of the island — everything from mangoes to breadfruit — out of business. Groaning resort buffets are obliterating the true Creole flavor of the island's cuisine.

Searching out Sint Maarten/St. Martin

Since 1648, this dual-nation island has claimed two colonial masters: the Netherlands (Sint Maarten) and France (St. Martin). Regardless of how you spell the name, both sides of the unguarded international border comprise the same island — though the two halves are quite different.

The Dutch side contains the island's major airport and more shops and tourist facilities than the other side, and the French side has some of the most posh hotels and superior food. Both sides are modern, urbanized, and cosmopolitan. And both suffer from traffic jams, a lack of parking space in the capitals, tourist-industry burnout (especially on the Dutch side), and a disturbing increase in crime. In spite of the drawbacks, Sint Maarten/St. Martin offers plenty to attract: great beaches, some of the best dining and shopping in the Caribbean, gambling, nightlife, self-contained resorts, and nonstop flights from the U.S. From this island, you can fly over for a daytrip to St. Eustatius or Saba.

We strongly suggest that you stay on the French side, as it has better restaurants, a more-authentic island atmosphere, and is more laid-back.

You can find shopping bargains galore on both sides of the island nations. What you rarely encounter, however, are inexpensive tariffs charged by hotels or low-cost restaurant prices. The cost of food and lodging makes Sint Maarten and St. Martin high-priced destinations. To save money, you might consider a package deal.

Top aspects of a vacation on Sint Maarten/St. Martin include

- ✔ **Prime beaches:** With a full range of water sports, the island is known for its white sandy beaches — more than three dozen. During your stay, you can try at least a different one every day, including **Cupecoy Bay Beach,** close to the Dutch-French border on the western side of the island.

- ✔ **Shopping bargains galore:** Dutch Sint Maarten is a free port, as it has no local sales tax. Prices on certain merchandise (such as watches and crystal) are often the lowest in the Caribbean — at times even better than St. Thomas. On French St. Martin, check out all those little shopping arcades carrying duty-free imports, such as jewelry and perfume, directly from Paris.

- ✔ **A gourmet adventure:** On the French side of the island, the cuisine is often sublime, although many quality meals can be had on the Dutch side as well. In the peak of the winter months, 747s wing in from Paris with cargoes of epicurean supplies. Some of the top chefs in France, wanting a winter vacation, become chefs here in high season.

But also consider the following:

- ✔ **A rising crime rate:** Crime has become a serious problem, and muggings are frequent, especially on little-traveled roads at night and on semideserted beaches.

- ✔ **Serious overdevelopment:** Both sides of the island are among the most populous in the Caribbean — so much so that traveling through the congested capitals is maddening. Developers have destroyed much of the island's natural scenic beauty.

- ✔ **Uneven hotel service:** Don't always expect top service, even at the finer resorts. Resorts on both sides of the island seem more interested at times in selling timeshare slots than in providing good service to their hotel guests. Some establishments depend on back-to-back charter bookings, which means personal service has more or less disappeared.

Venturing into the U.S. Virgin Islands

Blessed with about 300 sunny days a year, the U.S. Virgin Islands (USVIs) have deservedly been dubbed America's Paradise. The island group encompasses St. Thomas, St. John (our personal favorite), and St. Croix, plus another 50 islets and cays, most of them uninhabited.

As an American territory, the USVIs are a breeze for U.S. citizens to visit. English is spoken everywhere, the currency is the dollar, and you don't need a passport. What's also cool is that you can easily and conveniently visit more than one of these beautiful islands, which are awash in flowers ranging from brilliantly colored bougainvillea to fragrant jasmine to the cheekily named "jump-up-and-kiss-me" that has ruby-red blossoms. And you'll *want* to visit more than one, because they each have such distinctive personalities. In fact, we highly recommend arranging your trip with all three islands on the agenda. If you only have a week, though, pick two and save the third for next time.

In the U.S. Virgin Islands, you don't have the sheer number of islands of the neighboring British Virgin Islands, but you find plenty to roam.

Top aspects of a vacation in the USVIs include

- ✔ **Spectacular beaches:** All three islands have glorious ones, especially St. John. Both diving and snorkeling are generally excellent.

- ✔ **Duty-free shopping:** The islands — St. Thomas is king of the hill — are known for bargains on liquor, crystal, china, linens, and perfumes. The duty-free allowance is $1,200 a person, three times that of most other Caribbean islands.

- ✔ **American comfort:** If you're coming from the United States, you get an easy introduction to the Caribbean.

- ✔ **Top-notch water sports and sailing:** Consistent trade winds, deep cruising waters, and dozens of safe anchorages make the USVIs and neighboring BVIs a pleasure to sail or fish.

But also consider the following:

- ✔ **The (sometimes) madding crowds:** The shopping area in Charlotte Amalie (the capital of St. Thomas) is claustrophobic when the cruise ships disgorge.

- ✔ **The need to be on guard:** Travelers should use caution — and taxis — around Charlotte Amalie and Christiansted (the capital of St. Croix) at night.

- ✔ **Too much like home:** If seeing all-too-familiar fast-food joints clashes with your dream of the tropics, St. Thomas probably isn't for you. Pockets of St. Croix are industrial as well.

✔ **Hurricanes:** Unlike Aruba, the U.S. Virgins lie in the major path of hurricanes. These violent storms periodically sweep across the islands, destroying property, uprooting trees, and damaging beaches. Not only must you avoid the USVIs when hurricane warnings go up, but you often have to make other plans in the wake of massive destruction.

Check out the following sections for more details on each individual island.

A shopper's dream: St. Thomas

Known for its duty-free shopping, gourmet restaurants, busy nightlife, golf courses, and sandy beaches, St. Thomas is by far the most cosmopolitan of the trio — and the most touristy. Frenetic energy courses through the busy and historic capital, Charlotte Amalie (pronounced ah-*mahl*-yah), where jungle-thatched hills and red-tile roofed houses surround a sapphire-blue harbor punctuated with every kind of craft, from sailboats to gargantuan cruise ships.

The main shopping area is limited to a few congested waterfront streets, but it's great for strolling around. A mind-boggling number of jewelry shops clamor for your attention, giving away cheap gems to lure you in.

If you're the type who simply must feel a strong U.S. connection no matter where you are, St. Thomas will satisfy that need. Like any heavily populated U.S. city, Charlotte Amalie battles crime and grime, but commonsense precautions will suffice.

St. Thomas boasts one of the Caribbean's more famous beaches: **Magens Bay,** a broad, U-shaped inlet edged by a mile of sugar-white sand. Whether you crave the reliable luxury of the Ritz-Carlton or want to cook your own meals in a bare-bones condo, you can find something to suit your wallet.

Mother Nature's prized son: St. John

Although it's a mere 15-minute ferry ride away from St. Thomas, St. John feels like another world when you step onto the dock at Cruz Bay. Nature reigns supreme on lush St. John, which was largely transformed (two-thirds of it) into a national park in 1956 and boasts challenging hills ideal for hiking and turquoise waters perfect for snorkeling. On the island's North Coast, the necklace of pearl-white beaches ranks among the world's best, including **Hawksnest, Trunk Bay** (whose coral reefs have been trammeled by too many tourists of late), and **Cinnamon Bay.**

Although neighboring St. Thomas wins the prize for the most shops, St. John gets our vote for the most intriguing — especially those at **Mongoose Junction.** Almost 200 of the island's 5,000 residents put "artist" on their tax returns. You can find some real treasures here. And for such a small island, its restaurant scene is surprisingly happening — the laid-back nightlife has a collegial feel to it.

St. John is renowned for its eco-tents — visitors who are in the know reserve tents in its popular campgrounds at least eight months in advance. The island's selection of villas is dazzling, too. Its two traditional luxury resorts — the venerable, old-money **Caneel Bay** and newer **Westin St. John** — have plenty of fans as well. Count us among them. In other words, no matter where you stay on St. John, you'd have to be a grouch not to have fun.

For city slickers and tree huggers alike: St. Croix

The largest of the three islands, St. Croix sometimes gets overlooked, but we prefer it to the overdeveloped St. Thomas. St. Croix gives you the best of the other two. It has the beautiful architecture of Charlotte Amalie in its two towns, with a nice selection of shops and good restaurants. You can walk the streets and get a sense of history without being distracted by commercialism. St. Croix's natural beauty hasn't been swallowed up by development, either. In fact, its agricultural roots are still much in evidence.

Sixty-four kilometers (40 miles) and a 20-minute plane hop to the south of St. Thomas, St. Croix presents a dazzling montage of scenery: powdery, white-sand beaches; cactus-dotted plains; mangrove swamps; stands of mahogany trees; and rain forests. Christiansted, the capital, still has traces of architecture from 200 years ago when it was the centerpiece of the Danish West Indies, with waterfront arcades and an imposing ocher fort at its heart. Rent a car for at least a day or two and just explore. You'll find botanical gardens, abandoned sugar mills, an artist who uses naturally fallen trees to carve island-style furniture, and Great Houses in various stages of restoration. Another good way to see the island is by horseback or by bicycle.

Not as popular with the cruise ships, St. Croix yields more opportunities for finding your own little private strand of sand. About 3km (2 miles) off the Northeast Shore, you can rest assured of claiming uncrowded territory. Have a champagne picnic for two on the beach of uninhabited **Buck Island,** a wooded nature preserve administered by the U.S. National Park Service. Nearby is a coral reef that President Kennedy declared the nation's first underwater national park.

Visiting More than One Island

If you've never been to the Caribbean before, the thought of visiting more than one island can be overwhelming; besides, a visit to the Caribbean forces you to relax so that you may not want to leave the comfort of your chaise longue (or the convenience of your swim-up bar). But island hopping can be surprisingly easy, depending on where you decide to go. **American Airlines** and **Air Jamaica** have generous programs that make hitting more than one island quite reasonable (see Chapter 5). Or you usually can catch a small regional carrier for less than $100.

Both Puerto Rico and Jamaica are so large that you'll be too busy to go anywhere else, but here's the scoop on the islands that lend themselves to island hopping:

- **Aruba:** As we noted earlier in this chapter, two other Dutch islands are a short ride in a puddle-jumper away from Aruba. You can either visit Bonaire or Curaçao, but we wouldn't recommend trying to cram all three into your schedule.

- **Barbados:** Visitors to Barbados may consider spending a few days on St. Lucia (and vice versa), which is a quick flight away but an entirely different experience and one of our favorite islands for romance.

- **The British Virgin Islands and the U.S. Virgin Islands:** Indeed, in the BVIs you won't be able to keep yourself from island hopping. Boat travel between islands is frequent, and the islands lie so close to each other that you can literally see neighboring islands from the one you're standing on, a temptation that appeals to the explorer in all of us. With the USVIs, it's a tossup, but we recommend visiting at least two of the three. For that matter, as long as you have your passport, you can go back and forth between the BVIs and USVIs by boat or plane.

- **Grand Cayman:** Hard-core divers may be lured from Grand Cayman to one of its smaller, laid-back sister islands, Little Cayman or Cayman Brac.

Chapter 3

Deciding When to Go

- -

In This Chapter

▶ Evaluating the seasons
▶ Forecasting the weather, island by island
▶ Planning your trip around festivals and carnivals

- -

*W*hen most people think of the Caribbean, they think of a place where they can escape winter's chill. The truth is, the Caribbean makes a magnificent vacation destination year-round. In fact, summer is one of our favorite times to visit. We enjoy the quick shower bursts followed by beautiful skies, rainbows, and gorgeous sunsets. In the broadest terms, the weather in this part of the world is tropical, warm, humid, and sometimes rainy.

In this chapter, we demystify the hotel lingo about seasons and explain the connection between the timing of your trip and the related expenses that you can expect to pay. We also give you an honest assessment of the dreaded *h* word — *hurricane* — and what it means for your Caribbean getaway. Finally, we tell you about the climates of the different islands and about the timing of various festivals and carnivals.

Revealing the Secrets of the Seasons

When you plan a trip to the Caribbean, you can expect to encounter lots of talk about seasons: The Season (holiday season), high season, low season, shoulder season, and hurricane season. For a place where the leaves don't change and the temperature rarely budges more than a few degrees either direction from around 27°C (80°F), you'll hear the word *season* tossed about an awful lot. All the Caribbean islands have similar seasons with slight weather variations.

 The reason seasons matter in the Caribbean has virtually nothing to do with the weather and everything to do with your room rate. For example, published room rates for a resort may include as many as a half-dozen different prices listed for the exact same accommodations. What you pay depends on exactly when you visit; timing is everything when it comes to a Caribbean vacation.

Generally, seasonal differences break down something like this, but keep in mind that they have lots of variations:

- ✔ **Holiday season (also known as The Season):** December 15 to January 3

- ✔ **High season:** January 4 to April 14

- ✔ **Shoulder season:** April 15 to May 30 and September 1 to December 14

- ✔ **Low season:** May 30 to August 31

- ✔ **Hurricane season (overlaps with shoulder and low seasons):** June 1 to November 30

Holiday season and high season

The Caribbean's high season heats up right before Christmas and lasts through mid-April. During the holiday season, referred to on the upscale islands as simply "The Season," longtime guests often snatch up reservations for the best lodgings years in advance. At Christmastime, Jamaica's exclusive **Round Hill** once turned away James Bond — er, Pierce Brosnan, who once played the character originally conceived by author Ian Fleming at his home on Jamaica. So, if you're going to a resort in Barbados or the British Virgin Islands (BVIs) around the holidays, be prepared to make your plans well in advance.

The better hotels often have minimum-stay requirements in effect during the holiday season and stringent cancellation policies. If you plan a trip during the holidays, make your reservations as early as possible, expect crowds, and plan to pay top dollar for everything.

The last two weeks of January sometimes provide a slight lull in tourism, but high season shifts back into high gear in February and March, the busiest months in the Caribbean.

The forecast: If you're craving an escape and don't mind planning ahead and shelling out the bucks — rates reach their peak the last two weeks of December — this blast of sunshine will cure your midwinter blues.

In-season advantages

If you live in northern climes that are swept with wintry blizzards, nothing is more appealing in brutal February than visions of a white sandy beach, a brilliant sun, and a palm tree–studded Caribbean island. Here are a few advantages of fulfilling that desire:

- ✔ The winter weather in the Caribbean is considered as close to perfection as anywhere on the planet. The temperature rarely dips below 21°C (70°F).

✔ All restaurants, services, sports activities, entertainment, shops, and facilities operate at full blast from mid-December to mid-April.

✔ The timing is ideal for singles and honeymooners because families with children are gone and a more romantic atmosphere prevails.

✔ Both the rainy season and the hurricane season are over. Except for that rare cloudy day, you mostly have sand, sea, and sunshine.

✔ The cuisine at resorts is better than ever. Top chefs from both Europe and America are brought in during the winter months to tempt your palates.

In-season disadvantages

Of course, vacationing in the Caribbean during the in-season does have a downside:

✔ You'll have to get used to people crowding you in airport lounges, on the most popular beaches, at the all-inclusive resorts, at groaning buffet tables, at the best restaurants, and in the casinos.

✔ If you plan a winter visit, reservations are vastly important — at resorts, car-rental agencies, nightclubs, the best restaurants, and even sports activities such as scuba-diving courses.

✔ Hotel rates peak in-season, especially around the Christmas holidays. You'll pay top dollar for *everything,* from your bedroom to your car rental. Nothing, not even merchandise in shops, is reduced in winter.

✔ Expect a more frantic pace at the resorts when the house count reaches maximum capacity. Personalized service goes the way of the trade winds.

Shoulder season

In the shoulder seasons — late spring and the fall — prices are sometimes slightly reduced. Shoulder season is ideal if you want to go at a quiet time, because children are in school and few families are on the islands.

This rule has an exception, however: Between the Easter holidays and spring break, April is an extremely tough and expensive time to book a vacation on Puerto Rico. You may also have difficulties booking in Aruba, Montego Bay and Negril (Jamaica), and St. Thomas (U.S. Virgin Islands) at this time.

Some smaller resorts and restaurants close for repairs and maintenance in July, August, September, or October. So before you take an expensive taxi ride over to a top restaurant, call first to make sure it's open. You still need to make reservations for the most popular places anyway.

We've never found more than a few places shuttered, and lots of other options have always been available. The islands where closures could be a problem are the smaller ones like Nevis and Anguilla (we cover neither in this guide). We ran into a newlywed couple that had left The Four Seasons on Nevis to come to The Ritz-Carlton, St. Thomas, because they were so limited in their dining choices on tiny Nevis. "Everything was closed, and there wasn't anything to do," the young bride told us.

Rate reductions of 10 to 20 percent beat holiday season charges, but they're not as economical as in low season. In April and May, the weather barely differs from the bright sunshine of winter months, but in the early fall — especially September — you have to consider the possibility of hurricanes and tropical storms (unless you've decided on Aruba, which is below the hurricane belt).

Low season

If you come during the low season (or, as we call it, the slow season), rates drop like an anchor. Rates decrease as much as 60 percent in June, July, and August, making even some of the more exclusive resorts affordable. Travelers often make the assumption that because the Caribbean is so deliciously warm in the winter, it must be searingly hot in the summer. (That's not the case.)

Because school is out and bargains for families abound, you see lots of kids during low season — especially from Europe. On some islands, several hotels and resorts band together with the tourist boards during the summer months to offer super deals for families and honeymooners.

In the last few years, the Caribbean has finally begun convincing people that it's a year-round destination. Despite that self-promotion, finding a hotel room in the low season is pretty easy. Booking your flight, however, may not be as simple. Many nationals go home to visit during the summer — flights to Jamaica are especially full. And Europeans, who have much longer vacations than Americans, frequent the Caribbean in summer months. Reserve your flight as soon as you pick your destination.

If you have your heart set on a particular restaurant, call or e-mail ahead so you aren't disappointed. Chefs often take their vacations in the summer months (especially Aug).

Tropical storms can kick up quickly in Caribbean summers, but they usually pass just as fast, leaving brilliant blue skies in their wake.

Off-season advantages

Although the Caribbean may appear inviting during the winter to those who live in northern climates, your trip may be more enjoyable if you go in the off season:

✔ A less-hurried way of life prevails. You have a better chance to appreciate food, culture, and customs.

✔ Swimming pools and beaches are less crowded — perhaps not crowded at all.

✔ Resorts offer amenities, which may include snorkeling, boating, and scuba diving, year-round — often at reduced rates off season.

✔ Resort boutiques often feature summer sales, hoping to clear excess merchandise.

✔ You can often appear without a reservation at a top restaurant and get a table.

✔ The endless waiting game is over: no waiting for a rental car, tee time, or tennis court.

✔ Some package-tour fares are as much as 20 percent lower, and individual excursion fares are also reduced between 5 and 10 percent.

✔ Accommodations and flights may be easier to book.

✔ The very best of attractions — sea, sand, and surf, with lots of sunshine — remain undiminished in the off season.

Off-season disadvantages

We don't want to paint too rosy a picture, though. Although the advantages of off-season travel outweigh the disadvantages, summer travel has its drawbacks:

✔ You may be staying at a construction site. Caribbean hoteliers save serious repairs and major renovations until the off season.

✔ Hotels and resorts may be operating with reduced staffs, so services are often reduced.

✔ Not all restaurants and bars are fully operational at resorts.

Hurricane season

Part of the Caribbean's low season dovetails with the hurricane season, which officially runs from June 1 to November 30, with September being the peak time for a hurricane to hit. Of course, the rainy season also mirrors hurricane season, though it doesn't last as long on some islands. Fortunately, in the tropics, rainstorms typically pass over rapidly.

We travel to the Caribbean all the time during hurricane season, because we find the best bargains then. In all these years, we've only been evacuated once, and it turned out to be for nothing (luckily for St. Croix). Of course, you have no guarantee, and our good fortune certainly won't make you feel better if you're the one being sent packing by the storm.

Hurricane lingo

Confused by all the hurricane lingo tossed around on The Weather Channel (www.weather.com)? Here's a rundown of that weather-expert language.

Hurricanes are rated by the following categories:

- **Category 5** is the most dangerous, packing winds of more than 135 knots (155 mph), which produce storm tides of more than 5.4m (18 ft.). That's strong enough to drive a palm frond through a coconut tree.

- **Category 4** has winds of 113 to 135 knots (130–155 mph) with a storm surge of 3.9 to 5.4m (13–18 ft.).

- **Category 3** has winds between 96 and 113 knots (110 and 130 mph) and a storm surge of 2.7 to 3.6m (9–12 ft.).

- **Category 2** has winds from 83 to 96 knots (96–110 mph) with a storm surge of 1.8 to 2.4m (6–8 ft.).

- **Category 1** has winds of 64 to 82 knots (74–95 mph) with a storm surge of 1.2 to 1.5m (4–5 ft.).

When the weather forecasters talk about *tropical storms,* they mean a distinct circulation with winds not exceeding 64 knots (74 mph). Tropical storms can quickly turn into hurricanes and vice versa. As a hurricane loses strength, weathercasters define its intensity as a tropical storm.

Fortunately, modern tracking systems allow early warnings when a hurricane is approaching. So, unlike the old days when islanders were caught completely unaware, guests and residents alike can have at least four or five days' notice to get ready and decide what course of action to take. Other good news: Buildings have been reconstructed with more hurricane-resistant materials, enabling resorts in recent years to bounce back more quickly when they do get hit.

If a hurricane does threaten when you're in the Caribbean, hoteliers will provide as much information as possible so you can make an informed choice about whether to stay or go. If you decide to leave, ask your concierge to call the airport as soon as possible to get a flight out. Don't try to get a few more hours in at the pool, because flights fill up quickly.

The best source for detailed and up-to-date information is the **National Hurricane Center** Web site at www.nhc.noaa.gov. If you want to see what hurricane seasons have been like most recently, check the site at www.usatoday.com. You can find good advice on what to do in the event of a hurricane as well as predictions and current reports at www.fema.gov.

Finally, a great place to see what the weather experts are predicting is at http://typhoon.atmos.colostate.edu.

Here are some other good Web sites for weather information:

> ✔ **WeatherNet's Tropical Weather** is the largest collection of tropical weather Web site links. Find it at www.wunderground.com/tropical.

> ✔ **Caribbean Weather Man** is based on Tortola on the BVIs and gives good information about that region, particularly for sailors. Check out www.caribwx.com.

> ✔ **Caribbean Hurricane Network** has chat rooms and local correspondents on the islands where you can get the real scoop. Check out www.stormcarib.com.

 When you set up a trip months in advance, you have no way to predict the weather. However, you can take some precautions to make sure that you're not hung out to dry. If you're traveling to an island where hurricanes sometimes hit, ask the hotel to fax (or e-mail) you its hurricane policy — just in case. Larger, more affluent properties are much more likely to give credits toward future travel.

SuperClubs (☎ **877-GO-SUPER,** 877-467-8737; www.superclubs.com), which operates properties in Jamaica, The Bahamas, St. Kitts, Brazil, Dominican Republic, and Curaçao, introduced a No Hurricane Guarantee that gives guests full reimbursement for the total value of disrupted nights and issues a voucher for a future stay for the same number of nights to be used during the same month the following year. Meanwhile, the Blue Chip Hurricane Guarantee offered by **Sandals** (☎ **888-SANDALS** or 888-726-3257; 305-284-1300; www.sandals.com) and **Beaches** (☎ **888-BEACHES** or 888-232-2437; 876-975-7330; www.beaches.com) provides guests with a replacement vacation if a hurricane directly hits a property and the all-inclusive activities are disrupted. You can take the replacement vacation at the Sandals or Beaches resort of your choice, and you also get free round-trip airfare.

 Smaller properties often don't give refunds — no matter what. We strongly urge you to consider buying **trip interruption/cancellation insurance,** which covers everything from hurricanes to missed connections due to snowstorms snarling air traffic stateside. (See Chapter 8 for more on purchasing insurance.)

If you hear that a storm has struck the Caribbean, and your island vacation is on the horizon, don't panic. Remember that the region takes up 1 million square miles. Fretting over a hurricane on St. Thomas when you're going to Aruba is like someone in Chicago freaking out over a tornado in Texas. Unfortunately, U.S. weather reports are often vague and inflammatory and talk about the Caribbean as one big mass.

If you're truly concerned, put in a quick call directly to your hotel — not the toll-free reservation number, which is usually in the U.S. Don't ask a general question about hurricane damage to the island. Ask specifics such as

✔ Do you have any water damage?

✔ How's your beach? (Sometimes an island doesn't have to suffer a direct hit from a hurricane to have damage to its beaches.)

✔ Are all your facilities open? (Restaurants, bars, and water-sports facilities near the beach are often likely to suffer damage.)

✔ If the property has been damaged, when will everything be back in order?

The forecast: As long as a hurricane doesn't blow in and you don't arrive in the middle of a week of rain, this season is a good time to snag terrific deals.

Weathering an Endless Summer

Aruba is the hottest Caribbean island and the one where you'll find sunshine practically guaranteed. St. Croix is the runner-up in terms of the least rainfall. Aruba gets a mere 43cm (17 in.) of rain a year, while Jamaica gets 198cm (78 in.). Table 3-1 shows what you can expect weather-wise in 11 island locations.

Even on the greener islands like Jamaica and both sets of Virgin Islands, rain showers tend to be brief. We've never once found ourselves stuck inside for an entire day because of rain. But just in case, **SuperClubs** (☎ **877-GO-SUPER,** or 877-467-8737; www.superclubs.com) has a Jamaica Sunshine Guarantee, which means that for any day the sun doesn't show its face, guests are issued a credit voucher for that day's value (good for one year) toward another SuperClubs vacation.

The trade winds are always blowing in the Caribbean, keeping the temperatures mild. In fact, you may feel slightly cool walking on the beach at night, exploring a rain forest, hiking in the mountains, or dining in an overly air-conditioned restaurant.

The year-round average water temperature in the Caribbean is a warm 25°C (77°F) and reaches a bathlike 29°C (84°F) or so in summer. Surf conditions are localized, so if the waves or undertow are threatening on your beach, you can usually find sheltered, calmer waters by taking a short walk. Ask the hotel staff for recommendations.

Table 3-1

Weather Averages

Island	Summer Temperature	Winter Temperature	Annual Rainfall	Rainiest Months	Summer Water Temperature	Winter Water Temperature
Aruba	29°C (84°F)	27°C (81°F)	43cm (17 in.)	Oct–Dec	28°C (82°F)	28°C (82°F)
Barbados	28°C (82°F)	26°C (79°F)	119cm (47 in.)	June–Nov	28°C (82°F)	26°C (79°F)
BVIs	30°C (86°F)	27°C (81°F)	152cm (60 in.)	May–Nov	28°C (82°F)	26°C (79°F)
Grand Cayman	29°C (84°F)	24°C (75°F)	152cm (60 in.)	May–Oct	29°C (84°F)	26°C (79°F)
Jamaica	29°C (84°F)	27°C (81°F)	198cm (78 in.)	May–Oct	28°C (82°F)	26°C (79°F)
Puerto Rico	28°C (82°F)	25°C (77°F)	157cm (62 in.)	May–Nov	28°C (82°F)	26°C (79°F)
St. Croix	29°C (84°F)	26°C (79°F)	102cm (40 in.)	Aug–Oct	28°C (82°F)	26°C (79°F)
St. John	28°C (82°F)	25°C (77°F)	137cm (54 in.)	Aug–Oct	28°C (82°F)	26°C (79°F)
St. Lucia	28°C (82°F)	27°C (81°F)	152cm (60 in.)	July–Jan	28°C (82°F)	28°C (82°F)
Sint Maarten/St. Martin	29°C (84°F)	27°C (81°F)	104cm (41 in.)	July–Nov	28°C (82°F)	27°C (81°F)
St. Thomas	29°C (84°F)	26°C (79°F)	112cm (44 in.)	Aug–Oct	28°C (82°F)	26°C (79°F)

Perusing a Calendar of Events

As you consider when to go to the Caribbean, take a look at a calendar of ever-popular festivals — from jazz to reggae to Carnival — which can complicate the business of booking flights and hotel rooms. Because these dates change and more festivals seem to crop up each year, check with the tourist board of the island you intend to visit to make sure that you don't unexpectedly run into throngs of festival-goers — or to make sure you don't miss out on the fun.

Jamaica's **Ocho Rios Jazz Festival** (www.ochoriosjazz.com; mid-June) and **Sumfest** (July; see the listing later in this section) rank among the most popular events, while every Tuesday evening year-round Aruba celebrates the **Bonbini Festival** at Fort Zoutman with traditional dancing and music.

January

Barbados's **Paint-It-Jazz Festival** is one of the Caribbean's premier jazz events — a weekend jammed with performances by international artists, jazz legends, and local talent. For information, visit www.barbados.org/events; for tickets, e-mail bdosjazz@caribsurf.com. Mid-January.

The decade-old **St. Lucia Regatta** attracts yachties and others to Rodney Bay from throughout the Caribbean with its combination of racing and fun parties. For more information on the festival, visit www.slucia.com/regatta. Mid-January.

February

Colorful **Carnival** events whirl through Aruba's streets — kicked off by a children's parade — during a two-week period. Carnival usually occurs in February, but the dates vary from year to year. For the schedule of events, call ☎ **800-TO-ARUBA** (800-862-7822) or check the Web site at www.aruba.com.

The weeklong **Holetown Festival** (www.barbados.org) is held at the fairgrounds in Holetown to commemorate the date in 1627 when the first European settlers arrived in Barbados. Food, carnival rides, the Royal Barbados Police Force Band, and mounted troops add to the enjoyment. For further information, call ☎ **246-427-2623**. Mid-February.

San Juan residents *(Sanjuaneros)* and visitors alike eagerly look forward to the annual five-day **Casals Festival** (www.festcasalspr.gobierno.pr), the Caribbean's most celebrated cultural event. The bill at San Juan's Performing Arts Center includes a glittering array of international guest conductors, orchestras, and soloists who come to honor the memory of Pablo Casals, the renowned cellist and founder of the festival who was born in Spain to a Puerto Rican mother. Casals also founded the Puerto Rico Symphony Orchestra.

Ticket prices range from $25 to $50 per concert (you get a 20 percent discount if you purchase four or more tickets). Students, people over age 60, and those with disabilities can buy tickets at a 50 percent discount. Tickets are available through the Performing Arts Center in San Juan — call ☎ 787-620-4444. Information is also available from the **Puerto Rico Tourism Company,** 666 Fifth Ave., New York, NY 10103 (☎ 800-223-6530, 212-586-6262). The festivities take place late February to early March.

March

Barbados hosts three weeks of opera, concerts, and theatrical performances during **Holder's Opera Season.** The open-air theater at Holder's House, St. James, seats 600, and the program has won acclaim for its productions, which have included headliner Luciano Pavarotti. For information, call ☎ **246-432-6385** or fax 246-432-6461; www.holders.net. Throughout March.

The **International Rolex Cup Regatta** is one of three regattas in the Caribbean Ocean Racing Triangle (CORT) series. Top-ranked international racers come to the U.S. Virgin Island St. Thomas to compete in front of the world's yachting press. The St. Thomas Yacht Club hosts the three-day event. For more information, call ☎ **340-775-6320** or visit www.rolexcupregatta.com. Last week in March.

The British Virgin Islands' **Spring Regatta** is a sailor's dream, with three days of sailboat races surrounded by seven days of partying during the Spring Festival. It attracts boating enthusiasts from around the world (☎ **284-494-3286;** Fax: 284-494-6117; www.bvispringregatta.org). Late March through early April.

April

During Grand Cayman's colorful **Batabano Carnival,** revelers dress up as dancing flowers and swimming stingrays. For more information, call ☎ **345-949-7121** or visit www.caymancarnival.com. Mid-April.

Dubbed the "World's Greatest Street Party," Barbados's **De Congaline Carnival** is a festive celebration of music, dance, and local arts and crafts. The highlight is the Caribbean's longest conga line. For information, contact the Barbados Tourism Authority (☎ **246-427-2623;** Fax: 246-424-0909; www.barbados.org). End of April.

May

Gospelfest in Barbados features performances by gospel headliners from around the world. For information, contact the Barbados Tourism Authority (☎ **246-427-2623;** Fax: 246-424-0909; www.barbados.org). Last week in May.

June

If you want to see an utterly British parade spiced with island-style panache, check out the **Queen's Birthday Bash** (June 14) on Grand Cayman. At the sport-fishing competitions in **Million Dollar Month,** huge cash prizes are awarded, including one for a quarter of a million dollars given to the angler who breaks the existing Blue Marlin record. Contact the Department of Tourism for more information (☎ 345-949-0623; Fax: 345-949-4053; www.caymanislands.ky). Month of June.

For world-class windsurfing, check out the **Hi-Winds World Challenge at Hadakurari.** Contact the Aruba Tourism Authority at ☎ 800-TO-ARUBA (800-862-7822) or visit www.aruba.com. Last week in June.

The British Virgin Islands' **HIHO** (Hook In & Hang On), a windsurfing and sailing competition, welcomes a fleet of 100 windsurfers who cover 150 miles during races. Contact the tourist board at ☎ 800-835-8530 or 284-494-3134, or visit www.bviwelcome.com. End of June.

July

Elements of Carnival are combined with emancipation and independence celebrations in the festive **Carnival in St. John,** which culminates on July 4 with a big parade. Thousands of St. Thomas residents flock here for the parades, calypso bands, colorful costumes, and everything else leading up to the selection of Ms. St. John and the King of the Carnival. Call the St. John tourist office at ☎ 340-776-6450 for more details. First week of July.

Dating back to the 19th century, the **Crop Over Festival** in Barbados, a month-long event beginning in early July, marks the end of the sugar cane harvest with competitions, music and dancing, Bajan food, and arts and crafts. The grand finale of Crop Over is a huge carnival parade on Kadoonment Day (the first Mon in Aug), which is a national holiday and the biggest party day of the year; visitors are welcome to participate. Contact the Barbados Tourism Authority (☎ 246-427-2623; www.barbados.org). Early July to August.

Jamaica's **Reggae Sumfest** (www.reggaesumfest.com) is a reggae party that draws top names, including the late Bob Marley's children. For information, contact the Jamaican Tourist Board at ☎ 800-233-4JTB (800-233-4582) or 876-929-9200; www.visitjamaica.com. Mid-to-late July.

The British Virgin Islands' two-week **Emancipation Festival** features calypso shows, pageants, arts and crafts, and more. Contact the tourist board at ☎ 800-835-8530 or 284-494-3134, or visit www.bviwelcome.com. Late July to August.

October

The carnival-like atmosphere of **Pirates Week** on Grand Cayman actually lasts ten days and includes a mock invasion of Hog Sty Bay by a mock

Blackbeard and company. Visitors and locals dress up like pirates and wenches; music, fireworks, and a variety of competitions take place islandwide. Kids participate, too. Contact the tourism department (☎ **345-949-0623;** Fax: 345-949-4053; www.caymanislands.ky). End of October.

November

Parades and a joint ceremony officiated by French and Dutch leaders at Border Monument obelisk commemorate the long-standing peaceful coexistence of both countries during **Sint Maarten Day/St. Martin's Day.** The 20-mile "Around the Island" race is based on historical folklore about how the island's two-nation border was established. It also denotes the start of high season. Contact the tourist office for Sint Maarten (☎ **599-542-2337;** www.st-maarten.com) or St. Martin (☎ **590-590-87-57-21;** www.st-martin.org). November 11.

December

The best local *fungi* (Caribbean folk music performed with homemade instruments) bands compete at the **Scratch/Fungi Band Fiesta** on Tortola, BVI. Contact the tourist board at ☎ **800-835-8530** or 284-494-3134, or visit the Web site at www.bviwelcome.com. Late December.

Part II

Planning Your Trip to the Caribbean

The 5th Wave   By Rich Tennant

"Don't worry, they may be called St. Croix, St. Thomas, and St. John, but you're not required to act like a saint while you're there."

In this part . . .

So you've decided which islands you want to visit and what time of year to go. Now what? In this part, we give you advice for booking the trip of your dreams. We help you determine the fastest and most economic ways to travel to your destination.

We also show you how to estimate the cost of your trip and keep it within your budget. We walk you through the details you need to know to have a smooth travel experience. Finally, we give some advice for travelers who have special interests.

Chapter 4

Managing Your Money

*W*e know that money can be a delicate subject, so we've tried to make this chapter as painless as possible. We think that you'll be pleasantly surprised to know how *un*complicated money issues are when vacationing in the Caribbean. Making purchases is really no more difficult than when vacationing in, say, Las Vegas.

In this chapter, we work through the basic elements of planning a budget for your vacation by unveiling the hidden costs that could trip you up. We also show you how to cut costs without trimming your fun.

Planning Your Budget

We know that thinking about how much all this Caribbean fun is going to cost is probably the last thing you want to do. We don't want to throw a wet beach towel on your exotic dreams, but we actually think you'll be relieved after you work through the numbers.

Budgeting for your Caribbean vacation isn't difficult, but keeping a close eye on costs is another matter. A good way to get a handle on potential costs is to start the tally from the moment you leave home. Walk yourself mentally through the trip:

✔ Transportation to your nearest airport

✔ Flight cost

✔ Transportation from the airport to your hotel

✔ Hotel rate per day

✔ Meals (exclude these if they're included in the hotel rate)

✔ Activities, shopping, and nightlife

After you've done all that, add on another 15 to 20 percent for good measure.

In Table 4-1, we tell you what things cost on Puerto Rico, one of the Caribbean's most popular spots and a moderately priced destination. Estimate costs to be roughly 20 percent less for a lower-priced destination like Jamaica and roughly 20 percent more for a pricey destination like Barbados. For tax info, see "Taking Taxes into Account," later in this chapter, and to find out which currencies are (and aren't) accepted on the islands, see "Handling Money," later in this chapter.

Table 4-1	What Things Cost in Puerto Rico		
	US$	**UK£**	**CD$**
Taxi from Airport to Condado	$13	£6.85	CD$14.95
Average Taxi Fare within San Juan	$6	£3.20	CD$6.90
Typical Bus Fare within San Juan	25¢–50¢	13p–26p	29¢–57¢
Local Telephone Call	10¢	5p	11¢
Double Room at the Condado Plaza (very expensive)	$350	£184	CD$401
Double Room at El Canario by the Lagoon (moderate)	$115	£60.95	CD$132
Double Room at Wind Chimes Inn (inexpensive)	$99	£52	CD$113
Lunch for One at Amadeus (moderate)	$16	£8.40	CD$18.30
Lunch for One at Fatty's (inexpensive)	$10	£5.25	CD$11.45
Dinner for One at Ramiro's (very expensive)	$50	£26.30	CD$57.30
Dinner for One at Ostra Cosa (moderate)	$26	£13.78	CD$28.60
Dinner for One at La Bombonera (inexpensive)	$12	£6.30	CD$13.80
Bottle of Beer in a Bar	$3	£1.60	CD$3.45
Glass of Wine in a Restaurant	$4	£2.10	CD$4.60
Roll of ASA 100 Color Film (36 exp.)	$8.50	£4.50	CD$9.75
Movie Ticket	$5	£2.60	CD$5.75
Theater Ticket	$15–$75	£7.90–£39.45	CD$17.20–CD$86.25

Lodging

In the Caribbean, accommodations expenses take the largest bite out of your budget. Keep in mind that when you look at the price of an all-inclusive resort versus the price of a hotel, the all-inclusive rate appears inflated. Make sure to compare mangoes to mangoes, and take into account that you'll be shelling out extra for meals, drinks (though many all-inclusives include premium alcohol in their rates), and activities if you're at a hotel or resort where the price covers only your room. (For more on the different types of accommodations, see Chapter 6.)

In each of the island accommodations sections later in this book, we list dollar signs that indicate the price categories for lodging options. See the introduction for an explanation of those rate ranges.

Picking a rate range

Many Caribbean properties have up to a half-dozen different rates during the year based on the season. Rates frequently plunge as much as 60 percent in the summer (low season), though the norm is more in the 20 to 40 percent range. Luxury resorts typically offer the biggest discounts, because their stratospheric rates have farther to come down. In this book, we let you know if a property is known for having special package deals worth asking about. (In particular, see the section on package deals in Chapter 5.)

You won't find many entries in the "dirt-cheap" category in this book, because most of the places that are that cheap in the Caribbean we wouldn't feel comfortable sending anyone to. (Exceptions that spring to mind are **Jake's** in Jamaica and **Hilty House** on St. Croix.) Low-end properties exist, but you're likely to be sharing a bathroom with strangers, and the cleanliness and service issue will be a big question mark. And, you're almost guaranteed not to get air-conditioning.

Many accommodations fall in the middle (still reasonable) price range, and if we mention a particular feature in the review, take that as an indication that the property had something noteworthy in that area. For example, if we mention the balconies, terraces, or sea views, those features are somehow a little or a lot better than similar properties on the island. (Many hotels offer sea views, for example, but those panoramas differ significantly from place to place.)

In the high-end categories, you can expect all the extras you'd get at a four- or five-star hotel anywhere in the world. We've had gargantuan Jacuzzis in our rooms, fruit trays and champagne on arrival, private butler service where they unpacked our suitcases for us, and all kinds of other extravagances. The expensive hotels often throw in the full use of all workout and nonmotorized water-sport facilities (sometimes even including lessons for snorkeling and windsurfing). You often find CD players and dataport phones in the rooms. Several hotels and resorts have added extensive business facilities and free Internet kiosks so that their guests can stay connected easily.

People often wonder whether they should shell out a lot of extra money for a sea view or a big room. That decision depends on the property and your own agenda. If you're almost never in the room anyway, why add that cost? But at some facilities, a sea view is vital to the experience. In our individual property reviews, we mention the places where the views and suites are really worth the additional expense.

Beating the rack rate

The *rack rate* is the official published rate that a hotel charges for a room. It's the rate you'd get if you walked in off the street and asked for a room for the night.

In all but the smallest accommodations, the rate you pay for a room depends on many factors, not the least of which is how you make your reservation. A travel agent may be able to negotiate a better price with certain hotels than you could get on your own (see Chapter 6 for details), because the hotel gives the agent a discount in exchange for steering business toward that hotel. Airlines frequently team up with hotels to give package deals, too, which can also mean more lopped off that rack rate.

Of course, hotels are happy to charge you the rack rate, but with minimal effort and planning you can easily do better. Reserving a room through the hotel's toll-free number may sometimes result in a lower rate than if you called the hotel directly. However, we've found that when it comes to the Caribbean, the people manning the central reservations number sometimes don't know about the latest special packages or deals on the island. In fact, the reservations agent is usually sitting at a desk in Florida or New Jersey and has never set foot on the island.

We strongly recommend that you make initial comparisons by using the toll-free hotel reservation numbers or Web sites, narrowing your choices down to three properties. Then contact each resort directly via e-mail, phone, or fax to check the rates again. (Faxes or e-mails work best with islands like Puerto Rico and Jamaica, where the unfamiliarly accented English may be difficult to follow on the phone.) Make sure to ask about last-minute specials, and double-check to be certain that you're not missing some fantastic package that the U.S.-based reservation service hasn't been told about yet — that happens all the time. Many Caribbean resorts also offer Internet-only specials, so don't forget to check for those deals.

When you agree on a rate, make sure to get a confirmation either by fax or e-mail that outlines in its entirety the agreed-upon rate along with what's included — and what's not. Be sure the room category is what you asked for, too. Hoteliers are often loath to promise a particular room assignment, but if you're able to extract such a promise, get it in writing. Bring the confirmation of the deal you've worked out with you on your trip to avoid nasty surprises at checkout time.

Outsmarting the seasons

Room rates also change with the season and as occupancy rates rise and fall. (See Chapter 3 for a full discussion of how time of year affects hotel rates.) If a hotel is almost full, it likely doesn't extend discount rates. If it's empty, you may be able to negotiate. With many Caribbean hotels, you probably need to call nine months or more in advance to get a room during the popular winter months. In summer, you can almost always snag a deal.

 Although you may feel a little like an ambulance chaser, if you're willing to put up with some hassle, you can try to book a trip to an island soon after a hurricane has hit. Resorts and airlines are left scrambling for customers. Hotels are often back on track quickly, but because of the media-induced panic, guests don't come back for weeks or even months. The palm trees will be tattered, and you may have to put up with the sound of hammers, but the sun still shines.

 If you travel with a group, consider staying in a villa. With three couples, you can easily rent a villa for under $1,000 per person for a week. **Unusual Villas & Island Rentals,** 409F North Hamilton St., Richmond, VA 23221 (☎ **800-846-7280,** 804-288-2823; Fax: 804-342-9016; www.unusual villarentals.com), represents a large number of desirable properties in the Caribbean.

Transportation

Most of the time, aside from your airfare to the Caribbean (see Chapter 5 for tips on how to decrease this particular expense), your transportation costs should be relatively low during your Caribbean stay. This is especially true if you passed on the rental car or received a couple of free days of car rental as part of your package deal.

Many package tours include transfers from the airport to your resort or hotel. Several fine restaurants arrange free transportation, too; be sure to inquire when you make a reservation. In either case, you still need to tip the driver. See Chapter 5 for more details on booking a package trip.

 Taxi fares add up quickly, even on a moderately priced island like Puerto Rico, because attractions are often spread out. If you want to cover a lot of ground for the best price, you're usually better off lumping most of your touring into a single day and hiring a driver for the entire day at a rate ranging from $60 to $100 (not including tip).

Don't plan on taking public transportation except on Aruba and Barbados, where the bus service between the beach resort areas and the main towns is easy and cheap, but not always frequent. The public ferries are the most reasonably priced way to get from one island to the next in the British Virgin Islands and between the BVIs and St. Thomas or St. John.

As much as possible, take advantage of the free transportation that your hotel offers. If you pay attention to schedules, you can often find a free shuttle to the nearest place for shopping or a good beach.

Dining

In each of the dining sections in the destination chapters, we include reviews of our favorite restaurants, ranging from the pick of the high-end resort choices to local finds with rock-bottom prices. Each has a dollar-sign symbol to indicate its price category; see the introduction for an explanation of those categories.

Where, when, and what you eat in the Caribbean make a big difference in your final vacation tab. To save money, we generally suggest signing up for some sort of dining plan at your resort if it offers one. Choose whatever plan makes the most sense for you and your tastes. For example, if breakfast is the most important meal of the day to you, don't sign on for a plan that only serves a continental spread.

Investing in a dine-around plan

If you visit Aruba, Barbados, Jamaica, Puerto Rico, or St. Thomas, you probably want to try some of the good local restaurants that each island is known for. But you also want to keep costs in check, so ask if your hotel offers a *dine-around plan*. That way you won't get stuck in a culinary rut or shell out tons of money for food. Even some of the all-inclusives — like Aruba's **Allegro** — now offer dine-around plans, recognizing that travelers crave variety.

Dine-around plans aren't all identical, but the way they usually work is that you pay a flat fee for a certain number of gourmet meals (say, three to five for the week). You then get to use your dine-around credits with the hotels or restaurants that are part of the program.

Dining at your resort

Most hotels offer a *European Plan* (EP), which means that no meals are included. If you see a *Continental Plan* (CP) listed, you get only a continental breakfast — juice, coffee, and some kind of bread. A *Breakfast Plan* (BP) signifies a full American-style breakfast. Another popular option, which leaves couples to figure out only the evening meal on their own, is the *Modified American Plan* (MAP), which provides two full meals daily. With the three daily meals of the *Full American Plan* (FAP), that's exactly what you'll be — full. Finally, *all-inclusive* means that you get three all-you-can-eat meals a day and (often) all the alcohol you can guzzle — sometimes including premium liquors and fine wines.

Dining options have improved at all-inclusive resorts in the last few years because travelers have become more sophisticated in their tastes. Now most all-inclusive dining packages feature local dishes at least one night a week, and often you can find several local specialties amid more-familiar fare.

If you have special dietary restrictions and are staying at an all-inclusive or at a resort where you've signed on for an extensive meal plan, ask the reservation agent for the executive chef's name and send an e-mail or fax with your special requests about a month before you arrive. Most chefs consider pleasing their guests a point of pride, and they bend over backward to accommodate you. However, because ordering special items on the islands can take time, you need to give chefs advance notice.

If you go for the popular à la carte breakfast buffet, including coffee and juice, expect to pay a high $20 or much more per person — before tipping. And unless your cash flow is extremely good, don't even think about ordering room service. For one thing, the wait is often interminable, but you also have to add a tip on top of an already pricey way to eat.

Buying meals outside your resort

Outside the resorts, your dining choices generally fall into two categories: expensive and cheap. Dinner main courses at finer restaurants routinely start at around $20, and a three-course meal for two with cocktails can easily soar past the $100 mark — before the tip. Why so much? Many products must be brought from outside the island, and the high costs of importing are passed along to you. On some islands, even the seafood is frozen and shipped in; we've had Maine lobster served to us in the Caribbean more than once. If that fact bothers you, be sure to ask your server about the origin and freshness of the fish before you order.

Also, keep in mind that the European connection is strong on these islands, and many of them attract some of the world's finest chefs, who consider spending time in the tropics a career perk. Although you may pay the same amount you'd pay at the best restaurants in Atlanta (and on pricey-to-dine islands like Aruba, Barbados, and Grand Cayman, your dinner tab may be closer to New York prices), you're legitimately getting a gourmet meal. Plus, you get the kind of killer view that is in short supply at home.

Happily, on the other end of the payment scale, eating cheaply in the Caribbean doesn't mean risking your health the way it sometimes does in Mexico. You rarely have to be concerned about the safety of the food and water in the Caribbean. If you're willing to eat where the locals do, you can find some good meals for around $12.

In terms of cheap joints, you can follow our recommendations or, if you're feeling adventurous, ask a local where to go. Don't expect much in the way of surroundings; you may sit on a plastic chair at a wobbly plastic table enlivened with plastic flowers. But you'll get to bask in the friendly Caribbean atmosphere, *limin'* (island slang for "hanging out") with the locals, and enjoying treats like jerk chicken with *bammy* (a fried Jamaican bread) or a bowl of *sopa de pollo con arroz* (Puerto Rico's answer to Grandmother's chicken with rice soup).

Going for do-it-yourself meals

If you plan to stay in a villa, condo, or guesthouse, you can cut costs by cooking your own meals. Some islands, such as St. Thomas, have super-stores where you can pick up supplies at moderate costs.

Before you lug items such as salt and pepper with you, ask management to send you a list of what's already stocked in the kitchen. Remember that spices are cheaper on some islands, such as lush Jamaica.

Toasting top prices for drinks

Unless you're at an all-inclusive where drinks are part of your upfront tab, or you're content to drink water, another big expense is drinks. Paying $2.50 for a soda isn't uncommon, and you don't get refills without paying again. If you have a minibar or fridge in your room, find out whether the drinks are complimentary before swigging them down. Some places put bottled water in your room, but then they expect you to pony up a pretty penny for every one you chug. If you're not sure, call the front desk.

On many islands, import duties raise the prices of wines and imported beers sky-high. We've found that wines are often barely drinkable because they're improperly stored en route (sitting in the broiling tropical sun on a dock somewhere) or, after they arrive, the bottles aren't kept cool enough. Save money and your taste buds by drinking local. The Caribbean is noted for its rums and beers.

Tapping more cost-cutting tips

Here are a few more ways to trim your dining costs:

- ✔ **Fill up at the breakfast buffet at your hotel.** If you eat late and eat well, you'll eliminate the need for a big lunch, especially if all you're going to be doing is lazing on the beach.

- ✔ **Share.** Portions are often pretty hefty, and if you eat everything on your plate, you may get that way, too. At least try splitting appetizers and desserts.

- ✔ **Take advantage of happy hours and the manager's welcoming cocktail party.** You usually get free nibbles, too.

- ✔ **Forget about the lobster; it's the most pricey item on the menu.** The freshly caught local fish is less expensive and often just as good or better.

- ✔ **Avoid your minibar, or use it to stash the less-expensive drinks and snacks that you buy outside your resort.**

If your kids don't react well to too much sugar, beware of ordering juice on the islands. Often "juices" are actually fruit drinks, made up largely of corn-syrup sweeteners rather than pure juice.

Sightseeing

You want to spend at least one day touring the island, even if you're on Grand Cayman, where you won't find many interesting attractions. Sightseeing tours vary according to destination, duration, and extras such as meals and snacks. But here's a rough estimate of cost: Expect to spend a minimum of $50 (including tip) for a half-day island tour of Aruba or Grand Cayman. For a full-day guided tour that includes lunch and a stop for snacks on bigger islands with more to see — Barbados, Jamaica, and Puerto Rico (where you have *lots* to see) — you're looking at about $80 minimum, including tip.

Shopping

Shopping is the wild card. You can easily get away with buying a few inexpensive souvenirs at the crafts markets, where you may pick up a hand-woven straw hat for about $15 or a small basket of spices for $7. But at the other end of the spectrum, artwork by notable Caribbean artists can go for thousands of dollars. Don't miss the fantastic art galleries in Old San Juan; the duty-free scene in Charlotte Amalie on St. Thomas; the funky boutique shops on St. John; or the hip art galleries in Jamaica.

 If you're eager to load up on luxury items from china to perfume, check out the duty-free shops that dot the islands. However, if you intend to shop for major items such as jewelry, we urge you to do some comparative pricing at home first. You may have a very hard time determining which items are truly bargains in the duty-free shops; don't be fooled by signs trumpeting terrific deals.

Nightlife

Even the smallest resorts usually roll out a reggae or steel pan band sometime during the week. Nightlife in the Caribbean runs the gamut from resort-sponsored theme nights (available on every island) to glitzy casinos (on Puerto Rico and Aruba). You can find high-class nightclubs where merengue and salsa rule (Puerto Rico and Aruba) and reggae rocks (St. Thomas), and you can enjoy Jamaica's street parties where locals mingle with visitors to the thumping beat of rock-steady reggae and *soca* (reggae dance music).

The action in Barbados is in the rum shops, and the funky beach bars in the British Virgin Islands are renowned for their rollicking impromptu parties. The best part is that the beach and street parties are free, and you usually only have a small cover charge ($5–$10 per person) to gain entry into clubs. As for casinos, well, that all depends on whether you're feeling lucky.

Outdoor activities

Of course, the two main activities in the Caribbean — swimming in that beautiful blue sea and basking on those sandy beaches — are absolutely free. However, if you're interested in activities such as scuba diving, snorkeling, windsurfing, and water-skiing, they usually cost extra.

More and more of the all-inclusives have started offering freebies such as scuba and windsurfing lessons, water-skiing, and snorkeling gear for the week. Some even toss in a round of golf.

Water sports

Although the charges vary slightly from island to island, we've generally found that a two-tank boat dive runs around $50 to $60. Snorkeling trips vary widely in cost, but if you go out on a boat, you pay at least $30; just renting snorkeling equipment at a beach usually costs about $15 to $18. Windsurfing lessons and gear cost close to $50 an hour, and water-skiing also goes for about $60 an hour. You also need to factor in the cost of a tip if you receive instructions.

Many variables are involved in calculating the costs of deep-sea fishing, but assuming that you don't mind mingling your lines with people you haven't met before, you'll probably pay at least $100 per person, including bait, a fishing license, and ice to preserve your catch.

Golf

For golf in the Caribbean, greens fees run from about $100 at Jamaica's **Sandals Golf and Country Club** to about $145 at Aruba's **Tierra Del Sol** and Jamaica's **Half Moon Bay.** You also pay at least $15 for club rentals and a minimum of $15 for a manual golf cart. In Jamaica, you also have the quirky rule that you must have a caddy, who, of course, you need to tip. (The show makes the cost worthwhile: Your caddy carries your golf bag by balancing it sideways on his head.)

Cutting Costs — But Not the Fun

The Caribbean delivers plenty of thrills if you get a rush out of being a savvy consumer. Following are our best money-saving tips:

> ✔ **Go off season.** If you can travel at nonpeak times (from mid-Apr to mid-Dec, for example), you find hotel prices at almost half the price of peak months.

✔ **Travel midweek.** If you can travel on a Tuesday, Wednesday, or Thursday, you may find cheaper flights to your destination. When you ask about airfares, see if you can get a cheaper rate by flying on a different day. For more tips on getting a good fare, see Chapter 5.

✔ **Try a package tour.** For many destinations, you can book airfare, hotel, ground transportation, and even some sightseeing just by making one call to a travel agent or packager, for a price much less than if you put the trip together yourself. (See Chapter 5 for more on package tours.)

✔ **Reserve a room with a refrigerator and coffeemaker.** You don't have to slave over a hot stove to cut a few costs; several motels have minifridges and coffeemakers. Buying supplies for breakfast saves you money — and probably calories.

✔ **Always ask for discount rates.** Membership in AAA, frequent-flier plans, trade unions, AARP, or other groups may qualify you for savings on car rentals, plane tickets, hotel rooms, and even meals. Ask about everything; you may be pleasantly surprised.

✔ **Ask if your kids can stay in the room with you.** A room with two double beds usually doesn't cost any more than one with a queen-size bed. And many hotels don't charge you the additional-person rate if the additional person is pint-size and related to you. Even if you have to pay $15 extra for a rollaway bed, you save hundreds by not taking two rooms.

✔ **Try expensive restaurants at lunch instead of dinner.** Lunch tabs are usually a fraction of what dinner costs at a top restaurant, and the menu often boasts many of the same specialties.

✔ **Walk a lot.** A good pair of walking shoes can save lots of money on taxi fares and other local transportation. As a bonus, you get to know your destination more intimately as you explore at a slower pace.

✔ **Skip the souvenirs.** Your photographs and your memories could be the best mementos of your trip. If you're concerned about money, you can do without the T-shirts, key chains, salt-and-pepper shakers, and other trinkets.

✔ **Carry your own bags.** Travel light and with wheels on your suitcases. Politely but firmly decline porters, no matter how persistently they reach for your luggage.

✔ **Steer clear of the hotel minibar and room service.** Don't even open that little refrigerator in your room. Likewise, don't order room service. If you do, you have to pay a service charge and tip — for what is often lukewarm food — on top of already-inflated prices. Also, some hotels provide complimentary bottled water, while others charge $5 or even more.

✔ **Use a pay phone to call home.** Avoid using the phone in your hotel room to call outside the hotel. Charges can be astronomical, even for local calls, which are sometimes at least $1 a pop (instead of 25¢ at a pay phone). When you call long distance, you may think you're saving money by using the toll-free number of your calling card instead of dialing direct. However, most hotels charge you at least $1 to connect you to an outside line for the toll-free call. On top of whatever your calling card bills you, the hotel also charges you just for picking up the phone — whether or not you reach the person you wanted.

✔ **Get a room off the beach.** Accommodations within walking distance of the shore can be much cheaper than those right on the beach. Beaches are public, so you don't need to stay in a hotel on the sand to spend most of your vacation at the beach.

✔ **Steer clear of the casinos.** If you can't resist gambling, head to an island without casinos.

Handling Money

All the Caribbean islands that we cover in this book accept the Yankee dollar. On such U.S.-controlled islands as Puerto Rico and the U.S. Virgins, the U.S. dollar, of course, is the coin of the realm.

Islands such as Jamaica have their own currency, but for the most part dollars are accepted. Therefore, obtaining a small amount of the local currency before you go is unnecessary.

Of course, if you pay for something in U.S. dollars, at some shops or small restaurants you may receive change in a mix of U.S. dollars and Jamaican or Eastern Caribbean dollars. If so, use the island currency for tipping and try to use up your supply before heading home.

Caribbean establishments don't accept European and Canadian currencies, but you can readily exchange them into the local money at banks, currency exchange offices, or at your hotel. The rate of exchange fluctuates daily according to international monetary markets. For the most recent exchange rates on a variety of currencies, check out www.xe.net/ucc. When exchanging currency, seek out the bigger banks; commercial money-changers and airport facilities can charge 10 percent or more in fees for each transaction.

You're the best judge of how much cash you feel comfortable carrying or what alternative form of currency is your favorite, and those preferences don't change much on your vacation. True, you'll probably be moving around more and incurring more expenses than you generally do (unless you happen to eat out every meal when you're at home), and you may let your mind slip into vacation gear and not be as vigilant about your safety as when you're in work mode. But, those factors aside, the only type of payment that isn't quite as available to you away from home is your personal checkbook.

Using ATMs and carrying cash

The easiest and best way to get cash away from home is from an ATM (automated teller machine). The **Cirrus** (☎ 800-424-7787; www.master card.com) and **PLUS** (☎ 800-843-7587; www.visa.com) networks span the globe; look at the back of your bank card to see which network you're on, and then call or check online for ATM locations at your destination. Be sure you know your personal identification number (PIN) before you leave home, and be sure to find out your daily withdrawal limit before you depart. Also keep in mind that many banks impose a fee every time you use your card at a different bank's ATM, and that fee can be higher for international transactions (up to $5 or more) than for domestic ones (where they're rarely more than $1.50). On top of this charge, the bank from which you withdraw cash may charge its own fee. To compare banks' ATM fees within the U.S., use www.bankrate.com. For international withdrawal fees, ask your bank.

Charging ahead with credit cards

Credit cards are a safe way to carry money: They provide a convenient record of all your expenses, and they generally offer relatively good exchange rates. You can also withdraw cash advances from your credit cards at banks or ATMs, provided you know your PIN. The exchange rate for a cash advance on a credit card is better than you receive when exchanging currency in the banks. On the downside, interest rates for cash advances are often significantly higher than rates for credit card purchases. Also, you start paying interest on the advance the moment you receive the cash. On an airline-affiliated credit card, a cash advance doesn't earn frequent-flier miles.

 If you've forgotten your PIN or didn't even know you had one, call the number on the back of your credit card and ask the bank to send it to you. It usually takes five to seven business days, though some banks provide the number over the phone if you tell them your mother's maiden name or some other personal information.

MasterCard and Visa are the most widely accepted credit cards in the Caribbean, followed by American Express. Some places accept Discover, but many resorts and restaurants don't. Diners Club isn't widely accepted. We recommend that you carry at least two credit cards with you, in case you hit a snag with one. We like paying with credit cards, because then we have a paper trail to look at for budgeting purposes. We also have purchase protection, too, if one of our island treasures doesn't pan out.

Keep in mind that when you use your credit card abroad, most banks assess a 2 percent fee above the 1 percent fee that Visa, MasterCard, and American Express charge for currency conversion on credit charges. But credit cards still may be the smart way to go when you factor in things like exorbitant ATM fees and higher traveler's check exchange rates (and service fees).

Some credit card companies recommend that you notify them of any impending trip abroad so that they don't become suspicious when the card is used numerous times in a foreign destination and block your charges. Even if you don't call your credit card company in advance, you can always call the card's toll-free emergency number if a charge is refused — a good reason to carry the phone number with you.

Toting traveler's checks

These days, traveler's checks are less necessary because most cities have 24-hour ATMs that allow you to withdraw small amounts of cash as needed. However, on smaller islands, such as Saba or Statia (which we don't cover in this book), ATMs are few and far between — or else non-existent. Keep in mind that the bank you're taking money from (and your own bank) likely charges an ATM withdrawal fee if the bank isn't your own, so if you're withdrawing money every day, you may be better off with traveler's checks — provided that you don't mind showing identification every time you want to cash one. Also note that, in the Caribbean, some restaurants tack on an additional service charge if you pay with traveler's checks.

You can get traveler's checks at almost any bank. **American Express** offers denominations of $20, $50, $100, $500, and (for cardholders only) $1,000, with a service charge ranging from 1 to 4 percent. You can also get American Express traveler's checks over the phone by calling ☎ **800-221-7282;** Amex gold and platinum cardholders who use this number are exempt from the 1 percent fee.

Visa offers traveler's checks at most banks nationwide. The service charge ranges from 1.5 to 2 percent; checks come in denominations of $20, $50, $100, $500, and $1,000. Call ☎ **800-732-1322** for information. AAA members can obtain Visa checks without a fee at most AAA offices or by calling ☎ **866-339-3378. MasterCard** also offers traveler's checks. Call ☎ **800-223-9920** for a location near you.

When cashing or exchanging traveler's checks, the bigger the bank, the better. Beware of commercial money-changers or facilities in airports; you can pay 10 percent or more in fees for each transaction.

If you choose to carry traveler's checks, be sure to keep a record of their serial numbers separate from your checks in the event that they're stolen or lost. You get a refund faster if you know the numbers.

Taking Taxes into Account

On your hotel bill, you also pay resort taxes and gratuities and sometimes an energy surcharge. Some hotels include these extras in the
quoted rates, while others add them to your bill. Make sure to clarify
any extra charges, because they can easily swell your hotel bill by $20,
$30, or even $60 or more per night, depending on the cost of your room.

Total charges vary from hotel to hotel, but you can roughly expect to
pay a 12 percent resort tax and about an $8 to $10 per day, per guest
(over age 12) housekeeping gratuity and energy surcharge for use of
electricity.

A lot of visitors forget that a government tax, which ranges from 6 percent on Aruba to Jamaica's whopping 23 percent, applies to their final
hotel bill. When you ask for lodging rates, clarify whether the tax is
included in the quote; obviously, that can make a big difference. We
strongly urge you to ask the hotel for a written outline of everything that
the rate includes — faxed, if possible. We've run into people who were
extremely annoyed because they thought they had a set rate, and the
government tax came as a nasty surprise. The rates quoted in this book
don't include government tax and service charges.

Tipping Tips

For the most part, tipping is much the same in the Caribbean as in the
rest of the world. Plan to tip 15 percent of the bill in a restaurant, $1 per
bag to a bellhop, and $2 per night for a maid at a resort. (If your hotel
isn't very expensive, leave $1 a night on your pillow; leave it each day
because the maids often rotate out.) Taxi drivers and tour guides get a
10 to 15 percent tip.

Tips are often automatically included in a bill (in European fashion). If
you're in doubt, ask before you accidentally overtip. Bring along lots of
small-denomination bills; otherwise, you're likely to end up giving a much
larger tip than the situation calls for — or, worse, stiffing someone.

Telephone Traps

Making long-distance calls from the Caribbean is extremely expensive.
Don't ever dial direct from your hotel room, unless forking over $50
or so for a five-minute call is okay with you. Also, be aware that many
Caribbean hotels charge even for attempted calls, and toll-free numbers
aren't free.

Keep the following tips in mind before attempting to reach out and
touch someone:

✔ **Calling cards are the way to go.** In your room, you usually find long-distance instructions that give you some options, but you're best off using your calling card. However, we've had problems on some islands connecting to the appropriate operator, so call the front desk at the first sign of trouble and ask the hotel operator to guide you through their particular system.

✔ **Buy a phone card locally.** This can reduce your long-distance costs significantly, too. Ask your concierge for the best place to purchase one.

✔ **Fax it to 'em.** Unless a call is urgent, we've found faxing to be much less expensive. That way, neither party has to worry about the other person's availability to answer.

✔ **E-mail sparingly.** Sometimes hotels have free Internet kiosks for their guests in the lobby area. If you do bring your laptop, remember that it costs you a mint to connect, so e-mail addicts, beware. We heard one fellow laughing at his own stupidity. He downloaded a bunch of e-mails using the dataport in his room and got slapped with a $120 charge.

✔ **Cellphones let you down.** Many U.S. cellphones and services don't work in the Caribbean, but you can rent them on the island if you're desperate.

Dealing with a Lost or Stolen Wallet

Be sure to block charges against your account the minute you discover that a card has been lost or stolen along with your wallet. Then be sure to file a police report.

Almost every credit card company has an emergency toll-free number to call if your card is stolen. Yours might be able to wire you a cash advance off your credit card immediately, and in many places, credit card companies can deliver emergency credit cards in a day or two. The issuing bank's toll-free number is usually on the back of your credit card — though of course, if your card has been stolen, that won"t help you unless you recorded the number elsewhere.

For your convenience, we give you the major credit card company emergency telephone numbers:

✔ **Citicorp Visa's** U.S. emergency number is ☎ **800-847-2911.**

✔ **American Express** cardholders and traveler's check holders should call ☎ **800-221-7282.**

✔ **MasterCard** holders should call ☎ **800-307-7309.**

✔ For other companies, call the toll-free number directory at ☎ **800-555-1212** to get the number of your card issuer.

Odds are that if your wallet is gone, the police won't be able to recover it for you. However, it's still worth informing the authorities. At the very least, it helps protect your credit rating. Your credit card company or insurer may require a police report number or record of the theft.

If you need emergency cash over the weekend when all banks and American Express offices are closed, you can have money wired to you from **Western Union** (☎ 800-325-6000; www.westernunion.com). You generally must present a valid ID to pick up the cash at the Western Union office. However, on most islands, you can pick up a money transfer without valid identification as long as you can answer a test question provided by the sender. Be sure to let the sender know in advance that you don't have an ID. If you need to use a test question instead of an ID, the sender must take cash to his or her local Western Union office rather than transfer the money over the phone or online.

Chapter 5

Getting to the Caribbean

● ●

In This Chapter

▶ Locating the right airline for your destination

▶ Grabbing a great deal on a flight

▶ Flying from island to island

▶ Deciding if package tours are right for you

▶ Cruising to the Caribbean

● ●

*N*aturally, traveling to your dream destination in the cheapest, most comfortable, and fastest way possible is a chief concern when you start to plan a trip. You may save a bundle if you read this chapter before making reservations the old-fashioned way.

We tell you which airlines fly to which destinations and give you the latest tips on locating the best airfare. We explain package tours, including what they mean for your wallet and what impact they have on your Caribbean experience, and we also recommend some specialists who sell them. And, for those of you who think you'd rather float than fly, we offer some information on cruises, too.

Flying to the Caribbean

Getting to the Caribbean from the United States and Canada is relatively easy. And with improved connections from the West Coast, many islands are seeing more visitors from that area who want to experience islands other than Hawaii. That said, we recommend you do a few things to make sure that your flight goes smoothly:

✔ **Reserve early.** Flights to the Caribbean tend to be extremely full. During the summer months, islanders who live in the United States go home to visit, and during the winter months, visitors flock to the warm weather, so seats go quickly year-round. If you want to use frequent-flier miles to the Caribbean, you have to plan well in advance. Only a small number of seats on flights are devoted to frequent fliers, and they get snapped up quickly.

✔ **Scout out less-mainstream airlines.** Your quickest route and best price to the Caribbean may be on an airline that you don't normally fly or on one that you've never even heard of before. For example, Air Jamaica often is both the quickest and the cheapest means to Jamaica, but many travelers have never heard of that option. Others are too intimidated to book a foreign carrier like Cayman Airways or Dutch-owned Martinair.

✔ **Be willing to make a connection.** From your part of the country, your best bet may be to get a cheap flight to Miami or San Juan and change to another carrier from there. Or, the best way to get to your destination may be via another island. For example, visitors going to the British Virgin Islands (BVIs) can fly into St. Thomas in the U.S. Virgin Islands and then take a ferry over to the BVIs, which are extremely close.

If you have a connecting flight, make sure you allow ample time to make your connection. For example, many American Airlines flights connecting to American Eagle flights in Puerto Rico allow travelers only 55 minutes. That's too narrow a margin for error with all the additional security checks and delays that travelers have to deal with.

Finding out which airlines fly to your destination

New York and Miami are the most popular gateway cities to the Caribbean from the continental United States. Atlanta is another major traffic hub for the Southeast. In Canada, the two most popular gateways to the Caribbean are in Montreal and Toronto. Flights from Britain to the Caribbean commence in London. In Australia, the Sydney airport has the best connections to the Caribbean and in New Zealand, it's the Auckland airport. In the Caribbean itself, San Juan, Puerto Rico, is the major traffic hub for points throughout the Caribbean, north and south.

Aruba

Air Canada (☎ 888-247-2262 in the U.S. and Canada; www.aircanada. ca) has connections from Toronto and Quebec to Miami. After stopping in Miami, Canadians and other passengers can fly nonstop to the island (weekends only).

On **American Airlines** (☎ 800-433-7300; www.aa.com), Aruba-bound passengers can catch a daily nonstop 4½-hour flight from New York's John F. Kennedy (JFK) Airport. American also offers nonstop flights from Boston, Miami, and San Juan, Puerto Rico.

Continental Airlines (☎ 800-525-0280; www.continental.com) flies to Aruba via nonstop flights from Newark and also from Houston three times a week.

Delta Airlines (☎ 800-221-1212; www.delta.com) flies from New York's JFK Airport with a stop in Atlanta, where flights depart for Aruba. This airline offers a direct flight from JFK on Saturday only.

Dutch Caribbean Express (☎ 800-327-7230; www.flydca.net) has good connections into Aruba from Miami, but it offers no direct flights — all flights stop first in Curaçao.

United Airlines (☎ 800-241-6522; www.united.com) offers weekend service from Chicago with a stop in Atlanta and Washington's Dulles.

US Airways (☎ 800-428-4322; www.usairways.com) offers nonstop flights from Charlotte, North Carolina, and Philadelphia several days a week, plus Boston on Saturday.

Barbados

Air Canada (☎ 888-247-2262 in the U.S. and Canada; www.aircanada.ca) has daily flights from Toronto in winter. From Montreal, you can make a connection through Toronto. In summer, when demand wanes, fewer flights are available. All flights are nonstop from Toronto to Barbados.

Air Jamaica (☎ 800-523-5585; www.airjamaica.com) offers daily flights that link Atlanta, Baltimore, and Miami to Barbados through the airline's Montego Bay hub. Air Jamaica offers service between Los Angeles and Barbados on Friday and Sunday, but an overnight stay is required in Montego Bay. Nonstop flights from New York to Barbados are available five days a week, daily in winter.

American Airlines (☎ 800-433-7300; www.aa.com) has dozens of connections passing through San Juan, plus daily nonstop flights to Barbados from Miami.

British Airways (☎ 800-AIRWAYS, or 800-247-9297; www.britishairways.com) flies nonstop service to Barbados from London's Gatwick Airport.

BWIA (☎ 800-538-2942; www.bwee.com), the national airline of Trinidad and Tobago, offers daily flights from New York and Miami, plus many flights from Trinidad.

US Airways/AmericaWest Airlines (☎ 800-428-4322; www.usairways.com) flies daily from New York's La Guardia to Philadelphia, and then on to Barbados. They don't offer any direct flights from New York to Barbados.

Virgin Atlantic (☎ 800-821-5438 in the U.S.; www.virgin.com) has one daily direct flight from London to Barbados.

British Virgin Islands

No direct flights are available from anywhere in the U.S. or Canada to the British Virgin Islands (BVIs), but you can make connections from San Juan and St. Thomas to Beef Island/Tortola.

Air Sunshine (☎ **800-327-8900,** 284-495-8900; www.airsunshine.com) is a minor airline, flying between San Juan or St. Thomas to Beef Island/ Tortola and Virgin Gorda.

American Eagle (☎ **800-433-7300** in the U.S.; www.aa.com) is your best bet to reach Beef Island/Tortola. This airline has dozens of flights to its hub in San Juan, and then at least four daily trips from San Juan to Beef Island/Tortola.

Clair Aero (☎ **284-495-2271**) flies from St. Thomas to Tortola on Monday, Wednesday, and Friday, with flights continuing to Virgin Gorda and Anegada.

LIAT (☎ **888-844-5428** or 268-480-5601; www.liatairline.com) is much less reliable but is a good choice if you're on one of Tortola's neighboring islands. This Caribbean carrier makes the short hop to Tortola from St. Kitts, Antigua, Sint Maarten, St. Thomas, and San Juan in small planes not known for their frequency or careful scheduling. You can make reservations through travel agents or through the larger U.S.-based airlines that connect with LIAT hubs.

Grand Cayman

Air Canada (☎ **888-247-2262;** www.aircanada.ca) offers direct twice-weekly service from Toronto on Sunday and Wednesday.

American Airlines (☎ **800-433-7300;** www.aa.com) offers three daily nonstop flights from Miami.

British Airways (☎ **800-AIRWAYS;** www.britishairways.com) offers twice-weekly service from London's Gatwick Airport with a stopover in Nassau.

Cayman Airways (☎ **800-GCAYMAN** in the U.S. and Canada, 345-949-2311; www.caymanairways.com) offers the most frequent service to Grand Cayman, with three daily flights from Miami, five flights a week from Tampa, two flights a week from Orlando, and three nonstop flights a week from Houston.

Continental Airlines (☎ **800-525-0280;** www.continental.com), the newest carrier to fly to the Caymans, offers service between its Houston hub and Grand Cayman on Wednesday, Friday, Saturday, and Sunday, and daily from Newark.

Delta (☎ 800-221-1212; www.delta.com) flies daily into Grand Cayman from its hub in Atlanta.

Northwest Airlines (☎ 800-225-2525; www.nwa.com) flies to Grand Cayman from Detroit and Minneapolis.

Spirit Airlines (☎ 800-772-7117; www.spiritair.com) offers flights daily from Ft. Lauderdale.

US Airways (☎ 800-428-4322; www.usairways.com) offers daily non-stop flights from Charlotte, North Carolina and Philadelphia.

Jamaica

Air Canada (☎ 888-247-2262 in the U.S. and Canada; www.aircanada.ca) flies to Jamaica daily, either nonstop from Toronto or via Montreal or Winnipeg with a stop in Toronto.

Air Jamaica (☎ 800-523-5585 in the U.S.; www.airjamaica.com) operates about 14 flights per week from New York, most of which stop at both Montego Bay and Kingston, and even more frequent flights from Miami. The airline offers less-frequent service from such cities as Atlanta, Baltimore, Boston, Chicago, Fort Lauderdale, Houston, Los Angeles, Newark, Orlando, Philadelphia, Phoenix, San Francisco, and Washington, D.C.

American Airlines (☎ 800-433-7300 in the U.S.; www.aa.com) wings in via its hubs in New York and Miami. One daily nonstop flight departs from New York's JFK airport for Montego Bay, continuing on to Kingston. Return flights to New York usually depart from Montego Bay. From Miami, at least two daily flights depart for Kingston and two daily flights for Montego Bay.

British Airways (☎ 800-247-9297; www.britishairways.com) has three nonstop flights weekly to Montego Bay and Kingston from London's Gatwick Airport.

Copa Airlines (☎ 876-926-1762; www.copaair.com) flies between Miami and Kingston three times a week.

Northwest Airlines (☎ 800-225-2525, 876-952-9740; www.nwa.com) flies directly to Montego Bay from Detroit, Minneapolis/St. Paul, and Memphis.

US Airways/AmericaWest (☎ 800-428-4322; www.usairways.com) has several daily flights from New York, Newark, Charlotte, North Carolina, and Philadelphia. One daily flight leaves out of Baltimore, stopping in either Charlotte or Philadelphia before continuing to Jamaica.

Puerto Rico

Puerto Rico is by far the most accessible of the Caribbean islands, with frequent airline service.

Air Canada (☎ 888-247-2262; www.aircanada.ca) flies from both Montreal and Toronto to San Juan.

American Airlines (☎ 800-433-7300 in the U.S. and Canada; www.aa.com) has designated San Juan as its hub for the entire Caribbean. American offers nonstop daily flights to San Juan from Baltimore, Boston, Chicago, Dallas–Fort Worth, Fort Lauderdale, Hartford, Miami, Newark, New York (JFK), Orlando, Philadelphia, Tampa, and Washington (Dulles), plus flights from both Montreal and Toronto with changes in Chicago or Miami. At least two daily flights from Los Angeles to San Juan stop in Dallas or Miami. The airline's **American Eagle** (same contact info) is the undisputed leader among the short-haul local commuter flights of the Caribbean. Collectively, American Eagle and American Airlines fly to dozens of destinations on more than 30 islands of the Caribbean.

British Airways (☎ 0870-850-9850 in the U.K.; 800-AIRWAYS, or 800-247-9297, in the U.S.; www.britishairways.com) offers a daily flight from London's Gatwick and Heathrow airports to New York and then a connection to San Juan.

Continental Airlines (☎ 800-231-0856; www.continental.com) flies nonstop daily from Newark, New Jersey, Houston, and Cleveland. The airline also flies five times a week direct to the northwestern airport outside Aguadilla, in case you want to begin your tour of Puerto Rico in the West. In winter, they offer daily flights.

Delta (☎ 800-221-1212 in the U.S. and Canada; www.delta.com) has four daily nonstop flights during the week, and five on Saturday and Sunday, from its international hub in Atlanta, and daily flights from New York and Orlando.

JetBlue (☎ 800-538-2583; www.jetblue.com) flies two times a day from New York's JFK airport to San Juan, daily from Orlando to San Juan and Aguadilla.

Northwest Airlines (☎ 800-225-2525 in the U.S. and Canada; www.nwa.com) has one daily nonstop to San Juan from Detroit, as well as at least one (and sometimes more) connecting flights to San Juan from Detroit. Northwest also offers flights to San Juan, some of them nonstop, from both Memphis and Minneapolis, with a schedule that varies according to the season and the day of the week.

Spirit Air (☎ 787-772-7117; www.spiritair.com) offers two daily nonstop flights from Fort Lauderdale to San Juan.

United Airlines (☎ 800-241-6522 in the U.S. and Canada; www.united.com) offers daily nonstop flights from Chicago to San Juan.

US Airways (☎ 800-428-4322 in the U.S. and Canada; www.usairways.com) has daily nonstop flights between Charlotte, North Carolina, and

San Juan. The airline also offers two daily nonstop flights from Philadelphia, and one from Pittsburgh.

St. Lucia

You'll probably have to change planes somewhere else in the Caribbean to get to St. Lucia. A few carriers fly directly into St. Lucia's airports, though.

Air Canada (☎ **888-247-2262,** 758-454-6038; www.aircanada.ca) has two nonstop weekly flights to St. Lucia's Hewanorra Airport that depart from Toronto.

Air Jamaica (☎ **800-523-5585,** 758-453-6611; www.airjamaica.com) serves the Hewanorra Airport with nonstop service from either New York's JFK or Newark daily, except Wednesday and Friday.

American Airlines (☎ **800-433-7300;** www.aa.com) has daily flights from Miami.

American Eagle (☎ **800-433-7300** in the U.S., 787-791-5050; www.aa.com) serves George Charles Airport with nonstop flights from San Juan. Connections from all parts of the North American mainland to the airline's enormous hub in San Juan are frequent and convenient.

British Airways (☎ **0870-850-9850** in the U.K.; 800-AIRWAYS, or 800-247-9297, in the U.S.; www.britishairways.com) offers three flights a week from London's Gatwick Airport to St. Lucia's Hewanorra Airport.

BWIA (☎ **800-538-2942;** www.bwee.com) offers two weekly flights to George Charles Airport on Sunday and Tuesday from London's Heathrow Airport. All flights make a quick stopover in Barbados. At least, we hope it's quick.

Delta (☎ **800-221-1212;** www.delta.com) offers daily nonstop flights from Atlanta.

LIAT (☎ **888-844-5428;** www.liatairline.com) has small planes flying from many points throughout the Caribbean into George Charles Airport. Points of origin include such islands as Barbados, Antigua, St. Thomas, Sint Maarten, and Martinique. On some LIAT flights, you may visit all these islands before arriving in St. Lucia.

US Airways (☎ **800-428-4322,** 758-454-8186; www.usairways.com) flies from Philadelphia to George Charles and Hewanorra airports twice a week.

Sint Maarten/St. Martin

American Airlines (☎ **800-433-7300** in the U.S. and Canada; www.aa.com) offers more options and more-frequent service into Dutch Sint Maarten than any other airline — two daily nonstop flights from both New York's JFK and Miami. Ask about American's package tours, which can save you a bundle.

Continental Airlines (☎ **800-525-0280** in the U.S. and Canada; www. continental.com) has daily nonstop flights out of its hub in Newark, New Jersey, during the winter months. However, in low season, flight times vary.

US Airways (☎ **800-428-4322** in the U.S and Canada; www.usairways. com) offers nonstop service from Philadelphia and from Charlotte, North Carolina.

U.S. Virgin Islands

American Airlines (☎ **800-433-7300** in the U.S and Canada; www.aa. com) offers frequent service to St. Thomas and St. Croix from the U.S. mainland, with five daily flights from New York to St. Thomas in high season. Passengers originating in other parts of the world are usually routed to St. Thomas through American's hubs in Miami or San Juan, both of which offer nonstop service (often several times a day) to St. Thomas. (**American Eagle** has 11 nonstop flights daily from San Juan to St. Thomas.)

Continental Airlines (☎ **800-525-0280** in the U.S. and Canada; www. continental.com) has daily nonstop flights from Newark International Airport to St. Thomas.

Delta (☎ **800-241-4141** in the U.S and Canada; www.delta.com) offers two daily nonstop flights between Atlanta and St. Thomas year-round.

United Airlines (☎ **800-241-6522** in the U.S. and Canada; www.united. com) has nonstop service on Saturday to St. Thomas from Chicago (one flight) and Washington, D.C. (two flights).

US Airways (☎ **800-428-4322** in the U.S. and Canada; www.usairways. com) has one nonstop daily flight from Philadelphia to St. Thomas, and an additional flight on Saturday.

If you're traveling from Australia or New Zealand, you must take a flight to London, where you can make a connection to the U.S. Virgin Islands. It's a long and difficult link.

Getting the best deal on your airfare

Good airfares to this part of the world can disappear in the time it takes the ice in your drink to melt in the Caribbean sun. If you find a fare that sounds good, book it immediately. Generally speaking, you're most likely to find discounted fares to the Caribbean from May through December 15, which is the low season (see Chapter 3 for more on travel seasons).

Competition among the major U.S. airlines is unlike that of any other industry. Every airline offers virtually the same product (basically, a coach seat is a coach seat is a coach seat), yet prices can vary by hundreds of dollars. Don't fool yourself into thinking that the passenger sitting in an identical seat next to you paid the same fare as you. He or she may have shelled out a whole lot more — or a whole lot less — depending on when, where, and how he or she purchased the seat. While planning a trip, we've often called the same airline three times in a single day and received three different fares for the same dates and destination. What's up with that?

Because of cancellations and ever-changing specials, the number of seats available for a particular flight in a particular fare category can fluctuate wildly from hour to hour, so get a feel for what you're willing to pay. If you come across a fare that looks good, jump on it. Otherwise, you snooze, you lose, because that handsome deal can disappear in a flash.

Booking in advance and being flexible

Business travelers who need the flexibility to buy their tickets at the last minute and change their itineraries at a moment's notice — and who want to get home before the weekend — pay (or at least their companies pay) the premium rate, known as the *full fare.* But if you can book your ticket far in advance, stay over Saturday night, and are willing to travel midweek (Tues, Wed, or Thurs), you can qualify for the least expensive price — usually a fraction of the full fare. On most flights, a 7- or 14-day advance purchase ticket may cost less than half the amount of a full flight. Obviously, planning ahead pays.

The airlines also periodically hold sales, in which they lower the prices on their most popular routes. These fares have advance purchase requirements and date-of-travel restrictions, but you can't beat the prices. As you plan your vacation, keep your eyes open for these sales, which tend to take place in seasons of low travel volume — that is, mid-April to mid-December.

Make your reservations right after midnight. Cinderella knew that things start to shake up 'round midnight. In the middle of the week, just after the clock strikes 12, many airlines download low-priced airfares to their computers, so this is a great time to buy newly discounted seats. Midnight is also the cutoff time for holding reservations, which means that you can snag cheap tickets that were just released because someone reserved them but never purchased them. Because most travel agents are in dreamland at this hour, you're on your own here (meaning that you can't call an agent to ask questions).

Buying from a consolidator

Consolidators, also known as bucket shops, are a good place to check for the lowest fares. Their prices are much better than the fares you can get yourself, and they're often lower than what your travel agent can get you. How can they do it? They buy the seats in bulk, far in advance. You can see their ads in the small boxes in your Sunday newspaper's travel section.

However, using a consolidator is sometimes very time-consuming. After you finally get past the busy signal, plan on hanging on hold for a good while before you get to an agent — and then he may take your name and number and take his sweet time getting back to you. (To comparison shop, you have to go through this process a few times.) When you finally get through, some consolidators may not even have the Caribbean flights that you requested at the moment. But, that's the penalty you pay for the great deal you may receive. Some of the most reliable consolidators include **800-FLY-4-LESS** and **800-FLY-CHEAP.**

Before you pay, request a confirmation number from the consolidator and then call the airline to confirm your seat. Be aware that bucket shop tickets are usually nonrefundable or rigged with stiff cancellation penalties, often as high as 50 to 75 percent of the ticket price. Protect yourself by paying with a credit card rather than cash. Keep in mind that if an airline sale is going on, or if it's high season, you can often get the same or better rates by contacting the airlines directly, so do some comparison shopping before you buy. Also check out the name of the airline; you may not want to fly on some obscure Third World airline, even if you're saving $10. And check whether you're flying on a charter or a scheduled airline; the latter is more expensive but more reliable.

Flying on a charter plane

You may want to book a seat on a charter flight. Lots of the most popular Caribbean destinations have charter flights, though discounted fares have clipped the wings of some. However, you can still find them. Most charter operators advertise and sell their seats through travel agents, so check with the pro you've selected with our help (see the section "Locating Caribbean specialists," later in this chapter).

Before deciding to take a charter flight, check the ticket restrictions: You may be asked to purchase a tour package, to pay in advance, to be amenable if the day of departure changes, to pay a service charge, to fly on an airline you're not familiar with (this usually isn't the case), and to pay harsh penalties if you cancel — but be understanding if the charter doesn't fill up and is canceled up to ten days before departure. Summer charters fill up more quickly than others and are almost sure to fly, but if you decide on a charter flight, seriously consider buying **cancellation and baggage insurance.** Also be prepared for late departure hours and long airport delays, because charters usually don't have priority.

Join a travel club such as **Moment's Notice** (☎ 888-241-3366; www. moments-notice.com) or **Travelers Advantage** (☎ 800-835-8747 to join; www.travelersadvantage.com), which supply unsold tickets at discounted prices. You pay an annual membership fee to get the club's hot-line number. Of course, you're limited to what's available, so you have to be flexible.

Booking your flight online

The "big three" online travel agencies, **Expedia** (www.expedia.com), **Travelocity** (www.travelocity.com), and **Orbitz** (www.orbitz.com), sell most of the airline tickets bought on the Internet. (Canadian travelers should try www.expedia.ca and www.travelocity.ca; U.K. residents can go for www.expedia.co.uk and www.opodo.co.uk.) Each has different business deals with the airlines and may offer different fares on the same flights, so shopping around is wise. Expedia and Travelocity will also send you an e-mail notification when a cheap fare becomes available to your favorite destination. Of the smaller travel agency Web sites, **SideStep** (www.sidestep.com) receives good reviews from users. It's a browser add-on that purports to search 140 sites at once, but in reality only beats competitors' fares as often as other sites do.

Great last-minute deals are available through free weekly e-mail services provided directly by the airlines. They announce most of these deals on Tuesday or Wednesday, and you must purchase them online. Most tickets are only valid for travel that weekend, but you can book some weeks or months in advance. Sign up for weekly e-mail alerts at airline Web sites or check megasites that compile comprehensive lists of last-minute specials, such as **Smarter Travel** (www.smartertravel.com). For last-minute trips, **Site59** (www.site59.com) in the U.S. and **lastminute.com** (www.lastminute.com) in Europe often have better deals than the major-label sites.

E-ticketing

Only yesterday, *electronic tickets* (E-tickets) were the fast and easy ticket-free alternative to paper tickets. E-tickets allowed passengers to avoid long lines at airport check-in, all the while saving the airlines money on postage and labor. With the increased security measures in airports, however, an E-ticket no longer guarantees an accelerated check-in. You often can't go straight to the boarding gate, even if you have no bags to check. You probably need to show your printed E-ticket receipt or confirmation of purchase, as well as a photo ID, and sometimes even the credit card with which you purchased your E-ticket. Besides that, for Caribbean travel, we've found that E-tickets aren't necessarily the ticket for smooth travel. Wise travelers still insist on the old paper version for Caribbean travel, especially if they're changing airlines en route or are planning on island hopping. Computer systems on the islands are sometimes slow or down, so paper tickets are easier. Plus, having that paper trail can become critical if you run into cancellations or delays; you may need to have a gate agent endorse your ticket or receipt so that you can hop the next flight on another airline.

If you're willing to give up some control over your flight details, use a service like **Priceline** (www.priceline.com; www.priceline.co.uk for Europeans) or **Hotwire** (www.hotwire.com). Both offer rock-bottom prices in exchange for travel on a mystery airline at a mysterious time of day, often with a mysterious change of planes en route. The mystery airlines are all major, well-known carriers — and the possibility of being sent from Philadelphia to Chicago via Tampa is remote; the airlines' routing computers have gotten a lot better than they used to be. But your chances of getting a 6 a.m. or 11 p.m. flight are pretty high. Hotwire tells you flight prices before you buy; Priceline usually has better deals than Hotwire, and you no longer have to play their "name your price" game. You also have the option to pick your flight, time, and airline from a list of low prices they offer. If you're new at this, the helpful folks at **BiddingForTravel.com** do a good job of demystifying Priceline's prices. Priceline and Hotwire are great for flights within North America and between the U.S. and Europe. But for flights to other parts of the world, consolidators almost always beat their fares.

 Great last-minute deals are also available directly from the airlines themselves through a free e-mail service called *E-savers*. Each week, the airline sends you a list of discounted flights, usually leaving the upcoming Friday or Saturday and returning the following Monday or Tuesday. You can sign up for all the major airlines at one time by logging on to **Smarter Travel** (www.smartertravel.com), or you can go to each individual airline's Web site. Airline sites also offer schedules, flight booking, and information on late-breaking bargains.

Hopping between Islands

Island hopping in the Caribbean is easy via the numerous small carriers servicing the islands. You can often find alternative routes to get where you want to go even if an airline says a certain itinerary is booked. In particular, Air Jamaica, BWIA, and LIAT all offer bargain fares that make visiting more than one island extremely affordable.

Puerto Rico is the major transportation hub of the Caribbean, with the best connections for getting anywhere on the islands.

With **Air Jamaica's** (☎ **800-523-5585;** www.airjamaica.com) "Island Hopping" package, you can visit two islands for the price of your ticket to the farthest destination. With Air Jamaica/Air Jamaica Express's "Caribbean Hopper" for $565, you can visit three or more islands on one trip.

Air St. Thomas (☎ **877-776-4315,** 340-776-4315; www.airstthomas.com) has service from St. Thomas to San Juan and Fajardo, Puerto Rico, and from San Juan and St. Thomas to Virgin Gorda.

American Airlines (☎ 800-433-7300; www.aa.com) and its local affiliate, **American Eagle** (same contact info), offer additional nonstop daily flights into Sint Maarten from San Juan. American Eagle also has nine to ten flights a day traveling between St. Thomas and St. Croix.

BWIA (☎ 800-538-2942; www.bwee.com) flies from Trinidad, Antigua, and Barbados to Dutch Sint Maarten.

Cape Air (☎ 800-352-0714 in the U.S. and Canada, 508-771-6944; www.flycapeair.com), based in St. Thomas, offers 12 flights daily between St. Thomas and Puerto Rico. This Massachusetts-based airline has expanded its service to include flights from San Juan to St. Croix and flights between St. Croix and St. Thomas.

Cayman Airways and **Air Jamaica** have joined forces to provide an air link from Grand Cayman to Barbados and Trinidad, going via Kingston in Jamaica. Flights depart Grand Cayman on Monday, Tuesday, Saturday, and Sunday, linking up in Kingston with continuing flights to Barbados and Port-of-Spain, with daily return flights. For reservations and information, contact Air Jamaica (☎ 800-523-5585; www.airjamaica.com).

Dutch Caribbean Airlines (☎ 800-327-7230; www.flydca.net) flies from San Juan to Aruba, Bonaire, and Curaçao — the so-called ABC islands — in the southern Caribbean, and to Jamaica.

Caribbean-based **LIAT** (☎ 800-744-5428 in the U.S. and Canada, 866-549-5428; www.liatairline.com), provides generally poor service to Barbados (one of its major hubs) from a handful of neighboring islands, including St. Vincent & the Grenadines, Antigua, and Dominica. The airline offers one flight to Dutch Sint Maarten from San Juan. Other flights to Sint Maarten stop first at Tortola in the British Virgin Islands. Even so, the trip usually takes only 90 minutes. From Sint Maarten — not on French St. Martin — LIAT, often with connections, offers ongoing service to Anguilla, Antigua, St. Croix, San Juan, St. Kitts, St. Thomas, and Dominica.

Seaborne Airlines (☎ 888-FLY-TOUR, or 888-359-8687; 340-773-6442; www.seaborneairlines.com) offers 10 to 17 round-trip flights traveling between St. Thomas and St. Croix daily. Flight time is only 25 minutes. It also offers daily links between St. Croix and St. Thomas with San Juan. The one-way cost from the U.S. Virgin Islands to Puerto Rico is a reasonable $85 per person. The planes are small and frequent, carrying 15 to 19 passengers. They often offer more than 50 flights a day.

Choosing a Package Tour

Package tours (also known as *package deals*) aren't the same as escorted tours, so we're not referring to a herd of tourists being jostled around to six islands in five days. Most vacationers wouldn't want to visit the

Caribbean in such a manner anyway even if such escorted tours existed. Package tours are simply a way of buying your airline ticket and hotel room (and sometimes more) in one transaction.

Opening your package

A package tour includes your flights, accommodations, land transportation to and from your hotel, taxes, meals (sometimes, but not always), and rental cars (if you want), as well as both travel and cancellation insurance. It allows you the convenience of buying everything at the same time and saves you a lot of money in the process.

Your air/hotel package costs you less, and often *much* less, than the hotel and airfare if you book them yourself separately. In some cases, these packages are even cheaper than the hotel alone. If this sounds too good to be true, it isn't. Packages are sold in bulk to tour operators, who resell them to the public. It's like buying your vacation at a membership discount club, except that the tour operator is the person buying the boxes of paper towels and reselling them at a cost that undercuts what you'd pay at your average neighborhood supermarket.

So what's the catch? These economical vacation packages vary as much as paper towels do. Because some packagers buy in bigger bulk than others, they can offer the same hotels for lower prices. Some feature a better class of hotels than others, and some offer flights on scheduled airlines, while others book charters. Also, some packages book only non-stop flights, while others make you change planes.

Nabbing the best deal

The best place to start looking for package deals is the travel section of your local Sunday newspaper. Also, check the ads in the back of national travel magazines such as *Travel & Leisure, Caribbean Travel & Life, Islands,* and *Condé Nast Traveler.* **Liberty Travel** (☎ **888-271-1584,** or check your local phone book for a location near you; www.libertytravel.com) is one of the biggest packagers in the country and usually runs a full-page ad in Sunday papers. You may not get much in the way of personalized, first-hand knowledge with the service (so familiarizing yourself with some choices beforehand is particularly important), but you get a good deal.

Some packagers specialize in types of trips, such as scuba-diving adventures, golf getaways, or casino excursions. Likewise, a few of the larger hotels, such as all-inclusive Club Med resorts, offer money-saving hotel packages that include charter flights. If you already know where you want to stay, call that resort and ask whether it offers land/air packages.

Airlines are another good resource because they package their flights together with accommodations. All the airlines, plus American Express, offer comparable packages and often use the same first-class hotels. Therefore, you can book your package through the airline that features the best transportation link through your hometown (and perhaps one on which you accumulate frequent-flier miles). Although disreputable packagers are uncommon, they do exist. By buying your package through the airline, you can be almost certain that the company will still be in business when your departure date nears.

Locating Caribbean specialists

The **Caribbean Tourism Organization** provides names of its recommended travel agents at www.doitcaribbean.com. You can go online to find travel agents specializing in the Caribbean at the **Association of Retail Travel Agents** (www.artaonline.com) or the **American Society of Travel Agents** (www.astanet.com).

TourScan (☎ **800-962-2080,** 203-655-8091; www.tourscan.com) has specialized in the Caribbean since 1987. Twice a year, it compiles information on all the different packages offered by tour operators, who often have prices that vary by hundreds of dollars for the exact same resort. Then it factors in the rack rates of upscale Caribbean hotels, smaller boutique hotels, guesthouses, and inns often not known by travel agents or carried by tour operators. The company also inputs information on bulk package airfares. Through its computerized system, the agency can then scan for the absolute best bargain package and come up with customized packages including airfare — even for unique and upscale places that normally don't offer any packages. All this information makes bargain hunting a breeze. This agency offers the lowdown on 1,800 properties on 56 islands in the Caribbean, the Bahamas, and Bermuda. The information is available by catalog or on its Web site, which answers common questions.

If you can pack up and go at the drop of a straw hat, try **Changes in L'Attitudes,** 3080 East Bay Dr., Largo, FL 33771 (☎ **800-330-8272,** 727-437-1177; Fax: 727-573-2497; www.changes.com). This agency, which has specialized in the Caribbean since 1985, has a terrific Web site that connects you to tons of resorts. It also lists specials and promotions with a heavy concentration on Jamaica with offerings on Aruba, the Cayman Islands, the U.S. Virgin Islands, and Barbados, as well as Bermuda and The Bahamas. Honeymooners and sailors will find some good deals here. If you register your e-mail address, the agency frequently sends out notices of deeply discounted, last-minute trips if you're able to travel within 21, 14, or 7 days.

If you think that you want to stay at an all-inclusive resort, **Bill Fox All-Inclusive Vacations,** 21999 Van Buren St., Suite 6, Grand Terrace, CA 92313 (☎ **800-944-3862,** 909-824-8825; www.billfoxtravel.com) has specialized in discounted all-inclusive packages since 1991 and handles Sandals, Beaches, and Club Med. Its excellent Web site answers many common questions about all-inclusives.

Here are some other packagers we like:

- ✔ **Caribbean Dive Tours,** 732 Johnson Ferry Rd., Marietta, GA 30068 (☎ **800-786-3483;** www.caribbeandivetours.com), arranges dive trips to Aruba, Puerto Rico, the Cayman Islands, the British Virgin Islands, the U.S. Virgin Islands, and other Caribbean islands.

- ✔ **Caribbean Inns, Ltd.,** P.O. Box 7411, Hilton Head Island, SC 29938 (☎ **800-633-7411;** www.caribbeaninns.com), which has been in business since 1987, puts together Caribbean cruise packages and honeymoon packages if you're interested in a small, intimate inn in the three- to five-star range or in villas.

- ✔ **Island Destinations** (☎ **888-454-4422,** 914-833-3300; Fax: 914-833-3318; www.islanddestinations.com) is a tour operator for upscale travelers that represents some of the more exclusive properties on 15 Caribbean islands, including 30 hotels and three groups of villas. This agency sends representatives to each property annually so that they can match clients to the best place.

- ✔ For dive, leisure, and soft adventure packages (like kayaking), try **Maduro Dive Fanta-Seas,** 4500 Biscayne Blvd., Suite 320, Miami, FL 33137 (☎ **800-327-6709,** 305-981-9113; Fax: 305-981-9397; www.maduro.com). The company has offerings in Barbados, the Cayman Islands, and Puerto Rico, as well as on Bonaire, Curaçao, Tobago, Tortola, Saba, St. Croix, St. Lucia, and Dominica.

- ✔ One of the leading Caribbean packagers for Canadian travelers is **Signature Vacations,** 160 Bloor St. E., Suite 400, Toronto, Ontario, Canada M4W 1B9 (☎ **866-324-2883,** 416-967-1510; Fax: 416-967-7154; www.signaturevacations.com).

- ✔ If you want to stay at a villa, try booking through **Unusual Villas,** 409F North Hamilton St., Richmond, VA 23221 (☎ **800-846-7280,** 804-288-2823; Fax: 804-342-9016; www.unusualvillarentals.com). This company has more than 100 villas for rent in Barbados and Jamaica, and about 50 on St. Thomas, with a total of 2,500 represented throughout the Caribbean.

- ✔ **WIMCO,** P.O. Box 1461, Newport, RI 02840 (☎ **800-449-1553,** 401-849-8012; www.wimco.com), a Caribbean villa and hotel expert for 20 years, represents 1,000 villas and 30 hotels in the region. Most of the properties are on St. Barts, Sint Maarten/St. Martin, the British Virgin Islands, Barbados, the Cayman Islands, and the U.S. Virgin Islands. Forbes.com recently honored its Web site by naming it the best vacation rental site on the Web.

Other good resources are the airlines themselves, which package their flights together with accommodations. Your options include

- ✔ **Air Canada Vacations** (☎ **888-247-2262;** www.aircanada.com)

- ✔ **Air Jamaica Vacations** (☎ **800-LOVE-BIRD;** www.airjamaica vacations.com)

- ✔ **American Airlines Vacations** (☎ 800-321-2121; www.aa
  vacations.com)

- ✔ **Continental Airlines Vacations** (☎ 800-301-3800; www.co
  vacations.com)

- ✔ **Delta Vacations** (☎ 800-221-6666; www.deltavacations.com)

- ✔ **Northwest Airlines World Vacations** (☎ 800-800-1504; www.
  nwaworldvacations.com)

- ✔ **United Vacations** (☎ 888-854-3899; www.unitedvacations.com)

- ✔ **US Airways Vacations** (☎ 800-455-0123; www.usairways
  vacations.com)

Cruising the Islands

A great way to see more than one island is on a cruise. Request a Q&A
booklet from **Cruise Lines International Association** (www.cruising.
org). Some lines that sail in the Caribbean include the following:

- ✔ **American Canadian Caribbean Line** (☎ 800-556-7450; www.
  accl-smallships.com)

- ✔ **Carnival** (☎ 888-CARNIVAL; www.carnival.com)

- ✔ **Club Med Cruises** (☎ 888-WEB-CLUB; www.clubmed.com)

- ✔ **Disney** (☎ 800-951-3532; www.disneycruise.com)

- ✔ **Holland America Line** (☎ 877-SAIL-HAL; www.hollandamerica.
  com)

- ✔ **Royal Caribbean** (☎ 866-562-7625; www.royalcaribbean.com)

- ✔ **Seabourn Cruise Line** (☎ 800-929-9391; www.seabourn.com)

- ✔ **Windjammer Barefoot Cruises** (☎ 800-327-2601; www.
  windjammer.com)

- ✔ **Windstar** (☎ 800-258-7245; www.windstarcruises.com)

Cruise lines operate like airlines, setting rates for their cruises and then
selling them in a rapid-fire series of discounts, offering almost whatever
it takes to fill their ships. Because of this, great deals come and go in the
blink of an eye, and most are available only through travel agents.

If you have a travel agent you trust, leave the details to him or her. If not,
try contacting a travel agent who specializes in booking cruises. Some of
the most likely contenders include the following:

✔ **The Cruise Company,** 10760 Q St., Omaha, NE 68127 (☎ **800-289-5505,** 402-339-6800; www.thecruisecompany.com)

✔ **Cruises, Inc.,** 1415 NW 62 St., Fort Lauderdale, FL 33009 (☎ **866-325-6893,** 800-854-0500, 954-958-3681; www.cruisesinc.com)

✔ **Cruises Only,** 1011 E. Colonial Dr., Orlando, FL 32803 (☎ **800-CRUISES;** www.cruisesonly.com)

✔ **Hartford Holidays Travel,** 129 Hillside Ave., Williston Park, NY 11596 (☎ **800-828-4813,** 516-746-6670; www.hartfordholidays.com)

✔ **Kelly Cruises,** 1315 W. 22nd St., Suite 105, Oak Brook, IL 60523 (☎ **800-837-7447;** www.kellycruises.com)

✔ **Mann Travel and Cruises,** 4400 Park Rd., Charlotte, NC 28209 (☎ **866-591-8129;** www.manntravelandcruises.com)

Because we could fill a large barge with information on cruising — and we have somewhat less space in this book — we suggest that you check out *Cruise Vacations For Dummies* (Wiley), for more help in this area.

Chapter 6

Booking Your Accommodations

* *

In This Chapter

▶ Understanding your lodging options
▶ Becoming familiar with hotel symbols
▶ Booking the best room in the house — for the best rate

* *

*A*ccommodations options in the Caribbean run the gamut from your desert island beach-hut fantasy (don't expect air-conditioning) or a small guesthouse for less than $80 a night to accommodations so fancy that they include a maid, gardener, cook, laundress, and butler, all in starched uniforms, standing ready to anticipate your every whim. Our tastes lie somewhere in the middle of these two extremes.

Getting to Know Your Options

Expectation and reality often clash for first-time travelers in the tropics. Life moves languidly in the Caribbean, and change comes slowly and in small increments — radically different from the instantaneous responses we expect from our point-and-click world. In the Caribbean, concerns are different. In recent years, enormous battles have been waged at some of the region's finer resorts over whether to install phones and air-conditioning in the rooms at all. However, many hoteliers have given in and are adding direct-dial phones with dataports. Some small resorts now offer free places to check your e-mail, too, but others charge for the service.

Although most of our recommended choices in the individual island accommodations chapters are located on the beach and have air-conditioning (unless otherwise noted), understand that some of the sexiest resorts in this region have no air-conditioning, no phone, no television, no alarm clock — not even *USA Today* or CNN.

Hotels and resorts: A variety of options

The Caribbean offers a tremendous range of hotel and resort accommodations, from small-budget places that provide a basic room with a bed and a bathroom all the way up to exclusive resorts owned and managed by some of the world's finer chains. The latest trend among Caribbean hotels is the addition of spa services and upgraded workout facilities. On most islands, building ordinances require that structures be no taller than the tallest coconut tree. On Puerto Rico, St. Thomas, Jamaica, and Aruba, however, you can see high-rise hotels like those on Miami Beach. Chains operate the best properties on Aruba (Marriott, Hyatt, and Radisson), Grand Cayman (Westin, Hyatt, and soon The Ritz-Carlton), and St. Thomas (Marriott and The Ritz-Carlton). But many of the hotels listed in this book have fewer than 100 rooms, and several are boutique hotels, stylized and unique in character. We tend to favor these kinds of places.

Hotels and resorts often include meal plans and the use of facilities in their rates. We discuss meal plans later in this chapter and in Chapter 4. Even if a hotel or resort doesn't offer all-inclusive packages (which we explain in the next section), you can usually count on full use of the pool and nonmotorized water sports. However, you may have to pay for use of a lounge chair on the beach and snorkeling or other equipment.

We recommend hotels and resorts for

- ✔ Honeymooners or couples who want to focus on each other

- ✔ Families who want programs and babysitters close at hand

- ✔ Sports lovers who want all the facilities

- ✔ First-time visitors to the Caribbean

- ✔ Travelers with disabilities, because these places are much more likely to have appropriate facilities

But staying at a hotel or resort also has its drawbacks:

- ✔ Many resorts and hotels lack island atmosphere.

- ✔ You may feel obliged to spend your time on the property, because you've paid so much to be there.

- ✔ Extra expenses for meals, drinks, and water sports add up quickly, and you're likely to get a shock at checkout if you've been charging everything to your room.

All-inclusive resorts: Simplifying your vacation

The all-inclusive concept, where you shell out the dough for your vacation in advance (with no tipping allowed after you arrive at the property), is essentially a one-price-buys-all package that includes your hotel room, meals, drinks, and activities. All-inclusive resorts have found their niche because travelers want to simplify their lives. The Caribbean's version of the concept started in Jamaica and now dominates the accommodations scene on that island. You'll run into the all-inclusive concept in Barbados, St. Thomas, St. Lucia, and Aruba, and in a smattering of places across most of the other islands, too.

Recently, the top-tier all-inclusive resorts have been duking it out by adding more and more extras. For instance, stung by criticism in the early days that they were cheapskates when it came to food and drink, the big players all now serve premium-brand alcohol and have been hiring better and better chefs for their restaurants. Now you may find yourself with half a dozen or so restaurants from which to choose — without ever leaving your resort.

The new battleground, however, appears to be in the spa arena. The words *and Spa* after the name of the all-inclusive resort are becoming almost as ubiquitous as the words *and Casino* after the name of almost every hotel on Aruba. Guests at many spa resorts get one spa treatment (full-body massages and facials are the most popular) per day included in their all-inclusive package.

We like all-inclusive resorts and include our favorites in this book, along with several smaller boutique hotels and resorts that don't have the big advertising budgets.

The main operators of all-inclusive resorts in the Caribbean are

- ✔ **Sandals** (☎ 888-SANDALS; www.sandals.com), which operates several couples-only properties

- ✔ **SuperClubs** (☎ 877-GO-SUPER; www.superclubs.com), which owns numerous properties in Jamaica and a few on other islands, including Curaçao

- ✔ **Beaches** (☎ 888-BEACHES; www.beaches.com), which has several family-oriented properties in Jamaica with four upscale properties geared to adults and older children

- ✔ **Divi Resorts** (☎ 800-367-3484; www.diviresorts.com), which operates nine resorts on six Caribbean islands: Aruba, Barbados, Bonaire, Cayman Brac, Sint Maarten, and St. Croix

- ✔ **Club Med** (☎ 888-WEB-CLUB; www.clubmed.com), which has a few "villages" in the Caribbean

Each all-inclusive company offers packages that allow you to get married for free when you book a honeymoon with them.

One of our favorite features of Sandals and SuperClubs is a user-friendly program that lets you split your time between resorts within each company's range of accommodations. To us, that's the resort equivalent of ordering the fisherman's platter. You get to sample the best of everything. For example, SuperClubs allows you to book a stay at the slightly less-expensive couples **Sans Souci Resort & Spa** and then spend a few days of your minimum six-night stay at the more expensive **Grand Lido Negril.**

What you get at an all-inclusive resort varies dramatically, and the differences can be confusing. One Web site that rates all-inclusive resorts is www.all-inclusive.com. It operates similarly to AAA Diamond Awards, which uses a ten-star rating, assigning point values to all the services and amenities. Sandals, which obviously has a vested interest, is a partner in the undertaking.

 Many guests at all-inclusive resorts are under the mistaken impression that they don't need to tip baggage handlers at the airport and drivers who get you to and from your resort. That isn't the case, and this misunderstanding has unfortunately created tension on both sides. Unless the person helping you is an employee of the resort, assume that you *do* need to tip.

Good candidates for all-inclusive resorts are

- ✔ Honeymooners
- ✔ Families
- ✔ Inexperienced travelers
- ✔ The budget conscious
- ✔ The super stressed

 The drawbacks to staying at an all-inclusive resort?

- ✔ You may feel obligated to spend all your time on the property, because you've paid so much to be there. Every island is exactly the same when you view it from the cushy confines of an all-inclusive. You miss what makes the island special after you've traveled so far to get there.
- ✔ Rah-rah activity instructors can wear on your nerves.

Villas: Vacationing with the comforts of home

Villa is a broad word in the Caribbean. Basically, it means a rental property. Properties ranging from princely digs to modest bungalows fall into this category.

A villa promises two luxuries: space and good kitchen facilities. Villas offer more privacy than hotels and resorts and are tucked away on gated lots with either sea or mountain views. If you like the comforts of home, a villa is the way to go. Villas are particularly popular in the Virgin Islands (U.S. and British), Jamaica, and Puerto Rico.

Villas rent for anywhere from less than $1,000 a week all the way up to thousands of dollars a day. Three couples traveling together can rent a villa for a week for less than $1,000 per person. We've been amazed at how reasonably priced some drop-dead gorgeous villas are, particularly on St. John. You can also find some good deals in Jamaica. Many villas require that you book for a minimum of a week.

We recommend booking a villa through a professional management company that's responsible for renting out and maintaining the house when the owner isn't on the island. (See our recommendation in the next paragraph or look at the back of the ad sections in *Caribbean Travel & Life* or *Islands* magazines.) Renting a villa from an individual can be a little iffy, because the Caribbean has a way of taking a toll on even the finest resorts. Unless an owner is extremely diligent about upkeep, a place can quickly slip below par. You also run the risk of renting a place where the décor looks like leftovers from a yard sale. In this book, we include only villas that we've inspected personally and recently.

For the preeminent source on villas, try **Unusual Villas,** 409F North Hamilton St., Richmond, VA 23221 (☎ **800-846-7280,** 804-288-2823; Fax: 804-342-9016; www.unusualvillarentals.com). Owner John Greer, who's been specializing in villas since 1992, has an award-winning Web site with more than 1,500 pages dedicated to villas. He has more than 100 villas for rent in Barbados and Jamaica. On St. Thomas, he handles rentals for about 50 villas, and he deals with rentals on a total of 30 Caribbean islands.

Two other good sources for villas are

- ✔ **WIMCO** (☎ **800-449-1553;** www.wimco.com), which represents villas in Barbados, Grand Cayman, the Virgin Islands, and several other Caribbean isles

- ✔ **Island Destinations** (☎ **888-454-4422,** 914-833-3300; Fax: 914-833-3318; www.islanddestinations.com), which represents villas in Jamaica, Puerto Rico, and the Virgin Islands as well as a few other Caribbean islands, and offers wedding and honeymoon coordinators

So that you don't waste time and money on duplicate supplies, check with the management company about what the villa has on hand for your use. Depending on the unit, you may be treated to a welcome platter of fresh fruit and a bottle of wine. You may find that you get access to a vehicle as part of the rental as well.

We recommend villas for

- ✔ Families.

- ✔ A group of friends — you'd better be close, though, or you run the risk of fights over the master bedroom, which invariably has some cool feature that everyone covets.

- ✔ Honeymooners or couples craving privacy.

- ✔ Independent travelers who want to connect independently with the island.

But staying at a home-away-from-home can also have a downside:

- ✔ You don't get the extensive dining facilities and other amenities of a resort.

- ✔ A villa may not offer daily maid service and other niceties (like a pool or Jacuzzi) that you consider vital to your relaxation.

- ✔ Few are located right on the beach; resorts usually snag the prime real estate.

- ✔ You definitely won't get (or be subjected to, depending on your point of view) the nightly entertainment that almost every Caribbean hotel trumpets.

- ✔ A villa can be isolating, so you'd better really like your traveling companion(s).

- ✔ Of all the travel options, villas are least likely to live up to their brochure promises.

Condos and timeshares: Apartment-style living

Condos and timeshares are popular options on Aruba, Grand Cayman, and the U.S. Virgin Islands (mainly St. Thomas). With these properties, you get apartment-style accommodations in a hotel setting. The amenities vary greatly. At busy La Cabana on Aruba, for example, the experience isn't much different from staying at a large resort. **The Ritz-Carlton** on St. Thomas, the **Westin St. John,** and the **Aruba Marriott** have all entered the timeshare business in recent years with units that are on the same property as their respective resorts. Prices are comparable to what you'd pay at a hotel, but you almost always have kitchen facilities.

We recommend condos and timeshares for

- ✔ Families. You can feed your kids what you want and not have to suffer disapproving looks from the honeymooners at the next table when Junior flips his soggy cereal on the floor.

- ✔ A group of friends. Try to choose friends that you're familiar traveling with or with whom you feel comfortable discussing some ground rules before you go.

- ✔ Older couples looking for quiet.

- ✔ Long-term vacationers. Cooking your own meals is a money-saving tactic for an extended stay on an island.

- ✔ Independent travelers who want to connect with the island and its people.

What are some drawbacks of staying at a condo or timeshare?

- ✔ You have all the comforts of home, *plus* all the work.
- ✔ The amenities are limited.
- ✔ You're trusting your tropical dream to someone else's decorating taste.
- ✔ When dinnertime comes, you're the staff as well as the diner.

Guesthouses: Living la vida local

If you want lodging that resembles a bed-and-breakfast, a guesthouse is the Caribbean's answer. In a guesthouse, only a few rooms are available for rent, and the owner/manager lives on the property.

Guesthouses work well for bargain hunters and for those who like being under someone else's roof. You may get a light breakfast as part of your rate, which is usually $100 or less per night. If you plan to explore a great deal, this option may be good for you, too — you have a place to come home to after satisfying your wanderlust.

We recommend guesthouses for

- ✔ Older couples who like the bed-and-breakfast concept
- ✔ Long-term vacationers on tight budgets
- ✔ The independent traveler who needs a home base

Here are some of the drawbacks of staying at a guesthouse:

- ✔ You may be far from the beach, without a pool.
- ✔ The digs may not be glamorous.
- ✔ You may not get along with your host.
- ✔ Housekeeping standards vary widely.
- ✔ If you have a problem, you're stuck dealing one-on-one with the house owner.

Deciphering Hotel Symbols

As you speak with hotel reservationists, search the Web, or discuss your vacation desires with a travel agent, you encounter various symbols that are common to the travel industry. Those symbols may be Greek to you unless you've traveled a lot.

To familiarize yourself with the terms you'll likely come across, check out the following quick rundown of what the symbols mean and what the plans entail. "All-inclusive" means what it says, leaving no room for negotiation. However, if you have a particular preference for one meal plan, which will probably save you money, you can review the options before booking a room and settle on what seems to fit you and your budget.

- ✔ **European Plan (EP):** All Caribbean resorts offer a European Plan, which means that you pay for the price of a room only. That leaves you free to dine at various other resorts or restaurants without restrictions.

- ✔ **Continental Plan (CP):** Includes a light breakfast — juice, coffee, pastry or bread, and perhaps a piece of fruit. This plan is popular because most guests don't like to dine around at breakfast time.

- ✔ **Breakfast Plan (BP):** Includes a full traditional American-style breakfast (eggs, bacon, pancakes, French toast, hash browns, and so on).

- ✔ **Modified American Plan (MAP):** Includes breakfast (usually a full one) and lunch or dinner.

- ✔ **Full American Plan (FAP)** or **American Plan (AP):** Either plan means three meals a day.

- ✔ **All-inclusive:** You get three all-you-can-eat meals a day, plus soft drinks and alcoholic beverages, which sometimes include premium liquor and excellent wine, and, usually, snacks throughout the day.

At certain resorts, you save money by booking either the MAP or FAP/AP because they offer discounts. If you dine à la carte for lunch and dinner at various restaurants, your final dining bill will no doubt be much higher than if you stayed on the MAP or FAP/AP.

Meal plans can have drawbacks, particularly if you enjoy eating out as part of your holiday. You virtually face the same dining room every night, unless the resort you're staying at has many different restaurants on the dining plan. Often they don't. Many resorts have a lot of specialty restaurants, serving, say, Japanese cuisine, but these more-expensive restaurants aren't included in the MAP or FAP/AP and charge à la carte prices.

Dining at your hotel at night cuts down on transportation costs. Taxis especially are expensive. Nonetheless, if dining out and having many different culinary experiences is your idea of a vacation, and you're willing to pay the higher price, avoid FAPs/APs or at least make sure that the hotel where you're staying has more than one dining room.

One option is to ask whether your hotel has a **dine-around plan.** You might still keep costs in check, but you can avoid a culinary rut by taking your meals in some other restaurants if your hotel has such a plan. (See Chapter 4 for more on dine-around plans.)

Before booking a room, check with a good travel agent or investigate on your own what you're likely to save by booking with a dining plan. Under certain circumstances, such as visiting during the high season, you may not have a choice if MAP is dictated as a requirement for staying there. It pays to investigate, of course.

Price ranges in Table 6-1 are for standard guest rooms based on double occupancy in high season and one-night bookings. These are the highest rates charged. Expect discounts ranging from 20 to 60 percent for the same room if you book between mid-April and mid-December. For easy reference, these dollar-sign symbols appear with each hotel review in the destination chapters. You can stick within your hotel budget by seeking out the hotels with a symbol that matches your price range.

Table 6-1		Key to Hotel Dollar Signs
Dollar Signs	*Price Range*	*What to Expect*
$	$100 or less	These accommodations are relatively simple and inexpensive. Rooms are likely small, and they don't necessarily have televisions. Parking isn't provided but instead catch-as-you-can on the street.
$$	$101–$200	A bit classier, these midrange accommodations offer more room, more extras (such as an iron, hair dryer, or microwave), and a more convenient location than the preceding category.
$$$	$201–$300	Higher-class still, these accommodations begin to look plush. Think chocolates on your pillow, a classy restaurant, underground parking garages, and maybe even expansive views of the water.
$$$$	$301–$500	These top-rated accommodations come with luxury amenities such as valet parking, on-premise spas, and in-room hot tubs and CD players — but you pay through the nose for 'em.
$$$$$	$501 and up	These properties are the most deluxe in all the Caribbean, with the best rooms, the best facilities, and the best of everything. This category is for those travelers who insist on putting on the Ritz.

Finding the Best Room at the Best Rate

One of the frustrating aspects of Caribbean travel is meeting people that are staying in accommodations similar to yours but are paying far less for the privilege. Here are some ways to get the most bang for your buck (or euro, pound, or whatever).

Finding the best rate

The *rack rate* is the maximum rate a hotel charges for a room. It's the rate you get if you walk in off the street and ask for a room for the night. You sometimes see these rates printed on the fire/emergency exit diagrams posted on the back of your door.

Hotels are happy to charge you the rack rate, but you can almost always do better. Here are a few tips for starters:

- ✔ **Just ask for a cheaper or discounted rate.** You may be pleasantly surprised.

- ✔ **Buy a package deal.** Package deals abound, and they're always cheaper than rack rates. So, sometimes you're better off going to a reliable travel agent to find out what, if anything, is available in the way of a land-and-air package before booking into a particular accommodations. For more on package deals, see Chapter 5.

- ✔ **Go during the off season.** The off season in the Caribbean — roughly from mid-April to mid-December, although this varies from hotel to hotel — amounts to a sale. In most cases, hotel rates are slashed a startling 20 to 60 percent. This deal is a bonanza for cost-conscious travelers, especially for families who can travel in the summer. Be prepared for very strong sun, though, plus a higher chance of rain. Also note that hurricane season runs through the summer and fall. (See Chapter 3 for more on seasons.)

 The winter season in the Caribbean runs roughly from the middle of December to the middle of April, and hotels charge their highest prices during this peak period. Winter is generally the dry season in the islands, but heavy rainfall can occur regardless of the time of year. During the winter months, make reservations two months in advance if you can. You can't book early enough if you want to travel over Christmas or in February.

Even within a given season, room prices are subject to change without notice, so the rates quoted in this book may be different from the actual rate you receive when you make your reservation.

You'll also find that, in all but the smallest accommodations, the rate you pay for a room depends on many factors — chief among them being how you make your reservation. A travel agent may be able to negotiate a better price with certain hotels than you can get by yourself, because the hotel often gives the agent a discount in exchange for steering his or her business toward that hotel.

 Reserving a room through the hotel's toll-free number may also result in a lower rate than calling the hotel directly. On the other hand, the people answering the phones at the central reservations number may not know about discount rates at specific locations. For example, local franchises may offer a special group rate for a wedding or family reunion, but they may neglect to tell the central booking line. Your best bet is to call both the local number and the toll-free number and see which one gives you a better deal.

When you call to book a room, be sure to mention membership in AAA, AARP, frequent-flier programs, any other corporate rewards programs you can think of — or your Uncle Joe's Elks lodge in which you're an honorary inductee, for that matter. You never know when the affiliation may be worth a few dollars off your room rate.

For more tips on saving money on your accommodations, see our list of pointers in Chapter 4.

Surfing the Web for hotel deals

Although the major travel booking sites such as Travelocity.com, Expedia.com, and Orbitz.com offer hotel booking, you may be better off using a site devoted primarily to lodging. You can often find properties that more-general online travel agencies don't list. Some lodging sites specialize in a particular type of accommodations, such as bed-and-breakfasts (B&Bs), which you won't find on the more-mainstream booking services. Others, such as TravelWeb (see the following list), offer weekend deals on major chain properties, which cater to business travelers and have more empty rooms on weekends. A few of the sites worth checking are

- ✔ **All Hotels on the Web** (www.all-hotels.com): Although the name is something of a misnomer, the site does have tens of thousands of listings throughout the world. Bear in mind that each hotel has paid a small fee ($25 and up) to be listed, so this list is less objective and more like a book of online brochures.

- ✔ **hoteldiscount!com** (www.hoteldiscount.com): This site lists bargain room rates at hotels in more than 50 U.S. and international destinations, including the Caribbean. Because these folks prebook blocks of rooms, you can sometimes reserve rooms at hotels that are otherwise sold out. Select a place, input your dates, and you get a list of the best prices for a selection of hotels. The site often delivers deep discounts at resorts where hotel rooms are expensive. Call the toll-free number (☎ 800-715-7666) if you want more options than those that are listed online.

- ✔ **InnSite** (www.innsite.com): InnSite has B&B listings in all 50 U.S. states and more than 50 countries around the globe, including the

Caribbean. Find an inn at your destination, see pictures of the rooms, and check prices and availability. This extensive directory of B&Bs includes listings only if the proprietor submitted one (getting an inn listed is free). The descriptions are written by the innkeepers, and many listings link to the inn's own Web sites.

✔ **TravelWeb** (www.travelweb.com): Listing more than 26,000 hotels in 170 countries, including the Caribbean, TravelWeb focuses mostly on chains (both upper and lower end), and you can book almost 90 percent of these online. TravelWeb's Click-It Weekends, updated each Monday, offers weekend deals at many leading hotel chains.

Reserving the best room

Somebody has to get the best room at a hotel or a resort, so it may as well be you. Here's how to go about it:

✔ Ask detailed questions when booking a room. Don't just ask for a certain hotel, but specify your likes and dislikes.

✔ Find out what the rates include — a so-called expensive hotel that includes beach chairs, snorkel rentals, or whatever may cost less than a moderate hotel that charges you every time you breathe.

✔ Ask how far your hotel is from the beach.

✔ Question whether the price includes transportation from the airport.

✔ Find out about meal plan options.

✔ Inquire about ceiling fans, air-conditioning, and whether the windows open.

✔ Discover whether the room faces the water or the garage in back — if you're not going to spend time a lot of time in your room, the back view makes sense because it costs less. Upper-floor rooms with views are more pricey.

✔ Ask for a room, floor, or annex that is newly renovated.

✔ Check to see if the hotel is in the midst of renovation; if it is, request a room away from the work site.

✔ If the kids are along, find out whether they can stay with you for free — and look into a suite, which may cost less than two rooms.

✔ Ask about nonsmoking rooms.

✔ Inquire about your room's proximity to any of the hotel's open-air restaurants, the lounge or bar, beach bars with steel pan bands, family pools with screaming kids, and discos blaring reggae — all sources of irritating noise that can be torture if you're a light sleeper.

✔ Find out how much lower the rates are in the off season.

Specify what size bed you want, or you may find yourself with two twins — especially on British islands like Barbados.

If your resort isn't air-conditioned and relies on trade winds and ceiling fans for cooling, try to get a room as close to the sea as possible. You get more of a breeze if you're on the second floor or higher. Corner rooms with more windows give you that much more breeze coming through. At **The Ritz-Carlton** on St. Thomas, for example, the suites occupy the far-end corner of the building overhanging the bluff with a view of the harbor. Although the suites are air-conditioned, you can also open the windows out to the sea, as well as the doors onto the private wrap-around decks.

If you aren't happy with your room when you arrive, talk to the front-desk manager. Recently, I, Danforth, stayed at a resort where I was given a lovely room right on the beach. However, when I walked out the front door of my room, the trash receptacle for the hotel was behind a nearby wall and the smell was overpowering. If the wind hadn't shifted, I would've been in the manager's office. In a case like that, speak up. If the hotel has another room, they'll accommodate you, within reason.

Chapter 7

Catering to Special Travel Needs or Interests

- -

In This Chapter

▶ Planning a family trip
▶ Searching for senior discounts
▶ Selecting the best sites for travelers with disabilities
▶ Locating gay- and lesbian-friendly businesses
▶ Taking the plunge (and we don't mean snorkeling)
▶ Enjoying an island honeymoon

- -

*C*aribbean travel planning seems to inspire some common questions: How family-friendly are the islands? Where can couples honeymoon or even tie the knot? What discounts and privileges are available for seniors? Which islands have the best facilities for travelers with disabilities? And which put out the welcome mat for gay and lesbian travelers? If you're among those who have special needs or concerns about your Caribbean visit, read on — our discoveries can help you prepare for a delightful, rather than disappointing, getaway.

Traveling with the Brood: Advice for Families

These days, a growing number of families spend their summer and holiday vacations in the Caribbean. Eager to take advantage of this trend, hotels and resorts are scrambling to add facilities and services appealing to pint-size customers. And that's not a tough task: Between the pool and the warm Caribbean Sea, the kids are already enthralled. Add in games like limbo, crab races, and reggae dance contests, and they're over the moon. Relatively new programs offering cultural and ecological exploration impress parents and children alike. For example, your child could spend the morning learning from a marine biologist how to protect coral reefs or with an archaeologist digging for Indian artifacts.

Flying with kids

The toughest part of traveling with kids is that time-worn question, "Are we there yet?" Getting there with kids in tow is definitely not half the fun, but for most island destinations, the trip really isn't that bad. It sure beats a long car trip.

 Don't forget that when traveling internationally, children — babies, too — must have either a certified copy of a birth certificate (with a raised seal) or an official passport (see Chapter 8). Here are some other points to keep in mind when traveling with young children:

✔ Children's airfares are typically discounted 50 percent, but during peak season, the reduction may be as little as 33 percent.

✔ You can't expect many empty seats on Caribbean flights, so don't gamble on being able to seat your infant (under age 2) beside you. If you both want to be comfortable, buy a seat for your child. Ask about special children's fares.

✔ Order a kid's meal when you reserve your flight and ask about the airline's rules regarding car seats.

✔ Because Caribbean flights are so full, and because of the stringent new rules, you'll probably have to check your child's stroller. Make sure that you label the stroller with your name and where you're staying on the island.

✔ Families should arrange to be seated together on the plane. Double-check with your travel agent or with the airline directly. If you don't have boarding passes, get to the airport extra early to ensure that you get seats together. Caribbean flights are usually packed, and we've seen families separated by several rows.

✔ The bulkhead, which has extra space, is in high demand, but you may get lucky if you request it early.

✔ Pack four times the amount of favorite snacks you think you'll need. Delays can be lengthy these days, and airport food prices are sky-high. Baby wipes (even if your children are older) come in handy, too. Also bring a good supply of water for each child — especially if you're changing planes. For babies and toddlers, bring a large supply of diapers onboard with you, too.

✔ To relieve painful pressure on eardrums, bring chewing gum for older children. Nurse or give babies a bottle on takeoff and landing to keep their ears from hurting.

✔ Let your child bring his or her favorite small toys. But don't bring expensive electronic ones that are likely to get misplaced or stolen. On islands with high poverty levels, including Jamaica, we like to bring boxes of crayons and small items that we can leave behind for island children.

✔ If you rent a car, request a car seat in advance. If a hotel is arranging transportation for you, ask if the vehicle being sent will have seat belts. We've found that even family-friendly resorts often send vans and cars with nary a seat belt in sight.

✔ For the return trip, ask at the hotel what food the airport serves. If it doesn't sound like something your child would eat, request a packed lunch for the plane from the resort, which is often happy to accommodate you. Even if you have to pay a small fee, it's worth it, because food service is often pretty skimpy at island airports.

Choosing a family-friendly resort

Most major resorts claim to have children's programs, but the offerings differ greatly. Take a tour of the facilities before dropping off your kids. Some of the ritzier resorts accept children only at certain times of year, and then the staff's attitude may be one of tolerance rather than enthusiasm. A children's program in such a place may consist of a bored sitter stuck in a small room with several kids. We actually got a press release from one place trumpeting its kids' program, which consisted of setting out cookies and milk for children each evening.

 Always check on the children's program before you book at a resort to make sure you're getting what you think you are. Here are some good questions to ask:

✔ What is the ratio of program counselors to children?

✔ How are the ages divided?

✔ How much beach or pool time do they get (with expert supervision, of course)?

✔ Where and what do the children eat?

 Be sure to alert the workers to any food allergies your child has and double-check to make sure they really understand.

Some programs don't accept children who aren't potty trained. Others have skimpy or nonexistent offerings for teens. If you travel during a slow period, you may find that the kids' program hours have been cut or even eliminated entirely in response to diminished numbers of participants. If you've made special reservations for an evening out, double-check the day before with the kids' program to be sure it'll be operating. Babysitting services often require 24-hour notice, so you don't want to be caught scrambling at the last minute.

 Make sure to let the children's program workers know where to find you in case of an emergency. If your children sunburn easily, slather on waterproof sunscreen first thing in the morning (it takes about a half-hour before it starts working), because the child-care workers probably won't have time to apply it as painstakingly as you do.

Overall, rest assured that islanders love children. So, even if your resort doesn't have a formal children's program, you can find a reliable babysitter through your concierge or hotel manager if you want an evening out. Always give at least 24 hours notice and expect to pay $8 to $10 per hour for one or two children. Ask how the sitter will get home, too. Always give extra money for cab or bus fare if you're out late.

If your kids are older, almost all the islands have enough adventure activities to entice even the most stubborn teen or 'tween. Of course, water sports are plentiful everywhere in the Caribbean. We especially recommend the ATV riding and hiking in Jamaica; hiking and sailing in both sets of the Virgin Islands; spelunking and surfing on Puerto Rico; and windsurfing, horseback riding, and *SNUBA* (a combination of snorkeling and scuba diving where participants breathe through an air line that is connected to a boat on the surface; certification isn't necessary, and children can participate in the activity as well) on Aruba. Teens who are into scuba diving will enjoy Grand Cayman, but we've heard complaints of boredom from those who don't go for water sports. We think Barbados would be too buttoned up for teens as well.

You may want to warn teens that drug offenses are taken extremely seriously on the islands, and that if they get into trouble, they're considered guilty until proven innocent.

At family-friendly resorts, kids 12 and under usually stay and eat for free, although you may have to pay a daily fee for using the children's program. (Check when you reserve; it usually costs about $30–$80 per day.) During the summer low season (approximately mid-April through early December), rates drop anywhere from 15 to 60 percent. Islands that offer excellent summer specials for families include Aruba, Barbados, Grand Cayman, St. Croix, and St. Thomas.

Unfortunately, the typical kids' menu in the Caribbean is the greasy diet you find in the U.S.: burgers, fries, chicken fingers, and pizza. Fresh fruit is cheap and plentiful on most islands and makes a good snack. Just be sure to wash or peel it before your kids partake.

You can find good family-oriented vacation advice on the Internet from sites like the **Family Travel Network** (www.familytravelnetwork. com); **Traveling Internationally with Your Kids** (www.travelwith yourkids.com), a comprehensive site offering sound advice for long-distance and international travel with children; and **Family Travel Files** (www.thefamilytravelfiles.com), which offers an online magazine and a directory of off-the-beaten-path tours and tour operators for families.

For more information on traveling with kids, pick up Paris Permenter and John Bigley's book *Caribbean with Kids* (Open Road Publishing). *How to Take Great Trips with Your Kids,* by Sanford Portnoy and Joan

Flynn Portnoy (Harvard Common Press), is also full of good general advice that applies to travel anywhere. For information about passport requirements for children, flip ahead to Chapter 8.

Making Age Work for You: Tips for Seniors

Older people are treated with great respect in Caribbean cultures. However, you usually don't get special privileges or discounts for being over a certain age. Your best bet at getting discounts is on the front end by making reservations through a travel club for seniors.

If you're over 50, join **AARP,** formerly the American Association of Retired Persons, 601 E. St. NW, Washington, DC 20049 (☎ **888-687-2277,** 202-434-2277; www.aarp.org). Always mention your AARP membership (which costs $12.50 a year) when you make reservations. You get discounts ranging from 5 to 20 percent on car rentals with Avis, Hertz, and National, as well as with cruises, hotels, and airlines.

Some car-rental agencies have maximum age limits; if you're over 65, you may not be able to rent with certain agencies in the Caribbean.

Many airlines, including American, United, Continental, and US Airways, offer discount programs for senior travelers (ages 62 and above), but restrictions often apply on popular Caribbean routes. Rate reductions are worth asking about whenever you book a flight.

If you're thinking of cruising to the Caribbean, **SAGA Cruise & Tours,** 100 Cummings Center, Suite 120B, Beverly, MA (☎ **800-343-0273;** www.sagaholidays.com), offers cruises in the Caribbean for those 50 and older. **Grand Circle Travel,** 347 Congress St., Suite 3A, Boston, MA 02210 (☎ **800-959-0405,** 800-321-2835; www.gct.com), is a travel agency specializing in vacations for seniors, including Caribbean cruises. Traveling companions must be age 13 or older.

In some Caribbean cities, people over the age of 60 receive a slightly reduced admission at theaters, museums, and other attractions, and they can often get discount fares on public transportation. Carry identification with proof of age, just in case.

Recommended publications offering travel resources and discounts for seniors include

- ✔ *101 Tips for the Mature Traveler,* available from Grand Circle Travel, (see contact info earlier in this section)

- ✔ *Travel 50 & Beyond* **magazine** (www.travel50andbeyond.com)

- ✔ *Travel Unlimited: Uncommon Adventures for the Mature Traveler* (Avalon)

> ✔ *The 50+ Traveler's Guidebook* (St. Martin's Press)
>
> ✔ *Unbelievably Good Deals and Great Adventures That You Absolutely Can't Get Unless You're Over 50* (McGraw-Hill)

Accessing the Caribbean: Advice for Travelers with Disabilities

Generally speaking, most of the islands in this book offer some options for travelers with disabilities. Of course, the law requires public spaces on Puerto Rico and the U.S. Virgin Islands to be wheelchair accessible, but San Juan, St. Thomas, and St. Croix are the only Caribbean destinations that offer services from wheelchair-accessible van companies.

Aruba, Barbados, Jamaica, St. Lucia, Sint Maarten/St. Martin, and Grand Cayman have some wheelchair-accessible hotel and restaurant facilities, but for the most part, wheelchair-bound travelers will find accessibility still at Third World standards in the Caribbean — with the exception of San Juan, St. Thomas, and St. Croix. The mountainous British Virgin Islands (BVIs) present very challenging travel and lack easy access — traveling on those islands requires going up and down lots of steps and getting on and off a variety of modes of transportation. You don't find sidewalks here, and many roads are unpaved.

The cruise industry is slowly recognizing that much of the Caribbean has overlooked the needs of travelers with disabilities. New cruise ships typically have a larger number of wheelchair-accessible cabins than in the past. However, many of the Caribbean's ports still remain inaccessible.

 Howard McCoy, R.N., is a tour operator and planner who runs **Accessible Journeys,** 35 West Sellers Ave., Ridley Park, PA 19078 (☎ **800-846-4537,** 610-521-0339; Fax: 610-521-6959; www.disabilitytravel.com). The agency focuses primarily on travelers with mobility challenges and is now the largest cruise wholesaler in the world for wheelchair vacations. The company sponsors five to eight Caribbean cruise groups with guaranteed space and guaranteed departure annually.

Travelers with disabilities may want to use a travel agent who specializes in special-needs trips. One of the better outfits that books Caribbean cruises is **Flying Wheels Travel,** 143 West Bridge or P.O. Box 382, Owatonna, MN 55060 (☎ **507-451-5005;** www.flyingwheelstravel.com).

A World of Options, a 658-page book of resources for travelers with disabilities, covers everything from biking trips to scuba outfitters. It costs $18 and is available from Mobility International USA, P.O. Box 10767, Eugene, OR 97440 (☎ **541-343-1284,** voice and TTY; Fax: 541-343-6812; www.miusa.org). For information by phone, call the **MossRehab Travel Information Service** at ☎ **800-CALL-MOSS,** 215-456-9900 (voice); www.mossresourcenet.org.

Organizations that offer assistance to travelers with disabilities include

- ✔ **SATH (Society for Accessible Travel & Hospitality)** (☎ 212-447-7284; www.sath.org), which offers a wealth of travel resources for all types of disabilities and informed recommendations on destinations, access guides, travel agents, tour operators, vehicle rentals, and companion services. Annual membership fees are $45 for adults and $30 for seniors and students.

- ✔ **The American Foundation for the Blind (AFB)** (☎ 800-232-5463; www.afb.org), which provides information on traveling with Seeing Eye dogs.

- ✔ **The Oxygen Traveler** (☎ 800-308-2503, 407-438-8010; www.theoxygentraveler.com), which supplies oxygen and durable medical equipment for international and cruise travel. For them to supply the oxygen, you must provide advance notice as well as a doctor's prescription. The company makes arrangements for transporting equipment to ships, airports, or hotels by working with travel agencies, healthcare providers, and the cruise-line industry, maintaining contacts on Aruba, Barbados, Jamaica, Puerto Rico, and the U.S. Virgin Islands. The Oxygen Traveler may also be able to make arrangements on Tortola in the British Virgin Islands.

For more information specifically targeted to travelers with disabilities, check out the following:

- ✔ *Emerging Horizons* ($16.95 per year, $21.95 outside the U.S.; www.emerginghorizons.com), a quarterly magazine about accessible travel

- ✔ *Open World Magazine,* published by the Society for Accessible Travel & Hospitality (☎ 212-447-7284; www.sath.org; subscription: $13 per year, $21 outside the U.S.)

Following the Rainbow: Resources for Gay and Lesbian Travelers

Don't confuse the Caribbean with New York, London, or any other metropolis where gays and lesbians enjoy relatively open lifestyles. In much of the Caribbean, homophobic attitudes are common. Most islands, like some U.S. states, have antigay laws on the books. The former British colonies in particular (particularly Jamaica and the Cayman Islands) frown on gay and lesbian relationships.

But this is not to say that gays and lesbians can't vacation comfortably in the Caribbean. Shortly after the Grand Cayman flap (a cruise ship carrying a gay and lesbian group was denied docking rights), community members from St. John welcomed with love beads a small cruise ship carrying lesbian travelers. In general, the discreet can travel virtually anywhere in the

Caribbean without fear of hassle. Most hotels are indifferent to the issue. Prominent exceptions are the Sandals and SuperClubs chains and a few other all-inclusive outfits. They call themselves "couples-only" resorts, defined in strictly male/female terms.

Puerto Rico is home to the region's most visible gay scene and features a robust nightlife in San Juan. The U.S. and British Virgin Islands are other places that we cover in this book where gays and lesbians will feel most comfortable — St. Croix in particular.

A handful of Caribbean lodgings, although not necessarily gay-owned, have won the endorsement of many readers as gay-friendly resorts.

In San Juan, Puerto Rico:

Atlantic Beach Hotel (☎ **787-721-6900**; Fax: 787-721-6917; www. atlanticbeachhotel.net)

Hosteria del Mar (☎ **877-727-3302**, 787-727-3302; Fax: 787-268-0772; www.hosteriadelmarpr.com)

L'Habitation Beach Guesthouse (☎ **787-727-2499**; Fax: 787-727-2599; www.habitationbeach.com)

Numero Uno (☎ **866-726-5010**, 787-726-5010; Fax: 787-727-5482; www.numero1guesthouse.com)

On the U.S. Virgin Islands:

The Palms at Pelican Cove, St. Croix (☎ **800-548-4460**, 340-778-8920; www.palmspelicancove.com)

Inn at Blackbeard's Castle, St. Thomas (☎ **800-344-5771**, 340-776-1234; www.blackbeardscastle.com)

Maho Bay and its sibling properties, St. John (☎ **800-392-9004**, 340-715-0501; www.maho.org)

Sandcastle on the Beach, St. Croix (☎ **800-524-2018**, 340-772-1205; www.sandcastleonthebeach.com)

In the British Virgin Islands:

Fort Recovery Resorts (☎ **800-367-8455**, 284-495-4467; www.fort recovery.com)

Cooper Island Beach Club (☎ **800-542-4624**, 413-863-3162; www. cooper-island.com)

In Jamaica:

Hotel Mocking Bird Hill (☎ **876-993-7267**; Fax: 876-993-7133; www. hotelmockingbirdhill.com)

In St. Lucia:

Anse Chastanet (☎ **888-GO-LUCIA,** 800-223-1108, 758-459-7000; Fax: 758-459-7700; `www.ansechastanet.com`)

On St. Martin:

La Samanna (☎ **800-854-2252,** 590-590-87-64-00; Fax: 590-590-87-87-86; `www.lasamanna.com`)

Getting Hitched in the Caribbean

According to *Brides Magazine,* more and more couples are choosing to get married abroad. With the exception of Aruba, the Caribbean offers great options.

Almost all the larger hotels that we mention in this book have on-site wedding planners, as do many of the smaller ones. Even better, basic weddings at most of the all-inclusive resorts are free. A company called **Weddings on the Move, Inc.** (☎ **800-444-6967,** 262-629-4499; Fax: 262-629-1740; `www.weddingsonthemove.com`) specializes in planning island weddings. If you prefer to handle everything yourself long distance, check out **The Knot** (`www.theknot.com`), where you can find free listings of wedding vendors, plus advice on good wedding locations and tips on choosing vendors.

On St. Thomas, which hosts many, many weddings each year, Debra Williams, founder of **Fantasia Weddings & Honeymoons,** 168 Crow Bay, St. Thomas, USVI 00802 (☎ **800-326-8272,** 340-777-6588; `www.fantasia weddings.com`), has been coordinating wedding services from the simplest ceremonies to lavish affairs on yachts since 1990.

For the basic legalities of a Caribbean wedding, contact the **Caribbean Tourism Organization** (☎ **212-635-9530;** `www.doitcaribbean.com`) to request its "Weddings Requirement Chart," which tells you everything you need to know at a glance. Because the rules of a foreign wedding can change suddenly, though, call the tourist board about two months ahead of time for any last-minute updates. Generally speaking, the waiting period — if one exists — is only a day or two. The license fees range from $20 (and the price of a stamp) on Puerto Rico to $200 on the Cayman Islands.

Planning the Perfect Honeymoon

The Caribbean is a paradise for couples in search of romance. Honeymoon packages at most resorts are generous, even creative. Some all-inclusive resorts — in Jamaica in particular — are devoted exclusively to couples. The downside is that you'll be just two faces in a flock of lovebirds. In other words, don't expect anyone to go to great lengths and deliver beyond what your honeymoon package promises. Often, the package is good enough, though, because you can be assured that you won't encounter conventioneers, family reunions, or young children.

If you have any special requests, fax them to the concierge about a month before your arrival; you want to give your hotel or resort plenty of time to make your dreams come true. Don't worry — they're up to the challenge. One concierge told us of a groom who requested different-colored satin sheets and matching rose petals for each night of his honeymoon. The staff had to call all over the place to find king-size satin sheets in a rainbow of colors, but they did it.

Chapter 8

Taking Care of the Remaining Details

*A*lthough we can't cover everything from *ackee* (a Jamaican fruit) to *zouk* (African-influenced Caribbean music) in this book, we can address a few of the more important must-knows, such as how to get your passport in order, how to get through Customs smoothly, and how to stay healthy during your stay in the Caribbean. We also help you decide whether to rent a car on the islands. Read on for more.

It's always wise to have plenty of documentation when traveling in today's world with children. For changing details on entry requirements for children traveling abroad, keep up-to-date by going to the U.S. State Department Web site: http://travel.state.gov.

To prevent international child abduction, governments have initiated procedures at entry and exit points. These often (but not always) include requiring documentary evidence of relationship and permission for the child's travel from the parent or legal guardian not present. Having such documentation on hand, even if not required, facilitates entries and exits. All children must have their own passport. To obtain a passport, the child *must* be present — that is, in person — at the center issuing the passport. Both parents must be present as well. If not, then a notarized statement from the parents is required.

Any questions or guardians might have can be answered by calling the **National Passport Information Center** at ☎ 877-487-6868 Monday to Friday 8am to 8pm eastern standard time.

New Passport Requirements

During the lifetime of this book, a change in Homeland Security will require Americans returning from the Caribbean to show passports when reentering the United States. At press time, the new rules were set to go into effect on January 8, 2007. Visit http://travel.state.gov for more information on this change.

Citizens from the U.K. must have passports and return-trip tickets to visit Aruba, Barbados, the British Virgin Islands, Jamaica, Puerto Rico, and the U.S. Virgin Islands. To visit the Cayman Islands, British citizens need a passport or a birth certificate and current photo ID.

U.S., U.K., and Canadian visitors don't need any special visas to enter the islands that we describe in this book. Citizens of other countries should call the tourism authority of the country they want to visit to find out what documents they need in hand when they travel to the Caribbean. For contact info, look under the appropriate country's listing in the Appendix.

Identifying requirements for kids

Children from the U.S. who are under 18 must present a passport or both a birth certificate and official photo identification. We recommend bringing a passport photo of babies and preschool children or a current school photograph of older children and teens. If you're traveling with kids, be sure to start the process of getting the passport or birth certificate at least three months ahead to avoid expediting fees and nail biting over whether it'll arrive in time.

If a child is traveling with only one parent or with grandparents, we also suggest bringing a notarized permission letter (with the child's photo attached) from the other parent or parents as a precaution. Be sure to authorize the person who has charge of the children to seek medical attention if the need arises.

Minor children from countries other than the U.S., including Canada, are allowed to travel on their parent's passport. However, if you plan to bring children to the Caribbean, we suggest that you call the tourism authority

Planning ahead for the BVIs

If you're a U.S. citizen visiting the U.S. Virgin Islands, bring your passport if you want to make the popular jaunt over to the neighboring British Virgin Islands. That thought holds true even if you're arriving by boat. Many visitors have been turned away disappointed because they forgot the required identification. You can't set foot on the BVIs — not even from a privately chartered yacht — without that all-important passport.

of the island you plan to visit (see the Appendix for more information) and confirm any special documentation you need for anyone under 18.

Applying for a U.S. passport

If you're applying for a first-time passport, follow these steps:

1. **Complete a passport application in person at a U.S. passport office; a federal, state, or probate court; or a major post office.** To find your regional passport office, either check the U.S. State Department Web site (www.travel.state.gov) or call the National Passport Information Center (☎ 877-487-2778) for automated information. For general information, you can also call the National Passport Agency (☎ 202-647-0518).

2. **Present a certified birth certificate as proof of citizenship.** Bringing along your driver's license, state or military ID, or social security card is also a good idea.

3. **Submit two identical passport-size photos, measuring 2 x 2 inches in size.** You often find businesses that take these photos near a passport office. *Note:* You can't use a strip from a photo-vending machine because the pictures aren't identical.

4. **Pay a fee.** For people 16 and over, a passport is valid for ten years and costs $97. For those 15 and under, a passport is valid for five years and costs $82.

 Allow plenty of time before your trip to apply for a passport; processing normally takes three weeks but can take longer during busy periods (especially spring).

If you have a passport in your current name that was issued within the past 15 years (and you were over age 16 when it was issued), you can renew the passport by mail for $67. Whether you're applying in person or by mail, you can download passport applications from the U.S. State Department Web site at www.travel.state.gov. For more information, contact the organizations listed earlier in Step 1.

Applying for other passports

The following list offers more information for citizens of Australia, Canada, New Zealand, and the United Kingdom.

- ✔ **Australians** can visit a local post office or passport office, call the **Australian Passport Information Service** (☎ **131-232** toll-free from Australia), or log on to www.passports.gov.au for details on how and where to apply.

- ✔ **Canadians** can pick up applications at passport offices throughout Canada, post offices, or the central **Passport Office, Department of Foreign Affairs and International Trade,** Ottawa, ON K1A 0G3 (☎ **800-567-6868;** www.ppt.gc.ca). You must also present two identical passport-size photographs (2 x 2 inches) and proof of Canadian citizenship. Processing takes five to ten days if you apply in person, or about three weeks by mail.

✔ **New Zealanders** can pick up a passport application at any New Zealand Passports Office or download it from their Web site. Contact the **Passports Office** (☎ **0800-225-050** in New Zealand, 04-474-8100), or log on to www.passports.govt.nz.

✔ **United Kingdom** residents can pick up applications for a standard ten-year passport (five-year passport for children under 16) at passport offices, major post offices, or a travel agency. For information, contact the **United Kingdom Passport Service** (☎ **0870-521-0410;** www.ukpa.gov.uk).

Dealing with Customs and Duties

If you have a ticket and a photo ID or passport, going through Customs before leaving the United States should be pretty simple.

If you carry an expensive camera, computer gear, or jewelry, don't forget to register these items with Customs before you leave the country. Otherwise, upon your return, you may wind up being charged a duty for them.

To register your valuables, take the items to the nearest U.S. Customs and Border Protection (CBP) office and request a certificate of registration (CBP Form 4457). It shows that you had the items with you before leaving the U.S., and all items listed on it will be allowed duty-free entry. CBP officers must see the item you are registering to certify the certificate of registration. You can register items with CBP at the international airport from which you're departing. Keep the certificate for future trips.

For more information, contact the **U.S. Customs & Border Protection (CBP),** 1300 Pennsylvania Ave., NW, Washington, DC 20229 (☎ **877-287-8867**), and request the free pamphlet, *Know Before You Go.* You can also find it on the Web at www.customs.ustreas.gov. (Click on "Traveler Information," then "Know Before You Go.")

Dealing with Customs when you arrive overseas and when you return to your homeland doesn't have to be a daunting undertaking. Following are a few tips to make the process go as smoothly as possible.

Arriving at a foreign port

When you arrive overseas:

✔ Have your passport or other photo ID ready before you get into the Customs line.

✔ Have available your return ticket (ship or airline) or an ongoing ticket to another destination.

✔ If you're bringing in items not intended for your personal use, have documentation available.

✔ If possible, have your hotel reservation available in case a Customs official requires it.

✔ If you're on medication that contains controlled substances or requires an injection, carry an original prescription or note from your doctor.

Clearing Customs upon your return to the U.S.

Unless Puerto Rico is your vacation spot, you have to go through U.S. Customs. (If you go to Puerto Rico, you can skip U.S. Customs and bring back as much stuff as you want, except plants, fruits, and vegetables that may not be allowed on the U.S. mainland.)

What's cool about Aruba and the USVIs is that you pass through U.S. Customs via the islands' airports. From all other points, you have to go through stateside. If you bought more than $800 worth of merchandise on your trip, you must fill out a simple form stating how much you spent on the goods you're bringing back. Save receipts from duty-free stores, just in case. Each family member can bring a whopping $1,600 worth of goods back from the U.S. Virgin Islands — double the allowable amount from the other islands.

Here are a few things to keep in mind for your return trip:

✔ Have your passport or photo ID ready before you get into the Customs line.

✔ Declare all items from abroad and be prepared to pay duty if the value of those articles exceeds established guidelines. (You can bring back limitless booty if you're arriving from Puerto Rico, $1,600 worth from the U.S. Virgin Islands, or $600–$800 worth from most other islands.)

✔ Remember that *duty-free* purchases on the islands means that you don't pay tax in the country of purchase. It doesn't mean, however, that you're exempt from U.S. tax.

✔ Keep receipts of all goods acquired while abroad.

✔ Pack purchases together in an easily accessible place.

✔ Don't even think of bringing illegal substances into the U.S. You may be strip-searched and arrested!

✔ Fresh fruit and prohibited products such as Cuban cigars will be seized — don't try to bring them home.

✔ No matter what a local tells you, you'll also get in trouble with U.S. Customs (and have your purchases confiscated) if you try to bring back any live souvenirs. Coral, sea-turtle shells, and even shells from the beach are contraband.

Dressing for acceptance

Don't dress sloppily when you go to the Cayman Islands. If the Customs officers think you don't look like you have the money to bankroll your visit, they'll question you and may even demand proof that you have the bucks to lavish on your island getaway. Remember that until you pass through U.S. Customs, you technically don't enjoy the same rights as you do on U.S. soil. Customs officials are allowed to pull anyone out of line and even order a strip search without having any reason beyond how you look.

Traveling from countries other than the U.S.

If you're traveling from other countries, you can get Customs information from the following sources:

- ✔ **U.K. citizens** should contact **HM Customs** (☎ **0845-010-9000,** 020-8929-0152 from outside the U.K.), or consult their Web site at www.hmrc.gov.uk.

- ✔ **Canadians** can find a clear summary of rules by requesting the booklet *I Declare,* issued by the **Canada Border Services Agency** (☎ **800-461-9999** in Canada, 204-983-3500; www.cbsa-asfc.gc.ca).

- ✔ **Australian citizens** should request a helpful brochure, *Know Before You Go,* available from Australian consulates or Customs offices. For more information, call the **Australian Customs Service** at ☎ **1300-363-263,** or log on to www.customs.gov.au.

- ✔ **New Zealand** Customs information is available through the **New Zealand Customs Service** (☎ **0800-428-786,** 04-473-6099; www.customs.govt.nz).

Keeping Up with Airline Security Measures

With the federalization of airport security, security procedures at U.S. airports are more stable and consistent than ever. Generally, you're fine if you arrive at the airport two hours before a flight to the Caribbean.

Bring a **current, government-issued photo ID** such as a driver's license or passport, and if you've got an E-ticket, print out the **official confirmation page;** you need to show your confirmation at the security checkpoint and your ID at the ticket counter or the gate.

Security lines are getting shorter than they were immediately following 9/11, but long ones still remain. If you have trouble standing for long periods of time, tell an airline employee; the airline will provide a wheelchair. Speed up security by not wearing metal objects such as big belt buckles or clanky earrings. If you've got metallic body parts, a note from your doctor can prevent a long chat with the security screeners. Keep in mind that only ticketed passengers are allowed past security, except for folks escorting passengers with disabilities or children.

 Passengers with E-tickets and without checked bags can still beat the ticket-counter lines by using electronic kiosks or even online check-in. Ask your airline which alternatives are available, and if you're using a kiosk, bring the credit card you used to book the ticket. If you're checking bags, you'll still be able to use most airlines' kiosks; again, call your airline for up-to-date information. Curbside check-in is also a good way to avoid lines, although a few airlines still ban curbside check-in entirely; call before you go.

Federalization has also stabilized what you can carry on and what you can't. The general rule is that sharp things are out, nail clippers are okay, and food and beverages must be passed through the X-ray machine — but security screeners can't make you drink from your coffee cup. Bring food in your carryon rather than checking it, as explosive-detection machines used on checked luggage have been known to mistake food (especially chocolate, for some reason) for bombs. Travelers in the U.S. are allowed one carry-on bag, plus a personal item such as a purse, briefcase, or laptop bag. Carry-on hoarders can stuff all sorts of things into a laptop bag; as long as it has a laptop in it, it's still considered a personal item. The Transportation Security Administration (TSA) has issued a list of restricted items; check its Web site (www.tsa.gov/public) for details.

The TSA also recommends that you leave your checked luggage unlocked so screeners can search it by hand if necessary. The agency says to use plastic zip ties instead, which you can buy at hardware stores and which can easily be cut off.

Renting a Car — Or Not

Living in a car-crazed society, you may have a hard time imagining a place where you don't necessarily need wheels. But just as you wouldn't rent a car in New York City (unless you were training to become a cabdriver), you may not want to rent a car on certain Caribbean islands either.

However, renting a car is a good idea in Barbados, Puerto Rico, St. Lucia, Sint Maarten/St. Martin, and St. Thomas. Puerto Rico and St. Thomas are large enough that you need your own wheels if you want to get a full flavor of the island. You'll be dealing with the big U.S.-based chains in those locations. Barbados also begs for motorized exploration, and you can rent from local companies on that island.

 Rent a car for a day or so to take a tour if the rental is part of a package, if you're a scuba diver, or if you're staying in a villa or condo on Aruba, Grand Cayman, or St. Croix.

You don't need a car in the British Virgin Islands or St. John. Renting a car in the BVIs is really more trouble than it's worth. The main mode of transportation between the various BVIs is via boat. If you stay in a villa on St. John, you may want to rent a Jeep — but that island is small, and you can easily get a taxi.

Rent at your own risk in Jamaica. If you're the adventurous type, renting a car in Jamaica can be fun. The driving style is supposedly British, but it's best described as Third World craziness. The country has the third-highest accident rate in the world, the roads are often in disrepair or under construction, and the police stop drivers frequently for infractions both real and imagined. See Chapter 13 for additional details.

Taking some tips for the road

When you ask about package deals to the Caribbean, find out if a few days' car rental is included; this perk is common, especially in summer. The car-rental value-added feature is a good deal, because most of the islands are small enough that you can easily see everything worth seeing in that time frame.

If you decide that you want to rent a car, do so well in advance of your trip and make sure that the reservation agent faxes or mails you a confirmation, including the specifications on the car you were promised. Rental cars can be snapped up quickly during high season or during a festival or other event, so that piece of paper could become important. On more than one occasion, we've seen tired, angry people at car-rental desks arguing with clerks that they had indeed reserved a car with the company. But because they had nothing to back up their claim, well, let's just say we don't think they got anywhere fast.

Because import taxes on vehicles are usually outrageous in the Caribbean, be assured that your rental-car choices are going to be fairly limited. You'll probably be issued a Toyota Corolla or a similar small car. On many of the islands, though, Jeeps and small trucks are becoming increasingly popular with visitors. If you have dive gear or lots of water-sports toys to haul around, paying a few extra dollars for a Jeep or truck probably makes sense.

Don't forget your driver's license if you're going to rent a car. Seniors and students should bring proof of age and status, though discounts are limited in the Caribbean. You may also have to pay a nominal fee for a temporary local license. We discuss car-rental procedures in each island chapter.

If you need a car seat, be sure to ask if one is available when you reserve the car; request that it be put on reserve as well. However, if you have young children, we strongly recommend that you bring your own car seat(s) for the highest level of safety.

Getting the best deal

Car-rental rates vary even more than airline fares. The price depends on the size of the car, the length of time you keep it, where and when you pick it up and drop it off, where you take it, and a host of other factors. Asking a few key questions may save you hundreds of dollars.

- ✔ Weekend rates may be lower than weekday rates. Ask if the rate is the same for pickup Friday morning as it is Thursday night. If you're keeping the car five or more days, a weekly rate may be cheaper than the daily rate.

- ✔ Check whether the rate is cheaper if you pick up the car at a location in town rather than at the airport.

- ✔ Find out whether age is an issue. Many car-rental companies add on a fee for drivers under 25, while some don't rent to them at all.

- ✔ Don't forget to mention membership in AAA, AARP, and trade unions. These memberships usually entitle you to discounts ranging from 5 to 30 percent.

- ✔ Check your frequent-flier accounts. Not only are your favorite (or at least most-used) airlines likely to have sent you discount coupons, but most car rentals add at least 804km (500 miles) to your account.

- ✔ As with other aspects of planning your trip, using the Internet can make comparison shopping for a car rental much easier. You can check rates at most of the major agencies' Web sites. Plus, all the major travel sites — **Travelocity** (www.travelocity.com), **Expedia** (www.expedia.com), **Orbitz** (www.orbitz.com), and **Smarter Travel** (www.smartertravel.com), for example — have search engines that can dig up discounted car-rental rates. Just enter the car size you want, the pickup and return dates, and location, and the server returns a price. You can even make the reservation through any of these sites.

Adding up the charges

In addition to the standard rental prices, other optional charges apply to most car rentals (and some not-so-optional charges, such as taxes). Many credit card companies cover the *Collision Damage Waiver* (CDW), which requires you to pay for damage to the car in a collision. Check with your credit card company before you go so you can avoid paying this hefty fee (as much as $20 a day).

Car-rental companies also offer additional *liability insurance* (if you harm others in an accident), *personal accident insurance* (if you harm yourself or your passengers), and *personal effects insurance* (if your luggage is stolen from your car). Your insurance policy on your car at home probably covers most of these unlikely occurrences. However, if your own insurance doesn't cover you for rentals, or if you don't have auto insurance, definitely consider the additional coverage (ask your car-rental agent for more information). Unless you're toting around the Hope diamond, and you don't want to leave that in your car trunk anyway, you can probably skip the personal effects insurance, but driving around without liability or personal accident coverage is never a good idea. Even if you're a good driver, other people may not be, and liability claims can be complicated.

Generally, you don't have to worry about drop-off charges in the Caribbean. In fact, most companies are so eager for your business that they offer complimentary delivery and pickup to and from your resort. Mileage is usually unlimited. (We guess the companies figure, "How far can they go? We're surrounded by an ocean!")

Some companies also offer *refueling packages,* in which you pay for your initial full tank of gas upfront and can return the car with an empty gas tank. The prices can be competitive with local gas prices (which are much higher than what you find in the U.S., by the way), but you don't get credit for any gas remaining in the tank. If you reject this option, you pay only for the gas you use, but you have to return the car with a full tank or face charges of $4 or more a gallon for any shortfall. If you like to squeeze in every last second on the beach or at the pool, then finding a gas station on the way to the airport, messing with lines, and paying the clerk may make you miss your plane. We'd rather take advantage of the fuel-purchase option.

Playing It Safe with Travel and Medical Insurance

Three kinds of travel insurance are available: trip-cancellation/interruption insurance, medical insurance, and lost-luggage insurance. The cost of travel insurance varies widely, depending on the cost and length of your trip, your age and health, and the type of trip you're taking, but expect to pay between 5 and 8 percent of the total cost of the vacation itself. In this section, we give our advice on all three.

Insurance policies offered through cruise lines and tour operators tend to be skimpy. Compare prices and policies with one of the companies listed here and get advice from your travel agent. If you're interested in purchasing travel insurance, try one of the following companies:

- ✔ **Access America** (☎ 866-807-3982; www.accessamerica.com)
- ✔ **Travel Guard International** (☎ 800-826-4919; www.travel guard.com)
- ✔ **Travel Insured International** (☎ 800-243-3174; www.travel insured.com)
- ✔ **Travelex Insurance Services** (☎ 888-457-4602; www.travelex-insurance.com)

Don't pay for more insurance than you need. For example, if you need only trip-cancellation/interruption insurance, don't buy coverage for lost or stolen property.

Trip-cancellation/interruption insurance

Trip-cancellation/interruption insurance, which costs about 6 to 8 percent of your vacation's total value, helps you get your money back if you have to back out of a trip, if you have to go home early, or if your travel supplier goes bankrupt. You can also get refunds on the unused portion of your trip and reimbursements on your airfare home if your trip is cut short for covered reasons. Allowed reasons for cancellation can range from sickness to natural disasters to the State Department declaring your destination unsafe for travel. (Insurers usually won't cover vague fears, though, as many travelers discovered who tried to cancel their trips in Oct 2001 because they were wary of flying.)

Optional add-ons for these types of policies include medical and dental expenses, tour-operator bankruptcy, and bad weather. (Weather problems don't just include hurricanes — missed connections due to winter snowstorms in the U.S. may be covered as well.)

Are you booked into a small boutique hotel during hurricane season? Then trip-cancellation/interruption insurance is vital. Most small places don't give refunds even if the hotel is severely damaged by a hurricane. Even if you're vacationing with SuperClubs or Sandals, both of which offer generous guarantees against having your trip ruined by a hurricane (see Chapter 3), we still recommend trip-cancellation/interruption insurance because so many other things can cause problems.

A good resource is **Travel Guard Alerts,** a list of travel companies that Travel Guard International (www.travelguard.com) considers high-risk. Protect yourself further by paying for the insurance with a credit card — by law, consumers can get their money back on goods and services not received if they report the loss within 60 days after the charge is listed on their credit card statement.

Lost-luggage insurance

Lost-luggage insurance isn't necessary for most travelers. On domestic flights, checked baggage is covered up to $2,500 per ticketed passenger. On international flights (including U.S. portions of international trips), baggage coverage is limited to approximately $9.07 per pound, up to approximately $635 per checked bag. If you plan to check items more valuable than the standard liability, see if your valuables are covered by your homeowner's policy or get baggage insurance as part of your comprehensive travel-insurance package. Don't buy insurance at the airport, as it's usually overpriced. Be sure to take any valuables or irreplaceable items with you in your carry-on luggage, as airline policies don't cover many valuables (including books, money, and electronics).

If your luggage is lost, immediately file a lost-luggage claim at the airport, detailing the luggage contents. For most airlines, you must report delayed, damaged, or lost baggage within four hours of arrival. The airlines are required to deliver luggage, once found, directly to your house or destination free of charge.

Medical insurance

Buying medical insurance for your trip doesn't make sense for most travelers. Most U.S. health insurance plans and HMOs — with the exception of certain HMOs and Medicare/Medicaid — cover at least part of the out-of-country hospital visits and procedures if insurees become ill or are injured while out of the country. (If you belong to an HMO, check to see whether you're fully covered while in the Caribbean.) Most plans require that you pay the bills upfront at the time of care, issuing a refund after you return and file all the paperwork. Be sure to carry your insurance card in your wallet.

If you have any serious health problems, if you're adventurous, or if you're a diver, make sure you have coverage that will pay for medical evacuation in case of an emergency, in addition to your regular insurance. **Divers Alert Network (DAN),** 6 W. Colony Place, Durham, NC 27705 (☎ **800-446-2671,** 919-684-2948; www.diversalertnetwork.org), offers plans than range in cost from $25 to $70 (after the $29 annual membership). Depending on which option you choose, your plan can cover such emergencies as dive accidents, decompression illness, accidental death and dismemberment, permanent and total disability, lost diving equipment, and diving vacation cancellation. Coverage is available for individuals or families. For emergencies worldwide, members can call collect at ☎ 800-446-2671.

Another excellent resource for medical evacuation coverage is **International SOS Assistance,** 3600 Horizon Blvd., Trevose, PA 19053 (☎ **800-523-8930;** www.internationalsos.com). This agency provides evacuation to the closest medical care facility that would be equivalent to what you'd get in the U.S. For $60 per person for up to ten days ($110 per couple or $165 per family), you're covered for air evacuation and all travel-related expenses. This insurance doesn't cover hospitalization or other charges related to medical care.

You might also try one of the following companies:

- **MEDEX International,** 8501 LaSalle Rd., Suite 200, Towson, MD 21286 (☎ **410-453-6300;** Fax: 410-453-6301; www.medexassist.com).
- **Travel Assistance International,** 9200 Keystone Crossing, Suite 300, Indianapolis, IN 46240 (☎ **800-821-2828;** www.travel assistance.com).

Talk to your doctor before leaving on a trip if you have a serious and/or chronic illness. For conditions such as epilepsy, diabetes, or heart problems, wear a **MedicAlert Identification Tag** (☎ **888-633-4298;** www.medic alert.org), which immediately alerts doctors to your condition and gives them access to your records through MedicAlert's 24-hour hot line.

Staying Healthy When You Travel

The Caribbean is generally considered an easy place to travel. You don't have to get special shots to go to the islands that we recommend, and you don't need to worry about consuming the food and water. If you have any concerns about these issues, you can check the State Department's Web page for travel warnings (www.travel.state.gov) or check with the **Centers for Disease Control and Prevention** at its Web site (www. cdc.gov/travel).

Even so, vacations aren't always smooth sailing when it comes to your health. Bring all your medications with you, but keep them in their original bottles so you don't run into problems with Customs. Carry a prescription for more if you worry that you'll run out.

 If you suffer from motion sickness, bring a remedy like Dramamine, even if you're not planning to be on a boat. You may suddenly decide that a sunset sail is irresistible. Plus, we've often found that the combination of heat and winding roads can cause problems even if we're not on the water.

If you do get sick, ask the concierge at your hotel to recommend a local doctor. You'll get a better recommendation from a concierge than from any national consortium of doctors available through a toll-free number. If you can't get a doctor to help you right away, try the emergency room at the local hospital. You can find contact info in the "Fast Facts" section of each destination chapter.

Island creatures great and small

Be prepared to see lots of lizards, geckos, and iguanas. You may even find the first two in your room, but they're harmless. They eat bugs, which is good, because you'll see those also. If you're one of those unlucky people who are mosquito magnets, bring repellent or Avon's Skin So Soft, which seems to do the trick. What we almost always find on any fresh flowers or fruit trays in our room are tiny little ants, which are harmless. In any event, keep a few tips in mind about those not-so-harmless creatures:

✔ **Keep pooches and kitties at bay.** Expect to see stray animals strolling in and out of even the nicer restaurants on the islands. As tempting as it is to pet and feed them, keep a safe distance from the many dogs and cats that you see on the islands — some heart-breakingly thin. Teach your children to do the same. We've seen youngsters get scratched and bitten when they disregarded the rules that apply back home. Rabies is rare in the Caribbean, but it still exists.

✔ **In the water, the best policy is to look but not touch.** Some marine life inhabiting these waters can inflict nasty stings. Don water shoes so that you don't step on something painful. Coral inflicts cuts that almost always become raw and infected, and you can easily damage this living organism with just the slightest touch.

✔ **Beware of stinging ocean organisms.** If you step on a sea urchin — the ocean's answer to a porcupine — its spines deliver a painful prick. Apply vinegar to the places where the spines go in, which look like giant splinters. The vinegar neutralizes the poison and helps draw out the spines.

Jellyfish stings are infrequent but can be painful. If you see what looks like a plastic baggie with tentacles floating on the water surface, *move away immediately.* If you get stung, don't rub the wound. Gently put baking soda on it (vinegar for a Portuguese man-of-war, which is more severe), and then remove any tentacles clinging to the spot.

✔ **Don't worry about sharks, but take precaution.** Barracuda and shark attacks are extremely rare. We've often seen barracudas and sharks on our dives, but we've never felt threatened. Avoid wearing shiny jewelry in the water, which can attract them.

Water, water everywhere, but is it safe to drink?

It's wise to bring bottled water on the plane to keep hydrated en route to the Caribbean, especially if you have a long ride to the hotel after you arrive on the island.

After you arrive, follow these tips to help prevent any illnesses from drinking contaminated water:

✔ **Drink bottled water if you're on an island after a major storm.** Tap water is safe to drink in the Caribbean, but sewage can sometimes seep into the water supplies during major storms.

✔ **Never drink from a freshwater stream, no matter how tempting it looks, because the water can contain dangerous parasites.** We've been with local guides who told us the water was fine, but we knew that running water had potential problems.

Some of the ritzier island resorts provide you with bottled water at no charge if you request it, while others charge for it. Before you swig those bottles in the minibar or the ice bucket, be crystal clear on whether the resort intended the bottled stuff as a freebie or not. You might wind up paying about $75 for a week's worth of bottled Evian and Perrier that you mistook as complimentary.

Observing some underwater rules

When you're underwater, remember to observe the following rules:

✔ **Look, but don't touch.** Coral reefs are extremely sensitive, and some coral grows less than an inch per year. Breakage by careless divers can take decades for Mother Nature to repair. You're asked not to bump, stand on, break, or even touch the coral.

✔ **Don't feed the fish (or the stingrays).** We know you'll see other people doing it, but marine research has demonstrated that feeding by humans is doing serious damage to the fish population by throwing off the delicate balance of the coral reefs. Besides, you may wind up with a "stingray hickey." These graceful, buttery soft creatures vacuum the food out of your hands (their mouths are in the middle bottom part of their bodies), and sometimes the suction can be uncomfortable. We saw one fellow give the rays squid handouts and then wipe his hands on his swim trunks. He got much closer to these creatures than he intended — not a good move.

Protecting You and Your Valuables

 Even if you're fairly street savvy, keep your danger antennae up in Jamaica's craft markets (where vendors are overly aggressive), in Jamaica's airports (where drug dealers lurk), and on the beach in Negril (where drugs and sex are openly peddled). Of all the islands, be the most guarded in Jamaica, where poverty is an extreme problem. Also be on guard in the more densely populated areas of St. Thomas, Sint Maarten, Puerto Rico, and St. Croix — in descending order of concern.

What we mean by "guarded" is that you shouldn't walk about freely at night — first, check with your hotel to see if you should avoid any specific areas. Also, be wary while browsing in the markets. At the same time, you may want to do some shopping on the islands, because the vendors in the markets are desperately poor. Understand that bargaining is the norm in island markets, so don't be rattled at the back-and-forth. On the other hand, don't be bullied into buying something. If you aren't interested, politely and firmly say "no," and move on.

That said, even in Jamaica, sticking behind the guarded gates of an all-inclusive hotel or resort and refusing to venture out is hardly adventurous. In fact, we highly recommend getting out to see the country and experience the culture. Just be smart. Don't take a stranger up on an offer to guide you around. Stick with guides known to your hotel.

 Use your room or hotel safe to store any valuables. Never leave valuables lying on the beach or in a beach chair. We know that sounds obvious, but you wouldn't believe how many vacationers tuck their wallets in their towels and go for a stroll on the beach. Of course, don't flash expensive baubles, cash, or credit cards.

Before you travel, make two copies of the key information pages of your passports, as well as your airline tickets and credit cards. On the same sheets, jot down international help line numbers to report lost or stolen cards. Leave one copy with a relative or friend back home. Keep the other copy with you — in a safe spot separate from your actual passport. If you do lose your passport or it gets stolen, the copy helps speed the replacement process. Also bring two extra passport photos. If you bring traveler's checks, record the serial numbers and keep a copy in a safe place separate from the checks so that you can be ensured a refund in case of theft.

Scuba divers should keep a list of all equipment and their serial numbers. If your gear gets lost or stolen, file a police report immediately. You need both that list and a copy of the report to collect on your insurance after you return home.

Getting the Straight Dope on Drugs

Although the Caribbean has a reputation for being a laid-back region as far as drug use goes, in reality, marijuana (ganja), cocaine, and other illicit substances are just as illegal there as they are in the United States. The islands have drug informants who turn people in to the authorities all the time, and the drug dogs in the airport are highly skilled at finding illegal drugs and other contraband. We've seen many people pulled out of line.

Using drugs or trying to smuggle them back are serious infractions, and in other countries you have no rights as a U.S. citizen. In fact, your hometown lawyer can't even represent you unless he or she is licensed to practice in the Caribbean. Penalties are severe, prison conditions are downright nasty, and you won't get bail.

Jamaica's reputation as a freewheeling place causes some people to think that they can get away with drug use on this island. In fact, that's where we've seen the strictest controls: two checkpoints with drug dogs before you get on a plane, and then another when you land.

Staying Connected by Cellphone or E-mail

Travelers have a number of ways to check their e-mail and access the Internet on the road. Of course, using your own laptop — or even a PDA (personal digital assistant) or electronic organizer with a modem — gives you the most flexibility. But even if you don't have a computer, you can still access your e-mail. In lieu of the cybercafes that exist in most cities today, in the Caribbean you may have to rely on the good graces of your hotel to get your mail.

Without your own computer

To find cybercafes in your destination, check www.cybercaptive.com and www.cybercafe.com.

Aside from formal cybercafes, most **public libraries** have Internet access. Avoid hotel business centers unless you're willing to pay exorbitant rates.

Most major airports now have **Internet kiosks** scattered throughout their gates. These give you basic Web access for a per-minute fee that's usually higher than cybercafe prices.

With your own computer

More and more hotels, cafes, and retailers are signing on as Wi-Fi (wireless fidelity) "hotspots." Mac owners have their own networking technology: Apple AirPort, T-Mobile. **Boingo** (www.boingo.com) and **Wayport** (www.wayport.com) have set up networks in airports and high-class hotel lobbies. IPass providers also give you access to a few hundred wireless hotel lobby setups. To locate other hotspots that provide free wireless networks in destinations around the world, go to www.personaltelco.net/index.cgi/WirelessCommunities.

For dial-up access, most business-class hotels throughout the world offer dataports for laptop modems. In addition, major Internet Service Providers (ISPs) have **local access numbers** around the world, allowing you to go online by placing a local call. The **iPass** network also has dial-up numbers around the world. You'll have to sign up with an iPass provider, who will then tell you how to set up your computer for your destination(s). For a list of iPass providers, go to www.ipass.com and click on "Individuals Buy Now." One solid provider is **i2roam** (www.i2roam.com; ☎ **866-811-6209,** 920-235-0475).

Wherever you go, bring a **connection kit** of the right power and phone adapters, a spare phone cord, and a spare Ethernet network cable — or find out whether your hotel supplies them to guests.

Using a cellphone outside the U.S.

The three letters that define much of the world's wireless capabilities are **GSM (Global System for Mobiles),** a big, seamless network that makes for easy cross-border cellphone use. If your cellphone is on a GSM system, and you have a world-capable multiband phone such as many Sony Ericsson, Motorola, or Samsung models, you can make and receive calls across civilized areas around much of the globe. Just call your wireless operator and ask for "international roaming" to be activated on your account. Unfortunately, per-minute charges can be high.

For many, **renting** a phone is a good idea. While you can rent a phone from any number of overseas sites, including kiosks at airports and at car-rental agencies, we suggest renting the phone before you leave home. North Americans can rent one before leaving home from **InTouch USA** (☎ **800-872-7626;** www.intouchglobal.com) or **RoadPost** (☎ **888-290-1606,** 905-272-5665; www.roadpost.com). InTouch will also, for free, advise you on whether your existing phone will work overseas; simply call ☎ **703-222-7161** between 9am and 4pm EST, or go to http://intouchglobal.com/travel.htm.

Part III
Exploring the Islands

The 5th Wave

By Rich Tennant

The resort said it had its own beach. This must be it.

In this part . . .

*B*efore you pack your bags and head off for the Caribbean, check out our recommendations for the best among a wide array of accommodations. We give you tips for arriving at your destination and for setting out to see an island's landscape.

On islands where food is an art form, you want to make the best of your dining experiences; our recommendations guide you to some prime choices. Finally, we show you how to live it up while the sun shines — and after it sets — with a guide to the best activities.

Chapter 9

Aruba

● ●

In This Chapter

▶ Knowing what to expect when you arrive

▶ Getting around the island

▶ Deciding where you want to stay

▶ Sampling the local cuisine at the best restaurants

▶ Scoping out good beaches and diving into water sports

▶ Satisfying the landlubber: Shopping and nightlife

● ●

*G*reat sandy beaches put Aruba on the tourist maps in the 1970s. Up to then, the island was known for its desertlike terrain and almost lunar interior landscapes. Considered an almost-forgotten outpost of the Netherlands, Aruba blossomed with high-rise luxury resorts followed by gambling casinos. Imagine 11km (7 miles) of palm-shaded white beachfront opening onto a sea that's a mecca for water sports, especially scuba diving. But wait — we have more good news. Aruba lies outside the hurricane belt, so you can visit the island at any time of year.

Aruba's declaration of independence from the Kingdom of the Netherlands on July 1, 1986, coincided with this small island's enthusiastic embrace of tourism as its future. Its warm, friendly people — among the Caribbean's most highly educated, because a quarter of the national budget is devoted to education — are known for their hospitality. In fact, many Arubans study at Europe's finest hotel schools before returning home to work in the catering trade.

Aruba hosts a large share of U.S. travelers looking for an easy sun-and-sand vacation package in the Caribbean. A sprinkling of European tourists come as well, but most Europeans opt for neighboring Curaçao, which has far more architectural charm and is almost unknown to most U.S. tourists. Wealthy South Americans like Aruba for its proximity — only a few miles north of Venezuela — as well as its nightlife and casinos. The island is clean, easy to navigate, and one of the safest destinations in the Caribbean.

Arriving at the Airport

Arriving in the Caribbean doesn't get any easier than this. Welcoming more than a million visitors a year, tiny Aruba sure knows what it's doing. After you get off the plane and whet your appetite with the sunshine, you'll whisk right through Customs and passport control.

Thanks to a much-needed, $64-million expansion that tripled its capacity, Aruba's busy Queen Beatrix International Airport (☎ **297-524-2424;** www.airportaruba.com) handles jumbo jets and charters that arrive from all over the world, delivering visitors from the U.S., South America, and Europe. The airport is well maintained, bright, and well staffed.

You'll be presented immediately with armloads of tourist information — all free. Pick up copies of the excellent magazines ***Aruba Experience*** (☎ **297-583-4467;** www.aruba-experience.com) and ***Aruba Nights*** (www.nightspublications.com) — they're packed with coupons, including some for car rentals. Cheerful tourist-board representatives chirping *bon bini* (the Papiamento phrase for "welcome") patrol the orderly lines looking for visitors to assist. You'll also find ATMs in the arrivals hall.

Right after you've claimed your bags and cleared Customs, you'll find spiffy taxis lined up at the curb. Courteous drivers quickly approach when you beckon. The capital of Aruba, Oranjestad, is a five- to ten-minute ($10) ride from the airport. The Aruba Marriott, an easy 20-minute ($22) ride, is the farthest hotel from the airport. The average tab runs $18 along the hotel strip. All fares are set by the government. You can tip from 10 to 15 percent of the fare, but doing so isn't mandatory.

If you rented a car in advance, you can pick it up across from the arrivals terminal, along with easy-to-follow directions to your hotel. Unless you've arranged with your hotel to send a shuttle, no airport bus service is available.

Choosing Your Location

What Aruba lacks in range of accommodations choices — no secluded hideaways or unique inns here — it makes up for with good service and guaranteed sun at familiar U.S.-based chains, condos, and timeshares, and a few small, individually owned hotels. Virtually none of the accommodations on Aruba capitalize on the island's surreal natural beauty, but rather most congregate on the southwest edge of the island. Businesspeople, and some tourists, prefer Aruba's capital, Oranjestad.

The Southwest Coast

Almost all of Aruba's hotels (with more than 7,000 hotel rooms) are jammed adjacent to the wide, white-sand beaches on the island's calm

Southwest Coast. Abutting a string of high-rise resorts is Aruba's most famous and aptly named beach — **Palm Beach** — which is popular with North and South Americans.

Low-rise hotels (as the locals call them) hug the **Eagle** and **Manchebo beaches,** a quieter area on the Southwest Coast that appeals more to Europeans. The most tranquil and widest point of Eagle Beach is in front of one of our favorite hotels, **Bucuti Beach Resort.** Because the hotel doesn't encourage families as vacation visitors and the resort is popular with Europeans, this part of the beach is the one spot where you may see a few topless sunbathers. (However, the practice is officially frowned upon on conservative Aruba.)

You can find some timeshares and hotels slightly inland from the beach, but we don't feature any of them. We figure that if you go to Aruba, you go for the beach. The savings gained by staying inland are so negligible that we don't think it's worth the five-minute walk to get there. (We make one exception for the Renaissance Aruba Beach Resort and Casino in Oranjestad — see the next section.)

Oranjestad

Oranjestad is the capital of Aruba but is more a destination for shoppers and sightseers than those seeking a resort. Most hotels lie west of the city along L.G. Smith Boulevard.

Businesspeople prefer the central location of Oranjestad, but chances are you won't. From a resort on the Southwestern Coast beachfront, you can take a 15- to 20-minute journey by taxi or bus for a day of shopping and sightseeing in Oranjestad.

If you do want the convenience of a downtown location, make it the **Renaissance Aruba Beach Resort and Casino,** which stands adjacent to the waterfront. In lieu of a beachfront location, this hotel has its own small island for guests, with a plethora of water sports on its beach and other good amenities. See the section "The Top Resorts" for more information.

Getting Around Aruba

Because most of the hotels are lined up along the island's fabulous beaches, you may not feel the need to wander far from the hotel pool and the milky teal blue calm of the Caribbean.

You definitely don't need a car to tour downtown Oranjestad. A leisurely stroll through the town with its charming Dutch architecture is all that's required.

On foot

The hassle-free, pristine beaches of Aruba are perfect for walks. Oranjestad is a good spot, too. Nature lovers and adventurers may want to take the easy hike around **Arikok National Park.** Ask your hotel to refer you to a guide, or call the park at ☎ **297-582-8001;** www.aruba travelinfo.com/arikok.html.

By bus

Aruba has the Caribbean's most reliable public bus system, which runs hourly trips between the hotels fronting Palm and Eagle beaches and Oranjestad, as well as down the coast between Oranjestad and San Nicolas. Each trip costs $1 each way, and you can pay with U.S. dollars. Your hotel's front desk should have current schedules available. The terminal is on Oranjestad's main drag across from the waterfront, next to the Royal Plaza shopping center. For schedules and bus information, call **Arubus Company** (☎ **297-588-2300;** www.arubus.com).

By taxi

The government set fixed fares for taxis, so there's no need to anxiously watch the meter. After midnight, you pay an additional $1 surcharge for trips. Tell the driver where you want to go before you climb in, and he or she will tell you the fare. Make sure to ask for the rate in U.S. dollars.

Taxis are also available for sightseeing tours; an hour-long tour for one to four people costs $40. For the airport dispatch office, dial ☎ **297-582-2116.** Or, ask your hotel to call a taxi for you. In town, you can easily flag one by raising your hand.

By car

Car-rental companies on Aruba are eager for your business, and they often roll a free day's rental into package deals, especially during generous summer promotions. We think that renting a car for a day here — especially if it's a freebie — is a fun idea, because this island is so safe and friendly. You'll likely get extras such as free pickup and delivery. In winter, call ahead to reserve.

Whether you've reserved your car ahead of time or not, look for coupons in the tourist guides you grabbed when you got off the plane (see the section "Arriving at the Airport," earlier in this chapter) and present them when you start the transaction, or simply ask about any special discounts. All rental companies offer unlimited mileage; with an island measuring 31km (19 miles) long by 9.6km (6 miles) wide, they have a no-lose proposition. Without a coupon, expect to spend about $50 a day. Local car-rental agencies are sometimes slightly less expensive. You'll mainly see Toyotas and Suzuki Samurais on the road.

Car-rental operators include the following:

- **Budget** (☎ **800-527-0700,** 297-582-8600; www.budget.com)
- **Dollar** (☎ **800-800-4000,** 297-583-0101; www.dollar.com)
- **Econo Car Rental** (☎ **297-582-0920** main office; www.econo aruba.com)
- **Hedwina Car Rental** (☎ **297-582-6442**)
- **Hertz** (☎ **800-654-3131,** 297-582-1845; www.hertz.com)
- **National** (☎ **800-CAR-RENT,** 297-586-3768, 297-582-5451; www.nationalcar.com)

  Request a four-wheel-drive vehicle if you plan on touring the island's less-developed countryside, the *cunucu,* which is kind of like Australia's outback. The weather's hot, so don't forget to request air-conditioning.

A few tips before you cruise:

- **Don't worry; be cautious.** All the roads in Oranjestad and toward the hotels are well marked and in good shape. On other parts of Aruba, though, the signage quickly dwindles down to sketchy at best, and the same goes for the roads at certain points. In fact, locals often tack up homemade signs on the fences, made out of cactus, directing hopelessly lost visitors to the spot they're likely seeking. You'd think it'd be tough to get lost on such a small island, but we've even been with a few local drivers who appeared confused sometimes.

- **Remember that you're not in the U.S. of A.** You may be unfamiliar with the road signs here, which use international symbols, and the European-style traffic lights. And speaking of signs, keep an eye out for one-way directionals in Oranjestad — the capital is a collection of one-way streets.

 If you do rent a car, study the local rules of the road before setting out, bring a map (but feel free to ask directions), drive defensively, and remember — *no right turns on red.*

Parking is free, and traffic isn't bad. You get a few mild jam-ups in Oranjestad when people get off work or during a celebration, which, come to think of it, happens with great frequency because Arubans love to celebrate. Aruba is safe, so if you do get lost, pull over and ask a local. Just be prepared to get directions in landmarks, rather than by street signs.

By bicycle, moped, and motorcycle

The flat terrain makes Aruba a fun place to bike or ride, but because of the ferocious intensity of the sun and wind, we recommend bicycles only for masochists or for those in good shape. Stay off Routes 1 and 2, which have busy traffic around the hotel strip and town. And take plenty of water and sunscreen.

Bicycles are available through many hotels. You can also find them at these places:

- ✔ **Semver Cycle Rental,** Noord 22 (☎ **297-586-6851**) rents motor scooters beginning at $25 a day.

- ✔ **George's Scooter Rentals** (☎ **297-582-5975**) and **Nelson Motorcycle Rentals** (☎ **297-586-6801**) both rent motor scooters and motorcycles for $40 to $100 a day.

- ✔ **Big Twin Aruba,** L.G. Smith Blvd. 124-A (☎ **297-582-8660;** Fax: 297-583-9322), rents Harleys for motorcycle mamas and papas who want to go whole hog. At the very least, have your picture taken with Big Twin's 1939 Harley Davidson Liberator.

Staying in Style

Most of Aruba's large resorts have attached the words *and Casino* to their names in the past several years. The latest race is to attract the growing spa market. The **Marriott,** the **Hyatt,** the **Renaissance,** and **Playa Linda Beach Resort** all offer full-service spas, and the **Intermezzo Day Spa,** which specializes in garden-fresh Aruban aloe in its wraps and the exfoliating marine salt body scrub, is now at **The Mill, Allegro,** and **Holiday Inn.** For families or budget travelers who prefer to save money by preparing some or all of their own meals, Aruba offers several timeshares, condos, and guesthouses that are equipped with kitchen facilities.

All our choices are air-conditioned (you have that luxury on one of the Caribbean's hottest islands) and all, except the Renaissance, are on Palm, Eagle, or Manchebo beaches.

 Good Web sites for trip reports and a mother lode of information about resorts on Aruba include **Aruba Bound!** (www.arubabound.com), **Visit Aruba** (www.visitaruba.com), and **Aruba Bulletin Board** (www.aruba-bb.com). Cruise-ship passengers may also want to log on to www.cruisearuba.com, sponsored by the Cruise Tourism Authority Aruba.

 Aruba's **One Cool Honeymoon, One Cool Family,** and **One Cool Summer** packages are extremely generous programs — the most comprehensive we've seen on the islands. Each package gives participants more than two dozen freebies and deep discounts, including better room rates at several participating hotels. The honeymoon deal is offered year-round, but the packages for families and summer specials, which give goodies such as free breakfast, free stays, and free snorkeling and sailing for kids, are valid only from June 1 to September 30. Newlyweds, families, and summer visitors just need to ask about the programs when they make reservations and remind the hotel (almost all participate) upon check-in that they want to take part in the package. You'll be given a card that you then show participating merchants on Aruba.

For more possible discounts, contact **Travel Unlimited** (☎ **800-228-1502;** www.travelunlimited.com), which specializes in packages that can get you good discounts.

The Top Resorts

The rack rates that appear for each accommodations are in U.S. dollars, and they represent the price range for a standard double room during high season (mid-Dec through mid-Apr), unless otherwise noted. Much-lower rates are available during the off season and shoulder season (see Chapter 3 for information on travel seasons).

Before booking a room, refer to Chapter 6 for more recommendations.

Aruba Marriott Resort and Stellaris Casino
$$$$ Palm Beach

The name "Marriott" doesn't usually register on our romance meter, but this eight-story stunner is an exception. This high-rise resort with 413 guest rooms, including 20 suites, occupies the most far-flung spot at the end of the high-rise hotel district on Palm Beach. The biggest plus here is the oversize, sun-drenched guest rooms at 46 sq. m (500 sq. ft.) apiece with roomy 9.3-sq.-m (100-sq.-ft.) balconies that give you views of the island's best waters for windsurfing and Aruban fishing boats bobbing in the teal sea. (Request a room on the higher floors for a more dramatic vista; some have views all the way to the California Lighthouse.)

The rooms offer big bathrooms with dual sinks, deep tubs with showers, and full-length mirrors. They also have large walk-in closets. The Marriott and its adjacent timeshare property, Ocean Club, form a U-shape around the well-landscaped (though not lush like the Hyatt or Radisson) pool area. Also next to the pool are an iguana habitat, **Red Sail Sports Water Sports/ Retail Shop,** workout facilities, and a small children's playground and center. However, the kids' program still comes across as an afterthought here. The fact that the children's playground is in the broiling sun high-lights the lack of attention. Families should look elsewhere, unless you have older kids who mainly want to windsurf. Some complain about the rockiness of the beach at this end, but we're too busy having fun wind-surfing to focus on that. Wear water shoes, and you're fine.

See map p. 144. L.G. Smith Blvd. 101, Palm Beach. ☎ *800-223-6388, 297-586-9000. Fax: 297-586-0649.* www.marriott.com. *Rack rates: $390–$600 double; $520–$1,299 suite. AE, DC, MC, V.*

Aruba Accommodations

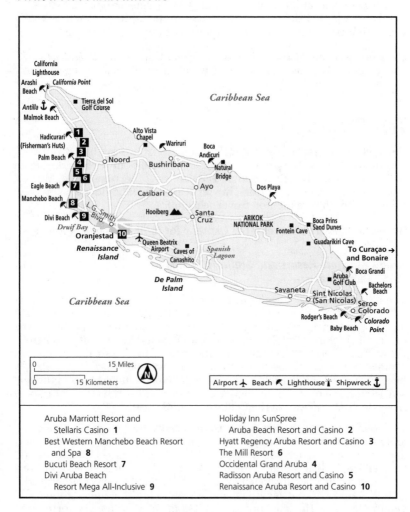

California
Lighthouse
Arashi
Beach   California Point
Antilla
Malmok Beach
Tierra del Sol
Golf Course

Caribbean Sea

Hadicurari
(Fisherman's Huts)   Alto Vista
Chapel   Wariruri   Boca
Palm Beach   Noord   Andicuri
Bushiribana   Natural
Bridge
Eagle Beach   Ayo   Dos Playa
Manchebo Beach
Casibari
Divi Beach   Hooiberg   Santa   ARIKOK
Cruz   NATIONAL PARK   Boca Prins
Druif Bay   Fontein Cave   Sand Dunes
Oranjestad   Guadarikiri Cave
Renaissance   Queen Beatrix   Caves of   Spanish   To Curaçao →
Island   Airport   Canashito   Lagoon   and Bonaire
Boca Grandi
De Palm   Aruba
Island   Golf Club   Bachelors
Savaneta   Sint Nicolas   Beach
Caribbean Sea   (San Nicolas)   Seroe
Colorado
Rodger's Beach   Colorado
Baby Beach   Point

0   15 Miles
0   15 Kilometers   N

Airport ✈ Beach ↖ Lighthouse 👁 Shipwreck ⚓

Aruba Marriott Resort and Stellaris Casino **1**	Holiday Inn SunSpree Aruba Beach Resort and Casino **2**
Best Western Manchebo Beach Resort and Spa **8**	Hyatt Regency Aruba Resort and Casino **3**
Bucuti Beach Resort **7**	The Mill Resort **6**
Divi Aruba Beach Resort Mega All-Inclusive **9**	Occidental Grand Aruba **4**
	Radisson Aruba Resort and Casino **5**
	Renaissance Aruba Resort and Casino **10**

Best Western Manchebo Beach Resort & Spa
$$$ Eagle Beach

If you can't afford the Bucuti (see the following listing), then the Best Western Manchebo, set in the middle of 4 hectares (10 acres) of palms and brightly blooming bougainvillea, is your best bet with access to that same wide, quiet Eagle Beach. Also popular with Europeans, who have a knack for finding bargains, this sprawling low-rise — one of Aruba's first resort projects started in 1966 — appeals to divers and those looking for a low-key beach vacation. **PADI Gold 5-star Mermaid Divers** is on-site, offering scuba from custom-made dive boats, beginners' courses, and snorkeling excursions. This resort has comfortable, midsize guest rooms (some open onto the beach) that are freshened with tropical floral prints. The staff gives friendly, personal attention in a relaxed atmosphere, and the resort offers live entertainment. It has a small, freshwater pool and a dive shop. The beachfront chapel/pavilion is popular for weddings. Alhambra Casino and shopping complex is adjacent.

See map p. 144. J.E. Irausquin Blvd. 55. ☎ *800-223-1108, 297-582-3444. Fax: 297-583-2446.* www.manchebo.com. *Rack rates: $219–$269 double. Children under 12 stay free. Extra person charge $20 a night. AE, DC, DISC, MC, V.*

Bucuti Beach Resort
$$$ **Eagle Beach**

If you don't feel like shelling out for one of the top-drawer hotels, this gracious European-style managed place is a great lower-priced alternative. It's also one of the few resorts that's geared to couples (children are discouraged entirely) and has a perfect location on the widest section of pristine Eagle Beach, far from the madding crowds. Constructed in a low-slung, hacienda style, the 63-room Bucuti has big, sunny rooms, all stylishly decorated in bright Caribbean colors, with handmade furnishings custom-designed for the resort. Its guest rooms meld contemporary luxury with tropical chic and come with ceiling fans, microwave ovens, minibars, refrigerators, and coffeemakers. All have either queen- or king-size beds. It features an on-site grocery store, a place to do laundry, and a well-equipped workout area shaded under a huge palapa beach hut. The open-air, beachfront **Pirates' Nest** serves good food with generous portions.

See map p. 144. L.G. Smith Blvd. 55B (P.O. Box 1299, Eagle Beach). ☎ *297-583-1100. Fax: 297-582-5272.* www.bucuti.com. *Rack rates: $285–$320 double; $375 bungalow or junior suite; for MAP (two meals daily), add $33 per person daily. AE, DISC, MC, V.*

Divi Aruba Beach Resort Mega All-Inclusive
$$$$ **Druif Beach**

You can't miss this awkwardly named, low-rise resort with its multicolored exterior. Divi made a comeback with the refurbishment of its open-air lobby with Jerusalem stone tiles and greenheart hardwoods, topping off an extensive redo of its restaurants, snack bar, and pool area. Dark wood Balinese panels and benches add to the look. The oceanfront lanais got king- and queen-size beds, televisions, bedspreads, and curtains. Kept spick-and-span, the rooms — our picks are in the Vista II building — aren't luxurious, but they're mere feet from the exquisite, wide, white-sand beach. This busy all-inclusive had lost its luster, but it's quickly found its audience again, primarily with honeymooners and families looking to cap their costs. Most evenings a live DJ spins tunes out by the pool with dancing on the pool deck. Oranjestad is a five-minute drive. Also included in the package is complete use of the **Tamarijn Aruba Beach Resort Mega All-Inclusive** next door, as well as nightly entertainment, theme nights, tickets to the **Bon Bini Festival,** and *Funbook!* coupons for the adjacent Alhambra Casino. One caveat: Guests hoard the skimpy supply of free floats and snorkels and save the grass huts overnight, even though it's against policy.

See map p. 144. L.G. Smith Blvd. 93, Manchebo Beach. ☎ *800-554-2008 in the U.S., 297-525-5200. Fax: 297-525-5203.* www.diviaruba.com. *Rack rates: $375–$475 per couple double. All-inclusive includes all tax and service charges except airport transfers. Children (maximum two per room with parents) up to age 17 stay and eat free year-round. AE, DISC, MC, V.*

Holiday Inn SunSpree Aruba Beach Resort and Casino
$$–$$$ Palm Beach

This sprawling resort — which had a $13-million face-lift along with a redo of its Excelsior Casino — now boasts more than 600 guest rooms, and you need a map to figure out where everything is. This Holiday Inn is a busy place, right on a 0.4km (quarter-mile) stretch of the island's most popular beach, but it's great for families thanks to an excellent kids' program — complimentary and with longer hours than others — and the fact that children 17 and under stay and eat free. Kids have their own center and a big, shady playground, too, adjacent to a special pool and the beach. Teens have access to a game room.

The friendly staff is eager to please, and the spartan guest rooms are unusually large and come with direct-dial phones with dataports, hair dryers, coffeemakers, irons, and ironing boards. Altogether, this Holiday Inn boasts three restaurants and five bars. However, management apparently thinks quantity makes up for quality. Even the solicitous wait staff can't bridge the gap between the good presentation and what the food actually tastes like. Gourmands should dismiss the all-inclusive option and consider the **Dine-Around Program** (get the scoop in the "Dining Out" section, later in this chapter). Several meal plans are available. A car-rental and tour desk, concierge, and shopping arcade are all on-site.

See map p. 144. J.E. Irausquin Blvd. 230. ☎ *800-315-2621, 297-586-3600. Fax: 297-586-5165.* www.sunspreeresorts.com. *Rack rates: $350–$400 double. AE, DC, MC, V.*

Hyatt Regency Aruba Resort and Casino
$$$$–$$$$$ Palm Beach

Set on 5 hectares (12 acres) fronting one of the more action-packed stretches of Palm Beach, this $57-million Mediterranean-style tropical oasis attracts families and couples. Built in 1990, it's centered around a $2.5-million, three-level, lushly landscaped pool water park. It gets our vote as one of the top-ten most luscious pools in the Caribbean. Black swans, flamingos, and scarlet macaws inhabit its 465-sq.-m (5,000-sq.-ft.) lagoon, and the tri-level pool boasts cascading waterfalls, two secluded hot tubs, and a two-story water slide. (*Warning:* The stone around the pool gets too hot for bare feet.) Families love this beautiful place, and romantics do, too.

If you're the active type who loves options but you hate the frantic, circuslike atmosphere that sometimes plagues resorts pedaling numerous activities, this excellently managed place is sure to sate your restlessness without sacrificing privacy. You rarely feel overrun by other guests — except during high season, when you're trying to get a shade hut on the beach. Service overall is excellent, with our only less-stellar encounters happening at the front desk. Guests in the 29 Regency Club rooms get a private concierge, upgraded linens, and other bells and whistles. The resort has five first-class restaurants and four bars; a beautiful pool area; a lively casino; on-site shops; the full-service Stillwater Spa with sauna, steam, and massage; and **Red Sail Sports** — in case you want to scuba dive, Jet Ski, or windsurf.

See map p. 144. J.E. Irausquin Blvd. 85. ☎ *800-233-1234, 297-586-1234. Fax: 297-586-1682.* www.hyatt.com. *Rack rates: $505–$655 double; $700 suite. AE, DISC, MC, V.*

The Mill Resort
$$–$$$ Palm Beach

This 200-room complex of two-story red-roofed concrete buildings is set in an arid, dusty location inland from famed Palm Beach, near the Wyndham and the start of the high-rise hotel section. The resort is adjacent to a large, modern re-creation of a Dutch windmill, a kitschy Aruban landmark. Units surround a free-form, freshwater pool and wading pool for kids. The sliver of beach used by Mill guests lies across the busy highway, a five-minute walk away, with its own beach facilities including a towel hut, chaise longues, and a beach attendant. The room décor is bright tropicals, with white rattan furniture and white floor tiles; studio units have king-size beds and sofa beds, full kitchens, and dining corners. The royal suites offer king-size beds, whirlpool tubs, and balconies, as well as minifridges and coffeemakers. Junior suites feature two double beds and a sofa bed or a king-size bed along with a kitchenette and balcony. The resort also has one- and two-bedroom suites with full kitchens available. The Intermezzo Spa, a morning coffee hour, and a free weekly scuba lesson are some of the extras.

See map p. 144. L.G. Smith Blvd. 330, Palm Beach. ☎ *800-992-2015, 297-586-7700. Fax: 297-586-7271.* www.millresort.com. *Rack rates: $189–$207 double; $209 junior suite. Children up to 14 years old stay for free with their parents. AE, DC, DISC, MC, V.*

Occidental Grand Aruba
$$$ Palm Beach

Well positioned on a lushly landscaped spot on Palm Beach next to the Hyatt, this nine-story, 417-room all-inclusive calls itself "a cruise ship on land." The upbeat mood is punctuated by the hubbub — water aerobics, volleyball, and scuba clinics — in and around the gigantic free-form pool enhanced with a swim-up bar, cascading waterfalls, and two nearby bubbling hot tubs. However, the popular pool area, studded with palm trees, gets crowded and loud during high season, with chairs and lounges on the beach and pool tough to snag. Iguanas roam the property freely, looking for handouts. Of the all-inclusives, though, this one is top-notch, and it's a favorite of young honeymooners. Its children's programs are among the best on the island, with a wide range of programs for the 4-to-12 set. Entertainment six nights a week in the Jardins Brasilien nightclub and the on-site casino's action win raves (free bingo twice a night and friendly dealers at the blackjack tables).

The small, carpeted bedrooms have light rattan furniture, comfortable beds, small, white-tiled bathrooms (in need of an update) along with combo tub/showers, and tiny balconies overlooking the beach. Upgrades to the higher floors yield only slightly better views and aren't worth the extra cost. The food (house wine served with dinner and all alcohol included) is a cut above what you find at most all-inclusives, and you'll get attentive service with a smile — which is definitely not always the case at all-inclusives. The resort gets kudos for joining the **Dine-Around Program,** which gives guests discounts and vouchers for approximately 35 local restaurants. That effectively eliminates one of our main beefs with all-inclusives on Aruba: being cuffed to a resort's restaurants when so many on the island are worth a visit.

See map p. 144. J.E. Irausquin Blvd. 83, Palm Beach. ☎ **800-858-2258** *in the U.S., 297-586-4500. Fax: 297-586-3191.* www.occidentalhotels.com/grandaruba. *Rack rates: $280–$304 double; $760 suite. Rates are all-inclusive. AE, MC, V.*

Radisson Aruba Resort & Casino
$$$$–$$$$$ Palm Beach

The 358-room resort sits on a 457m (1,500-ft.), less-crowded strand of Palm Beach's sugar-white sand with 50 shade palapas for guests (we didn't have a problem getting one, whereas at the Hyatt and Marriott, guests stake out every inch of shade by 8:30 a.m., leaving late-risers to bake). Chill out on one of the comfortable cushioned chaise longues by one of the twin beach-front handicap-accessible free-form swimming pools. They're gargantuan and surrounded by ornamental grasses and swaying palm trees. Two bubbling whirlpools are hidden away at the property's far edge. Radisson's elegant, 1,486-sq.-m (16,000-sq.-ft.) casino attracts a more-upscale crowd than some of the others on the island. The 6-hectare (14-acre) tropical landscaping is laced with lagoons and waterfalls, replete with parrots and macaws squawking from their gigantic cages. The stylish guest rooms, which are the most elegant on the island, have extra-roomy marble bathrooms with separate showers/tubs equipped with islandmade aloe vera toiletries. Ultraluxe, comfortable, four-poster beds are plush with high-count linens. All rooms have spacious balconies with teak patio furniture — a big plus over the Hyatt. For sea views, you need to be above the fourth floor. Watch out for the high cost of breakfast here. It'll quickly push up your final tally.

This resort's extensive **guest-enrichment program** is one of the best we've experienced. It helps visitors make the most of their Aruban vacation with fun extras such as cooking classes to prepare local dishes, *papiamento* (the local language of Aruba) lessons, and family days (kite flying, sand castle–building lessons, and more). Even though kids aren't as much of a focus as at some of the other resorts, kudos to the Radisson for not canceling its children's activities if only a few children show.

See map p. 144. J.E. Irausquin Blvd. 81, Palm Beach. ☎ *800-333-3333 in the U.S., 297-586-6555. Fax: 297-586-3260.* www.radisson.com/palmbeachaw. *Rack rates: $400–$665 double; $650 suite. AE, DC, DISC, MC, V.*

Renaissance Aruba Resort and Casino
$$$ Oranjestad

If you like to be in the heart of the action, this 550-room hotel with a 24-hour casino and 130 shops adjacent will suit you. Located in downtown Oranjestad and within walking distance of fun discos and good restaurants, the Renaissance is good for couples and families looking for lots to do combined with a little privacy. The resort fronts a marina rather than a beach, but the Renaissance cleverly turned a negative into an asset by acquiring a small private island just five minutes away by motorboat and transforming it into a lovely alternative to Aruba's somewhat crowded beaches. You step off the elevator in the lobby to a waiting motorboat launch, which speeds you to the Renaissance's island where full facilities await. The island offers all the usual water sports. One path on the island leads to the adults-only section, where hammocks beckon and couples can have their own private butler for the day. Another path takes you to an area reserved for families. The resort's regular Marina Tower guest rooms are on the small side (crowded for families taking advantage of the good children's program) and the tubs are liliputian. Go for the much-roomier suites across the street if your budget permits.

See map p. 144. L.G. Smith Blvd. 9, Oranjestad. ☎ *800-421-8188, 297-583-6000. Fax: 297-588-4389.* www.marriott.com. *Rack rates: $260–$285 double; $325 suite. AE, DC, DISC, MC, V.*

Dining Out

In the mood for Indonesian food? How about a nice Argentine steak? Or sushi so fresh that it's practically swimming? You name it; you can expect it to be good here. Aruba is one of those islands where you'll really miss out if you just stick with the meals served at your all-inclusive resort. Many of the chefs on the island were trained in Europe's best hotel schools and restaurants. Some attained additional seasoning by working on cruise ships and in other hotels abroad. In other words, your palate reaps the full benefit of Aruba's melting pot.

Indeed, with more than 40 nationalities represented on this small island, finding a restaurant isn't the problem — you have more than 100 to choose from. Deciding on a restaurant is the hard part. We give you a head start in this chapter by reviewing some of our favorites.

In casual and most inexpensive and moderately priced restaurants, patrons often arrive in shorts. In more expensive places, casual resort wear is advised — that is, collared shirts for men.

Aruba's **Dine-Around Program** allows visitors to vary their dining choices and save money in the process. Select your restaurant from a list of participating hotels and restaurants that accept the dine-around coupons. Packages available range from three dinners ($115 per person) to seven dinners ($250 per person). Another plan offers five breakfasts or lunches, plus four dinners, for $220 per person.

If you'll be visiting during high season, we strongly recommend that you phone ahead with reservation requests before you're on the island to avoid disappointment.

Be aware that many of the restaurants follow the European custom of not presenting the bill until you request it, and that your bill likely includes a 15-percent service charge, so be sure you don't overtip.

Enjoying a Taste of Aruba

The local cuisine is a combination of Dutch and Caribbean. Dutch cuisine tends to use a lot of fine cheeses and meats with heavy sauces, and the Caribbean influence adds fresh seafood and curries. We love the result and urge you to try at least one of the local specialties, such as *sopito de pisca* (fish chowder made with tomatoes, garlic, peppers, and onion), *pastechi* (meat-filled turnover), *stoba* (beef, goat, or lamb stew), or *funchi* (a sort of cornmeal pudding). Sensitive stomachs, however, may find local food too rich.

You'll also find a strong South American influence lending additional spice, because Aruba is so close to that part of the world. You'll have no problem getting a good steak here; the meat is imported from Argentina, which is noted for its beef.

Outrageous import taxes on wine render getting a decent bottle without paying sky-high prices virtually impossible. If you're a wine drinker, the excellent and more reasonably priced Chilean wines from nearby South America are your best bet. Beer drinkers are in luck: The local brew called Balashi (now you can get Balashi Light, too) has won an international gold medal, and Amstel and Heineken are brewed on neighboring Curaçao.

Two excellent liqueurs are brewed on the island: Ponche crema, which tastes rather like eggnog, and Coe Coe, made from the agave plant. You'll find these two as ingredients in a number of tropical libations, lending them an Aruban spin.

During Aruba's "One Cool Summer" celebration — May through September — the **Watapana Food and Arts Festival** allows you to sample specialties from several different restaurants while you browse works by local artists and take in some local entertainment. Staged every Wednesday from 6 to 8 p.m., the festival is located outdoors between the Allegro and Hyatt Regency on Palm Beach.

The Best Restaurants

 ### Brisas del Mar
$$–$$$$ Savaneta   SEAFOOD/TRADITIONAL ARUBAN

For fresh seafood prepared down-home Aruban style, take the 20-minute drive (bus or cab) to get you to this locally owned, open-air seaside restaurant. Housed in what was formerly a police station in the 1800s, this spot is nothing special in the looks department. But when we tasted the indigenously flavored fish stew and classic Aruban fish cakes, called *kerri kerri,* from the old family recipes of diminutive proprietress Lucia Rasmijn, we were hooked. She pops out of the kitchen throughout the evening to mingle with her guests, sharing an Aruban folk tale or island history with anyone who asks. Request a table right by the water overlooking Boca San Carlo, where the local fishermen arrive daily with their catches. You can order whatever they've brought to Lucia while enjoying the sounds of the sea. On the weekends, live music draws hordes of local families, and it's a fun place to bring your children, too.

See map p. 152. Savaneta 222A. 20 minutes from downtown Oranjestad. ☎ *297-584-7718. Reservations required. Main courses: $12–$26. AE, MC, V. Open: Tues–Sun noon to 2:30 p.m. and daily 6–10 p.m.*

Chalet Suisse
$$$–$$$$$ Eagle Beach   SWISS

A citadel of Teutonic *gemütlichkeit* (well-being), this restaurant is an alpine chalet that brings the cuisine of a mountainous country to a desertlike island — and does so exceedingly well. The restaurant is conveniently located on Eagle Beach. Soothed by romantic lighting and an exceptionally attentive wait staff, we enjoyed such scrumptious creations as the hot Chalet Suisse appetizer (shrimp, crabmeat, fish, lobster, and fresh mushrooms), lobster bisque, roast duckling with orange sauce, and a Caribbean seafood platter, which included lobster. Each dinner comes with fresh vegetables and home-baked bread. Save room for a local fave: Toblerone chocolate fondue served with pound cake and fresh, perfectly ripened fruit.

See map p. 152. J.E. Irausquin Blvd. 246. ☎ *297-587-5054. Reservations recommended. Main courses: $20–$55. AE, DC, DISC, MC, V. Open: Mon–Sat 5:30–10:30 p.m.*

Aruba Dining

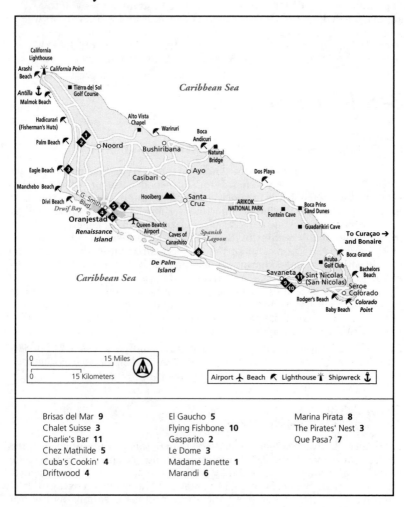

California
Lighthouse
Arashi ⚓ California Point
Beach
Antilla ⚓ ☈ Tierra del Sol
Malmok Beach   Golf Course

Caribbean Sea

Hadicurari ☈
(Fisherman's Huts)   Alto Vista
Chapel   ☈ Wariruri   Boca
Palm Beach ☈   Andicuri
2❶❶ ○ Noord Bushiribana   ■ Natural
Bridge
Eagle Beach ☈ ❸   Casibari ○   ○ Ayo   Dos Playa
Manchebo Beach ☈   ☈
Divi Beach ☈ *L.G. Smith Blvd* Hooiberg ▲▲ Santa   ARIKOK   Boca Prins
Druif Bay ❺ ❼   Cruz   NATIONAL PARK Sand Dunes
Oranjestad ❻   ■ Fontein Cave
Renaissance ✈ Queen Beatrix ■ Guadarikiri Cave
Island   Airport Caves of *Spanish*   To Curaçao →
Canashito *Lagoon*   and Bonaire
❽   ■ Boca Grandi
De Palm   ■ Aruba   Bachelors
Island   Golf Club Beach
Caribbean Sea   Savaneta ☈ Sint Nicolas Seroe
❾ ⑪ (San Nicolas) ○ Colorado
❾⑩ Colorado
Rodger's Beach ☈   Point
Baby Beach ☈

| 0 | | 15 Miles | Ⓐ |
| 0 | | 15 Kilometers |

Airport ✈ Beach ☈ Lighthouse 🗼 Shipwreck ⚓

Brisas del Mar **9**	El Gaucho **5**	Marina Pirata **8**
Chalet Suisse **3**	Flying Fishbone **10**	The Pirates' Nest **3**
Charlie's Bar **11**	Gasparito **2**	Que Pasa? **7**
Chez Mathilde **5**	Le Dome **3**	
Cuba's Cookin' **4**	Madame Janette **1**	
Driftwood **4**	Marandi **6**	

Charlie's Bar
$$$–$$$$ San Nicolas   CREOLE/INTERNATIONAL

On the day you head to **Baby Beach** or **Boca Grandi,** stop in at Charlie's Bar, which has been operating since 1941 and is now run by the late Charlie's grandson Charlito. Forget about the food; you're here to soak up the atmosphere. You can spend an entire afternoon or evening with the locals, artists, sailors, musicians, and other visitors drinking Amstels and getting to know each other. For your "tuck in," you can order platters of

---

Satisfying picky Ricky and choosy Susie

If your kids' favorite refrain is "Euuuw, Mom, do I have to eat that?!", try **Tony Roma's**, L.G. Smith Blvd. 230 (☎ **297-586-7427**), for ribs.

Creole-style calamari, jumbo shrimp, and other dishes, each plate accompanied by homemade bread (baked fresh daily) and Aruban-style french fries (that is, fat and freshly cut).

The walls are cluttered with oddities left behind — from tennis shoes to license plates. Think American attic. Make a point of chatting with the friendly staff; you can pick up all kinds of fascinating island trivia. Kids are welcome at this authentic Caribbean-meets-Cheers hangout.

See map p. 152. Main St., San Nicolas (a 25-min. drive east of Oranjestad). ☎ 297-584-5086. Reservations not accepted. Main courses: $22–$30, daily soup $7. AE, DISC, MC, V. Open: Mon–Sat 11:30 a.m.–9:30 p.m. (bar to 10 p.m.)

Chez Mathilde
$$$$–$$$$$ Oranjestad   FRENCH

If you're going to splurge, go for it at Chez Mathilde, one of the island's best restaurants. In an elegant house built in the 1800s — one of the few fine examples remaining on the island — you can enjoy French specialties focusing on fresh local seafood and imported aged beef. We suggest starting with the rich bouillabaisse and escargots escoffier. For a main course, try the mildly flavored sole with a delectable sauce or the *tournedos au poivre* (beef filet with a pepper sauce). Make a reservation as soon as you're on the island and ask for a private nook in the ultraromantic Pavilion Room, awash in tasteful beiges and decorated in Italian and French antiques. An elegant fountain serves as the tropical garden's centerpiece.

See map p. 152. Havenstraat 23. ☎ 297-583-4968. Reservations recommended. Main courses: $24–$38. AE, DISC, MC, V. Open: Daily 11:30 a.m.–2:30 p.m. and 6–11 p.m.

Cuba's Cookin'
$$ Oranjestad   CUBAN

One of the oldest buildings on Aruba, constructed as a private home in 1877, is the setting for a restaurant where Batista-era Havana seems to come back to life. The most popular drink at its bar is a mint, rum, and sugar-laced *mojito*. There's a main dining room, plus three smaller areas, each lined with paintings inspired by the urban life in the tropics and, in some cases, imported from Cuba. Lunch is simple, usually heaping platters of fish, chicken, or steak garnished with salad and vegetables. Dinners are more elaborate, and more representative of old-time Cuban cuisine. Try *ropa vieja* (shredded skirt steak fried with green peppers, tomatoes, and onions) or a succulent version of *picadillo de res* (ground beef garnished with olives and raisins). Cuban or Dominican cigars are available at the end of the meal. Every Monday to Saturday night this downtown Oranjestad place is mobbed with islanders coming for the live merengue, salsa, and Cuban jazz that go from 7:30pm until at least 1am.

See map p. 152. Wilhelminastraat 27 (across from the police station). ☎ *297-58-80627. Reservations recommended. Main courses: Lunch $10, dinner $15–$26. AE, DC, MC, V. Mon–Sat noon to 2:30 p.m. and 5:30–11 p.m.*

Driftwood
$$$ Oranjestad   SEAFOOD

The married partners who run this restaurant have an unusual setup: He (Herbert Merryweather) spends the day on the high seas catching the fish served that night in the restaurant, while she (Francine Merryweather) stays on-site, directing the sometimes busy traffic in the dining room. The setting is an antique Aruban house in the center of Oranjestad, with interior walls covered with (guess what) irregular pieces of driftwood. The menu items that are always available include Argentine filet mignon served with a bacon-flavored mushroom sauce; boneless breast of chicken with Parmesan and linguine; stewed conch; and shrimp in Creole sauce. But the composition of the fish menu varies according to the day's catch. It might include mahi-mahi, wahoo, kingfish, grouper, and lobster. These will be prepared in ways that you'll discuss with a staff member, usually Francine, who will propose any of several methods of preparation, either blackened, meunière, fried, or baked, along with appropriate garnishes and sauces.

See map p. 152. Klipstraat 12. ☎ *297-58-32515. Reservations recommended. Main courses $18–$35. AE, MC, V. Open: Wed–Mon 5:30–10:30 p.m. (last order).*

El Gaucho
$$$–$$$$$ Oranjestad   ARGENTINE STEAKHOUSE

Located in an old town house infused with the traditional décor of Argentine gaucho (cowboy), this rustic but cozy restaurant has been a prime stopover for steak lovers since 1977. These walls — half leather and half stone — talk, telling the legendary story of the Argentine cowboy life. An upstairs dining room expands the space. Celebrating its quarter century on Aruba, El Gaucho serves up thick slabs of juicy steaks charcoal-grilled Argentine-style. The specialties of the house are an 18-ounce sirloin and a well-seasoned shish kebab called *Pincho Torro Caliente.* Of course, the food is paired with Argentine wines. Across the street at **Garufa,** El Gaucho's Cigar and Cocktail Lounge, an extensive variety of premium single malt scotch, cognacs, brandy, and the fine port wine, along with a selection of cigars (including Cubans), provides the topper for the evening.

See map p. 152. Wilhelminastraat 80. ☎ *297-582-3677. Fax: 297-583-0123. Reservations required. Main courses: $16–$35. DISC, MC, V. Open: Mon–Sat 11:30 a.m.–11 p.m.*

Flying Fishbone
$$$–$$$$$ Savaneta   SEAFOOD

The name alone attracted us to this beach-bordering eatery in the old fishing village of Savaneta, which lies between Oranjestad and San Nicolas. For dining to the sound of a crashing surf, there's no better place on Aruba, especially on a starlit night. Tables are placed on a wooden deck with a view of the moonlit surf. The menu is defined by what's fresh at the market. Dishes are innovative and characterized by refined yet definite flavors — witness such appetizers as a coconut shrimp salad with horseradish mayonnaise, and a crabmeat, apple, and celery salad studded with sunflower seeds. No other appetizer, however, tastes as good as the freshly made lobster soup. The chefs appeal to your palate with such expertly rendered main dishes as an array of fresh fish in a creamy curry sauce or *poulet de Bresse* (French chicken breast grilled and served with a honey mustard sauce). For the vegetarian, they offer a truffle tortilla rolled with vegetables and truffles and served with a creamy mustard sauce.

See map p. 154. Savaneta 344. ☎ 297-584-2506. Reservations required. Main courses: $16–$30. AE, DISC, MC, V. Open: Daily 5:30–10 p.m.

Gasparito
$$$–$$$$$ Noord   TRADITIONAL ARUBAN

Across from the high-rise district in a traditional country house, a restaurant featuring works by local artists turns out some of the best local cuisine. Relax and enjoy the excellent service while sampling such favorites as *keshi yena*, a wheel of Dutch Gouda cheese filled with seafood, spiced chicken, or beef. (Trust us, it tastes much better than it sounds.) You'll see why the chef frequently wins awards in Caribbean cooking competitions.

See map p. 154. Gasparito 3, near the high-rise hotel section. ☎ 297-586-7144. Reservations recommended. Main courses: $18–$35. AE, DISC, MC, V. Open: Daily 5:30–11 p.m.

Le Dome
$$$ Eagle Beach   BELGIAN/FRENCH

Owners from Belgium operate this elegant restaurant on Eagle Beach where some 12,000 bricks were shipped from Belgium to create an "Antwerp atmosphere." The menu is sumptuous and excellently prepared, beginning with bold cold and hot appetizers. Delights are duck-liver mousse served with a blueberry compote or a lobster-based vegetable soup. The chef's signature dishes are his game specialties, including breast of pheasant with cranberry compote or a venison-sirloin chop pan-fried and glazed with a Poivrade sauce. One of the delights of dining in Aruba is to partake of the four-course "once in a lifetime" game menu served here. You can order other main courses as well, including *le passion du jour,* your platter depending on whatever the local fishermen caught that day.

J. E. Irausquin Blvd. 224. ☎ 297-58-71517. Reservations recommended. Main courses: $20–$44. AE, DC, DISC, MC, V. Daily noon to 3 p.m. and 5:30–10:30 p.m.

Madame Janette
$$–$$$$$ Cunucu Abao   INTERNATIONAL/CARIBBEAN

A favorite hot spot with the hip, young windsurfing crowd, this restaurant was an instant hit in 1999 when it opened the doors of the casual, low-slung *cunucu* house it occupies a short drive from **Palm Beach.** Most of the tables are outside in the small desert courtyard, sparkling with strands of tiny white lights and candles. Request one at the outer edge for the most privacy. The casual mood and a guitarist who sings American folk classics (Wed–Sun) make for a convivial evening. The courtyard can be a little warm on a still night, but that's the only drawback. European Master Chef and co-owner Karsten Gesing continue to generate a buzz with creative menus which make good use of the freshest seafood, herbs, vegetables, and fruit. Although trained in old-school ways, Gesing brings Caribbean flair to such appetizers as Madame's hot shrimps in petit casserole, and Caribbean rock lobster in a light creamy sauce with fine cognac. He employs his father's secret marinade on his savory rack of lamb. The well-trained service staff lets patrons linger as long as they want. Settle in with the big wine list. It has a wide range veering from classic European to New World selections. For dessert, our favorite is *Mama Jamaica,* fresh pineapple marinated in aged Appleton rum topped with vanilla ice cream and roasted coconut flakes.

See map p. 154. Cunucu Abao 37. ☎ *297-587-0184. Reservations required. Main courses: $15–$34. AE, MC, V. Open: Wed–Mon 6–11 p.m.*

Marandi
$$$–$$$$$ Oranjestad   INTERNATIONAL

Marandi is often called Aruba's "sunset restaurant," celebrated for its fine view. Fortunately, the restaurant can count on a lot more than a pretty setting for its allure. Next to the Havana nightclub, this is an elegantly casual place, noted for its tranquil atmosphere, good service, and well-prepared food. Lots of wood and bamboo provide the décor. Appetizers come both hot and cold, ranging from stir-fried shrimp with green asparagus to "wild" lasagna with cherry tomatoes, mussels, and calamari. Robust, flavorful main courses include the grilled catch of the day with a tapenade of olives, anchovies, fresh basil, and a tomato garlic sauce. Chefs roam the world for inspiration, evidenced in such dishes as a Japanese pork tenderloin rolled and stuffed with prunes or grilled tuna steak in a teriyaki sauce and tempura vegetables.

See map p. 154. L.G. Smith Blvd. 1. ☎ *297-582-0157. Reservations required. Main courses: $18–$38. AE, DISC, MC, V. Open: Daily 5:30–10:30 p.m.*

Marina Pirata
$$$–$$$$ South of Oranjestad   SEAFOOD

South of Oranjestad, and worth the drive, this restaurant lies right on the water with open-air (but shaded) tables and a sunset vantage point that is among the most panoramic in town. Reliably good seafood keeps visitors coming back — that and the deliciously tender, well-flavored steaks. The strong repertoire of dishes includes such savory appetizers as conch in oyster sauce or a bowl of one of the best-tasting fish soups on the island. You can order the fresh fish filet of the day prepared in garlic sauce, with almonds, or grilled to your specifications. Other specialties include garlic shrimp or a *shore platter* (a little bit of everything). If you don't want fish, know that the chefs import some of the best beef on the island, ranging from T-bone steaks to filet mignon.

See map p. 154. Spaanslagoenweg z/n. ☎ *297-585-7150. Reservations recommended. Main courses: $16–$25. AE, MC, V. Open: Wed–Mon 6–10:30 p.m.*

The Pirates' Nest
$$$–$$$$$ Eagle Beach   STEAKS/SEAFOOD

At first glance, the kitschiness of this hotel restaurant may be a turnoff. The grand scheme is a fake Dutch galleon designed to look as if it's sinking in the sand. But the place is also open-air and situated on the best part of Eagle Beach. By day, this is a fun spot to take the kids for good sandwiches and tasty salads. By night, the twinkling lights, moonlight, and torches transform the place. Chef Patrice Coste specializes in fresh seafood and U.S. steaks. We suggest Captain Kidd's shrimp treasure (jumbo Caribbean shrimp sautéed in a spicy chili sauce and flamed with cognac). For the best dinner deal, try the five-course chef's choice for two served away from the dining area on the beach. In the morning you can get a lavish champagne buffet breakfast here, too, and during the happy hour (4–6 p.m.), live music entertains guests.

See map p. 154. Bucuti Beach Resort, L.G. Smith Blvd. 55B. ☎ *297-583-1100. Reservations recommended. Main courses: Buffet breakfast $9, dinner $16–$49. AE, DISC, MC, V. Open: Daily 7 a.m.–10:30 p.m.*

Que Pasa?
$$–$$$$ Oranjestad   CARIBBEAN/ARUBAN

This quaint, casual restaurant, tucked in a downtown side street, attracts a young, hip European crowd, along with locals and in-the-know U.S. visitors who like to dine here before an evening of dancing. Chef specials are scrawled on the blackboard, but the menu is an eclectic mix of Aruban favorites, spicy American appetizers, and Caribbean standards like jerk chicken. The wait staff here greets everybody like they're long-lost friends. The island art on display and the wildly colored interior create a hipper version of what you'll find at Gasparito (see the listing earlier in this section).

See map p. 154. Wilhelminastraat 2. ☎ *297-583-4888. Reservations recommended. Main courses: $12–$22. DISC, MC, V. Open: Daily 5 p.m.–midnight.*

Enjoying the Sand and Surf

Aruba offers water sports galore, including world-class windsurfing and wreck scuba diving. Check out your options in the following sections.

Combing the beaches

Aruba's main draws are its powder-white beaches (all public) and its virtually guaranteed sunshine. The glossy photos that you've probably seen are accurate — impossibly white sand juxtaposed against the turquoise and cobalt blues of the calm sea. The beaches are generally spotless, too.

Leaning toward the leeward side

You'll find Aruba's best-known beaches — Palm, Eagle, and Manchebo — on the leeward side. The low-rise and high-rise hotel districts are located here as well. Our favorite stretch of the famed **Palm Beach** — lined by the island's finest hotels and an abundance of imported palms — lies in front of the **Aruba Marriott.** Despite the constantly blowing trade winds, the Caribbean's clear waters are smooth and boast visibility up to 30m (100 ft.). Even children can safely play in the surf here.

Anywhere along Palm Beach, you can find beach and swim-up bars, casual restaurants, and public restrooms galore. If you decide to go for a long stroll, take along some money in case you work up a thirst.

An idyllic place to stop and get a bite or an icy Amstel or Balashi (the local brew) is **Hadicurari Fisheries Center,** the fishermen's co-op right on Palm Beach. By law, the food prices must be low enough that the fishermen can afford to eat here, so you can get fresh fish (caught that day) at an affordable price.

You don't have to limit yourself to the beach right in front of your hotel. On Palm Beach, which gets crowded during high season, you can jockey for a position in front of the larger hotels. Competition is especially fierce for shade-providing cabanas, which are reserved for the hotel's guests. Expect to pay about $5 a day for a beach chair if you aren't a guest at the hotel where you want to lounge, and during high season even guests sometimes find them in short supply.

For sheer tranquillity and open space, **Manchebo Beach,** also known as Punto Brabo, is top-notch. Because the sand here stretches 110m (360 feet) from the shore to the hotels, congestion is never a problem. The handful of smaller resorts that occupy this coveted location next to Eagle Beach offers beverages and food, and the discreet atmosphere makes Manchebo one of Aruba's few tops-optional beaches. The white-powder sand is spectacular, but the surf is steady and brisk. With no water sports in the area, serenity is guaranteed. The premier spots are in front of the **Bucuti Beach Resort** and **Manchebo Beach Resort.**

On Arashi, parts of Eagle Beach, and Baby Beach, at the southern tip of the island, the government provides cabanas for visitors. The quietest and widest point of **Eagle Beach** is in front of the **Bucuti Beach Resort.** The surf here is a tiny bit rougher, and the beach drops off much more quickly. If you aren't staying here, reserve lunch or dinner at its restaurant, **The Pirates' Nest** (see the review earlier in this chapter), and hang out at the beach before or after your meal.

On **Fisherman's Hut Beach,** which is littered with the battered remains of conch shells, several water-sports outfitters casually but expertly give windsurfing lessons. This spot is ideal for watching the neon-colored sails of the windsurfers as they skim across the aquamarine sea. You'll think you're watching a butterfly ballet.

At night, you can safely stroll along the beaches and hotel hop until you settle on a "theme night" — pirates, anyone? — that best fits your mood. **Holiday Inn**'s theme nights are kitschy fun and have been popular on the island for more than two decades.

Breezing toward the windward side

On the windward side of the island, the pounding waves and wild surf crashing against odd rock formations translate into only a few beaches that are worth investigating. But some of the beaches here offer a unique experience. On the southeastern tip of the island, **Boca Grandi** (Big Cove) is one of the prettiest and least crowded of Aruba's beaches. Skilled windsurfers and snorkelers are drawn to this beach, but you need to be a strong swimmer to go in the water here because the undertow can be fierce. **Dos Playa** is a good place for a picnic and for swimming in the waves, but you should beware of the undertow here as well.

Wariruri, found near Alto Vista, is the island's hottest surfing/bodyboarding spot. Extreme-sports enthusiasts also use the beach coves of **Boca Andicuri,** which is an advanced shore dive site, meaning that you can wade to the dive site from the shore, instead of taking a boat. (Boca Andicuri is located near the **Natural Bridge,** which we describe in the "Exploring on Dry Land" section, later in this chapter.) **Alto Vista,** Dos Playa, and Boca Grandi are other sought-after shore dive sites.

The aptly named **Baby Beach** is a family favorite. Located on the southeast shore near San Nicolas, this beach makes a semicircular curve around bath-water calm, shallow waters sheltered by a promontory of rocks. You can buy cold drinks and food at the beach's concession stand, as well as rent snorkeling equipment. Baby Beach has a fun, festive vibe, thanks to the locals, who gravitate to this spot.

On **Rodger's Beach** (just up the coast from Baby Beach), you can find slightly better facilities with showers, restrooms, picnic tables, food vendors, and shade. Rodger's also has a shallow reef close to shore. Brave souls can venture farther out, where the coral reef offers decent snorkeling.

Picnicking Aruba-style

If you want to have a down-home picnic Aruba-style, try an Aruba barbecue. Every Sunday afternoon, home-style barbecue shops set up to sell a cholesterol jamboree: takeout platters groaning with slabs of ribs, chicken drumsticks and thighs, fish filets, and blood sausages, along with sides of rice, potato salad, and macaroni salad. If your hotel concierge can't direct you to a favorite stop, a quick drive around an Aruban neighborhood should turn up something. The average price is about $8.

Playing in the surf

When you tire of soaking up the rays on the beach, Aruba offers plenty of other options for having a good time — in, on, and around its bountiful beaches.

Putting wind in your sails

With its steady, strong trade winds (which average 15 knots year-round), Aruba is a natural location for windsurfing and one of the better places in the world to learn the sport. The calm waters off **Fisherman's Hut** (also known as Hadicurari) and the beaches of **Arashi** and **Malmok** are the most desirable windsurfer hangouts. Fisherman's Hut is where the annual Hi-Winds World Challenge is held each June. But its waters aren't so crowded that beginners feel intimidated. Learners stick close to the beach while more experienced surfers are much farther out.

Vela Windsurf Aruba (Aruba Marriott Resort, ☎ **800-223-5443;** www. velawindsurf.com) rents boards for $60 a day. Beginner lessons run $50 an hour and include a board.

Good news for parents with adventuresome kids: Windsurfing instruction starts for children as young as age four. Miniaturized boards for tots are available.

Sailboard Vacations (☎ **800-252-1070,** or 781-829-8915 stateside; www. sailboardvacations.com) offers windsurfing and accommodations packages. You can find it on Malmok Beach along with fully equipped shops with good instructors. This section of the beach has a little more of the surfer dude feel to it.

Diving right in

Aruba ranks right behind Bermuda for its wreck diving. For several years running, *Rodale's Scuba Diving* magazine has rated Aruba in the top five for the best wreck diving in the Caribbean/Atlantic region category. The magazine also notes that Aruba has one of the "world's favorite dive sites," the ***Antilla,*** a hulking German freighter that sank off Malmok Beach during World War II. This site is one of the most remarkable in the

Caribbean as well as the largest in the region, at 122m (400 feet). The *Antilla* is encrusted with coral and giant tube sponges, and its cathedral-like hold is easy even for a beginning diver. You'll often see schools of silversides, horse-eyed jacks, tarpons, and lobsters at the site. Check the cruise-ship schedule because this site can get extremely crowded. The *Antilla* is also popular for night dives.

The *California,* a wooden cargo ship that sank while trying to deliver general merchandise from Liverpool to South America, is also a popular wreck dive. (In the midst of a midnight party, the *California* crew let the ship get a little too close to the dark Aruban coast.) If you're a qualified diver interested in wreck diving, contact **De Palm Tours,** L.G. Smith Blvd. 142 (☎ **800-766-6016,** 297-582-4400), and don't forget to bring your proof of certification.

Another excellent operator, centrally located on Palm Beach between Holiday Inn and Playa Linda, is **Pelican Adventures N.V. Tours and Watersports,** P.O. Box 1194, Oranjestad (☎ **297-587-2302;** Fax: 297-587-2315; www.pelican-aruba.com). Pelican has a PADI Gold Palm 5-Star Facility with custom-built dive boats and numerous dive packages (beginners scuba course, $75; PADI Open Water Certification, $350; one-tank dive, $40; two-tank dive, $60; night dive, $45).

Other good operators include **Unique Sports of Aruba,** J.E. Irausquin Blvd. 79 (☎ **297-586-0096**); **Fly 'n Dive,** Shiribana 9-A Paradera (☎ **297-588-1150**), which offers multidive sites on Aruba as well as on neighboring islands; and **Native Divers,** Washington 19, Noord (☎ **297-586-4763**), run by a husband-and-wife team with personality plus that takes small groups (two to six) of experienced divers and offers far more flexibility than other operators.

Snorkeling adventures

Aruba yields some of our favorite snorkeling trips, too, although opportunities right offshore are limited. Your best bet is to take a snorkeling trip with one of the many boats offering excursions. They typically make three stops, including one at the *Antilla* (see the previous section), which is one of the few wrecks close enough to the surface for snorkelers to really enjoy.

Mi Dushi (☎ **297-586-2010;** www.arubaadventures.com/midushi), a 24m (78-ft.) Swedish sailing vessel built in 1925, has a rope swing and specializes in four-hour guided snorkeling trips crowned with an exceptional hot barbecue lunch — the trip is $59 for adults, $20 for children. The crew is attentive, fun, and helpful with children. The first snorkeling stop at **Boca Catalina** is in the smoothest water, so if you're timid about trying snorkeling or have inexperienced youngsters with you, take the plunge at Catalina. The seas can be rough around the *Antilla,* but it's worth braving — though we wouldn't recommend it for young children unless they're confident swimmers. Silversides, tarpons, and lots of macro life are visible on the coral-encrusted hull.

Fishing the local waters

In the deep waters off the coast of Aruba, you can test your skill and wits against the big ones — wahoo, marlin, tuna, bonito, and sailfish. **De Palm Tours,** L.G. Smith Blvd. 142, in Oranjestad (☎ **800-766-6016,** 297-582-4400), takes a maximum of six people (four can fish at the same time) on one of its five boats, which range in length from 8 to 12m (27–41 ft.). Half-day tours, with all equipment included, begin at $275 for up to four people. Extra persons are $20 each. The price for a full-day trip is $550. Boats leave from the docks in Oranjestad. De Palm maintains 13 branches, most of which are located in Aruba's major hotels.

Another fun crew operates the *Jolly Pirates* (☎ **297-586-8107;** www.jollypirates.com), a Brazilian schooner. It offers two snorkel expeditions to **Malmok Reef** (you can access this one from the beach, but you need water shoes because lots of rocks are at the entry), where you'll see giant brain coral and colorful barrel sponges; **Boca Catalina** (calm waters and lots of reef fish); and the *Antilla.* One expedition goes out daily from 9:30 a.m. to 2 p.m. and costs $50 per person for a barbecue lunch, open bar, snorkeling gear, and use of the rope swing. The other sails Tuesday, Wednesday, Thursday, and Saturday from 3 to 6 p.m. You get time at the same three sites but no lunch. That trip costs $30 per person.

Another good snorkeling spot, especially for children, is at **De Palm Island.** The operator ferries you out to its private island from Balashi, about ten minutes from Oranjestad. The island has full facilities with volleyball and basketball, a tiny man-made beach, a kids' playground, fair food (nothing special), and a full bar. As soon as you step off the dock to snorkel, you'll encounter several large blue parrotfish waiting for handouts. Snorkel beyond the crowd at the small pier and near the stepladder where the water gets really murky from the silt, and you'll find reefs in relatively good shape, teeming with six different types of parrotfish, as well as sergeant majors, squirrel fish, trunk fish, and much more. De Palm sells its island as all-inclusive with additional charges for SNUBA (a Sea Trek option whereby you wear a helmet — in appearance, not unlike the old-time dive helmet — and walk along the sea floor). Dive certification isn't necessary.

Climbing aboard

A party mood prevails on Aruba. Reserve an evening for dirty dancing to live music on *Tattoo* (☎ **297-586-2010;** www.arubaadventures.com/tattoo), a party boat with an unfortunately awful buffet dinner. It's $39 *a person* for a four-hour tour; drinks are $1 to $2 apiece. If you're feeling frisky, wear your swimsuit under your clothes and take a plunge from the boat's rope swing. *Jolly Pirates,* 21 Emanstraat in Oranjestad (☎ **297-586-8107;** www.jollypirates.com), has a $26 sunset cruise (5–7 p.m.) aboard a Brazilian teakwood 26m (85-ft.) gaff-rigged sailing boat with an open bar and a rope swing.

San Francesco, at the Seaport Marina in Oranjestad near the Renaissance hotel (☎ 297-582-3044; www.sanfrancesco.nl), an authentic romantic wooden schooner built in 1870, makes Aruba its home port and offers sails, too. Prices are per person: $60 for half-day snorkeling trips; $35 for two-and-a-half-hour sailing jaunts; and $40 for two-hour sunset cruises.

Exploring on Dry Land

If you just stick to the hotel strip, you'll think that Aruba's not much more than an overbuilt sandbar. Traveling across the island's unusual landscape or visiting its cultural attractions can paint an entirely different — and far more intriguing — tropical picture.

Admiring the Aruban landscape

You may enjoy driving into the *cunucu,* which in Papiamento means "the countryside." Here Arubans live in modest, colorful, pastel-washed houses, decorated with tropical plants that require expensive desalinated water. Visitors who venture into the center of Aruba will want to see the strange divi-divi tree, with its trade wind–blown coiffure.

Aruba's most outstanding landmark is **Hooiberg,** affectionately known as "The Haystack." From Oranjestad, take Caya G. F. Croes (7A) toward Santa Cruz. Anybody with the stamina can climb steps to the top of this 162m-high (541-ft.) hill. On a clear day, you can see Venezuela.

Aruba is studded with massive boulders. You'll find the most impressive ones at **Ayo** and **Casibari,** northeast of Hooiberg. Diorite boulders stack up as high as urban buildings. The rocks weigh several thousand tons and puzzle geologists. Ancient Amerindian drawings appear on the rocks at Ayo. At Casibari, you can climb to the top for a panoramic view of the island or a close look at rocks that nature has carved into seats or prehistoric birds and animals. Pay special attention to the island's unusual species of lizards and cacti. Casibari is open daily from 9 a.m. to 5 p.m.; admission is free, and souvenirs, snacks, soft drinks, and beer are for sale.

Guides can also point out drawings on the walls and ceiling of the **Caves of Canashito,** south of Hooiberg. You may see some giant green parakeets here, too.

On the jagged, windswept North Coast of Aruba, the unrelenting surf carved the **Natural Bridge** out of coral rock. You can order snacks in a little cafe overlooking the coast and check out the souvenir shop.

You can spend the remainder of your time touring through **Arikok National Park,** north of the road between the Boca Prins and San Fuego and bound on the east by the coastline as far as Boca Keto. Here you can see more cacti and birds such as *shoko* (owls) and *prikichi* (the Aruban parakeet). You may also see the almost extinct Aruban rattlesnake, called *cascabel.*

Driving the rugged North Coast can be a sunny, dusty trip. Bring some bottled water, sunglasses, extra sunscreen, and a bandanna. Then get ready to eat some trail dust.

Soaking up some Aruban culture

The **Bon Bini Festival** takes place every Tuesday starting at 6:30 p.m. at small **Fort Zoutman,** Zoutmanstraat z/n, Oranjestad (☎ **297-582-6099**), which houses an even smaller historical museum in its tower. The festival is well worth an hour or so of your time. The folkloric dancing and music give you a feel for Aruba's warm-hearted people and their culture. The event is perfect for families and is only $3 per person. Skip the museum, though: The faded labeling is all in Dutch.

Keeping active

If you're a tennis buff, a golfer, or a horseback rider, you'll find all these activities and others highly organized on Aruba. Take your pick from our recommendations in this section.

Swinging a round of golf

Aruba's deluxe hotels offer golf at the island's **Tierra del Sol,** Malmokweg (☎ **297-586-0978;** www.tierradelsol.com), an 18-hole championship course designed by Robert Trent Jones, Jr., and one of the Caribbean's top courses. You can view the sea from an astounding 15 holes. Located near the California Lighthouse, this 6,130m (6,811-yard), par-71 course allows you to admire the rugged beauty of Aruba's Northwest Coast. The sights include cacti, a saltwater marsh inhabited by egrets, a bird sanctuary with rare burrowing owls, and odd rock formations.

After playing this course, you may think that the *A* in Aruba stands for *air ball,* because the trade winds add an extra challenge to your swing. Fortunately, Tierra del Sol isn't an overly difficult course, so it's still a lot of fun to play. The surroundings are beautiful, and the pros have a sense of humor. (If you don't know your eight irons from your Tiger Woods, check out the club's "No Embarrassment" golf clinics.)

The $98-to-$145 greens fee includes a golf cart (low season fees offer discounts, as do afternoon rounds). Club rentals are an extra $35. The golf clinic is a real bargain: $45 for an hour-and-a-half lesson including an excellent lunch at **Ventanas del Mar,** where floor-to-ceiling windows overlook the course.

During the low season, you can rent beautiful villas that surround the course (starting at $250 a night) and get free greens fees and cart fees as well as access to the club swimming pool. To book a villa, contact the Executive Office at ☎ **297-586-7800.**

The most recent feature at Tierra del Sol is the **Body & Soul Spa** overlooking the ocean. The spa, with views of the California Lighthouse, offers a state-of-the-art fitness center, exercise classes including yoga and outdoor aerobics, nature walks, aqua aerobics, tennis, and more and is open daily from 8 a.m. to 8 p.m. For more information, call ☎ **297-586-4861.**

Playing a game of tennis

Most of the island's beachfront hotels offer tennis courts, often swept by trade winds, and some have top pros on hand to give instruction (although some hotels only allow their guests on their courts). Many of the courts can also be lit for night play. We don't advise playing in Aruba's hot noonday sun.

The best tennis is at the **Aruba Racket Club** (☎ **297-586-0215**), the island's first world-class tennis facility, which has eight courts, an exhibition center court, a swimming pool, a bar, a small restaurant, an aerobics center, and a fitness center. The club is open Monday to Friday 6 a.m. to 9 p.m., Saturday 8 a.m. to 5 p.m., Sunday from 10 a.m. to 5 p.m. Rates are $10 per hour per court, and lessons are available by appointment only. The location is Rooisanto 21 on Aruba's Northwest Coast, near the California Lighthouse.

Riding horseback

De Palm BF Tours, L.G. Smith Blvd. 142 (☎ **800-766-6016,** 297-582-4400), will make arrangements for you to ride at Rancho Del Campo (☎ **297-585-0290**). Two daily rides last three hours each and cut through a park to a natural pool, where you can dismount and cool off with a swim. The price is $60 to $100 per person, and the minimum age is ten years old.

Taking a guided tour

Getting there is half the fun. That phrase certainly applies to Aruba's requisite island tour. Our favorite is the tour provided by **ABC Tours** (☎ **297-582-5600;** www.abc-aruba.com). Free pickup and drop-off, beverages, lunch, and snorkeling equipment are all included in your $70-per-person fee. Many special stops unique to this tour include the Shark's Mouth, California Lighthouse, Wish Garden, Arikok National Park, Alto Vista Chapel, Natural Bridge, Gold Mine Ruins, Indian Caves, Boca Prins Dunes, and snorkeling at the famous Baby Beach.

Shopping the Local Stores

Aruba manages to offer goods from six continents along the 0.8km-long (½-mile) **Caya G. F. Betico Croes,** Oranjestad's main shopping street. Technically this isn't a free port, but the duty is so low (3.3 percent) that prices are attractive — and Aruba has no sales tax. You'll find the usual array of Swiss watches; German and Japanese cameras; jewelry; liquor; English bone china and porcelain; Dutch, Swedish, and Danish silver and pewter; French perfume; British woolens; Indonesian specialties; and Madeira embroidery. Delft blue pottery is an especially good buy. Other good buys include Dutch cheese (Edam and Gouda), Dutch chocolate, and English cigarettes in the airport departure area.

The high-end shops are tucked into **Royal Plaza Mall,** a colorful building designed in traditional Dutch architecture, rendering it as pretty as a wedding cake. You can find some cool outlets across the street at the 90-shop **Seaport Village Mall** and the 60-shop **Seaport Marketplace.** The local market is right on the waterfront, too, but it doesn't offer much.

Alhambra, J. E. Irausquin Blvd. 47 (☎ **297-588-9000**), located along the strip at **Manchebo Beach,** is a complex of buildings and courtyards designed like an 18th-century Dutch village. About a dozen shops here sell souvenirs, leather goods, jewelry, and beachwear. From the outside, the complex looks Moorish, with serpentine mahogany columns, arches, and domes.

Living It Up After Dark

The famous casinos are a sure-fire after-dinner diversion, attracting both casual and serious players. Many casinos have Las Vegas–style shows, most of them very professional and entertaining. Aruba's bar and club scene is robust, though less dazzling, beginning early with happy hour at various places when drink prices are reduced.

Trying your luck at the casinos

Feeling lucky? Almost every major Aruban hotel comes with a casino attached. Most offer blackjack, poker, craps, roulette, baccarat, slot machines, and an island original called Caribbean Stud Poker. This high-stakes game is like blackjack but tempts players with a progressive jackpot.

The Renaissance's **Crystal Casino** stays open all day and all night. We like it because it draws a more-upscale crowd and is centrally located in downtown Oranjestad. This attraction is also handy to the discos, in case you tire of blackjack. We recommend dinner, then gaming, and winding up the evening at whichever disco is the rage at the moment. Other casinos worth checking out if you're feeling lucky include **Casino Masquerade,** at the Radisson Aruba Caribbean Resort and Casino, J. E. Irausquin Blvd. 81, Palm Beach (☎ **297-586-4045**), which is the best casino on Aruba.

Finding the local hot spots

Put on your dancing shoes and your best resort wear for a night (or two) on the town. Most dance clubs don't charge a cover, and alcohol isn't legal until you're age 21. Revelers 18 and over are admitted with ID. Go late — the Latin influence means the action doesn't even get started until around 11 p.m. Aruban club hoppers are fickle, so check with your concierge before setting out. The current hot spots include **Mambo Jambo,** Royal Plaza Mall, L. G. Smith Boulevard (☎ 297-583-3632); and the open-air restaurant **Carlos and Charlies,** Weststraat (☎ 297-582-0355). **Kukoo Kunuku** (☎ 297-586-2010) are wildly decorated party buses that blare festive Caribbean music and transport party goers from one bar to the next ($55 a person); they're a big hit with 20-something visitors. The bus takes you to three local bars where the first drink is free, then $2 to $3 apiece. Of course, you start with dinner.

Taking in Las Vegas–style revues

Aruba hosts more stage spectacles than any other island in the Caribbean. Some of the best shows are at the **Seaport's Crystal Theatre,** at the Aruba Renaissance Beach Resort, L.G. Smith Blvd. 82, Oranjestad (☎ 297-583-6000). "Let's Go Latin," its current and long-running revue, features some two dozen Cuban performers in an array of lavish costumes. Tickets for just the show cost $44 or $22 for children under 12. A dinner-show package costs $75 for adults. Showtimes are Monday to Saturday at 9 p.m.

The biggest stage shows on Aruba are at **Las Palmas Showroom,** in the Allegro Resort & Casino Aruba, J.E. Irausquin Blvd. 83, Palm Beach (☎ 297-586-4500). Shows are Monday through Saturday, starting at 9 p.m.; the cost is $53 per person and includes dinner and one show. The show is different every night.

You'll think you've arrived in Havana when you attend performances at the **Cabaret Royal Showroom,** Wyndham Aruba Beach Resort & Casino, J.E. Irausquin Blvd. 77, Palm Beach (☎ 297-586-4466). It stages hot Cuban revues, with dancing and salsa music, every Tuesday through Saturday. The dinner show (seating at 7 p.m.) includes a three-course menu for $50 per person, but for $30 you can enjoy the "cocktail show," which seats at 8:15 p.m.; the revue begins at 8:30 p.m.

Fast Facts: Aruba

Area Code

The area code for Aruba is **297.**

ATMs

About 50 ATMs are located on the island in hotels, markets, malls, gas stations, and casinos. Casino ATMs usually have very high surcharges. You'll find two ATMs at the airport. Several machines are available in town in the shopping areas: Noord

Branch Palm Beach 4B; Seaport Marketplace, L.G. Smith Boulevard; Playa Linda Beach Resort, L.G. Smith Blvd. 87; Sun Plaza Building, L.G. Smith Blvd. 160. For a complete listing, look in the back of one of the handy guides you get at the airport, such as *Aruba Nights, Aruba Experience, Aruba Events, Menu,* or *Island Temptations.* You can choose to get your money in either U.S. dollars or *florins* (Aruba's currency).

Babysitters

Most hotels are happy to help you arrange babysitting. The average cost per hour is $10 to $12.

Currency Exchange

The official currency is the Aruban *florin* (also called the Aruban *guilder*), written as Af or Afl. U.S. dollars are happily accepted everywhere: U.S. $1 = Afl $1.77. You really don't need to exchange money, unless you want pocket change for soda machines or a few coins to collect because they're cool-looking.

U.S. dollars are the only foreign currency readily accepted on Aruba; however, you can easily convert other monies at any local bank. All exchange rates are posted in the bank, or check the Internet at www.xe.net/ucc.

Doctors

Hotels have doctors on call.

Emergencies

For police, dial ☎ **911**. For fire and ambulance, dial ☎ **911**.

Hospitals

You can reach Horacio Oduber Hospital, J.E. Irausquin Boulevard, at ☎ 297-587-4300.

Information

See the Appendix for helpful Web sites and locations of U.S.-based and local tourist offices.

Internet Access and Cybercafes

Most hotels have an internal terminal in their lobbies.

Pharmacies

For prescriptions and other needs, visit Botica Eagle (☎ 297-587-6103) at L.G. Smith Blvd.

Police

Call ☎ **911**.

Post Office

The post office is located at 9 J.E. Irausquin Blvd., Oranjestad (☎ 297-582-1900), but your hotel's front desk can also mail your letters and postcards.

Restrooms

Public toilets are located along the Aruban beachfront west of Oranjestad. If you're shopping in Oranjestad, you'll have to rely on facilities in restaurants and bars, where, technically speaking, you should be a patron.

Safety

Crime is extremely rare on Aruba, which is a prosperous island. You can walk about freely, but common-sense rules apply. Don't leave valuables wrapped in your towel on the beach or have your camera dangling behind you while you look at the shops along the waterfront.

Smoking

To cater mainly to their large American clientele, many resorts designate nonsmoking sections. In Aruban dives, the air is often thick with smoke. If you have a problem with smoke, you can always call ahead and inquire about the policy.

Taxes

The government room tax is 6 percent, and hotels sting you for an additional 10 percent service charge for room, food, and beverages. The Departure Tax is $34, plus $3.25 for those making use of the U.S. Departure terminal and, therefore, U.S. INS/Customs services on Aruba. The Departure Tax, officially referred to as the Passenger Facility Charge, is included in the airline ticket price.

Taxis

Fixed fares are set by the government. After midnight, you pay an additional $1 surcharge for trips. Tell the driver where you want to go before you climb in, and he or she will tell you the fare. Make sure to ask for the rate in U.S. dollars.

Weather Updates

Visit www.weather.com for updates.

Chapter 10

Barbados

● ●

In This Chapter

▶ Knowing what to expect when you arrive
▶ Getting around the island
▶ Deciding where you want to stay
▶ Sampling the local cuisine at the best restaurants
▶ Scoping out good beaches and diving into water sports
▶ Satisfying the landlubber: Shopping and nightlife

● ●

*B*arbados has steadily been gaining popularity with the U.S. market, though tourists from the States still account for only 20 percent of the island's visitors. Barbados is by far the most urban of the islands that we cover in this book. Indeed, almost all of Barbados's quarter million–plus residents live in and around the capital of Bridgetown. For the first hour you're on the island, you may be jangled at how crowded and congested it is. Relax. When you get away from the airport area and through Bridgetown, you start to find more of what you'd expect on a Caribbean island, and when you make it to your hotel and are offered a cool tropical punch (perhaps with a splash of rum), you know you're in the right place.

Arriving at the Airport

Thoroughly modern **Grantley Adams International Airport** is located on the South Coast about 4.9km (8 miles) east and a half-hour drive from the bustling, sprawling capital of Bridgetown. You won't find crinkly, sun-bleached tourist posters taped to the walls at this immaculate airport.

Getting oriented at the airport

By 2005, Barbados had plunked down upwards of $70 million to ensure that its airport is oh-so-right. In addition, they added air-conditioning to the Customs, baggage claim, and departure lounge areas, and doubled the airport's duty-free shopping area to more than 929 sq. m (10,000 sq. ft.). In fact, the Barbados airport is one of the few we've encountered that has an **Arrivals Duty-Free Shop** (☎ 246-428-0189) so you don't have to wait until you're in a hurry at the end of your trip to pick up mementos.

The **Barbados Tourism Authority** operates a welcome kiosk from 8 a.m. to whenever the last flight arrives at night at the airport terminal (☎ **246-428-5570**). And for those who arrive cash-poor, an ATM is handily stationed at the kiosk.

Navigating your way through passport control and Customs

Going through passport control and Customs takes far longer in Barbados than on most islands. Expect to spend at least a half-hour in line if you're on a full flight. Plus, the paperwork is the most detailed we've seen, and you must fill it out in triplicate. Be sure to get it on the plane and fill it out en route to save time. The neatly uniformed Customs officials are crisply efficient. If you're carrying valuables like expensive jewelry and camera equipment, don't forget to register those items with the Customs officials as you're entering the country. Otherwise, you may find yourself paying an import duty on your belongings at the end of your stay. For more information on going through Customs and registering your valuables, flip back to Chapter 8.

Getting from the airport to your hotel

Official taxis have a *Z* on their license plates, and they operate 24 hours a day. A large sign at the airport announces the fixed rate for a taxi ride to each hotel or parish (district), giving rates in both Barbados and U.S. dollars. Count on about $35 to **Bridgetown** (the capital of Barbados) for a 30-minute ride, $40 to $70 to hotels on the West Coast, and $24 to St. Lawrence Gap and less-expensive hotels. Drivers are usually chatty and full of details about the island.

Airport bus service into Bridgetown (Bds$1.50/U.S. 75¢; Barbados currency only) departs about every 10 minutes, but it takes 45 minutes to get into town.

This island is a good one on which to rent a car (see "Getting Around Barbados," later in this chapter, for more details), but the roads are confusing. After a long day of travel, unless you're really good with a map, we suggest that you take a cab to your hotel and have the rental car delivered the next day.

If you're doing your own driving, get detailed directions on how to get to the **Adams-Barrow-Cummins (ABC) Highway.** It bypasses Bridgetown and saves you travel time to the West Coast, where most of the hotels are. Going along the coastal highway is much prettier but much slower, and because it'll likely be nightfall by the time you arrive, make it easy on yourself with the ABC.

Arriving by Cruise Ship

More than half a million visitors — many of them making a return trip — come to Barbados each year, and another half million arrive via cruise ship. The Barbados Cruise-Ship Terminal, located on Bridgetown's waterfront, is one of the Caribbean's finest, thanks to a $6-million renovation. Bridgetown's Deep Water Harbour is on the northwest side of Carlisle Bay, and as many as eight cruise ships can dock simultaneously at its cruise-ship terminal, whose interior features a faux island street scene with storefronts, brightly colored chattel houses, tropical flowers, benches, and pushcarts. Postal and banking facilities are also available at the terminal.

As soon as you clear Customs and immigration, which is usually an easy entry, you can whip out your plastic. The port facility has 20 duty-free shops, more than a dozen retailers, and dozens of vendors. You can also find car and bike rentals, a florist, dive shops, and a communications center with fax machines and telephones. Downtown Bridgetown is an easy 0.8km (½-mile) walk from the pier; a taxi costs about $5 each way.

The **Barbados Tourism Authority** operates a welcome kiosk at the cruise terminal (☎ 246-427-1817) from 8 a.m. to 4 p.m. An ATM is available at this kiosk.

Choosing Your Location

The island is divided, for administrative purposes, into several parishes. The most interesting for visitors include the ones we describe in this section.

St. Michael (including Bridgetown)

The **St. Michael** parish traditionally has been the hub of Bajan business activity and culture. Although Barbados has far-more-interesting parishes from a traveler's point of view, many people visit St. Michael in order to shop in Bridgetown and to visit the **Barbados Museum,** directly south of Bridgetown. Standing across the street from the museum is **Garrison Savannah,** one of the finest parade grounds in the Caribbean. This parish is the beginning of the **Gold Coast,** which comprises the St. James and St. Peter parishes as well.

The capital of **Bridgetown,** in the southwestern corner of St. Michael's parish and the island, is small but pulsating with life — in fact, it's one of the liveliest capitals in the Caribbean, although it has nowhere near the activity (or danger) of bustling Kingston, Jamaica. Colonial buildings and contemporary office blocks go hand in hand — for some, mere backdrops to the vendors hawking their wares. You can reach the city by two bridges, both in the east — one spans the Constitution River (not actually a river) and the other, Chamberlin Bridge, takes you to the waterfront, called the Careenage. Although some hotels are in Bridgetown, nearly all visitors are here on daytrips — either for shopping or sightseeing. For hotels, they either head north or south of the city.

St. James (the Gold Coast)

St. James is the heart of the West Coast tourist district, sometimes referred to as the **Gold Coast** or the Platinum Coast. Most of its posh hotels and restaurants stretch along Highway 1, which runs up the West Coast from Bridgetown. Nearly all the deluxe resorts have made their home here, including **Sandy Lane,** where the rich and famous hang out. Over the years, everyone from Princess Margaret to Mick Jagger and Jackie Onassis to Claudette Colbert has passed along this coast's too-narrow highway. The parish embraces some of the best beaches along the coast and the town of **Holetown,** where an obelisk marks the spot on which the British ship *Olive Blossom* landed the first settlers in 1627.

St. Peter

Wedged between the **Gold Coast** and the seldom-visited St. Lucy parish at the top of the island, fashionable St. Peter spans Barbados and opens onto the Caribbean Sea in the west and the Atlantic Ocean in the east. Many of the finest homes on the island are located here, along with such attractions as **St. Nicholas Abbey, Farley Hill National Park,** and **Barbados Wildlife Reserve,** home of the rare green monkey. St. Peter is also home to the town of **Speightstown,** once a major sugar port and now a fishing center with a bustling waterfront, old houses, and a restored **Church of St. Peter's.** People on the north end of the island do their shopping in Speightstown. You can find some chic, elegant, and expensive hotels in this parish.

Christ Church

South and east of Bridgetown, the southernmost parish of Christ Church embraces **Oistins,** the fishing capital of the island, and **Hastings** and **Worthing,** where you find many of the least expensive accommodations and restaurants in Barbados. Accordingly, Christ Church attracts vacationers of more-modest means than does posh St. James. It has a string of white sandy beaches and a surf that lures windsurfers from around the world. The parish is also a center of commercial activity, although nothing to equal that of St. Michael.

St. Philip

In the southeastern corner of Barbados, bordered by Christ Church to the west and St. John to the north, St. Philip is geographically the biggest parish in Barbados. It's a long way from Bridgetown, however, so it has been allowed to sleep. Because it borders the rough Atlantic Ocean — not the tranquil Caribbean Sea — developers' bulldozers haven't overtaken it. St. Philip hosts mainly travelers who want to see **Sam Lord's Castle,** one of the major attractions of Barbados. However, developers are coming in fast, so you'd better go now before its rural charms disappear.

St. John

Site of the East Coast sugar plantations, St. John is home to **Hackleton's Cliff,** which at 304m (1,000 ft.) offers some of the most panoramic Atlantic Ocean vistas. In many ways, this parish is the most ideal for wandering about, or even getting lost. You always have something to discover down every road. Highways 4 and 3B split through the parish. Follow 3B to **St. John's Parish Church,** set upon a cliff fronting the Atlantic. One of the major attractions here is **Villa Nova,** an elegant hotel that Queen Elizabeth II and Prince Philip visited.

St. Joseph

Windswept St. Joseph, in the middle of the East Coast, is the site of **"Little Scotland,"** with rolling hills, tiny hamlets, grazing sheep, and valleys. Its main target is the fishing village of **Bathsheba** and nearby **Tent Bay,** major destinations for both visitors and Bajans who head here for Sunday picnics at the beach, with its often turbulent waters. Visitors often pass through here heading for lunch at the world-famous (although extremely modest) **Atlantic Hotel.** The parish is also the site of **St. Joseph Anglican Church,** above Horse Hill, and **Andromeda Gardens,** one of the island's choice beauty spots.

Getting Around Barbados

After you've settled into your hotel, you'll want to check out the island's sites, shops, restaurants, and landscape. This section shares some sight-seeing options.

By car

On the pro side for renting a car in Barbados is the fact that it's one of the most intriguing islands in the Caribbean to explore. It has historic Great Houses, practically deserted beaches in some places, a bucolic countryside, unusual caverns, and riotous tropical gardens. The negatives include some of the most poorly marked, confusing roads in the Caribbean. The roads — most of which are paved but have potholes in the outlying areas — give new meaning to the word *narrow.* On the West Coast and in the more-urban areas, they have no shoulder, just a deep gully between the road and the sidewalk. In the country, the dense sugarcane fields and lush growth can make it difficult to see around corners and at stop signs. And don't venture into the rural areas after dark — not because danger lurks, but because it's pitch black and you can barely see where you're going.

On top of all that, you're dealing with driving on the left, British style. In more-rural areas, sheep and goats sometimes wander into the road. The only signs are tiny — sometimes hand-lettered — and point in a some-times-undecipherable direction. Locals are generally helpful, though, when you ask for directions.

Rental prices are high even for the unimaginably minuscule minimokes, a putt-putt popular on the island. For a little more money, you can rent a four-wheel-drive Jeep or a convertible. All that said, if you want to rent a car, you must have a valid driver's license or an international driver's license, be 25 or older, and buy a $5 temporary driving permit for Barbados, obtainable at the airport, police stations, and car-rental firms. The permit is valid for one year.

You can pick up your vehicle at the airport. The rental process is smooth, but you may encounter another long line at the airport rental counters. We recommend having your vehicle brought to you where you're staying, which is a free service companies provide. Be sure to request that they fill it up with gas before bringing it to you. None of the familiar major firms offer rentals in Barbados, but about 30 local agencies — National is the one that U.S. visitors are familiar with — rent cars, Jeeps, or small open-air vehicles for $60 to $90 a day (or $250–$325 a week), depending on the vehicle and whether it has air-conditioning. The rental generally includes insurance. Before you turn down the **collision damage waiver,** be absolutely certain you're covered on either your auto insurance at home or by the credit card company with which you're paying. Proceed carefully with rentals on this island. Inspect the vehicle thoroughly, and point out even the smallest scratch before you drive away.

Among the car-rental agencies in Barbados are the following:

- ✔ **Coconut Car Rentals,** St. Michael (☎ **246-437-0297**): This agency gets high marks from travelers for friendly service and good prices.
- ✔ **Corbins Car Rentals,** St. Michael (☎ **246-427-9531,** 246-426-8336).
- ✔ **Courtesy Rent-A-Car,** Grantley Adams International Airport (☎ **246-431-4160**).
- ✔ **Drive-a-Matic,** St. James (☎ **246-422-3000**).
- ✔ **National Car Rentals,** Lower Carlton, St. James (☎ **246-426-0603**).
- ✔ **P&S Car Rentals,** Pleasant View, Cave Hill, St. Michael (☎ **246-424-2052**).
- ✔ **Stoutes Car Rentals,** St. Philips (☎ **246-435-4456**).
- ✔ **Sunny Isle Motors,** Worthing (☎ **246-435-7979**).

The speed limit is 60kmph (roughly 37 mph) on the highway, 50kmph (about 30 mph) in the country, and 30kmph (20 mph) in town. Remember that kilometers per hour are the norm here; a shift in mental gears can keep you out of trouble if you're accustomed to miles per hour.

In Bridgetown and at The Gap on the South Coast, where a great deal of construction is always going on, parking can be virtually impossible. Near the waterfront, the roads are snarled with construction and several of them are one-way streets. Never turn your car over to a local who offers to find you a parking space for a small finder's fee. Visitors who've done so often find out the hard way that the space was illegal, which makes them the target of a ticket. Bridgetown's rush hour runs from 7:30 to 8:30 a.m. and 4:30 to 5:30 p.m.

By taxi

Taxis aren't metered; the government set fixed rates, and one cab can carry up to four passengers for the same fare. Taxis are plentiful and easily identifiable by the letter *Z* on their license plates. Drivers produce a list of standard rates ($15–$30 per hour, subject to change). To call a taxi, contact **Lyndhurst Taxi Service** (☎ 246-436-2639), **Paramount Taxi Service** (☎ 246-429-3718), or **Royal Pavilion Taxi Service** (☎ 246-422-1260).

By bus

Taking a bus in the Caribbean can be more hassle than the savings is worth, but Barbados (as well as Aruba and Grand Cayman) is an exception. If you don't want to rent a car, you can explore this island cheaply by relying on the bus system.

The fare is Bds$1.50 (U.S. 75¢) for any one destination, and you must have exact change in Barbados currency ready when you board. Barbados has a reliable bus system fanning out from Bridgetown, leaving from Fairchild Street for the south and east, and from Lower Green and the Princess Alice Highway for the north going along the West Coast, to almost every part of the island. The nationally owned buses (☎ 246-427-2623) of Barbados are blue with yellow stripes. They're not numbered, but their destinations are marked on the front. On most major routes, they run between 6 a.m. and midnight about every 30 minutes.

Privately operated minibuses run shorter distances and travel more frequently. They're bright yellow with blue stripes, with their destinations displayed on the bottom-left corner of the windshield. You board minibuses in Bridgetown at River Road, Temple Yard, and Probyn Street. The fare is Bds$1.50 (U.S. 75¢).

Small signs that say TO CITY or OUT OF CITY (meaning Bridgetown) are tacked on roadside poles to indicate bus stops. Ask a local to be sure you're heading in the right direction if you're uncertain. Flag down the bus with your hand, even if you're standing at the stop or think you are. Drivers don't always stop automatically at the stops.

By scooter or bicycle

Scooters or bikes are a viable option for more-adventurous travelers on this lush island — just be extremely careful in more-urban areas. **Flex Bicycle Tours and Rentals** (☎ 246-419-2453, 246-231-1518) matches bikes and routes to riders' skills and preferences. Rates are $15 per day with a discount of two days free for every seven days of rental.

By helicopter

Bajan Helicopters (☎ 246-431-0069; Fax: 246-431-0086) at the Bridgetown Heliport offers an eagle's-eye view of Barbados. The price per person ranges from $140 for a 20- to 25-minute Discover Barbados flightseeing tour to $180 for a 30- to 35-minute full Island Tour that makes a full circuit of the coastline. Though the Island Tour is only 5 to 10 minutes longer, many visitors want to see the entire coastline and are willing to pay a lot more for the privilege of doing so.

Staying in Style

Barbados boasts an impressive range of accommodations — villas, small boutique hotels, timeshares, small guesthouses, and a handful of all-inclusive resorts — along with some of the Caribbean's most over-the-top resorts, places that are luxurious to the point of absurdity. The ultraexclusive **Sandy Lane** leaps to mind. Barbados isn't the place for romantic secluded retreats like you can get on the British Virgin Islands or Jamaica. Nor is Barbados the place to find stunning structures; most hotels have fewer than 100 rooms, and, with few exceptions, the architects who designed them didn't go for the cutting-edge look. Most resorts rely instead on Barbados's beautiful beaches and lush gardens to enchant visitors. Barbados can claim some of the region's more sophisticated and charming hoteliers. Many properties are exquisitely managed with a careful eye toward making guests feel welcome.

Barbados is developed, so don't expect to find a little gem tucked into the edge of junglelike growth. Most of our favorite resorts are in the fashionable St. James, St. Peter, or St. Michael parishes. All three are on Barbados's western shore, where Caribbean waters are calm. This area is nicknamed the **Gold Coast** — supposedly for the color of the sand, but we think it's because you need a bag of gold to pay your hotel bill. The resorts here tend to be self-contained. If you stay on the Gold Coast, don't expect to walk to a nearby restaurant; two-lane Highway 1 runs along the coast, and it's too busy to safely stroll for any distance. Hotels on the South Coast in the **Christ Church** parish (near Bridgetown) tend to be a bit less pricey. If you like to restaurant-hop and enjoy nightlife, we recommend staying near here. On the scenic Atlantic side, where the waves crash against the shoreline, you find a few rustic little places, popular with windsurfers. Villas, private homes, and condos are available south of Bridgetown, in the Hastings-Worthing area, and along the West Coast in St. James and in St. Peter.

Many of the resorts, though on good beaches, are also near busy roads. If traffic noise bothers you, make sure you ask for a room as close to the sea as possible. Unfortunately, some truck drivers on the island apparently find it great fun to merrily toot their horns as they roll by the hotels — especially in the wee hours of the morning.

If you're on a budget, Barbados isn't the best choice, unless you go during the summer low season. Ask for a room price for an approximate time in the distant future, and a reservations agent is likely to tell you crisply, "Those rates haven't been set yet," or, "The rate will depend on availability." Translation: We'll charge as much as we possibly can, depending on how business shakes out. Your best bet is to have several exact dates in mind before you call to extract a quote.

Barbados does have some bargains, but you have to hunt for them. Try small efficiency condos where you can whip up your own meals. Or pick from a dozen or so guesthouses where you'll be treated to Bajan hospitality and traditional Bajan cooking.

Many Barbados hotels insist that you take their meal plans if you visit in winter. We find this limiting, especially because Barbados is known for having many fine restaurants.

You're always better off with at least a weeklong package. Hotel prices in Barbados are geared to the longer vacation times of Europeans, not the U.S. vacationers' habit of popping onto an island for three or four days. As a result, several per-night rates listed in this chapter may curl your hair — or even shock it into dreadlocks.

If you're thinking about a private home, contact the **Barbados Tourism Authority (BTA)** (☎ **888-BARBADOS,** 246-427-2623; Fax: 246-426-4080; www.barbados.org). The BTA maintains a list of apartments and rates.

The **Best of Barbados Program** (☎ **246-228-4221**), which runs from April 15 to June 30 and September 1 to December 14, offers discounts on airfare, hotels, meals, car rentals, and attractions. Guests who book the package receive a range of information helpful for busy travelers including a full-color ticket-size voucher that includes a summary of the package, a list of discount specials, a 24-hour hot-line number, a list of participating hotels, a full description of all the "Meet and Mingle" options, and reservation numbers to book any of the offers. The package also contains a sheet of tickets that you can redeem for free meals and discounts at participating vendors. The program includes round-trip air on American Airlines, Air Jamaica, or BWIA; transfers in Barbados; the first night free with a minimum five-night stay; full breakfast daily; and a "Bajan Meet-and-Mingle Meal Event." More than 20 hotels participate in the program.

Between Barbados's hefty room tax and the 10 percent surcharge, expect your final hotel bill to jump by about 18 to 25 percent of the subtotal.

The Top Resorts

The rack rates listed in this section are in U.S. dollars and are for a standard double room during high season (mid-December through mid-April), unless otherwise noted. Lower rates are often available during the off season and shoulder season (see Chapter 3 for information on travel seasons).

Before you book your accommodations, check out Chapter 6 for more information.

Accra Beach Hotel and Resort
$$–$$$ **Christ Church**

In a West Indian mega style, the three-story, 125-room property is tastefully laid out, fronting white-sand **Accra Beach,** and it offers spacious rooms opening onto a view of the lovely pool or the sea. The units have large balconies and wooden shutters, plus full-size bathrooms with tubs; the suites are good for families. The look is a bit sterile, more like a businessperson's hotel than a resort inn, and the rooms show some wear. Steer clear of rooms marked "island view" — the panorama is of the parking lot. This hotel is one of the best in Barbados for those with disabilities. One drawback: Much of the hotel is open-air, and the man-eating mosquitoes appreciate that fact. The food in the restaurants is lackluster, with breakfasts especially poor and pricey. Children under 12 stay free with a paying adult. A beauty salon, exercise room, squash court, and shops round out the facilities.

See map p. 180. Highway 7 (Box 73W), Rockley, Christ Church. ☎ *246-435-8920. Fax: 246-435-6794.* www.accrabeachhotel.com. *Rack rates: $191–$240 double; from $250 suite. Meal plans available. AE, MC, V.*

Bougainvillea Beach Resort
$$$ **Christ Church**

This 100-room resort, on a broad, sandy beach with good swimming and bodysurfing, is one of the best South Coast deals. A family favorite with friendly service, this low-rise timeshare offers an assortment of studios and suites. It features all-suite first-class rooms and studios with one-, two-, and three-bedroom suites, each with a private balcony opening onto a seafront view; four units have plunge pools. However, be aware that all rooms face the pool and the popular swim-up bar, which stays open late, so it's pretty noisy day and night. Bedrooms are furnished along modern lines, with a medley of pastels that makes the rooms comfortable and tasteful without being too exciting. Each unit has a small bathroom containing a shower. Deluxe suites have full kitchens but no dishwasher. Waterfalls flow into the pools. Bougainvillea is just minutes away from the hip strip in **St. Lawrence Gap** with its many restaurants. This hotel participates in the **Best of Barbados Program** (see the "Staying in Style" section, earlier in this chapter, for more information).

Barbados Accommodations

Accra Beach Hotel and Resort **6**
Bougainvillea Beach Resort **9**
Casuarina Beach Club **7**
Cobblers Cove Hotel **1**
Coral Reef Club **3**
Divi Southwinds Beach Resort **8**
Little Arches **10**
Sandpiper **2**

Sandy Lane Hotel &
 Golf Club **4**
Silver Rock Resort **11**
Tamarind Cove Hotel **5**
Time Out at The Gap **8**
Traveller's Palm **3**
Turtle Beach **7**

Caribbean Islands

Barbados

North Point

Archer's Bay
River Bay
Stroud Bay
Harrison Point
ST. LUCY
Cuckold Point
Gay's Cove
Maycock's Bay
Fairfield
Pico Teneriffe
Coleton
Half Moon Fort
Morgan Lewis Beach

Six Men's Bay
ST. PETER
Greeland
Heywoods Beach
Speightstown
ST. ANDREW
St. Andrew's Church
SCOTLAND

Atlantic Ocean

Mullins Beach
Weston
Chalky Mount
Gibbs Beach
Turner's Hall Woods
Cattlewash
Lower Carlton
Tent Bay
ST. JAMES
Flower Forest
Bathsheba
Church Point
Welchman Hall Gully
ST. JOSEPH
Martin's Bay
FOLKSTONE UNDERWATER PARK
Welchman Hall
Congor Rocks
Holetown
Hackleton's Cliff
Consett Bay
Sunset Crest
Blackmans
ST. JOHN
CULPEPPER ISLAND
Ragged Point Lighthouse
Paynes Bay
Harrison's Cave
ST. THOMAS
Lazaretto
Locust Hall
Groves
Francia Plantation
Three Houses
Kitridge Point
Prospect
Warrens
ST. GEORGE
Gun Hill Signal Station
Sunbury Plantation House
Bushy Park
Sandford
Bottom Bay
Paradise Beach
Brighton Beach
ST. MICHAEL
Sandford
ST. PHILIP
Brandon's Beach
Black Rock
Sam Lord's Castle
Deep Water Harbour
Long Bay
Heritage Factory & Rum Park
Marchfield
Beachy Head
Queen's Park
CHRIST CHURCH
Crane Beach
Bridgetown
Tyrol Cot Heritage Village
Crane Beach Hotel
Carlisle Bay
Hastings
Worthing
St. Lawrence
Tom Adams Hwy
Grantley Adams Int'l Airport
Needham's Point
Maxwell
Rockley Beach
Sandy Beach
Casuarina Beach
Oistins
Long Bay
Caribbean Sea
South Point
Silver Sands Beach

Airport ✈ Beach ☚ Church ⊥ Lighthouse ☀

0   5 Miles
0   5 Kilometers

See map p. 180. Maxwell Coast Road, Christ Church. ☎ **246-418-0990.** *Fax: 246-428-2524.* www.bougainvillearesort.com. *Rack rates: $277 double; from $344 suite. European Plan. AE, DC, MC, V.*

Casuarina Beach Club
$$$ Christ Church

Family-owned and -operated Casuarina Beach Club, which has won numerous awards for its environmental efforts, manages to be an oasis of calm in the midst of the frenetic South Coast, 6.4km (4 miles) from Bridgetown and close to **St. Lawrence Gap.** The 160-room Casuarina, which has wedding, honeymoon, and golf packages, is popular with honeymooners, families, and package groups from Canada and the U.K. Its oversize pool is perfect for swimming laps, and the 457m (1,500-ft.) strand of white, powder-soft sand it fronts has plenty of inviting lounge chairs for sunbathers. The surf can be a little rough, depending on the time of year (Jan and Feb, especially). You can sit out on your balcony overlooking the tropical gardens and see a myriad of birds each morning. You may also catch a glimpse of a monkey climbing the palms in the early evenings. The hotel has tennis courts lit for night play and air-conditioned squash courts. All rooms and one- and two-bedroom suites offer large balconies and kitchenettes, and several have interconnecting doors, making them good for families. You can arrange for scuba diving, golf, and other activities through the hotel. The hotel has a supervised children's playroom, and all facilities are wheelchair accessible.

See map p. 180. St. Lawrence Gap, Christ Church. ☎ **246-428-3600.** *Fax: 246-428-1970.* www.casuarina.com. *Rack rates: $195–$210 double; 1 BR and 2BR $225–$390. Children under 12 stay free in parent's room. European Plan, Continental Plan. AE, DISC, MC, V.*

Cobblers Cove Hotel
$$$$$ St. Peter

Originally a plantation house, this intimate 40-suite resort, shielded from traffic by a high, coral stone wall, is adjacent to a small but pleasant crescent beach in a protected cove situated on Barbados's famed **Gold Coast.** Cobblers Cove, one of only five Caribbean hotels to achieve the vaunted designation of Relais & Châteaux, is a favorite of honeymooners, gourmets, and genteel U.K. visitors. The resort isn't splashy, but it's ripe with a cozy elegance. Afternoon tea is served poolside. Situated on 3 lush and fragrant garden acres dotted with coconut and traveler's palms, ten two-story cottages house four suites each. Only bedrooms are air-conditioned. Suites have wide sitting areas with louvered shutters opening to furnished balconies or patios, spacious bathrooms, and wet bars with a small fridge and hot pot. (Some suites are a bit too close to the busy highway; ask for Suites 1 through 8, toward the sea.)

See map p. 180. Road View, Speightstown, St. Peter. ☎ **800-890-6060** *in the U.S., 020-8350-1001 in London, or 246-418-0990. Fax: 246-428-2524.* www.cobblerscove.com.

Rack rates: $405–$875 double; $1,800–$2,400 suite. Rates include breakfast. AE, MC, V. Closed end of July to mid-Oct. Children under 12 aren't allowed during high season.

Coral Reef Club
$$$$$ St. James

This gracious 88-room luxury hotel is set on 4.8 hectares (12 acres) of elegantly landscaped property beside a white-sand swath of beach that's ideal for swimming and snorkeling adjacent to the underwater marine park. Guests, who meet around the hotel's two swimming pools, are housed in luxury cottages or suites with their own private plunge pools in a natural rock setting. These units contain vaulted pickled ceilings, a living room, and an elegant bathroom with a separate dressing room. Four garden rooms, which can accommodate only one adult, are also available, although they're much smaller. We recommend splurging on the ultraspacious luxury plantation suites if your budget allows. Each has a private bougainvillea-draped terrace or balcony and an open sun deck with a 2.7m-x-3.6m (9-x-12-ft.) private plunge pool. Canopied four-poster beds and oversize marble-decked tubs appeal to romantics. A beauty salon, a massage therapist, three tennis courts, an exercise room, billiards, windsurfing, boating, and water-skiing are also available.

See map p. 180. Highway 1, Holetown, St. James. ☎ **800-223-1108**, *246-422-2372. Fax: 246-422-1776.* www.coralreefbarbados.com. *Rack rates: $685–$1,375 double; from $2,095 suite. No children under 12 in Jan–Mar. AE, MC, V.*

Divi Southwinds Beach Resort
$$$ Christ Church

Busy Divi caters to couples who like being in the center of the action — the resort is a short stroll through a palm grove to a 0.8km (half-mile) stretch of sandy white beach in the heart of the bustling and happening **St. Lawrence Gap** nightlife/restaurant district. The buildings on 8 lush hectares (20 acres) are plain vanilla, but this renovated (in 2001) Divi (much larger and more modern than sister property Divi Heritage) is the sort of place where you don't spend much time in your room anyway. The friendly staff goes out of its way to make sure that you're having fun. Request a larger suite in the newer section with a full kitchen and a balcony overlooking the gardens and L-shaped pool. The older section is closer to the beach, but in this case, our vote goes to the roomier digs. The hotel has two restaurants and two bars, or you can cook in your room. On-site you also find two free-form pools, a beauty salon, a putting green, two lighted tennis courts, basketball and volleyball courts, a dive shop, and other shops.

See map p. 180. St. Lawrence Gap, Christ Church. ☎ **800-367-3484**, *246-428-7181. Fax: 246-428-4674.* www.diviresorts.com. *Rack rates: $219–$282 double; $335 suite. Children 16 and under stay free in parent's room. AE, DC, MC, V.*

Little Arches
$$$–$$$$ **Christ Church**

This family-owned, ten-room boutique hotel is a real discovery. Overlooking white sandy Enterprise Beach on the South Coast, it's a charmer for those who seek out personalized hotels. The oceanview bedrooms are individually styled with four-poster king-size beds, along with such extras as private Jacuzzi sun decks. Italian fabrics and well-chosen furnishings grace the bedrooms. The colorful rooms look like an arranged set waiting for the *House & Garden* photographers. The extras make this place really thrive: a roof-deck swimming pool, a holistic massage therapist, an alfresco restaurant run by an international chef, free use of mountain bikes, and the hotel's own private 13m (42-ft.) yacht. The location is a short walk from the village of Oistins and a short ride from **St. Lawrence Gap** (2.4m/4 miles) and the airport (4.9m/8 miles).

See map p. 180. Enterprise Coast Road, Christ Church. ☎ ***800-860-8013***, *246-420-4689. Fax: 246-418-0207.* www.littlearches.com. *Rack rates: $347–$480 double. AE, MC, V.*

Sandpiper
$$$$$ **St. James**

The Coral Reef Club (covered earlier in this section), owned by the same family, offers plushier digs but may be full, so consider this more-casual West Indian resort on the beach. Similar to Cobblers Cove, this 45-room resort is self-contained and intimate, with a cascading waterfall to greet arriving guests. Set in a small grove of coconut palms and flowering trees, the place is dramatically lit at night. A cluster of rustic-chic units surrounds the lushly landscaped pool ringed by cushioned wrought-iron chaise longues; some rooms have fine sea views of the white-sand beach edged by mature palms. The newly redone rooms open onto little terraces that stretch along the second story, where you can order drinks or have breakfast. Accommodations are generous in size, consisting of superior rooms and one- and two-bedroom suites with white-tile floors. All are beautifully furnished with tropical pieces. Each has a private terrace, luxurious bed, and small fridge. The medium-size bathrooms are equipped with combination shower/tubs. The hotel restaurant's award-winning Mediterranean/provincial cuisine with a Caribbean twist ensures that diners won't be bored.

See map p. 180. Holetown (a 3-minute walk north of town), St. James. ☎ ***800-223-1108*** *in the U.S., 800-567-5327 in Canada, or 246-422-2251. Fax: 246-422-0900.* www.sandpiperbarbados.com. *Rack rates: $630–$805 double; from $880 suite. Rates include breakfast and dinner. Children under 12 not accepted Jan–Mar. AE, MC, V.*

Sandy Lane Hotel & Golf Club
$$$$$ **St. James**

The 112-room Sandy Lane is one of the most luxurious places to stay in the southern Caribbean, as its horrifying prices attest. When Ronald Tree, an heir to the Marshall Field's department-store fortune, constructed it in the 1960s, Sandy Lane enjoyed a celebrity-haunted heyday. After it fell into neglect, Irish investors rescued the resort in 1997, pouring $350 million into its reconstruction. Fortunately, its pristine beach set against a backdrop of swaying palms needed no such rehabilitation. The Palladian-style Sandy Lane is practically identical to its first incarnation, with the addition of a mammoth spa, better restaurants, and a trio of golf courses. You'll feel like royalty when checking in — especially when your valet unpacks your suitcase. On request, guests arrive in style — you'll be picked up at the airport in the hotel's Bentley. The rooms are furnished grandly, with lots of extras not found at any of the hotel's competitors — such as a motion-sensor alarm to alert maids that you're in the room, and a marble shower with seven adjustable nozzles. Accommodations are decorated mostly with redwood furnishings, each with a king-size bed or two twin beds. The bathrooms are the most luxurious on the island, and in addition to the shower, also contain oversize tubs and a bidet.

Four on-site restaurants offer the finest hotel dining in Barbados and serve a mostly French or Mediterranean cuisine; a Spa Cafe caters to the weight conscious.

See map p. 180. Highway 1, Paynes Bay, St. James. ☎ *246-444-2000. Fax: 246-444-2222.* www.sandylane.com. *Rack rates: $1,100–$2,700 double; from $2,300 suite. AE, DC, MC, V.*

Silver Rock Resort
$$ Christ Church

Ideal for professional windsurfers and adventure seekers, this beachfront hotel opened in 2000 on **Silver Sands Beach.** A range of beachfront, oceanview, and gardenview accommodations — some with soaring, white pickled ceilings and louvered windows — is available. The hotel's open-air restaurant, Jibboom, serves tasty local and international dishes and has occasional theme nights. Guests frequently take part in the Friday Night Street Party at nearby Time Out at The Gap. Scuba diving, snorkeling, body boarding, surfing, hiking, beach volleyball, and sea kayaking are also popular here. All guests receive reduced greens fees and preferential tee times at the **Barbados Golf Club,** the island's only public championship golf course.

See map p. 180. Silver Sands, Christ Church. ☎ *246-428-2866. Fax: 246-428-3687.* www.gemsbarbados.com. *Rack rates: $145–$180 double. AE, DISC, MC, V.*

Tamarind Cove Hotel
$$$$–$$$$$ St. James

On 240m (800 ft.) of prime sandy beachfront, this flagship of a British-based hotel chain (St. James Properties) challenges the Coral Reef Club/Sandpiper properties, attracting the same upscale clientele, thanks to an $8-million restoration in the 1990s. Designed in Mediterranean style with pale-pink walls and red terra-cotta roofs, the rambling 105-unit resort occupies a desirable location on St. James Beach, 2km (1¼ miles) south of

Holetown. The stylish and comfortable rooms are in a series of hacienda-style buildings interspersed with vegetation. The well-appointed bathrooms boast dual basins, spacious Roman tubs, stall showers, and long marble counters. Each unit has a patio or balcony overlooking the gardens or ocean, which has a reef for good snorkeling. The water-sports staff is helpful.

Management overall has slipped, especially the concierge desk and restaurants, which are pricey and have slow service. Make sure to request a room near the sea; otherwise, you'll be disturbed by noise from the nearby highway. Room walls are somewhat thin, too, so you may also hear your neighbors.

See map p. 180. Paynes Bay, St. James. ☎ *800-326-6898, 246-432-1332. Fax: 246-432-6317.* www.tamarindcovehotel.com. *Rack rates: $420–$675 double. AE, DC, MC, V.*

Time Out at The Gap
$$ **Christ Church**

Across the road from Dover Beach, a wide, white-sand beach, this 76-room hotel is popular with an active, younger crowd looking for an affordable yet happening place. The friendly staff adds to the party atmosphere that prevails, arranging water sports, submarine rides, cricket matches, and nature walks. Rooms are attractively furnished in neutrals with splashes of bright yellow and teal and overlook the pool, surrounded by lush tropical plantings or the equally lush gardens. Honeymoon suites and services are also available. Water-sports options are sometimes limited because the beach gets extremely windy. Food and drinks are excellent. On Friday nights, jazz plays at the popular Whistling Frog on-site, and the hotel makes itself party central with happenings throughout the week.

See map p. 180. St. Lawrence Gap, Christ Church. ☎ *800-868-9429, 246-435-9473. Fax: 246-435-8822.* www.gemsbarbados.com. *Rack rates: $140–$170 double; $180–$260 deluxe. Children 12 and under stay free when staying with two full-paying adults. AE, MC, V.*

Traveller's Palm
$$ **St. James**

Within a 10-minute walk of a good beach, this is for self-sufficient types who are not too demanding and want to save money. There's a choice of 16 simply furnished, one-bedroom apartments with fully equipped kitchens and well-maintained bathrooms with shower units. They're simple, slightly worn apartments, with bright but fading colors, but they're quite a deal in this high-rent district. The apartments have living and dining areas, as well as patios where you can have breakfast or a candlelit dinner you've prepared yourself (no meals are served here). To run the in-room air conditioners you must purchase tokens. ☎ *246-432-6750. Fax 246-432-7229.* www.barbadostraveler.com. *Rack rates $155 apt for two. MC, V.*

See map 180. 265 Palm Ave., Sunset Crest, St. James.

Turtle Beach
$$$$$ Christ Church

Set on a wide, 457m-long (1,500-ft.) white strand of beach on the South Coast, this plush all-inclusive, three-story hotel opened in 1998 as the flagship of London-based Elegant Hotel Group. Guests from Great Britain account for 75 percent of the business, with many families coming on packages to take advantage of the Kids Club (for ages 3–11), which runs from 9 a.m. to 9 p.m. daily and features computer games and lots of activities. Included in the price, you get instruction and use of the equipment to participate in scuba diving, water-skiing, snorkeling, kayaking, sailing, and body boarding. Set amid lush gardens, the hotel opens onto ocean views from every suite. Tennis equipment is provided; golfers get special rates and times at Royal Westmoreland Golf and Country Club. Ask about the hotel's excellent children's packages, which let one child between the ages of 2 and 12 stay free in the off season. (Additional children stay at 50 percent off the adult rate.) The downside? The restaurants here have slow service and short hours. Also, several stray cats wander around the grounds and in the restaurants.

See map p. 180. Dover, Christ Church. ☎ *800-326-6898, 246-428-7131. Fax: 246-428-6089.* www.turtlebeachresortbarbados.com. *Rack rates: $863–$1,072 suite for two. Rates are all-inclusive. AE, DC, MC, V.*

Dining Out

Barbados, the easternmost island of the Lesser Antilles jutting out into the Atlantic, was often the first stop for ships carrying goods either from Europe or South America, so Bajans are used to having first pick of the bounty flowing into and out of the Caribbean. That long tradition of expecting the best of the best extends to food and has contributed to making this a sophisticated island where the dining experience has been elevated to a fine art. Many of the zippy young chefs coming out of London in order to make a name in the food world come to the Caribbean — chiefly Barbados and the British Virgin Islands — to hone their talents. These chefs, often trained in France and at the finest English country estates, design experimental and fun menus.

Like the island itself, however, eating out in Barbados is a study in contrasts. You can go as fancy (and pricey) as you want, with tuxedoed waiters at your elbow. Or you can get delicious down-home Bajan cooking at a funky little beachside cafe or at a weekly Friday-night village fish fry for a reasonable price.

Pack your tiara and your jacket and tie for dining out on this island. Okay, it's not quite that formal at most places, but in Barbados, you'll likely have the urge to dine at some swank spot at least once, and dressing up is the way it's done here. Shorts generally elicit raised eyebrows (at the least) in the evenings. Guys should wear collared shirts, and women should wear smart resort wear.

Following British custom, the waiters on this island don't bring your final bill until you signal that you're ready for it. Also, the service charge is usually already included, so make sure that you don't overtip.

 During high season, many of the best places get booked up, so we suggest that you phone, fax, or e-mail reservation requests before you arrive.

Enjoying a Taste of Barbados

Interestingly enough, Barbados has a strong culinary connection with South Carolina, so if you're familiar with Low Country cooking, you'll have a good handle on the native cuisine of Barbados — lots of seafood and fresh vegetables like okra and tomatoes. Of course, catches from the Atlantic and Caribbean figure heavily into the menus here. Flying fish, the national bird — oops, we mean fish — leaps onto menus all over the island. Sides of rice and peas are important, as are spicy stews. Desserts often feature fresh fruit.

Most restaurants here offer a strong taste of local flavor, and even franchises such as KFC have adjusted their offerings to Bajan tastes. Order a side order of the Colonel's mashed potatoes, and you'll get sweet potatoes spiked with local herbs. Chefette is the local answer to McDonald's, and the local chain has nearly two dozen locations around the island. It has playgrounds for kids at half a dozen locations. If you want a quick bite, it offers good salads and burgers.

In-the-know visitors join the throng of locals at **Oistins Fish Fry** on Friday nights, where $12 and up gets you a whopping helping of crisply fried or grilled and deboned flying fish or chicken, macaroni pie, and a salad. Arrive by 7 p.m. and several vendors will be frying up fish. Our pick is the one with the longest line: **Fisherman's Net.** You pay a reasonable price for good food and a fun time with festive music blaring and locals scrambling to buy freshly caught fish to cook at home.

The Best Restaurants

Angry Annie's Restaurant & Bar
$$ **Holetown   INTERNATIONAL**

Don't ask Annie why she's angry — she might tell you! Annie and Paul Matthews, both from the United Kingdom, run this friendly, cozy, 34-seat joint. It's decorated in tropical colors with a circular bar, and rock classics play on the excellent sound system. The dishes are tasty with lots of local flavor. The place is known for its "famous" ribs, the most savory on the island. We like the garlic-cream potatoes and the fresh local vegetables. Annie also turns out fresh fish and excellent pasta dishes. Get your meal to go if you'd like to dine back in your room.

Barbados Dining

Angry Annie's Restaurant and Bar **5**	Nico's Champagne Wine Bar
Bellini's Trattoria **13**	and Restaurant **8**
Bombas Beach Bar **7**	Olives Bar and Bistro **5**
Brown Sugar **11**	Pisces **13**
Carambola **6**	Ragamuffins **5**
The Cliff **10**	Round House Inn Restaurant and Bar **15**
Daphne's **9**	The Ship Inn **13**
The Emerald Palm **3**	The Terrace Restaurant
Lone Star Restaurant **4**	at Cobblers Cove **2**
Mango's by the Sea **1**	Waterfront Cafe **11**
Naniki **14**	

North Point

Archer's Bay
River Bay

Caribbean Islands

Stroud Bay

Harrison
Point
ST. LUCY
Cuckold Point

Barbados

Fairfield
Gay's Cove
18
Pico Teneriffe
Maycock's Bay
Coleton
1C
Half Moon Fort

Morgan Lewis Beach

Six Men's Bay
ST. PETER
Greeland

Atlantic Ocean

Heywoods Beach
1
2
St. Andrew's
Church
Speightstown
ST. ANDREW
SCOTLAND
Mullins Beach
2
Weston
Chalky Mount
Gibbs Beach
1
Turner's Hall
Woods
Cattlewash
2A
Lower Carlton
Tent Bay
3
ST. JAMES
Flower Forest
Bathsheba
15
Church Point
4
Welchman Hall
Gully
ST. JOSEPH
Martin's Bay
FOLKSTONE
UNDERWATER PARK
Welchman Hall
3A
14
Hackleton's Cliff
Congor Rocks
5
1A
Holetown
3
Consett Bay
Blackmans
ST. JOHN
6
Sunset Crest
Harrison's
Cave
CULPEPPER
ISLAND
Ragged Point
Lighthouse
Paynes Bay
7
2A
ST. THOMAS
3B
8
Lazaretto
9
Locust Hall
Groves
Francia
Plantation
Three Houses
Kitridge
Point
10
Prospect
Warrens
Paradise Beach
ST. MICHAEL
3
ST. GEORGE
Gun Hill
Signal Station
Sunbury
Plantation
House
Bushy Park
Sandford
Bottom Bay
Brighton Beach
2
4
4B
ST. PHILIP
5
Brandon's Beach
Sam Lord's
Castle
Black Rock
3
5
Long Bay
Deep Water Harbour
Heritage Factory
& Rum Park
Marchfield
Beachy Head
Queen's Park
11
Tyrol Cot
Heritage Village
CHRIST CHURCH
7
Crane Beach
Bridgetown
Crane Beach Hotel
Carlisle Bay
Hastings
St. Lawrence
6
Tom Adams Hwy
Grantley Adams
Int'l Airport
Needham's Point
12
Worthing
13
Maxwell
7
Rockley
Beach
Sandy
Beach
Casuarina
Beach
Oistins
Long Bay

Caribbean
Sea
South
Point
Silver
Sands Beach

Airport ✈ Beach 🏖 Church ⛪ Lighthouse 🗼

0		5 Miles
0		5 kilometers

See map p. 188. First St., Holetown, St. James. ☎ 246-432-2119. Reservations not required. Main courses: $15–$50. MC, V. Daily 5–10pm.

Bellini's Trattoria
$$$–$$$$ Christ Church   NORTHERN ITALIAN

South of Bridgetown, this trattoria, on the main floor of Little Bay Hotel, evokes the Mediterranean in a beautiful setting that opens onto a veranda overlooking the water. The menu has a changing array of freshly made antipasti, plus well-prepared seafood dishes. The pasta menu with succulent sauces is extensive. After an appetizer — perhaps a small pizza — you can order tender and well-flavored beef tenderloin, chicken parmigiana, or jumbo shrimp in white wine, lemon, and garlic sauce. The Italian desserts, such as tiramisu, are velvety smooth. Most main courses are priced at the lower end of the scale (see below).

See map p. 188. Little Bay Hotel, St. Lawrence Gap, Christ Church. ☎ 246-435-7246. Reservations required. Main courses: $24–$69. AE, DC, MC, V. Open: Daily 6–10:30 p.m.

Bombas Beach Bar
$$–$$$ St. James   BAJAN/INTERNATIONAL

This colorful beach bar, tucked between **Sandy Lane** and **Tamarind Cove** hotels on the West Coast, serves tasty simple fare turned out by Scottish chef/owner Gay Taaffe, whose partner is a Bajan Rastafarian named Wayne Alleyne. Both locals and visitors favor this funky little place for dining alfresco on casual decking shaded by tall palm trees (lit by spotlights at night), right on the wide sandy beach. For lunch, they serve beach-style snacks — jalapeño poppers, Bajan fishcakes, and the black-and-blue chicken sandwich (grilled with blue cheese). In front of Bombas is a good place to swim in the sheltered bay, rent a beach chair, and watch the sun go down. In the evening, the chef cuts loose with lamb meatloaf served with mint and apple chutney or char-grilled steakfish marinated in rum and lime with a hint of ginger. All main courses come with local veggies, rice, and crisp greens.

See map p. 188. Paynes Bay Beach, St. James. ☎ 246-432-0569. Reservations not required. Main courses: $8–$40. MC, V. Open: Daily noon to 9:30 p.m.

Brown Sugar
$$–$$$ St. Michael   BAJAN

Brown Sugar, on the outskirts of Bridgetown, serves the tastiest Bajan specialties on the island. The alfresco restaurant, opened in 1977, is hidden behind lush foliage in a turn-of-the-20th-century coral limestone bungalow. The latticed ceiling is punctuated with slow-turning fans, and on the open veranda you dine by candlelight beneath hanging plants, listening to waterfalls that feed into small ponds. We suggest starting with gungo-peak soup (pigeon peas cooked in chicken broth and zested with fresh coconut milk, herbs, and a touch of white wine). Among the main dishes we like, Creole orange chicken is the best, or you may prefer stuffed crab backs. You can also choose from a selection of locally grown vegetables. Only the lobster is expensive; most of the other dishes are reasonably priced. For dessert, we recommend walnut-rum pie with rum sauce. The restaurant is known for its buffet-style, three-course lunches, popular with local businesspeople for its good value, and it now offers takeout. Sometimes they offer live entertainment at night.

See map p. 188. Aquatic Gap, Bay Street, Bridgetown, St. Michael. ☎ *246-426-7684. Reservations recommended. Main courses: $16–$36; fixed-price lunch buffet $20 weekdays, $24 Sun. AE, DC, DISC, MC, V. Open: Sun–Fri 12:30–2:30 p.m. and daily from 6–9:30 p.m.*

Carambola
$$$$ St. James CLASSIC FRENCH/CARIBBEAN/ASIAN

Named for one of our favorite tropical fruits, Carambola is also one of our favorite Caribbean restaurants. Stationed beside the road that runs along the island's western coastline, this stunningly elegant restaurant, with crisp-white-linen-topped tables and white canopies, sits atop a 6m (20-ft.) seaside cliff and offers one of the most panoramic dining terraces in the Caribbean. The Cliff (see the next listing) has the edge in the looks department, but both are stellar on all counts. The prizewinning cuisine is creative, with modern, French-nouvelle touches. Try the chef's lobster and spring rolls, or his grilled teriyaki of scallop and jumbo shrimp. Another spectacular dish is rack of lamb, coated in parsley and mustard with a truffle/sesame-seed/sweet-potato purée and caramelized root vegetables. The priciest items are the seafood platter and the grilled Caribbean lobster, but either is as succulent as you can imagine. Save room for one of the luscious desserts, such as lime mousse. Try to be seated by 6:30 p.m. to see the staff feed the manta rays that glide through the illuminated sea just below.

See map p. 188. Derricks (2.4km/1½ miles south of Holetown), St. James. ☎ *246-432-0832. Reservations required. Main courses: $33–$63. AE, MC, V. Open: Mon–Sat 6:30–9 p.m. Closed Aug.*

The Cliff
$$$$$ St. James INTERNATIONAL/CARIBBEAN

Hands down, this romantic restaurant is our all-time favorite in Barbados. Custom-made, wrought-iron torches and candelabras punctuate the already dramatic setting, a series of open-air terraces spilling down to a 3m (10-ft.) coral cliff, overlooking the illuminated sea, waves gently lapping the rocks below. Request a torch-lit table on the outer edge for the biggest wow factor. Flambeaus are rolled out to cover guests should it begin to rain. Ensconced at a table, you can sip a complimentary glass of Laurent Perrier Rose Champagne and watch fish glide by. Chef Paul Owens constantly changes the menu and offers nightly specials. Of late, his offerings have often had an Asian touch to them. Start with rocket salad with char-grilled vegetables, herbed goat cheese, and balsamic vinaigrette; or snow crab cake with coriander cream, vinaigrette, and red curry oil. Masterful entrees include the seared tuna on wasabi mash with spicy Asian vinaigrette, Japanese ginger, and soy, as well as the red snapper on jasmine rice with a Thai yellow curry coconut sauce. For dessert, keep cool with the homemade sorbet served in a ginger basket.

See map p. 188. Derricks, St. James. ☎ *246-432-1922. Reservations required in winter. Prix-fixe menu $88. AE, MC. V. Open: Mon–Sat 6:30–10 p.m. Dec–Apr daily 6:30–10 p.m.*

Daphne's
$$$$ St. James   MEDITERRANEAN/CARIBBEAN

This sexy, intimate restaurant — operated by the owners of The House hotel and custom-made for the glitterati — is an outpost of the fabled eatery attracting chic London. The service is flawless and the beach setting idyllic for dining in the tropics. The interior evokes Bali with its Indonesian batiks and lampshades fashioned from coconut shells. For greater privacy, tables are surrounded by silk curtains. Chef Nick Bell is a whiz, turning out memorable dishes based on fresh ingredients. The pasta dishes rate a rave, especially the linguine with spicy crab and the pappardelle with braised duck in a red-wine sauce. On a recent visit, the chef's most successful main dishes were grilled mahi-mahi with Marsala, peperonata, and zucchini and the char-grilled tuna with rocket (arugula). We also enjoyed the spicy mussels with chickpea broth.

See map p. 188. Paynes Bay, St. James. ☎ *246-432-2731. Reservations required. Lunch main courses: $28–$36. Dinner main courses: $34–$50. AE, MC, V. Open: Daily 12:30–3 p.m. and 6:30–10:30 p.m. Closed Mon off season.*

The Emerald Palm
$$$$ St. James   INTERNATIONAL

The only noise at this 4-hectare (10-acre) tropical oasis is the trickling of waterfalls and the rustling of palms. The centerpiece: a massive coral stone house, where you'll pass under an arbor and quickly be offered a drink to sip as you settle on one of the many comfortable lounges while your table — we suggest those in the fragrant garden — is prepared. You'll have to reserve early if you want the best table, the middle one of a trio of gazebos. The restaurant, which mainly attracts older Europeans, often has bookings a year in advance. The menu changes three times a year, and the chef turns out flavorful and intriguing combinations. Begin with a marinated shrimp in soy and ginger served with a cucumber and pink grapefruit salad. Specialties include his grilled dolphin filet with a shrimp fritter; fondant potato and a grain mustard butter sauce; or red snapper with fettuccine, buttered bok choy, and red pepper cream. For the grand finale, go with the dark chocolate crème brûlée spiked with Mount Gay Extra Old Rum served with a clementine confit.

See map p. 188. Porters (3.2km/2 miles north of Holetown), St. James. ☎ *246-422-4116. Reservations required. Main courses: $18–$36. AE, MC, V. Open: Tues–Sun 6:30–10 p.m. Closed Sept.*

Lone Star Restaurant
$$$–$$$$$ St. James   BAJAN/INTERNATIONAL

Situated in a hotel converted from a 1940s garage, Lone Star delivers refined dining without stiff formality. In spite of its former role, it is today a pocket of posh — for example, offering the island's widest selection of pure Iranian caviar. Beautifully appointed, it is decorated with muslin curtains and polished wood floors. The main restaurant fronts the beach, maintaining a casual atmosphere during the day that is transformed to elegance in the evening. Top chefs cooking for a discerning international clientele turn out Caribbean fish pie (especially delectable with its cheesy mashed potatoes), blackened dolphin, and such fusion dishes as a Thai green king prawn curry. Mediterranean and modern European dishes, along with Barbadian specialties, are the focus, but the culinary delights of Southeast Asia are also served — mainly Thai, Vietnamese, and Chinese dishes. You can even get Japanese dishes such as sushi and sashimi. Such *fruits de mer* as king prawns, crab legs, and fresh oysters add to the utterly delightful but frighteningly expensive seafood selections, but the average dish is affordable.

See map p. 188. Hwy. 1, Mount Standfast, St. James. ☎ 246-419-0599. Reservations required. Lunch main courses: $23–$33. Dinner main courses: $23–$90. AE, MC. V. Open: Daily 7:30 a.m.–11 p.m. (closing hours can vary).

Mango's by the Sea
$$ St. Peter   SEAFOOD/INTERNATIONAL

This romantic hideaway restaurant and bar overlooking the lapping waves is best known for its seafood; the owners buy the catch of the day directly from the fishermen's boats. The food is exceedingly tasty, and they use market-fresh ingredients to good advantage. Appetizers may be anything from an intriguing green peppercorn pâté to pumpkin soup. If you don't want fish, opt for the 8-ounce U.S. tenderloin steak cooked to perfection or the fall-off-the-bone barbecued baby-back ribs. Top off your meal with passion-fruit cheesecake or star-fruit torte. Live entertainment is offered on some nights. After 10 p.m., cigar aficionados make their selection from a collection of Cubans from Pierre's humidor and puff away at the bar or their tables. This restaurant is also one of the few in the Caribbean to have a wine cellar.

See map p. 188. 2 West End, Queen Street, Speightstown, St. Peter. ☎ 246-422-0704. Reservations required. Main courses: $25–$34. AE, MC, V. Open: Daily 6–9:30 p.m.

Naniki
$$ St. Joseph   CARIBBEAN/ORGANIC

A little greenheart house at the Lush Life Nature Resort, outside the village of Suriname, is home to this restaurant. Naniki is all about healthy cooking; the chef is committed to serving fresh vegetables, most of which are organic, along with Bajan and other Caribbean treats. He pays meticulous attention to the presentation of creations, using delicacies like *lambie* (conch) and blue crab and grilled Bajan black belly lamb. Sweet potatoes, yams, and breadfruits are menu staples. This place is our top pick if you're heading to **Bathsheba** for the day. The Sunday Bajan buffet has become so popular that you need a reservation. The surroundings are refreshingly beautiful, too. Light streams through the mostly glass walls, making optimal use of the rolling hills, the stands of cabbage palms, and the Atlantic Coast beyond.

See map p. 188. Suriname, St. Joseph. ☎ *246-433-1300. Reservations recommended. Main courses: $29–$44. Sun buffet: $65. MC, V. Open: Tues–Sun 12:30–3 p.m. Dinner served on moonlit nights only.*

Nico's Champagne Wine Bar and Restaurant
$$ St. James   INTERNATIONAL

Set on the side of a road away from the sea that bisects some of the most expensive residential real estate in Barbados, Nico's is a great value with friendly service — a cozy, informal bistro inspired by the wine bars of London. In an atmospheric 19th-century building, originally constructed as the headquarters for a plantation, is its air-conditioned tropical bar. Meals are served at tables under a shed-style roof in the back garden. About a dozen wines are available by the glass; the flavorful food is well-matched to the wines. The finest plates include deep-fried Camembert with passion-fruit sauce, chicken breasts stuffed with crab, and some of the best lobster (grilled simply and served with garlic butter) in Barbados.

See map p. 188. Derricks, St. James. ☎ *246-432-6386. Reservations recommended. Main courses: Dinner $26–$75; Sun brunch $30–$48. AE, DISC, MC, V. Open: Mon–Sat 6:30 p.m.–midnight; Sun brunch 11:30–3 p.m.*

Olives Bar and Bistro
$$ St. James   MEDITERANNEAN/CARIBBEAN

Olive oil is used to prepare almost all the good-value, imaginative dishes here, and olives are the only snack served in the large breezy bar upstairs that has become a popular hangout. The street-level, air-conditioned, and unpretentious dining room (where no smoking is permitted) spills out from its original coral-stone walls and scrubbed-pine floorboards into a pleasant garden. (On a warm evening, stick to the inside air-conditioning.) The cuisine, featuring fresh ingredients and a beautiful presentation, celebrates the warm climates of southern Europe and the Antilles, and does so exceedingly well. Even some local chefs like to dine here on their nights off. Service is proficient and friendly. The best items include yellowfin tuna, marinated and seared rare and served with green peppercorn mustard cream sauce. Next door is a sandwich bar that serves light lunch fare, Monday through Friday from 8 a.m. to 4 p.m.

See map p. 188. 2nd Street, Holetown, St. James. ☎ *246-432-2112. Reservations required in winter. Main courses: $25–$65. AE, MC, V. Open: Light fare Mon–Fri 8:30 a.m.–4 p.m., dinner nightly 6:30–10 p.m.*

Pisces
$$ Christ Church   BAJAN

This beautiful restaurant with a tropical décor offers alfresco dining at water's edge. Begin with one of the soups, perhaps split pea or pumpkin, or a savory appetizer such as flying fish Florentine. Seafood lovers enjoy the Pisces platter — charcoal-broiled mahi-mahi, fried flying fish, broiled kingfish, and butter-fried prawns. You may also be drawn to the seasonal Caribbean fish, which you can order broiled, blackened, or pan-fried, served with lime-herb butter. The restaurant offers a limited but good selection of poultry and meat, including roast pork with traditional Bajan stuffing.

See map p. 188. From Bridgetown, take Highway 7 south for about 6.4km (4 miles), then turn right at the sign toward St. Lawrence Gap. St. Lawrence Gap, Christ Church. ☎ *246-435-6564. Reservations recommended. Main courses: $21–$55. AE, DC, MC, V. Open: Daily 6–10:30 p.m.*

Ragamuffins
$$$ St. James   CARIBBEAN

This affordable, lively place — packed most nights — serves authentic island cuisine in a brightly colored, authentic chattel house, the humble abode of the slaves and laborers who worked the sugar-cane fields. The broiled T-bones, the most pricey menu item, are juicy and perfectly flavored. Take heart, vegetarians. The cooks are always willing to stir-fry some vegetables with noodles, and a vegetarian stew is on the menu, too. Other menu highlights are blackened fish with *garlic aioli,* the local version of a spicy West Indian curry, and a zesty jerk chicken salad. On Sunday nights, this restaurant features the only drag show — often sold out, so reserve early — in Barbados. (Request seats in the garden for the best view.)

See map p. 188. 1st Street, Holetown, St. James. ☎ *246-432-1295. Reservations recommended. Main courses: $15–$25. AE, MC, V. Open: Daily 6:30–10 p.m.*

Round House Inn Restaurant and Bar
$–$$$ St. Joseph   BAJAN

The small historic inn is perched on a hill overlooking the dramatic Soup Bowl in Bathsheba where surfers like to battle the waves of the Atlantic. From the small tables beside the large open windows, you can watch families playing in the tidal pools at the water's edge. The Round House attracts locals who love the reggae and surf scene. The Bajan food here is excellent, with tasty homemade bread, a decent selection of wines, and good, though casual, service. For lunch, go with the grilled flying fish sandwich served with breadfruit chips. The soups, served with saltbread, and the salads are good, too. Request some of the Bajan hot sauce on the side for an extra kick. At night, go with the fishermen's catch, including dolphin, flying fish, and shrimp, complemented by peas and rice. The homemade banana bread with ice cream is a fine ending to the meal. In the evenings, live reggae bands often play. The rooms at the inn have been redone, too, and are a reasonably priced choice if you're into the surf scene or want to stay on this quiet coast.

See map p. 188. Bathsheba, St. Joseph. ☎ *246-433-9678. Reservations required on Sun and recommended on other days. Main courses: $12–$23. MC, V. Open: Mon–Sat 8:30–10 a.m., 11:30 a.m.–3:30 p.m., and 6–9 p.m.; Sun 8–10 a.m. and 11:30 a.m.–5 p.m.*

The Ship Inn
$ Christ Church   ENGLISH PUB/BAJAN

South of Bridgetown between Rockley Beach and Worthing, The Ship Inn is a traditional English-style pub with an attractive, rustic nautical décor. You can also enjoy a drink in the garden bar's tropical atmosphere. Many guests come to play darts, meet friends, and listen to top local bands. The Ship Inn, which has popular happy hours (4–6 p.m. and 10–11 p.m.), serves substantial bar food, such as homemade steak-and-kidney pie, shepherd's pie, and chicken, shrimp, and fish dishes.

See map p. 188. St. Lawrence Gap, Christ Church. ☎ *246-435-6961. Reservations not required. Main courses: $15–$30; all-you-can-eat Carvery meal $15 at lunch, $21 at dinner, plus $6.50–$8.50 for appetizer and dessert. DC, MC, V. Open: Daily noon to 10:30 p.m.*

The Terrace Restaurant at Cobblers Cove
$$$$ St. Peter   BRITISH HAUTE/CARIBBEAN

This English-style country house on a beach is one of only five restaurant/hotels in the Caribbean to receive the Relais & Châteaux designation, which recognizes excellent small hotels with top-notch dining. This elegant yet casual dining spot has an open-air terrace, allowing sea breezes to waft through. The chefs use local market-fresh produce whenever it's available. Your palate will adore such starters as a sauté of shrimp with ginger, coconut, and coriander, or shaved breast of duckling with mango chutney and a lemon-grass dressing. Perfectly prepared are the roast loin of pork with garlic cream potatoes and a Calvados sauce and the roasted breast of chicken flavored with fresh thyme and garlic. You can order the catch of the day — perhaps your best bet — blackened, grilled, or pan-seared. A bit of heaven is the raspberry tiramisu with mascarpone cheese steeped in a raspberry liqueur.

See map p. 188. Cobblers Cove, St. Peter. ☎ *246-422-2291. Reservations required. Main courses: $60–$90. Prix-fixe menu: $150. AE, MC, V. Open: Daily 8–10 a.m., 12:30–2:30 p.m., and 6:30–9 p.m. Closed Aug 31–Oct 13.*

Waterfront Cafe
$$–$$$ St. Michael   INTERNATIONAL

The Waterfront Cafe is your best bet if you're in Bridgetown shopping or sightseeing. In a turn-of-the-20th-century warehouse originally built to store bananas and freeze fish, this cafe serves international fare with a strong emphasis on Bajan specialties. Try the fresh catch of the day prepared Creole-style, the peppered steak, or the fish burger made with kingfish or dolphin. Vegetarians can choose from such dishes as pasta primavera, vegetable soup, and usually a special of the day. Both diners and drinkers are welcome here for Creole food, beer, and pastel-colored drinks. Tuesday nights bring live steel-band music and a Bajan buffet. To see the Thursday-night Dixieland bands, reserve about a week in advance. Come for jazz on Friday and Saturday.

See map p. 188. The Careenage, Bridgetown, St. Michael. ☎ *246-427-0093. Reservations required. Main courses: $17–$38. AE, DC, MC, V. Open: Mon–Sat 10 a.m.–10 p.m.*

Enjoying the Sand and Surf

George Washington (and his younger brother) slept here. Really. Lots of places make such a claim, but in this case, it's true. Indeed, Barbados has been giving the royal treatment to the wealthy and the famous for centuries — from the British royals to U.S. presidents, from the Rolling Stones to the Rockefellers. The upscale appeal comes from its outstanding golf courses, its historic Great Houses and gardens, its stellar dining scene, and the pampering of the Gold Coast's resorts with water sports in the calm Caribbean.

In the last several years, however, Barbados has become a popular holiday choice with regular folks as well, especially younger Brits and Canadians, who come for the pub-hopping and dance scene on the South Coast in an area known as **The Gap,** as well as for Barbados's rollicking music festivals. The younger set also likes the surfing on the rugged Atlantic side and the windsurfing on the South Coast.

Combing the beaches

With more than 113km (70 miles) of coastline, the coral island of Barbados is ringed by a great selection of soft white to pale golden sand beaches with ample opportunities for water play from snorkeling to skiing to surfing. If you love nothing better than hanging out on the quintessential Caribbean beach, this island is a good pick. Most of the beaches — all are public, though you may have to cross a resort's property or find a small public path to access them — are relatively litter free. Although vendors selling pareus (wraparound skirts), shark-tooth necklaces, dolls, baskets, and carvings do approach you on the more populated beaches, they aren't overly aggressive. If you aren't interested in what they're selling, a simple but firm "No, thank you" should preserve your peace. Private boat owners may also approach you, offering to take you water-skiing, parasailing, or snorkeling.

 A euphemism that beach vendors who are selling drugs use is asking if you're interested in any local pottery. Tell them you'll be checking out the wares at Earthworks, a well-known local maker of pottery.

West Coast

If you're picturing the calm, clear kaleidoscope of blues that are the signature of the Caribbean, you'll likely find the beaches on the West Coast — commonly referred to as the **Gold Coast** or Platinum Coast — to your taste. It's no accident that Barbados's toniest resorts and grand homes are located here. This part of the island is breathtakingly beautiful with tropical gardens, stands of palm trees, and little coves with shallow reefs close to shore for snorkeling. The Caribbean is often so smooth (especially early in the morning) that you can water-ski, and swimming conditions are generally excellent.

We recommend **Mullins Beach** because it has a scenic reef for snorkeling. Park on the main drag or take the bus.

An even better spot for snorkeling — and good for other water sports, too — is the somewhat crowded but panoramic **Paynes Bay,** accessed from the Coach House, south of Holetown. You can rent beach chairs and water-sports equipment at **Bombas Beach Bar,** a colorful gathering spot and watering hole. Famous for snorkeling on this side of the island is **Folkestone Marine Park** (see later in this chapter for more information). The lovely strand fronting **Sandy Lane** offers excellent swimming conditions.

On this coast, you may encounter what looks like an apple tree with little green apples. Several such trees are on Almond Beach Village's beach. Watch out and warn your children, too, because the fruit of this manchineel tree is not only poisonous to eat but also toxic to the touch. Even taking shelter under the tree when it rains can give you blisters. Most manchineels are identified with signs or with a red ring painted on the tree trunk.

East Coast

Although the West Coast of the island boasts white-sand beaches and calm, turquoise Caribbean water, you may want to head toward the crashing waves of the Atlantic pounding the East and craggy North Coasts. Your first stop: windswept **Bathsheba/Cattlewash,** where magnificent boulders frame crashing waves, to watch the sunrise.

Bajans ride the waves here almost daily. (Barbados is the location of the Independence Classic Surfing Championships, held each November.)

On the sleepy East Coast, you'll see miles of untouched beach along the island's wildest, hilliest, and most beautiful stretch. But swimming at Bathsheba or along the Atlantic Coast can be extremely dangerous, so you may want to stick to sightseeing in these areas and save your swimsuit for the South or West Coast beaches. If you like to stroll on the beach, the area north of Cattlewash is your best bet, and you can also find several idyllic spots — often deserted — for a picnic. You can get picnic fixings in Holetown, or stop by one of the local restaurants and ask for a boxed lunch.

If you're wading along the shore, watch out for sea urchins among the rocks. Locally called *cobblers,* these critters look like small dark porcupines underwater, about the size of a hockey puck. Wearing water shoes in the Caribbean is wise, but if you're barefoot and step on one, its needle-sharp spines feel like a giant splinter embedded in your foot. Apply vinegar immediately to neutralize the poison. The spines aren't life threatening, just painful.

South Coast

Known for small waves and strong trade winds, the area, with its wealth of nightclubs, pubs, and reasonably priced seaside beach bars, attracts a young crowd looking for a good time. Windsurfers and body boarders head to this area, which is also good for swimming. Windsurfers are especially fond of wide, windswept **Casuarina Beach,** which you access from Maxwell Coast Road, going across the property of the **Casuarina Beach Hotel.** You can order food and drinks at the hotel.

Silver Sands Beach, to the east of Oistins, is near the southernmost point of Barbados, directly east of South Point Lighthouse and near the Silver Rock Hotel. This white-sand beach is a favorite with many Bajans (who probably want to keep it a secret from as many visitors as possible). Drinks are available at the Silver Rock Bar. **Silver Rock Beach** is where the more-expert windsurfers go, primarily between November and June. **Maxwell Beach** (in front of the Windsurf Beach Hotel) is best for flat-water windsurfing.

Sandy Beach, reached from the parking lot on the main road in Worthing, has tranquil waters opening onto a lagoon, the epitome of Caribbean charm. A favorite of families, this beach is especially boisterous on weekends.

Carlisle Bay, which also has a new marine reserve and exceptionally calm waters for swimming, as well as changing facilities with restrooms, is popular with day-tripping cruise-ship passengers.

Ultrapopular **Accra Beach** in Rockley is a hot spot with body boarders, and you can rent boards and snorkeling gear, as well as gear for other water play. A wide interlocking brick promenade, several additional palms, and better parking facilities have made this area even prettier.

Southeast Coast

The Southeast Coast is the site of the big waves, especially at **Crane Beach,** the white-sand strip set against a backdrop of palms that you see in all the travel magazines. It offers excellent bodysurfing, and you can rent a board on the beach — but at times the waters may be too rough for all but the strongest swimmers. The beach is set against cliffs, with the **Crane Beach Hotel,** which has undergone complete renovation, towering above it.

We suggest booking lunch at **Crane Beach Hotel Restaurant** (☎ 246-423-6220) overlooking the beach. On Sundays from 10 to 11 a.m., it sponsors a gospel brunch. Later that afternoon, it has a traditional Bajan spread with a steel pan (drum) band playing. The prices are reasonable, the food is good, and the view is panoramic.

 Bottom Bay, north of Sam Lord's Castle Resort, is one of our all-time Bajan favorites. Park on the top of a cliff, and then walk down the steps to this much-photographed tropical beach with its grove of coconut palms; it even has a cave. The sand is brilliantly white against the aquamarine sea, a picture-postcard perfect beach paradise.

Foul Bay is the longest beach on this coast, with dramatic cliffs framing either end of the white sandy beach. In the first half of the year, you'll often see sea turtles coming up for air just beyond the waves.

Playing in the surf

Though it's a coral island surrounded by fringing and banking reefs, Barbados hasn't become known among divers for good reason. First of all, fishing is still big business around this island, and you rarely see any large fish on its reefs. But if you're a beginning diver who wants to get in a few dives between rounds of golf, or you're into wreck diving, you'll likely enjoy the experience. Snorkelers will find plenty to make renting the gear worth it. Visibility is generally around 24 to 27m (80–90 ft.), but during the rainy season (June–Jan), it may be greatly diminished.

Locating dive and snorkeling sites

Many wrecks are submerged in the shallow waters off the South and West Coasts. The most popular wreck to explore is the south's *Berwyn* — a coral-encrusted French tugboat that sank in Carlisle Bay in 1916 — which attracts photographers for its variety of reef fish, shallow depth, good light, and visibility. The **Carlisle Bay Marine Reserve** has eight wrecks — three shallow enough for snorkeling — in a concentrated area for divers to explore. The bay is noted as a place to see hawksbill turtles, elusive sea horses, and rare frogfish.

The most beautiful site on the West Coast is **Dottin's Reef,** which stretches 8km (5 miles) from Bridgetown to Holetown. It's accessible at 12m (40 ft.) and is festooned with sea fans, gorgonians, and brain coral. You'll see parrotfish, barracuda, snappers, and maybe a sea turtle or two.

Also on the West Coast is the *Stavronikita,* a 108m (356-ft.) Greek freighter whose hull rests 40m (130 ft.) underwater with one mast just 6m (20 ft.) beneath the surface. The freighter is often crowded with tourist divers, but it's a good wreck to explore. In 1978, the ship was intentionally scuttled 0.4km (a quarter-mile) off the West Coast to become an artificial reef in **Folkestone Marine Park,** north of Holetown.

The **Folkestone Marine Park,** located at Church Point, Holetown, St. James (☎ 246-422-2314; free admission), has a Marine Museum with a large minireef, saltwater aquarium, and marine artifacts and specimens. The park also has an underwater snorkeling trail around Dottin's Reef, and you can rent snorkeling gear and lockers for the day. A glass-bottom boat ride allows youngsters and nonswimmers to get a good look, too, at the *Stavronikita* freighter. The facilities are open daily from 9 a.m. to 5 p.m.

Atlantis Submarines, Shallow Draught, Bridgetown, St. Michael (☎ 246-436-8929; www.atlantisadventures.com), offers the ***Rhino Rider Water Safari,*** a two-person boat that's equipped with snorkel gear. The guided jaunt from a white-sand beach up the West Coast for snorkeling costs $58 for adults and $40 for children. Trip time is two hours.

Renting underwater gear

The good news for divers is that, because diving isn't as popular on this island, the dive-shop operators are eager to please. If they sense that you're interested in a unique experience, dive masters will go out of their way to take you to interesting sites and point out the small marine life that you may otherwise overlook. The boats aren't overcrowded, so you can get more-personalized attention.

A one-tank dive in Barbados runs about $55, a two-tank dive about $80. All gear is supplied, and you can purchase multidive packages. You can rent snorkeling gear for a small charge from most hotels. Snorkelers can usually accompany dive trips for $20 to $25 for a one- or two-hour trip.

Both **Dive Boat Safari,** located at the Grand Barbados Beach Resort, Aquatic Gap, St. Michael (☎ 246-427-4350), and **The Dive Shop, Ltd.,** located at the Aquatic Gap near Bay Street, St. Michael (☎ 246-426-9947; www.divebds.com), are in the Carlisle Bay area, with five wrecks and 15 reef sites nearby. The latter is the oldest dive shop in Barbados and teaches all levels of certification.

Dive Blue Reef Barbados, next to The Lone Star, St. James (☎ 246-422-3133; www.divebluereef.com), and **Hightide Watersports,** Coral Reef Club, St. James (☎ 800-970-0016; Fax 246-432-6628; www.divehigh tide.com), are both known for highly personalized dives catering to small groups. Hightide offers one- and two-tank dives, night reef/wreck/drift dives, the full range of PADI instruction, specialties including underwater photography, and free transportation. It also has a new custom-built, high-speed, 9m (30-ft.) dive boat with dry storage and a camera table.

Taking a ride under the sea

Atlantis Submarines, Shallow Draught, Bridgetown, St. Michael (☎ 246-436-8929; www.atlantisadventures.com), offers minisubmarine voyages good for families with youngsters and those who are curious about what's under the sea but don't want to dive or snorkel. The 48-passenger, 19m (65-ft.) *Atlantis III* gives you a 45-minute tour of wrecks and reefs as deep as 46m (150 ft.). Special nighttime dives, which use high-power searchlights, are spectacular. The cost for adults is $89; $57 for teens, $45 for children. Be sure to make a reservation in advance, as this dive books up quickly.

Water-skiing around Barbados

We recommend water-skiing early in the day, because the waters can get a little rough in the afternoons. Many hotels on the West and South Coasts of the island offer water-skiing, sometimes at no additional cost. If your hotel doesn't provide this service and you're staying on the West Coast, book with **Hightide Watersports,** Coral Reef Club, St. James (☎ **800-970-0016;** Fax 246-432-6628; www.divehightide.com). Its Moomba World-Class 300-horsepower mid-drive inboard tournament ski boat — the only one in Barbados — gives a powerful pull. The instructors offer lessons and work with kids, too. This outfit also rents gear for windsurfing, banana and biscuit rides, sea kayaks, Hobie Cats, Sunfish, and water bikes.

Private speedboat owners troll for business along the St. James and Christ Church waterfront, but you water-ski at your own risk with these operators.

Riding the wind

Experts say that the windsurfing off Barbados is as good as any this side of Hawaii. Judging from the crowds that flock here, they're right. Windsurfing in Barbados has turned into big business between November and April, attracting windsurfers from as far away as Australia, Argentina, and Japan. The shifting of the trade winds between November and June and the shallow offshore reef of **Silver Sands Beach** create unique conditions of wind and wave swells, which allow windsurfers to reach speeds of up to 50 knots and do complete loops off the waves. Silver Sands is rated the best spot in the Caribbean for advanced windsurfing. Barbados Windsurfing Championships are held in mid-January. Here's where to rent gear ($55–$65 a day) or get instruction ($65 for an hour):

 ✔ **Beginners or less experienced windsurfers: Club Mistral Windsurfing School,** now in two locations — Club Mistral Oistins and Club Mistral Silver Sands (☎ **246-428-7277;** www.clubmistral barbados.com)

 ✔ **Advanced windsurfers: Silver Rock Windsurfing Club,** in the Irieman Action Shop, Silver Rock Hotel on Silver Sands Beach, Christ Church (☎ **246-428-2866**)

Boards and equipment are often free for guests at the larger hotels, and you may even get lessons as part of your package. Several smaller hotels specialize in windsurfing packages.

Reeling in the big one

Barbados is deep-sea-fishing paradise. If you dream of hooking that big one, this island is a good place to book a full charter in your hunt for blue and white marlin, billfish, and sailfish — or a half-day if you're satisfied with sticking closer to shore for dorado, tuna, wahoo, and barracuda. Charter fishing trips depart from the Careenage in Bridgetown.

You're in good hands with captain and owner Winston "The Colonel" White, who's been plying the waters around Barbados for more than a quarter of a century. His **Billfisher II,** Bridge House, Cavans Lane, the Careenage, Bridgetown (☎ 246-431-0741) is a 12m (40-ft.) Pacemaker — with five rods and three chairs — that accommodates up to six people. Half-day charters get you drinks (rum, beer, and soft drinks) and sandwiches. Full-day charters include a full lunch with drinks, and the confident captain even guarantees fish. You can keep everything you catch, and the crew will clean and cook your catch for you at day's end. The affable captain will even match you with other people who want to share the cost of the charter.

The Blue Jay, St. James (☎ 246-429-2326), is a 14m (45-ft.) fully equipped Sports-Fisherman with a huge cockpit and four fishing chairs. The fishing party is limited to four, guaranteeing that everyone gets to cast a line. Captain "Callie" Elton's crew knows the waters where the bigger game fish frolic. You may hook into such game fish as blue marlin, sailfish, barracuda, and kingfish. Each person fishing can invite a guest free. Drinks and snacks are provided.

Climbing aboard

Most popular and fun are the **Jolly Roger "Pirate" Cruises** (☎ 246-430-0900), operating out of Bridgetown Harbour. Passengers can rope-swing, swim, snorkel, and suntan on the top deck. Even mock weddings are staged. A buffet lunch with rum punch is available Thursday and Saturday from 11 a.m. to 3 p.m. Lunch cruises cost $53 per person.

You can also sail on a catamaran lunch cruise, a four-hour cruise offered daily from 10 a.m. to 3:30 p.m. (cruises depart every 45 minutes), costing $70 per person. Children 12 and under sail for half price. Catamaran cruises are available on **Tiami** (☎ 246-430-0900), which is part cruise ship, part nightclub, and on the **M/V Harbour Master** (☎ 246-430-0900), which is a 31m (100-ft.), four-story vessel with theme decks, a modern gallery, and three bars. It boasts a dance floor and a sit-down restaurant and also offers formal buffets on its Calypso Deck. On the Harbour Master Deck, sports buffs can enjoy watching a bank of TVs. The showpiece of the vessel is an onboard semisubmersible, which is lowered hydraulically to 1.8m (6 ft.) beneath the ship. This is, in effect, a 30-seat boat within a boat. Lunch and dinner cruises cost $65 per person on Wednesday; on Thursday, the dinner cruise is $70. The semisubmersible experience goes for another $10.

Exploring on Dry Land

If your sea legs need a break from all that fun in and on the water, check out some of the options you'll find on dry land.

Touring historic sites

History-rich Barbados has much to offer to those interested in the past. To encourage you to tour the island's many historic sites, the Barbados National Trust has designed the **Heritage Passport,** a free pass that gives you discounts to some of Barbados's most popular attractions and historic sites. Full Passports, which cost $35, provide 50 percent discounts to 15 different sites. The Full Passport also gives you invitations to the open-house program (a look into the island's most historic and beautiful private homes) in the winter months. The Mini Passport ($18) provides 50 percent discounts to five historic sites. Contact the **Barbados National Trust,** Wildey House, Wildey, St. Michael (☎ **246-426-2421**), for more information.

Thanks to the British influence, Barbados also boasts some of the Caribbean's finest gardens. Here are our favorite picks to get a flavor for both the historical and natural aspects of Barbados:

- ✔ **Andromeda Botanic Gardens,** Bathsheba, St. Joseph (☎ **246-433-9384**): You can spend an entire afternoon here, admiring the fascinating collection of unusual and beautiful plant specimens from around the world assembled by the late Iris Bannochie and willed to the Barbados National Trust. Limestone boulders make for a natural 3.2-hectare (8-acre) rock-garden setting for this impressive 2.4-hectare (6-acre) garden, nestled among streams, ponds, and rocky outcroppings overlooking the sea above the Bathsheba coastline. Thousands of orchids, hundreds of hibiscus and heliconia, and many varieties of ferns, begonias, palms, and other species grow here in splendid profusion. You'll occasionally see frogs, herons, lizards, hummingbirds, and sometimes a mongoose or a monkey. You may want to eat a picnic lunch from the Hibiscus Café. The well-stocked gift shop on-site also offers some of the island's best prices. Admission is $7.50 for adults, $3.50 for children. The gardens are open daily from 10 a.m. to 3:30 p.m.

- ✔ **Barbados Wildlife Reserve,** Farley Hill, St. Peter (☎ **246-422-8826**): Across the road from Farley Hill National Park, in northern St. Peter parish, the reserve is set in a mahogany forest maintained by the Barbados Primate Research Center. Visitors can stroll through what is primarily a monkey sanctuary and an arboretum. Aside from the uncaged monkeys — watch your sunglasses, because these little thieves love to swipe them — you'll see wild hares, deer, otters, and wallabies (which were imported into Barbados). The best time to see the monkeys is in the afternoons after 3 p.m. The admission allows you to visit Grenade Hall Forest, too. Walk through a rain forest with displays that explain why rain forests are important and what Barbados looked like before its land was so heavily cultivated. The Grenade Hall Forest has a good snack bar with shady tables for lunch. Admission is $12 for adults and $6 for children age 12 and under. The reserve is open daily from 10 a.m. to 5 p.m. (last entrance is at 4:45 p.m.).

✔ **Farley Hill National Park,** Farley Hill, St. Peter (no phone): This park surrounds what used to be one of the greatest houses of Barbados — Farley Hill, a mansion in ruins with a view of Barbados's Scotland District. The park lies in the north of the St. Peter parish, directly across the road leading into the Barbados Wildlife Reserve. You can bring in a picnic and wander in the park, overlooking the turbulent waters of the Atlantic. You can enter the park for free if you're walking, but it costs $3.50 to bring a car in. The park is open daily from 8:30 a.m. to 6 p.m.

✔ **Harrison's Cave,** Welchman Hall, St. Thomas (☎ **246-438-6640**): You view the underground world here, the number-one tourist attraction of Barbados, from aboard an electric tram and trailer. On the tour, you see bubbling streams, tumbling cascades, and subtly lit deep pools, while all around stalactites hang overhead like icicles, and stalagmites rise from the floor. Visitors may disembark and get a closer look at this natural phenomenon at the Rotunda Room and the Cascade Pool. Although it's interesting, it may not impress Americans who've been to the far more spectacular Carlsbad Caverns. Tour reservations are recommended. Admission is $16 for adults and $7 for children. The cave is open daily from 9 a.m. to 4 p.m. and is closed Good Friday, Easter Sunday, and Christmas Day.

Keeping active

In Barbados, you can pursue many of the outdoor pursuits that you may not have time for at home. Golf, hiking, horseback riding, tennis, squash — it's all here.

Hitting the links

Open to all is the Tom Fazio 18-hole championship golf course of the **Sandy Lane Hotel,** St. James (☎ **246-444-2000**), on the West Coast. Greens fees for 18 holes are $220 for nonguests and $185 for guests in winter, and $175 for nonguests and $140 for guests in summer. Or you can play its famed "Old Nine" holes, which wind through the estate grounds — the year-round cost is $90 for nonguests and $80 for guests. Carts and caddies are available. In 2004, its new Green Monkey championship course, carved from a former quarry, was slated to open.

The **Royal Westmoreland Golf and Country Club,** located in Westmoreland, St. James (☎ **246-422-4653**), has become the island's premier golf course. Designed by Robert Trent Jones, Jr., this $30-million,

18-hole course is spread across 200 hectares (500 acres) overlooking the Gold Coast. It is part of a private residential community, and only guests of the Royal Pavilion, Glitter Bay, Colony Club, **Tamarind Cove, Coral Reef,** Crystal Cove, **Cobblers Cove, The Sandpiper,** and **Sandy Lane** can play it. The course costs $200 for 18 holes in winter, including a cart. Fees in off season are $125.

Barbados Golf Club, located in Durants, Christ Church (☎ **246-428-8463;** Fax: 256-420-8205; www.barbadosgolfclub.com), on the South Coast, opened as Barbados's first public championship golf course in 2000. The 6,313m (6,905-yard), par-72 course, designed by Ron Kirby, hosted the PGA Seniors Tournament in 2002. Greens fees for 18 holes are $125 in the high season and $85 in the low season, plus $16 for cart rental and $25 for Cobra club rentals. A three-day unlimited golf pass during high season is $300, $203 in low season.

Taking a hike

The **Barbados National Trust** (☎ **246-426-2421**) offers Sunday morning hikes throughout the year, often attracting more than 300 participants. Led by young Bajans and members of the National Trust, the hikes cover a different area of the island each week, giving you an opportunity to discover the natural beauty of Barbados. The guides give brief talks on subjects such as geography, history, geology, and agriculture. The hikes, free and open to participants of all ages, are divided into fast, medium, and slow categories, with groups of no more than ten. All hikes leave promptly at 6 a.m. and take about three hours to complete. You can also take hikes at 3:30 and 5:30 p.m., the latter conducted only on moonlit nights. For the more fit, the Trust sponsors a three-hour trek through the Arbib Nature and Heritage Trail.

The **Arbib Nature and Heritage Trail,** which won *Islands* magazine's 1999 Ecotourism Award, takes you through Speightstown, once a major sugar port and even today a fishing town with old houses and a bustling waterfront; the mysterious gully known as "the Whim"; and the surrounding districts. The first marked trail is a 7.6km (4.7-mile) trek that begins outside St. Peter's Church in Speightstown, traverses the Whim, crosses one of the last working plantations in Barbados (Warleight), and leads to the historic 18th-century Dover Fort, following along white-sand beaches at Heywoods before ending up back in town. You must book a spot for the three-hour guided walk by 3 p.m. through the Barbados National Trust the day before you want to go. Hikes take place on Wednesday, Thursday, and Saturday starting at 9 a.m. and 2:30 p.m. The fee is $8 for adults, $3.70 for children.

Riding horses

Caribbean International Riding Centre, St. Andrew, Sarely Hill (☎ **246-422-7433**), offers a different view of Barbados. With nearly 40 horses, Mrs. Roachford and her daughters offer a variety of trail rides for all levels of experience, ranging from a 1½-hour jaunt for $60 to a 2½-hour trek for $90. You'll ride through some of the most panoramic parts of Barbados, including the hilly terrain of the Scotland district. Along the way, you can see wild ducks and water lilies, with the rhythm of the Atlantic as background music.

Playing tennis and squash

Most of the larger hotels have tennis courts that you can reserve even if you're not a guest. In Barbados, most tennis players still wear traditional whites. The public tennis court at **Folkestone Park,** Holetown (☎ 246-422-2314), is available for free on a first-come, first-served basis. The **National Tennis Centre,** Sir Garfield Sobers Sports Complex, Wildey Street, St. Michael (☎ 246-437-6010), charges $15 per hour; you must reserve in advance. You can also reserve courts at the **Barbados Squash Club,** Marine House, Christ Church (☎ 246-427-7913), for $18 for 45 minutes.

Watching from the sidelines

Barbados's spectator sports include several thoroughly British options. **Cricket,** Barbados' national sport, is played from May to late December. For information, call the **Barbados Cricket Association** (☎ 246-436-1397). **Horse racing** takes place year-round (except during Apr) every other Saturday at the **Garrison Savannah** (☎ 246-426-3980; www.barbadosturfclub.com) in Christ Church. The track opens at 1:30 p.m. on race days, and admission is $5. **Polo** matches in Barbados are much more casual than at other places, so spectators are more than welcome — for a $2.50 fee. Matches take place at the **Barbados Polo Club** in Holders Hill, St. James (☎ 246-432-1802), on Wednesday and Saturday from October to April.

Taking a guided tour

For those who are adventurous or for families, our pick is **Island Safari,** Bush Hall, St. Michael (☎ 246-429-5337; Fax: 246-429-8147), which offers a daylong land/sea tour for $112 per person, $55 for children 12 and under. You start out tooling around the Bajan countryside in a Land Rover and spend the afternoon on a catamaran doing a sail/snorkel.

Bajan Tours, Shak-Shak Complex, #4 Frere Pilgrim, Christ Church (☎ 246-228-6000), is a locally owned and operated company. The best bet for the first-timer is the Exclusive Island Tour, departing Monday to Friday between 8 and 8:30 a.m. and returning between 2:30 and 3 p.m. It covers all the island's highlights, including the Barbados Wildlife Reserve, the Chalky Mount Potteries, and the rugged East Coast. All tours cost $63 per person and include a full buffet lunch. **Boyce's Tours,** Gazette Court, St. Michael (☎ 246-425-1103; Fax: 246-424-1455; www.boycestours.com), offers a craft tour ($35 per person) that takes visitors to some of our favorite artisans, a history and high-tea tour ($45 per person), and a photographer's dream tour ($40 per person) of Barbados's most dramatic vistas.

Shopping the Local Stores

Bridgetown's Broad Street, in St. Michael, is the capital's primary shopping area, littered with signs advertising duty-free goods. The upscale offerings here may remind you of Bermuda.

To get duty-free prices, you need to show your passport and airline ticket, so bring them with you on any shopping adventure.

Our idea of a fun shopping excursion is sampling Barbados's famed liquid gold — rum — after a fun tour of the **Mount Gay Rum Factory** (☎ 246-425-8757). The factory is a quick drive outside of Bridgetown, and you can pick up a smattering of the island's history there. Island music blares over the loudspeaker while a gleeful bartender enjoys pouring samples from Barbados's oldest distillery.

The quintessential Barbados handicrafts are black-coral jewelry and clay pottery. The latter originates at **Highland Pottery, Inc.** (☎ 246-422-9818), which is worth a visit. Potters turn out different products, some based on designs that are centuries old. The potteries (which are signposted) are on the East Coast, in St. Joseph Parish near Barclay's Park. In shops across the island, you'll also find a selection of locally made vases, pots, pottery mugs, glazed plates, and ornaments.

Island craftspeople weave wall hangings from local grasses and dried flowers and also turn out straw mats, baskets, and bags with raffia embroidery. You can also find leatherwork, particularly handbags, belts, and sandals, in Barbados.

Living It Up After Dark

Just a quarter of a century after Barbados was settled in 1627, Bridgetown already had more than 100 bars. That tradition continues today. You'll never find a Caribbean island with so many watering holes — Barbados averages 12 per square mile. The nightclubs open around 9:30 p.m., but the action doesn't really heat up until at least 11 p.m. and may go on until 3 a.m. For most nightlife venues, women wear dresses or skirts, although nice pants are fine. Men often wear khaki pants, collared shirts, and dress shoes.

Always exercise caution, especially if you're out late after the wallop of a few Planter's Punches has settled in. Take a cab back to your resort if you've had much to drink — the roads on Barbados are narrow and dark.

St. Lawrence Gap, called simply The Gap and situated on the South Coast in the Worthing area, has long had a reputation as the place for late-night limin'. Its hip strip, which has been a construction zone of late, boasts a mind-boggling 40 bars, pubs, clubs, and restaurants. **Café Sol,**

St. Lawrence Gap, Christ Church (☎ 246-435-9531), has a wraparound terrace with a scenic view of the St. Lawrence Gap strip. One of the best-known nightspots is **The Ship Inn,** St. Lawrence Gap, Christ Church (☎ 246-435-6961), a friendly pub with live local bands every night for dancing.

On the South Coast, the hot spot is the **Boatyard,** located on Bay Street on Carlisle Bay, five minutes from Bridgetown (☎ 246-436-2622). It has a pub atmosphere with both a DJ and live band music. From happy hours (twice daily: 3–6:30 p.m. and 10–11 p.m.) until the wee hours, the Boatyard is packed with mingling locals and visitors.

On the West Coast, **Baku Beach,** Holetown, St. James (☎ 246-432-2258; cover charge $5 or $10, depending on the night), and its sibling night-club **The Casbah,** a Moroccan theme with Euro flair, are hot spots, though the action doesn't heat up until after 11 p.m. The trendy crowd at Baku, open nightly from 6:30 p.m. to 2 a.m., consists of locals and visitors alike. Some of the hottest bands on the island perform at its cocktail bar. The Casbah, open nightly from 10 p.m. to 3 a.m. (no cover), resembles a New York City lounge with a DJ spinning tunes all night. **Vintage Wine Bar,** also at the Baku complex, serves light tapas and a choice of champagnes, wines, and cigars.

Fast Facts: Barbados

Area Code

The area code for Barbados is **246.**

ATMs

About 50 ATMs are available 24 hours a day at bank branches, transportation centers, shopping centers, and other convenient spots throughout the island. ATMs dispense Barbados dollars, of course. The major banks of Barbados, all with ATMs, are located along Broad Street in Bridgetown.

Babysitters

You won't find a central babysitting service in Barbados, but check with your hotel to see if they offer the service.

Currency Exchange

The Barbados dollar (Bds$1) is tied to the U.S. dollar at the rate of Bds$1 to U.S. 50¢.

The currency exchange rate fluctuates daily and is posted at banks or online at www.xe.com/ucc. U.S. dollars are readily accepted all over the island. Be sure that you know which currency you're dealing in when making a purchase. Neither euros nor British pounds are accepted.

Doctors

Hotels have doctors on call.

Electricity

The electric current in Barbados is 115/230 volts 50Hz. Hotels generally have adapters/transformers available.

Embassies and Consulates

The Embassy of the United States is on Broad Street, Bridgetown, St. Michael (☎ 246-436-4950), and the Canadian High Commission is at Lower Bishop's Court,

Pine Road, Bridgetown, St. Michael
(☎ 246-429-3550). The British High
Commission is found at Lower Collymore
Rock, St. Michael (☎ 246-430-7880).

Emergencies

Call ☎ **211**. For an ambulance, dial ☎ **511**;
in case of fire, ☎ **311**.

Hospitals

Two modern facilities are on the island:
Bayview Hospital, St. Paul's Avenue,
Bayville, St. Michael (☎ 246-436-5446), and
Queen Elizabeth Hospital, Martindales
Road, St. Michael (☎ 246-436-6450).

Information

See the Appendix for helpful Web sites and
locations of U.S.-based and local tourist
offices.

Internet Access & Cybercafes

Go to the Global Business Centre, West
Coast Mall, Sunset Crest (☎ 246-432-6508).
Hours are Monday to Friday 9 a.m. to 5 p.m.
and Saturday 9 a.m. to 2 p.m. Prices are
U.S. 25¢ per minute. You can also make
international calls here at a substantial
discount.

Newspapers and Magazines

Island Newsstand, 1st floor, Dacostas Mall,
Bridgetown, St. Michael (☎ 246-431-0011),
and Pages, 1st floor, Cave Shepherd, Broad
Street, Bridgetown (☎ 246-431-2120), sell
local papers and magazines, plus the *New
York Times* and the *Miami Herald.*

Pharmacies

Collins Pharmacy, Broad Street, Bridgetown
(☎ 246-426-4515), is open Monday to
Saturday from 8 a.m. to 5 p.m.

Police

In an emergency, call ☎ **211**; otherwise,
call ☎ 246-430-7100.

Post Office

The main post office, in Cheapside,
Bridgetown, is open Monday to Friday
7:30 a.m. to 4:30 p.m.; branches in each
parish are open weekdays 8 a.m. to 3 p.m.
One branch is handily located at the airport.

Restrooms

Public toilets are located in both of
Bridgetown's bus terminals. They include
the Princess Alice Terminal (on the Route
Princess Alice) and the River Bus Terminal
(on Fairchild Street). Public toilets are also
available within a prominent and centrally
located Bridgetown department store, Cave
Shepherd, at the corner of Broad Street and
Swan Street, immediately across from the
statue of Lord Nelson. Most of the major
public beaches maintain cinder-block
dressing rooms with toilets, including Accra
Beach, St. Lawrence Gap, Miami Beach,
and many more. In addition, hotels, casinos,
bars, and restaurants in Barbados long ago
grew used to the constant flow of visitors
using their toilets, and no one is likely to
stop you if you try.

Safety

Although Barbados is generally prosperous,
poverty does exist here. Visitors have
reported purse snatching, pickpocketing,
armed robbery, and sexual assault on
women. Most of the incidents have been
around Bridgetown and St. Lawrence Gap.
Take normal precautions: Don't leave cash
or valuables in your hotel room, beware of
purse snatchers when walking, exercise
caution when walking on the beach (we
avoid it at night altogether) or visiting
tourist attractions, and be wary of driving
in isolated areas.

Smoking

Smoking policies are left to the discretion
of the individual establishments, and most
restaurants have designated nonsmoking
sections within their restaurants and bars.

With so many open-air establishments, the natural ventilation of the trade winds helps resolve conflicts.

Taxes

A 7.5 percent government tax is added to all hotel bills. A 15 percent value-added tax (VAT) is imposed on restaurant meals, admissions to attractions, and merchandise sales (other than duty-free). Prices often include the tax, but if not, the VAT is added to your bill. A departure tax of U.S. $13 (Bds$26) is payable in either U.S. or Barbadian currency.

Taxis

To call a taxi, contact one of the following services: Paramount Taxi Service (☎ 246-429-3718), Royal Pavilion Taxi Service (☎ 246-422-1260), or Lyndhurst Taxi Service (☎ 246-436-2639).

Weather Updates

Call ☎ 246-976-2376 for current conditions.

Chapter 11

The British Virgin Islands

In This Chapter

▶ Knowing what to expect when you arrive
▶ Getting around the islands
▶ Deciding where you want to stay
▶ Sampling the local cuisine at the best restaurants
▶ Scoping out good beaches and diving into water sports
▶ Satisfying the landlubber: Shopping and nightlife

The British Virgin Islands (BVIs), still in peaceful slumber, are what the United States Virgin Islands (USVIs) were some three decades ago before overdevelopment. Only the Grenadines (owned by St. Vincent) are as favored by the yachting crowd. Sailing in the BVIs has been a tradition ever since the Arawak Indians first arrived back when Europe was getting through the Dark Ages.

You don't have to be a sailor, like former visitor Sir Francis Drake, to enjoy these idyllic islands. They seem to have been designed for R & R — perfect for those who plan only to go to the beach. In an overcrowded world, like the harbor at Charlotte Amalie on St. Thomas, the BVIs are sparsely populated. You may even have the beach all to yourself — especially if you find some hidden cove.

The BVIs comprise at least 40 islands (some people tally up a larger count, but they're including mere islets or rocks projecting up from the sea). Of these, no more than a dozen or so are inhabited. Some remain waiting for discovery. One, in particular, Norman Island, is so remote that it was said to have inspired Robert Louis Stevenson's novel *Treasure Island.* For megaresorts and round-the-clock entertainment, the USVIs should be your choice. But for the tranquil, laid-back lifestyle, make it the BVIs. It's estimated that nearly half of the so-called rooms occupied in these islands are actually found on boats lying peacefully at anchor at night.

Arriving at the Airport

If you were hoping to fly directly into Tortola (the capital of the BVIs) from the U.S., forget about it: No direct flights arrive there from the U.S. mainland. San Juan, Puerto Rico, which is a half-hour flight to Tortola, is the main gateway into the British Virgin Islands. More flights arrive in San Juan from the U.S. mainland than anywhere else in the Caribbean; New York and Miami have the most frequent flights. Another gateway is Charlotte Amalie, the capital of the U.S. Virgin Islands, on St. Thomas. You can fly to St. Thomas, and then make another connection into Tortola. To get to Virgin Gorda, you can take a direct flight from St. Thomas. If you don't make that connection, you can land on Tortola and take a shuttle flight over to Virgin Gorda.

Getting oriented at the airport

Although recently expanded, **Beef Island Airport** (☎ 284-494-3701) on Tortola is relatively modest. Congestion often occurs when several flights are scheduled to take off within 20 to 30 minutes of each other. If you've checked into a major hotel, you'll often find a welcome desk right at the airport to make your transition easy. If you've booked more modest digs, you'll see a fleet of taxis waiting to take you either to your hotel on Tortola or to one of the ferry departure points if you're going on to another island such as Virgin Gorda. The little Queen Elizabeth Bridge connects Beef Island with "mainland" Tortola. You can find ATMs in Road Town, the capital of Tortola.

With a quick phone call, e-mail, or fax, you can alert your hotel of your arrival time. All reception desks know the easiest transportation link, which is especially important if you're staying on one of the islands other than Tortola. Transfer costs, most often by ferry service, may be included in your hotel bill, with you signing a voucher or two en route to your final destination.

Navigating your way through passport control and Customs

To enter Tortola, you must pass through Customs and passport control (☎ 284-495-2235). No large jets land here, but the line at Customs can take a long time because officials are thorough, often insisting that arriving passengers open up all their luggage for a detailed search. For more on going through Customs, see Chapter 8.

Getting from the airport to your hotel

The taxi lobby is powerful enough on Tortola to have pickup of rental cars banned at the Beef Island Airport. After you clear Customs, a fleet of taxis or open-air shuttles awaits you to take you anywhere on the island. Taxis are often shared, the cabbie crowding in as many passengers and as much luggage as he can. After you're at your hotel, you can make arrangements for picking up a rental car if you want one.

Taxis from the Beef Island Airport travel to Tortola's capital, Road Town, in about 20 minutes. Rental of the entire taxi costs $18, and, as mentioned, is often shared, which cuts down the tariff per person. The taxi driver will often make you wait until he corrals more customers to share the ride.

Arriving by Ferry

Even though a plane is quicker and more efficient, many passengers prefer the sea route from St. Thomas or St. John in the USVIs. A sail from island to island becomes part of the Caribbean experience. From Charlotte Amalie (on St. Thomas) or Cruz Bay (on St. John), public ferries ply these sometimes-choppy waters to Road Town (about an hour) and the West End (about a 45-minute ride) on Tortola.

Unless sailing conditions are bad, ferries depart daily at 6:15 a.m. Depending on the season, departures are scattered throughout the day until the last ferries leave at 5:30 p.m. A one-way fare is $21 to $23 per person or $35 to $40 round-trip. Everything depends on the weather, so schedules are subject to change. You often have to check boat departures upon your arrival on St. Thomas.

Here are the major ferry operators in the BVIs:

- ✔ **Native Son, Inc.** (☎ 284-495-4617) connects St. Thomas and St. John (pickups in Charlotte Amalie and Red Hook, respectively) to Road Town and West End, Tortola, daily.

- ✔ **Smith's Ferry Services** (☎ 284-494-4495) operates daily to connect St. Thomas (pickups in Red Hook and Charlotte Amalie) and St. John to Road Town and West End, Tortola. It also connects Tortola to Virgin Gorda.

- ✔ **Inter-Island Boat Services** (☎ 284-495-4166) connects St. John (Cruz Bay) and West End, Tortola, daily.

From either St. Thomas or St. John, ferries traverse the Sir Francis Drake Channel, named after the English seafarer whom the Spanish still call a "pirate." Waters can be choppy or downright rough, especially in winter, and the ferries are relatively stable. Even so, seasickness is commonplace, and many prudent passengers take Dramamine to ward off this malady.

While based in the BVIs, many visitors become day-trippers to the USVIs. Don't go just in your bikini; take a photo ID. You are, in effect, crossing through international waters. If you've left your identification in your hotel room in the BVIs, you may not be able to get back into the country.

BVI patrol boats from the Port Authority monitor local waters and may demand to see your passport when traveling between the two sets of Virgins. The three main entry ports into the BVIs where Customs and immigration booths are set up are at the ferry docks on Tortola, Virgin Gorda, and Jost Van Dyke.

Choosing Your Location

Except for some scattered accommodations on the remote islands such as **Anegada,** the choice narrows between **Tortola,** the islands' capital, and **Virgin Gorda.** We tilt toward Virgin Gorda because it's even slower paced than Tortola, and it's also more beautiful. We're also drawn to Virgin Gorda's more-secluded beaches — almost two dozen in all — and we like hiking its mountain peak. Don't write off Tortola, though. It has more activities than Virgin Gorda and some equally good inns and powdery beaches.

Many of the finest places to stay on either Tortola or Virgin Gorda aren't on the beach. If staking your post on a beach is a requirement of your vacation, you'll find great properties in the USVIs and most definitely on Aruba and Puerto Rico.

Instead of a beach location, you often get a panoramic view. The BVIs are mountainous islands, having been the tops of volcanoes in unrecorded times. From nearly every island inn or hotel, you can be on a good, white-sand beach within a ten-minute commute.

The greatest number of hotels, from bare-bones to first class, are located on Tortola. If you're shopping for villas to rent or seeking the lowest priced rooms available, you'll also do better on Tortola. Virgin Gorda is more exclusive, which translates into higher rates, of course.

Housing two to ten guests, private villas are available for rent through **Virgin Gorda Villa Rentals Ltd.,** P.O. Box 63, The Valley, Virgin Gorda (☎ **800-848-7081,** 284-495-7421; Fax: 284-495-7367; www.virgingorda bvi.com). Maid service, cooks, and staff are arranged.

For that ultimate escape evocative of *Gilligan's Island,* we nominate **Jost Van Dyke.** This rugged 10-sq.-km (4-sq.-mile) island is the West Indies as it used to be.

Because most inns are small, as are most island hotels, they fill up fast during the winter months, beginning around Christmas and lasting until mid-April. The Christmas holidays and February are the hardest times to get reservations.

From mid-April through mid-December, plenty of rooms are available, and prices are slashed on all the islands, usually around 20 percent but at some properties as much as 60 percent.

Getting Around the BVIs

You'll quickly get the hang of island hopping in the BVIs. It's a way of life for the locals, many of whom work on one island but commute by ferryboat to their home on another island in the late afternoon.

Getting around the BVI archipelago is part of the fun of making a trip here. Many visitors, for example, often like to go to a different island every day during their stay to sample the beaches on a neighboring island — for example, sailing from Tortola to Jost Van Dyke in the morning with a return in the late afternoon.

By taxi

The local government dictates taxi rates, so you don't have to negotiate them as on most Caribbean islands. The good news is that the cabbies in the BVIs are the most honest we've encountered in the islands. Taxis meet incoming planes at the Beef Island Airport and at all the ferry docks at Road Town and West End. They also operate like tour guides and can take you to all the major beauty spots on Tortola in about three hours for $50. Your hotel will book you a taxi, which will pick you up at your front door, or you can call the **B.V.I. Taxi Association** directly (☎ **284-494-1982,** 284-494-0550).

Don't let the name of the company scare you away. **Deadman's Taxi Service** (☎ **284-495-2780,** 284-495-2041) is one of the most reliable companies. You not only get where you want to go, but you also discover a lot about the legend and lore of Tortola from the drivers. Your hotel desk can also call a taxi for you.

 Cheaper than a taxi are the so-called open-air safari buses, which are ideal for a group of people sharing a ride. These buses are the least expensive way to get around Tortola or Virgin Gorda for a look at either island. For details, call the B.V.I. Taxi Association.

When you're on Virgin Gorda, **Mahogany Taxi Service** (☎ 284-495-5469) or **Potter's Taxi** (☎ **284-495-5329,** 284-495-5960) will meet you at the airport for the ten-minute, $24 roller-coaster ride to the North Sound, where your hotel's launch will pick you up and ferry you across a small bay.

By ferry

The former pirates' haven of the BVIs is not only the Caribbean's favored sailing grounds for yachties, but also the most practical means of getting around. Because public ferries are the main transportation link for the islanders themselves, they're the cheapest and easiest way to get from island to island or even to St. Thomas or St. John. See the section "Arriving by Ferry" earlier in this chapter for a few recommendations if you plan to island hop.

Arrive at the ferry dock at least 15 minutes before departure time to get the best seat. Unless the weather is bad, ferries leave on time. Some of the larger resorts, such as **Little Dix Bay** on Virgin Gorda, have their own ferryboats; ask if this is the case when you're making arrangements with your hotel for your arrival.

If you miss the boat and another one isn't sailing for a long time, or even until the next day, you still can get to where you're going by renting a private water taxi at a fare that you can negotiate. You can be certain that it'll be at least ten times the rate of the public ferry, which is about $12 to $15 one-way.

Many arriving passengers at the Beef Island Airport are actually going to a hotel on neighboring Virgin Gorda. Open-air shuttle buses await incoming flights and will transport you over to the **North Sound Express Ferry** (☎ 284-495-2138; Fax: 284-495-1639). You could walk this route if you didn't have luggage. A small, high-speed ferry will drop you either at Bitter End or Biras Creek's dock. Along the way, you get a panoramic look at some of the islands. You'll see why Virgin Gorda is often compared to a large pregnant woman lying prone on her back.

You need a reservation to take the North Sound Express Ferry, which departs daily at 6:15 a.m., 10:30 a.m., 3:30 p.m., 5:30 p.m., and 7:15 p.m.; it costs $22 each way and takes about 45 minutes. If you arrive after 7:15 p.m., you can still get to Virgin Gorda, but you have to arrange in advance and fork over a $30 surcharge per person.

If you're going to Virgin Gorda's Spanish Town or a resort nearby, take a taxi to Road Town's ferry dock and board **Smith's Ferry Services** (☎ 284-495-4495) or **Speedy's** (☎ 284-495-5240) for the half-hour ride, which costs $15 to $23 each way.

By plane

If you're going to one of the remote islands, such as Jost Van Dyke or Anegada, you can board a small puddle-jumper (seaplane) for a quick flight. Be sure to make your hotel arrangements before you arrive on either of these islands.

If you don't mind a small aircraft and want to skip the ferryboat, you can arrange a booking on either **Clair Aero Services** (☎ 284-495-2271; www. clairaero.com), which offers scheduled flights from Tortola to Anegada on Monday, Wednesday, and Friday or **Air Sunshine** (☎ 800-327-8900, 284-495-8900; www.airsunshine.com), which takes you from Tortola to the minuscule Virgin Gorda Airport, which closes at dusk. (The trip is so brief it's virtually a takeoff-and-land flight.)

On foot

Until the muggers learn about the BVIs, the islands are still one of the safest places to walk either day or night in the Caribbean.

Hiking is a rather tame undertaking here — nothing like Jamaica's Blue Mountains — except for the national parks such as the **Sage Mountain National Park** on Tortola or **Gorda Peak National Park** on Virgin Gorda.

By car

The roads — that is, when you can find roads — are a disaster; driving is on the left as in the U.K., and steering wheels are commonly on the left as well, as in the U.S. Maneuvering a vehicle here can be disconcerting unless you're used to it. You also don't have much to see on an actual driving tour. Usually, you can get by on a visit by using taxis when needed. Those who plan to spend part of their vacation hopping from island to island don't have much need for an auto, anyway. You'll probably be on the beach most of the time or else out on the waters in a boat. Our advice is to save your money on a car rental during your BVI trip.

If you feel you must always have wheels wherever you go, and you rent a car, you'll rarely encounter a traffic jam except in Road Town when people are going to or getting off from work, or when cruise-ship arrivals generate more traffic two or three times a week. If you're staying in a remote villa or hotel on Tortola, you may feel that a car is best. Check first with your hotel to see if they'll include a rental car in a package deal. If the hotel doesn't offer a specific package, ask if they can arrange a car for you after you arrive.

You need your own driver's license from back home, and you also have to pay $10 for a temporary BVI permit (the rental company will arrange this for you). Most car rentals cost around $55 per day. Make reservations before arriving on the island, especially if you'll be visiting from Christmas through February, when rental cars are in short supply. Sticking with international firms is safer than dealing with some under-financed and often unreliable local companies. On Tortola, you have three choices: **Avis** (☎ **800-331-1212**, 284-494-3322), **Hertz** (☎ **800-654-3131**, 284-495-6228), and **Itgo** (☎ **284-494-5150**).

By motorcycle or bicycle

Tortola's terrain is mountainous or at least hilly — no problem if you're an Olympic athlete, but a bit difficult for most folks. Mountain bikes and helmets are available for $20 a day at **Boardsailing B.V.I.** (☎ **284-495-2447**) at Nanny Cay and Trellis Bay on Tortola, and **Last Stop Sports** (☎ **284-494-1120**; www.laststopsports.com) in Road Town on Tortola (bike/helmet rental: $30). Last Stop also arranges bike/hike excursions.

The Top Resorts

The rack rates listed in this section are in U.S. dollars and are for a standard double room during high season (mid-Dec through mid-Apr), unless otherwise noted. Lower rates are available in spring, summer, and fall. See Chapter 3 for more information on travel seasons and Chapter 6 for more on booking accommodations.

Accommodations in the British Virgin Islands

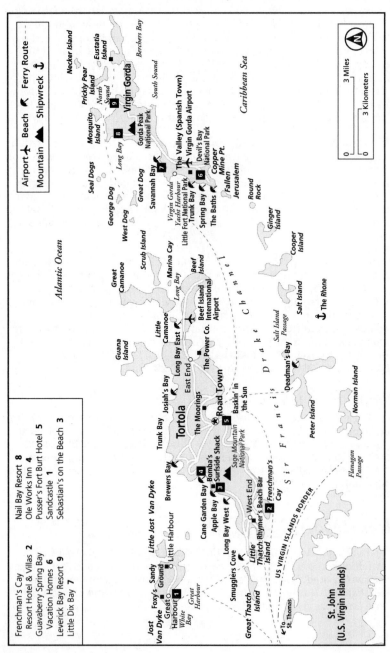

On Tortola

Frenchman's Cay Resort Hotel & Villas
$$$–$$$$ **Tortola**

Ideal for honeymooners, Frenchman's Cay Resort Hotel & Villas is a col-
lection of first-class one- and two-bedroom condos opening onto the scenic
Drake's Channel on a 4.8-hectare (12-acre) site. On the windward tip of
Frenchman's Cay, this nine-villa casual resort is a sleek retreat. Life
revolves around an octagonal, peak-roofed structure, open to the breezes,
that conceals everything from the restaurant to the library to the enter-
tainment area, with a pool and tennis court nearby. Each with a shady ter-
race, accommodations come with full kitchens and one or two bathrooms;
all are imbued with a tropical motif featuring bamboo furnishings. The aura
of a barefoot elegance settles here. The adjoining beach is small, but the
snorkeling is ideal. As this book went to press, the resort was preparing to
reopen under new management; be sure to call them for more details
before booking your stay.

See map p. 218. P.O. Box 1054, West End, Tortola. ☎ **800-235-4077** *in the U.S., 800-
463-0199 in Canada, or 284-495-4844. Fax: 284-495-4056.* www.frenchmans.com.
Rack rates: $250–$285 villa; $385–$430 two-bedroom villa. AE, DISC, MC, V.

Ole Works Inn
$–$$ **Tortola**

On the premises of a three-century-old sugar mill, this 18-room inn is a
good alternative to Tortola's pricey resorts. Across the road from a wide,
well-maintained, white-sand beach, it isn't for the demanding but is a
worthy choice. In a setting of foliage and flowers, the bedrooms are in a
lackluster modern structure of wood, glass, and stone, and units range
from hillside accommodations with air-conditioning and refrigerators to
simple and older yet comfortable doubles. A honeymoon suite nestles in
an old tower. The hotel's owner, Quito Rymer, is a famous island recording
star, and it's always party time at the on-site bar, a hush settling only when
Quito performs.

See map p. 218. P.O. Box 560, Cane Garden Bay, Tortola. ☎ **284-495-4837.** *Fax: 284-
495-9618.* www.quitorymer.com. *Rack rates: $90–$235 double. AE, MC, V. Closed
Sept.*

Pusser's Fort Burt Hotel
$–$$ **Tortola**

Pusser's, famous for its rum, operates this 19-room unit on the site of a
fort constructed by the Dutch in the 17th century. It offers no beach but
does have a freshwater pool with a panoramic view of the harbor. The
hotel is only a three-minute stroll to two of the island's best beaches:
Garden Bay Beach and **Smuggler's Cove.** Bedrooms are set at a higher
elevation than any others around Road Town. The regular doubles are

spacious and newly renovated. The on-site Fort Burt Restaurant and Pub, run by the BVI Culinary School, is popular with both visitors and Road Towners.

See map p. 218. P.O. Box 3380, Fort Burt, Road Town, Tortola. ☎ *284-494-2587. Fax: 284-494-2002. Rack rates: $99–$385 double. AE, MC, V.*

Sebastian's on the Beach
$–$$ Tortola

This hotel is located at Little Apple Bay, about a 15-minute drive from Road Town, on a long beach that offers some of the best surfing in the British Virgin Islands. The 30 rooms are housed in three buildings, with only one on the beach. All come with rattan furniture and balconies or porches. You should be careful here about room selection, as accommodations vary considerably. Most sought after are the beachfront rooms, only steps from the surf; they have an airy tropical feeling, with tile floors, balconies, patios, and screened jalousies. The rear accommodations on the beach side are less desirable — not only do they lack views, but they're also subject to traffic noise. Also avoid the two noisy bedrooms above the commissary. The dozen less-expensive, rather spartan rooms in the back of the main building lack views, but they're only a short walk from the beach.

See map p. 218. Little Apple Bay (P.O. Box 441), West End, Tortola, B.V.I. ☎ *800-336-4870 in the U.S., 284-495-4212. Fax 284-495-4466.* www.sebastiansbvi.com. *Rack rates: $135–$285 double. Breakfast and dinner $45 per person extra. AE, DISC, MC, V.*

On Virgin Gorda

Guavaberry Spring Bay Vacation Homes
$$–$$$ Virgin Gorda

Guavaberry Spring Bay is a special property in a tropical setting of flowers and trees. From here, you can walk right over to **The Baths,** the top sight-seeing attraction of Virgin Gorda with its giant boulders and tranquil pools (ideal for a swim). You're also near the golden sands of **Spring Bay.** Guests occupy one of 18 hexagonal redwood houses, with louvered windows open to catch the trade winds. Each accommodations is a home away from home, with one or two bedrooms, a living room with a combined kitchenette and dining area, a private bathroom with a shower, daily maid service, and an open sun deck with views of Sir Francis Drake Channel. For emergency supplies, there's an on-site commissary.

See map p. 218. P.O. Box 20, Spring Bay, Virgin Gorda. ☎ *284-495-5227. Fax: 284-495-5283.* www.guavaberryspringbay.com. *Rack rates: $210–$275 one- or two-bedroom home. Cash only.*

Leverick Bay Resort
$$ Virgin Gorda

Less well-known than Guavaberry and not as dramatically situated, this complex of 18 spacious hillside villas lies at the southern edge of Virgin

Gorda's North Sound. The resort has two small beaches, but it's only a ten-minute ride to the far-superior beach at Savannah Bay. The units are breeze-swept and comfortable with their waterfront balconies or patios. Each comes with such essentials as a refrigerator and safe. Furnishings are far more luxurious, but they're designed for comfort and easy living. You can cool off in a small pool. On-site is a little spa offering the usual — massages, both manicures and pedicures, and body treatments.

See map p. 218. P.O. Box 63, The Valley, Virgin Gorda. ☎ *800-848-7081, 284-495-7421. Fax: 284-495-7367.* www.leverickbay.com. *Rack rates: $119–$149 double. AE, MC, V.*

Little Dix Bay
$$$$$ **Virgin Gorda**

Those who want a posh retreat head for this winning choice — the original creation of Laurance Rockefeller himself in 1964 — far superior to all the first-class hotels on Tortola. The 98-unit resort opens onto a half-moon-shaped private bay with a white-sand beach, set against a backdrop of a 200-hectare (500-acre) preserve. Units are spacious and breezy, decorated with Caribbean style, and some of the rooms — our favorites — are in two-story *rondavels* — like Tiki huts on stilts, very South Pacific. As this book went to press, the resort's owners were completing enhancements to all rooms at the resort, as well as building six villas on the hillside. If you like a lot of facilities, such as fitness centers, tennis courts, snorkeling, and sailing a Sunfish, this resort is for you. You even get a daily *New York Times* fax. The children's program here is the best in the BVIs.

See map p. 218. P.O. Box 70, Virgin Gorda. ☎ *888-767-3966, 284-495-5555. Fax: 284-495-5661.* www.littledixbay.com. *Rack rates: $650–$825 double; $1,800 suite. AE, MC, V.*

Nail Bay Resort
$$–$$$ **Virgin Gorda**

Nestled near **Gorda Peak National Park,** this 20-room resort lies on the site of a 19th-century sugar plantation. The enclave comprises luxurious rooms, apartments, and two- to five-bedroom villas, all with sweeping views of the water. You'll feel at home with Nail Bay's array of amenities such as CD/cassette/radios, TV/VCRs, fridges, microwaves, toaster ovens, and coffeemakers; a few feature espresso machines. Facilities include pools replete with a waterfall and swim-up bar (a rarity in the laid-back BVIs), a tennis court, and bocce and croquet lawns. Three crescent beaches are within easy walking distance of the 59-hectare (147-acre) estate. If you don't want to cook, a chef can come to your villa and prepare meals.

See map p. 218. P.O. Box 69, Virgin Gorda. ☎ *800-871-3551, 284-494-8000. Fax: 284-495-5875.* www.nailbay.com. *Rack rates: $200–$250 double. Packages available. AE, DISC, MC, V.*

On Jost Van Dyke

Sandcastle
$$–$$$ Jost Van Dyke

Those with fantasies of being Robinson Crusoe retreat here. Six cottages, set in tropical gardens with views of the sea, open onto a white-sand beach. This colony of octagonal cottages is the ultimate retreat for escapists. Only two units are air-conditioned, but all are furnished in a simple but comfortable Caribbean motif, each with a large, tiled bathroom. This place is only for self-sufficient types who bring their own amusement with them, although windsurfing and snorkeling are complimentary. On-site is one of our favorite hangouts, **The Soggy Dollar Bar,** located in the **Sandcastle** restaurant (see the recommendation later in this chapter).

See map p. 218. White Bay, Jost Van Dyke. ☎ *284-495-9888. Fax: 284-495-9999.* www.sandcastle-bvi.com. *Rack rates: $160–$295 double. MC, V.*

Dining Out

The British Virgin Islanders have lived from the sea for centuries, and fresh fish is still the focus of most menus. Grouper here is as good as that in The Bahamas. The lobster caught off the island of Anegada is justly fabled among foodies and is imbued with a sweet flavor, more so than the coveted lobsters from Maine.

Except in a few restaurants on Tortola and Virgin Gorda, cookery is rather straightforward, because no real native cuisine exists. In general, you'll find far grander restaurants on St. Croix and St. Thomas than anywhere in the BVIs.

Most visitors dine at their hotel, especially at night, when traveling around the islands on badly lit roads is difficult. For the most part, at least for our recommendations, the food is competently prepared. Because the BVIs don't grow much of their foodstuff, and nearly everything in the larder has to be imported, prices are high.

 If you book into a resort on the MAP (breakfast and dinner plan), you can save money. Renting a taxi every night to go to independently run restaurants on Tortola and Virgin Gorda is a lot of fun, but you can run up a big bill in a short time. The drawback to taking MAP is that you're confined to one hotel every night unless you can book on a dine-around plan.

Unlike the old days, more and more places take credit cards. But in some of the smaller joints, you need cash (U.S. dollars are actually the official currency of the BVIs). Many local cooks set up little dives offering amusing dining, calling their places "Naughty Thelma's" or whatever (and they rarely take plastic). They make for a sense of adventure when dining out if you can escape from your hotel dining room for the night.

Dress is casual but not totally laid-back. That is, men should wear shirts with collars, but no restaurants require a jacket. A man's tie is a memory of yesterday. Women appear in fashionable resort wear at the finer places. Out at the funky little beach shacks, show up dressed as you would to clean up the backyard on a hot summer day.

Enjoying a Taste of the British Virgin Islands

Making your own discoveries, finding those little treasures like **Mrs. Scatliffe's** famous baked chicken in coconut served with her own garden vegetables, is fun. You can locate this treasure on the second-floor terrace of Mrs. Scatliffe's home, a yellow-and-white building across from Carrot Bay in Road Town, Tortola (☎ **284-495-4556;** lunch Mon–Fri 10 a.m.–4 p.m.; dinner nightly 7–9 p.m.; reservations required; prix-fixe menu $25–$32). A lively fungi band performs some evenings. Another delight is **Sandcastle** (☎ **284-495-9888**), on Jost Van Dyke, a candlelit beachside restaurant where four-course menus like duck l'orange and stuffed grouper are regularly served. (See our complete review of Sandcastle later in this chapter.)

Of course, fresh seafood seasoned with local herbs is invariably part of the menu on these islands. You'll also find spicy West Indian cooking, with curries of every description, at small, locally owned places.

The Best Restaurants

In this archipelago, you can't always dine where you want at night unless you're willing to take a boat or a puddle-jumper, and few want to do that just for dinner. Most guests opt for at least the MAP (breakfast and dinner plan) at their hotel. Some of the restaurants recommended in this section are ones you'll want to visit only for lunch as you're hopping about the islands. The first-class resorts employ either the most talented of local chefs or else cooks trained in America or Europe (mostly Britain).

If you're on a boat, you can still make reservations at many of the restaurants in the BVIs by contacting them via radio on VHF (very high frequency) Channel 16. Ask the captain to call ahead for you.

On Tortola

Brandywine Bay
$$$$–$$$$$ Tortola   TUSCAN

With tables opening to a panoramic view of Sir Francis Drake Channel, Brandywine Bay is your best bet for romantic dining. The location is a ten-minute ride by car or taxi east of Road Town. You arrive at an elegant hillside house where the chef and owner, David Pugliese, welcomes you like a private guest in his home. This isn't a discovery — gourmet magazines

Dining in the British Virgin Islands

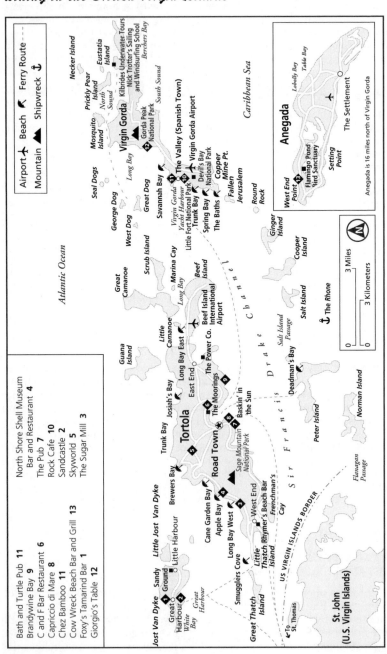

Bath and Turtle Pub **11**
Brandywine Bay **9**
C and F Bar Restaurant **6**
Capriccio di Mare **8**
Chez Bamboo **11**
Cow Wreck Beach Bar and Grill **13**
Foxy's Tamarind Bar **1**
Giorgio's Table **12**

North Shore Shell Museum
Bar and Restaurant **4**
The Pub **7**
Rock Cafe **10**
Sandcastle **2**
Skyworld **5**
The Sugar Mill **3**

such as *Bon Appétit* have already found it (and featured it in their magazines). As a former fashion photographer, Pugliese believes in presentation, and he sets an elegant table. Begin, perhaps, with his homemade mozzarella served with fresh basil and tomatoes, going on to grilled grouper graced with fresh herbs or a succulent homemade pasta. Beautifully sauced duck is a regular feature. One of the island's finest wine *cartes* is presented to you.

See map p. 224. Brandywine Estate, just outside of Road Town on Sir Francis Drake Highway, Brandywine Bay. ☎ *284-495-2301. Reservations required. Main courses: $26–$30. AE, MC, V. Open: Mon–Sat 6:30–9:30 p.m. Closed Aug–Oct.*

C and F Bar Restaurant
$$–$$$ Tortola   WEST INDIAN

Near **The Moorings** (see later in this chapter for details on this yachtie haven), C and F is one of Tortola's most laid-back eateries. The chef enjoys a local following. Here's an excellent place to order that sweet Anegada lobster that everyone talks about as they smack their lips. Locally caught fish is prepared as you like it. Try Clarence's spicy curried conch or his zesty barbecue chicken, finishing off with a piece of his real homemade Key lime pie.

See map p. 224. Purcell Estate. ☎ *284-494-4941. Reservations necessary in winter. Main courses: $13–$45. AE, DISC, MC, V. Open: Nightly 6:30–11 p.m.*

Capriccio di Mare
$–$$ Tortola   ITALIAN

Brandywine Bay restaurant (see the listing earlier in this chapter) is more upmarket, but its developers, in what they called "a flight of fancy," opened this laid-back, informal *caffè*, which almost overnight became a favorite with both islanders and visitors. No more-authentic Italian *caffè* exists in the Virgin Islands. It's open all day, so from cappuccino in the morning to the last succulent pasta or zesty pizza at night, this address is a good one with which to be familiar. For lunches, the sandwiches are well stuffed, and the salads are made of fresh greens. You can also stop in here and get the fixings for a picnic on your favorite beach.

See map p. 224. Waterfront Drive, Road Town. ☎ *284-494-5369. Reservations not necessary. Main courses: $15–$25. MC, V. Open: Mon–Sat 8 a.m.–9 p.m.*

North Shore Shell Museum Bar and Restaurant
$$$ Tortola   WEST INDIAN

Mrs. Scatliffe (see "Enjoying a Taste of the British Virgin Islands," earlier in this chapter) is the most celebrated local chef in the BVIs. Her daughter, Mona, took her recipes with her when she married Egberth Donovan and opened this West Indian tavern where they serve a savory Caribbean cuisine. We like to drop in early for breakfast, sampling the island's best pancakes, which are made with such ingredients as guava, mango, and coconut. For dinner, we also arrive early for one of those soursop daiquiris (no better ones exist). From the authentic island menu, you can enjoy such main dishes as grilled lobster, barbecued chicken, and spicy conch fritters, along with some zesty chicken and tender ribs. Mona's mama taught her well. After dinner, an impromptu fungi band entertains in this concrete-block building with its modest museum of shells.

See map p. 224. Carrot Bay, North Shore, Tortola. ☎ *284-495-4714. Reservations recommended at dinner. Main courses: $15–$35. No credit cards. Open: Daily 8 a.m.–9:30 p.m.*

The Pub
$$ Tortola   INTERNATIONAL

This establishment is housed in a low-slung timbered building on a narrow strip of land between the coastal road and the southern edge of Road Town's harbor. It has a barnlike interior and a rambling veranda built on piers over the water. The pub attracts many of the island's yachties, as well as the local sports teams, who celebrate here after their games. More than 25 different kinds of beer are available. If you're here for a meal, some of the best options include Bahamian fritters, Caesar or Greek salads, pastas, four kinds of steaks, and burgers. Locals who frequent this place are especially fond of the chef's jerk chicken and his combo platter of spareribs, chicken, and fried shrimp. The chef also prepares a catch of the day. Happy hour brings discounted drinks Saturday to Thursday from 5 to 7 p.m. and from 11 a.m. to 7 p.m. on Friday, when hot wings and raw vegetable platters are offered.

See map p. 224. Fort Burt Marina, Harbour Road. ☎ *284-494-2608. Reservations recommended. Main courses $15–$32. AE, DISC, MC, V. Mon–Sat 6 a.m.–10 p.m.; Sun 5 a.m.–noon.*

Skyworld
$$$$ Tortola   INTERNATIONAL

The equal of Brandywine (maybe even better on some nights), Skyworld is aptly named, because it commands the grandest view of any restaurant on the island, at a windswept 408m (1,337 ft.). You can even see the U.S. Virgins from here if the weather is clear. You can dine in a more-formal section or in a casual, laid-back garden atmosphere. The menu is the same in both areas of the restaurant, and over the years we've found this place the most reliable choice for dining on the island. We always go for the fresh catch of the day, preferably grilled. We like to begin with a savory fresh fish chowder or a delightful appetizer such as mushrooms stuffed with conch meat. For dessert, the chef makes the best Key lime pie on the island.

See map p. 224. Ridge Road, Road Town. ☎ *284-494-3567. Reservations recommended. Main courses: $24–$30. AE, MC, V. Open: Daily 10 a.m.–2:30 p.m. and 5–11 p.m.*

The Sugar Mill
$$$$ Tortola   CARIBBEAN/CALIFORNIAN

Have you ever wished that those food critics would just put down their laptops, pick up their sauté pans, and launch their own restaurant if the task is so easy? Former *Bon Appétit* columnists Jeff and Jinx Morgan did just that when they bought The Sugar Mill, a 350-year-old former plantation in Apple Bay, which they subsequently transformed into Tortola's most atmospheric restaurant. Candles cast a golden glow on the thick walls of ballast stone and coral of this former rum distillery, and fine examples of Haitian art decorate the walls. The handful of menu offerings rotates nightly and includes wine pairings recommended by Jeff. The West Indian influence is evident, but the experimental duo doesn't stop there. Standouts are the Cajun oyster étouffée (stew), grilled mahi-mahi in banana leaves with a peppery Creole sauce, and Jamaican jerk pork roast with pineapple chipotle sauce. The liberally used vegetables and herbs come from the hotel's garden. The mango and pineapple mousse or banana crepes are a sweet and scrumptious delight to end the meal.

See map p. 224. Apple Bay. ☎ *284-495-4355. Reservations required. Main courses: $26–$36. AE, MC, V. Open: Lunch daily at the Islands Beach Bar noon to 2 p.m.; dinner nightly 7–9 p.m.*

On Virgin Gorda

Bath and Turtle Pub
$$–$$$ Virgin Gorda   PUB GRUB/INTERNATIONAL

The busiest pub on Virgin Gorda, this local favorite lies at the end of the waterfront shopping plaza in Spanish Town. You can come here to drink, to listen to the live music on Wednesday and Sunday nights, or to select an indoor or courtyard table and fill up on the grub of the day. Portions are large and affordable. The spiciest chicken wings on the island are made here and flavored with ginger and tamarind. The chili is spicy, as is the barbecue chicken. Steak, lobster (prepared as you wish), and daily seafood temptations round out the menu. The bartender's mango coladas are addictive.

See map p. 224. Virgin Gorda Yacht Harbour, Spanish Town. ☎ *284-495-5239. Reservations recommended. Main courses: $15–$32. AE, MC, V. Open: Daily 7:30 a.m.–11 p.m.*

Chez Bamboo
$$$–$$$$ Virgin Gorda   CAJUN/CREOLE

Chez Bamboo is as close as Virgin Gorda comes to evoking a New Orleans supper club. Make a night of it. It lies a five-minute walk north of the Virgin Island Yacht Club. Here you can enjoy food prepared with zesty flair, full of flavor as evoked by the conch gumbo. Nassau grouper comes *en papillotte* (baked in foil), and the New Orleans strip steak is served in a creamy

Worcestershire sauce. The crème brûlée is the island's best. Friday night on the terrace, you can listen to live blues or jazz music.

See map p. 224. Near the Virgin Gorda Yacht Club, Spanish Town. ☎ *284-495-5752. Reservations recommended. Main courses: $20–$50. AE, MC, V. Open: Daily 3–10 p.m.*

Giorgio's Table
$$$$ **Virgin Gorda** **ITALIAN**

A 15-minute drive north of Spanish Town, Giorgio's is the only authentic Italian restaurant on Virgin Gorda. The interior evokes a yacht, but most guests ask for a table on a large covered terrace, where the stars will get in your eyes. Giorgio is proud that his style of cooking is Italian as opposed to Italian-American. He seeks flavor in all his dishes from the succulent pastas to the freshly caught fish, and he gets the pick of the catch that the fishermen bring in. Lunch offers a filling array of pizzas and sandwiches.

See map p. 224. Mahoe Bay. ☎ *284-495-5684. Reservations recommended. Main courses: $30–$40. AE, MC, V. Open: Lunch daily noon to 3 p.m.; dinner daily 6:30–9 p.m.*

Rock Cafe
$$$ **Virgin Gorda** **ITALIAN/CARIBBEAN**

Unlike the name suggests, this restaurant isn't some island clone of the ubiquitous Hard Rock Cafe. It's better in our view than that overrated international chain. You can stop for a drink in the bar before going to the rear, where a different world unfolds. The setting is amid boulders like the ones at **The Baths,** the number-one sightseeing attraction on Virgin Gorda. The recessed lighting and boardwalks add to the theatrical allure at night. Fortunately, the chefs don't depend just on the setting. The menu is wisely balanced, the dishes well prepared — and well consumed with affordable wine from a respectable list whose vintages range from Italy to California. Freshly caught red snapper comes in a tangy marinade, and we're especially fond of the chicken piccata. Homemade cakes and fudge sundaes finish the meal nicely.

See map p. 224. The Valley. ☎ *284-495-5482. Reservations recommended. Main courses: $26–$50. MC, V. Open: Nightly 4 p.m.–midnight. Special Tequila bar upstairs.*

On Jost Van Dyke

Foxy's Tamarind Bar
$$$ **Jost Van Dyke** **WEST INDIAN**

"Foxy," also known as Philicianno Callwood, is a legend among yachties in the Virgin Islands. It's always party time at his Tamarind Bar, especially on New Year's Eve, when this place is the hottest and most happening in the BVIs. Known for more than three decades for his little bar and restaurant,

Foxy will feed you well. Drop in at lunchtime and he'll tempt you with *rotis* (flat, African-style bread stuffed with curried fillings). He also grills a mean burger. If you're coming for dinner, reserve a table by 5 p.m. Grilled meats and freshly caught seafood such as lobster are prepared with zest and flair. Foxy also has a way with barbecue. Bands play from Thursday to Saturday nights when the joint jumps.

See map p. 224. Great Harbour. ☎ **284-495-9258.** *Reservations recommended. Main courses: $14–$26. MC, V. Open: Daily 9 a.m.–9 p.m. or "until everyone goes home."*

Sandcastle
$–$$$ Jost Van Dyke   WEST INDIAN

Corporate escapees Debby Pearse and Bruce Donnath came to run this small resort in 1996. Until then, the only access to the bar-restaurant was via a small dinghy, and invariably guests took a dunk up to their waists, thus the name of the restaurant's bar, the Soggy Dollar. By day, flying fish sandwiches, rotis, and jumbo burgers keep guests sated at the unassuming open-air spot. On Sunday afternoons, calypso and reggae tunes draw charter yachts to the small beach. By night at the beachfront dining room, you're treated to linen-and-silver-set tables by candlelight and a four-course affair accompanied by homemade bread. The menu is changed daily but may include such dishes as mahi-mahi Martinique (marinated in citrus juice and cooked with fresh dill, onions, and fennel). The sesame-coated snapper is also excellent, as are the fresh pastas.

See map p. 224. White Bay, Jost Van Dyke at Sandcastle Resort. ☎ **284-495-9888.** *Reservations for dinner must be made by 4 p.m. for 7 p.m. seating. Lunch: $8–$12. Prix-fixe dinner $40–$45. MC, V. Open: Bar lunch daily 9:30 a.m.–3 p.m.; dinner daily at 7 p.m. (one seating).*

On Anegada

Cow Wreck Beach Bar and Grill
$$$ Anegada   WEST INDIAN

Flat as a johnny cake, the remote island of Anegada is fabled for its lobsters. Here they're kept in a cage underwater, waiting their turn to do service in the pot. Informal and funky, this family-owned eatery is laid-back and a lot of fun. A straw roof shelters you from the elements, and rough wood tables are placed on a terrace with an oceanview. At lunch you can snorkel before eating, or at night enjoy a sundowner or two. Those who drop in for lunch often order sandwiches. But if you're here in the evening, go for that lobster. There's none better in the West Indies.

See map p. 224. Lower Cow Wreck Beach, Anegada. ☎ **284-495-8047.** *Main courses: $15–$45. Reservations required for dinner. Open: Lunch daily 10:30 a.m.–midnight; dinner seatings daily 6–7 p.m. (Open daily unless no reservations are made, in which case the restaurant closes, so be sure to make a reservation.)*

Enjoying the Sand and Surf

You'd have to go to the South Pacific to find sailing waters to equal those of the British Virgin Islands, and you can find places for swimming and snorkeling around every bend on every island. Or, you could always just delight in the blissfully uncrowded beaches, many of which you can have all to yourself.

Combing the beaches

Sometimes on a remote beach in the BVIs, you don't have the golden sands all to yourself. You may have to share the beach with a family of iguanas out for some late-morning sun. Some of the best beaches are on deserted islands appealing to the Robinson Crusoe in you. These islands are reachable only by boat trips, which you can arrange with locals on both Tortola and Virgin Gorda.

Even on the remotest beach, signs of encroaching civilization crop up unexpectedly. Our party of eight had booked an island all to ourselves. One day as we were sunning ourselves, a boatload of some 100 gay male tourists arrived and took over the beach, running nude up and down its long stretches. Getting into the spirit of it, our party ordered kegs of beer brought over for the men and invited them to our own hastily arranged Oktoberfest. Chances are that won't happen to you. You'll probably wander for miles without encountering another beachcomber.

 Some people do go nude on the beaches, but officially it's against the law. If you want to show off your assets, you'd be more comfortable going to Negril, Jamaica, or one of the French islands such as Martinique. Most British Virgin Islanders are deeply religious and are offended by public nudity.

All beaches are public in these islands, including such exclusive enclaves as the 343-hectare (850-acre) island **Guana Island Club** or the 30-hectare (74-acre) hideaway **Necker Island.** We don't recommend going to either one of them unless someone like Bill Gates and his family invited you. You're allowed to use the beaches, but they don't really want you there — in fact, a security guard may ask you to move on.

 If you want to sample the high life, the nearest beach to Tortola that will give you a preview of it is **Deadman's Bay** on the exclusive **Peter Island.** This 728-hectare (1,800-acre) island is one of the most beautiful and romantic palm-fringed beaches in the BVIs, as well as the setting for the most expensive resort in the BVIs, **Peter Island Resort** (☎ **800-346-4451,** 284-495-2000). You can easily reach the resort's beach by boat from Tortola.

On Tortola

West of Road Town, **Cane Garden Bay Beach** is the island's finest strip of fine white sands with sheltering palm trees, a Caribbean movie cliché.

This beach is also the best in regard to facilities — you'll find kiosks renting kayaks, sailboards, and Hobie Cats. Windsurfing is also possible. Cane Garden Bay is a favorite anchorage for the yachting crowd and is the site of food shacks, bars, and shops. If a cruise ship is in port, avoid this beach, because passengers invariably are taken here.

On cruise-ship days, you may want to head to remote **Elizabeth Beach,** with its wide, palm-fringed sands. This beach lies off Ridge Road. Also reached along Ridge Road is the never-crowded **Josiah Bay Beach** in the East End.

A small, sandy beach at the West End, **Smuggler's Cove,** opposite the offshore island of Great Thatch, is one of our favorites. A half-moon of white sand, it lies at the end of the bumpy Belmont Road and is a popular spot for snorkelers because of its great visibility and its underwater parade of rainbow-hued fish and brain and elkhorn corals.

Another good beach, **Brewers Bay Beach,** lies east of Cane Garden Bay along the hilly Brewers Bay Road and is the site of a campground. Both snorkelers and windsurfers come to this beach of white sand. This spot is popular in the late afternoon when beach buffs gather for their sundowners at one of the two beach-bar shacks found here.

For the most fun beach party in all the Virgins, both U.S. and British, head for **Bomba's Surfside Shack** (☎ 284-495-4148). Its construction of flotsam and jetsam du jour looks like a train wreck. Both visitors and locals in equal numbers flock to this rollicking haven of reggae music and the most lethal rum punches on the island. Revelers dance barefoot in the sands all night. Its Full Moon parties are legendary, and local fungi bands entertain on Wednesday and Sunday nights. The free house tea is spiked with hallucinogenic mushrooms, and the barbecue isn't bad either.

On Virgin Gorda

First, the good news. Called the "Stonehenge of the BVIs," **The Baths** are the most fabled spot on all the Virgin Islands for swimming and spectacular beauty. The boulders here are massive, in some cases like a mammoth truck, and no one knows how they got here — although scientists speculate that volcanic explosions pushed them to the surface in dim, unrecorded times.

Tranquil pools and grottoes are flooded with seawater, and the snorkeling can be excellent. What's the downside? Because The Baths are so magnificent, they're on everybody's itinerary, including the cruise-ship charters from St. Thomas and St. John, which start rolling in by 10 a.m. You'll have to hang out until 4 p.m. before the crowds thin out.

We like to come here for a swim shortly after the sun comes up when we can enjoy the mysticism and surreal beauty of this place before the hordes invade.

Even if you arrive during overcrowded periods, you can look around and then retreat to **Spring Bay Beach,** a nearby strip of white sand and turquoise clear water. This beach, which you can walk to from The Baths, is rarely crowded because it's not known. The snorkeling is also idyllic here. For even more privacy, you can take a difficult 15-minute trail to **Trunk Bay Beach,** another wide, sandy beach nearby.

Another good beach is **Mahoe Bay Beach** at the Mango Bay Resort (☎ **284-494-5672**), a complex of villas set on landscaped grounds fronting the islets of the Sir Francis Drake Channel. The sands are good here, and the waters have long-range visibility for snorkelers. Swimming conditions are also ideal.

Good beaches on the northern end of Virgin Gorda include those at the very pricey **Bitter End Yacht Club** (☎ **284-494-2746**), which is far too expensive for the average pocketbook. Windsurfers are especially fond of this spot, and it also offers the best water-sports rentals on the island, including Sunfish and Boston Whaler rentals. The offshore reefs feature some of Virgin Gorda's best snorkeling opportunities. Via a footpath from Bitter End, you can explore **Bercher's Bay Beach,** which attracts the shellcomber, with its delicately hued shells found among the rocks here.

On Jost Van Dyke

Getting more discovered every year, this 10-sq.-km (4-sq.-mile) island is named for a Dutch pirate. It didn't get electricity until the early '90s. Because this spot is one of the most favored in the BVIs by yachties, a series of ramshackle bars and food joints have been opened to cater to this burgeoning trade. Our favorite of these joints is the justifiably famous **Foxy's Tamarind Bar** (see the review earlier in this chapter), known for its New Year's Eve parties but a lively venue throughout the year.

The best beach, reached by a little road, is **White Bay Beach.** This beach is on the southern rim of the island, lying west of the only real settlement here, and is pompously called "Great Harbour." Lined with palm trees, the beach also has some really funky bars; in some of these, a Rasta man may try to sell you ganja (marijuana).

Local boatmen, for a fee that you negotiate, may take you over to the uninhabited **Sandy Cay,** a beach of perfect white sand and clear water with some of the best snorkeling in the BVIs. Find them at Little Harbour or East End Harbour.

On Anegada

Home of the Caribbean's sweetest lobsters, Anegada is the most remote and the most northerly of the British Virgins, lying at a point 48km (30 miles) east of Tortola. Most of the BVIs are hilly or even mountainous, but Anegada is so flat that ships or boats don't even see it on the horizon until they're almost upon it.

It's estimated that some 500 ships went down on Anegada's dangerous Horseshoe Reef. Reports are floating around of vast sunken treasures to be found here. At its loftiest point, Anegada manages to rise 8.5m (28 ft.). The island itself is 4.8km (3 miles) wide and 18km (11 miles) long.

The best beaches lie at the island's northern and western tiers, and these white sands are the reason that most visitors come here in the first place. Anegada has little else except the bird sanctuary of the **B.V.I. National Parks Trust** with its flamingo colony.

The best beach of white sand facing beautiful living coral reefs is located at the amusingly named **Loblolly Bay,** with its funky little food joints and raffish bars. Snorkelers swim among the caverns offshore to see the rainbow-hued marine life. Sea turtles and the unwelcome barracuda also make an appearance here. We've never done a scientific experiment, but we think that the sand here is whiter and more powdery than elsewhere in the BVIs.

The greatest delight is to order a freshly caught lobster cooked on the beach. We like to head over to **Big Bamboo** at Loblolly (☎ **284-495-2019**) for this succulent treat. The wafting aromas from the grill will entice you. If you've downed too much beer, a hammock is waiting.

Another amusing place is the **Cow Wreck Beach Bar and Grill** on **Lower Cow Wreck Beach** (see earlier in this chapter for more details). "Cow Wreck?" you ask. A century or so ago a boat loaded with cow bones to be used in making buttons ran afoul on these notorious reefs and split apart, those bovine bones scattering into the sea. For years to come, cow bones washed ashore.

Playing in the surf

Whether swimming at the boulder-strewn Baths or island hopping from Virgin Gorda to Tortola or from Cooper Island to Guana, this island chain is your best chance to live that mermaid (or merman) fantasy.

Diving and snorkeling delights

The BVIs are number one for sailing but not for diving. If you want a strictly diver's holiday, head for Grand Cayman (see Chapter 12). But if you want to work some diving into your vacation, the BVIs are a potent underwater attraction, mainly because of their chief dive site, the wreckage of the **RMS *Rhone.*** This 94m (310-ft.) royal mail steamer sank in 1867 in waters near the western point of Salt Island. *Skin Diver* magazine called it "the world's most fantastic shipwreck dive," teeming with a wide variety of marine life and stunning coral formations. A film based on Peter Benchley's *The Deep* was shot at this site.

The second-most intriguing dive site is the wreck of the ***Chikuzen,*** an 81m (270-ft.), steel-hulled refrigerator vessel that went down on Tortola's East End in 1981. It lies in 24m (80 ft.) of water, home today to an array of tropical fish, including black-tip sharks and octopus. Off Ginger Island is another premier dive site, **Alice in Wonderland,** known for its coral wall that slopes from 12m (40 ft.) to a sandy bottom of 30m (100 ft.). Monstrous overhangs and mammoth corals, plus an array of graceful sea animals from the garden eel to the long-nose butterfly fish, make it a diver's favorite.

In addition to the celebrated dive sites mentioned, the island chain also has more than two dozen other popular dive sites filled with coral for-mations and abundant marine life. The BVIs are especially known for their wreck diving, because before Doppler weather reports, hurricanes could sweep in without warning, sending ships to watery graves. Visibility underwater is among the clearest in the Caribbean.

Nearly all dive sites are within a 56km (35-mile) reach, so you can have a varied underwater program without boating over long stretches of sea. Even the most distant dive sites lie within a 30-minute boat ride of either Tortola or Virgin Gorda.

Norman Island, the legendary setting for Stevenson's *Treasure Island,* is eagerly sought out by divers for its series of four sea caves, one idyllic for snorkelers at Treasure Point. Bring the fixings for a picnic and make a day of it. The aptly named **Angelfish Reef** lives up to its promise. You can also see schools of eagle rays here.

 The clear visibility underwater makes the BVIs a mecca for snorkelers as well. Snorkelers can even see some of the *Rhone,* because its rudder lies in shallow water about 4.5m (15 ft.) below the surface.

For snorkelers, marine life is abundant, and the living reefs are in better shape than in the USVIs. You'll find thousands of brilliantly colored fish such as parrot fish, queen angelfish, damselfish, wrasses, and a variety of soft corals and incredible sponges in all shapes and sizes. On Norman Island, one snorkeler discovered a purple tube sponge that was nearly 1.5m (5 ft.) long.

If waters get choppy, as they often do, snorkelers can easily move on to a neighboring cove or even sail to another island nearby. Waters, of course, are more tranquil in summer. All dive operators and all resorts, including the super-expensive **Bitter End Yacht Club** (North Sound, Virgin Gorda; ☎ 800-872-2392), have snorkeling gear near prime snor-keling sites with gear to rent to nonguests. Snorkeling costs $30, a one-tank dive is $65, and a two-tank dive, $95.

Also on Virgin Gorda, you can get a history lesson on the RMS *Rhone* wreck from **Kilbrides Sunchasers Scuba,** at the Bitter End Yacht Club (☎ 800-932-4286, 284-495-9638; www.sunchasersscuba.com), which takes divers to 50 different sites and offers resort dive courses and PADI certification. Rates are $80 for a one-tank dive and $95 for a two-tank dive.

PADI five-star **Dive B.V.I. Ltd.** (☎ **800-848-7078,** 284-495-5513; Fax: 284-495-5347; www.divebvi.com) operates out of Leverick Bay, Virgin Gorda Yacht Harbour, Peter Island, and Marina Cay. Owner Joe Giacinto has been diving the BVIs for more than three decades, charging $120 for a two-tank dive if they provide equipment and $105 if you have your own equipment.

Paddling your own kayak

You can wave at the yachties as you go by piloting your own kayak at a fraction of the cost. A typical kayak itinerary starts at Peter Island and goes to Norman Island, said to have been the inspiration for Stevenson's *Treasure Island.* The jaunt by sea continues on to Tortola before reaching the more-remote Jost Van Dyke, coming to an end at St. John, the most beautiful of the USVIs. You can book five-day trips, costing $1,050 per sailor, with Arawak Expeditions (☎ **800-238-8687;** www.arawakexp.com).

Reeling in the big one

The waters washing up in the BVIs are some of the richest game-fishing channels in the world, especially the 80km (50-mile) so-called Puerto Rican Trench near Anegada. Record catches of tuna, marlin, sailfish, shark, bluefish, and wahoo are on the books. Your hotel will help you make arrangements.

Bonefishing (fishing for small but feisty catches in the saltwater flats) is a popular sport. Be warned: These fish are skittish — one wrong move can send the school fleeing. Try your hand at snagging these elusive critters on Anegada. **Anegada Reef Hotel** at Setting Point (☎ **284-495-8002**) can hook you up.

Climbing aboard

The BVIs, especially Tortola and Virgin Gorda, are imbued with the best marinas and shore facilities of any other country in the West Indies. Tortola is the charter-boat center of the Caribbean. It's estimated that about 65 percent of all visitors come here for the sailing (whether novice or veteran sailors), with the added allure of swimming, diving, and snorkeling — a virtual water wonderland.

Instead of long overnight sea jaunts, you can sail with ease from island to island in a short time. With island outcroppings everywhere, major waves rarely spring up (good news for those prone to seasickness), and most of the waters are tranquil. You're in sight of some landmass virtually wherever you sail in the BVI chain.

The premier charter-boat operator in the Caribbean is **The Moorings** (☎ **888-535-7289,** 284-494-2226; www.moorings.com), which has a flagship base on the protected side of Tortola in Road Town and is home to 18 crewed yachts and 150 bareboats (including 9.7–15m/32–50-ft. sloops and catamarans). Bareboats run $3,200 for six people for five days; crewed yachts cost $1,300 per day for six people for five days. Other outfitters on Tortola that may put you out to sea include **Catamaran Charters,** Nanny Cay, just west of Road Town (☎ 284-494-6661), which charters catamarans with or without captains. **BVI Yacht Charters,** Inner Harbour Marina, Road Town (☎ 284-494-4289), offers 12 to 16m (38–51-ft.) sailboats for charter.

Old salts and beginning sailors flock to the well-heeled **Bitter End Yacht Club** (☎ 800-872-2392, 284-494-2746; Fax: 284-494-4756), which operates in the tranquil waters of the North Sound. This place is the most idyllic in the BVIs to learn to windsurf or sail. At the yacht club, seek out **Nick Trotter's Sailing and Windsurfing School.** The staff here is the best on the island; they're patient with neophytes. You can also charter boats here.

Exploring on Dry Land

In spite of their tiny size, the BVIs offer more nature reserves and national parks than any other island nation in the Caribbean except Jamaica.

Our favorite trails are in the hilly remnants of a primeval rain forest in the 37.2-hectare (92-acre) **Sage Mountain National Park** on Tortola, where the BVIs reach their loftiest citadel at 542m (1,780 ft.). A trio of trails leads up to the summit as you make your way along lush growth such as the elephant-ear philodendron, prickly ferns, and hanging vines. Trails begin west of Road Town. Secure the makings of a picnic before setting off. As you enjoy your picnic, you can take in the same view enjoyed by Sir Francis Drake of Ginger Island, Peter Island, Jost Van Dyke, Sandy Cay, and Salt Island.

On Virgin Gorda, the 107.2-hectare (265-acre) **Virgin Gorda Peak National Park** is riddled with well-marked trails. Here you can climb the "belly" of the woman that suggests the geographic shape of Virgin Gorda — that is, a pregnant woman lying flat on her back. The "navel" in the belly sits at 418m (1,370 ft.). Laurance Rockefeller built the lookout point at the summit, which is a continuation of the paved road to **Little Dix Bay.** Also on Virgin Gorda, you can hike through the **Devil's Bay National Park** in the southwest corridor of the tiny island. This area embraces the much-touted Baths with their mammoth boulders. If it's not too crowded, you can explore the caverns, labyrinths, and passageways created by these huge rocks. As the waves surge and retreat, they create shimmering pools where you can enjoy a cool splash — hence, the name of **The Baths.** Trails begin south of The Baths.

Contact the **British Virgin Islands Tourist Board** for more information. The office is above the FedEx office on the AKARA Building's second floor on DeCastro Street, in Wickham's Cay in Road Town (☎ 284-494-3134; www.bviwelcome.com).

Shopping the Local Stores

Shopping is mildly amusing in the BVIs, and most shops are centered along Main Street in **Road Town** on Tortola. The shopping here isn't duty-free. If you make a purchase, it's the same as if you'd bought an item in London.

You can look for imports from the U.K. and can often find some bargains in such items as Wedgwood china. The BVIs aren't a place to bargain, however.

Pusser's Rum, island spices and herbs, local handicrafts, certain botanical skin-care products, terra-cotta pottery, and plenty of T-shirts and sandals are for sale. And keep in mind that you have to smoke those Cuban cigars before you return to the U.S., because U.S. Customs won't allow them entry.

Living It Up After Dark

Nightlife in the BVIs often means dinner, lots of rum drinking, and early retirement to bed.

Many locals — and visitors, too — eagerly anticipate happy hour, when all bars offer two drinks for the price of one. Sometimes, free snacks are included. In general, happy hours are from 4 to 7 p.m., but this can vary.

On Tortola, you can tank up on the BVIs' "Painkiller," made from the local Pusser's Rum at **Pusser's Road Town Pub** on Waterfront Drive (☎ 284-494-3897). Orange and pineapple juice and a dash of coconut crème are added to the libation. You can stick around for some English pub grub such as fish and chips or shepherd's pie.

The hottest spot on the island is **Rhymer's Beach Bar** on Tortola's West End (☎ 284-495-4639). At this beach bar and restaurant, you'll meet the most convivial gang of locals and visitors of any age hanging out in the BVIs, enjoying the camaraderie, the tropical rum punches, and the native menu of conch chowder, tasty ribs, and the like. Steel-drum bands entertain in the evenings.

Funky little beach bars are nestled throughout the inhabited islands. Our favorites include **The Soggy Dollar** at the **Sandcastle,** White Bay on Jost Van Dyke and **Foxy's Tamarind Bar,** our favorite watering hole in all the BVIs (see the reviews for all three earlier in this chapter). Come here for a limin' time (*limin'* means "hanging out" — just what you do here, for hours on end).

Fast Facts: The BVIs

Area Code

The area code is **284**.

ATMs

Only Tortola and Virgin Gorda have ATMs. On Tortola, try Banco Popular (☎ 284-494-2117) on Main Street next to the Customs office in Road Town, or the Bank of Nova Scotia at Wickhams Cay (☎ 284-494-2526), also in Road Town.

Babysitters

Most hotels will make arrangements for babysitters at $10 an hour and up.

Currency

The U.S. dollar is the official currency of the BVIs, much to the surprise of many a Brit who views the archipelago as a colony.

Doctors

Check with your resort for a referral; serious emergencies may require an airlift to St. Thomas or San Juan. The nearest decompression tank is on St. Thomas.

Emergencies

For fire, police, and ambulance, dial ☎ **999**.

Hospitals

Peebles Hospital (☎ 284-494-3497), on Porter Road in Road Town, Tortola, is the only hospital in the BVIs.

Information

See the Appendix for helpful Web sites and locations of U.S.-based and local tourist offices.

On the island, pick up the latest copy of *The British Virgin Islands Welcome Tourist Guide,* published bimonthly. For a good beach read, *Treasure Island* by Robert

Louis Stevenson, is supposedly based on the BVIs' Norman Island.

Internet Access

Check with your hotel about Internet access.

Newspapers and Magazines

The more-deluxe resorts offer the *New York Times* by fax. Otherwise, you'll be hard-pressed to find either the *Times* or *USA Today.*

Pharmacies

J.R. O'Neal Drugstore is at 75 Main St., Road Town, Tortola (☎ 284-494-2292). Hours are Monday to Friday 8:30 a.m. to 5 p.m. and Saturday 8:30 a.m. to 1:30 p.m.

Police

Dial ☎ **999** for emergencies.

Post Office

Where else? Main Street in Road Town, Tortola (☎ 284-468-3701 or 284-494-3701, ext. 4996). Hours are Monday through Friday 8:30 a.m. to 4:30 p.m. and Saturday 9 a.m. to noon.

Restrooms

All public drinking and dining facilities in the BVIs are required, by law, to admit members of the public into their restrooms. Restaurant owners, however, always appreciate it when outsiders sociably stop for a cold drink, before or after using the toilet.

Safety

Take normal precautions in town, even though crime is rare on these islands. A few hotels still don't have locks on their doors. You can walk about freely, but don't leave valuables wrapped in your towel on the beach or dangle your camera behind you while you look at the shops along the waterfront.

Smoking

Smoking policies are left to the discretion of the individual establishments. Some restaurants have designated nonsmoking sections within their restaurants and bars. With so many open-air establishments, the natural ventilation of the trade winds helps resolve conflicts.

Taxes

Room tax is 7 percent; departure tax is $10 by air and $5 by sea (not included in the price of your ticket).

Taxis

Call the B.V.I. Taxi Association (☎ 284-494-2322).

Weather Updates

Check out www.weather.com for updates.

Chapter 12

Grand Cayman

• •

In This Chapter

▶ Knowing what to expect when you arrive
▶ Getting around the island
▶ Deciding where you want to stay
▶ Sampling the local cuisine at the best restaurants
▶ Scoping out good beaches and diving into water sports
▶ Satisfying the landlubber: Shopping and nightlife

• •

*I*f you come to Grand Cayman expecting to encounter an upper-crust attitude to coincide with the island's reputation as an offshore banking mecca, you'll be pleasantly surprised. Despite its wealth and status as a British Overseas Dependent Territory — we know, even the designation sounds stuffy — Grand Cayman is relaxed and casual.

The cost of living is about 20 percent higher on Grand Cayman than in the United States; one U.S. dollar is worth only about 80 Cayman cents. Nonetheless, many of the 40,000 islanders are wealthy, and they wear their millionaire status without any ostentation. If you run into any problem while on the island, the warm and friendly folks on Grand Cayman are happy to point you in the right direction.

Arriving at the Airport

With more than 100 flights landing at **Owen Roberts International Airport** (☎ 345-949-7811) weekly — 70 direct flights from Miami alone — officials are adept at handling a continuous stream of visitors. This clean, modern airport with its good air-conditioning system is one of the more comfortable in the Caribbean. Even if you're coming in on a packed flight, you'll likely encounter few lines and barely feel that you're entering a foreign country.

The airport is centrally located for points east and west. After you clear Customs (see Chapter 8) and gather your luggage, you'll note stacks of free tourist information. Grab a copy of everything you see — especially useful is **"Key to Cayman,"** available at the airport, hotels, and shops. These giveaways often contain coupons for meals, attractions, and car rentals.

Flights going on to Cayman Brac land at **Gerrard-Smith Airport** (☎ 345-948-1222); flights to Little Cayman land at **Edward Bodden Airfield** (☎ 345-948-0021). Air service from Grand Cayman to Cayman Brac and Little Cayman is offered via **Cayman Airways** (☎ 800-422-9626, 345-949-2311; www.caymanairways.com).

The other way to reach Grand Cayman is by ship. Most major cruise lines call on Grand Cayman, docking in George Town. However, the Cayman Islands limit cruise visitors to a maximum of 6,000 cruise passengers or three ships per day, whichever is greater. Tuesdays, Wednesdays, and Thursdays tend to be the busiest days.

Check with your hotel ahead of time to see if it offers free pickup at the airport. All arriving flights are met by taxis, which line up neatly, awaiting an agent to assign them to deplaning passengers.

Taxis are usually vans (capable of transporting divers and all their accompanying gear) or Toyota Corollas. Taxi rates are fixed, and you can get fare information from the dispatcher at the curb. Drivers are generally pleased to share island lore. Typical one-way fares from the airport to **Seven Mile Beach** range from $15 to $20, depending on which end of the beach you're traveling to.

Taxis are also readily available from all resorts and from the taxi stand at the cruise-ship dock in George Town. A sign with current rates is posted at the dock.

Local minibuses run along main routes between 7 a.m. and 6 p.m. from George Town parallel to Seven Mile Beach. The fare is $1.90.

If you rented a condo but not a car and you need provisions, have **McCurley's Tours** (☎ 345-947-9626) pick you up at the airport. The driver will gladly take you by a grocery store en route.

If you rent a car, getting to your hotel from the airport should be easy on this flat island. The roads are well marked and in good shape, and your car-rental agent can pencil in the route for you on a map. The major car-rental companies all have offices in a plaza across from the airport terminal, where you can pick up and drop off vehicles.

Choosing Your Location

As with Aruba, almost all 50 of Grand Cayman's hotels and condos are crowded along the island's famous **Seven Mile Beach.** Even if you go to the island for diving, you may want to be close to this lovely beach. From here, you have broad dining options; you can walk to town from many resorts.

Hard-core divers like to stay on the **East End,** near Grand Cayman's best diving. If you want to skip the crowds and Cayman Cowboys (as the dive operators who pack people on their boats are derisively called), head to the much-more-secluded north side, which also offers good diving.

Divers who want more of an escape will do better on Cayman Brac or Little Cayman. But if you think nightlife is limited on Grand Cayman, you'll be bored out of your wet suit on those quiet islands.

Getting Around Grand Cayman

Grand Cayman is one of the easiest islands in the Caribbean to navigate. The terrain is flat, and the easygoing locals are ready to help if by some weird happenstance you get lost.

By taxi

Taxi service is available on Grand Cayman 24 hours a day, and fares are set by the director of civil aviation (☎ 345-949-7811). Always inquire, however, about the estimated fare before getting in, although most Caymanian cabbies are honest — unlike taxi drivers on some other islands. If you want to be sure about the fare, you can always ask for a chart that gives the regulated fees drivers can charge. Most taxis can hold as many as five passengers, and visitors can inquire about private around-the-island tours. Taxis on 24-hour call include **Cayman Cab Team** (☎ 345-926-8294) and **A.A. Transportation** (☎ 345-949-7222).

By car

You'll have to pay for a $7.50 rental permit to drive any vehicle on the island. You can get a permit from either the rental agent or the central police station in George Town if you have a valid driver's license. You must have a credit card and be at least 21 years of age — 25 with some companies — to rent a car. In summer you'll have no problem renting a car, but in winter during the heavy tourist traffic, we recommend that you rent a car before leaving the mainland.

Rates range from $35 to $75 a day; remember to use coupons and ask about special promotions. Some agencies offer additional discounts for booking via the Internet. Car-rental companies include **Budget** (☎ 800-527-0700, 345-949-5605), **Cico Avis** (☎ 800-331-1212, 345-949-2468), **Coconut** (☎ 345-949-4377), **Economy** (☎ 345-949-9550), **Hertz** (☎ 345-949-2280), **Soto's 4 x 4** (☎ 345-945-2424), and **Thrifty** (☎ 800-367-2277, 345-949-6640).

Most firms have a range of models, from compacts to Jeeps to minibuses. Divers who are staying a bit farther afield and have gear to haul will definitely need a larger vehicle; we suggest a Jeep or van with plenty of sprawl room. Whatever kind of car you choose, you're sure to encounter lots of other people who've rented the exact same model. Put something in your car window so that you'll be able to distinguish your car easily. Otherwise, you may find yourself staring at a sea of small, white, four-door Toyotas.

Everyone drives on the left side of the road — British style — and the steering wheel is on the right, so when pulling out into traffic, look to your right. The car's setup may be slightly different in other ways, too. The local joke is to watch out for tourists with their windshield wipers on, because they're about to make a turn.

When you get away from the airport and heavy traffic along **Seven Mile Beach,** traffic thins out and driving is simple. You can't get lost, because you'll travel Grand Cayman's one main road, a route that offers a few little offshoots. George Town has several one-way streets marked with international signs. Ask the rental agent to show you what the signs look like.

If you're behind a bus that stops to let off passengers, be sure to stop or you may run over a fellow traveler — the exit doors swing out into traffic. Always watch for pedestrians; Grand Cayman attracts visitors from around the world, and you never know what the pedestrian rules are on their home turf.

You may want to tour the island for a day; you won't need more than that for a complete tour. For that day, rent a car — unless picking up local history and color from a taxi driver, who will gladly serve as a guide, is really important to you. If you tour by taxi, though, the tab will likely exceed what you'd pay for a one-day car rental.

On foot

If your accommodations are in the midst of Grand Cayman's Seven Mile Beach, your feet will get you where you need to go. You can walk to the shopping centers, restaurants, and entertainment spots along West Bay Road. **George Town** is small enough to see on foot.

By bicycle, moped, or motorcycle

Biking is popular on this flat, safe island where drivers tend to take it easy; bikes, mopeds, and motorcycles are good means to explore. When renting a motor scooter or bicycle, don't forget to wear sunscreen. Also remember to drive on the left. You can rent bicycles ($10–$15 a day) and scooters ($25–$30 a day) from **Bicycles Cayman** (☎ 345-949-5572), **Cayman Cycle** (☎ 345-945-4021), and **Soto Scooters** (☎ 345-945-4652). Some resorts also offer free bicycles.

Ask whether your speedometer is in kilometers per hour or miles per hour. They're often in kilometers, but the speed signs (circles with 25, 30, 40, or 50) are posted in miles per hour.

Staying in Style

Grand Cayman is a curious place. Although tourism is huge here, and its famous **Seven Mile Beach** (like Aruba's hotel strip) features a lineup of every type of hotel and condo imaginable, the island still manages to exude a certain laid-back charm. Maybe that's because its residents by-and-large have the security of wealth — they're glad you're vacationing here, but nobody's desperate for your money. In fact, Grand Cayman's wealth isn't based just on tourism. It's built on banking, and with the prices you pay for the privilege of staying on this island (unless you get a great low-season package or dive package), islanders may need to build more banks to hold all the dough rolling in.

This peaceful, safe, and upscale island takes all the work out of your vacation if you just want to hang at the beach or swim among the fishes. That's why it's a favorite with honeymooners, cruise-ship passengers, and seniors — despite warnings from previous visitors to "take half as many clothes as you think you'll need and twice as much money."

Families with young children have discovered that huge summer discounts make the cost of a week on this clean, safe island about the same as a week at Disney World. We've heard grousing from teens who are bored because of the dearth of nighttime activities. For families with young children, though, the gentle waters are ideal; your little wannabe mermaids and mermen won't be disappointed. Both the **Hyatt** and the **Westin** have strong children's programs.

Despite its British ways, Grand Cayman has veered toward being too Americanized for some tastes. In recent years, many fast-food chains, cutesy boutiques in restored buildings in **George Town** (the capital), and homogenized timeshares have increased the Florida-comes-to-the-Caribbean look. You can find local color, thanks to some of the quirky artists who live on the island, but you have to look for it.

You'll find about as broad a range of accommodations here — from big chains to condos, villas, and modest guesthouses — as on the much-larger islands of Puerto Rico, Jamaica, and St. Thomas. In fact, the Cayman Islands have more than 2,000 hotel rooms and an equal number of units in condos (timeshares), guesthouses, and dive lodges. You'll see tons of "For Sale" signs on the island, and you'll probably be pitched to buy a timeshare at least once if you're on the island for more than a day. A new wave of construction is going on, bringing even more timeshares and condos.

Because Grand Cayman doesn't have extensive nightlife, shopping, or even much sightseeing, you'll probably spend much of your time around the property at which you're staying. Therefore, the amenities and what your room, pool, and particular stretch of beach are like are very important.

Guesthouses may be some distance from the beach and short on style and facilities, but in addition to being a bargain, they're a great choice for families with older children. (With babies and toddlers, we'd stick to the hotels with established children's programs.) Some guesthouses have outdoor grills and picnic tables.

Most guesthouse owners don't accept personal checks or credit cards but do take reservations through **Friendly Management** (☎ 345-949-3900; Fax: 345-949-3944). This service can also describe and book most condominiums and villas on the islands. **Cayman Villas** (☎ 800-235-5888, 345-945-4144; Fax: 345-949-7471) and **Hospitality World Ltd.** (☎ 800-232-1034, 345-949-3458; Fax: 345-949-7054) are local agencies that make reservations.

Gays and lesbians often avoid this island, which has a reputation for homophobia (see Chapter 7 for better options).

Before you spring for a dive package upfront, make sure you know what you're getting with your bucks. Some dive operators are more geared toward experienced divers, whereas others are better suited to beginners.

The Top Resorts

The rack rates listed in this section are in U.S. dollars and are for a standard double room during high season (mid-Dec through mid-Apr), unless otherwise noted. Lower rates are often available during the off season and shoulder season (see Chapter 3 for more information on travel seasons and Chapter 6 for more on booking accommodations).

The Avalon Condominiums
$$$$$ Seven Mile Beach

One of the best condo options on Seven Mile Beach, the Avalon has one of the plum spots on the famed strand. We like the oversize tub and separate shower in the spacious bathrooms, as well as the tropical décor of the roomy units. It also has daily maid service except on Tuesday. The handsome property consists of 27 three-bedroom/three-bathroom units (15 of which are available to rent and book up fast; call at least six months in advance to avoid disappointment). All are located right on the Caribbean. Only a short distance from restaurants and a five-minute drive from George Town, the Avalon has style that's disappointingly rare on Grand Cayman. Each condo has a fully equipped open kitchen and a large, screened lanai overlooking the glorious beach. Fitness buffs are bound to be pleased with the tennis court, fitness center, swimming pool, and hot tub.

See map p. 246. West Bay Road (P.O. Box 31236). ☎ *345-945-4171. Fax: 345-945-4189.* www.cayman.org/avalon. *Rack rates: $740–$815 (higher at Christmas and Easter holidays). AE, MC, V.*

Grand Cayman Accommodations

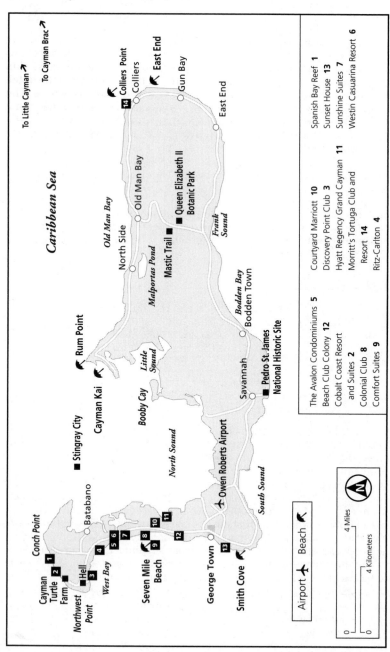

The Avalon Condominiums **5**
Beach Club Colony **12**
Cobalt Coast Resort
and Suites **2**
Colonial Club **8**
Comfort Suites **9**

Courtyard Marriott **10**
Discovery Point Club **3**
Hyatt Regency Grand Cayman **11**
Morritt's Tortuga Club and
Resort **14**
Ritz-Carlton **4**

Spanish Bay Reef **1**
Sunset House **13**
Sunshine Suites **7**
Westin Casuarina Resort **6**

Airport ✈ Beach ↖

Beach Club Colony
$$$$ Seven Mile Beach

About 4.8km (3 miles) north of George Town, the Beach Club — with its 41 rooms, built in the early 1960s — snagged one of the finer spots on Seven Mile Beach. Over the years, the Club has established a loyal following among divers who return year after year. Unfortunately, the cruise-ship day-trippers have also discovered the strand of beach in front of the hotel. So on days when the ships are in, you'll wish you were elsewhere. The center of activity is designed like a large colonial plantation villa with a formal Doric portico. A popular beach bar featuring Grand Cayman staples of calypso and rum draws both guests and outsiders. The resort has a dive shop on-site and offers all types of water sports.

See map p. 246. West Bay Road (P.O. Box 903G). ☎ *800-482-3483, 345-949-8100. Fax: 345-945-5167. Rack rates: $500 double. Ages 4–6 $25. Rates are all-inclusive. Children 3 and under stay free in parent's room; ages 7–12 $75 daily; ages 13–17 $103 daily. Honeymoon and dive packages available. AE, MC, V.*

Cobalt Coast Resort and Suites
$$$$ Boatswains Bay

Fans of this 18-room resort liken it to a bed-and-breakfast where most of the clients are deeply involved with diving. It's the best resort for divers on Grand Cayman. Don't expect a sand beach or any strong link to the glittery tourist scene of Seven Mile Beach, whose extreme northern terminus lies 4.8km (3 miles) to the south. The accommodations, ranging from oceanfront suites to standard rooms, are comfortable. Bedrooms are roomy, modern, cozy, and soothing, with Marimekko fabrics from Finland and European plumbing fixtures. On-site is an excellent restaurant called Dupplies, which offers light fare.

See map p. 246. 18 Seafan Dr., Boatswains Bay. ☎ *888-946-5656 or 345-946-5656 for hotel or 345-946-5658 for Divetech dive center. Fax 345-946-5657 for hotel or 345-946-5659 for dive center.* www.cobaltcoast.com *or* www.divetech.com. *Rack rates: $265 double, $305 one-bedroom suite for 2,$495 two-bedroom suite or villa for four. Many dive packages available. AE, DC, MC, V.*

Colonial Club
$$$$–$$$$$ Seven Mile Beach

Pretty-in-pink Colonial Club occupies a highly desirable stretch of Seven Mile Beach. The main appeal of these 24 standard condos, built in 1985, is the good upkeep and service of the neat-as-a-pin accommodations. The three-story building is conveniently located ten minutes from the airport and 6.4km (4 miles) north of George Town. Your choices are units with two bedrooms and three bathrooms or units with three bedrooms and three bathrooms. Besides a pool, you have a tennis court (lit at night) and Jacuzzi at your disposal. One drawback: It doesn't have an on-site restaurant.

See map p. 246. West Bay Road (P.O. Box 320W). ☎ *345-945-4660. Fax: 345-945-4839.* www.thecolonialclub.com. *Rack rates: $520–$580 apartment for two;*

$595–$665 apartment for three–four; $670–$750 apartment for five–six. Minimum stay five nights Dec 16–Apr 15. AE, MC, V.

Comfort Suites
$$$–$$$$ Seven Mile Beach

Streamlined, efficient, and cost-effective, this hotel, which opened in February 2000, is one of the more-modern lodgings along Seven Mile Beach. Rising five sand-colored stories near the southern end of the fabled beach, it follows a time-tested generic layout that has proven successful in hundreds of other Wyndham locations throughout North America. Bedrooms are outfitted in tones of blue and white, and each is standardized in a generic format that, while not particularly Caribbean, is nonetheless very comfortable. Unfortunately, none of the rooms have a balcony or veranda to let the light in. All 109 units have refrigerators, coffeemakers, and microwaves. One- and two-bedroom suites also contain stoves and dishwashers. On-site is **Don Foster's Dive/Scuba Centre.**

See map p. 246. West Bay Road. ☎ **345-945-7300.** *Fax: 345-945-7400.* www.cayman comfort.com. *Rack rates: $270–$375. 10 percent discount for booking online. AE, DISC, MC, V.*

Courtyard Marriott
$$$ Seven Mile Beach

This less-budget-busting option lies across the street from its portion of Seven Mile Beach. It's not within walking distance of restaurants and shopping, so the bad news is that you'll need to either take the bus or rent a car. The good news is that the beach here is wide and rock-free, with decent snorkeling and fine swimming. Best of all, the beach is typically not very crowded — yet. The rooms are basic but inviting (definitely request an oceanview). It has a full-service dive shop and two restaurants, e-mail and Internet access, and on-site laundry facilities.

See map p. 246. 1590 West Bay Rd. (P.O. Box 30364-SMB). ☎ **800-HOLIDAY** *(800-465-4329), 345-946-4433. Fax: 345-946-4434.* www.marriott.com. *Rack rates: $250–$290. AE, MC, V.*

Discovery Point Club
$$$–$$$$ Seven Mile Beach

This ultrasecluded complex, at the far north end of Seven Mile Beach in West Bay (9.6km/6 miles from George Town), has a white-sand beach and ideal snorkeling in the tranquil waters of **Cemetery Reef.** This place is great for families and often offers some good deals during the low season. The suites and villas are freshly redone with pastel colors and summery furniture. If you're the independent type who wants to stay far off the beaten path, you're assured a quiet spot here. There's no nightlife and no restaurant, so you'll need to rent a car. But what you do get is a screened patio, coin laundry, two tennis courts, a hot tub, and a beautiful pool.

See map p. 246. West Bay (Box 439). ☎ *800-327-8777, 345-945-4724. Fax: 345-945-5051.* www.cayman.org/discoverypoint. *Rack rates: $395 studio for two; $445 one-bedroom apartment for two; $495 two-bedroom apartment for four. AE, DISC, MC, V.*

Hyatt Regency Grand Cayman
$$$$–$$$$$ Seven Mile Beach

Hugging one of the best sections on famed Seven Mile Beach and housed in grand, low-slung British colonial–style buildings amid beautifully land-scaped gardens with tall royal palms, this elegant Hyatt Regency has no real competition on the island. Of the choices in this book, we'd put it in our top-20 for its great beach location, some of Grand Cayman's best restaurants (see later in the chapter), over-the-top water sports (the top-notch **Red Sail Sports** even caddies your gear for you), fantasy-inducing water oases (seven pools, a rooftop sun deck, a footbridge, and two swim-up gazebo bars), a full-service spa, two health clubs, and the breathtaking **Britannia Golf Club.** The international staff, attentive without being fussy, makes you feel like you're part of a fun global village. Guests in the Regency Club get VIP service, and you can also rent a villa or one of the beachfront suites (built to the tune of $15 million). The suites look out over the beautiful pool area and are mere feet from the beach.

The children's program is top-notch, but with the food and beverage prices here, we think a condo with kitchen facilities is a better choice for families. Under age 18, kids stay free if they share a room with their parents. This resort is more suitable for couples on a getaway or a honeymoon.

See map p. 246. West Bay Road (P.O. Box 1588). ☎ *800-233-1234, 345-949-1234. Fax: 345-949-8528.* www.hyatt.com. *Rack rates: $850 one-bedroom suite; $1,685–$2,185 two-bedroom suite. Additional fee for meal plans. AE, DC, DISC, MC, V.*

Morritt's Tortuga Club and Resort
$$$ East End

These plantation-style, three-story condos, about half timeshares, are just over 9m (about 30 ft.) from the water. The surrounding 3.2 beachfront hectares (8 acres) are on the idyllic East End, about 42km (26 miles) from the airport and known for some of Grand Cayman's best diving. Some people would say this location is isolated, and that's exactly what the clien-tele here is after. Nothing is within walking distance, unless you count the scuba diving, snorkeling, and windsurfing. A rental car is an absolute must. Home to **Tortuga Divers,** which offers resort courses, and **Cayman Windsurfing,** which offers snorkeling and windsurfing and rents sailing craft and catamarans, this well-managed complex is perfect for athletic types eager to get the most from the sun, sand, and surf in a laid-back atmosphere. The snorkeling off the dock here is idyllic thanks to a protec-tive outer reef just 0.4km (about a quarter-mile) offshore. One of the two pools has a swim-up bar and a waterfall. Each of the comfortably furnished one- and two-bedroom town houses — most facing one of two pools — has a fully equipped kitchen, but many guests eat at the restaurant on-site (where the food is pricey). The next closest restaurant is about 3.2km (2 miles) away.

Morritt's has a metered electricity charge, which averages about $50 extra for a week's stay (unless you do something silly like leave the sliding door open with the air-conditioning running).

See map p. 246. East End (P.O. Box 496GT). ☎ *800-447-0309, 345-947-7449. Fax: 345-947-7669.* www.morritt.com. *Rack rates: $195–$205 studio; $255–$285 one-bedroom apartment; $345–$385 two-bedroom apartment. AE, DISC, MC, V.*

Ritz-Carlton
$$$$$ West Bay Rd.

At long last and after many delays and setbacks, this prestigious hotel chain has opened a citadel of deluxe living in the Caymans. Fronting Seven Mile Beach, the 365-room Ritz-Carlton has become the island's most prestigious and glamorous address, even outpacing Hyatt.

Spanning 144 acres from Seven Mile Beach to North Sands, the resort is graced with such stellar features as a Greg Norman–designed golf course, children's programs designed by Jean-Michel Costeau, and even the world's first spa inspired by La Prairie's Silver Rain. Of its five restaurants, two are supervised by Eric Ripert of Le Bernardin, Zagat's number-one rated restaurant in New York.

You expect — and get — posh accommodations with comfortable, elegant, and most tasteful furnishings. All the rooms are blissful, but luxury living is found at The Reserve, an exclusive collection of two dozen oceanfront condos with large living and dining areas and vast terraces (units can be booked as one, two, or three bedrooms).

See map p. 246. West Bay Rd. ☎ *800-241-3333 or 345-943-9000. Fax 345-943-9001.* www.ritzcarlton.com. *Rack rates: $649 double; from $1,300 suite. Off season $349 double; from $1,250 suite. AE, DC, MC, V.*

Spanish Bay Reef
$$$$–$$$$$ North West Bay

This 67-room intimate resort — one of Grand Cayman's few all-inclusives — lies on a sliver of sandy beach in an isolated location amid the scrublands of the island's northwest tip. Rather informally run, the pale-pink, two-story stucco units are favorites with divers. The reef out front has a steep drop-off, which makes for superior diving and good snorkeling. Don't expect a lot of comfort. If you're seeking resort-style accommodations and extras, this place may not appeal to you. The accommodations, which are rather simple, have balconies or patios with garden- or oceanviews. Beds are comfortable, and bathrooms are a bit cramped but contain shower/tub combinations. The casual furnishings are in a Caribbean motif. Rates include all meals and beverages, island sightseeing, entertainment, bicycle use, intro-ductory scuba and snorkeling lessons, unlimited snorkeling or scuba diving from the shore (including tanks and weight belt), round-trip airport trans-fers, taxes, and service. If you're a diver, ask about **Certified Divers Packages** when making your reservations. Guests lounge around **Calico Jack's Poolside Bar** and later enjoy an array of food (with lots of fish) in the Spanish Main Restaurant.

See map p. 246. North West Bay (P.O. Box 903). ☎ *800-482-3483, 345-949-3765. Fax: 345-945-1842.* www.caymanresortsonline.com/spanishbay. *Rack rates: $230–$280 per person double. Children under 12 each $50 when staying in parent's room. Rates are all-inclusive. AE, MC, V.*

Sunset House
$$–$$$ Seven Mile Beach

Low-key describes this spartan diver's resort with 58 rooms — okay, so they look like 1950s-era strip motels — on the ironshore (sharp, hard, cal-cified black coral) south of George Town and about 6.4km (4 miles) from Seven Mile Beach. Some rooms have kitchenettes, and all contain data-ports and e-mail access. The congenial staff, a happening bar, and a top-notch seafood restaurant match with the full-service dive operation (including six dive boats) to make this place popular with scuba divers. Full dive services include free waterside lockers, two- and three-tank dives with a fleet of six dive boats, and use of the excellent Cathy Church's Underwater Photo Centre. Perhaps to make up for not being on the beach, the hotel has two pools (one right by the sea), plus a whirlpool. It's a five-minute walk to a sandy beach and a ten-minute walk to **George Town.** All-inclusive dive packages are the way to go here with great rates via **Cayman Airways** and **American Airlines.**

See map p. 246. South Church Street (P.O. Box 479). ☎ *888-854-4767, 345-949-7111. Fax: 345-949-7101.* www.sunsethouse.com. *Rack rates: $175–$310 double. Meal plans available for extra charge. Dive packages available. AE, DISC, MC, V.*

Sunshine Suites
$$$ West Bay Rd.

Built in 1998 on a flat-as-a-pancake stretch of scrubland that requires a five-minute trek to the beach, this is a well-designed 132-unit compound. It evokes either a private country club or a condo complex, depending on your point of view. Both inside and out, the design reflects British colonial architecture. Each of the units has its own kitchenette, so many guests pre-pare their meals on-site, avoiding the high cost of many of the nearby restaurants. Each of the accommodations is equipped with a midsize pri-vate bathroom with tub and shower. Nestled in the compound's center are a handful of gazebos and the resort's simple restaurant, the Sunshine Grill.

See map p. 246. 112 West Bay Rd. ☎ *877-786-1110, 345-949-3000. Fax 345-949-1200.* www.sunshinesuites.com. *Rack rates: $240–$305 double. Rates include conti-nental breakfast. AE, MC, V.*

Westin Casuarina Resort
$$$$–$$$$$ **Seven Mile Beach**

Like the Hyatt, the low-slung Westin has 213m (700 ft.) on palm-fringed Seven Mile Beach. This beautiful and large (343-room) British Caribbean–style resort, which we'd rate second to the Hyatt, occupies one of the better stretches of Seven Mile Beach. A full-service spa is an attractive feature. The staff is cheerful and energetic. Like many other hotels on Grand Cayman, the Westin offers a plethora of water sports including scuba diving through **Red Sail Sports.** You'll find a challenging 18-hole golf course across the street, as well as a salon and a spa. **Camp Scallywag** is available for kids ages 4 to 12. Bright, airy rooms (on the small side) with private balconies face either the Caribbean or the lovely gardens. This elegant resort is one of those places where the sea view is worth the extra money. Two free-form pools with a happening swim-up bar, and poolside decks (465 sq. m/5,000 sq. ft. of them) are appealingly lined with palm and date trees. Cruise-shippers sometimes try to crash the scene. If you love the nightlife, you aren't going to love the Westin. This resort is the kind of place where everybody goes to bed early. If you haven't slept in Westin's Heavenly Bed, though, you're in for a treat.

See map p. 246. Seven Mile Beach Road (Box 30620). ☎ *800-WESTIN-1 (800-937-8461), 345-945-3800.* www.westin.com. *Rack rates: $349–$499 double; from $1,050 suite. AE, MC, V.*

Dining Out

Dining out on Grand Cayman can put a serious dent in your budget, so consider whether some sort of meal plan at your hotel makes sense for you. You can easily blow $20 or more per person at breakfast. To cut costs, many people buy groceries on the island and cook for themselves in their condos — some even bring groceries from home. The island has several fast-food chains, too, if you aren't looking for anything fancy.

For fast, low-cost Internet, hot coffee, and good cheesecake, head to **Café del Sol** (Marquee Shopping Centre, Harquail Bypass; ☎ **345-946-2233;** www.cafedelsol.ky). Lunch prices are $4 to $6.

For the best and cheapest hearty brunch (opens at 10 a.m.) on the island, head to **Fidel Murphy's Irish Pub Restaurant,** Queens Court Plaza, Seven Mile Beach, West Bay Road (☎ **345-949-5189**), which has an Irish breakfast with bacon, sausage, tomato, black-and-white pudding, baked beans, and two fried eggs for $8.95.

Despite the high prices and British influence, you don't have to spend money on fancy duds for dinner. Casual attire is suitable at most places.

Enjoying a Taste of Grand Cayman

In culinary schools, students are sometimes asked to create a meal with a box of miscellaneous ingredients — in a limited amount of time. Many days, chefs on Grand Cayman are forced to perform that same drill. The small coral island doesn't produce much in the way of fresh fruits and vegetables. About the only fruit around here is *las frutas del mar:* fish, conch, lobster, turtle, octopus, and squid.

Although the local ingredients may be limited, your restaurant choices aren't. Like Aruba, this small island boasts a surprising number of restaurants — more than 200 all told — featuring everything from Caribbean classic to New World, Thai, Asian, and American cuisine.

Using what they have on hand, Caymanian cooks have created their own distinctive cuisine, which prominently features a version of conch fritters, spicy pepperpot soup, Cayman patties (filled with lobster, chicken or other meat, or vegetables), fish "rundown" (fresh catches simmered in coconut milk), and the national dish, turtle stew. (Turtle, which tastes somewhat like beef and is slightly chewy, is farmed here.) Local lobster is in season from summer's end until January.

The Best Restaurants

Bamboo
$$$$ Seven Mile Beach   SUSHI/JAPANESE

The hippest thing to hit Grand Cayman in a long time is this swank sushi joint where a sushi master presides over the festivities like an MTV host. The handsome wait crew pads around in sleek, all-black attire, and appears just as you need the next rainbow roll. In a room with walls paneled in warm woods and with recessed colored lighting, the chef cheerfully turns out the most succulent sushi and sashimi. We especially like the *white snake,* a special hand roll with barbecue freshwater eel, cucumber, tobiko, and thinly sliced avocado. The drink of the house is *sakatini* — sake-meets-martini. Try the *red dragon* (vodka, plum sake, and cranberry juice). Every Wednesday night Hi Tide plays live from 6:30 to 10:30 p.m.

See map p. 254. In the Hyatt Regency, West Bay Road. ☎ *345-949-1234. Reservations recommended. Main courses: $21–$29. AE, DISC, MC, V. Open: Daily 5:30 p.m.–1 a.m.*

Chicken! Chicken!
$ Seven Mile Beach   CARIBBEAN CHICKEN

Known as one of the best values on the island for tasty Caribbean-style wood-roasted chicken, this superbusy little shop offers daily lunch specials until 3 p.m. that give you an entire meal for $7 to $10. It's the

Grand Cayman Dining

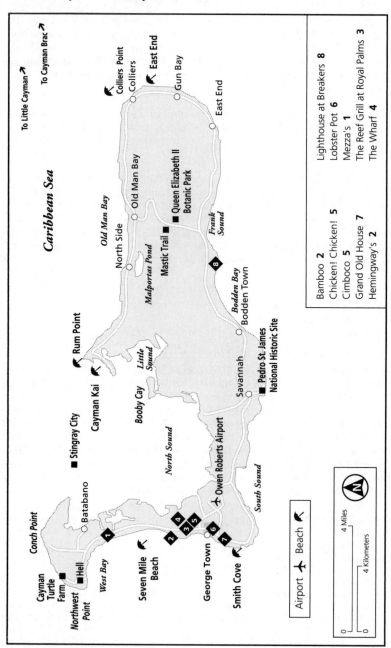

To Little Cayman ↗

To Cayman Brac ↗

Caribbean Sea

Colliers Point
Colliers
East End

Gun Bay

East End

Old Man Bay

Old Man Bay

Queen Elizabeth II
Botanic Park

North Side

Frank Sound

Mastic Trail ■

Malportas Pond

8

Bodden Bay
Bodden Town
Bodden Town

Rum Point

Little Sound

Savannah

Pedro St. James
National Historic Site

Cayman Kai

■ Stingray City

Booby Cay

North Sound

Owen Roberts Airport ✈

South Sound

Conch Point

Batabano ○

Cayman
Turtle
Farm ■ ■ Hell

Northwest
Point

West Bay

Seven Mile
Beach

2

3 5
4   5
6
7

George Town

Smith Cove

Bamboo **2**
Chicken! Chicken! **5**
Cimboco **5**
Grand Old House **7**
Hemingway's **2**

Lighthouse at Breakers **8**
Lobster Pot **6**
Mezza's **1**
The Reef Grill at Royal Palms **3**
The Wharf **4**

Airport ✈ Beach ↖

N

0 ——— 4 Miles
0 ——— 4 Kilometers

Caribbean's answer to Boston Market, but lots better. The chicken is marinated in citrus and herbs, and then slow roasted. Sides include jicama coleslaw, sweet tarragon carrots, buttermilk mashed potatoes, and several other good dishes. Takeout makes the perfect solution when you want a picnic lunch for beach hopping.

See map p. 254. West Shore Centre. ☎ *345-945-2290. No reservations needed. Complete meal: $7–$10. AE, DISC, MC, V. Open: Daily 11 a.m.–10 p.m.*

Cimboco
$ Seven Mile Beach   CARIBBEAN

The exhibition-style kitchen of this place — dolled up in Caribbean brights — turns out creative fire-roasted pizzas, Caribbean-style sandwiches (roti and jerk chicken), rustic pastas, and simply prepared catch-of-the-day seafood, all well priced. The appetizers are equally as creative: plaintain-wrapped callaloo with a Cayman sauce and coconut- or Caribbean fire-roasted shrimp with local greens, bacon, tomatoes, and black-eyed peas. This restaurant offers some of the best bargains on Grand Cayman.

See map p. 254. Next to the Cinema, Seven Mile Beach. ☎ *345-947-2782. Reservations not accepted. Main courses: $8–$13. Sunday brunch: $8.50–$10. AE, MC, V. Open: Daily 7 a.m.–10 p.m. (until 11 p.m. on Sat); Sun brunch 11 a.m.–3 p.m.*

Grand Old House
$$$$ George Town   CARIBBEAN/NEW WORLD

Although the dining scene on Grand Cayman has changed considerably in the last few years, this Grand Dame, set in a former early-20th-century plantation house where legend has it that you can spot a *duppy* (island-speak for "ghost"), still lives up to its own legend. Reserve a romantic table in one of the seaside gazebos with fans swirling lazily overhead. Chef Mathai, who counts presidents and royalty among his guests, adds Caribbean flair to his fun-to-read menu with offerings like Cayman-style turtle steak in spicy tomato sauce with Bermuda onions and bell peppers, or baked shrimp "Grand Old House" with local herbs, white wine, and hollandaise sauce with a mousseline potato ring. The starter can be the classic conch fritter or something a little more exotic like terrine of fresh foie gras and smoked wild boar. He's equally good with both.

See map p. 254. 648 S. Church St. ☎ *345-949-9333. Dinner reservations essential. Main courses: $20–$35. AE, DISC, MC, V. Open: Lunch Mon–Fri 11:45 a.m.–2 p.m.; dinner daily 6–10 p.m.*

Hemingway's
$$$$$ Seven Mile Beach   NOUVELLE CARIBBEAN

We love the amber glow emanating from this romantic, right-on-the-beach place with French doors giving view to the sea beyond. Diners don elegant resort wear for this retreat where the air-conditioning is welcome after a day in the sun. A classical guitarist serenades diners. The paella with broiled Caribbean lobster and pan-fried snapper with vanilla sweet-potato cake, goat cheese, and thyme brûlée are winners. If you want a tropical drink, try the Seven Mile Meltdown, with dark rum, peach schnapps, pineapple juice, and fresh coconut. Or sample the Papa Doble, a daiquiri fashioned like those Hemingway preferred in Havana. Some grouse about the high prices here, but you'll find the experience, the food, and the price you pay comparable to other restaurants we recommend. At lunch the salads are generous and well priced.

See map p. 254. West Bay Road, on the beach in the Hyatt complex. ☎ *345-949-1234. Reservations required. Main courses: $28–$36. AE, DC, DISC, MC, V. Open: Daily 11:30 a.m.–2:30 p.m. and 6–10 p.m.*

Lighthouse at Breakers
$$$ Breakers   CARIBBEAN/ITALIAN/SEAFOOD

On the south shore of the island, this local landmark lies about a 25-minute drive from George Town. Its creative menu features mainly fresh local seafood. A well-trained chef, backed up by a skilled staff, offers well-prepared meals, attracting both locals and visitors. Ask for a table with an oceanview and sit back to enjoy such tempting appetizers as portobello mushroom carpaccio with Gorgonzola or tuna sushi rolled in sesame seeds. For your main course, opt for the tender veal chop topped with Gorgonzola and pancetta, or else a mixed seafood grill in a lemon-butter sauce. The pastas are good; fettuccine Mediterranean with seasonal vegetables is a particular favorite. The restaurant has one of the best wine cellars on island.

See map p. 254. Breakers. ☎ *345-947-2047. Reservations recommended. Main courses: $18–$50. AE, DISC, MC, V. Open: Daily 11:30 a.m.–3:30 p.m. and 5:30–10 p.m.*

Lobster Pot
$$$ George Town   SEAFOOD/INTERNATIONAL

Though not as good as Hemingway's, Lobster Pot is still an island favorite. It overlooks the water from its second-floor perch at the western perimeter of George Town, near what used to be Fort George. True to its name, it offers lobster prepared in many different ways: Cayman style, bisque, and salad. Braised jerk chicken, turtle steak, and stuffed Chilean salmon are also on the menu. Sometimes the seafood is a bit overcooked, but most dishes are right on the mark. The place is also known for its prime beef steaks. For lunch, you might like the English fish and chips or perhaps lobster quesadillas or a pasta dish. The Lobster Pot's wine bar is a pleasant place for a drink.

See map p. 254. N. Church St. ☎ *345-949-2736. Reservations recommended in winter. Main courses: Lunch $8.75–$30, dinner $24–$43. AE, MC, V. Mon–Fri 11:30 a.m.–2:30 p.m.; daily 5–10 p.m.*

Mezza's
$$ West Bay Rd. INTERNATIONAL

Hip, breezy, and urban, this restaurant sits one floor above a landmark liquor store and microbrewery (Big Daddy's and the Old Dutch Brewery). Much of the beer produced at the brewery is sold within Mezza's. This is a venue that you might expect to encounter in South Beach, Miami. Mugs of Old Dutch beer come in at least six shades ranging from pale to dark amber. Lunches are simple, featuring steak sandwiches, burgers, Caesar salads, and seafood pasta. The dinner menu is more artful, with dishes that include sautéed shrimp with wine sauce and asparagus, grilled sword-fish with papaya salsa, sautéed lobster with curry-flavored cream sauce, marinated conch, and fettuccine with jerk chicken. It's estimated that 90 percent of the diners here order the caramel pecan fudge cake, claiming "it's to die for." Most dishes are priced at the lower end of the scale.

See map p. 254. West Bay Rd., above Big Daddy's Liquor Store. ☎ *345-949-8511. Reservations recommended. Main courses: $19–$38. AE, DC, MC, V. Mon–Sat 11 a.m.–10 p.m.*

The Reef Grill at Royal Palms
$$$ Seven Mile Beach SEAFOOD

The current hot spot for dining and one of our top-five picks on the island, the seaside Reef Grill — where live local bands like CoCo Red play on the beach — has deservedly earned a reputation as one of the best places for spanking-fresh fish. The honey-soy-glazed sea bass with Thai curry and tuna sashimi over a rice cake with wasabi ponzu dipping sauce rate among our most memorable dishes from Grand Cayman. Meat eaters rave about the grilled rib-eye. Go with the coconut ice cream or mango sorbet for dessert. The wine list has 20 selections, and the service is top-notch. You can dine in the elegant, air-conditioned bistro with flickering candles and sconces, but we suggest a garden patio table where the mood is more casual.

See map p. 254. Seven Mile Beach (between the Hyatt and the Marriott). ☎ *345-945-6358. Reservations essential. Main courses: $21–$40. AE, DC, MC, V. Open: Mon–Sat 11 a.m.–3 p.m. and 6:30–10 p.m.*

The Wharf
$$$$$ Seven Mile Beach CARIBBEAN/CONTINENTAL

About 3km (2 miles) north of George Town, the 375-seat Wharf has been everything from a dinner theater to a nightclub. Try to catch the tradi-tional 9 p.m. feeding of the tarpon, which are kept in a large tank on the premises — it's quite a show. The restaurant is decorated in soft pastels and offers dining inside, out on an elevated veranda, and on a beachside terrace. The sound of the surf mingles with music from the strolling Paraguayan harpist and pan flute player and chatter from the Wharf's Ports of Call Bar. Many diners wisely begin with the blue crab and shrimp salad with cucumber and mango or the golden fried Caribbean lobster cake with a roasted corn relish. Main dishes are a delight, especially the basil and pistachio-crusted seabass in a creamy champagne sauce or the grilled turtle and lobster pie with rice and vegetables. A local favorite is the pork tenderloin Tortuga marinated with cumin and coriander and served with a dark rum sauce. The kitchen makes a laudable effort to break away from typical, often dull menu items — for the most part, they succeed.

See map p. 254. West Bay Road, Seven Mile Beach. ☎ *345-949-2231. Reservations recommended. Main courses: $25–$38. AE, MC, V. Open: Daily 6–10 p.m. Also Dec–Mar daily 11:30 a.m.–2:30 p.m.*

Enjoying the Sand and Surf

Besides scuba diving, Grand Cayman is noted for other water sports such as windsurfing and deep-sea fishing, as well as for golf and decent shopping.

Combing the beaches

Grand Cayman's **Seven Mile Beach** — one of the Caribbean's finer bands of sand — begins north of George Town. This famed stretch, which is actually only 9km (5½ miles) long (but who's counting?), boasts sparkling white sand edged by casuarina pines and a variety of palms. Toward the southern end, the landscape becomes quite rocky. Low-rise deluxe resorts, condos, and small hotels are strung all along the beach, much like Aruba's immensely popular but crowded Palm Beach.

The surf is that milky teal color that invites you to loll on a raft. You don't have to worry about being swept out to sea, either. The wave action along this beach mirrors the calm of the island, and the bath-warm water barely laps at your ankles.

Thankfully, you don't have to be a guest at a particular hotel to use the beach, and you're welcome to use the beach bar and toilet facilities at most spots. Note, however, that the Hyatt gets understandably persnickety about nonguests overtaking its pools and beach chairs. And Hyatt security can spot nonguests a mile away. (For starters, you won't have the plush Hyatt-issued blue beach towel tucked under your arm.)

Be discreet if you're not a registered guest and you decide to venture beyond a hotel's beach bar or toilet facilities. We don't recommend trying to use the pool at a place where you're not staying; however, if you eat lunch at the hotel restaurant, that's your ticket to splash in the pool if you want.

About the only time Seven Mile Beach gets crowded is when the cruise ships dock; no more than 6,000 passengers are allowed per day, but that's still a lot of folks. You'll never see the crush of people you find on the most popular beaches on Puerto Rico or Aruba, though. You also don't have to worry about vendors asking to braid your hair or inviting you to toss out the toll for cheap jewelry and tie-dyed T-shirts like you do in Jamaica or Puerto Rico. And panhandling is outlawed, so forget about being hassled. In fact, Grand Cayman, with one of the lower crime rates in this hemisphere, is among the few islands where we could actually visualize ourselves napping on the beach without worrying about what would be gone when we woke up. Of course, the annoying buzz of Jet Skis plying the waters off Seven Mile Beach makes snoozing unlikely.

The rockier beaches on the **East and North Coasts,** a good 20- to 30-minute drive, are protected by an offshore barrier reef and offer good snorkeling. They're much less congested, and their reefs are in better shape than Seven Mile Beach, which has suffered from its popularity. On the **Southwest Coast** you can find small sandy beaches, but they're better for sunning than snorkeling because blankets of ribbonlike turtle grass have proliferated in the water.

Playing in the surf

Water sports in the Cayman Islands — diving, fishing, swimming, and water-skiing — are among the finest in the Caribbean.

Diving right in

Grand Cayman, ringed by glorious coral reefs teeming with marine life, has earned its reputation as a world-class diving destination. Underwater visibility often exceeds 30m (98 ft.) in these crystalline teal waters where you can indulge your Jacques Cousteau fantasies at more than 130 sites — everything from wall dives and wreck dives to cave dives, coral garden dives, and shore dives. The island has won kudos from every diver's publication and is the Caribbean's premier dive spot.

Grand Cayman's diving is literally a mountaintop experience. The coral island sits at the top of an underwater mountain, the side of which — known as the **Cayman Wall** — plummets straight down for over 152m (500 ft.) before becoming a steep slope falling away for 1,828m (6,000 ft.) and eventually plunging 7,010m (23,000 ft.) to the ocean floor.

You may have heard rumors that Grand Cayman isn't what it used to be and that the popular dive sites have been overrun. We're happy to report that you can still find gorgeous corals, diverse marine life, and great wall diving, but if you want more-pristine diving, you need to go to the east or north of the island. Sadly, the diving hordes have damaged the corals, particularly to the west of the island.

Divers seem to be everywhere. (When a tiny island has more than 60 dive operators, what do you expect?) But thanks to the good practices of the professional operators and conservation efforts, the diving experience here rates a definite thumbs-up. (The Grand Cayman operators make sure divers' professed expertise really is up to snuff and that a diver has a current card from one of the national diving schools.)

If something does go wrong during a dive, the island has a decompression chamber; local doctors can successfully treat most cases of decompression sickness (or "the bends").

Taking a scuba course

If you've never tried scuba diving, Grand Cayman is the ideal place to get your feet wet. You can take a *resort,* or introductory, course in the morning and make your virgin dive that afternoon. You don't have to worry about strong currents, and the (usually) patient dive instructors are used to dealing with beginners. A resort course allows you to sample the sport (which is expensive) without committing to the much more costly and lengthy process of getting certified.

One resort course designed to teach the fundamentals of scuba to beginners who already know how to swim costs $140. It requires a full day: You spend the morning doing some classroom work and learning skills in the pool, and in the afternoon you take a one-tank dive. All necessary equipment is included. Contact **Bob Soto's Diving Ltd.** (☎ **800-262-7686,** 345-949-2871) or **Red Sail** (☎ **877-733-7245,** 345-945-5965; www.redsail cayman.com) at the Hyatt or Treasure Island Resort.

If you aren't in good physical shape, or if you have a great deal of anxiety about the prospect of being under the sea, we don't recommend a resort course. Unless you're the type who catches on quickly, you'll feel pushed, and we wouldn't want a bad initial experience to sour you on a great sport. If you have any sort of medical condition that may preclude you from diving, such as high blood pressure, frequent ear infections, or sinusitis, you need to obtain clearance from a doctor on the island who specializes in dive medicine. The dive shop will give you a referral.

If you're interested in becoming a certified diver, we strongly urge you to do all your coursework at home. Otherwise, you may be certifiable after you realize how much precious beach and dive time you have to waste. Your local YMCA probably teaches a certification course with necessary pool work. Then you can simply do your checkout dives on Grand Cayman and get official.

Peeking into an underwater world

Snorkeling on Grand Cayman allows you to see much of the same scenery as diving, thanks to the incredible clarity of the water. More than 400 species of fish and more than 100 species of coral have been identified in these reefs. Popular spots where you can snorkel right off the beach include the **West Bay Cemetery Reef, Public Beach, Wreck of the *Cali*, Smith's Cove, Devil's Grotto,** and **Eden Rock.**

The snorkeling is excellent off the North Coast. Many fish have taken to the Russian warship that was scuttled offshore. (Look for the beautiful queen angelfish that make their home between two of the guns.)

If you book a tour to **Stingray City,** which is 3.2km (2 miles) east of Grand Cayman's northwestern tip, forget walking shoes — you need your swimsuit. At this unusual underwater attraction (accessible via an easy dive in the 3.6m-deep, or 12-ft., waters of North Sound or by snorkeling across the surface), you'll see hordes of graceful creatures. We absolutely love this place. Seeing all these beautiful creatures flitting about is surreal.

In the mid 1980s, when local fishermen cleaned their catches and dumped the leftovers overboard, they noticed swarms of southern stingrays (which usually eat marine crabs) feeding on the debris, a phenomenon that quickly attracted local divers and marine zoologists. Today, between 30 and 70 relatively tame stingrays hover for daily handouts of squid from increasing hordes of snorkelers and scuba enthusiasts.

All the dive operators listed in the previous section offer snorkeling trips, but one of our favorites is **Captain Marvin's Water Sports** (☎ 866-978-0022, 345-945-6975; Fax: 345-945-5673; www.captainmarvins.com). Octogenarian Captain Marvin Ebanks, who's been in business since 1951 and who unofficially founded Stingray City, is still operating an all-day snorkel tour of the north shore, taking guests out on his 40-passenger *Miss Jackie* every day except Sunday. The boat leaves at 9 a.m. for Conch Point, where you can see live queen conch (pronounced *conk* — as in what you'll get on the head if you try to remove any of these shells). The second stop is at a colorful shallow barrier reef. Lunch is Caymanian fare on Kaibo Beach. After lunch, it's full-speed ahead to Stingray City, with a final stop at Coral Gardens. The price is $63 for ages 12 and older, $31 for ages 4 to 11, and free for children under age 4.

Captain Sterlin Ebanks of **Stingray City Charters** (☎ 345-949-9200; www.stingraycitycharters.com) gives a three-hour Stingray City snorkel trip, which stops at Stingray City, Coral Garden, and the shallow barrier reef. For $39, you get snorkeling equipment, drinks, and a free pickup across from the Waterfront Center. Ages 4 to 11 are half price and children under 3 are free. Trips depart daily at 9:30 a.m. and 1:30 p.m.

Reeling in adventure

Sport fishermen come to Grand Cayman from all over the world for a chance at reeling in one of the big ones: tuna, wahoo, and marlin. Most hotels can make arrangements for charter boats; experienced guides are also available. **Red Sail Sports,** in the Hyatt regency Cayman on West Bay Road (☎ 877-733-7245), offers deep-sea fishing excursions in search of wahoo, tuna, marlin, on a variety of air-conditioned vessels with an experienced crew. Tours depart daily at 7 a.m. and noon, last half a day, and cost $700 (a full day goes for $900). The fee can be split among four to six people.

Navigating the waves

The best-known water-skiing outfitter is **Red Sail Sports** in the Hyatt Regency Cayman on West Bay Road (☎ **877-733-7245,** 345-949-8745). Water-skiing outings are $75 per half-hour, with the cost divided among several skiers. Parasailing, which yields a great view of George Town, is $60 per ride. You can find other outfitters at the **Westin Casuarina** (☎ **345-949-8732**), **Red Sail Sports at Rum Point** (☎ **345-947-9203**), and the **Marriott Grand Cayman Beach Resort** (☎ **345-949-6343**), all charging comparable prices.

Speed freaks looking for some thrills will be glad to know that Jet-Skiing is allowed off Seven Mile Beach, where you can skip over the surf at more than 48kmph (30 mph). You'll be several yards offshore. After a quick lesson in operating the watercraft and a review of some safety tips, you'll be on your way. Many islands have banned Jet Skis because of the damage they wreak on the reefs, not to mention the noise they produce. Check with your resort's front desk for the nearest water-sports operator offering Jet-Skiing — if you must.

Some Jet-Skiers ignore swimmers and divers in the area and come too close — we know you won't be that careless.

If you prefer a gentler approach to the waves, you can glide quietly along the water enjoying the warm Cayman breezes from your rented sailboat. Anchor in a shallow spot and snorkel or swim to cool off. Red Sail Sports rents 4.8m (16-ft.) Prindle catamarans for $32 per hour, depending on the time of day.

Climbing aboard

If you're yearning for a peek under the sea but don't want to dive, you still have plenty of options. *Atlantis XI* on Goring Avenue (☎ **345-949-7700;** www.atlantisadventures.net) is a $3-million submersible that's 20m (65 ft.) long, weighs 80 tons, and was built to carry 48 passengers. You can view the reefs and colorful tropical fish through 26 wide windows as the vessel cruises at a depth of 30m (100 ft.) through a coral garden maze. *Atlantis XI* dives Monday through Saturday; reservations are recommended 24 hours in advance.

You have two options when boarding the *Atlantis XI:*

- ✔ *Atlantis Expedition* lets you see the famous **Cayman Wall,** lasts an hour and a half (45 minutes underwater), and costs $84 for adults, and $42 for kids 91cm (36 in.) tall to 12 years old; no children under age 4 allowed.

- ✔ *Atlantis Odyssey* features such high-tech extras as divers communicating with submarine passengers by wireless underwater phone. The 45-minute dive costs $82 and is available on Wednesdays only.

Seaworld Explorer, which costs $32 for adults, is a semisubmarine that introduces viewers to the marine life of Grand Cayman. Children ages 4 to 12 are charged $16; younger children ride for free. The *Deep Explorer,* which takes two passengers, is a submersible that goes 182m (597 ft.) offshore and then drops to 243m (800 ft.) for $395 per person, or 305m (1,000 ft.) for $450 per person.

Exploring on Dry Land

Underwater delights are the main attraction on Grand Cayman, but sea-based exploration only scratches the surface of available activities on this island.

Wandering around George Town

The good news on Grand Cayman is that you can feel safe walking anywhere on the island. The bad news? You don't have much to look at in your wanderings. You can easily explore the tiny capital of George Town in an afternoon. About the most exciting thing here is the post office on Edward Street, where you can buy the beautiful and highly collectible stamps of the Cayman Islands.

Originally built as a house in 1833, the **Cayman Islands National Museum,** at Harbour Drive (☎ **345-949-8368**), was used as a courthouse, a jail (now the gift shop), a post office, and a dance hall before reopening in 1990 as a museum. It's a good entry point to the island's history and way of life. The museum is small but fascinating with good displays and videos that illustrate local geology, flora, and fauna. Admission is $5 for adults, $2.50 for seniors and children 7 to 12, and free for 6 and under; it's open Monday to Friday from 9 a.m. to 5 p.m. and Saturdays from 10 a.m. to 2 p.m. Last admission is 30 minutes before closing.

Pick up a walking-tour map of George Town at the museum gift shop before leaving.

Going to Hell and back

Hell really does exist on Grand Cayman. And we don't mean being caught on a dive boat on a rough day without Dramamine. On Grand Cayman, Hell is a surreal craggy landscape at the far northwest end of West Bay Beach Road, about a half-hour from George Town. When you've reached Hell, that's the end of the line. The area got that nickname in the 1930s thanks to the otherworldly rock formation of dolomite and limestone. Caymanians, always looking for a business opportunity, turned the natural sculpture into a tourist attraction. If you want to thrill your friends back home, the postmaster will stamp your postcard with "Hell, Grand Cayman" — a certain hit with those who envied your travel plans.

You'll only want to spend 15 minutes tops in Hell. The place doesn't offer much to do, and the biggest excitement is getting the postmarked proof that you've been there.

Ivan Farrington, the proprietor of the **Devil's Hangout Gift Shop,** dresses up like the demon himself. While you're buying your postcards, he'll crack lots of jokes about the place — "It's a hell of a town, isn't it? But it's hotter than hell here." He'll also tell you where to go when you leave.

The **Cayman Turtle Farm** (☎ 345-949-3894; www.turtle.ky), on Northwest Point near Hell, is the only green sea turtle farm of its kind in the world. At one time the islands had a multitude of turtles in the surrounding waters (which is why Columbus called the islands "Las Tortugas"), but today these creatures are sadly few in number, and the green sea turtle has been designated an endangered species (you can't bring turtle products into the United States). The turtle farm exists to provide the local market with edible turtle meat (preventing the need to hunt them in the wild) and to replenish the waters with hatchling and yearling turtles. Visitors today can observe 100 circular concrete tanks in which these sea creatures exist in every stage of development; the hope is that one day their population in the sea will regain its former status. Turtles here range in size from 170 grams (6 ounces) to 170 kilos (600 lbs.). At a snack bar and restaurant, you can sample turtle dishes. The turtle farm is open daily from 8:30 a.m. to 4:30 p.m. Admission is $7.50 for adults, $4 for children 7 to 12, and free for children age 6 and under.

Enjoying a dose of local history

At the end of a quiet, mango and mahogany tree–shaded road in Savannah, Grand Cayman (about a 20-minute drive from George Town), high atop a limestone bluff, lies one of the Caribbean's most spectacular historic restorations. The **Pedro St. James Historic Site** (☎ 345-947-3329) is a historically accurate reconstruction of a 1780 Great House, which was the birthplace of democracy in the Cayman Islands and its first national landmark. The visitor center offers a 20-minute film that gives a zippy overview of the Cayman Islands' 200-year history. Hours are 10 a.m. to 4 p.m. daily. Admission is $8 for adults, $4 for children 6 to 12 years old, and free for children under 6.

Hop in your rental car or onto the ferry at the Hyatt Regency dock and head to **Rum Point** on Grand Cayman's quiet north side, a favorite destination for residents and visitors alike. Experience island atmosphere the way it used to be (Rum Point was first documented on a 1773 map, and one can only speculate how it got its name) in a scenic spot known for its clear, calm waters and tall pines. Swim, snorkel, sink into a hammock (tough to snag during high season) or a lounge chair with a book, or try a glass-bottom-boat trip. **The Wreck Bar and Grill** (☎ 345-947-9412), a Rum Point landmark, serves lunch and frosty drinks at picnic tables on the beach.

Communing with wildlife

For a scenic walk, do it up royally at **Queen Elizabeth II Botanic Park** (☎ 345-947-9462) at Frank Sound Road on the North Side, about a 45-minute drive from George Town. The short trail (less than 1km/0.6 mile long) slices through 24 hectares (60 acres) of wetland, swamp, dry thicket, mahogany trees, orchids, and bromeliads. The trail is easy enough for children, and you can see it all in under an hour. You may spend two hours if you want to meander through the Heritage Garden and other new additions.

 Time your visit for early in the day when the animals are more active. You'll probably see *hickatees,* the freshwater turtles found only on the Cayman Islands and in Cuba. Occasionally you'll spot the rare Grand Cayman parrot or the anole lizard with its cobalt-blue throat pouch. Even rarer is the endangered blue iguana, but you can see 40 of them here. Your best chance to see them in motion is from 8:30 to 10:30 a.m. on a sunny day.

The park is open daily from 9 a.m. to 6:30 p.m.; last admission is at 5:30 p.m. Admission is $7.50 for adults, $5 for children, and free for children 5 and under.

A visitor center offers changing exhibitions, a good gift shop, and a canteen for food and refreshments. We like the **Heritage Garden** with its restoration of a traditional early-19th-century Caymanian home, garden, and farm, and its floral garden with one hectare (2½ acres) of flowering plants and traditionally grown fruit trees (mango, breadfruit, tamarind, plum, cherry, and ackee). Around the small lake you'll find many birds.

If you're more athletic and an eco-hound to boot, visit **Mastic Trail** (west of Frank Sound Road, a 45-minute drive from George Town). This restored 200-year-old footpath winds through a two-million-year-old woodland area leading to the North Sound. *Islands* magazine gave this site one of its top eco-preservation awards. Named for the majestic mastic tree, the rugged 3.2km (2-mile) trail showcases the reserve's natural attractions, including a native mangrove swamp, traditional agriculture, and an ancient woodland area, home to the largest variety of native plant and animal life found in the Cayman Islands.

 The hike isn't recommended for children under 6, the elderly, or persons with physical disabilities. Wear comfortable, sturdy shoes and carry water and insect repellent.

For $45 per person, you can take a 3½-hour guided tour of **Mastic Trail** that includes transportation and cold soft drinks. Tours are available Monday through Saturday at 8 a.m. and 1 p.m. For reservations, call ☎ 345-945-6588 Monday to Friday from 10 a.m. to 4 p.m.

Golfing Grand Cayman

Grand Cayman offers an unusual golf experience at the **Britannia Golf Club** (☎ 345-525-7901), next to the Hyatt Regency on West Bay Road. The course, the first of its kind in the world, was designed by Jack Nicklaus. It incorporates three different courses in one: a 9-hole championship layout, an 18-hole executive setup, and an 18-hole Cayman course. The last was designed for play with the Cayman ball, which goes about half the distance of a regulation ball.

The Britannia's greens fees run $80 for 18 holes and $60 for 9 holes. Cart rentals are included; club rentals are $20 for 9 holes and $30 for 18 holes.

Shopping the Local Stores

The duty-free shopping in **George Town** encompasses the types of luxury items that you'll also see in the USVIs: silver, china, crystal, Irish linen, and British woolen goods. Unfortunately, you'll also run into such local crafts as black coral jewelry. (We're disappointed to see this sold, especially on an island that relies on pristine corals to entice visitors.)

The prices on many items aren't that much better than in the United States. Our advice is to comparison shop before you come so you'll know if you're truly getting a deal. Don't purchase turtle products or any shells, because you can't bring them back into the United States.

Living It Up After Dark

Divers expend a lot of energy on their sport, plus some of them would rather see nature's nighttime light show on the coral reefs than hang out in a disco. So if you're looking for a cranking nightlife, you're on the wrong island.

Barhopping is about as crazy as it gets here, particularly during happy hour (usually from 5–7 p.m.). Watching the sunset and trying to see the mysterious green flash that people say they see on the horizon right at the moment the sun sizzles into the sea is the big entertainment. Bars close at 3 a.m. weeknights and at midnight on Saturday and Sunday nights (seems odd that the bar would close at midnight on Sat — but it's true). Many are shuttered on Sundays. For other options, look at the freebie magazine *What's Hot* or check the Friday edition of the *Caymanian Compass.*

Sports nuts who can't live without ESPN head to the **Lone Star Bar and Grill** (☎ 345-945-5175) on West Bay Road. Here, they can see sports events simultaneously on 15 different TV screens and sip lime and strawberry margaritas. This popular watering hole is a favorite gathering spot for local dive masters, too. Mondays and Thursdays are fajita nights — all-you-can-eat affairs. Tuesday is all-you-can-eat lobster night, virtually unheard of in the Caribbean. Whenever we're on Grand Cayman, we always head here for lobster night. The lobsters caught off the coast of the Cayman Islands tend to be exceptionally sweet and succulent.

Legendz, West Bay Road (☎ 345-945-1950), is a nice lounge bar with mahogany paneling, polished brass, and stiff drinks. Another good spot is the **Royal Palms Beach Club,** West Bay Road (☎ 345-945-6358), offering a bar open to the trade winds where you can dance the night away in the moonlight. Local bands play here Thursday, Friday, and Saturday nights.

A nightclub with dancing is **O bar** (☎ 345-943-6227), a sleek nightclub at Queen's Court lair on Seven Mile Beach.

Fast Facts: Grand Cayman

Area Code
The area code is **345**.

ATMs
ATMs are everywhere. What else would you expect on an island with more than 500 bank offices?

Babysitters
Hotels can readily help you arrange babysitting, but make arrangements as far in advance as possible because getting a babysitter at the last moment isn't always easy. Expect to pay at least $8 an hour.

Currency Exchange
Although the U.S. dollar is accepted everywhere, you'll save money if you go to the bank and exchange U.S. dollars for Cayman Island (CI) dollars, worth about U.S. $1.25 at press time. The Cayman dollar is divided into a hundred cents with coins of 1¢, 5¢, 10¢, and 25¢ and notes of $1, $5, $10, $25, $50, and $100 (no $20 bills). Prices are often quoted in Cayman dollars, so it's best to ask. You'll also be given change in Caymanian money. All prices quoted in this book are in U.S. dollars, unless otherwise noted.

Doctors
Healthcare on the island is excellent. Ask your hotel concierge for a referral or call professional Medical Centre at ☎ 345-946-6066.

Emergencies
For fire, police, and ambulance, call ☎ 911.

Hospital
The Cayman Islands Hospital, Hospital Road, George Town (☎ 345-949-8600), has a state-of-the-art accident and emergency unit, staffed 24 hours a day. It has a two-man double-lock hyperbaric chamber and is staffed on a 24-hour on-call basis by trained staff from the Cayman Islands Divers chapter of the British Sub Aqua Club. A doctor trained to treat diving injuries supervises the unit.

Information
See the Appendix for helpful Web sites and locations of local tourist offices.

Internet Access

Contact your hotel for information about Internet access.

Newspapers and Magazines

To find out what's happening on the island, check out any of the local newspapers: *Cayman Net News, Cayman Free Press, Ltd.,* or *Cayman Compass.*

Pharmacies

Try **Cayman Drug** at Kirk Freeport Centre, George Town (☎ 345-949-2597).

Police

In an emergency, call ☎ **911.**

Post Office

Post offices are generally open Monday to Friday from 8:30 a.m. to 5 p.m. and Saturday from 8:30 a.m. to noon. Beautiful stamps are available at the General Post Office in downtown George Town and at the philatelic bureau in West Shore Plaza.

Restrooms

Every public bar and restaurant in the Cayman Islands is required to provide clean and well-maintained restrooms for anyone in need. At beaches throughout the island, you can always find a bar or snack shack nearby with facilities that are available to the public. We usually try to buy a cold drink as part of the experience, just to be sociable. In-the-know Caymanians who spend significant time in George Town tell us that at least three public toilets are located within the densest concentration of stores and office buildings of central George Town: 1) within the south terminal of the cruise-ship docks on Harbour Street, 2) within the Public Library on Edward Street, and 3) near the corner of Cardinal Avenue and Harbour Drive, behind The Craft Market souvenir shop.

Safety

This island doesn't suffer from the crime that plagues some other Caribbean islands. You can walk wherever you want. Nonetheless, don't tempt fate: Don't leave valuables in plain sight in rental cars, be sure to lock your hotel room when you leave, and don't leave valuables unattended on the beach.

Frankly, Caymanians are law-and-order types. They're more concerned about you breaking the law than they are about islanders taking something or harming another person. Penalties for drunk driving or for drugs include jail time and large penalties.

One of the few dangers comes from the manchineel trees, which have fruit that look like little green apples. They're poisonous to touch. Even raindrops dripping from them can cause painful blisters if they hit your skin. Most of these trees are marked with a red ring on the trunk or a small warning sign. Warn your children not to touch the fruit.

Smoking

Smoking policies are left to the discretion of the individual establishments, and many restaurants have designated nonsmoking sections within their restaurants and bars. With so many open-air establishments, the natural ventilation of the trade winds helps resolve conflicts.

Taxes

All accommodations add a 10 percent government tax, and you'll encounter a departure tax of $25 when you leave the island.

Otherwise, you don't face any tax on goods or services. But most hotels and restaurants tack on a 15 percent service charge to your bill.

Taxis

Taxis are readily available from all resorts and from the taxi stand at the cruise-ship dock in George Town. A sign with current rates (set by the director of civil aviation) is posted at the dock.

Weather Updates

Check out the following Web sites: `www.weather.com` or `www.caymanislands.ky`.

Chapter 13

Jamaica

● ●

In This Chapter

▶ Knowing what to expect when you arrive
▶ Getting around the island
▶ Deciding where you want to stay
▶ Sampling the local cuisine at the best restaurants
▶ Scoping out good beaches and diving into water sports
▶ Satisfying the landlubber: Shopping and nightlife

● ●

*S*ailing around the lush coasts of Jamaica, Christopher Columbus got it right when he said, "It is the fairest island eyes have beheld; mountainous and the land seems to touch the sky." That was way back in 1494, but the words are still true today.

Except for the island of Grenada, Jamaica is the lushest island in the West Indies, its Blue Mountains reaching a peak at 2,225m (7,400 ft.). This land is one of countless cascading waterfalls (such as Dunn's River in Ocho Rios) and more than 150 rivers, the most fabled of which is the Rio Grande near Port Antonio on which you can go river rafting.

For such a relatively small landmass — about the size of the state of Connecticut — the terrain is widely varied, from tropical rain forests to an arid Southern Coast that evokes, in parts, an African savanna. Jamaica is blessed with some of the best sandy beaches in the Caribbean, most often golden, but sometimes white, and, on occasion, black volcanic sand (found on the South Coast).

No one knows exactly how many people inhabit the island of Jamaica, but estimates put the population at 2½ million, of which some 850,000 live in the capital of Kingston. Of these, some 95 percent claim Africa as their ancestral home.

Although dominated by persons of African descent, Jamaica has such a large polyglot population that its national slogan is, "Out of Many, One People." Thousands of Germans, Irish, Welsh, and English live on the island along with Chinese, Middle Easterners, and East Indians. The locals refer to Middle Easterners as "Syrian." The leader of the Jamaican Labour Party, Edward Seaga, a former prime minister, is Lebanese.

In the West Indies, Jamaicans are known for their sardonic wit and their humor, often using sarcasm as the ultimate putdown, especially of pretentious people. The humor is often lusty, tinged with sexual connotations.

Arriving at the Airport

Most resort-bound foreign visitors land at the **Donald Sangster International Airport** (☎ 876-952-3124), 3.2km (2 miles) east of the center of Montego Bay, the island's leading resort city. This airport not only serves Montego Bay itself, but all the other major resort cities, including Ocho Rios and Runaway Bay to the east, Negril to the southwest, and even such remote South Coast villages as Treasure Beach.

Visitors who seek more of an experience with Jamaican culture or who have business there wing into the **Norman Manley International Airport** (☎ 876-924-8452) at Kingston. The Kingston airport is also the closest to those planning a hiking tour of the Blue Mountains or a stay at the small North Coast resort city of Port Antonio.

Flying into Montego Bay

After you deplane on the tarmac in Montego Bay, you walk into the burning heat of the terminal of Jamaica's most efficient airport, which has been expanded and improved in recent years for your convenience. You head directly down a long, air-conditioned corridor to Jamaican Customs and Immigration.

Surprisingly, winter visitors often clear the rather thorough Jamaican Customs faster than summer visitors. The summer months are virtually homecoming months for Jamaicans living abroad. They often arrive with massive luggage, which local officials insist on probing thoroughly. The wait can seem endless, particularly if disputes arise about what Jamaicans are trying to bring back home.

With many exceptions, you can usually clear Customs in less than half an hour. While you wait, a live band will often serenade you with everything from reggae to calypso. At their desks, the Jamaican Tourist Board dispenses meager literature about the island. They supply plenty of coupons touting discounts at attractions, restaurants, bars, and car-rental outfitters.

After Customs and Immigration gives you the green light, a currency exchange office awaits you. Here is where you can exchange the Yankee dollar for the Jamaican dollar.

 U.S. money is widely accepted in Jamaica, although sometimes the Jamaican dollar comes in handy. We recommend that you exchange at least $100 into Jamaican dollars for those times you'll need the local coin of the realm.

The currency exchange kiosk at the airport offers better exchange rates than at most banks. Your hotel invariably offers the worst exchange rates. The airport has some ATMs, but don't count on these. Readers report that the machines are either out of order or out of cash.

 After you've secured your checked luggage, your problems aren't over yet. Guard it carefully both within the airport and when leaving the airport to get into some form of transport. Stolen luggage is a commonplace occurrence, so keep your eagle eye on alert.

Flying into Kingston

Montego Bay hosts the international Donald Sangster airport in the west of Jamaica, with the Norman Manley airport, 18km (11 miles) southeast of Kingston, receiving visitors to the eastern shores of Jamaica. Domestic flights — say, from Montego Bay to Kingston — fly into the smaller commuter airport, **Tinson Pen Airport** (☎ 876-923-0022), on the west side of Kingston.

The Norman Manley International Airport lies on the Palisadoes, a narrow strip of land that projects into the Caribbean Sea. After going through Customs and Immigration, you enter the main terminal.

On-site are rental desks for **Island Car Rentals** (covered later in this chapter) and **Jamaica Union of Travelers Association (JUTA),** the official taxi company for Kingston. The Jamaican Tourist Board operates a small kiosk here, which usually opens to meet major international flights and dispense *Discover Jamaica,* a booklet with an islandwide map.

 As in Montego Bay, keep your eye out for your luggage. Many visitors report having their luggage stolen after they clear Customs and during the time they're arranging ground transportation — either taxi or car — into the center of Kingston.

Getting from the airport to your hotel

After your luggage has been inspected at the Donald Sangster airport at Mo Bay (the nickname the locals use for Montego Bay), you're officially cleared to enter Jamaica. If you're staying at one of the megaresorts or the all-inclusives, chances are a hotel van will be waiting to take you to its grounds and check you in. Make sure you notify your resort of choice in advance before your arrival in Jamaica. The big resorts have desks at the airport where you can go, or look for your resort's name on a placard held up by a hotel van operator.

The attendant for the resorts will have a list of all the arrivals due in at the same time as you, and you won't roll until everyone has been accounted for. Baggage handlers will hoist your luggage onto the hotel bus or into the van. Tip them $1 per bag and watch to be sure that all your luggage makes it on the vehicle. This process for all passengers can take another 20 to 30 minutes.

If you're arranging to rent a car or hire a taxi, only deal with an official baggage handler with a badge. Don't hand your luggage over to just anyone who comes up to help you, or you may fall prey to the "Mo Bay hustle." The so-called porter could actually be a thief, and you'll never see your baggage again. Also, many pirate taxi drivers in unmarked and uninsured cars will try to hustle you into their vehicles. Don't go for it. You may leave the airport and head down some back street where a robber — prearranged with the "innocent" taxi driver — will suddenly emerge and steal your possessions from the pirate cab.

If you're staying at one of the smaller, more affordable hotels, you'll have to get to your destination on rented wheels. Use only taxis or buses operated by JUTA (☎ 876-957-4620). The union's emblem, a red license plate with the initials PPV (for "public passenger vehicle"), indicates an official cab. Unlike pirate cabs, these air-conditioned taxis are insured and licensed to carry you.

If you don't have prearranged transportation, an airport taxi dispatcher in front of the terminal holds a clipboard and arranges a ride to where you're going in the Greater Montego Bay area.

The best way to get to the center of Kingston from the Norman Manley Airport or Tinson Pen is aboard an officially sanctioned **JUTA Taxi** (☎ **876-957-4620**). The cost of the ride is about $22 per person from Norman Manley or $14 per person from Tinson Pen. No airport buses make this run.

Choosing Your Location

Nowhere else in the Caribbean will you find such an array of accommodations. Whatever your needs are, you can probably find a bed waiting for you in Jamaica at a price you can afford. You can live here for $30 a night or $1,000 a night — the choice is yours.

Honeymooners fly in by the planeload to stay at the all-inclusive mega-resorts, which were pioneered here before sweeping across the West Indies to such islands as St. Lucia. Some resorts cater to families; others, especially all the Sandals properties, to couples only, defining a loving duo as male and female. Some resorts, especially those in Montego Bay, attract the poshest and most demanding traveler. After staying at **Half Moon,** the first President Bush recommended it to Junior and his wife, Laura.

Jamaica also rents some of the grandest villas in the West Indies. Harrison Ford or Eddie Murphy may have warmed your bed before you checked in. Some beds for the night are found in funky shacks on the beach, others in palaces like the swank Ritz-Carlton at Mo Bay. And some places in Jamaica (not our recommendations) are so bone-bare that only the most die-hard backpacker doing Jamaica on $5 a day would contemplate a stopover.

Romantic bargains

Jamaican resorts such as SuperClubs or Sandals compete like Olympic athletes for the honeymoon, anniversary, or even "Romantic Duo" business. All these chain resorts are all-inclusives centered in Negril, Mo Bay, or Ocho Rios/Runaway Bay. Offerings can change from year to year.

SuperClubs (☎ 877-467-8737; www.superclubs.com) presents a wedding for free if you stay at one of its hotels. If you book a honeymoon package, the staff handles the paperwork of the actual wedding arrangements. If you book six nights, you get a seventh night free. A wedding cake, champagne, the flowers, and even a nondenominational marriage officer are part of the deal.

Also touting honeymoon packages, **Sandals** (☎ 800-SANDALS, or 800-726-3257; www.sandals.com) consistently wins as the "world's number-one all-inclusive honeymoon destination" from *Bride's* magazine. Sandals also features a package for renewal of marriage vows. Subject to change, prizes such as a free 20-piece Wedgwood china set is offered to couples who book for six nights or more. The basic wedding package is free, though restrictions may apply. This could represent a savings of up to $1,500.

If you're going to Half Moon in Mo Bay, you may want to take along a casually elegant collection of resort wear, especially for dining or entertainment at night, whereas if you're heading for a hedonistic resort in Negril, all you need to bring are a bathing suit, a bed sheet for toga night, and not a lot of luggage.

The largest concentrations of hotels are in Montego Bay, Negril, and Ocho Rios/Runaway Bay, with Port Antonio on the North Coast running a distant fourth. Most visitors don't venture outside these large resort cities, although a few offerings, such as **Jake's** on the Southern Coast or a Hilton stopover for a business or cultural trip to Kingston, are worth considering, depending on your interest. When you see what each resort city has to offer in the pages ahead, you can determine which place and location you're going to honor with your business.

Montego Bay

If you arrive like most visitors, your plane will land at the Donald Sangster airport outside Montego Bay, your gateway onto the troubled but fascinating island of Jamaica. The party crowd rushes through the airport and on to Negril in the southwest. Those who stay behind can sample Jamaica's second-largest city (Kingston is number one).

A cruise-ship mecca and a growing industrial base, Mo Bay is also the major resort city on the island, with more hotels, more restaurants, and more sightseeing attractions, especially on its periphery, than any other resort area. In that regard, it's rivaled only by Ocho Rios.

Montego Bay is the most cosmopolitan and sophisticated of the island's resort cities, and it has been ever since its touristic future was launched back in the 1940s when rich travelers came to test the spring-fed waters at **Doctor's Cave Beach,** still Mo Bay's number-one beach (see the section "Combing the beaches," later in this chapter).

Mo Bay never won any port city beauty contests, like the panoramic harbor at Charlotte Amalie on St. Thomas or the historic, restored old city of San Juan, Puerto Rico. The city is completely undistinguished architecturally, yet it's the center for exploring the most historic sights in western Jamaica. It also has some of the Caribbean's finest golf courses, dwarfing all other competition on the island. It offers the island's best shopping and opens onto a marine park of turquoise waters and underwater formations along its coral reef.

Kingston may be rioting and killing policemen, the countryside languishing in poverty, but Mo Bay puts on a smiling face for its visitors, the mainstay of its economy.

College students started coming to Mo Bay for spring break, but when word spread about the nudity and ganja smoking in Negril, they rushed to the Southwest.

Negril

Kick-back-'n-groove Negril, on the arid western tip of the island, is a 50-minute drive southwest of Montego Bay (usually a two-hour drive), but is a world apart. This once-sleepy fishing village was discovered by the hippies of the 1960s, who took to its ganja smoking and nudity, two cultural pastimes of that era that still flourish here. In those days, the counterculture press heralded Negril as a "groovy outpost," with no phones, no electricity, and plenty of free sex.

Culture clash: The Jamaican hustle

If you're going to walk along any resort in Jamaica on your own, chances are you'll acquire an unwanted companion or two. Hustlers hawking everything from ganja to sex, or offering their services as a "guide," attach themselves to you like those leeches that clung to Bogie in the film classic *The African Queen*. Getting rid of them can take some powerful persuasion on your part — a simple "no" rarely turns off these battle-hardened veterans. You may have to call one of the resort police (if you can spot one) to get rid of these uninvited walking companions.

Old reputations take a long time to die, and Negril still has somewhat of a '60s aura, especially at a handful of raunchy resorts such as **Hedonism II.** But another, more-sophisticated Negril exists, evoked by its first-class resorts that are bringing a more mature dimension to the city, even attracting the family trade.

 Negril's white-sand **Seven Mile Beach** is what put it on the tourist map in the '60s and keeps it there — that and three sheltered bays, including **Negril Harbour** (still nicknamed Bloody Bay from its whale-slaughtering days), **Orange Bay,** and **Long Bay.** Negril has few sightseeing attractions other than its Seven Mile Beach, which is all it needs.

You'll find two faces to Negril. The beachfront is home to the mega-resorts, which lie along **Norman Manley Boulevard.** This two-lane high-way is flanked by restaurants, shops, and hotels and is bordered by the seemingly endless sands, some of which are for nudists. The **West End,** the setting for the film *How Stella Got Her Groove Back,* lies south of Negril River and is a journey back to the resort's '60s heyday. Here the little inns are more intimate and raffish. Instead of a beach, visitors swim off the limestone cliffs honeycombed with caves.

As it moves deeper into the 21st century, Negril is improving and becoming more of a world-class resort city, although it's leagues away from overtaking Mo Bay in exclusivity. Negril has none of the world-class resorts that Mo Bay has — nothing like Half Moon (covered later in this chapter), for example.

 From the end of February through Easter weekend, thousands of students from America's East Coast colleges descend on Negril for one massive hell-raising good time. It's called "Don't Stop the Carnival," with action round-the-clock, including reggae concerts, wet T-shirt competitions, and dancing in foam flavored with piña colada, to name a few. If you're not a spring breaker, you may want to steer clear of Negril at this time. You'll be in the minority. "When the students leave," a local vendor, Cosmos, told us, "our fields are stripped of ganja, and all the Red Stripe beer and Appleton Rum are gone."

Ocho Rios/Runaway Bay and Port Antonio

A trio of resort areas lures visitors to the lush North Coast of Jamaica, which records far more rainfall than the arid, partly desertlike south.

Nicknamed *Ochi,* **Ocho Rios** is the cruise capital of Jamaica, drawing more visitors by sea than Montego Bay. It isn't named for eight rivers, as its name suggests. The Spanish called the section of flowing rapids *los chorreros* (river rapids), which was corrupted by the English into "ocho rios." Ocho Rios doesn't even have eight rivers. The resort city lies about a two-hour drive east of Mo Bay. You first approach the satellite resort town of **Runaway Bay** as you drive in from the west in a car, van, or bus from Mo Bay. Runaway Bay is the site of several all-inclusive resorts but is removed from most of the action and the cruise-ship hordes dominating the center of Ocho Rios.

The tiny little banana and fishing port of Ocho Rios itself has virtually disappeared in a sea of bad commercial architecture and megaresorts, most of which extend to the east of the center. Ocho Rios opens onto Ocho Rios Bay, dominated by a decaying bauxite-loading terminal evocative of Ohio's Rust Belt.

Many hip jazz aficionados who would head for the more fun-loving resort of Negril instead of Ocho Rios go here anyway for the most important jazz festival in the Caribbean. The weeklong **Ocho Rios Jazz Festival** presented at various venues takes place annually during the second week in June. Some of the biggest names in jazz from both America and the West Indies perform at this time. For details, call ☎ **323-857-5358** in the U.S. or go online to www.ochoriosjazz.com.

The busy port town of Ocho Rios may be meager on attractions within its central core, but it's set against a lush section of the North Coast. Easy half- or full-day trips are possible east, west, or south. Waterfalls, grottoes, some of Jamaica's most luxuriant gardens, and old plantations can occupy your time when you're not on the beach.

Most of the all-inclusives lie on the beach-studded coast east of Ocho Rios. If you demand a hotel on the beach, these are for you. Others prefer to be more remotely located; properties on the hillsides, most of which are within a 10- to 15-minute commute of a good beach, fill that need. Ocho Rios also harbors various secret nooks and crannies where you can stay, places not known to the masses that descend on the center.

The beach strip between Ocho Rios and Port Antonio to the east put the North Coast on the tourist maps of the world when it was discovered by such celebrated figures as Sir Noel Coward. Here, Coward and his lover, Graham Payn, erected a home referred to as Firefly that attracted everybody from the Queen Mother of England to Sir Winston Churchill, along with Coward's "bloody loved ones" such as Katharine Hepburn. Errol Flynn claimed that he personally discovered the glories of Port Antonio when his yacht washed ashore in a storm. In 1946, Ian Fleming constructed Goldeneye at Oracabessa, where he created the character of "007," James Bond, in 1952. Today this property (☎ **800-688-7678,** 876-975-3354) is open to the public — that is, those who can afford it, and we're talking the likes of Jim Carrey, who can shell out 6,000 big ones a night to rent the entire property.

To the east of Ocho Rios, **Port Antonio** is still an elite retreat for some film stars, such as Tom Cruise, although it no longer has the cache it did in the '50s and '60s when some of the golden-age movie stars showed up. Still used as a film site every year or so, Port Antonio positively slumbers when compared to the other resorts just previewed, and it is for this reason we like it so.

Set against a lush background with some of the best beaches in Jamaica, the hotels here suffer a low occupancy rate. That means that many of the glamour addresses of yesterday aren't kept in state-of-the-art condition, because the hotels can't generate enough money to maintain them properly. Still, the place has a lovely, nostalgic, and evocative decay that can make for a charming interlude for those who require tranquillity on their holiday and who want to escape the masses overrunning the other resorts such as Mo Bay.

Getting Around Jamaica

If you've booked a package at one of the big resorts, airport transfers are probably part of the deal. Many resorts on the island send buses or vans to pick up and drop off arriving and departing guests. If you're on your own, you have the option of domestic airplanes for some limited routings, a taxi, or a private car. Public transportation, such as it is, is recommended only for the most adventurous.

By taxi

Island taxis, even the official ones, generally have no meters; if they do, they rarely work. The official transport agency is the **Jamaica Union of Travelers Association (JUTA),** with offices in all the major resorts and at the two international airports at Mo Bay and Kingston. JUTA prices its tariffs by the car, not by the passenger, and adds a 25 percent jump to fares between midnight and 5 a.m. (For more information, see the section "Getting from the airport to your hotel," earlier in this chapter.)

For longer jaunts such as trips from Mo Bay to Ocho Rios, or for half- or full-day tours, you may be quoted what sounds like ridiculously high tariffs. Taxi fares are posted at the airports, but agreeing on prices before you get in is best. Regrettably, you can't always trust the tour desk or even the reception desk of your own hotel. Sometimes staff members or desk personnel, especially at some of the all-inclusives such as Sandals, have made deals with a driver, perhaps one of their cousins. If you agree to the inflated rate, the cabbie often gives a kickback to the hotel staff member who booked the deal. This is a widely practiced scam.

Pirate taxis — called *robots* on the island — will also solicit your business, often aggressively. Many people, especially locals, ride these cabs successfully. They stop at random and pick up as many passengers as they can fit in. You'll often have a stranger piled right on top of you. Pickpockets often work these illegal cabs, and keeping control of your belongings is difficult. Robots almost invariably lack three elements: seatbelts, air-conditioning, and car insurance.

JUTA drivers are also trained to take you on sightseeing tours in a resort town, including Mo Bay, Negril, and Ocho Rios. Depending on where you want to go and for how long, half- to full-day tours range from $50 to $100 per vehicle, a cost that you can split among three or four passengers.

The staff at your hotel reception desk can call a cab for you. If you're staying in one of the major resort areas, such as Mo Bay, and patronizing certain first-class restaurants, the establishment will often provide a private van to pick you up, take you to dinner, and bring you back. Call the restaurant of your choice to see if they offer such a luxury. If so, you save all that transport money. If you do hire a taxi, asking the driver to return for you at a certain time and bring you back to your hotel is customary. Most drivers easily agree to that, because it's a guaranteed fare for them.

You can also flag down JUTA taxi drivers on the street. Agree on the fare before getting in, however.

On foot

Even though you may be hassled by hustlers trying to make some sort of deal with you, you still may want to explore the heart of your resort area on foot. If you do, go walking during the daytime and keep your guard up. Avoid, whenever possible, wandering around at night, even in a small group. If you ever needed some street smarts and a keen eye, it's walking the teeming streets of Jamaican towns, especially Kingston. Except for some annoying vendors or volunteers wanting to be your guide, the following districts shouldn't be a problem for strollers:

- ✔ Mo Bay's Gloucester Avenue or Hip Strip, where you'll find lots of restaurants, clubs, shopping, and beaches

- ✔ Ocho's shopping district, near where the cruise ships unload their passengers

- ✔ Negril's Seven Mile Beach or West End

The preceding sections in town are tourist zones and are often patrolled by security police. Even so, taking out a fat wallet to make a purchase, carrying around expensive camera equipment, or wearing pricey jewelry puts you at risk. Wandering off and getting lost on some back street, especially in a slum, is at your own risk.

 The most dangerous place for a stroll is downtown Kingston near the waterfront, although this district isn't without its fascination. Even the cruise ships had to stop coming here because of muggings. Yet many visitors walk around unmolested every day, taking in the sights in this history-rich part of Kingston. The choice is yours, and it depends on how adventurous you are. Our only advice is that you're better off with a guide, which you can arrange through your hotel. And stay out of the district at night. Many Kingstonians avoid downtown Kingston after dark.

Wherever you are, be aware of your surroundings at all times and don't walk around alone — especially if you're a woman. Jamaican men apparently have heard about the book and movie *How Stella Got Her Groove Back* (the story of an author who falls in love with a young Jamaican man while she's on vacation). You'll get lots of offers if you're walking unaccompanied. Just say no, firmly but politely, and stride on.

By car

If you routinely rent a car and race across Nigeria, or drive through Calcutta without a blink, driving around Jamaica will be like eating a piece of island rum cake. But if you're a first-timer to Jamaica, and not used to the Jamaicans' own rules of the road (or lack of them), try to avoid a car rental.

Many veteran visitors to Jamaica rent a car at the airport and head out for Ocho Rios, some 120km (75 miles) to the east, or Negril, 104km (65 miles) to the southwest. But we don't recommend it for the timid driver for these reasons:

- ✔ Bad roads
- ✔ Bad drivers
- ✔ Bad characters
- ✔ Bad directions
- ✔ Bad vibes

When you've gone through the hassle of arranging a car rental, some 16,093km (10,000 miles) of roads await you in Jamaica. Of those, only a third are likely to be paved, if that's what you call it. Many of the others, especially in the hard-to-reach hinterlands, don't seem to have been worked on since the Arawaks blazed these trails hunting for some wild animal for the nightly roast.

The creator of "007," Ian Fleming, lived on the North Coast of Jamaica and hatched the character of his master spy there. James Bond, according to all those movies, would have no trouble driving in Jamaica. But you may be challenged by it, and it is for that reason that we don't recommend renting a car, even though Jamaica has considerable charms that you may not see unless you have your own wheels for exploring on your own.

To make matters worse, accidents are a routine occurrence, and car break-ins are commonplace. The potholed roads and the British-imported custom of driving on the left with a steering wheel also on the left make driving a bit chancy.

Securing a rental car

If you still want to rent wheels after all our words of warning, here's the scoop. At most agencies, a driver has to be at least 25 years old; a few may rent you a car if you're 21, although insurance will be higher. You must also possess a valid driver's license (those from home are fine for short-term visits) and a credit card, and you'll have to put down a security deposit — not in cash but as a guarantee on your credit card. If you return the car undamaged, the agency refunds your security deposit or, rather, removes it from your credit card charge.

Because disputes often break out about whether you've actually reserved a car during seasons when they get snapped up quickly, we strongly recommend booking through a familiar company before you leave your home country and insisting on a confirmation number. Several agencies offer free delivery and pickup of your vehicle to your hotel or villa.

Because they don't have to pay the added cost of an airport rental desk, car-rental agencies outside the airports are less expensive, but these rentals are much more difficult to arrange because of their lack of accessibility. In general, car rentals in Jamaica are more expensive than in the average U.S. city. Travelers from such countries as England won't be surprised at the high tariffs, which may well match those you pay back home.

A few tour operators offer good fly/drive packages that include rental cars. If you're determined to have your own wheels, consider that route to conserve funds.

Many car-rental agencies offer unlimited mileage. If yours doesn't, look for one that does. Inspect your car carefully before taking off, and make sure that any dents are recorded. In Jamaica, you often have to pay for any damage or scratch discovered on a vehicle even though you rented it that way. The slightest mark on a car can mean extra charges for you.

U.S.-based operators in Jamaica include the following:

- ✔ **Avis** (☎ 800-331-1212), with branches at the two major airports — in Montego Bay and in Kingston.

- ✔ **Budget International** (☎ **800-472-3325,** 876-952-3838 at the Montego Bay Airport, 876-924-8762 in Kingston; www.budgetrentacar.com) is a good choice. With Budget, a daily **collision-damage waiver** costs another $15 and is mandatory.

- ✔ **Dollar International** (☎ **800-800-4000** in the U.S.).

- ✔ **Hertz International,** which operates branches at the two major airports (☎ **800-654-3131;** www.hertz.com for reservations; 876-979-0438, Montego Bay's Donald Sangster airport; or 876-924-8028, Kingston's Norman Manley airport).

- ✔ **Thrifty Car Rental** (opposite the Mo Bay airport, ☎ 800-367-2277).

Local car-rental companies include

- ✔ **Island Car Rentals** (☎ 876-952-7225 in Montego Bay; ☎ 876-926-5991 in Kingston)

✔ **Jamaica Car Rental** (☎ **876-952-5586** in Montego Bay; www. jamaicacar.net)

✔ **United Car Rentals** (☎ **876-952-3077** in Montego Bay)

Driving time for the 80km (50 miles) from the center of Montego Bay to Negril is two hours. From Montego Bay to Ocho Rios, expect a minimum drive of 2½ hours; from Ocho Rios to Port Antonio, 2½ hours; and from Ocho Rios to Kingston, two hours. Be especially cautious at night. Speed limits in town are 48kmph (30 mph), 80kmph (50 mph) outside towns. Speed traps are common.

Toyota Corollas and Suzuki Sidekicks are the most popular rentals. Rates average $50 to $150 a day, but on top of that, several agencies also insist that you carry their pricey insurance (as much as $50 a day), even if your home auto insurance covers rentals. You'll also get socked with a 15 percent government tax on your car rental. If you need a baby seat or anything special, be sure to ask when you reserve.

Gas stations are open daily; few accept credit cards, and most of them require payment in Jamaican dollars. Gas costs roughly J$180 (U.S. $2.90) a gallon and is measured in the imperial gallon (a British unit of measure that is 25 percent larger than a U.S. gallon).

Covering your tracks with insurance

If you hold a private auto insurance policy in the U.S., check to see if you're covered in Jamaica for loss or damage to the car and liability in case a passenger is injured. The credit card you used to rent the car also may provide some coverage. Policies vary widely from holder to holder. Most American Express cardholders, for example, don't need a **damage waiver** option, because most Jamaican car-rental agencies recognize Amex's policy, especially if you're dealing with a U.S.-affiliated firm such as Hertz. Many local car-rental companies in Jamaica don't recognize the policy; therefore, you may feel safer in dealing with a U.S. affiliate than a domestic car-rental agency.

Car-rental insurance probably doesn't cover liability if you caused the accident. Check your own auto insurance policy, the rental company policy, and your credit card coverage for the extent of coverage: Is Jamaica covered? Are other drivers covered? How much liability is covered if a passenger is injured? (If you rely on your credit card for coverage, you may want to bring a second credit card with you, because damages may be charged to your card, and you may find yourself stranded with no money.)

Car-rental insurance costs at least $20 a day. Hiring a guide at a daily rate for sightseeing works out much cheaper. Plus, you'll be with someone who knows where the potholes are; where schoolchildren tend to congregate right by the road; where persnickety farm animals tend to be on the loose, grazing with their hindquarters occupying half the lane; and where construction goes on for miles and for years with no end in sight.

By air

The wild rides in speeding vehicles along bumpy, potholed roads leading either to Negril or Runaway Bay/Ocho Rios have, over the years, earned notoriety among travelers to Jamaica. You can skip them by taking a small domestic commuter plane to the landing strips at Negril or Ocho Rios.

Flights are aboard **Air Jamaica Express** (☎ **800-523-5585;** www.air jamaica.com) with local offices in Montego Bay at ☎ 876-940-9054 and in Kingston at ☎ 876-FLY-AIRJ. Flights are often fully booked, so make reservations before you leave home, either directly through Air Jamaica or through a travel agent. You have to confirm your departure a full 72 hours in advance, so be duly warned.

Air Jamaica Express flies more than 50 scheduled cross-island flights per day. The airline will fly you to all the airstrips at the major resort areas, including Montego Bay, Ocho Rios/Runaway Bay, and Negril. If you land in the west at Mo Bay, you can take a domestic flight east across the island to Kingston. On most flights, you're airborne for only 20 to 30 minutes. A typical fare on one of the most popular air routes, Mo Bay to Ocho Rios, costs $70 one-way, with no reduction if you book round-trip.

 Sometimes getting a booking aboard Air Jamaica Express isn't possible — either the flight departed without you or you didn't make a reservation far enough in advance. In that case, the charter carrier **International AirLink** (☎ **800-523-5585** in the U.S., 876-940-6660 in Jamaica), like Superman, may come to your rescue. Alert the airline of your arrival in Mo Bay, and a staff member will meet you and help you through Customs, guiding you to the aircraft. Although charter planes can be terribly expensive, International AirLink is reasonable if you can collect a party of four. The airline will do that for you. If two of you are looking to fly, the staff can quickly arrange for another couple to fly on the same trip. In that case, a one-way fare is $66 per person from the Mo Bay airport to Negril ($128 round-trip), or $91 per person from Mo Bay to the more distant Ocho Rios ($178 round-trip).

By bus

Only the most die-hard world-traveling backpackers ride on local buses, especially those linking one Jamaican town with another. Many Jamaicans themselves won't ride these buses. The only good thing about public bus travel in Jamaica, as distinguished from privately arranged bus travel for visitors, is that fares are remarkably cheap. Buses and private minibuses, called *coasters,* traverse the island.

 Buses are invariably overcrowded, drivers often take dangerous chances, they're a haven for pickpockets, possessions are easily lost as they're carelessly thrown on top of the bus and held together by rope, people hang out from open doors because of overcrowding, and latrine stops are so foul you can smell the toilets a mile away. Not only that, but drivers routinely overcharge foreign visitors. If you disregard our advice and ride buses anyway, don't be surprised to find yourself sharing a seat with a woman carrying a little pig to market, or perhaps a plump chicken. The Jamaican government is slowly attempting to make improvements in bus travel — but they're on an uphill journey.

Two major outfitters operate buses from the Mo Bay airport to Negril and Runaway Bay/Ocho Rios. Both **Tour Wise** (☎ 876-952-4943) and **Caribic Vacations/Ire Tours** (☎ 876-953-2600) run buses from the Mo Bay airport and will drop you off right at the doorstep of your hotel, not a mile or two away. Fares are affordable: A one-way fare from Mo Bay to a resort on Negril's Seven Mile Beach costs $20 per person for the two-hour trip. You can even be taken to a little inn at the West End cliffs in Negril for $20 per person.

By bicycle, moped, and motorcycle

Most hotel concierges or tour desks can arrange the rental of bicycles, mopeds, and motorcycles. Daily rates run from about $50 for a moped to $85 (helmets and locks included) for a Honda 550. Deposits of $100 to $300 or more are required. However, we highly recommend that you don't rent a moped or motorcycle because of Jamaica's status as the country with the third-highest accident rate in the world (behind India and Ethiopia) combined with the hassle factor of fending off aggressive vendors and drug dealers at traffic lights.

If you ignore our advice, at least check on your medical insurance before you leave and have proper identification handy in case you land at a healthcare facility.

Mountain biking has become popular around the Blue Mountains, Negril, Port Antonio, and the rural Treasure Beach area on the South Coast, where traffic and other hazards aren't as pronounced.

Tykes Bike Rental and Tours, on West End Road near Rick's Café and at the visitor information office in Negril (☎ 876-957-0388), offers free pickup and drop-off service. You need your valid driver's license to rent anything motorized.

If you're staying at a resort in Mo Bay or Ocho Rios, you can sometimes arrange a rental at your hotel. Independent outfitters open and shut down so frequently that no guidebook can keep abreast. Because bike and motor-scooter rentals in these resorts aren't popular, few independent operators can make a go of it.

Staying in Style

Resorts in Jamaica run the gamut from small inns with personal attention to all-inclusive megaresorts. Which resort is right for you depends
on how you like to travel.

All-inclusives aren't for the independent traveler: You pay upfront for all
your meals and most activities as part of a package. Like a mother hen,
the all-inclusive pampers you during your entire stay — it even picks
you up at the airport and hauls you back there for your return flight.
Some dine-around plans help you break the monotony of eating at the
same resort every night. Also, with their 24-hour security force, these
all-inclusives give you more protection than the smaller, independent
inns without such expensive patrolling.

If you're an adventure traveler, you may not want such womblike security. You may prefer to stay at a small inn or little hotel where you're free
to roam throughout the day, returning to your bed after a night of rum
and reggae on the town.

Of all the resorts in Jamaica, the all-inclusive has virtually taken over
Ocho Rios, although Mo Bay and Negril have their fair share. The concept was pioneered by Jamaica's Butch Stewart with his Sandals properties (☎ **800-SANDALS,** or 800-726-3257) and has since swept the
Caribbean.

If you don't want to stick to the all-inclusives, one of the best travel
agencies specializing in hotel deals is **Changes in L'Attitudes** (☎ **800-
330-8272;** www.changes.com). For villas in Mo Bay, Ocho Rios, and Port
Antonio, contact **Elegant Resorts International,** P.O. Box 80, Montego
Bay, Jamaica (☎ **800-237-3237;** www.elegantresorts.com).

The Top Resorts

The rack rates listed are in U.S. dollars and are for a standard double
room during high season (mid-Dec through mid-Apr), unless otherwise
noted. Lower rates are available in spring, summer, and fall. See Chapter
3 for more information on travel seasons.

Banana Shout Resort
$ Negril

This intriguing accommodations takes its name from the best-selling novel
yet on Negril — *Banana Shout,* a racy story of hippies, voodoo, drug smug-
glers, and a displaced wild counterculture. The resort is a colony of seven
handsomely furnished cottages set on 2½ acres of tropical gardens, with
waterfalls and fruit trees opening onto a cliff in the West End. Concrete
steps crossing tiered decks lead down to the garden. All the bedrooms,
furnished with handcrafted pieces, contain kitchenettes and ceiling fans.

Jamaica Accommodations

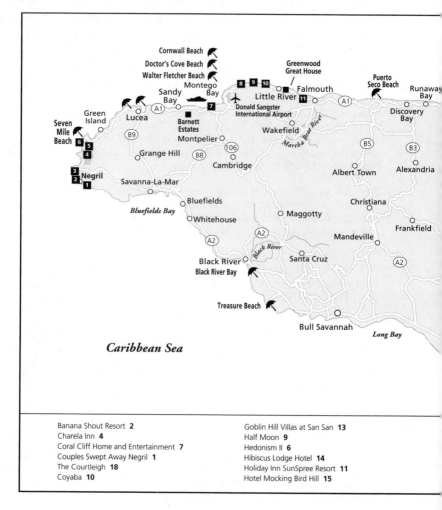

Banana Shout Resort **2**
Charela Inn **4**
Coral Cliff Home and Entertainment **7**
Couples Swept Away Negril **1**
The Courtleigh **18**
Coyaba **10**

Goblin Hill Villas at San San **13**
Half Moon **9**
Hedonism II **6**
Hibiscus Lodge Hotel **14**
Holiday Inn SunSpree Resort **11**
Hotel Mocking Bird Hill **15**

See map above. 4 West End Rd. (P.O. Box 4), Negril. ☎ *and fax* **876-957-0384.** www.bananashout.com. *Rack rates: $100–$120 cottage for one or two; $150 cottage for four. MC, V.*

Charela Inn
$$–$$$ Negril

On a choice 1.2-hectare (3-acre) plot of landscaping on **Seven Mile Beach,** this 49-room resort was designed to evoke an Iberian hacienda. It has long been the market leader in the moderately priced field, and it caters to an

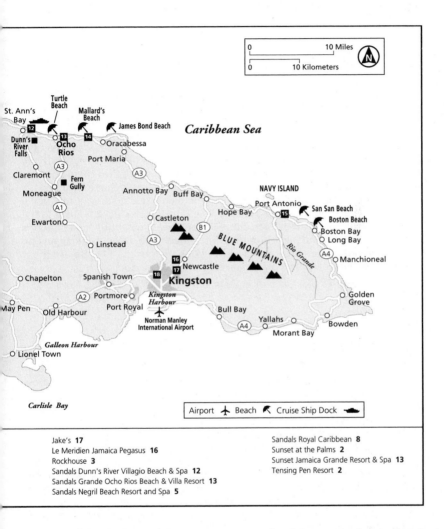

Caribbean Sea

Jake's **17**
Le Meridien Jamaica Pegasus **16**
Rockhouse **3**
Sandals Dunn's River Villagio Beach & Spa **12**
Sandals Grande Ocho Rios Beach & Villa Resort **13**
Sandals Negril Beach Resort and Spa **5**

Sandals Royal Caribbean **8**
Sunset at the Palms **2**
Sunset Jamaica Grande Resort & Spa **13**
Tensing Pen Resort **2**

independent traveler not wanting to book into one of the all-inclusives. Close to Sandals, Charela Inn is a world apart in aura from that couples-only resort (covered later in this section). A self-reliant guest checks in to one of the rooms overlooking the water or the garden. Accommodations are full of character, often with a four-poster bed. We try to avoid the rooms on the ground floor with their barred patios. The on-site **Le Vendôme** restaurant serves one of the finest prix-fixe meals in Negril and offers live music on Thursday and Saturday nights. Children under ten stay free in their parent's room. On-site is a pool; windsurfing and Sunfish sailing can be arranged.

See map p. 286. Norman Manley Boulevard (P.O. Box 33), Negril. ☎ **876-957-4277.**
Fax: 876-957-4414. www.charela.com. *Rack rates: $166–$221 double. AE, MC, V.*

Coral Cliff Home and Entertainment
$$ Montego Bay

For good value, the Coral Cliff may be your best bet in Montego Bay, lying only a two-minute walk from **Doctor's Cave Beach.** The hotel grew from a colonial-style building that used to be the private home of Harry M. Doubleday (of the famous publishing family). It's located about 2km (1 mile) west of the center of town. Many of the light, airy, and spacious bedrooms open onto seaview balconies. The rooms, as befits a former private house, come in a wide variety of shapes and sizes, most of them containing old colonial furniture, wicker, and rattan. Most units have twin beds. If you'd prefer a double, ask at the time you make your reservations; they'll accommodate you if a double is available. The bathrooms are small in the older bedrooms but more spacious in the newer wing out back. Each is tidily maintained and has a combination shower/tub. Decent Jamaican and international dishes are served at **Ma Loos** restaurant. On-site are a bar and fitness center, plus a small spa and a small casino.

See map p. 286 168 Gloucester Ave., Montego Bay. ☎ **876-952-4130.** *Fax 876-952-6532.* www.coralcliffjamaica.com. *Rack rates: $110–$180 double; $120–$190 triple. AE, MC, V.*

Couples Swept Away Negril
$$$$$ Negril

Midway along **Seven Mile Beach,** Couples Swept Away is one of the most elegant of the all-inclusive properties in Negril. A special feature is a 4-hectare (10-acre) adult playground across the boulevard, featuring Negril's best health club and tennis courts along with aerobics classes, yoga, and the like. Locally the place is known for attracting "health nuts," whereas Hedonism II and Sandals lure the most sexually active. A total of 134 well-furnished bedrooms are spread across 26 two-story villas with large balconies overlooking the water. At the beach is a grill offering spicy Jamaica fare, but a veggie bar is also on the premises. Water sports are strong here, including sailing, scuba, windsurfing, water-skiing, kayaking, and snorkeling. In all, more taste and style is reflected here than at the other all-inclusives along the strip.

See map p. 286. Norman Manley Boulevard, Long Bay (P.O. Box 77), Negril. ☎ **800-COUPLES** *(800-268-7537) in the U.S. and Canada; 876-957-4061. Fax: 876-957-4060.* www.couples.com. *Rack rates: $590–$833 double. Rates are all-inclusive, including airport transfers. AE, MC, V.*

The Courtleigh
$$ Kingston

More personal and welcoming than the Pegasus (which we cover later in this section), this 127-unit, six-story hotel is also more affordable.

Sandwiched between the Jamaica Hilton and the Pegasus in the heart of the business and diplomatic district of New Kingston, The Courtleigh is a much safer place to be at night than the historic quarter bordering the waterfront. Bedrooms are well furnished, often with hardwood pieces such as mahogany and the occasional four-poster bed. We especially recommend the suites because they have walk-in closets and large desks. The on-site restaurant, **Alexander's,** serves both Jamaican and international food and is a worthy choice for dining. Two bars, a swimming pool, and a gym round out the list of amenities.

See map p. 286. 85 Knutsford Blvd. ☎ *876-929-9000. Fax: 876-926-7744.* www. courtleigh.com. *Rack rates: $145 double. AE, DISC, MC, V.*

Coyaba
$$$$ Montego Bay

Only a 15-minute ride east of Mo Bay, but a world apart, Coyaba opens onto a beautiful strip of white sand along a private beach. All-inclusive, the 50-unit gem evokes a colonial atmosphere with its plantation-style décor and Great House. Personally managed by the Robertson family, it offers well-furnished units in the main structure or, even better, in a three-floor complex near the beach. Mahogany furnishings and hand-carved bedsteads are grace notes, and junior suites come with refrigerators. A fishing dock with a cabana juts out into the bay. Children are welcome and have their own programs and video library with babysitting arranged. Good food is available at two restaurants, and facilities also include a pool, three bars, a tennis court, a health club and spa, plus water sports.

See map p. 286. Mahoe Bay, Little River (P.O. Box 88), Montego Bay. ☎ *877-232-3224, 876-953-9150. Fax: 876-953-2244.* www.coyabaresortjamaica.com. *Rack rates: $300–$400 double. Meal options (price per person): Breakfast, $14; breakfast and lunch,$60; all-inclusive, $110. Three-night minimum stay required in winter. Honeymoon packages available. Kids ages 11 and under get a 50 percent discount on meals. AE, MC, V.*

Goblin Hill Villas at San San
$$ Ocho Rios

This green and sunny hillside — once said to shelter goblins — is now filled with Georgian-style vacation homes on San San Estate. The pool is surrounded by a vine-laced arbor, which lies just a stone's throw from an almost impenetrable forest. A long flight of steps leads down to the crescent-shaped sands of San San Beach. This beach is now private, but guests of the hotel receive a pass. Everything has the aura of having last been renovated in the 1970s, but the 28-unit resort is still comfortable. The accommodations are town-house style; some have ceiling fans and king-size beds (some have twin beds), but none have phones. The generally roomy units are filled with handmade pine pieces, along with a split-level living and dining area with a fully equipped kitchen. All units have well-maintained bathrooms with shower-tub combinations. Housekeepers attend to chores in the villas and prepare and serve meals (at an extra charge, depending on what you want). The hotel isn't ripe with amenities but does have a bar and an outdoor pool, plus two tennis courts.

See map p. 286. San San, Port Antonio. ☎ *800-472-1148, 876-925-8108. Fax: 876-925-6248.* www.goblinhill.com. *Rack rates: $115–$195 double or one-bedroom villa; $170–$265 two-bedroom villa. AE, MC, V.*

Half Moon
$$$$$ Montego Bay

For the visitor seeking a deluxe resort without the stuffiness of some of Mo Bay's grand dames, Half Moon is the finest choice in all of Jamaica. This well-landscaped, sprawling 419-unit colony is set on 161 hectares (400 acres) with 0.8km (a half-mile) of white crescent-shaped sandy beach that's 13km (8 miles) east of the center of Mo Bay. Half Moon is consistently ranked as one of the world's leading resorts, a luxurious hideaway of refinement and style. It's one of those amazing compounds that can appeal to everybody from golfers or horsemen (or -women) to honeymooners or families. Golfers flock to its Robert Trent Jones, Sr.–designed 18-hole golf course. Everyone from the queen of Jamaica (Elizabeth II of England) to the first President Bush has temporarily called Half Moon home. Villas with private pools are the posh way to go, but even the standard doubles are luxuriously furnished, often with Queen Anne or Chippendale reproductions.

The on-site **Sugar Mill** serves the resort's finest food, but Half Moon has 5 other restaurants as well, along with 6 bars and 13 tennis courts. You can even arrange to take part in such sports as horseback riding or deep-sea fishing. Children view Half Moon as a Shangri-La, with their special pool, playhouses, tennis courts, and donkey rides.

See map p. 286. Rose Hall, Montego Bay. ☎ *800-626-0592, 876-953-2211. Fax: 876-953-2731.* www.halfmoon.com. *Rack rates: $410–$645; from $695 suite. Meal options (price per person): Breakfast only, $25; breakfast and dinner, $85; breakfast, lunch, and dinner, $90. Wedding and honeymoon packages available. AE, DC, DISC, MC, V.*

Hedonism II
$$$–$$$$$ Negril

Hedonism II is called the "human zoo" — and nowhere in the Caribbean is a resort so aptly named. The resort's 280 units are filled with a hell-raising crew intent on fun in the sun, naked or otherwise. Located 3km (2 miles) east of the town center, the resort colony lies at the northern tip of **Negril Beach.** Racy, wild, and woolly, the resort invites you to go wicked for a week. The notorious toga parties would make Nero feel right at home. Singles (mostly male) coexist with couples on the beach with its nude and prude sides. Its five bars stay busy day and night, and a trio of restaurants serves standard fare — but plenty of it. Other facilities include two pools and six tennis courts, plus a dive shop and fitness center. As for the rooms, the more time you spend outside, the better. They're not special, with tired furnishings and beds that have seen much gymnastics in their day.

See map p. 286. Negril Beach Road (P.O. Box 25), Negril. ☎ *800-859-7873* in the U.S., 876-957-5070. Fax: 876-957-5214. www.superclubs.com. Rack rates: $449–$589 double. Rates are all-inclusive. AE, DC, DISC, MC, V.

Hibiscus Lodge Hotel
$$ Ocho Rios

Long the choice of the frugal traveler, this 26-room venerated old inn is built on a cliff three blocks from the Ocho Rios Mall and overlooks the wide sands of **Mallards Bay Beach.** Run in a personable, welcoming way, it's near the center of town, with its shops and restaurants, although the on-site restaurant itself, the **Almond Tree** (reviewed later in this chapter), is one of the finest in the area and is known for its Jamaican fare. The bedrooms are large and well furnished, and many are suitable for three people. Units open onto the sea, and on-site is a pool suspended over the cliffs and enveloped by a spacious sun deck.

See map p. 286. 83 Main St. (P.O. Box 52), Ocho Rios, St. Ann. ☎ *876-974-2676*. Fax: 876-974-1874. Rack rates: $140 double; $184 triple. AE, MC, V.

Holiday Inn SunSpree Resort
$$$$ Montego Bay

This family-friendly all-inclusive lies on 0.8km (a half-mile) of white-sand beach set on 4.8 landscaped hectares (12 acres). After a $13-million renovation, Holiday Inn SunSpree Resort is shipshape once again, especially its 76 oceanfront rooms. The 523-unit hotel is one of the island's largest and is housed in a seven-floor structure. Rooms are tastefully and comfortably furnished, ranging from midsize to spacious and opening onto balconies. Nonstop action is the keynote here, so try to book away from the dining and nightlife sections. Kids are favored here with their own play area that has splashing fountains and children's programs. The resort offers standard but well-prepared food in its restaurants, and its four bars are always active. Four tennis courts, a dive shop, three pools, a fitness center, and other facilities, plus entertainment and nearby golf, add to its allure.

See map p. 286. P.O. Box 480, Rose Hall (8km/5 miles east of Montego Bay). ☎ *800-HOLIDAY* (800-465-4329); 876-953-2485. Fax: 876-953-9480. www.holiday-inn.com. Rack rates: $400–$500 double. Rates are all-inclusive. AE, DISC, MC, V.

Hotel Mocking Bird Hill
$$$ Port Antonio

For the eco-conscious traveler, Hotel Mocking Bird Hill is the number-one choice in Jamaica. This welcoming ten-room inn lies a five-minute drive from the golden sands of **Frenchman's Cove Beach** and 10km (6 miles) east of Port Antonio in the foothills of the Blue Mountains. On 2.8 "natural" hectares (7 acres) of land, 180m (600 ft.) above the coastline, Barbara Walker and Shireen Aga created this little charmer, which is like a B&B.

Rooms have either air-conditioning or ceiling fans, and the water is solar heated. The furniture is locally made from bamboo. The on-site restaurant, **Mille Fleurs,** is worth a special trip even if you're a nonguest (see the review later in this chapter). Don't expect phones or TVs in the bedrooms — it's not that kind of place. Drop into the on-site art gallery for a look at some of Ms. Walker's art along with that of other artists.

 If you don't like dogs or are allergic to them, you'd better book elsewhere. The owners' lovable but large mutts have the run of the joint and add to the cozy charm of the place — that is, for those who, like us, love dogs.

See map p. 286. Mocking Bird Hill, east of Port Antonio on North Coast Highway (P.O. Box 254), Port Antonio. ☎ *876-993-7267. Fax: 876-993-7133.* www.hotelmocking birdhill.com. *Rack rates: $245–$295 double. AE, MC, V.*

 ### Jake's
$–$$$ Treasure Beach

Jake's is the ultimate escapist's retreat, lying on the undeveloped and arid South Coast of Jamaica east of Negril. Constructed on a cliff overlooking a scenic bay, this special, 18-cottage, eight-villa retreat lies adjacent to a rocky beach below. It's funky and fun, the colony of buildings seemingly inspired by some Moroccan Casbah. Sally Henzell, a Jamaican of British ancestry, and her husband, director/producer of that reggae classic *The Harder They Come,* created this hip joint, finding inspiration from anyone, but especially from Antoní Gaudí, the controversial Barcelona architect. If you like outdoor showers, painted concrete floors, saltwater pools where guests appear in "the minimum" if that, and green glass bottles embedded in stucco, this is your kind of place. This retreat is too laid-back for the crowd that books into such resorts as Sandals. Even if you don't stay here, try to visit for its restaurant, **Jake's,** on a daytrip down from Negril. If ever an inn in Jamaica deserved to be called rustic chic, it's Jake's. It's our kind of place.

 If you need to live in a refrigerator when visiting Jamaica, Jake's isn't for you. This is cactus country, and its hot ceiling fans aren't adequate at times. Mosquito nets are provided for good reason, because those sand flies will find you a tasty morsel.

See map p. 286. Treasure Beach, Calabash Bay P.A., Saint Elizabeth. ☎ *800-OUT-POST (800-688-7678); 876-965-0635. Fax: 876-965-0552.* www.islandoutpost.com. *Rack rates: $115–$225 double; $250–$800 villa. AE, MC, V.*

Le Meridien Jamaica Pegasus
$$–$$$ Kingston

For the business traveler or for the visitor who wants to absorb some of the cultural attractions of Jamaica's capital, Le Meridien Jamaica Pegasus is the finest choice in New Kingston. A 17-floor, 300-room high-rise (at least in Kingston skyscraper terms), the hotel lies at the core of the business and diplomatic center of Kingston, offering the finest dining and leisure facilities in the city, with a trio of restaurants, two bars, two tennis courts, a swimming pool, and a gym. From its pizzas to its seafood, its **Columbus Restaurant** is a good dining choice even for nonguests visiting New Kingston. The accommodations are medium in size but well equipped with such amenities as safes and coffeemakers. Try for a guest room with a balcony overlooking the bay or the Blue Mountains in the distance. Note that the nearest beach is at Lime Cay, about a 30-minute ride from the hotel. The staff here is better trained than at any other hotel in Kingston.

See map p. 286. 81 Knutsford Blvd., off Oxford Road, Kingston. ☎ *876-926-3690. Fax: 876-929-5855.* www.jamaicapegasus.com. *Rack rates: $120–$150 double; $230 junior suite; $530 royal suite. AE, DC, DISC, MC, V.*

Rockhouse
$$ Negril

The Rolling Stones checked out in 1970, but under its Aussie owners this funky 28-unit "boutique inn" is better than ever. With its thatched roof, it looks like something on a remote South Pacific island. Opening onto a small cove, you're perched on a cliff side in Negril's West End. A ladder leads down to the cove for snorkeling and swimming, and the inn also has a cliff-side pool. This place is hip, and so are the outdoor showers for showing off your physical assets. You sleep in a four-poster bed romantically draped in mosquito netting in the colonial style. Four cottages offer sleeping lofts. The on-site Rockhouse Restaurant serves zesty Jamaican food featuring freshly caught fish.

See map p. 286. West End Road (P.O. Box 3024), Negril. ☎ *876-957-4373. Fax: 876-957-0557.* www.rockhousehotel.com. *Rack rates: $150 studio; $275 villa. AE, MC, V.*

Sandals Dunn's River Villagio Beach & Spa
$$$$$ Ocho Rios

One of the best members of the Sandals chain in Jamaica, this couples-only (as in male/female combos only) resort opens onto a wide beach of white sand lying between Ocho Rios and St. Ann's Bay. The 250-unit complex is set on 10 landscaped hectares (25 acres) and is very activity-oriented, with complimentary use of an 18-hole, par-71 championship course, the largest hotel pool in Jamaica, 12 tennis courts, and a health club and spa. An estimated three-fourths of the guests are young honeymooners, but this Sandals resort also attracts the silver-haired, some of whom are celebrating a 25th anniversary or whatever. The décor evokes the Mediterranean, with marble columns in its Italian *palazzo*-styled lobby and in the design of its architecture. The resort also carries out this Italianate motif in the spacious bedrooms with their walk-in closets and panoramic balconies. The food is superior to many Sandals resorts and is widely varied, ranging from Caribbean to Japanese.

See map p. 286. Mammee Bay, Route A3 (P.O. Box 51), Ocho Rios. ☎ *800-SANDALS (800-726-3257) in the U.S. and Canada; 876-972-1610. Fax: 876-972-1611.* www.sandals.com. *Rack rates start at $350–$425 double; $450–$740 suite. A two-night minimum stay required. Rates are all-inclusive. AE, DISC, MC, V.*

Sandals Grande Ocho Rios Beach & Villa Resort
$$$$$ Ocho Rios

One of the largest resorts in Jamaica — a total of 522 rooms — was created in 2004 when the Sandals chain combined two of its North Coast resorts, Sandals Ocho Rios and Grande Sport Villa Golf Resort and Spa — into one sprawling resort. In the summer of 2004, the Grande Sport Villa closed for a $10-million refurbishment to bring it up to par with Sandals Ocho Rios. The all-inclusive lies 2km (1½ miles) southeast of town on 20 hectares (50 acres) of landscaped grounds. All the facilities have been renovated, including the villas, restaurants, spas, and the 90 private pools. Ocean- or gardenviews are offered, and most units are spacious with king-size beds and good-size bathrooms with shower/tub combinations. The resort opens onto the white sands of a private beach. Thirty-six units are on the third floor of the Great House, at the core of the property. The best accommodations are in one-, two-, or three-bedroom villas. Other facilities include two full-service spas, six tennis courts, five Jacuzzis, two steam rooms, and two saunas, and you can arrange on-site scuba diving. Some of the accommodations have such amenities as kitchenettes and private safes. As with all Sandals resorts, this property only accepts straight couples.

See map p. 286. Main Street (P.O. Box 771), Ocho Rios. ☎ *800-SANDALS (800-726-3257) in the U.S. and Canada; 876-974-1027. Fax: 876-974-5838.* www.sandals.com. *All-inclusive daily rates per person: $200–$370; $390–$715 suite. AE, MC, V.*

Sandals Negril Beach Resort and Spa
$$$$ Negril

Entrepreneur Butch Stewart long ago invaded Negril with his couples-only (meaning male/female couples) concept of an all-inclusive vacation. Occupying a prime location on Negril's **Seven Mile Beach,** this 5-hectare (13-acre), 223-unit resort attracts many first-timers to Jamaica, some booked on a honeymoon package. The resort is strong on water sports, such as scuba diving and snorkeling. The best rooms open right onto the sands or have balconies with a sea view. The aura is casual and laid-back, not as raunchy as the notorious Hedonism II (covered earlier in this section). Four restaurants give you some variety for on-site dining, including Kimonos, a Japanese teppenyaki cuisine prepared table-side. With its five bars, Sandals attracts the drinking crowd.

See map p. 286. Norman Manley Boulevard (Box 12), Negril. ☎ *800-SANDALS (800-726-3257) in the U.S. and Canada; 876-957-5216. Fax: 876-957-5338.* www.sandals.com. *Rack rates: $360–$435 double; $445–$750 suite. Three-night minimum stay required. Rates are all-inclusive, including airport transfers. AE, DISC, MC, V.*

Sandals Royal Caribbean
$$$$$ **Montego Bay**

The flagship of all the on-island Sandals resorts, this male/female couples-only all-inclusive is a tiny resort on its own private beach. Some of its former British colonial aura remains, and Sandals Royal Caribbean is a more refined resort than its sibling, Sandals Montego Bay (☎ **876-952-5510**), which has a better beach than the Royal Caribbean but unfortunately lies at the edge of the airport. The 190-unit RC attracts more of an international crowd than the more American-oriented Sandals Montego Bay. We prefer the luxe beachfront accommodations with their private balconies or patios, but all the units are well kept and comfortably furnished. The resort's four restaurants, including **Bali Hai** (on a private offshore islet, Sandals Cay), serve a variety of cuisine. Four bars, three pools, a trio of tennis courts, water sports, entertainment, and a health club keep you action oriented.

See map p. 286. Mahoe Bay, North Coast Highway (Box 167), Montego Bay. ☎ *800-SANDALS (800-726-3257); 876-953-2232. Fax: 876-953-2788.* www.sandals.com. *Rack rates: $305–$390 per person; from $420 suite. Rates are all-inclusive. AE, DISC, MC, V.*

Sunset at the Palms
$$$ **Negril**

This all-inclusive 85-room hotel appeals to travelers who want to get away from it all. It's an especially good choice for families with kids. The feeling overall is like something in the South Pacific, thanks to its design as a compound of low-rise wooden buildings set within a forest, across the coastal road from a beach called Bloody Bay, an eastern extension of Seven-Mile Beach. The 4 hectares (9 acres) of gardens are planted with royal palms, bull thatch, and a rare variety of mango tree. Photos of the layout have been featured within *Architectural Digest*. The simple but stylish cabins are small timber cottages, none more than two stories high, rising on stilts. Each offers two spacious and comfortable bedrooms, plus a balcony a shower-only bathroom, and dark-grained furniture, including four-poster beds and big armoires, that evoke Indonesia.

See map p. 286. Norman Manley Boulevard. (P.O. Box 118), Negril, Jamaica, W.I. ☎ *800-234-1707 in the U.S., 876-957-5350. Fax 876-957-5381.* www.sunsetatthepalms.com. *Rack rates: $375 double, $575 suite. Rates are all-inclusive. Children under age 2 stay free in parent's room; children age 2-12 are $25 extra. AE, MC, V.*

Sunset Jamaica Grande Resort & Spa
$$$–$$$$ **Ocho Rios**

This is one of the largest hotels in Jamaica with 730 rooms, a blockbuster all-inclusive that originated as a pair of high-rise beachfront properties in the 1970s. In 2005, it reopened after the most radical of its many reincarnations under the supervision of a locally owned chain, the Sunset Group, which poured many millions of dollars into a dramatic overhaul. The result is hugely appealing — a Jamaica-inspired cluster of waterfalls, serpentine and lagoon-shaped swimming pools, majestic staircases, and a carload of Disney-inspired theatrics. Set closer to the cruise ship docks than any other hotel in town, and painted in two vivid tones of canary yellow, it's impossible to miss. It boasts more beachfront (in this case, along Mallard's Beach) than any other hotel in Ocho Rios and a comfortably rambling series of high-ceilinged, open-sided public rooms. Spa facilities, a choice of restaurants, a high-energy sense of fun, and a large pavilion are dedicated to the amusement of adults and the care, feeding, and maintenance of children of all ages. Best of all, the resort choreographs the best children's programs in Ocho Rios. Bedrooms are tasteful and well-upholstered, with tropical-inspired fabrics, crown moldings, tiled floors, and mostly mahogany and rattan furniture. Each opens onto a private balcony. There's even a disco (Jamaica Me Crazy).

See map p. 286. Main St. (P.O. Box 100), Ocho Rios, St. Ann. ☎ *800-234-1707, 876-974-2200. Fax 876-974-2289.* www.sunsetjamaicagrande.com. *Rack rates: $350–$410 double; $590 one-bedroom suite for two. Rates are all-inclusive. Nonresidents can use the facilities, dine, and drink if they buy a Day Pass, priced at $60 per person, and valid from 7 a.m.–6 p.m. AE, DC, MC, V.*

Tensing Pen Resort
$$–$$$ Negril

Along West End Road, a ten-minute taxi ride from **Seven Mile Beach,** Tensing Pen Resort is an inn of character and a certain raffish charm. The 15-unit colony is set in a botanical garden with orchids and bromeliads among other luxuriant growth. An independent-type traveler is attracted to the beautifully furnished bedrooms with tile floors, beds of tropical wood, and refrigerators. Muslin netting drapes some of the beds in an evocative touch. You sleep in a rustic hut bungalow or a cut-stone cottage with outdoor showers. A Great House sleeps friendly groups or families (up to five guests). Guests meet fellow guests when using the large communal kitchen.

See map p. 286. West End Road (P.O. Box 13), Negril. ☎ *800-957-0387, 876-957-0387. Fax: 876-957-0161.* www.tensingpen.com. *Rack rates: $175–$554 double. AE, MC, V.*

Dining Out

It takes a sense of adventure to go out at night and sample cuisine at the local taverns. Taxis are expensive, and a certain danger of wandering around after dark is always present.

For that reason, many guests prefer to stay at their hotel at night. If it's an all-inclusive, dinner comes as part of the package. You'll be safe and secure in your Sandals or SuperClubs dining room, but will you eat well? You'll certainly get heaping amounts of food. Although Jamaican resorts have improved their cuisine in recent years, offering more variety, even Japanese food, they still lag behind comparable food served at top-rated American or European resorts. Much of the foodstuff, such as beef, served in these resort hotels is imported from the U.S. or elsewhere, including Mexico.

Because more and more guests are staying in their hotel at night, or booked into an all-inclusive where they've already paid for their meals, a death pallor has fallen over many an independent restaurant. The independent restaurants used to prosper in resort areas such as Ocho Rios before the all-inclusives came in and virtually ate up all the customers. A few (see our recommendations in "The Best Restaurants" later in this chapter) struggle valiantly on in the face of the all-inclusive onslaught. To survive, some of these restaurants have raised their prices, which does little to attract customers. It's a vicious cycle with no sign of relief on the way.

To break the monotony of dining at the same resort every night, some of the all-inclusives offer a dine-around plan. **Sandals** features the most, allowing a guest to dine at a different restaurant every night, providing it falls under the vast Sandals umbrella of resort restaurants.

Because so many potential diners resist paying an expensive taxi there and back, many upmarket restaurants have their own minivans, taking you to the restaurant and back to your hotel at night. That makes it easy for you and has greatly increased business to some independents. We feel, however, that they've covered the cost of the free transportation by raising their menu prices.

Almost no place in Jamaica requires men to wear ties at night, although a limited few request a jacket. More and more, even in the fanciest joints, a collared shirt for men will suffice. Women appear in fashionable resort wear ranging from a sundress to slacks and a blouse. If a restaurant or dining room is air-conditioned, women should bring a wrap, perhaps a shawl or sweater. If a Jamaican has air-conditioning, he believes in turning it on at full blast.

 Reservations in winter are important at the top-ranked restaurants. Even if you're staying at an all-inclusive, you may not find a free table at the hotel's best restaurant. To guarantee that you, too, have a table, make dinner reservations when booking your room.

Enjoying a Taste of Jamaica

Nyam is a word the slaves brought from Africa. It means "to eat," and that is what you can do rather well throughout Jamaica. Yes, you can find McDonald's, Burger King, and even KFC franchises, but the island has so much more to offer.

From curried goat to jerk pork, the pungent and aromatic cuisine of Jamaica, borrowed freely from all its settlers, creates a unique "pepperpot stew" of savory dishes. Some of the ethnic dishes would grow hair on your chest, even if you're a woman, but others are undeniably excellent and inventive.

From Africa, slaves brought recipes in their memories along with *yabbas,* or clay pots, in which to cook their stews. Some of the "descendants" of those clay pots are still in use in Jamaica today.

East Indians brought their hot curries, and immigrants arriving from the Middle East and China, especially Hong Kong, added more flavor and spice to the cuisine. Some of the dishes were inspired by the Arawak and Taíno Indians. And the Rastafarians have added their *I-tal* cuisine of natural ingredients. No meat, no liquor, not even salt — and still the Rasta cuisine tastes marvelously good.

Even if a dish is fiery hot, Jamaicans often sprinkle their own Pickapeppa Sauce over it, making it even hotter. This sauce can be addictive, and the formula for making it is a closely guarded secret. We've detected the taste of onions, raisins, tomatoes, mango, tamarind, red-hot peppers, cane vinegar, and spices such as thyme.

Many hotels still offer a bland international cuisine, although more and more island dishes appear on menus. On a recent swing through Jamaica, we even saw listed on a Sandals restaurant menu such soups as red pea (actually bean) and pepperpot, the latter a legacy of the Taínos with salt pork, okra, salt beef, and leafy callaloo, the local spinach.

If pepperpot is the national soup, then akee (also ackee) is the national dish. The red-skinned akee is poisonous until Mother Nature pops it open, releasing the dangerous gases. Chefs boil the lobes of the fruit and then blend them with salt cod, peppers, and onions. Akee is a breakfast favorite; it resembles scrambled eggs when cooked. The combination of akee and sal' (salt) fish is the way many a Jamaican fortifies himself or herself for the day — that and some *bammies* (cassava cakes), green bananas, or fried plantain.

Some of the truly local dishes you'll taste only in lowly food shacks, not in hotels. These include red beans cooked with pig's tail or salt beef and dumplings. Jamaicans have given their own colorful names to their most famous dishes — *Solomon Gundy* for spiced pickled herring; *stamp and go* for batter-fried salt-fish fritters; *rundown* for salt cod or mackerel boiled in coconut milk; *dip and fall back,* a salty stew made with bananas and dumplings; and *matrimony* for a dessert wedding — star-apple pulp with orange segments in cream.

Internationally, Jamaica's most famous dish is jerked (either pork or chicken). Bottles of jerk pork seasonings now line the shelves of American grocery stores. The pork is marinated in a wake-up-your-tongue hot sauce and then slowly barbecued over an open pit (usually in an oil drum). The fire is from pimento wood (allspice to most people), giving the meat its characteristic zest. Chicken, fish, and even lobster can also be jerked.

Jamaican beef is tough and is often ground into patties. The tender, juicy steaks served on the island are from the U.S. Go for fresh fish whenever you can, especially snapper, kingfish, grouper, and marlin. A typical offering is *escoveitched* fish, which is pickled and then fried with onions and peppers.

Side dishes include the starchy breadfruit, whose seedlings were brought to Jamaica by Captain Bligh; rice and peas; or the *cho-cho,* called *christophine* in most of the West Indies, a squashlike vegetable that grows on the vine like a cucumber.

Wandering in a Jamaican Garden of Eden, Eve wouldn't have settled for a mere apple. Instead she may have selected lush mangos, the yellow-rose papaya, the dark-purple star apple, the pink-fleshed and grapelike guinep, the fragrant soursop, or the musky sweet guava. The sight of the ugli fruit, like a warty, mottled, and deformed citrus, may have turned her off — that is, until she sampled its gushingly juicy golden pulp.

To finish a meal, you simply must partake of the Blue Mountain coffee. Ian Fleming had his master spy, "007" himself, proclaim it the most aromatic, exotic, and finest coffee in the world.

The Best Restaurants

Almond Tree
$$$ Ocho Rios   JAMAICAN/INTERNATIONAL

The restaurant at this small and affordable inn is named for the almond tree that grows through its roof. This place is especially dramatic at night when you can enjoy the twinkling lights and trade winds from its cliff-side location overlooking the sea below. For years, it was considered almost mandatory for visitors to come here and have a drink in one of the swinging rope chairs in the terrace bar. Candlelit dinners are served alfresco on the little pavilions set into the cliff side. Roast suckling pig is the specialty enjoyed by everybody from Keith Richards of the Rolling Stones to movie stars traveling incognito. Some habitúes claim the food isn't as good as it used to be (what is?), but it's still well flavored and prepared, everything from medallions of beef Anne Palmer named after the "white witch" of Rose Hall to a savory serving of Jamaican plantation rice. No one in the area does lobster Thermidor better than this chef.

See map p. 300. In the Hibiscus Lodge Hotel, 83 Main St., Ocho Rios. ☎ *876-974-2813. Reservations recommended for dinner. Main courses: $14–$31. AE, MC, V. Open: Daily 7:30–10:30 a.m., noon to 2:30 p.m., and 6–9:30 p.m.*

Jamaica Dining

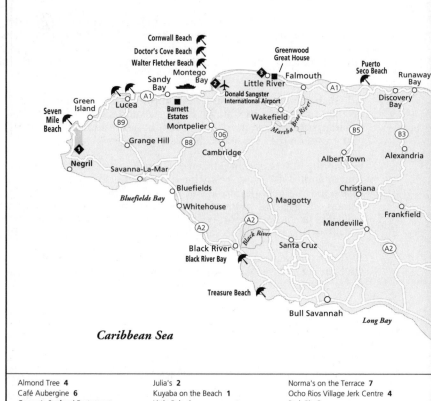

Almond Tree **4**	Julia's **2**	Norma's on the Terrace **7**
Café Aubergine **6**	Kuyaba on the Beach **1**	Ocho Rios Village Jerk Centre **4**
Cosmo's Seafood Restaurant	Little Pub **4**	Pork Pit **2**
and Bar **1**	Margaritaville **1**	Redbones-The Blues Café **7**
Day-O Plantation Restaurant **2**	Marguerite's Seafood by the Sea	Strawberry Hill **8**
The Dinner Terrace at the	and Sports Bar and Grill **2**	Sugar Mill **3**
Jamaica Inn **4**	Mille Fleurs **9**	Toscanini **5**
Evita's Italian Restaurant **4**	Norma's at the Marina **9**	
Hungry Lion **1**	Norma's on the Beach at Seasplash **1**	

Café Aubergine
$$ Moneague   FRENCH/ITALIAN

This most intriguing restaurant, 18km (11 miles) south of Ocho Rios (and a 40-minute drive), is an offbeat adventure. European-trained chef Neville Anderson converted an 18th-century tavern into a restaurant, serving food as good as (or better than) that in the best restaurants of Ocho Rios.

You're welcomed inside a gingerbread-trim house with cascading pink and red flowers. On our last visit, the cook was roasting half a cow. The dishes

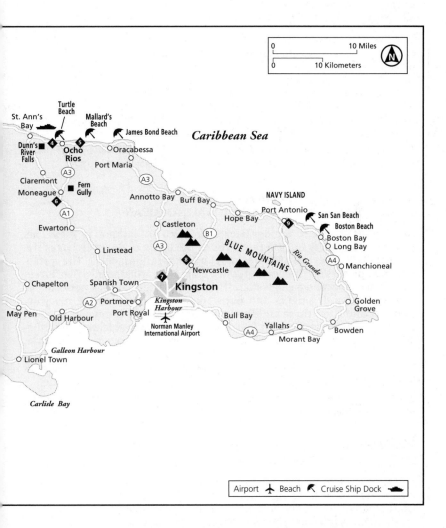

here would pass muster on the Left Bank: sautéed breast of chicken in a lemon caper sauce over a bed of linguine, or grilled lamb chops with a honey-mustard sauce, for instance. We're also fond of baked crab with white wine (seasoned with fresh herbs) and the smoked marlin with pineapple sorbet.

See map p. 300. Moneague, near Ocho Rios. ☎ 876-973-0527. Reservations required. Main courses: $15–$35. DC, MC, V. Open: Wed–Sun noon to 8:30 p.m. (last seating 8:30 p.m.).

Cosmo's Seafood Restaurant and Bar
$$ Negril SEAFOOD/JAMAICAN

The first time we dropped in at this East End dive, the owner and local character, Cosmo Brown, rushed over with a cup of conch soup. "Taste it," he said. "It's the best on the island." We must've agreed with him because we've been coming back ever since. He's not only a whiz with conch, which he also prepares stewed or curried, but he's also an expert with any number of seafood dishes, including grilled lobster. You eat under a thatched roof hut and may be tempted to use the beach facilities with changing rooms, costing $3 per person.

See map p. 300. Norman Manley Boulevard, Negril. ☎ *876-957-4784. Reservations not accepted. Main courses: $8–$18. AE, MC, V. Open: Daily 9 a.m.–10 p.m.*

Day-O Plantation Restaurant
$$–$$$ Montego Bay INTERNATIONAL/JAMAICAN

Here's your chance to wander back to Jamaica's plantation heyday. This place was originally built in the 1920s as the home of the overseer of the Barnett Plantation, one of the region's largest sugar producers. The restaurant occupies a long, indoor/outdoor dining room divided into two halves by a dance floor and a small stage. Here, owner Paul Hurlock performs as a one-man band, singing and entertaining the crowd while his wife, Jennifer, and their three children manage the dining room and kitchen. Every dish is permeated with Jamaican spices. Try the chicken plantation-style, with red-wine sauce and herbs; filet of red snapper in Day-O style, with olives, white wine, tomatoes, and peppers; or, even better, one of the best versions of jerked snapper in Jamaica. We also like the grilled rock lobster with garlic butter.

See map p. 300. Day-O Plantation, Lot 1, Fairfield. ☎ *876-952-1825. Reservations recommended. Main courses: $14–$33. AE, MC, V. Open: Tues–Sun noon to 11 p.m.*

The Dinner Terrace at Jamaica Inn
$$$$ Ocho Rios CONTINENTAL/CARIBBEAN

The timeless and discreetly upscale dining presentations at the Jamaica Inn seem to have endured better than many of this hotel's counterparts. Quite simply, there is nothing more upscale and dignified in town. Dinners, consequently, take on aspects of earlier, more graceful eras when guests actually gathered in the elegant, wood-paneled bar area, or on the moonlit terrace, for pre-dinner drinks before migrating into an open-sided (or, weather permitting, an open-air) dining room that's seeped in formal and undeniably upscale service rituals — the kind of venue where Sir Winston Churchill could (and frequently did) get in touch with colonial Jamaican posh. The menu changes nightly, and nonresidents who opt to dine here are expected to reserve a table in advance. In 2004, age-old rules were modernized, allowing men to abandon their jackets and neckties in favor of well-groomed shirts with collars and long pants, during the dinner hour.

See map p. 300. Main Street. ☎ *876-974-2514. Reservations required. Set-price five-course menu $65 without drinks. Daily 7:30–9 p.m.*

Evita's Italian Restaurant
$$$ Ocho Rios   ITALIAN

No, Evita Peron isn't alive and well and dispensing savory Italian food in Ocho Rios. The local Evita is actually the sophisticated international blonde-haired hostess, Eva Myers. When a hurricane blew down her place in Mo Bay, she moved her pots and pans to Ocho Rios and has been ensconced ever since, dispensing her cuisine to appreciative diners. She even grows her own herbs, which enhance many of her dishes such as homemade pastas that range from a Rastafarian version (no meat) to a "Viagra pasta" (oysters are the aphrodisiac). If you're not in the mood for pasta, try one of the fresh fish dishes. We recommend the enticingly pre-pared snapper stuffed with crabmeat. Lobster and scampi in a buttery white-cream sauce is another memorable dish. Come here early for a sun-downer, taking in the dramatic view from this hilltop 19th-century ginger-bread West Indian house overlooking **Mallards Bay.** Half orders of pasta are available, and kids under 12 eat for half price.

See map p. 300. Mantalent Inn, Eden Bower Road, Ocho Rios. ☎ *876-974-2333. Reservations recommended. Main courses: $12–$23. AE, MC, V. Open: Daily 11 a.m.–11 p.m.*

Hungry Lion
$$ Negril   ITALIAN/RASTAFARIAN

This hip local eatery draws the Bob Marley wannabe to its laid-back perch, an open-air hangout on the cliffs of the **West End,** far removed from the frenetic, organized activities of the megaresorts directly east. If you don't go in for Jamaican Red Stripe beer or a rum punch, a juice bar awaits you, turning out the most soothing, freshly squeezed drinks in Negril. For the first-time visitor, some of the fruit juice flavors may also be a first for you. Shepherd's pie, that staple choice of pub grubbers around the world, is all veggie here, as is the lasagna with the spinachlike leafs of the callaloo plant. Don't believe the waiter when he tells you the green is from the mar-ijuana plant. Some Rastas don't eat seafood, but Hungry Lion serves it. Especially recommendable are the pan-fried snapper, freshly caught that day, and the kingfish steak grilled just right. King lobster is prepared almost any way you want it. Save room for the pineapple-carrot cake, even better than Mama used to make.

See map p. 300. West End Road, Negril. ☎ *876-957-4486. Main courses: $10–$18. AE, MC, V. Open: Daily 5:30–11 p.m.*

Julia's
$$$$ Montego Bay   CONTINENTAL

Reached by a jolting ride up a hilly, rocky road, Julia's serves the best Italian cuisine in Mo Bay in a former private home built in 1840 for the Duke of Sutherland. The views of Mo Bay at night compete with the cuisine. Although fine in every way, Julia's still takes second billing to Evita's (see the listing earlier in this chapter) or Toscanini (see the listing later in this chapter), both competitors in the Ocho Rios area. Neville and Gisela Roe, a Jamaican-German couple who combine some of the best Continental cuisine with Jamaican flair, serve a finely honed prix fixe nightly. Look for about ten different types of pasta at night, even such Germanic dishes as pork schnitzel and goulash with noodles. The desserts are some of Mo Bay's best, especially the cheesecake of the day or Black Forest cake.

See map p. 300. Julia's Estate, Bogue Hill. ☎ *876-952-1772. Reservations required. Main courses: $20–$41. AE, DISC, MC, V. Open: Daily 5:30–11 p.m. Private van transportation provided; ask when you reserve.*

Kuyaba on the Beach
$–$$ Negril   INTERNATIONAL

Right near one of the most popular reggae joints in Jamaica is another joint projected out into the water. Laid-back, raffish, and funky, Kuyaba is the most evocative of those casual eateries that put Negril on the tourist map. People come here for the fun almost as much as they do for the food, finding a favored table on the wooden deck over the beach or a hammock seat at the bar and slugging down some of the tropical punches like screaming banana or Kuyaba rainbow. After a few of these, you'll be seeing more than rainbows. If an Arawak Indian were left on the island, he'd tell you that Kuyaba in his speak means "feasting, drinking, and dancing," so the eatery is aptly named. A mento band plays on some nights, and you can often hear Cuban salsa. Stop in for breakfast or stick around for a lunch of meal-sized, freshly made salads or big, juicy burgers. At night the cook gets more serious, grilling freshly caught red snapper, maybe even swordfish. Steaks from the U.S. are grilled to perfection, and sometimes lamb chops appear on the menu.

If you want to sleep in a party atmosphere, you can rent one of the 18 simply-furnished bedrooms that affordably cost $70 to $97 for a double per night.

See map p. 300. In the Hotel Kuyaba, Norman Manley Boulevard, Negril. ☎ *876-957-4318. Main courses: $10–$23. Burgers, sandwiches, and salads: $6–$9. AE, MC, V. Open: Daily 8 a.m.–11 p.m.*

Little Pub
$$ Ocho Rios   JAMAICAN/INTERNATIONAL

Little Pub is your best bet for combining drink, entertainment, and pub grub all under one roof. With its sports bar and a West Indian revue on most nights, this place is a lot of fun, featuring outdoor dining. Reggae bands enliven the scene on some nights. If you like steak and seafood (and plenty of it) at an affordable price, come here. As the waiter told us, "We don't get the fancy diners, but we feed you well." Dig into the barbecued chicken, grilled kingfish, freshly caught lobster, and, most definitely, jerk pork, curried chicken, or one of the succulent pastas. The pub also serves one of the heartiest breakfasts in town, and many locals like to stop in for a big burger with fries at lunch.

See map p. 300. 59 Main St., Ocho Rios. ☎ 876-974-2324. Reservations recommended. Main courses: $14–$30. MC, V. Open: Daily 10 a.m.–11 p.m.

Margaritaville
$$ Negril   AMERICAN/INTERNATIONAL

Inspired by the Jimmy Buffett song, it's party time here day or night. This restaurant is the leading sports bar of Negril, even luring some of the gang from **Sandals** and **Hedonism II.** It's relatively tame during the day, but the action begins after sundown. The complex is both a bar and a restaurant, plus an on-site gallery, gift shop, and dive center — very touristy but fun if you're in the mood. Live music rocks the joint after 9 p.m. When management doesn't want to pay for live entertainment, they give the entertainment job to you with karaoke. The food is better than you may expect. During the day you get good burgers and well-stuffed sandwiches. At night, try such good-tasting dishes as the Southern fried chicken or their "Pacific paella." The drink of choice? A margarita, of course, and the bartenders make a great selection — at least four dozen (we lost count after sampling 38) different varieties.

See map p. 300. Norman Manley Boulevard, Negril. ☎ 876-957-4467. Main courses: $12–$25. Burgers and sandwiches: $9–$10. AE, MC, V. Open: Daily 8 a.m.–11 p.m.

Marguerite's Seafood by the Sea and Sports Bar and Grill
$–$$ Montego Bay   INTERNATIONAL/SEAFOOD

Across from the **Coral Cliff Hotel,** this two-in-one restaurant and bar is both the best-known sports bar in Mo Bay and also one of the choice dining spots for fresh seafood. On a terrace swept by the trade winds, you can eat and drink either in the sports bar and grill, with its straightforward menu of seafood, sandwiches, pastas, and pizzas, or in the more-formal restaurant. The cuisine doesn't rate a rave, but it is competently prepared if you stick to the flambéed grilled dishes.

See map p. 300. Gloucester Avenue. ☎ 876-952-4777. Reservations needed only for restaurant. Main courses: $14–$42. Snacks and platters: $10. AE, MC, V. Restaurant open: Daily 6–10:30 p.m. Sports bar open: Daily 10:30 a.m.–5 a.m.

Mille Fleurs
$$$ Port Antonio   INTERNATIONAL/CARIBBEAN

With the scent of jasmine perfuming the air cooled by the distant **Blue Mountains,** and the sound of the sea below, this is not only a romantic interlude, but also a refined place to sample a well-prepared cuisine made with fresh ingredients. A delightful couple, artist Barbara Walker and her friend, Shireen Aga, welcome you into this homelike environment. Arrive early to enjoy one of their smooth tropical punches. Drawing largely a European clientele, they're becoming increasingly known to Americans thanks to the likes of us. Mille Fleurs in recent times has emerged as the number-one dining choice in the Greater Port Antonio area. By candlelight you enjoy your dinner, ending with a selection from a trolley of Sangster's Jamaican liqueurs. Some of the vegetables and herbs that the chefs use are from the hotel's own gardens. The menu is forever changing but includes a generous number of vegetarian dishes. If featured, we recommend the coconut and garlic soup, followed by fresh fish in a spicy mango-shrimp sauce. Breads, most jams, and ice creams are homemade. This place has lots of New Age charm.

See map p. 300. In Hotel Mocking Bird Hill, east of Port Antonio on North Coast Highway, Port Antonio. ☎ 876-993-7267. Reservations recommended. Main courses: $21–$40. Lunch platters: $10–$30. AE, MC, V. Open: Daily 8:30–10:30 a.m., noon to 2 p.m., and 7–9:30 p.m.

Norma's at the Marina
$$ Port Antonio   JAMAICAN/CONTINENTAL

This is the newest branch of an upscale, Jamaica-wide restaurant chain made famous by a Jamaica-born, Florida-trained matriarch (Norma Shirley), who has been the subject of more publicity in the culinary press than any equivalent entrepreneur in Jamaica. Established in 2005, the restaurant sprawls between two oversize gazebos that mark either end of a brick-floored beachside terrace inside the fenced-in compound of the Port Antonio marina. Your meal might be served outdoors, on the above-mentioned terrace, or one floor above ground level, within a high-ceilinged, mahogany-trimmed dining room that's open to the breezes on two sides. Menu items are elegant and flavorful, representing the best of modern and creative Jamaican cuisine, and include crab-back salad, elegant slices of smoked marlin, a "reggae salad" studded with sautéed shrimp, several different versions of grilled fish, teriyaki-flavored rib-eye steak, wood-smoked port riblets with a tamarind-flavored honey sauce; pan-seared butterfish filets, and grilled lobster with lime-flavored herb butter.

See map p. 300. At the Port Antonio Marina. ☎ 876-993-9510. Reservations recommended for dinner, not necessary for lunch. Main courses: $12–$20. MC, V. Open: Tues–Sat 10 a.m.–10 p.m.; Sun noon to 8 p.m.

Norma's on the Beach at Seasplash
$$–$$$ Negril   INTERNATIONAL/JAMAICAN

Norma Shirley is not only the best female chef in Jamaica, she's called the Caribbean's Julia Child. She formerly ran a popular restaurant in New York, but she moved back to Kingston to open the best restaurant there (see the following listing for Norma's on the Terrace). At a Negril outpost, she established this new outlet for herself, using her same recipes and flair for cookery. It's a sort of franchise. Because most visitors to Negril don't make it on to Kingston, she wanted local taste buds to know what a delight she is in the kitchen. Even without Norma on the premises all the time, you feel her culinary presence in the rich, bountiful dishes created here from the products of the Jamaican countryside. Seasonally adjusted, the menu offers beautifully prepared fare such as delicately poached salmon, a perfectly cooked and very tender rack of lamb, enticingly tasty lobster cocktails, and a well-sauced Cornish game hen. No one does grilled deviled crab backs better than Norma.

See map p. 300. In the Sea Splash Resort, Norman Manley Boulevard. ☎ *876-957-4041. Reservations recommended. Main courses: $7–$22 at lunch; $13–$24 at dinner. AE, DC, MC, V. Open: Daily 7:30 a.m.–10:30 p.m.*

Norma's on the Terrace
$$$$–$$$$$ Kingston   JAMAICAN

The celebrated female chef Norma Shirley welcomes guests to the finest restaurant in the center of Kingston. She showcases her culinary wares in Devon House, a striking, classic building erected in 1991 by George Stiebel, a Jamaican who became one of the first black millionaires in the Caribbean. Ms. Shirley changes her menus with the seasons, but you can always get something good here on her carefully balanced menu with well-chosen ingredients given her own innovative flair and zest for cooking. Her Jamaican chowder with crabmeat, conch, lobster, and shrimp is the finest we've had in Jamaica. You can dine in grand style if you order her grilled whole red snapper encrusted with herbs and served in a sauce studded with capers and laced with fresh thyme. The intense flavor of a grilled smoked pork loin is only enhanced by its ginger-laced teriyaki sauce with a side of caramelized apples.

See map p. 300. In Devon House, 26 Hope Rd. ☎ *876-968-5488. Reservations recommended. Main courses: $15–$40. AE, DISC, MC, V. Open: Mon–Sat 10 a.m.–10 p.m.*

Ocho Rios Village Jerk Centre
$ Ocho Rios   JAMAICAN

This dive, frequented by locals, is one of the best places to sample jerk pork on home turf, even if you're just visiting from a cruise ship for the afternoon. Jamaican jerk seasonings are used at their best to create hot, spicy dishes — both chicken and pork. We recommend consuming one of these main courses with a frosty Red Stripe beer (maybe more than one). A chalkboard menu lists the specials of the day, perhaps tangy barbecue ribs, also heavily spiced, or a freshly caught red snapper grilled to perfection.

See map p. 300. Da Costa Drive. ☎ *876-974-2549. Jerk pork $3.50 for a quarter-pound, $10 per pound. Whole jerk chicken $14. MC, V. Open: Daily 10 a.m.–11 p.m.*

Pork Pit

$ Montego Bay JAMAICAN

Locals and adventuresome visitors flock to this laid-back joint for a taste of the celebrated jerk pork and jerk chicken, said to have been a culinary gift of the Maroons, those slaves who escaped and fled into the hinterlands to escape bondage. If so, we owe them a debt. The jerk meats are fiery and full of zest and cooked in the old-fashioned method of barbecuing — and served on picnic tables. Coming here with a group (if you can corral one) is best, ordering the food along with such sides as baked yam or baked potato. As a change of pace, the restaurant features roast fresh fish of the day. You wash everything down with Red Stripe beer.

See map p. 300. 27 Gloucester Ave., a half-mile past the brewery and Walter Fletcher Beach, Montego Bay. ☎ **876-952-3663.** *One pound of jerk pork or chicken $10. MC, V. Open: Daily 11 a.m.–11 p.m.*

Redbones — The Blues Café

$$$ Kingston NOUVELLE JAMAICAN

The name alone lured us to this elegant place, which is the only restaurant in Kingston with cuisine as good as Norma's on the Terrace (see the review earlier in this section). All aglow in yellow and peach hues, Redbones is in a former Spanish colonial house. You're greeted with pictures of jazz greats on the wall, everybody from Billie Holiday to Louis Armstrong. A cozy bar, its ceiling studded with records, awaits in someone's former bedroom. Owners Evan and Betsy Williams give standard Jamaican dishes a new twist. Ask for *bammy,* a cassava dish crowned with sautéed shrimp, or a platter of stuffed crab backs, a delectable selection on a tricolor salad. A spinach callaloo with cream cheese is encased in a divine strudel. Seafood pasta is laden with shrimp, lobster, and salmon in a creamy coconut sauce. The best item on the menu is spicy lamb chops in a guava glaze. Live jazz or something is always going on.

See map p. 300. 21 Braemar Ave., Kingston. ☎ **876-978-6091.** *Reservations required. Main courses: $13–$32. AE, MC, V. Open: Lunch Mon–Fri noon to 11 p.m.; Sat 3 p.m.–midnight.*

Strawberry Hill

$$$$ Blue Mountains MODERN JAMAICAN

The Blue Mountain setting is charming. At this favored retreat of off-the-record celebrities, guests enjoy a refined cuisine while taking in the twinkling lights of Kingston at night. On chilly nights in the mountains, a bar with a crackling fire is a magnetic attraction. Diners prefer tables on the second-story enveloping porch or in the Great House with its tall ceilings and wrought-iron chandeliers. This restaurant is good for a long, leisurely meal — not fast service. Every dish is given island flavor, such as the freshly grilled catch of the day with a jerk mango and sweet pepper salsa, or rotis stuffed with herb-infused curried goat. Shrimp is perfectly grilled, its flavor enhanced by fresh cilantro. The Irish Town potato cakes with a passion-fruit salsa and mango chutney may precede a velvety crème caramel with a dash of Grand Marnier for an enticing aroma. The fashionable set from Kingston journeys into the hills for the big spread Sunday brunch.

See map p. 300. Irish Town, Blue Mountains. ☎ 876-944-8400. Reservations recommended. Main courses: Lunch $10–$24; Sun brunch $45. AE, MC, V. Open: Mon–Sat 8–10:30 a.m., noon to 3 p.m. and 6:30–10 p.m.; Sun brunch 11:30 a.m.–2:30 p.m.

Sugar Mill
$$$$$ Montego Bay   INTERNATIONAL/CARIBBEAN

As you sit at a private table by the waterfall, know that you've selected one of the most romantic places for dining in Mo Bay. You'll also get a more-polished cuisine here than anywhere else in the city. The restaurant is named for its former role when it was the site of a water wheel making sugar from cane for a nearby plantation. If you visit for lunch, you can sample what may be a first for you, an akee burger with bacon. Before ordering that, you can taste a velvety pumpkin soup. To finish? There's nothing finer than the homemade rum/raisin ice cream. For dinner, you might sample a refined version of jerk pork, fish, or chicken. The smoked marlin is one of the chef's specialties and is something to savor. The cookery is superbly crafted, and there's always something bubbling in the curry pot of the day, even curried goat served with a fruit-studded chutney.

See map p. 300. At Half Moon, 11km (7 miles) east of Mo Bay, Rose Hall. ☎ 876-953-2314. Dinner reservations required. Main courses: $30–$48. AE, MC, V. Open: Daily 7–9 p.m. Free minivan transportation provided; request when you make reservations.

Toscanini
$$$ Harmony Hall   ITALIAN

The chef (P.G. Ricci) and headwaiter (his sister, Lella Ricci) are co-owners. Both hail from Parma, Italy, and London. Coming from a long line of restaurateurs, they bring style and a continental sophistication to their food service and preparation. The restaurant occupies the airy and gracious street level of a 19th-century stone pavilion whose upper floors function as an upscale art gallery. It's located on the coastal highway, about 6.4km (4 miles) east of Ocho Rios. The menu offers many classic Italian dishes, supplemented by ever-changing specials, depending on what's fresh at the market. The best of the many specialties include spaghetti with lobster penne *all'ortolana* (vegetarian pasta with goat cheese and herbs); *crespelle* (oven-baked crepes with chopped callaloo and cheese), and local catch of the day with Acqua Pazza sauce (roasted tomatoes, fish reduction, white wine, and herbs). There's an ongoing strong emphasis on fresh fish and shellfish, especially lobster. The chef also caters to vegetarians. All this good food is backed up by a fine wine list.

See map p. 300. Harmony Hall, Towers Isle, Route 3, 6.4km (4 miles) east of Ocho Rios. ☎ 876-975-4785. Main courses: $9.50–$26. Pastas: $12–$19. AE, MC, V. Open: Tues–Sun noon to 2 p.m. and 7–10:30 p.m.

Enjoying the Sand and Surf

With all its political turmoil, a possible sense of danger, and a lot of hassle from the local vendors and hustlers, you may reasonably ask, "Why go to Jamaica?" For all its faults, it remains the most exotic island in the West Indies, with the possible exception of Haiti. Some islands have prettier beaches, but Jamaica's allure, ever since its swashbuckling days, has drawn a steady stream of visitors to this "Island in the Sun," and many came to visit and stayed forever.

As one old salt from England told us, "All islands in the Caribbean have sunsets. But carnal red sunsets?"

Combing the beaches

Jamaica offers a dazzling choice of beaches. Someone once took a ruler and discovered that there are 321km (200 miles) of beaches, ranging from white sand to black sand, encircling the island. Many of these are so secluded you'll have them all to yourself. Others such as those at Mo Bay and Ocho Rios are overrun, especially when cruise ships arrive.

Most of the beaches of Jamaica need not concern you. You'll happily settle for the strip of sand in front of your resort. For the most part, the megaresorts, including the all-inclusives, have grabbed up the best sands.

Pick and choose carefully if a beach is the reason you're coming to Jamaica. Montego Bay, Jamaica's second-largest city, has more hotels but only some relatively modest public beaches. Ocho Rios, site of the second conglomeration of hotels, has only two beaches, and they're crowded.

 For a beach holiday, make it Negril. No beach on the island can match its 11km (7 miles) of white sand. If you like to take it all off, Negril is the place to flaunt your charms. Some parts of its beachfront are clothing optional, dividing the prudes from the nudes.

In or near Negril

The XXX-rated beach attraction for Negril is **Booby Cay,** a tiny islet that the Walt Disney people used in their film *20,000 Leagues Under the Sea.* Today it's more likely to attract the cameramen from *Playboy* (or *Playgirl* as the case may be). This is the nude island of Jamaica, reached after an 0.8km (half-mile) boat ride from Rutland Point. First-time visitors assume the "booby" refers to a woman's breasts, because many of those are on exhibit here. "Booby" actually comes from the islet's original inhabitants, a colony of blue-footed booby birds. The crowd from **Hedonism II** is especially fond of visiting for the day. Barbecues are staged, and boatloads arrive, some of whose passengers take off their swimsuits before hitting the sands. If you visit, take plenty of suntan lotion to protect your vital assets.

Robinson Crusoe types may shun all these public and overrun beaches. For that uncrowded beachfront, you can head for the South Coast, an easy drive east of Negril along A2. After leaving the dreary port city of Savanna-La-Mar, the first good beach you'll approach is **Bluefields Beach,** where the famous reggae star Peter Tosh used to live. At the western fringe of Bluefields Bay is **Paradise Park,** a cattle and dairy farm with waters ideal for swimming and picnic tables and barbecue grills on-site.

Farther down the coast, past the settlement of Black River, you come to relatively undiscovered **Treasure Beach,** with its long, black sandy beaches flanked by rocky limestone headlands, suitable for mountain biking and hiking. Local fishermen along the shoreline will take you out either for fishing or cruising on the bay for a reasonable fee to be negotiated. In the evening, have dinner at our favorite stopover, **Jake's** (earlier in this chapter), check in, and drink and dance the night away in the moonlight.

In or near Montego Bay

The public beaches in Montego Bay are good but small and usually crowded. They lie right in the center of the resort area opening off Gloucester Avenue or "Hip Strip" as it's known. The 8km-long (5-mile) **Doctor's Cave Beach** (☎ 876-952-2566) launched Mo Bay as a resort city in the 1940s. Popular with families, it's the best all-around beach in Mo Bay. Also opening onto Hip Strip is **Cornwall Beach** (☎ 876-952-3463), a long stretch of white sand with excellent swimming all year. Both beaches have dressing cabanas and water-sports kiosks. You can rent chairs,

Splish-Splash in Mo Bay's Waterworld

AquaSol Theme Park (also known as Walter Fletcher Beach) (☎ 876-979-9447, 876-940-1344) opens onto a well-maintained beach, positioned a short walk from the heart of Montego Bay. In 2004, a team of entrepreneurs added a compound of entertainment options, fenced everything in, and renamed it "The Aquasol Theme Park." Now, its sands bustle with scantily clad sunbathers and swimmers throughout the day. Then, beginning at around 8 p.m. every Friday to Sunday, the site experiences a change of clientele when mobs of both Jamaicans and foreign visitors hang out for hours in the moonlight, jamming and gossiping until the wee hours. Foreign visitors pay a $5 entrance fee, which allows access to a water-sports kiosk, a pier where glass-bottomed boats are moored, a strip of sand, a beauty salon, a bar and grill-style restaurant, a gym/health club with a private local membership, and a disco/bar with views of the sea, a collection of caged macaws, and surges of reggae and soca. Admission is $5 for adults, $3 for children under 12. Regardless of which of the facilities you opt to patronize, the entire compound is open Monday to Thursday 9 a.m. to 7 p.m., and 9 a.m. to at least midnight, and sometimes, later, depending on business, on Friday to Sunday.

umbrellas, and rafts from 9 a.m. to 5 p.m. daily, and admission to either beach is $23 for adults and $1.65 for children 12 and under. Regrettably, vendors and hustlers annoy you throughout the day.

You'll pay more but can escape the hordes by going to **Rose Hall Beach Club** (☎ **876-680-0969**), 18km (11 miles) east of Mo Bay. Here you get 0.8km (a half-mile) of private white-sand beach and turquoise waters, better facilities, and a finer restaurant, along with clean toilets and changing rooms, even a full water-sports program. The cost is $6 for adults or $3 for kids 12 and under any time daily from 9 a.m. to 5 p.m.

In or near Ocho Rios

In spite of its many all-inclusive megaresorts, Ocho Rios isn't great beach country. Ochi is also the major cruise-ship entry port for Jamaica, and beaches are even more crowded when these mammoths dock. In the center of the resort is **Mallards Beach,** always overrun although the sands are idyllic here. To the south, the white sands of **Turtle Beach** are even more alluring, but it, too, is busy. Locals themselves, with children in tow, also swim here, and it gets very crowded on weekends.

We like to escape Ocho Rios entirely and follow 007's trail to **James Bond Beach** (☎ **876-726-1630**), lying at Oracabessa, east of Ochi. This beach is near the former home of Bond's creator, Ian Fleming. The sandy strip is open Tuesday through Sunday, charging $5 for adults and $3 for children. On-site is a water-sports concession as well.

It rains a lot in Port Antonio, but its beaches are among the most beautiful and most secluded in Jamaica. Elizabeth Taylor and Richard Burton have long left the beach at **Frenchman's Cove,** 8km (5 miles) east of Port Antonio, but this beach is still a romantic romp. These white sands and freshwater stream cost $3 to enter daily from 9 a.m. to 5 p.m.

While at Port Antonio you can also go for a dip in the **Blue Lagoon** where the 14-year-old Brooke Shields swam nude in the movie of the same name. You won't find a beach here, but a natural amphitheater feeds the always-stunning waters, and this place is one of the finest in all of Jamaica for a refreshing dip — without your bikini, of course.

Playing in the surf

Jamaica is hardly the scuba center of the Caribbean, and islands such as the Caymans or Bonaire have far more spectacular underwater worlds. Even so, this island has diving adventures to enjoy, especially at Negril.

Hurricanes have severely damaged many of Jamaica's once-stunning reefs — that and careless boaters, overzealous fishermen, and young boys robbing the shore of its shells and sea fans to hawk to tourists.

In spite of that, Jamaica still has plenty of marine life. The following outfitters feature dive trips and certification courses and will also rent snorkeling gear for the day.

In Montego Bay

North Coast Marine Sports (☎ 876-953-2211), located at the Half Moon resort, offers everything from scuba diving to rentals of Sunfish, snorkel gear, kayaks, and more. They can arrange for deep-sea fishing trips and snorkel cruises, too.

Seaworld Resorts, whose main office is at the Cariblue Hotel, Rose Hall Main Road (☎ 876-953-2180; www.diveseaworld.com), operates flying-bridge cruisers, with deck lines and outriggers, for fishing expeditions. A half-day fishing trip costs $400 for up to four participants.

In Negril

The best area for snorkeling is off the cliffs in the **West End,** where you can see stingrays, sergeant majors, and several parrotfish on the reef at a depth of about 3 to 4m (10–15 ft.). You can find dozens of shops along West End Road, where you can rent snorkeling equipment at modest prices.

Ochi and Runaway Bay offer good snorkeling, too, on its shoreline east of Ocho Rios to Galina Point, which is fringed by a colorful reef. The reef fish are making a slight comeback, and marine life is varied. Although some reefs are accessible from the shore, you can avoid the boats and beach activity if you take a short boat ride to the better reefs farther offshore. If you're going to Port Antonio, snorkel with **Lady Godiva's Dive Shop** in Dragon Bay (☎ 876-428-3437, 876-335-2663), 11km (7 miles) from Port Antonio. Lady Godiva offers two excursions daily to San San Bay, a colorful reef off Monkey Island, for $25 per person. Snorkeling equipment is included, and dive prices range from $40 to $60 per person.

Negril Scuba Centre, at the Negril Beach Club Hotel, Norman Manley Boulevard (☎ 800-818-2963, 876-957-9641), is the best-equipped scuba facility in Negril. They offer beginner dive lessons daily, as well as multiple-dive packages for certified divers. Full scuba certifications and specialty courses are also available. A resort course, designed for first-time divers with basic swimming abilities, includes all instruction and equipment, a lecture on water and diving safety, and one open-water dive. The course begins at 10 a.m. daily and ends at 2 p.m., costing $75. A one-tank dive costs $35 per dive plus $5 for equipment rental. More economical is a two-tank dive, which includes lunch; you must complete your dive in one day. It costs $30, plus the (optional) $5 rental of all equipment. This organization is PADI-registered, although it accepts all recognized certification cards. It specializes in night dives and has been in business for two decades.

Climbing aboard

Even if you don't know how to swim, you can enjoy close encounters with the water on this plush island known for its tranquil rivers and cascading waterfalls. One of the more-unusual ways to enjoy the water in Jamaica is to take one of its famed river-raft rides, popularized by the late Errol Flynn, the dashing, womanizing actor who used to challenge his friends to raft races.

Although a fading Hollywood memory, Flynn was spoofed by Mel Brooks as "the man in the green tights" — he was known for his swashbuckling roles, including Robin Hood. People in the Port Antonio area still talk about him.

Here's how to hook up with this amusing sport. A Jamaican raftsman will pole you down the Rio Grande. We're not talking Texas here — Jamaica's Rio Grande is only 13km (8 miles) long, stretching like a snake from Berrydale to Rafter's Restaurant. The trip takes three hours, and you can bring along a picnic to enjoy on the river's bank. Plenty of vendors will be on hand to hawk a frosty Red Stripe. Or you can wait and order lunch at Rafter's.

The following companies arrange rafting trips:

- ✔ **Rio Grande Experience**, Rafter's Restaurant, St. Margaret's Bay (☎ 876-993-5778), provides a fully insured driver who will take you in your rented car to the starting point at Grants Level or Berrydale, where you board your raft. The rafts, some 10m (33 ft.) long and only 1.2m (4 ft.) wide, are propelled by stout bamboo poles. The raised double seat set about two-thirds of the way back accommodates two passengers. The skipper guides the craft down the river, between steep hills covered with coconut palms, banana plantations, and flowers, through limestone cliffs pitted with caves, past the "Tunnel of Love" (a narrow cleft in the rocks), then on to wider, gentler water. Trips last two to three hours and are offered from 9 a.m. to 4 p.m. daily at a cost of $55 per raft, which is suitable for two people. The trip ends at Rafter's Restaurant, where you collect your car, which the driver has returned.

- ✔ **Martha Brae's Rafters Village** (☎ 876-952-0889) lies 45km (28 miles) to the east of Mo Bay at a point 4.8km (3 miles) inland from Falmouth. The rafts are similar to those on the Rio Grande. You sit on a raised dais on bamboo logs. Wearing a swimsuit isn't necessary because you're seated in dry comfort. The cost is $45, with two riders allowed on a raft, plus a small child if accompanied by an adult (but use caution). The trips last 1¼ hours and operate daily from 9 a.m. to 4 p.m. Along the way, you can stop and order cool drinks or beer along the banks of the river. The village has a bar, a restaurant, and two souvenir shops.

- ✔ **Mountain Valley Rafting** (☎ 876-956-4920) runs trips down the River Lethe, approximately 19km (12 miles) southwest of Mo Bay.

The hour-long trip is about $40 per raft (two per raft) and takes you through unspoiled hill country. You can also book through your hotel tour desk.

✔ If you're staying in Negril or on the South Coast, we recommend **South Coast Safaris,** 1 Crane Rd. (☎ 876-965-2513), where you can take a boat ride up Jamaica's largest river, navigated through mangrove swamps in savanna country. You'll see egrets and other water birds, as well as Jamaica's crocodiles. Locals call them alligators. The one-hour safari costs $15 per person.

Also in that area, you should check out the **Y.S. Falls;** a jitney (small bus) will drop you near the falls for $12 (☎ 876-997-6360 for information). It's an idyllic place to play in the cool waters and have a picnic. The site isn't nearly as touristy as Dunn's River Falls in Ocho Rios. The estate is open daily from 9:30 a.m. to 3:30 p.m.

✔ **Dunn's River Falls** (☎ 876-974-4767) is Ocho Rios's biggest attraction — its most touristy — and you should avoid it when cruise ships are in port. Forming a daisy chain, you climb to the top of the falls with a guide (tip expected, of course). After the climb, you stairstep down through tiers of cascades and cooling pools until you reach the beach. Admission to the falls is $15 for adults and $12 for children ages 2 to 11. They're open daily from 8:30 a.m. to 5 p.m. (7 a.m.–5 p.m. on cruise-ship arrival days).

Wear old tennis shoes or sports sandals/water shoes to protect your feet from the sharp rocks and to prevent slipping. Although very small children are allowed to climb the falls, consider carefully whether you want to take a risk, especially with toddlers.

Exploring on Dry Land

From horseback riding to wilderness hiking, from golf to tennis, the resorts of Jamaica and its hinterlands offer many chances for an athletic vacation for those who don't want to spend all their time lying on a beach.

Exploring the island's past

Like Tara in *Gone With the Wind,* the Great House in Jamaica was a large house at the center of a sugar plantation where the master lived with his wife and family, waited upon by house slaves. Some of these Great Houses are still preserved in Jamaica today, although islanders disdain their evocation of the days of slavery. The two most intriguing Great Houses lie outside Montego Bay.

Once the grandest Great House in Jamaica, **Rose Hall** (☎ 876-953-2323) is the stuff of legend and lore, fabled as the former abode of the notorious White Witch of Rose Hall. If you believe all those bodice-ripping Gothic novels, "the witch," Annie Palmer, murdered at least three husbands and various lovers. Actually this libel may be just so much paperback fodder.

The real Annie Palmer died peacefully at the age of 72 (she wasn't murdered in her bed) after a long and apparently happy marriage. The vastly restored Rose Hall was originally built between 1778 and 1790 as the center of a 2,428-hectare (6,000-acre) plantation with more than 2,000 slaves. Frankly, the legend of Annie Palmer overrides the decoration and architecture here, but it's well worth a visit to see how the landed gentry lived. On the outskirts of Mo Bay, Rose Hall lies 3.2km (2 miles) east of the little town of Ironshore across from the Rose Hall resorts. Admission is $15 per person, or $10 for children 11 and under. Hours are daily from 9 a.m. to 6 p.m.; last tour at 5:15 p.m.

Greenwood Great House, lying 24km (15 miles) east of Montego Bay (☎ 876-953-1077), also has literary associations, these for real. The Georgian-style Great House was the former abode of Richard Barrett, whose cousin was the famous poet Elizabeth Barrett Browning. The house was built between 1780 and 1800, when the Barrett family was the largest landholder in Jamaica, owning 33,993 hectares (84,000 acres) and 3,000 slaves. The house has been restored, and you can visit it, seeing its library and antiques, although the interior isn't as ornate as Rose Hall. Guides in costumes offer a narrated tour. The house charges $12 admission, or $6 for children under 12, and is open daily from 9 a.m. to 6 p.m.

At an elevation of 128m (420 ft.), the **Coyaba River Garden and Museum** (☎ 876-974-6235) lies 2.4km (1½ miles) south of Ocho Rios at the Shaw Park Estate on Shaw Park Ridge Road. Meaning "paradise" in Arawak, Coyaba is set on 1.2 hectares (3 acres) of beautifully landscaped gardens with some of the most evocative of the island's flora. The grounds are filled with cascades, carp pools, and streams. In a villa on-site, artifacts trace the history of Jamaica from the early Arawaks to independence from Britain. Taking about an hour, tours are conducted daily from 8 a.m. to 6 p.m., costing $5 for ages 12 and up (free for others).

Celebrities, many from the golden age of Hollywood, frequented the North Coast of Jamaica in the '50s and '60s, and one of them, Sir Noel Coward, liked the island so much that he erected a retreat from the world at **Firefly** (☎ 876-725-0920), lying in St. Mary, 32km (20 miles) east of Ocho Rios overlooking the little town of Oracabessa. Sir Noel, along with his longtime companion, Graham Payn, lived here until Noel's death in 1973. His friends, from Katharine Hepburn to the Queen Mother of England, dropped in for a visit. A closet still contains his Hawaiian-print shirts, and in his bedroom rests the original four-poster bed he once occupied. The library contains his collection of books, and two grand pianos mark the spot where he composed some of his famous show tunes. Coward is buried on the grounds. The house is open Monday to Thursday and Saturday from 9 a.m. to 5 p.m., charging an admission of $10 or $5 children under 12.

On the same day you visit Firefly, you can also drop in at **Harmony Hall** (☎ 876-975-4222), lying at Tower Isles on Route 3, 6.4km (4 miles) east

of Ocho Rios. Built in the 19th century as the center of a sugar plantation, the restored complex is today the site of an art gallery showcasing
some of the best paintings and sculpture by island artists. Seek out, in
particular, the "Starfish Oils" by Sharon McConnell. Arts, crafts, and
"reggae" resort wear are also sold. The complex is also the home of
Toscanini, one of the best restaurants in Greater Ocho Rios (see earlier
in this chapter). Harmony Hall is also the site of the Garden Café for
informal food and drink.

Taking in some culture

Kingston is not only the political capital of Jamaica, but also the island's
cultural center. The **National Gallery of Jamaica,** Roy West Building,
Kingston Mall (☎ 876-922-1561), showcases the most important art collection on the island. It's a treasure-trove of the nation's most talented
sculptors and painters, the most famous of whom is Edna Manley, a
sculptor, who was married to Norman Manley, a former prime minister. In
the entryway, you're greeted with a large statue of the late Bob Marley. A
gift shop with novelties and hooks has been recently added. Admission is
$1.50 and hours are Tuesday through Thursday 10 a.m. to 5 p.m., Friday
10 a.m. to 4 p.m., and Saturday 10 a.m. to 3 p.m.

While in Kingston, you can also see its most visited attraction, the **Bob
Marley Museum,** 56 Hope Rd. (☎ 876-927-9152), the reggae singer's
former home and recording studio where he lived until his death on May
11, 1981, in a Miami hospital. You can tour the house, filled with Marley
memorabilia, Monday through Saturday from 9:30 a.m. to 4 p.m.; admission is $8.30 for adults, $3.30 ages 13 to 18.

Getting a breath of fresh air

Follow up a morning spent at Dunn's River Falls (see the section "Climbing
aboard," earlier in this chapter) with the most scenic drive in the area,
reached by heading down A3 south into a lush gorge called **Fern Valley.**
Originally a riverbed, the main road through the valley now passes a profusion of wild ferns, a rain forest, hardwood trees, and lianas. The road
runs for 6.4km (4 miles), taking in a profusion of more than 600 species of
ferns. You can stop at any point at one of the roadside stands inspecting
carved wood souvenirs and basketwork or perhaps picking up some fresh
fruit at one of the stands.

Keeping active

Of course, you can lie on the beach for your entire trip, but if you want
to keep active you'll find an array of choices in Jamaica. Over the years,
the island has developed some of the Caribbean's most beautiful and
challenging golf courses, and it offers plenty of places to play tennis.
Many courts are lit for cooler nighttime play. A beautiful way to explore
Jamaica's backcountry of plantation lands and hills is to go horseback
riding. Hiking in the hills is yet another option, but only the strongest
and most athletic should attempt to climb the **Blue Mountain Peak.**

Riding the range on horseback

For the horseback rider, the best stables and the best trails are located near the resort city of Ocho Rios. **Chukka Caribbean Adventures** (☎ 876-972-2506) lies at Richmond Llandovery, 6.4km (4 miles) to the east of Runaway Bay. These stables are the best in Jamaica, a three-hour beach ride goes for $67. During weekends in winter, polo players, often from Britain, visit here. Polo lessons are $50 for 30 minutes. A more recent feature is a mountain-and-sea adventure on a bike (90 percent of which is downhill). The 2½-hour bike ride, priced at $65, ends with a swim and some snorkeling.

In the same area, you can also go horseback riding along a trio of scenic trails at **Prospect Plantation,** Route A3, 4.8km (3 miles) east of Ocho Rios (☎ 876-994-1058). A one-hour horseback ride goes for $58, although you can arrange longer trail rides. You can also tour a working plantation, at a cost of $27 per person, $20 for ages 12 and under. Tours are conducted Monday through Saturday at 10:30 a.m., 2 p.m., and 3:30 p.m.

In Negril, you can go riding through the Negril Hills to the south of the resort city. Several outfitters in the area can rent you a horse, but your best bet is **Rhodes Hall Plantation** (☎ 876-957-6334). They offer a two-hour ride across the scenic beauty spots of the outskirts of Negril. Cost averages $60 per hour.

In Montego Bay, the area around the resort city is heavily built up, but the people at **Rocky Point Riding Stables,** Half Moon Club, Rose Hall (☎ 876-953-2286), know the best trails. Their 30 horses are housed in Jamaica's most beautiful stables, where you can arrange for a 90-minute beach or mountain ride costing $60 per rider.

Linking up with a round of golf

The game of golf was imported from Scotland in the late 19th century, and the sport has been firmly entrenched in Jamaica ever since. Today the island offers some of the finest golf courses in the Caribbean, the best centered at Mo Bay.

Caddies are required, and rates are $12 to $25, but you'll get extra entertainment: They carry your golf bag and clubs balanced sideways on their heads.

Some of the best courses are in Mo Bay. The following are our favorites:

✔ **White Witch of Rose Hall Golf Course,** part of the new Ritz-Carlton Rose Hall grounds (☎ 876-518-0174), lies 11km (7 miles) east of Montego Bay and is Jamaica's most spectacular course. Designed by Robert von Hagge, the course is set on 80 landscaped hectares (200 acres), charging $139 for hotel guests, $159 for nonguests.

✔ The **Half Moon** golf, tennis, and beach club, Rose Hall, 11km (7 miles) east of Mo Bay (☎ 876-953-2560), has a championship

Robert Trent Jones–designed 18-hole course. Greens fees are $125 for guests, $130 for nonguests.

✔ **Ironshore,** at Ironshore, 4.8km (3 miles) east of the Donald Sangster International Airport (☎ 876-953-3681), is an 18-hole, par-72 course. The greens fee is $50.

✔ **Tryall Golf, Tennis, and Beach Club,** 24km (15 miles) west of Mo Bay on North Coast Highway (☎ 876-956-5660), has an 18-hole championship course on the site of a 19th-century sugar plantation. Guests of Tryall pay $85 in winter, $40 in the off season. Nonguests can play only in the off season, paying $155 for the privilege.

✔ **Rose Hall Resort & Country Club,** at Rose Hall, 6.4km (4 miles) east of the airport on North Coast Highway (☎ 876-953-2650), has a challenging seaside and mountain layout. Fees run $40 for one hour, $35 for 45 minutes, $30 for 30 minutes.

✔ **Sandals Golf and Country Club,** 2 miles (3.2km) east of Ocho Rios (☎ 876-975-0119), has an 18-hole course known for its panoramic scenery, 213m (700 ft.) above sea level. The greens fee is $100 for nonguests.

✔ **SuperClub's Runaway Golf Course,** North Coast Highway, Kingston (☎ 876-973-7319), is a challenging 18-hole course that has witnessed many championship tournaments. The greens fee is $80 for nonguests; guests of SuperClubs play for free.

✔ **Negril Hills Golf Club,** Sheffield Road (☎ 876-957-4638), is Negril's only golf course. Although it doesn't have the prestige of such Montego Bay courses as Tryall, this golf course is the only one in western Jamaica. The 91-hectare (225-acre) course lies in the foothills of Negril at Sheffield, 4.8km (3 miles) east of the center of the resort area, bordering the Great Morass. Opening in 1994, the course is known for its water hazards and its undulating fairways. This place is one where if your ball goes into the water, you don't try to retrieve it unless you want to fight over it with a crocodile. On-site is a restaurant (mediocre food) and a pro shop. Greens fees for 18 holes are $58.

Having a ball with tennis or squash

The megaresorts offer tennis courts, which are free to their guests. Most of them, except for the all-inclusives, let nonguests play if they reserve court space and pay to play. Nonguests are charged from $20 per day. Tennis pros on-site usually give lessons for about $14 per hour.

What follows is a sampling of some of the best courts:

✔ In Negril, tennis buffs book into **Couples Swept Away Negril,** Norman Manley Boulevard (☎ 876-957-4061), which offers ten courts, more than any other in the area. Half of these are clay, the others hard courts.

✔ **Half Moon,** outside Montego Bay (☎ 876-953-2211), has the finest courts in the area, even outclassing Tryall. Its 13 state-of-the-art courts, 7 of which are lit for night play, attract tennis players from around the world. Lessons cost $25 to $35 per half-hour, $50 to $65 per hour. Residents play free, day or night.

✔ **Tryall Golf, Tennis, and Beach Club,** St. James (☎ 876-956-5660), offers nine hard-surface courts, three lit for night play, near its Great House. Day games are free for guests; nonguests pay $30 per hour.

✔ **Rose Hall Resort & Country Club,** Rose Hall (☎ 876-953-2650), outside Montego Bay, is an outstanding tennis resort, though it's not the equal of Half Moon or Tryall. Rose Hall offers six hard-surface courts, each lit for night play. As a courtesy, nonguests are sometimes invited to play for free, but you have to obtain permission from the manager.

Going to the birds

Birdies flock to Jamaica, which offers some serious opportunities to observe our feathery friends. The island hosts more than 250 different species, including the verrain hummingbird, which you can see in the Blue Mountains. Only the famous "bee" hummingbird found in some places in Cuban forests is smaller.

Some 50 species of birds are found only in Jamaica, and in no other habitat in the world. Many of the species you're likely to see, including the Jamaican blackbird, are endangered.

In the 20th century, many exotic birds in Jamaica went the way of the dodo. If you're with a guide, don't be surprised if he shows fright at the sound of the *patoo,* an African word for owl. Superstitious Jamaicans believe that an owl's screech is a signal that the Grim Reaper is on his way.

The best place for concentrated bird-watching is at the **Rocklands Wildlife Station,** 1.6km (1 mile) outside Anchovy on the road from Montego Bay, St. James (☎ 876-952-2009). You can enjoy unique experiences like having a Jamaican "doctorbird" perch on your finger to drink syrup, feeding small doves and finches millet from your hand, and watching dozens of other exotic birds flying in for their evening meal. Don't take children age five and under to this sanctuary, because they tend to bother the birds. Admission is $10; the center is open daily from 9 a.m. to 5:30 p.m.

Taking a guided tour

The best guided hikes and the best guided ATV tours are offered along the lush North Coast, which gets more rain than elsewhere in Jamaica. In Port Antonio, **Valley Hikes** (☎ 876-993-3881) features a variety of hikes of various difficulties through the Rio Grande Valley, that luxuriant area between the John Crow Mountains and the Blue Mountains. The easiest trail is a one-and-a-half-hour waterfall tour for $35. You can also take a 6.4km (4-mile) hike (about four hours) into the Blue Mountains, taking in its flora and fauna at a cost of $35 per person.

Climbing every mountain

Reaching its peak at 2,255m (7,400 ft.) in the Blue Mountains, Jamaica offers the Caribbean's most dramatic mountain scenery and its most varied, with cascading waterfalls, roaring rivers, and vast, almost jungle-like rain forests filled with stunning flora. To watch the sun come up at the towering peak of the Blue Mountains is the goal of many a hiker in Jamaica. Even if you don't want to get up that early, you can enjoy organized hikes through this lush terrain. British soldiers first chopped many of the trails out of the wilderness. Today farmers carrying coffee by mule trains (sometimes the crop is ganja) are more likely to use the trails.

At the end of the trail, know that a steaming cup of Blue Mountain coffee — "the java of kings" — is waiting for you. Sometimes locals use wildflower honey instead of sugar to sweeten the brew.

You could get lost or mugged wandering around these Blue Mountain trails on your own. We recommend that you set out only with a guide. You can go with a group or else on your own with one or two other people in your party, but always, *always* with a guide.

You can book with Kingston's best-known specialists in eco-sensitive tours, **Sunventure Tours,** 30 Balmoral Ave., Kingston (☎ 876-960-6685). The staff here can always arrange an individualized tour for you and your party, but it also has a roster of mainstream offerings. The **Blue Mountain Sunrise Tour** involves a camp-style overnight in one of the most remote and inaccessible areas of Jamaica. For a fee of $75 to $120 per person, the guides retrieve participants at their Kingston hotels and drive them to an isolated ranger station, Wildflower Lodge, that's accessible only via a four-wheel-drive vehicle, in anticipation of a two-stage hike that begins at 2 p.m. A simple mountaineer's supper is served at 6 p.m. around a campfire at a ranger station near Portland Gap. At 3 a.m., climbers hike by moonlight and flashlight to a mountaintop aerie that was selected for its view of the sunrise over the Blue Mountains. Climbers stay aloft until around noon that day and then head back down the mountain for an eventual return to their hotels in Kingston by 4 p.m. A four-hour trek, costing from $25 to $30 per person, is also available.

Cycling is another option for touring the Blue Mountains. **Blue Mountain Bike Tours** in Kingston (☎ 876-974-7075; www.bmtours.com) offers all-downhill bike tours through the Blue Mountains — you peddle only about a half-dozen times on this several-mile trip. Guides drive visitors to the highest navigable point in the Blue Mountains, where they provide bikes and protective gear. They also provide lunch, snacks, and lots of information about coffee, local foliage, and history. The cost is about $93 per person.

Shopping the Local Stores

You literally can't go anywhere in Jamaica, even if lying on the beach, without some vendor coming around and hawking locally made crafts to you, most of dubious taste. Not only that, but every town, village, or hamlet has vendors along the roadsides, including Fern Gully, south of Ocho Rios. Hardwood carvings of Bob Marley are pure kitsch, and bead jewelry comes in Rasta colors of yellow, green, and red. If you're interested, remember to bargain. The asking price is merely the beginning of the negotiation. You can often get an item for about 25 percent less than what the vendor first asked.

Here's a thing or six you may want to bring back with you — all duty-free: Jamaican rum; Tia Maria, Jamaica's world-famous coffee liqueur; Blue Mountain coffee; hot sauces; woodcarvings; and handmade Macanudo cigars.

Most duty-free merchandise is sold at the major shopping plazas in Ocho Rios and Montego Bay. In Mo Bay, most of the duty-free shops are at **City Centre** or the **Holiday Village Shopping Centre.** Even better is **Half Moon Plaza,** on the coastal road 13km (8 miles) east of Mo Bay.

In Ocho Rios, all the major duty-free markets, easy to find, lie in the center of town, including **Ocean Village Shopping Centre, Coconut Grove Shopping Plaza,** and **Pineapple Place Shopping Centre.**

If you want to escape the hassle of the marketplace and shop in ease and comfort, visit the **Gallery of West Indian Art** at the exclusive Round Hill Hotel, Route 1A, west of Mo Bay (☎ 876-952-4547). Here the boutique owner has acquired some of the finest Jamaican and Haitian paintings, along with some locally made, painted pottery and carvings.

The best Jamaican art on the island is showcased at two galleries in Kingston: **Frame Gallery,** 10 Tangerine Place (☎ 876-926-4644), with more than 300 works on exhibit, and its main competitor, **Mutual Gallery,** Oxford Road (☎ 876-929-4302), a constantly changing showcase of the island's finest artists, both known and unknown.

Living It Up After Dark

When the sun goes down, sounds of reggae fill the air, and blenders whirl in the tropical bars mixing those lethal rum punches. For such large resorts, nightlife in Mo Bay and Ocho Rios is a bit skimpy, except for staged entertainment at the hotels such as limbo dancers, reggae bands, and the like. More happens in Kingston after dark (not the safest place to be) and Negril than anywhere else on the island. Because running around at night on your own is a bit risky, many visitors staying at one of the smaller inns can visit one of the all-inclusives just for the night with a purchase of a night pass, usually valid from 6 p.m. to 3 a.m. The cost varies but averages around $75 per person. Once inside, you're entitled to all the food and drink you can consume, with the entertainment thrown in as well.

One of the hottest venues after dark in Kingston is **Asylum,** 69 Knutsford Blvd. (☎ 876-929-4386), where the program changes nightly. Some nights are devoted only to reggae music, other nights to various contests, sometimes to the old hits of the '70s and '80s. A crowd mainly of locals in their 20s and 30s flocks here to enjoy the music, the dance, the entertainment, and even karaoke. This place is very tropical and very happening, open Tuesday through Sunday from 10 p.m. to 4 a.m., charging a cover ranging from $6 to $8.

In Ocho Rios, the place to head after dark is **Jamaica'N Me Crazy,** at the sunset Jamaica Grande Hotel & Spa (☎ 876-974-2200), which has the best lighting and sound system in Ocho Rios (and perhaps Jamaica). The crowd includes everyone from the passing yachter to the curious tourist, who may be under the mistaken impression that he's seeing an authentic Jamaican nightclub. Open nightly from 10 p.m. to 3 a.m.

In Montego Bay, **The Brewery,** Gloucester Avenue (☎ 876-940-2433), is one of the city's most popular nightlife hangouts, evoking a mixture of an English pub and an all-Jamaican jerk pork pit. It has a woodsy-looking bar where everyone is into Red Stripe and reggae, lots of neomedieval memorabilia à la Olde England, and a covered veranda in back where clients overlook the traffic on busy Hip Strip. This place mixes a brew of locals and visitors, usually in their 20s and 30s, and does so exceedingly well.

Fast Facts: Jamaica

Area Code

The area code is **876.**

ATMs

Traveler's checks, no longer used by some visitors, are still in wide use in Jamaica because few ATMs accept U.S. bank cards. You can receive cash advances by using a credit card — that is, if the ATM is working. The dollars spilling out will be Jamaican, of course.

Babysitters

Most charge about $8 an hour for one child. Your hotel can easily arrange sitters, and we've found that caregivers in Jamaica are among the best in the Caribbean. If you stay out late, though, please tip extra and ask how the sitter plans to get home.

Currency Exchange

The unit of currency in Jamaica is the Jamaican dollar, represented by the same symbol as the U.S. dollar ($). Both U.S. and Jamaican currencies are widely accepted. Always clarify which currency someone is quoting you. The rate of exchange for the Jamaican dollar isn't fixed. At press time, the exchange rate was about J$60 to U.S. $1.

Jamaican currency is issued in bank notes of J$10, J$20, J$50, J$100, and J$500. Coins are available in denominations of 5¢, 10¢, 25¢, 50¢, J$1, and J$5. We recommend carrying small change in Jamaican or U.S. dollars for tips, beach fees, and other incidentals.

Bank of Jamaica exchange bureaus are located at both international airports (Montego Bay and Kingston), at cruise-ship terminals, and in most hotels. You can get an immigration card, which you need for bank transactions and currency exchange, at the airport arrivals desks. Exchanging currency outside of the banking system is illegal.

Doctors

Hotels have doctors on call. If you need any particular medicine or treatment, bring evidence, such as a letter from your own physician.

Emergencies

To report a fire or call an ambulance, dial ☎ 110. For the police and air rescue, dial ☎ 119.

Hospitals

For dire situations, seek help in San Juan or Miami. St. Ann's Bay Hospital, St. Ann's Bay (☎ 876-972-0150), has a hyperbaric chamber for scuba-diving emergencies. In Kingston, Medical Associates Hospital (☎ 876-926-1400); in Montego Bay, the Cornwall Regional Hospital is at Mount Salem (☎ 876-952-5100); and in Port Antonio, the Port Antonio General Hospital is at Naylor's Hill (☎ 876-993-2646). Negril only has minor-emergency clinics.

Information

See the Appendix for helpful Web sites and locations of U.S.-based and local tourist offices.

Internet Access and Cybercafes

The best place to go, outside your hotel, is the Coral Seas Beach Hotel, Norman Manley Boulevard (☎ 876-957-3997), open daily 9 a.m. to 5 p.m. Nonguests are permitted to use the facilities.

Newspapers and Magazines

Resort gift shops carry a decent selection, including *USA Today,* and many hotels offer the *New York Times* via fax at no charge.

Pharmacies

Local pharmacies don't accept a prescription unless issued by a Jamaican doctor. One of the best pharmacies in Montego Bay is Clinicare Pharmacy, 14A Market St. (☎ 876-952-8510), open Monday to Saturday from 9 a.m. to 8 p.m. and Sunday 10 a.m. to 6 p.m. The most central pharmacy is Ocho Rios Pharmacy, Shop 27 in Ocean Village Plaza (☎ 876-974-2398), open Monday to Saturday 9 a.m. to 8 p.m. and Sunday 9 a.m. to 7 p.m.; and in Kingston, Moodie's Pharmacy, in the New Kingston Shopping Centre (☎ 876-926-4174).

Police

For the police and air rescue, dial ☎ 119.

Post Office

Jamaica issues stamps highly praised by collectors. The Montego Bay post office (☎ 876-952-7389) is at 122 Barnett St., and is open weekdays from 8 a.m. to 5 p.m. As you leave Negril Square, the post office is on Lighthouse Road.

Restrooms

According to Jamaica law, every restaurant and bar, in their capacity as a public place, must maintain, in good working condition, its public toilets. So even though the restaurant or bar you crash may not necessarily embrace you, they're obligated to at least let you in. (We usually consider it good form to buy a soda, some coffee, or a drink, just to be sociable.) But in reaction to complaints about the lack of public facilities on the streets of many Jamaican resorts, and to avoid overburdening the facilities of bars and restaurants, Jamaican law also requires every shopping center to provide clean, well-maintained restrooms for public use. Consequently, many Jamaicans head for the malls in whatever neighborhood they're in for access to public toilets. In Montego Bay, you'll find toilets in, among others, the huge Bay West Shopper Center on Harbour Street and the LOJ (Life of Jamaica) Shopping Center on Howard Cooke Boulevard. Public beaches in Jamaica almost always have port-o-potties or, in some cases, even more permanent toilet facilities. Examples include Long Bay Beach, positioned midway along the sandy stretch of Seven Mile Beach, and in Montego Bay, Doctor's Cave Beach, the most visible and prominent beach in downtown Montego Bay.

Safety

Most hotels and resorts, and even some villas, have private security guards, so you probably won't run into any problems. However, beaches are public, so if you go for a stroll, you can expect to be approached by people selling everything from woodcarvings and shells to drugs and sex to tours of the "real Jamaica." Safeguard your valuables and never leave them unattended on a beach. Likewise, never leave luggage or other valuables in a car or in the trunk. The U.S. State Department has issued a travel advisory about crime rates in Kingston, so don't go walking around alone at night. Caution is also advisable in many North Coast tourist areas, especially remote houses and isolated villas that can't afford security.

Drugs (including ganja, or marijuana) are illegal, and imprisonment is the penalty for possession. Also, you may well be buying ganja from a police informant, many of whom target visitors so that they aren't turning on their hometown buddies. Don't smoke pot openly in public, no matter who you see doing it. You may be the one who gets caught. Above all, don't even consider bringing marijuana back into the United States. Drug-sniffing dogs are stationed at the Jamaican airports, and they'll check your luggage. U.S. Customs agents pay keen attention to those arriving from Jamaica, and they easily catch and arrest those who try to take that sort of souvenir home.

Smoking

One wit in Negril said that the Jamaican government has enough trouble restricting the use of ganja in public places, and that if they ever imposed restrictions against tobacco, there might be a general revolution. Jamaica has no official restrictions against smoking in public places, so consequently, every restaurant in the country sets its own rules. In many cases, the venue is laissez faire, with clients lighting up whenever and wherever they want. In other cases, as in the restaurant at the hyperexclusive Round Hill, as well as within many of its less-exalted competitors, the moment a client complains about smoke from a neighboring table, he or she is moved to another table. We think it's wise, when you first enter the restaurant, to ask the host, hostess, or wait staff at any given restaurant where it's best to sit in reference to your particular smoking preference.

Taxes

Jamaica charges a general consumption tax of 15 percent on all goods and services, which includes car rentals and telephone calls. Additionally, the government imposes a 10 to 15 percent tax on hotel rooms. You'll also encounter a $37 departure tax at the airport, payable in either Jamaican dollars or in U.S. dollars. Don't count on getting cash at the airport, because few ATMs accept U.S. bank cards, and the machines are often out of money or service.

Taxis

Many visitors opt not to rent a car and to take a taxi to where they want to go. See the "Getting Around Jamaica" section earlier in this chapter for more details. Because even official taxis often have no meters, the important thing to keep in mind is to negotiate the fare before you get in and determine if payment is being quoted in Jamaican dollars or U.S. dollars. If the payment sounds fair, go for it. If you think it's too steep, try to negotiate it downward. If you can't agree on a price, walk away and try your luck with another cabbie.

Weather Updates

Try www.weather.com for current updates.

Chapter 14

Puerto Rico

- -

In This Chapter

▶ Knowing what to expect when you arrive
▶ Getting around the island
▶ Deciding where you want to stay
▶ Sampling the local cuisine at the best restaurants
▶ Scoping out good beaches and diving into water sports
▶ Satisfying the landlubber: Shopping and nightlife

- -

*R*ivaled only by Jamaica, Puerto Rico is the most diverse destination in the Caribbean. From its 415km (258 miles) of sandy beaches to its lush inland forest, Puerto Rico, a Commonwealth of the United States, is a happy melding of natural beauty and historical sights.

When stacked up against larger islands of the Caribbean such as Jamaica or Cuba, Puerto Rico is small, measuring 177km (100 miles) from east to west and 56km (35 miles) from north to south. It's the smallest of the easternmost islands known as *the archipelago of the Greater Antilles*. But the island is chock-full of activities — making it a perfect year-round destination.

The island offers miles of tennis courts, casinos galore, more dance clubs than any other place in the Caribbean, acres of golf, and almost as many shopping bargains as St. Thomas. Its restored **Old Town of San Juan** is the Caribbean's greatest living history book, far excelling its nearest rival, Santo Domingo, the capital of the Dominican Republic. Cruise ships also make San Juan the busiest port in the Caribbean, even more so than the clogged harbor of Charlotte Amalie on St. Thomas.

The little island lies some 1,609km (1,000 miles) southeast of the tip of Florida and opens onto both the sometimes-stormy Atlantic Ocean and the more-tranquil Caribbean Sea.

To see the real Puerto Rico, you need to leave San Juan, especially the high-priced **Condado Beach** area, and explore the narrow and steep roads, as well as meandering mountain trails, that lead to the Caribbean the way it used to be.

Arriving at the Airport

More airplanes arrive from the United States in San Juan, the capital of Puerto Rico, than on any other island in the Caribbean. San Juan is, in fact, the gateway to the northern Caribbean, and flights are not only frequent but also more affordable with many deals available.

San Juan is the major hub for **American Airlines,** which through that carrier or its subsidiary, **American Eagle,** offers more flights throughout the Caribbean than any other airline.

When you land in Puerto Rico, you're still in the United States, or at least an American territory. Flying time from Miami is only two hours.

The main airport for Puerto Rico, and the major air terminal in all of the Caribbean, is the **Luís Muñoz Marin International Airport** (☎ 787-791-1014), lying east of Isla Verde and east of the resorts of the Condado and the Old Town of San Juan. The airport is one of the finest in the Caribbean, evoking the Miami airport in some aspects. Half of all the flights to and from the Caribbean pass through here, making it a busy, bustling place.

American Airlines isn't only the only carrier flying into Marin International, although it does offer the most frequent and the largest number of flights from such U.S. cities as New York, Newark, Miami, Baltimore, Boston, Chicago, Dallas/Fort Worth, Tampa, Fort Lauderdale, and Washington (Dulles). **Delta** is the most convenient connection from Atlanta and points in the southeast, and **United Airlines** wings in from such cities as Detroit, Memphis, and Minneapolis. **US Airways** flies down from Charlotte, North Carolina; Pittsburgh; and Philadelphia.

Getting oriented at the airport

You'll find more ATMs in the San Juan airport than anywhere else in the Caribbean, as well as a helpful tourist information office dispensing useful material and discount coupons.

Passengers arriving in San Juan, often from an exhausting trip, or others facing lengthy waits for their next air connection can avail themselves of the **Diamond Point International Massage** (☎ 787-253-3063), located near gates four and five in the American Airlines terminal. A highly trained staff offers a variety of massages, including relaxing foot massages, which cost $50 for a 25-minute session. The shop is open daily from 9 a.m. to 6 p.m. and accepts MasterCard and Visa.

Families with children arriving at the San Juan airport with a layover between flights will find a centrally located video arcade, with games such as Cruisin' USA, Marvel Superheroes, and X-Men. A change machine dispenses quarters.

Those meeting scheduled flights soon learn that Puerto Rico is an hour ahead of the U.S. mainland when it's on eastern standard time. The only time that clocks in Puerto Rico and on the East Coast are coordinated is when the mainland goes on daylight saving time.

Navigating your way through passport control and Customs

Because Puerto Rico is a territory of the United States, U.S. citizens can fly in and out without a passport, although some photo ID is required. If your flight originated on the U.S. mainland, you don't have to clear U.S. Customs and Immigration. If you're flying into San Juan from elsewhere in the Caribbean, perhaps Barbados or Jamaica, you have to clear Customs and Immigration because you've been outside the United States.

Getting from the airport to your hotel

Some hotels, particularly the megaresorts, have a van waiting for you at the airport to take you to your hotel. You need to alert your hotel of your arrival time when making a reservation. If you're staying at one of the smaller, independent operators, you have to get to your hotel or resort on your own steam. Continue reading to find out how.

By taxi

Taxi drivers line up at the airport, meeting all incoming flights, so you rarely have to wait. Fares are about the same as in most major U.S. cities such as Miami. When you're on the sidewalk in front of the terminal with your luggage, tell the official dispatcher (he or she is in uniform and wears a badge) where you're going. The dispatcher hands you a slip of paper with the amount of your fare written on it. Give this slip to your driver, who's obligated to follow the fixed tariffs.

Airport taxis, called **Taxi Turísticos,** assess rates based on zones. The hotels of Isla Verde are close to the airport, so the taxis charge $8 per person. Heading to a hotel on the Condado costs $12. In the unlikely event you're staying in Old Town, the fare is the most expensive at $16.

If you're carrying more than two pieces of luggage, you have to pay an additional 50¢ per bag and another dollar for use of the trunk.

Bracero Limousine Ltd. (☎ 787-253-1133) offers limousine transport from the airport to various neighborhoods of San Juan for prices that are much higher than those that taxis charge (although the limousines are much more luxurious than taxis). The fare for two adults for transport (with luggage) to any hotel in Isla Verde or Condado is $105 and to Old San Juan is $125.

By car

If you reserved a car before you left the mainland, you're more likely to get a better rate, and you have the convenience of having your vehicle waiting for you at the airport. All major U.S. car-rental firms have desks at the airport. Look for your choice in the ground transportation section adjoining the baggage claim area. See "Getting Around Puerto Rico," later in this chapter, for more information on auto rentals.

If you need a wheelchair-accessible van, you can get such a vehicle via **Wheelchair Transportation** (☎ 800-868-8028).

Choosing Your Location

The room with your name on it in Puerto Rico could be in a high-rise opening onto San Juan's famous **Condado Beach,** or in a restored convent or an artist's studio in the historic **Old Town of San Juan.** Perhaps your dream nest is elsewhere on the island in a *parador* that was created out of a former coffee plantation, such as the 20-room Parador Hacienda Gripiñas in Jayuya. If you want a hotel with a casino, you'll find those, too, both in San Juan and in the satellite resorts out on the island.

Chances are you'll book a room on the North Coast in or around San Juan, because most resorts are centered here. The Southern Coast of Puerto Rico is relatively undeveloped. In this chapter, we provide our picks to help you keep your options simple.

San Juan: A tale of two cities

If Charles Dickens were writing about San Juan instead of London and Paris, he could still call it *A Tale of Two Cities,* because Puerto Rico's capital divides into two radically different zones.

The seven-block square known as *Viejo San Juan,* or **Old Town,** is the most historic and architecturally pure in all the Caribbean. Today a protected World Heritage Site, Old Town has buildings that date back 500 years, although vastly restored. The Spanish architectural style of carved wood or iron balconies prevails. Old Town not only offers some of the Caribbean's most historic museums, forts, and sightseeing attractions, but it is also one grand shopping bazaar. The square is also the site of **El Convento,** Puerto Rico's most venerated landmark hotel. With very few exceptions, accommodations are scarce in Old Town; it's much better as a dining choice.

The hotels stretch to the east of Old Town, beginning along the **Condado Beach** strip — the most famous in the Caribbean — long called "the Waikiki of the Caribbean." Beach resort life began at the Condado mainly in the 1920s, but now **Isla Verde,** lying farther east close to the airport, is challenging the Condado, many of whose hotels are looking stale.

Gamblers, families, commercial travelers, and cruise-ship passengers in San Juan for a brief layover prefer this long San Juan beachfront, with its high-rises, many dating from the dull architectural era of the 1960s. All the megaresorts open onto the beachfront.

All the large resorts also feature casinos. San Juan is hardly Las Vegas, but only Aruba equals it in gambling in the Caribbean. One big difference: In Las Vegas, gamblers often get liquor free. In San Juan, you have to pay not only your gambling debts, but your scotch bill as well.

Elsewhere on the island

Outside of San Juan, two other large resorts, the Westin Rio Mar Beach and Wyndham El Conquistador, lie to the east of San Juan. Other than those megaresorts, and with the exception of Horned Dorset Primavera at Rincón in the West, most hotels in Puerto Rico are relatively modest affairs. For small villas, inns, and condos, you can always escape to the offshore island of **Vieques.**

As an option to a sprawling megaresort, you can book into one of the rural inns of Puerto Rico, some of them government-sponsored *paradores*. Most of them are modest but the prices are very affordable. *Paradores* usually charge from $55 to $135 a night for a double room.

You can get information for all *paradores* by contacting the tourist board's **Paradores of Puerto Rico,** P.O. Box 4435, Old San Juan, PR 00902 (☎ **800-866-7827** for all of Puerto Rico) or visiting www.gotoparadores.com.

In hotels outside of San Juan, rates don't often include airport transfers. Be sure to ask when you book.

Getting Around Puerto Rico

San Juan offers the best and most varied means of getting about in the Caribbean. If you want to see the island itself, however, public transportation is woefully inadequate.

By car

If you're staying only in San Juan, you can get about by public transportation, foot, hotel shuttle, or taxi. But if you want to tour the island in any depth, especially that hidden beach or that mountain retreat, a car is necessary.

As the Caribbean goes, the highways or even smaller arteries of Puerto Rico are well marked and in passable or even good condition for the most part. Distances are posted in kilometers and not in miles. Surprisingly, speed limits are posted in miles. Avoid night driving whenever possible because of poor lighting.

Compared to Jamaica, motorists in Puerto Rico are practically driving-school instructors. That being said, they do have a tendency to indulge in dangerous passing and seem to hog the center of the road.

 If you plan to veer off the main highways on the island and head for remote destinations in the mountainous interior, don't rely on the maps that car-rental agencies hand out — they aren't adequately detailed. The maps sold at gasoline stations, such as those published by Rand McNally, are worth the investment.

In Puerto Rico, you can use a valid driver's license from your country of origin for three months. All major U.S. car-rental agencies are represented on the island, including **Avis** (☎ **800-331-1212,** 787-791-0600; www.avis.com), **Budget** (☎ **800-472-3325,** 787-791-3685; www.budget.com), **Dollar** (☎ **800-800-4000,** 787-791-5500; www.dollar.com), and **Hertz** (☎ **800-654-3131,** 787-791-0840; www.hertz.com).

Most car-rental agencies in Puerto Rico offer unlimited mileage. If yours doesn't, seek out a firm that does. Rental rates start as low as $23 per day, plus insurance. Check with your local insurer to see if you're covered in Puerto Rico. Extra insurance is often waived for those with American Express or certain gold bank credit cards. Check the tourist literature that the airport information desks hand out for car-rental discount coupons. Sometimes your AAA membership gets you a discount. Often, if you reserve three days or more in advance, you also get a discount.

The major car-rental firms such as Hertz or Avis offer a free shuttle service from the airport to their car depots where you can pick up your car.

 Gasoline stations in Puerto Rico sell by the liter, not by the gallon. Stations along major highways accept credit cards, but after you veer into the mountains, carry the Yankee dollar to purchase your fuel.

By taxi

Taxis are plentiful in San Juan and are more difficult to secure out on the island. In San Juan, airport taxis, called **Taxi Turísticos,** are painted white and are marked with the company's logo on their doors. These official taxis charge fixed tariffs based on the zones in which you travel. Depending on where you're going in San Juan, fares generally range between $8 and $16.

All authorized taxis, falling under the umbrella of the **Public Service Commission** (☎ 787-756-1401), should have a working meter. If not, agree on the price before getting in. Expect a minimum charge of $3, plus an extra charge of $1 at night. You're assessed 10¢ for each 2.1km (1⅓ mile) and 50¢ for every piece of luggage. You can call a cab in San Juan by dialing **Mejor Taxicabs** (☎ 787-723-2460) or in Puerto Rico's second city of Ponce by dialing **Ponce Taxi** (☎ 787-840-0088).

Taxis are lined up outside the entrances to most hotels; if not, a staff member can usually call one for you. If you want to arrange a taxi on your own, call **Rochdale Radio Taxi** (☎ **787-721-1900**).

By train

Tren Urbano, the first mass-transit project in the history of Puerto Rico, opened in 2005, linking San Juan to its suburbs such as Santurce, Bayamón, and Guaynabo. Costing $1.55 billion, the system provides an easy mode of transportation to the most congested areas of metropolitan San Juan. During rush hour (5–9 a.m. and 3–6 p.m.), the train operates every 5 minutes; otherwise, it runs every 10 minutes. Service is not available daily from 11p.m. to 5 a.m. The fare is $1.50 one-way. From the airport, it's possible to take the AMA-B40 bus to Tren Urbano, a 30-minute ride. For more information, call **866-900-1284;** www.ati.gobierno.pr.

On foot

If you stay in one of the major tourist zones in San Juan, you can walk about, especially in **Old Town.** If you get tired, you can always hop on Old Town's free trolley, which we describe later in this chapter.

Self-guided walking tours of Old San Juan are outlined in copies of *Qué Pasa,* the official information booklet issued by the tourism authority. If you don't pick up a copy at the airport, you should be able to get one from your hotel.

By bus

If your vacation budget is lean, you can rely on the *guaguas* or buses run by the **Metropolitan Bus Authority** (☎ **787-767-7979**). They're very crowded at rush hours; be careful of pickpockets who also ride these buses. The fare is really cheap, costing 50¢ on a standard bus or 75¢ on the more-modern and comfortable Metrobus.

Most of the large hotels of the Condado and Isla Verde maintain an air-conditioned bus that makes free shuttle runs into Old San Juan. Clients are usually deposited at the **Plaza de Colón.** Public buses also make the run along the Condado, stopping at clearly designated bus stops near the major hotels. Public buses usually deposit their clients at the Plaza de Colón and the main bus terminal across the street from the Cataño ferryboat pier. This section of Old San Juan is the starting point for many of the city's metropolitan bus routes.

A cheap way to get to Puerto Rico's second city, Ponce, or its third-largest city, Mayagüez, is aboard a *público* (public car). With fares fixed by the Public Service Commission, these *públicos* are marked with yellow license plates, which end in a P or PD. They carry about 18 passengers in vans running during the day and stop for boarding in San Juan's Old Town at the Plaza de Colón or at the airport.

Information about *público* routes between San Juan and Mayagüez is available from **Linea Sultana,** Calle Esteban González 898, Urbanización Santa Rita, Rio Piedras (☎ 787-765-9377). Information about *público* routes between San Juan and Ponce is available from **Choferes Unidos de Ponce,** Terminal de Carros Públicos, Calle Vive in Ponce (☎ 787-764-0540). English-speaking operators are available at both offices.

Fares from San Juan to Mayagüez run $30; from San Juan to Ponce, $30 to $50. Although prices are low, the routes are slow, with frequent stops, an often erratic routing, and lots of inconvenience.

By trolley

When you tire of walking around Old San Juan, you can board one of the free trolleys that run through the historic area. Departure points are the Marina and La Puntilla, but you can hop aboard along the route by flagging the trolley down (wave at it and signal for it to stop) or by waiting at any of the clearly designated stopping points. Relax and enjoy the sights as the trolleys rumble through the old and narrow streets.

By ferry

Aqua Expresso (☎ 787-729-8714) crosses San Juan Bay between Old San Juan (Pier 2) and costs only 50¢ one-way. It departs every 30 minutes from 6 a.m. to 9 p.m. If you want to visit one of the offshore islands of Puerto Rico — Culebra or Vieques — you can go to the eastern seaport of Fajardo. Here the **Fajardo Port Authority** (☎ 787-863-0705) runs a 400-passenger ferry to Vieques three times a day (Mon–Fri at 9:30 a.m., 1 p.m., and 4:30 p.m., and Sat and Sun at 9 a.m., 3 p.m., and 6 p.m.) costing $2 one-way (trip time: 1½ hours). It takes the same time to cross between Fajardo and Culebra, with ferries departing at 4 p.m. Monday to Friday and three times on weekends. A one-way fare costs $2.25.

Staying in Style

For such a small island, Puerto Rico has one of the greatest arrays of accommodations in the Caribbean. The choices range from high-rise beachfront hotels evocative of Miami Beach to a small *parador* up in the mountains for those who want to explore the island beyond San Juan. The largest concentration of hotels is in San Juan, along the **Condado** and **Isla Verde** beachfront strips. **Old Town,** though more historical and romantic than San Juan, offers limited choices. Those who want to escape the hustle and bustle of congested San Juan altogether can experience a more typical urban scene, while still being close to the sea, by booking into a hotel in **Ponce,** the second city of Puerto Rico.

Unlike islands such as Jamaica, the all-inclusive hotel — operating on the **American Plan** (AP) with all meals — hasn't overtaken Puerto Rico. Most of the island's hotels function on the **European Plan** (EP) — that is, a room but no meals. Nonetheless, you can still book into a meal plan at most of the island's resorts, and you can save money this way — it works out cheaper than if you dine à la carte at every meal.

For a meal plan, we recommend the **Modified American Plan** (MAP), which gives you breakfast and dinner at your hotel but leaves you free to eat elsewhere for lunch. Under MAP, you at least get out every day to sample some of the island's restaurants and aren't obligated to take every meal at the resort of your choice.

For families or friends traveling together, a short-term villa or condo rental is an attractive alternative to a hotel, especially when you can share the daily or weekly rate. Here are some contacts to make if you want to investigate this lodging choice:

- ✔ For information on nearly 200 properties in San Juan's Condado and Isla Verde, contact **Puerto Rico Vacation Apartments,** Marabella del Caribe Oeste S-5, Isla Verde, Carolina, PR 00979 (☎ **800-266-3639,** 787-727-1591; Fax: 787-268-3604).

- ✔ For weekly and monthly rentals in Rincón, contact **Island West Properties,** Route 413, Km 1.3, P.O. Box 700, Rincón, PR 00677 (☎ **787-823-2323;** Fax: 787-823-3254).

- ✔ For rentals on Vieques, try either **Connections,** P.O. Box 358, Esperanza, Vieques, PR 00765 (☎ **787-741-0023**), or **Acacia Apartments,** P.O. Box 1211, Esperanza, Vieques, PR 00765 (☎ **787-741-1059**).

The Top Resorts

The rack rates listed in this section are in U.S. dollars and are for a standard double room during high season (mid-Dec through mid-Apr). Rates are lower during the off season and shoulder season; see Chapter 3 for advice on when to go. Purchasing a package tour is another way to save on accommodations; see Chapter 5 for details.

At Wind Chimes Inn
$–$$ Condado, San Juan

Lying only a short block from Condado's sandy beaches, this 17-room hotel is one of the best and most affordable along the ocean-bordering strip. You get a real tropical feel here, as evoked by the patio where you can sit out and enjoy a rum punch while being shaded by swaying palm trees and flowering bougainvillea. The wind chimes hanging about the patio and playing breeze-induced melodies give the inn its name. Bedrooms are well furnished with tropical style and contain ceiling fans *and* air-conditioning, and even kitchens. The tiled bathrooms are small and have showers. A good, full breakfast is served every morning on the patio (though not included in the rate), and for other meals many restaurants are within a short walk of the Wind Chimes.

See map p. 337. 1750 McLeary Ave., Condado, San Juan. ☎ *800-946-3244 in the U.S., 787-727-4153. Fax: 787-728-0671.* www.atwindchimesinn.com. *Rack rates: $99–$140 double; $135–$150 suite. AE, DISC, MC, V.*

Copamarina Beach Resort
$$–$$$ Guánica

This 106-unit resort set on 7.2 hectares (18 acres) is a mecca for divers but attracts everybody from honeymooners to families. Between the sea and Guánica Dry Forest in a UNESCO-designated world biosphere reserve, it lures nature lovers as well. The reserve is home to more than 100 species of birds. The resort opens onto a wide public beach set against a backdrop of palms. Of the two pools, one comes with a Jacuzzi and the other is for kids. Much improved after a $5.5-million overhaul, the rooms are in one- and two-story wings radiating from a central core. They're very tropical, with tile floors and louvered doors and screens opening toward private terraces or verandas. A favorite of visiting *Sanjuaneros* (San Juan natives, that is), the resort's two restaurants serve some of the finest cuisine along the South Coast. Hot tip: Join one of the snorkeling excursions to an off-shore cay called **Gilligan's Island** (after the long-running TV sitcom). Two tennis courts and two bars are part of the facilities, and you can rent bikes, kayaks, and snorkeling gear.

See map p. 337. Route 333, Km 6.5, Caña Gorda (P.O. Box 805), Guánica. ☎ *800-468-4553, 787-821-0505. Fax: 787-821-0070.* www.copamarina.com. *Rack rates: $165–$270 double; $350–$450 suite. European Plan. AE, DC, DISC, MC, V.*

El Canario by the Lagoon
$$ Condado Beach

A relaxing, informal, 40-room European-style hotel, El Canario is in a quiet residential neighborhood just a short block from **Condado Beach.** The place is a bit run-down and the staff isn't too helpful, but it charges afford-able rates. The hotel is very much in the Condado styling, which evokes Miami Beach in the 1960s. The bedrooms are generous in size and have balconies. Most of them have twin beds (though you can try to reserve a double for your stay) and a sleek and contemporary bathroom, with a shower stall and enough space to spread out your stuff. If the hotel doesn't have room for you, it can book you into El Canario Inn.

See map p. 337. Calle Clemenceau 4. ☎ *800-533-2649, 787-722-5056. Fax: 787-723-8590.* www.canariohotels.com. *Rack rates: $120–$135 double. Rates include continental breakfast. AE, DC, DISC, MC, V.*

El Conquistador Golf Resort & Casino
$$$–$$$$ Fajardo

Mitsubishi, at a cost of $250 million, has given this old property a new lease on life in the 21st century. With 750 rooms, it's set on 202 hectares

Puerto Rico Accommodations

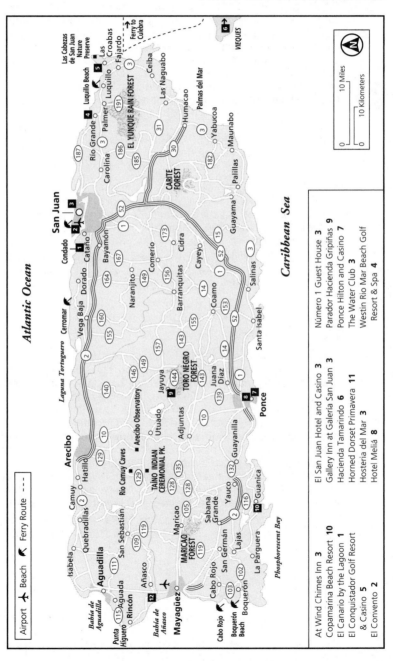

Atlantic Ocean

Caribbean Sea

Legend:
Airport ✈ Beach ⛱ Ferry Route ---

At Wind Chimes Inn **3**
Copamarina Beach Resort **10**
El Canario by the Lagoon **1**
El Conquistador Golf Resort
   & Casino **5**
El Convento **2**

El San Juan Hotel and Casino **3**
Gallery Inn at Galería San Juan **3**
Hacienda Tamarindo **6**
Horned Dorset Primavera **11**
Hostería del Mar **3**
Hotel Meliá **8**

Número 1 Guest House **3**
Parador Hacienda Gripiñas **9**
Ponce Hilton and Casino **7**
The Water Club **3**
Westin Río Mar Beach Golf
   Resort & Spa **4**

(500 acres) of forested hillside. To reach the hotel's private beach, you take a hotel ferry to the little fantasy island of Palomino, with its white sands, caverns, horseback riding, nature trails, and such water sports as scuba diving, windsurfing, snorkeling, and sailing. The megaresort is also a favorite among yachties because of its 32-slip marina. Accommodations come in four different sections, each with a Mediterranean theme. You stay in Spanish-style "villages," such as Las Olas. If you're hoping for a room with a balcony overhanging the water, ask for an accommodations in **La Marina Village.** A stylish tropical décor prevails, and rooms are handsomely equipped, often with kitchens. The resort's **Golden Door Spa** is the finest outside San Juan, and the 6,126m (6,700-yard), par-72, 18-hole golf course, the creation of Arthur Hills, is one of Puerto Rico's finest. A vast array of facilities includes eight restaurants, seven bars, a nightclub, a casino, three pools, six tennis courts, children's programs, and a dive shop for water sports.

Las Casitas Village is now a separate resort, though it is managed by El Conquistador and guests have access to many of that resort's facilities, including the Golden Door Spa (see www.lascasitasvillage.com for more information).

See map p. 337. 1000 Conquistador Ave. (P.O. Box 70001), Fajardo. ☎ *866-317-8932, 787-863-1000. Fax: 787-863-6500.* www.elconresort.com. *Rack rates: $600–$900 double; $600–$1,015 suite. AE, DC, DISC, MC, V.*

El Convento
$$$$ Old San Juan

El Convento is the most historic hotel in Puerto Rico, housed in what was the New World's first Carmelite convent. The building was restored and opened in 1997, each bedroom costing $275,000. Replete with a Spanish courtyard and a splashing fountain, it evokes old Spain. A total of 59 well-furnished rooms lie on the top three (of four) floors, each one different and individually decorated, and furnished for the most part with restored mahogany antiques. Suites are even more splendid with marble floors, colonial antiques, and black marble bathrooms, all with a Jacuzzi. A tiny splash pool on the fourth floor overlooks the historic port, and you're a 15-minute walk from the nearest beach. Even if you're not a guest, consider dining here in one of four restaurants (or have a drink in a pair of bars). We like to begin our evening with a tropical punch at **El Picoteo Tapas Bar.**

See map p. 337. 100 Cristo St., Old San Juan. ☎ *800-468-2779, 787-723-9020. Fax: 787-721-2877.* www.elconvento.com. *Rack rates: $355–$410 double; from $650 suite. AE, DC, DISC, MC, V.*

El San Juan Hotel and Casino
$$–$$$$ Isla Verde, San Juan

One of the grandest hotels in Puerto Rico, El San Juan is the favored hotel along the beachfront extending from Condado to Isla Verde moving toward the airport. It opens onto one of the island's best golden-sand beaches and is a monument to opulence and the good life. Sheathed in red marble and hand-carved mahogany paneling, the public rooms are luxurious, centered around a magnificent lobby with a massive chandelier where it's always party time. From cigar bars to live salsa music, this grand lobby of the hotel is the most glittering place to be at night along the beach strip. Accommodations come in a bewildering number of choices and locations, ranging from bungalows on the outer reaches of the gardens — they're called *casitas* — to oceanfront-bordering suites in the 17-story tower with an eagle's view of Greater San Juan. The facilities are impressive, with three bars, two pools, tennis courts, a health club and spa, water sports, and a children's club that's staffed by well-trained counselors who provide a series of activities from nature strolls to craft classes. What makes this hotel special is its selection of eight different restaurants, all serving a different type of cuisine, ranging from Mexican to Japanese, from Caribbean to Italian.

See map p. 337. 6063 Av. Isla Verde (P.O. Box 2872), Isla Verde. ☎ *866-317-8935, 787-791-1000. Fax: 787-791-0390.* www.thesanjuanhotel.com. *Rack rates: $315–$465 double; $795 suite. AE, DC, DISC, MC, V.*

Gallery Inn at Galería San Juan
$$–$$$ Old San Juan

This private home turned 22-room inn, the former abode of an aristocratic Spanish family, isn't for everyone, especially those who want a megaresort with casino. The most whimsically bohemian inn in the Caribbean, it's also an art studio and gallery, the domain of Jan D'Esopo and Manuco Gandia. Macaws and cockatoos are on hand to welcome you to this hilltop location in Old San Juan with panoramic views. You're a 15-minute ride to the nearest beach. Quirky details such as winding, uneven stairways give the inn its bohemian charm. Bedrooms are full of comfort and individually furnished. Lovers or honeymooners book into the top-floor suite with a panoramic view of El Morro, the fortress. At night, as the sun sets, the rooftop deck is the most romantic spot in Old Town.

See map p. 337. 204–206 Calle Norzagaray, Old San Juan. ☎ *787-722-1808. Fax: 787-724-7360.* www.thegalleryinn.com. *Rack rates: $175–$270 double. Rates include continental breakfast. AE, DC, MC, V.*

Hacienda Tamarindo
$$ Vieques

Built around a mammoth tamarind tree, two centuries old, this intimate, 16-unit inn was created by two Vermonters, Burr and Linda Vail, who gave it the look of a Spanish colonial hacienda. Less than a mile west of Esperanza, the inn is 0.2km (⅛ mile) inland from the ocean, with a footpath leading to a pool and the beach. Bedrooms have tiled floors and reflect Linda's decorating skills. Each is spacious and eclectically furnished, with a medley of art and antiques. Families with children under 12 are asked to book elsewhere. The inn features a convivial bar on-site, but for dinner, guests walk five minutes down the hill to the **Inn on the Blue Horizon,** which serves some of the best food on the island.

See map p. 337. Route 996, Km 4.5 Barrio Puerto Real (P.O. Box 1569), Vieques. ☎ *787-741-0420. Fax: 787-741-3215.* www.haciendatamarindo.com. *Rack rates: $135–$165 double; $210 suite. AE, DC, MC, V.*

Horned Dorset Primavera
$$$–$$$$ Rincón

The most elite retreat on the West Coast of Puerto Rico, this intimate, 52-unit resort is one of the special inns of the Caribbean — designed in the style of a Spanish hacienda and set among lush gardens overlooking the sea with a secluded beach, a small strip of narrow golden sand. The rooms deliberately don't have phones or TVs, because guests come here for a total retreat. Kids under 12 aren't even allowed. Bedrooms are beautifully furnished, often with mahogany four-poster beds evoking plantation days. In the bathrooms are brass-footed tubs and marble walls. The choice units are the eight suites in the separate Casa Escondida villa, some with their own private pools. The on-site restaurant is one of the finest in western Puerto Rico.

See map p. 337. Route 429, Km 3 (P.O. Box 1132), Rincón. ☎ ***800-633-1857,*** *787-823-4030. Fax: 787-823-5580.* www.horneddorset.com. *Rack rates: $600–$950 double; $900–$1,490 suite. AE, MC, V.*

Hosteria del Mar
$–$$ Ocean Park, San Juan

At Ocean Park, lying between the two major beachfronts of **Condado** and **Isla Verde,** is one of the finer affordable guesthouses in this residential seaside colony. Try for one of the attractively furnished bedrooms on the second floor, because they have private balconies open to the trade winds and views of the ocean. Those at ground level come with private patios. The eight bedrooms are done in a tropical motif with wicker furnishings and ceiling fans, although they have air-conditioning as well. Children 11 and under stay free in their parents' room. The hotel has no pool, but with the ocean close by, you don't need one. On-site is a busy local restaurant that serves tasty Puerto Rican cuisine and some vegetarian and macrobiotic specialties.

See map p. 337. 1 Tapia St., Ocean Park, San Juan. ☎ ***877-727-3302*** *in the U.S.. Fax: 787-268-0772.* www.hosteriadelmarpr.com. *Rack rates: $75–$277 double without oceanview; $165–$195 double with oceanview. AE, DC, DISC, MC, V.*

Hotel Meliá
$–$$ Ponce

Before the inauguration of the Ponce Hilton (covered later in this chapter), Hotel Meliá was the traditional favorite, lying in the bull's-eye center near the Ponce Cathedral and the landmark Parque de Bombas with its famous red-and-black firehouse. Not connected with the international hotel chain of Meliá, this 73-unit hotel is like what you'd find in some small provincial town in Castile. Spanish tiles of Moorish design reinforce that image. Upstairs the rooms are a bit cramped but tidily kept and well furnished. The only thing special about them is their affordable rates. At least you don't have far to go for dinner. Under separate management, the on-site restaurant, **Mark's at the Meliá,** is one of the finest dining spots in town. You're a 15-minute ride from the beach.

See map p. 337. 75 Calle Cristina (P.O. Box 1431), Ponce. ☎ *800-448-8355, 787-842-0260. Fax: 787-841-3602.* www.hotelmeliapr.com. *Rack rates: $90–$120 double. Rates include continental breakfast. AE, MC, V.*

Número 1 Guest House
$$–$$$ Ocean Park, San Juan

Even more inviting than Hosteria del Mar (covered earlier in this chapter), Número 1 is an intimate, 13-room, low-rise inn in the **Ocean Park Beach** section of San Juan, between the megaresorts of **Condado** to the west and **Isla Verde** to the east. A stylish boutique hotel evocative of Laguna Beach, California, this place attracts more repeat clients than any other in Ocean Park, both gay and straight. The atmosphere is laid-back and relaxed. The inn lies behind a walled-in compound, featuring a beautiful garden with splashing fountains and a swimming pool; the well-furnished bedrooms are comfortable and pleasing to the eye.

See map p. 337. Calle Santa Ana, Ocean Park, San Juan. ☎ *866-726-5010 in the U.S., 787-726-5010. Fax: 787-727-5482.* www.numero1guesthouse.com. *Rack rates: $115–$185 double; $265 apartment. Rates include continental breakfast. AE, MC, V.*

Parador Hacienda Gripiñas
$$ Jayuya

After just a 2½-hour drive southwest of San Juan, you can find yourself resting on the front porch of an old-world hacienda that was at the center of a former coffee plantation. This 20-room inn is one of the most atmospheric of the government-linked *paradores* of Puerto Rico, a chain of country inns scenically located. Eight hectares (20 acres) of aromatic coffee bushes still produce coffee beans, and the atmosphere itself evokes island life of long ago, with its landscaped gardens and whirling ceiling fans. On the open-air porch, a hammock is waiting for you. The small rooms are modest, but each comes with a shower-only private bathroom and a comfortable bed. Away from the main house are two pools. Of course, if you prefer to spend your days on the beach instead of in the mountains, you need to book elsewhere.

Warning: The mountain-fed pools are chilly. The staff will arrange boating or fishing trips for you at Lake Caonillas, a 30-minute drive from the *parador,* which is also situated near a major island attraction, **Río Camuy Cave Park.** On-site is a typical restaurant serving mainly a Puerto Rican cuisine. When you reach Jayuya, head east via Route 144. At the junction with Route 527, go south for 2.4km (1½ miles) until you see the *parador* signposted.

See map p. 337. Route 527, Km 2.5 (P.O. Box 387), Jayuya. ☎ *787-828-1717. Fax: 787-828-1719.* www.haciendagripinas.com. *Rack rates: $125 double. AE, MC, V.*

Ponce Hilton and Casino
$$$ Ponce

Even though it's not on a beach, this 148-unit hotel is the most luxurious along the South Coast of Puerto Rico, lying on 32 landscaped hectares (80 acres), a ten-minute drive north of the city of Ponce. A five-minute trip by private car or taxi delivers you to the closest beach of volcanic black sand, or in 20 to 30 minutes you reach the far more alluring golden sandy beaches west of Ponce. The island's newest Hilton is also the best equipped along the coast, with two restaurants, three bars, a small casino, four tennis courts, a fitness center, a lagoon-shaped pool, water sports, and a summer camp and playground for children, as well as a business center. Bedrooms are midsize to spacious and are typically attired in West Indian furnishings, each one exceedingly comfortable and opening onto a private terrace or balcony.

See map p. 337. 1150 Av. Caribe (P.O. Box 7419), Ponce. ☎ *800-HILTONS (800-445-8667), 787-259-7676. Fax: 787-259-7674.* www.hilton.com. *Rack rates: $180–$325 double; $400 suite. AE, DC, DISC, MC, V.*

The Water Club
$$$$ Isla Verde, San Juan

A refreshing change from the megachain resorts of San Juan, this ultrachic, 84-room hotel is hip and contemporary. It's the city's only "boutique hotel" on a beach. We find much to praise at this small and exclusive hotel because of its highly personalized and well-trained staff. Although avant-garde, the design is not daringly provocative. Behind glass are "waterfalls," even on the elevators, and inventive theatrical-style lighting is used to bring the outdoors inside. The one-of-a-kind glass art doors are from Murano, the famed center of glassmaking outside Venice. Overlooking Isla Verde's best beach area, all the bedrooms are spacious and contain custom-designed beds positioned to face the ocean. Bathrooms are tiled and elegant, with tub/shower combinations. Unique features are the open-air 11th-floor exotic bar with the Caribbean's only rooftop fireplace. The pool is a level above; it's like swimming in an ocean in the sky.

Calle José M. Tartak 2, Isla Verde, Puerto Rico 00979. ☎ *888-265-6699 or 787-728-3666. Fax 787-728-3610.* www.waterclubsanjuan.com. *Rack rates: $275–$330 double; $695 suite. AE, DC, DISC, MC, V.*

Westin Rio Mar Beach Golf Resort & Spa
$$$–$$$$$ Rio Grande

The Westin chain made an impressive debut in the Caribbean with this $180-million resort set on 195 landscaped hectares (481 acres) near Rio

Mar Beach and just a five-minute ride to **Luquillo,** the best and most popular beach in Puerto Rico. You're coddled in comfort here, in a setting of
artificial lakes and tropical flowering gardens. You're also just a 15-minute
drive from **El Yunque National Park,** the only rain forest in United States
territories. Rising seven floors, the 694-room megaresort also takes in the
Rio Mar Country Club with its two 18-hole golf courses, and has a vast
array of facilities, including eight restaurants, six bars, a casino, a health
club and spa, and 13 tennis courts. It also offers water sports and can
arrange sailing and deep-sea fishing. Its children's programs make it a
family favorite. The best and most expensive accommodations are on the
top floor with enhanced service and amenities, but all the units are exceedingly comfortable and well equipped, opening onto private balconies or
terraces, and furnished with a restful décor of Caribbean wicker, rattan,
and painted furniture.

Avoid suites 5099 and 5101 — the balconies overlook the hotel's noisy air-
conditioning ducts.

See map p. 337. 6000 Rio Mar Blvd., Rio Grande. ☎ *888-627-8556, 787-888-6000. Fax:
787-888-6600.* www.westinriomar.com. *Rack rates: $370–$405 double; from $695
suite. AE, DC, DISC, MC, V.*

Dining Out

In most of the Caribbean, we recommend that, if possible, you escape
from your hotel dining room unless you're booked at an all-inclusive
resort. Over the years, we've come to believe that the best and most
varied dining is outside the hotels in the independently operated little
restaurants. In Puerto Rico, either in San Juan or out on the island, that
isn't always true. Many of the finest restaurants are in hotels. Weekends
at these hotels can be particularly busy, as well-heeled islanders pack
into hotel restaurants, savoring the same cuisine as visitors.

As you travel around the island, look for restaurant signs indicating that
an establishment is one of the *mesones gastronómicos,* or preferred
dining establishments designated as such by the Puerto Rico Tourism
Company — more than 40 of these *mesones* exist islandwide. These
restaurants are known for serving *comidas criollas* (traditional Puerto
Rican and Creole food). Although we can't always guarantee top-quality
food in every one of these places, they invariably offer a good value.

Many Puerto Ricans, unlike in many other parts of the Caribbean, follow
the Spanish tradition of dressing up when they go out at night, either to
the clubs or to the top-rated restaurants. Men should wear their best
resort wear, and women in general appear in high heels and a sporty-
looking dress or pantsuit. You're still welcomed in most places regardless of your dress, but most visitors feel more comfortable when they're
dressed to fit in with the other diners. At the best restaurants, reservations are always preferred during the busy winter season.

Enjoying a Taste of Puerto Rico

Its restaurant scene hardly equals Miami, but in the Caribbean the cookery of Puerto Rico makes it *numero uno.* Even serious foodies agree. To create their unique *cocina criolla* (Creole cuisine), island chefs owe a debt to just about everybody, even the Taíno Indians, the original settlers.

The Spanish brought their own savory recipes, as did African slaves. The end result makes for a tantalizing *asopao* (the island's national soup, a delectable gumbo) of different delights to your palate. Puerto Rican cuisine, like that soup itself, can "feature a little bit of any and everything," a wise old island cook once told us.

Along with a cold beer or a glass of rum, Puerto Ricans like to begin their meal with some savory appetizers, such as crunchy cod fritters (called *bacalaitos*) or perhaps *empanadillas,* crescent-shaped turnovers stuffed with lobster, crab, conch, or beef. A basket of *tostones* (twice-fried plantains, sometimes delectably coated with honey) is likely to rest on your table. Puerto Ricans eat *tostones* the way Americans devour potato chips. Ripe plantains are also baked to make *amarillos* (fried in sugar and red wine, and flavored with cinnamon).

Called *arroz con habichuelas,* rice and beans accompany nearly every meal — lunch or dinner. Rice is often a main dish, especially when it's *asopao,* most often cooked with shrimp, lobster, chicken, or even octopus.

The aroma that wafts from kitchens throughout Puerto Rico comes from *adobo* and *sofrito* — blends of herbs and spices that give many of the native foods their distinctive taste and color. Chefs rub *adobo,* which they make by crushing together peppercorns, oregano, garlic, salt, olive oil, and lime juice or vinegar, into meats before roasting them. *Sofrito,* a potpourri of onions, garlic, and peppers browned in either olive oil or lard and colored with *achiote* (annatto seeds), imparts the bright yellow color to the island's rice, soups, and stews.

Most visitors to the island prefer the fresh fish and shellfish. A popular dish is *mojo isleno* (fried fish with Puerto Rican sauce). The sauce is made with olives and olive oil, onions, pimentos, capers, tomato sauce, vinegar, and a flavoring of garlic and bay leaves. Fresh fish is often grilled, and perhaps flavored with garlic and an overlay of freshly squeezed lime juice — a very tasty dinner indeed. Caribbean lobster is usually the most expensive item on any menu, followed by shrimp. Puerto Ricans often cook *camarones en cerveza* (shrimp in beer). Another delectable shellfish dish is *jueyes hervidos* (boiled crab).

If you're a frugal traveler, dining out on the island, you'll think that every meal in Puerto Rico serves *flan* (caramel custard) for dessert, and most of them do. Other popular desserts include a coconut pudding, *tembleque,* or another pudding, *dulce de leche,* which is really "candied milk." Served with an island white cheese, a fruit paste made of guava is another popular dessert that locals adore.

Finishing a meal with the strong, black aromatic coffee grown here is customary for most Puerto Ricans. Originally imported from the nearby Dominican Republic, coffee beans have been produced in the island's high-altitude interior for more than 300 years and still rank among the island's leading exports.

Rum is the national drink, and you can buy it in almost any shade. Because the island is the world's leading rum producer, it's little wonder that every Puerto Rican bartender worthy of the profession likes to concoct his own favorite rum libation.

The Best Restaurants

Ajili-Mójili
$$$ Condado, San Juan   PUERTO RICAN/CREOLE

Sanjuaneros come to Ajili-Mójili to dine on the food they enjoyed in their *mamacita*'s kitchen, but the chefs have elevated this *comida criolla* (traditional Puerto Rican and Creole food) to new heights, lightening the recipes and making island dishes more refined and sophisticated. Set against old brick walls, the restaurant and bar are evocative of a Spanish tavern of long ago. The food is a delight, and the waiters are helpful in explaining any dish with which you may be unfamiliar. The *arroz con pollo* (stewed chicken with saffron rice) shows a solid technique, as does the *mofongos* (green plantains stuffed with chicken, shrimp, pork, or veal). The kitchen takes full advantage of the island's bounty, especially in its meat dishes such as *medallones de cerdo encebollado* (pork loin sautéed with onions) and *carne machada* (rib-eye of beef stuffed with ham). The chefs will also regale you with *lechon asado con maposteado* (roast pork with rice and beans). The dish sounds ordinary, but the kitchen knows how to enliven it with real flair and flavor.

1052 Av. Ashford (at the corner of Calle Joffre). ☎ *787-725-9195. Reservations required. Main courses: $17–$39 lunch. AE, DISC, MC, V. Open: Mon–Thurs noon to 3 p.m. and 6–10 p.m., Fri noon to 3 p.m. and 6–11 p.m.; Sat 11:45 a.m.–3:30 p.m. and 6–11 p.m.; Sun 12:30–4 p.m. and 6–10 p.m.*

Amadeus
$$–$$$ Old San Juan   CONTEMPORARY PUERTO RICAN

A long-enduring favorite of both visitors and locals in Old Town, Amadeus lies in a restored 18th-century structure that was once the home of a rich merchant. More so than Ajili-Mójili (see the preceding listing), this restaurant gives a totally modern interpretation to classic island dishes. One appetizer alone, Amadeus dumplings with guava sauce and arrowroot fritters, will spark your taste buds. The chef creates a palette of flavors and originality in such dishes as pizza with smoked salmon and caviar or tender pork scaloppine in a sweet-and-sour sauce that had us asking for the recipe. The grilled fish such as mahi-mahi has real Cajun authenticity and is an excellent choice for a main course.

See map p. 347. 106 Calle San Sebastián. ☎ *787-722-8635. Reservations recommended. Main courses: $8–$25. AE, DISC, MC, V. Open: Mon 6 p.m.–midnight; Tues–Sun noon to 1 a.m.*

Aquaviva
$$$$ Old San Juan LATINO/SEAFOOD

The location of one of San Juan's finest restaurants is at the bottom of Calle Fortaleza, in Old San Juan, within a cool, turquoise-colored environment. Presiding above the sometimes-frenetic bar action and dining room hubbub of this place are replicas of three *aquaviva* (jellyfish), each manufactured from stained glass specifically for this site and quivering with illumination. Don't come here expecting calm or respite from the madding crowds. Its owners spend a small fortune on publicity and promotion, making it one of the hottest restaurants in Old San Juan.

The result verges on the chaotic, albeit in the most stylish of ways. Oysters and stiff drinks are available at the bar. Flowing from the open-to-view kitchens come dishes whose ingredients derive from the watery turquoise world which inspired this restaurant's color scheme. The best examples include six different seviches, including one made with mahi-mahi, mango juice, and lemons, and a different version from marlin and garlic. You might opt for a heaping tower composed of fried oysters, coconut-flavored shrimp, and fried octopus and calamari. The best main courses include grilled fresh mahi-mahi with smoky shrimp, salsa, and coconut-poached yucca; seared halibut medallions with a fondue of spinach and crabmeat; and a succulent version of paella garnished with seafood and pork sausage.

See map p. 347. 354 Calle Fortaleza. ☎ *787-722-0665. Reservations required. Main courses: $16–$45. AE, MC, V. Open: Mon–Wed 6–11 p.m.; Thurs–Sat 6 p.m.–midnight; Sun 4–11 p.m.*

Ciao Mediterranean Café
$$ Isla Verde, San Juan MEDITERRANEAN

This is the most charming restaurant in Isla Verde, and it is one of our enduring favorites. It's draped with bougainvillea and set directly on the sands, attracting both hotel guests and locals wandering in barefoot from the beach. The visual centerpiece is an open-air kitchen set within an oval-shaped bar. A crew of cheerfully animated chefs mingles good culinary technique with Latino theatricality. Pizzas and pastas are popular here, and even more appealing are such dishes as seafood salad, wherein

Old San Juan Dining

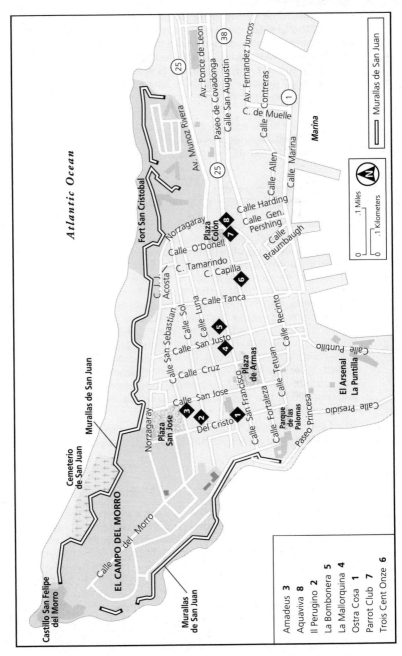

Amadeus **3**
Aquaviva **8**
Il Perugino **2**
La Bombonera **5**
La Mallorquina **4**
Ostra Cosa **1**
Parrot Club **7**
Trois Cent Onze **6**

shrimp, scallops, calamari, peppers, onions, and lime juice create some-thing you might expect in the south of Italy. *Kalamarakia tiganita* (Greek-style squid) consisting of battered and deep-fried squid served with ratatouille and spicy marinara sauce; rack of lamb with ratatouille, polenta, and Provençal herbs; and a mixed grill of seafood are evocative of what you'd expect in Marseilles, thanks to the roe-enhanced aioli and couscous. Compared to most of the restaurants around here, this cafe serves lighter fare that kids go for, especially in its selection of pizzas and pastas. The desserts are also some of the most luscious at Isla Verde, especially the ice cream.

See map p. 347. In the Inter-Continental San Juan Resort & Casino, Av. Isla Grande. ☎ *787-791-6100. Reservations recommended for dinner. Pizzas and salads $8–$20; main courses $14–$30. AE, MC, V. Daily 11:30 a.m.–11 p.m.*

Horned Dorset Primavera
$$$$$ Rincón   FRENCH/CARIBBEAN

The poshest restaurant in western Puerto Rico, which also serves the finest cuisine, is elegantly sheltered under the roof of this recommended Relais & Châteaux property. If you're touring the west, it makes a perfect luncheon stopover even if you're not a guest. At night, the intimate light-ing, elegant service, and sound of the ocean can put you in the mood for romance. Changed nightly, the menu is based on the inspiration of the chef that day and what he found fresh and good at the market. After he secures the produce, he comes back to the kitchen to concoct intelligent, imagi-native dishes of subtle flavors configured in four fixed-price menus. Starters have included an unusual chilled parsnip soup and a fricassee of wahoo with wild mushrooms. He's served a magnificent lobster medallion-style in an orange-flavored "white butter" sauce, and the grilled loin of beef was perfectly flavored in a zesty pepper sauce. A winning blend of flavors materialized in the mahi-mahi in a ginger-laced cream sauce served on a bed of al dente cabbage.

Route 429, Km 3, Rincón. ☎ *787-823-4030. Reservations recommended. Prix-fixe din-ners: $68 or $92 per person. AE, MC, V. Open: Daily noon to 2 p.m. and 7–9:30 p.m.*

Il Perugino
$$$–$$$$ Old San Juan   TUSCAN/UMBRIAN

This restaurant pleased Luciano Pavarotti, one of the world's most dis-cerning palates (he can also sing), and is likely to enchant you, too. Come here for the best Italian food in Old San Juan. Only La Piccola Fontana (see the listing later in this section) does it better, and the two run a close race. The setting is in the courtyard of a former private town house built three centuries ago, close to the Old Town Cathedral. The chef brought many of the most treasured recipes from his homeland of Perugia, deep in the heart of Umbria, a gastronomic center of Italy. The skillful cookery swoops from the classic to the inspired in such perfectly balanced dishes as marinated fresh salmon, medallions of beef flavored with balsamic vinegar, and a "black pasta" made with crayfish and eels that deserves an award. As in

Umbria, black and white truffles appear on the menu, but, as always, they're lethal in price.

See map p. 347. 105 Calle Cristo. ☎ **787-722-5481.** *Reservations required. Main courses: $18–$36. AE, DISC, MC, V. Open: Daily 6:30–11 p.m.*

La Bombonera
$ Old San Juan   CAFE

An Old San Juan tradition for 100 years, this cafe and restaurant is still going strong. Some of its oldest habitués have been eating here for 60 years. We like to join the throngs for breakfast — the pastries are unmatched in San Juan — where portions are so large that they'll practically fortify you for the day. The old men who hang out here order endless refills of *café con leche* (coffee with milk). You can return for lunch or dinner, enjoying a selection of flavorful and well-prepared island dishes such as rice with squid as good as your mama made for you. The tantalizing and aromatic roast legs of pork emerging from the oven move quickly. For decades, the chefs have pleased many with their savory kettle of seafood *asopao* (a gumbolike soup). How about a prune pie for dessert? Don't knock it until you've tried it.

See map p. 347. 259 Calle San Francisco. ☎ **787-722-0658.** *Reservations recommended. American breakfast $4.50-$6.45. Main courses: $6–$18. AE, MC, V. Open: Daily 7:30 a.m.–8 p.m.*

La Mallorquina
$$–$$$ Old San Juan   PUERTO RICAN

Puerto Rico's oldest restaurant dates from 1848, and little has changed — certainly not the recipe for the savory *paella* (the famous saffron rice dish) or one of Old Town's best *asopaos* (the gumbolike soup that comes with expensive lobster or more democratically priced chicken). The most ordered dish over the years? Classic *arroz con pollo* (chicken with rice). For a starter, the garlic soup leaves you with an aromatic taste in your mouth — and the breath to go with it. On a summer day, you may prefer the more-soothing gazpacho. Nearly everyone finishes his or her meal with an order of the chef's flan (caramel custard). That dessert is a tradition here, and tradition is what this place is all about.

See map p. 347. 207 Calle San Justo. ☎ **787-722-3261.** *Reservations not accepted for lunch, recommended for dinner. Main courses: $15–$36. AE, MC, V. Open: Mon–Sat 11:45 a.m.–10 p.m. Closed Sept.*

La Piccola Fontana
$$$$ Isla Verde, San Juan   NORTHERN ITALIAN

La Piccola Fontana is not only the best Italian restaurant along the beach strip of San Juan, it's also one of the leading Italian restaurants of the Caribbean. Even if you've dined Italian in New York, or gone to Italy, the chefs at La Piccola can hold their own against some stiff competition.

The setting is off the lobby of this magnificent *luxe* megaresort in two neo-Palladian rooms with frescoed walls of Italy's ruins and landscapes, a bit corny perhaps. But nothing else is corny here — certainly not the exquisite cuisine. Even if it's simply grilled veal chops, the chefs get it right. They grill fresh filets of fish perfectly, too. Our favorite pasta — and it's a succulent one — is tortellini San Daniele, made with tender veal, prosciutto, cream, and sage. Try also the grilled medallions of filet mignon served over a bed of freshly braised arugula. We applaud this restaurant for its fresh flavors, heady perfumes, and decisive seasonings.

At the Wyndham El San Juan Hotel and Casino, Avenida Isla Verde. ☎ 787-791-0966. Reservations required. Main courses: $18–$30. AE, MC, V. Open: Daily 6–11 p.m.

Mark's at the Meliá
$$$–$$$$ Ponce INTERNATIONAL/PUERTO RICAN

The finest dining along the island's South Shore in its "second city" is located at the Meliá Hotel. The viands here are even tastier than at the Ponce Hilton's best restaurants. Master chef Mark French roams the world for his repertoire, but he's inspired as much by produce of Puerto Rico, which he fashions into many dishes. For example, he serves fried green plantains, but his version comes with sour cream and a dollop of caviar. His tamarind-barbecued lamb with a yucca mojo deserves high praise, as does his corn-crusted red snapper with yucca purée, or his tempura jumbo shrimp with an Asian salad. Count yourself lucky if you save room for the vanilla flan layered with rum sponge cake and topped with a caramelized banana.

At the Meliá Hotel, Calle Cristina. ☎ 787-284-6275. Reservations recommended. Main courses: $16–$30. AE, MC, V. Open: Wed–Sat noon to 3 p.m. and 6–10:30 p.m.; Sun noon to 5 p.m.

Ostra Cosa
$$ Old San Juan ECLECTIC

Ostra Cosa is the most artfully promoted restaurant in San Juan, with a growing clientele who swear that the ambience here is one of the most sensual and romantic in Old San Juan. It was created by former advertising executive Alberto Nazario, now a lifestyle guru who mingles New Age thinking with good culinary techniques to promote love, devotion, and a heightened sexuality. Couples dine beneath a massive quenepe tree — waiters tell you to hug the tree and make a wish — in a colonial courtyard surrounded by a 16th-century building that used to be the home of the colony's governor. The atmosphere, enhanced by domesticated quail and chirping tree frogs, makes you feel far removed from the cares of the city. Featured foods are high in phosphorus, zinc, and flavor, designed to promote an "eat-up, dress-down experience." The seviche is superb, as are the grilled prawns. But it's the conch, known as Caribbean Viagra, that rates "Wow!!" or "Ay Ay Ay!!!"

See map p. 347. Calle del Cristo 154. ☎ *787-722-2672. Reservations recommended. Main courses: $13–$29. AE, MC, V. Open: Sun–Wed noon to 10 p.m.; Fri–Sat noon to 11 p.m.*

Parrot Club
$$$ Old San Juan   CONTEMPORARY PUERTO RICAN

If you're taking the mayor of San Juan or the governor of Puerto Rico out to dinner, head here to Old Town's hottest restaurant. In what was once a hair-tonic factory a hundred years ago, a beautiful restaurant tempts you into a long, lush evening of refined food and good times. The chefs are skilled at Nuevo Latino cuisine, blending elements of Spanish, Taíno, and even African influences into their tasty repertoire. Guests take their meals against a backdrop of live music — classic Cuban, wild salsa, or Latino jazz. The intensely flavored seviche of halibut is rich in texture, as are the crab cakes *caribeños,* one of our all-time favorites. The seared pork medallions with a sweet plantain chorizo or the sugar-cured skewered lamb with couscous will win you over, as will the pan-seared tuna served with a sauce made from dark rum and essence of oranges. The bartender's special drink is Parrot Passion, made from lemon-flavored rum, triple sec, and fresh oranges and passion fruit.

See map p. 347. 363 Calle Fortaleza. ☎ *787-725-7370. Reservations not accepted. Main courses: Lunch $10–$21, dinner $10–$36. AE, MC, V. Open: Mon–Fri 11:30 a.m.– 4 p.m.; Sat–Sun noon to 4 p.m.; Sun–Wed 6–11 p.m.; Thurs–Sat 6 p.m.–midnight. Closed for one week in Sept.*

Ramiros
$$$$$ Condado Beach   SPANISH/INTERNATIONAL

Ramiros boasts the most imaginative menu on the Condado. Its refined "New Creole" cooking is a style pioneered by owner and chef Jesús Ramiro. You might begin with breadfruit *mille-feuille* with local crabmeat and avocado. For your main course, any fresh fish or meat can be char-grilled on request. Some recent menu specialties have included paillard of lamb with spiced root vegetables and guava sauce, charcoal-grilled black Angus steak with shiitake mushrooms, and grilled striped sea bass with citrus sauce. Among the many homemade desserts are caramelized mango on puff pastry with strawberry-and-guava sauce, and "four seasons" chocolate.

Av. Magdalena 1106. ☎ *787-721-9049. Reservations required in winter. Main courses: $27–$39. AE, DC, MC, V. Open: Sun–Fri noon to 3 p.m.; daily 6–11 p.m.*

Trois Cent Onze (311)
$$$ Old San Juan   FRENCH

When the French and Puerto Rican owners of this place renovated this building in 1999, they discovered some of the most beautiful Moorish-Andalusian tilework in San Juan's Old Town buried beneath layers of later coverings. Because of those tiles, and because of the delicate Andalusian-style iron rosette above the door, they wisely decided to retain the area's Moorish embellishments during the reconfiguration of their restaurant's décor. What you'll get today is the premier French restaurant of San Juan, replete with a zinc bar near the entrance, a soaring and richly beamed ceiling, and a décor like what you might have expected in the Casbah of old Tangiers. Your hosts are Christophe Gourdain and Zylma Perez, who are proud to recite the building's former use as the photography studio that developed many of Puerto Rico's earliest movies. Colors, textures, and flavors combine here to produce an irresistible array of dishes. Menu items include a carpaccio of salmon marinated in citrus; sautéed sea scallops served with an almond-flavored butter sauce; mango and crabmeat salad; magret of duckling roasted with honey; and pork medallions served with caramelized onions, stewed white beans, and spicy *merguez* sausage.

See map p. 347. Calle Fortaleza 311. ☎ 787-725-7959. Reservations recommended. Main courses: $19–$30. AE, MC, V. Tues–Thurs noon to 2:30 p.m. and 6:30–10 p.m.; Fri–Sat noon to 2:30 p.m. and 6–11 p.m.; Sun 5–10 p.m.

Enjoying the Sand and Surf

You could easily spend all your time in Puerto Rico on the beach (or beaches), and we tell you where to go to find the best strips of sand. Of course, having fun in the sand and surf in Puerto Rico means a lot more than being a beachcomber. For those who like to be more active in the water, you'll find an array of other water-related activities that include windsurfing, diving, and snorkeling.

Combing the beaches

Puerto Ricans share with their visitors a love of their beaches, and on weekends, winter or summer, both Puerto Ricans and vacationers alike flock to the island's strips of golden sand. We'd dare to say that Puerto Ricans are the most beach-loving people of any country in the Caribbean. But with so many beaches — some crowded, some so isolated you'll have the sands all to yourself — the island has room for everyone.

On the North Coast, the Atlantic waters are more turbulent than those along the more-tranquil southern shore. Some stretches near San Juan and the major resorts are incredibly crowded, but you can still find a quiet, remote beach. The big resorts have claimed the best beaches, but even so, they're still open to the public — all the *playas* (beaches) on the island are free and open to the public. Of course, if you use a resort's facilities, you have to pay.

Public beaches in Puerto Rico are called *balnearios*. These beaches are government-run, with lifeguards, parking, and dressing rooms. They usually shut down on Monday but are open Tuesday to Sunday from 9 a.m. to 5 p.m. If Monday is a holiday, the *balnearios* are closed on Tuesday. For a report or any information on the island's beaches, call the Department of Recreation and Sports (☎ **787-728-5668**).

If you've booked a hotel on San Juan's Isla Verde or the Condado, chances are you can take off your mainland clothes, put on a swimsuit, and be on a white sandy beach within 30 minutes. Even if your hotel isn't right on the beach, it's probably no more than two or three blocks away.

The Condado/Isla Verde beaches are the best and most frequented in Greater San Juan. Good snorkeling is possible from either beach, and rental equipment is available at various kiosks. **Condado Beach,** where beach tourism to Puerto Rico began in the 1920s, evokes Miami Beach with its high-rises. Set near San Juan, this lively beach is punctuated with tall coconut palms and jammed with city folk mingling with resort guests. Boomboxes blare, young women dare with their barely-theres, and vendors sell colorful *pareos* (island wraps), anklets, T-shirts, and cheap eats.

Near the airport, **Isla Verde Beach** is a favorite of locals who share the golden sands with guests of the high-rise resorts found here. Isla Verde has picnic tables, so you can pick up the makings of a lunch and spend the day at the beach. This strip is also good for snorkeling because of its calm, clear waters. Isla Verde Beach extends from the end of Ocean Park to the beginning of a section called Boca Cangrejos. Most sections of this long strip have separate names, such as **El Alambique,** which is often the site of beach parties, and **Punta El Medio,** bordering the new Ritz-Carlton, which is also a great beach and very popular even with the locals. If you go past the luxury hotels and expensive condos behind the Luís Muñoz Marín International Airport, you arrive at the major public beach at Isla Verde. Here you find a *balneario* with parking, showers, fast-food joints, and water-sports equipment. The sands here are whiter than the golden sands of the Condado and are lined with coconut palms, sea-grape trees, and even almond trees, all of which provide shade from the fierce noonday sun.

One of the most attractive beaches in the Greater San Juan area is **Ocean Park,** 1.6km (1 mile) of fine gold sand in a neighborhood east of Condado. This beach attracts both young people and a big gay crowd. Access to the beach at Ocean Park has been limited recently, but the best place to enter is from a section called El Ultimo Trolley. This area is ideal for volleyball, paddleball, and other games. The easternmost portion, known as Punta La Marias, is best for windsurfing. The waters at Ocean Park are fine for swimming, although they can get rough at times.

One of the best beaches for windsurfers is at Rincón, 161km (100 miles) west of San Juan. Surfers from all over the world flock to the beach at **Punta Higuero,** along Route 413. Swells from the Atlantic Ocean in winter form waves averaging 1.5 to 1.8m (5–6 ft.) in height, with rideable rollers sometimes reaching 4.5 to 7.6m (15–25 ft.). This beach is also a winter venue for watching the endangered humpback whales, which pass in view off the coast from December through February. Some of the best snorkeling on the island is also possible offshore.

Rivaling Condado and Isla Verde beaches, **Luquillo Public Beach** is the grandest in Puerto Rico and one of the most popular, located 48km (30 miles) east of San Juan near the town of Luquillo. Here you'll find a kilometer-long (1-mile) half-moon bay set against a backdrop of coconut palms. This beach is another of the dozen or so *balnearios* of Puerto Rico. Saturday and Sunday are the worst times to go, because hordes of *Sanjuaneros* (San Juan residents) head here for fun in the sun. Water-sports kiosks offer everything from windsurfing to sailing. Facilities include lifeguards, an emergency first-aid station, ample parking, showers, and toilets. You can easily have a local lunch here at one of the beach shacks offering cod fritters and tacos.

Luquillo has a unique wheelchair-accessible program called **Mar Sin Barreras** or "sea without barriers," which allows physically challenged people to bask in the warm ocean waters. For more information, call ☎ 787-889-4329. The program is open from 8:30 a.m. to 5 p.m. daily.

Some of the best snorkeling in Puerto Rico is in and around Fajardo lying to the east of Luquillo. Its beach, **Playa Seven Seas,** isn't as alluring as Playa Luquillo, but it's an attractive and sheltered wide strip of sand shaded by coconut palms. The beach lies on the southwestern shoreline of Las Cabezas peninsula and is very crowded on weekends. The absolute best snorkeling, however, isn't here. Walk along this beach for about 0.8km (half a mile) to another beach called **Playa Escondido,** or "Hidden Beach." Beautiful coral reefs, ideal for snorkeling in clear waters, lie right off this *playa.*

We'll let you in on an even more alluring secret: East from Las Cabezas is a marine wildlife refuge known as **La Cordillera** or "The Spine." Off the mainland of the island, these waters are the most gin-clear and the most tranquil of any we've found in Puerto Rico. They're teeming with wildlife, including several species of fish such as grouper, but also lobster, moray eels, and even sea turtles. On these islets you may even see a rare crested iguana.

Lying 29km (18 miles) west of San Juan, the two **Dorado Beaches** are flanked by the now closed Hyatt Dorado Beach Resort & Country Club and the Hyatt Regency Cerromar Beach Hotel. These white sandy beaches are among the most desirable on the island.

Playing in the surf

Hardly a diving paradise, Puerto Rico does attract those interested in scuba diving offshore. You can hook up with this activity through most of the water-sports desks at several major San Juan resort hotels, or the big oceanfront resorts outside the capital. The calm, glasslike waters off the South Coast are better for snorkeling than those off the North Coast, which is overpopulated and faces the often-turbulent Atlantic. What Puerto Rico does excel in is windsurfing, its northwest beaches attracting the world's best windsurfers. The best months for surfing are October to February.

Taking a dive

The diving is better in the Cayman Islands, but if you want to include some diving in an otherwise full vacation agenda, Puerto Rican waters can tempt you. What makes the island an interesting dive site is that a continental shelf envelops it on three sides, creating coral reefs, sea walls, caves, and trenches.

Check out your dive operator thoroughly. Reaching some of the better sites requires a lengthy boat trip. Some operators have acquired a reputation for trying to pawn off more-accessible sites with little marine life when a little more effort would transport divers to pristine reefs with far more marine action. Plus, you don't want to be on an old boat spewing fumes if you have to travel far.

The best diving is offshore, with some fairly pristine sites. The 146-hectare (360-acre) **Isle Desecheo,** looking like it's from that long-running musical *South Pacific,* lies 24km (15 miles) off the coast of Rincón in the West. The fringe reefs of this wildlife preserve are among Puerto Rico's finest and are filled with coral and tropical fish, including rock terraces and caves.

Also in western Puerto Rico, diving is spectacular off the offshore **Isla Mona,** which is called Puerto's Rico's "Jurassic Park" because of all the wildlife found here, including gigantic rock iguanas with their big heads and powerful jaws. A 5,665-hectare (14,000-acre) nature preserve 80km (50 miles) off the coast, Mona offers overfished waters but visibility of 45m (150 ft.) with reef dives, wall dives, and nearly ten different kinds of living coral.

In eastern Puerto Rico, some two dozen of the best dive sites lie south of the fishing port of **Fajardo** within a 8km (5-mile) radius offshore. One of the best known and the most dramatic is called **The Cracks,** just off the coast from the town of Humacao. Large fissures in the reef create feeding grounds for rainbow-hued fish and other marine life.

Savvy divers also flock to the offshore island of **Culebra,** 29km (18 miles) east of the port of Fajardo (reached by ferry). A favored site here is called "Magical Mystery Tour," with a maze of tunnels and varied coral, lying in depths of 12m (40 ft.) with good visibility.

A number of outfitters on the island will take you on a two- to four-hour dive costing $50 to $115 for one- and two-tank dives, with all equipment thrown in. You can arrange some dive packages beginning at $50. Night dives generally cost twice as much. Most snorkeling excursions start at

$45, including boat transport (usually a sailboat), equipment rental, and maybe lunch. Either snorkelers or scuba divers can hook up with an outfitter by contacting **Caribbean School of Aquatics** in San Juan Bay Marina (☎ **787-728-6606;** www.saildiveparty.com) or **Dive Copamarina** in Guánica (☎ **787-821-0505;** www.copamarina.com).

Hooking up with one of these outfitters is always wiser than diving or snorkeling on your own, because you can easily become disoriented.

Advanced divers can head to the **Parguera Divers Puerto Rico Inc.,** Parador Posada Por la Mar, Route 304, La Parguera (☎ **787-899-4171;** www.parguueradivers.com). Dive master Angel Rovira has been diving the walls for more than a decade and knows every crevice of the walls. Angel and his wife, Roberta, put a premium on customer service, and they make sure that repeat guests don't repeat sites. Under their watchful eyes, you'll likely see nurse sharks, Atlantic spadefish, queen angelfish, and more.

Riding the surf

Winter storms in the North Atlantic Ocean have made the western city of **Rincón** a mecca for windsurfers from November through April. No landmass is around to break the swells. These gnarly waves roll into Rincón sometimes dangerously high at some 7.6m (25 ft.).

Windsurfers, take precautions. At Steps, Dogman's, and Tres Palmas, three major windsurfing sites just north of Rincón, several surfers have drowned in waves that shot up for at least 7.3m (24 ft.).

The best surfing beaches are along the Atlantic coastline from **Borinquén Point** south to Rincón, where you'll find several surf shops, including **West Coast Surf Shop,** 2 E. Muñoz Rivera St., Rincón (☎ **787-823-3935**). At these shops, you can rent surfboards for $20 and up for a full day. The reefs and rocks here mean that this "Surf City" is better for the experienced surfer. Beginners can check out **Aviones in Piñones** east of San Juan, **La Concha** beaches in San Juan, and **Casa de Pesca** in Arecibo, all summer surfing spots that have surf shops.

Reeling in the big one

In Puerto Rico, you can feel like you're in Hemingway's *The Old Man and the Sea,* pursuing the giant blue marlin. Puerto Rico's **Annual Billfish Tournament** is the world's largest consecutively held competition of its kind. The island's clear waters are home to game fish such as blue and white marlin (most prevalent in late summer), wahoo, dorado (best from Nov through early Apr), yellow and blackfin tuna, and barracuda. Catches have set more than 30 world records.

Boats range from 10 to 19m (34–61 ft.) in length. You can arrange half-day (four hours in the morning or four hours in the afternoon) and full-day charters through **Benitez Deep-Sea Fishing,** Club Nautico de San Juan, San Juan (☎ **787-723-2292;** Fax: 787-725-4344). Other options include **Castillo Watersports,** Isla Verde (☎ **787-791-6195**).

Outside of San Juan, try **Parguera Fishing Charters,** La Parguera (☎ **787-899-4698** or cellular 787-382-4698).

Your skipper provides food and drink, but it may not be what you want. Check in advance. If you don't like what the bar or menu offers, bring your own provisions. Fortunately, Puerto Pico doesn't hit you with extra taxes, nor does it require you to take out a fishing license.

Climbing aboard

If you can't imagine a trip to Puerto Rico without some close encounter with the sea, check out the ways you can take to the water without jumping in.

Puerto Rico's waters aren't the sailor's Valhalla that the British Virgin Islands are, but they're often idyllic. From the fishing port of **Fajardo** on the East Coast, a boater can reach such offshore, unspoiled cays as Icacos and Palomino in only an hour or two. Also lying to the east of Fajardo are the resort islands of Culebra and Vieques, and beyond that the islands that form the archipelago of the Lesser Antilles.

Unless you go far astray into the ocean, navigation is relatively easy because you're always in site of a landmass.

Marinas and charter boats are located all around the island, but the biggest concentration is in the vicinity of Fajardo. Catamarans, known for their stability, are especially popular. A typical charter starts from 9:30 a.m. for a leisurely sail to Icacos. (Prices begin around $75 per person. Many outfitters will arrange your transportation to Fajardo if you're staying in San Juan.)

Ocean kayaking along lagoons and through mangrove channels is yet another fun way to have an encounter with the island's waters without getting wet.

The megaresorts spread across the beachfront from the Condado (closest to Old Town San Juan) to Isla Verde in the east near the airport and rent all sorts of equipment: Sunfish, windsurfers, paddle boats, and kayaks. The waves here can be turbulent from November through April, but the constantly blowing trade winds delight sailors. Both the **Condado Plaza Hotel and Casino Water-Sports Center,** 999 Av. Ashford (☎ **787-721-1000**), and the **Wyndham El San Juan Hotel and Casino Watersports Center,** Avenue Isla Verde (☎ **787-791-1000**), will arrange water sports for their guests.

Boating and sailing trips of all kinds are available through **Caribbean School of Aquatics,** San Juan Bay Marina (☎ 787-728-6606), and **Castillo Watersports,** ESJ Towers, Isla Verde (☎ 787-791-6195, 787-726-5752).

Moving east of San Juan, **Iguana Water Sports,** at the Westin Rio Mar Beach Golf Resort & Spa, 6000 Rio Mar Blvd., Rio Grande (☎ 787-888-6000), stocks a wide selection of small craft. Sailing instruction is available at the **Palmas Dive Center,** Villas Palmas del Mar, 110 Harbour Dr. (☎ 787-852-6000). **East Wind Excursions** in Fajardo (☎ 787-860-3434) can fix you up with a catamaran snorkeling excursion.

To experience an oddity on the water at night, head for the little beach resort of **La Parguera,** lying in the southwestern sector of the island, reached by heading south of San Germán along Route 304. La Parguera is west of Ponce. This part of the island has been likened to Louisiana's bayous, with its mangrove swamps, secluded coves, and islets. The attraction is *Bahía Fosforescente,* or Phosphorescent Bay, where marine plankton, formally known as microscopic dinoflagellates, light up the waters when disturbed, but only on a moonless night. Gazing into the water is like looking at thousands of lightning bugs under the sea. Several boats leave from La Parguera for the hour-long trip nightly from dusk to midnight. The standard fee is $20 per person.

Exploring on Dry Land

If you don't want to spend all your time lazing on a beach, you'll discover that Puerto Rico has more natural attractions and historical sights than any other island in the Caribbean. Its chief attraction is **Viejo San Juan** (Old San Juan), which was once completely encircled by a city wall, part of which still stands. But the island has so much more — a world-class observatory, caves to explore, a rain forest, and some of the best art museums on the islands.

The top attractions

No city in the West Indies is more historic or more beautiful than **Old San Juan,** a seven-block-square zone that is best explored on foot or by the free **Old Town Trolley,** which you can hop on board and get off anytime something catches your fancy. Formerly encircled by a fortress wall, the area is now protected as both a UNESCO World Heritage Site and a U.S. National Historic Site.

To stroll the lamp-lit cobblestone streets of Old San Juan is to walk back in history 500 years, even though you'll see much that's commercial and often tawdry here. Nonetheless, for the history buff, this is as good as it gets in the Caribbean. The Spanish founded **Rich Port** (its English name) back in 1521. In the oldest capital city under the U.S. flag, at least 400 buildings have been restored to their colonial appearance. Many are decorated with iron balconies filled with potted plants in the Spanish

Old San Juan Attractions

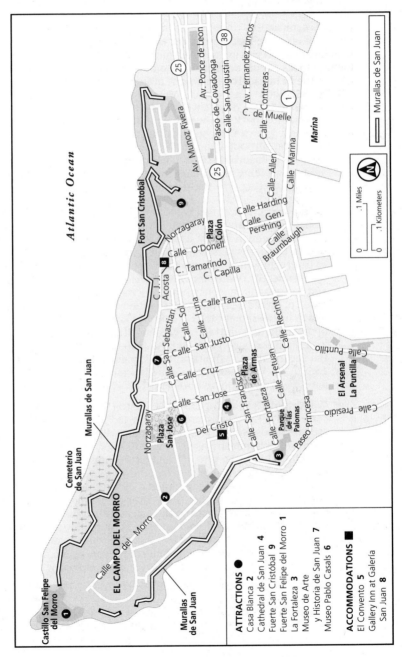

Atlantic Ocean

Marina

Murallas de San Juan

Castillo San Felipe del Morro

Cemeterio de San Juan

Murallas de San Juan

EL CAMPO DEL MORRO

Calle del Morro

Murallas de San Juan

Fort San Cristobal

Av. Ponce de Leon

Paseo de Covadonga

Calle San Augustin

C. Av. Fernandez Juncos

C. de Muelle

Calle Contreras

Calle Marina

Calle Allen

Calle Harding

Calle Harding

Calle Gen. Pershing

Calle Braumbaugh

Plaza Colón

Norzagaray

Calle O'Donell

C. Tamarindo

C. Capilla

C.J.J. Acosta

Calle Tanca

Calle Recinto

Calle San Sebastian

Calle Sol

Calle Luna

Calle San Justo

Calle Cruz

Calle Tetuan

Plaza de Armas

Calle San Francisco

Calle Fortaleza

Parque de las Palomas

Calle Puntilla

El Arsenal La Puntilla

Calle Presidio

Calle San Jose

Plaza San Jose

Norzagaray

Del Cristo

Calle San Jose

Calle del Cristo

Paseo Princesa

ATTRACTIONS ●
Casa Blanca 2
Cathedral de San Juan 4
Fuerte San Cristobal 9
Fuerte San Felipe del Morro 1
La Fortaleza 3
Museo de Arte
y Historia de San Juan 7
Museo Pablo Casals 6

ACCOMMODATIONS ■
El Convento 5
Gallery Inn at Galeria
San Juan 8

Murallas de San Juan

.1 Miles

.1 Kilometers

tradition. Some of the *adoquines* (bluish stones) that make up the streets originally arrived in port as ballast aboard Spanish galleons.

Churches, museums, shops, historic forts, hotels (a rather meager lot), restaurants (more than you'll ever need), bars, nightclubs, and taverns — Old Town has all you need to be amused. Exploring the major streets of the city takes about three or four hours (not counting any interior visits). Absorbing all of Old Town's unique atmosphere would take weeks.

We recommend that you walk the streets of Old San Juan both during the day and after dark, because the mood and atmosphere are remarkably different. You can see more during the day, but evening strolls are more romantic, although you should, of course, exercise caution walking down any dark, deserted street. Most of the streets are well lit, however, and filled with milling nighttime throngs. Highlights of Old San Juan include the following (see the "Old San Juan Attractions" map on p. 359):

- ✔ **Casa Blanca,** 1 Calle San Sebastian (☎ 787-725-1454): The "White House" of Old San Juan is sometimes mistaken as the residence of Ponce de León. Actually, it was built in 1521 after the famed explorer died in Cuba. His son-in-law, Juan García Troche, ordered the house to be erected on land given to Ponce by the Spanish Crown for services rendered. Two years after it was built, a hurricane destroyed it, and the present masonry home is a reconstruction. The descendants of Ponce de León occupied the house for 250 years, until the Spanish government took it over in 1779 as a residence for military commanders. An attractive garden with a refreshing fountain is located in the courtyard, and the Juan Ponce de León Museum, on the second floor, exhibits antiques, paintings, and artifacts from the 16th to the 18th centuries. Casa Blanca is open Tuesday through Saturday from 9 a.m. to noon and 1 to 4:30 p.m.; admission is $2.

- ✔ **Catedral de San Juan,** 153 Calle Cristo (☎ 787-722-0861): This cathedral is the ecclesiastical center of Puerto Rico, its most venerated religious edifice. A wood building with a thatched roof stood here until a hurricane blew it away in 1529. The present church was launched that same year, although the building has undergone many architectural changes over the years. Many of its once-treasured relics have been looted over the centuries. Most of what you see today is from the 19th century, although a quartet of vaulted rooms remains from the original structure. The greatest relic is the marble tomb of Ponce de León resting near the transept. Nearby is an alleged relic of San Pío, the Roman martyr. The cathedral is open Monday through Saturday 8 a.m. to 5 p.m., and Sunday 8 a.m. to 2 p.m. Admission is free. Masses held daily.

- ✔ **Fuerte San Cristóbal,** Calle Nozagaray (☎ 787-729-6960): The other major fort on the island in addition to El Morro (which we discuss next and is the best known) is this formidable fortress from the 18th century that protected Old San Juan from land-based attacks. Begun in 1634 and reconstructed in the 1770s, it's one of the largest forts ever built in the Americas by Spain, with walls rising more than 46m (150 ft.) above sea level. On 11 hectares (27 acres), it was linked to El Morro by a series of monumental walls and bastions riddled with cannons. You can visit on your own, although park rangers sometimes lead free tours. Admission is $3 for adults, $1 for ages 16 to 17, and free for 15 and under. Open daily from 9 a.m. to 5 p.m.

✔ **Fuerte San Felipe del Morro,** Calle Norzagaray (☎ 787-729-6960): "El Morro" (its local nickname), a U.S. National Historic Site, still stands guard on the rocky promontory overlooking the entrance to San Juan's harbor. With its round tower still intact, the fort has been guarding the bay since its founding in 1540. Built on six levels, about 46m (150 ft.) above the sea, the fort contains walls up to 4.5m (15 ft.) thick. The oldest Spanish fort in the so-called New World, this place is still an attraction with its tunnels, turrets, dungeons, ramps, and barracks. On-site is a small museum tracing the fort's history, and a video plays for all to view; tours are offered in English. You can also visit on your own. Admission is $3 for adults, $2 for students and seniors, $1 for ages 13 to 17, and free for children 12 and under. Open daily from 9 a.m. to 5 p.m.

✔ **La Fortaleza,** Calle Recinto Oeste (☎ 787-721-7000, ext. 2211): The oldest executive mansion in continuous use in the Western Hemisphere is today both the office and residence of the governor of Puerto Rico. Governors come and go, but this mansion seems to endure forever, having been the seat of government for centuries. The original structure that stood here dates from the mid–16th century. Guided tours conducted on the hour in English take you through the mansion, where you get to view the Moorish gardens, the dungeon, and a chapel. Informal but "proper" attire is required — no swimsuits. Admission is free. Open Monday through Friday 9 a.m. to 3:30 p.m.

✔ **Museo de Arte,** 299 Av. José de Diego, Santurce (☎ 787-977-6277): Puerto Rico's most important gallery, which opened in 2000 and cost $55 million to construct, is a state-of-the art showcase for the island nation's rich cultural heritage as reflected mainly through its painters. Housed in a former city hospital in Santurce, the museum features both a permanent collection and temporary exhibitions. Prominent local artists are the star — for example, Francisco Oller (1833–1917), who brought a touch of Cézanne or Camille Pissarro to Puerto Rico (Oller actually studied in France with both of these Impressionists). Another leading star of the permanent collection is José Campeche, a late-18th-century classical painter. The museum is like a living textbook of Puerto Rico, beginning with its early development and going on to showcase camp aspects such as the poster art created here in the mid–20th century. It also presents all the important modern island artists, including the best known, the late Angel Botello, but also such contemporaries as Rafael Tufiño and Arnaldo Roche Rabell. Come take a look one of these days: Tuesday, Thursday to Saturday 10 a.m. to 5 p.m., Wednesday 10 a.m. to 8 p.m., Sunday 11 a.m. to 6 p.m. Admission is $6 for adults, $3 for seniors and children under 12.

✔ **Museo de Arte y Historia de San Juan,** Calle Norzagaray at Calle MacArthur (☎ 787-724-1875): A bustling marketplace in 1855, this handsome building is now the modern San Juan Museum of Art and History. You'll find exhibits of Puerto Rican art and audiovisual shows that present the island's history. Concerts and other cultural events take place in the huge courtyard. Admission is free. Open Tuesday to Friday 9 a.m. to noon and 1 to 4 p.m., Saturday to Sunday 10 a.m. to noon and 1 to 4 p.m.

✔ **Museo Pablo Casals,** 101 Calle San Sebastián, Plaza de San José (☎ 787-723-9185): The famed cellist, Pablo Casals, lived in Puerto Rico for the last 16 years of his life. He came here in 1956 as a protest against the dictatorship of Federico Franco in Spain. Almost at once he became a major cultural figure on the island, and he contributed in part to a renaissance of music and the arts in Puerto Rico. Videotapes of major Casals Festival concerts are shown if requested. The museum displays much memorabilia of the great artist, including pictures, manuscripts, letters, and his favorite cellos. Even his beloved old sweater is on exhibit. Admission is $1 for adults, 50¢ for children and students. Open Tuesday through Saturday 9:30 a.m. to 4:30 p.m.

Taking a guided tour in and around San Juan

If you want to see more of the island but don't want to rent a car or deal with public transportation, perhaps an organized tour is for you. **Castillo Sightseeing Tours & Travel Services,** Calle Laurel 2413, Punta La Marias, Santurce (☎ 787-726-5752, 787-791-6195), maintains offices at some of San Juan's major hotels. They can also arrange pickup at other accommodations in one of their six air-conditioned buses. One of the most popular half-day tours runs from San Juan to El Yunque Rain Forest; it departs in the morning, lasts four to five hours, and costs $45 per person. The company also offers a four-hour city tour of San Juan that costs $40 and includes a stopover at the Bacardi rum factory. Full-day snorkeling tours to the reefs of a deserted island off Puerto Rico's eastern edge are aboard one of two sail- and motor-driven catamarans. These tours go for $79 and include lunch, snorkeling gear, and piña coladas.

The best tours of Old San Juan itself are available through **Legends** (☎ 787-605-9060). In a three-hour walking tour, Wednesday to Monday from 10 a.m. to 1 p.m., you visit the most intriguing sights in the old city as you listen to pirate stories, legends, and historical facts. The rate is $38 per person (children under 5 are free). Another intriguing tour is a night walk into Spanish colonial times. This two-hour tour, costing $30 per person, is conducted Sunday, Monday, Wednesday, and Thursday from 6 to 8 p.m. When calling for information, ask about other tours that may be available.

If you want a more-penetrating look at the city, you can book a tour from **Colonial Adventure,** 201 Recinto Sur (☎ 787-793-2992). The company offers a variety of informative walking tours for groups of ten or more; rates range from $18 to $24 per person.

Discovering the rest of the island

The only way to see Puerto Rico in any depth is to rent a car and get a good road map — and, even so, you may end up getting lost, but you can often make some fascinating discoveries that way. Many of the roads, especially those around the coastline, are well maintained. The north shore around San Juan is clogged at rush hours in the morning and again in the late afternoon.

Out and about: Nature, wildlife, and outer space

Families can bank on fun and education when they visit **Parque Zoologico de Mayagüez,** Route 108 at Barrio Miradero (☎ 787-834-8110), an 18-hectare (45-acre) tropical compound housing exotic animals from around the world. Admission is $6 for adults and $2 for children one to ten years old; parking is $2. Open Wednesday through Sunday from 8:30 a.m. to 4 p.m.

Mona Island, lying 80km (50 miles) across the treacherous Mona Passage, is called the "Galapagos of the Caribbean" because it's home to several endangered or unique indigenous species. The nearest town for embarkation is Puerto Rico's "third city" of Mayagüez. The heart-shaped island is 11km (7 miles) long. Formerly inhabited by the Taíno Indians, pirates later used it to stash their booty. Limestone cliffs reach a height of 61m (200 ft.) on the North Coast, where you'll find some pristine beaches that are home to mammoth iguanas or perhaps a nesting hawksbill turtle. In the coral reefs offshore, visibility is good up to 46km (150 ft.). Campsites are available, but otherwise Mona is uninhabited, except for the wildlife. Private boats from the West Coast of Puerto Rico visit the island daily. If you're staying at a West Coast hotel, check with reception to see if the staff knows someone willing to take you over. For data about the island or to reserve a campsite if you want to stay overnight, contact the **Department of Natural Resources** (☎ 787-724-3647).

If E.T. phones home, the scientists at **Observatorio de Arecibo,** Route 625 (☎ 787-878-2612; www.naic.edu), will pick up the phone. Some of the coolest scenes of James Bond's movies, as well as the Jodie Foster film *Contact,* were filmed here. This radio telescope is the largest in the world, with an 8-hectare (20-acre) curved reflector installed over a natural karst sinkhole. Lying 66km (41 miles) to the west of San Juan, it is dubbed "the ear to heaven." At this base, scientists can monitor natural radio emissions from distant galaxies, pulsars, and quasars. If some form of extraterrestrial intelligence is trying to send us a message, the scientists here are standing by. This facility, used for researching life in outer space, was launched October 12, 1992, the 500th anniversary of Columbus's arrival in the New World. You can take a self-guided tour through the observatory, which includes a visitor center with exhibits on the planetary systems. Admission is $4 for adults and $2 for children. Open Wednesday through Friday noon to 4 p.m., Saturday and Sunday 9 a.m. to 4 p.m.

Allow a half-day to tour this site — especially if you have budding astronomers in the family. This facility is part of the National Astronomy and Ionosphere Center of Cornell University.

Even if you don't like caves, you have much to be fascinated with at the 121-hectare (300-acre) **Río Camuy Cave Park,** Route 129, Km 18.9 (☎ 787-898-3100), set on a 101-hectare (250-acre) site just to the southwest of Arecibo Observatory. You can visit both Arecibo and Río Camuy on the same daytrip west of San Juan. The caves contain the third-largest underground river in the world, and the Taíno Indians knew them well. For years the caves lay undiscovered until their rediscovery in the 1950s. Visitors descend into the cool caverns 61m (200 ft.) underground on a trolley. At the entrance to the Clara Cave of Epalme, you hop out for a 45-minute nature walk where you view stalagmites, stalactites, and large natural "sculptures" formed over the centuries. Tours change slightly in the off season. Admission is $10 for adults and $7 for 4- to 12-year-olds; parking is $3. Open Wednesday through Sunday from 8 a.m. to 3 p.m.

Better known as *El Faro* or "The Lighthouse," **Reserva Natural las Cabezas de San Juan** in the northeastern corner of the island, north of Fajardo off Route 987 at Km 6.8 (☎ 787-722-5882, 787-860-2560), is one of the most beautiful and important areas on Puerto Rico. Here you find seven ecological systems and a restored 19th-century Spanish colonial lighthouse. From the lighthouse observation deck, majestic views extend to islands as far off as St. Thomas in the U.S. Virgin Islands. Surrounded on three sides by the Atlantic Ocean, the 128-hectare (316-acre) site encompasses forestland, mangroves, lagoons, beaches, cliffs, offshore cays, and coral reefs. A boardwalk trail winds through the fascinating topography. Ospreys, sea turtles, and an occasional manatee are visible from the windswept promontories and rocky beach. Under the tutelage of Las Cabezas guides, every visitor becomes a naturalist for a few absorbing hours. Call ahead to make a reservation to tour the reserve. Tours in English or Spanish are Wednesday through Sunday at 9:30 a.m., 10 a.m., 10:30 a.m., and 2 p.m. Admission is $7 for adults and $4 for seniors and children 4 to 12 years old.

Things of the past: Stepping back in time

Don't expect Stonehenge or any monumental ruins if you visit **Parque Ceremonial Indígena Barrio Caguana,** Route 111, Km 12.3 (☎ 787-894-7325). But this ceremonial site at Tibes, near Ponce, is one of the few reminders left by the early settlers of the island, the Taíno Indians. In a natural botanical garden, the Indians used these ball courts (called *batey*) as many as eight centuries ago. Stone monoliths still stand outlining many of the former courts, and a few weigh up to a ton. The Taínos used the 5.2-hectare (13-acre) site for both recreation and worship, and they left behind some petroglyphs to intrigue future generations. What kind of ball game did they play here? Some archaeologists have suggested that the game was the mother of soccer; others view it like playing volleyball without a net. Admission is $2 for adults and $1 for 6- to 12-year-olds. Open daily from 9 a.m. to 4:30 p.m.

The oldest cemetery in the Antilles, the **Tibes Ceremonial Center** is on Route 503 at Km 2.2 outside Ponce (☎ **787-840-2255**). Bordered by the Rio Portuguéz and excavated in 1875, it contains some 186 skeletons, dating from A.D. 300, as well as pre-Taíno plazas from A.D. 700. The site also includes a re-created Taíno village, seven rectangular ball courts, and two dance grounds. The arrangement of stone points on the dance grounds, in line with the solstices and equinoxes, suggests a pre-Columbian Stonehenge. Here you'll also find a museum, an exhibition hall that presents a documentary about Tibes, a cafeteria, and a souvenir shop. The museum is open Tuesday through Sunday from 9 a.m. to 4 p.m. Admission is $2 for adults and $1 for children. Guided tours in English and Spanish lead visitors through the grounds.

Breathing new life: The city of Ponce

The city of **Ponce,** second largest in Puerto Rico, makes for one of the island's most interesting stopovers, lying 120km (75 miles) southwest of San Juan. A once-decaying city, it has undergone a renaissance; hundreds of its buildings have been restored and given a new lease on life for the 21st century. Buildings ranging in style from European neoclassical to Spanish colonial are called *Ponce Créole,* a kind of colonial architecture with both interior and exterior balconies.

Ponce's Calle Reina Isabel is a virtual textbook of the different Ponceño styles. Many of the most historic buildings are on streets radiating from the stately **Plaza Las Delicias** (Plaza of Delights). The **Cathedral of Our Lady of Guadalupe,** Calle Concordia (☎ **787-842-0134**), dates from 1660 and stands on the western edge of the Plaza Las Delicias. The present building is Gothic inspired.

The major attraction of the city is **Museo de Arte de Ponce,** Av. Las Americas 25 (☎ **787-848-0505**). Donated to the people of Puerto Rico by Luís A. Ferré, a former governor, this museum has the finest collection of European and Latin American art in the Caribbean. The building itself, called the "Parthenon of the Caribbean," is the design of Edward Durell Stone, who also designed the John F. Kennedy Center for the Performing Arts in Washington, D.C. Its collection represents the principal schools of American and European art of the past five centuries. Among the nearly 400 works on display are exceptional pre-Raphaelite and Italian baroque paintings. Visitors also see artworks by other European masters, as well as Puerto Rican and Latin American paintings, graphics, and sculptures. On display are some of the best works of the two "old masters" of Puerto Rico, Francisco Oller and José Campeche. The museum also contains a representative collection of the works of the old masters of Europe, including Gainsborough, Velázquez, Rubens, and Van Dyck. Admission is $4 for adults and $2.50 for children under 12. Open daily from 10 a.m. to 5 p.m.

Keeping Active

Puerto Rico is a lot more than a beach, or even several beaches. It has one of the best organized-sports programs in the Caribbean, including great golf on fabled courses that often draw the champions. Tennis is big stuff throughout Puerto Rico, and all the major resorts feature courts, most of which are lit for night play when the sun isn't so hot. Because of its mountainous terrain and scenic beauty, Puerto Rico is one of the best islands for hiking in the West Indies. Not only that, but it also features some of the best stables in the Caribbean Basin, and trail rides are conducted along the beaches and through nature preserves.

Hitting the links

The comparison is a bit far-fetched, but Puerto Rico is often called "the Scotland of the Caribbean." It and Jamaica (see Chapter 13) have the best golf courses in the West Indies.

In recent years, the island has hosted the LPGA tour and the Hyatt PGA Matchplay Challenge. You can pick from 18 courses on the island, 14 of which are championship links designed by golf legends Greg Norman; Robert Trent Jones, Sr.; George Fazio; Arthur Hills; Greg Player; and, of course, local hero Chi Chi Rodríguez. Call ahead to reserve tee times. Some resorts limit their players to guests only (or at least favor guests). Greens fees begin at $65 but can run up to $185.

Some of Puerto Rico's best golf is located at the two Hyatt resorts at Dorado, 29km (18 miles) west of San Juan. Robert Trent Jones, Sr., is the famed designer of the quartet of 18-hole golf courses here, owned by the **Hyatt Dorado Beach Resort & Country Club** at Route 693, Km 10.8, Dorado (although the hotel is closed the courses remain open). The two original courses, known as East and West, are carved out of a jungle and offer tight fairways bordered by trees and forests, with lots of ocean holes. Call ☎ 787-796-1234 for tee times. The somewhat newer and less-noted North and South courses, now called The Plantation Club (call ☎ 787-796-8915 for tee times), feature wide fairways with well-bunkered greens and an assortment of water traps and tricky wind factors. Each course has a 72-par. The longest is the South course at 6,443m (7,047 yards).

Competing with the golf courses at the Hyatt is Chi Chi Rodríguez's own signature course at the **Dorado del Mar Golf Club,** 200 Dorado del Mar (☎ 787-796-3070). This course affords panoramic scenery, water on 12 holes, and tropical trade winds. Chi Chi's own favorite hole is 10, a long uphill par-5. A host of the Honda Classic, the 6,343m (6,937-yard), 18-hole course opened in 1998. Playing the course costs $102 in the morning until 1 p.m., $87 from 1 p.m. to 4 p.m., and $52 from 4 p.m. to 7:30 p.m.

Giving the Dorado courses serious competition these days are two world-class championship courses at **Westin Rio Mar Beach Golf Resort & Spa,** 6000 Rio Mar Blvd., Rio Grande (☎ 787-888-6000), as easily accessible from San Juan as the Dorado courses. Rio Grande is 31km (19 miles) east of San Juan. The older of the two, the Ocean Course, was designed by George and Tom Fazio as part of the original resort and has been a staple on Puerto Rico's professional golf circuit since the 1960s. In 1997, Westin opened the property's second 18-holer, the more-challenging River Course, which is the first Greg Norman–designed course in the Caribbean. Both courses are sandwiched between the ocean and the foot of El Yunque rain forest.

Few other real-estate developments in the Caribbean devote as much attention and publicity to their golf facilities as the **Palmas de Mar Golf Club** (☎ 787-285-2256). Today, both the older course (the Gary Player–designed Palm Course) and the newer course (the Reese Jones–designed Flamboyant) have pars of 72 and layouts of around 2,072m (2,266 yards) each. Crack golfers consider holes 11 to 15 of the older course among the toughest five successive holes in the Caribbean.

Having a ball with tennis

If you're staying at one of the large resorts, certainly if that hotel is outside of San Juan, your hotel will likely have its own tennis courts. If you're in a smaller inn, your hotel probably won't have a court. Most hotels allow nonguests to play for a fee, but you have to call to book a court time, and hotel guests naturally are given preference. The city of San Juan offers 17 lighted courts at **San Juan Central Municipal Park,** Calle Cerra, exit on Route 2 (☎ 787-722-1646). Fees run $3 per hour from 6 a.m. to 5 p.m. and $4 per hour from 6 to 10 p.m.

Our two favorite tennis facilities on island are the **Hyatt Dorado Beach Resort & Country Club,** Route 693, Km 10.8, Dorado (☎ 787-796-1234), open to the public even though the resort has closed, and the **Westin Rio Mar Beach Golf Resort & Spa,** 6000 Rio Mar Blvd., Rio Grande (☎ 787-888-6000), which rents courts to nonguests at $20 per person per hour.

Also good are **Ponce Hilton and Casino,** Route 14, 1150 Av. Caribe, Ponce (☎ 787-259-7676) and **Condado Plaza Hotel and Casino,** 999 Av. Ashford (☎ 787-721-1000), both open exclusively to hotel guests. **Palmas de Mar,** Route 906, Humacao (☎ 787-852-6000), rents courts for $24 to $34 per hour to nonguests.

Rooting for the home team

When it comes to baseball, Puerto Ricans reach a fever pitch. The island's season runs from October through February. Stadiums are in San Juan, Santurce, Ponce, Caguas, Arecibo, and Mayagüez; the teams also play once or twice in Aguadilla. Contact the **Puerto Rico Tourism Company** (☎ 800-223-6530) for details or call **Professional Baseball of Puerto Rico** (☎ 787-765-6285).

Hiking the island

The best place for hiking in the entire Caribbean is the Caribbean National Forest, nicknamed **El Yunque,** the only tropical rain forest in the U.S. National Park Service. The United Nations has designated El Yunque a Biosphere Reserve. The forest is riddled with 11,331 hectares (28,000 acres) of trails, lying only a 45-minute drive east of San Juan. You enter at **El Portal Tropical Forest Center,** Highway 3, then turn right on Route 191 (☎ 787-888-1810, 787-888-1880).

Granted national park status by President Theodore Roosevelt, El Yunque is an ideal spot for a picnic among rare flora and fauna, including 240 species of tropical trees, 20 kinds of orchids, and varied wildlife including millions of tiny tree frogs whose distinctive cry of *coquí* (pronounced koh-*kee*) has given them their name. Tropical birds include the greenish blue-and-red-fronted Puerto Rican parrot, once nearly extinct and now making a comeback. Other rare animals include the Puerto Rican boa, which grows to 2.1m (7 ft.) — but it's very unlikely that you'll encounter one. More than two dozen animal species found here don't live anywhere else in the world.

As you hike along the terrain, with its ropelike vines and feathery primeval ferns, you'll think you've entered Tarzan country. Towering over El Yunque is **El Toro,** its highest peak at 1,073m (3,523 ft.). At least 508cm (200 in.) of rain falls on El Yunque annually, and islanders thank the Indian god Yukiyú, the namesake of the forest, for this showering abundance of water, the envy of many a dry island in the Caribbean, particularly Aruba.

Because it's likely to rain down on you at any minute, bring along a lightweight rain slicker and some sturdy hiking boots. Along your trails, you'll find sheltered picnic tables and observation towers.

El Portal Tropical Forest Center features displays that explain El Yunque and tropical forests around the world. A theater presents video shows in English and Spanish. The visitor center is open daily from 7:30 a.m. to 6 p.m. and costs $3 to enter. You can obtain the best hiking information by contacting El Portal (see contact info earlier in this section). For more-general information, contact the **Department of Natural Resources**

(☎ 787-724-3724) or the **U.S. Forest Service** (☎ 787-724-3724). We suggest planning a full day of exploring this preserve. If you have kids along, you'll find plenty of easy trails for them to tackle.

Most San Juan hotels have a tour desk that can make arrangements for you to hike the forests. All-day tours ($35–$60) can include a trip to Ponce, a day at El Comandante Racetrack, or a combined tour of San Juan and El Yunque rain forest. Leading tour operators include **Rico Suntours** (☎ 787-722-2080), and **United Tour Guides** (☎ 787-725-7605, 787-723-5578).

Horsing around

Puerto Ricans not only love baseball, but they also have a passion for betting on horses. Just a 20-minute taxi ride or drive east of San Juan, **El Comandante Racetrack,** Route 3, Km 15.3, Canovanas (☎ 787-792-8306), is one of the major racetracks of the Caribbean. Post time varies from 2:15 to 5:30 p.m. on Monday, Wednesday, Friday, Saturday, and Sunday. The on-site restaurant is open on race days from 12:30 to 5:30 p.m. Entrance to the clubhouse is $3; no admission is charged for the grandstand.

If you'd rather ride a horse than watch one race, you've also arrived on the right island. Many locals are avid horsemen (or -women), and Puerto Rico is known in equestrian circles for its *paso fino* horses. These well-bred, graceful animals are small (but not miniature) and have a distinctive gait. You should always call to reserve before arriving at one of the stables.

One of the most convenient stables, and our favorite, is **Hacienda Carabali,** Route 992, Km 3.1, Luquillo (☎ 787-889-5820, 787-889-4954). This outfitter features the best of both worlds: rides along Puerto Rico's best beach at **Playa Luquillo** and rides through **El Yunque,** the rain forest. Prices are $60 for adults and $40 for children 11 and under for a two-hour ride.

While still in the eastern part of the island, you can also link up with forest trails and beach rides at the **Palmas de Mar Equestrian Center** at Rancho Buena Vista, Route 906, Humacao (☎ 787-852-6000). A unique place for riding is **Hacienda Restaurante Gaby's World,** Route 127, Km 5.2, Yauco (☎ 787-856-0381). Here you can ride the trails of an 81-hectare (200-acre) island ranch, which also has a restaurant and playgrounds on-site, making this a family favorite.

Pedaling around Puerto Rico

If you generally bike around New York City, then San Juan should be no daunting challenge. Not only San Juan, but also the major arteries along the North Coast are filled with cars and their fumes, no fun for bikers at all. In much of the interior, including the mountain-bike trails across the Cordillera Central, biking is for those in training for the Olympics.

The best areas we've found are along the small roads on the island's South Coast, both east and west of Ponce. This coastal plain area makes biking more fun than challenging. If you like to bike along a wide beach, we suggest **Boquerón Beach,** which fronts the town of Boquerón in the southwest.

In the southwest, you can rent bikes at **Boquerón Balnearios,** Department of Recreation and Sports, Route 101, Boquerón (☎ **787-722-1771**) and the **Ponce Hilton,** Route 14, 1150 Av. Caribe, Ponce (☎ **787-259-7676**).

Shopping the Local Stores

If you, like us, feel you were born to shop, then San Juan is your kind of city. Boutiques and specialized stores line the narrow streets of **Old San Juan.** Because, as a territory of the United States, Puerto Rico pays U.S. import taxes, from this island you can take back all you want in merchandise without extra duty. However, because the duty has been paid, it's reflected in the merchandise. Even so, you can find bargains; San Juan shops grant heavy discounts. (For those bargains in imported perfumes or expensive electronics, head for Charlotte Amalie, the capital of St. Thomas — see Chapter 17.)

The **Puerto Rico Tourism Company's Artisan Center** (☎ **787-721-2400**) and the **Fomento Crafts Project** (☎ **787-758-4747, ext. 2291**) offer advice about where to purchase high-quality works by island craftspeople.

Puerto Rican rum is the best in the world — just ask any local rum producer. Most visitors who like rum punches pick up a bottle or two before flying back or returning by ship to the mainland. Prices are lower than in the States, and you can bring back as many bottles as you want without paying duty. *Ron,* as locals call it, is the national drink of Puerto Rico, the world's largest producer. To many rum drinkers, no other brand than the famous Bacardi exists. To a lesser degree, we're also fond of Ronrico, Castillo, Don Q, and, for variety, a spiced rum called Captain Morgan.

Most impressive of the island's crafts are *santos,* carved religious figures that Puerto Ricans have produced since the 1500s. Craftspeople who make these are called *santeros.* Using clay, gold, stone, or cedar wood, they carve figurines representing saints, usually from 8 to 20 inches (20–50cm) tall.

Another Puerto Rican craft has undergone a big revival just as it seemed that it would disappear forever: lace. Originating in Spain, *mundillos* (tatted fabrics) are the product of a type of bobbin lace-making. This craft, five centuries old, exists today only in Puerto Rico and Spain. The first lace made in Puerto Rico was called *torchon* (beggar's lace). Early examples of beggar's lace were considered of inferior quality, but artisans today have transformed this fabric into a delicate art form, eagerly sought by collectors. Lace bands called *entrados* have two straight borders, whereas the other traditional style, *puntilla,* has both a straight and a scalloped border.

The most popular of all Puerto Rican crafts are the *caretas* papier-mâché masks worn at island carnivals. The menacing horns, fang-toothed leering expressions, and bulging eyes of these half-demon, half-animal creations send children running and screaming to their parents. At carnival time, costumed revelers called *vejigantes* don the masks. *Vejigantes* wear bat-winged jumpsuits and roam the streets either individually or in groups.

Puerto Rico, like the States, has its share of shopping malls. The greatest concentration of specialty stores is in Old San Juan, where you can get about on a free trolley if you don't want to walk. The best shops are on **Calle Cristo, Calle San Francisco,** and **Calle Fortaleza,** although dipping into the smaller side streets is fun as well. Here are our favorites: **El Alacazar,** Calle San José 103 (☎ 787-723-1229), the largest emporium of antique furniture, silver, and art objects in the Caribbean; **Galeria Palomas,** Calle del Cristo 207 (☎ 787-725-2660), one of the leading art galleries of Puerto Rico, carrying some of the major painters in Latin America; **Butterfly People,** Calle Fortaleza 152 (☎ 787-723-2432), which sells unique mounted butterflies that will last forever; **La Calle,** Calle Fortaleza 105 (☎ 787-725-1306), the best emporium for brightly painted papier-mâché carnival masks; **Club Jibarito,** Calle Cristo 202 (☎ 787-724-7797), which sells Puerto Rico's own excellent cigars, which some aficionados prefer to the more-famous Cubans; and **Spicy Caribbee,** Calle Cristo 154 (☎ 787-725-4690), which offers Old Town's best selection of Puerto Rican coffee (our favorite brands are Café Crema, Café Rico, Rioja, and Yaucono, in that order).

Living It Up After Dark

Puerto Ricans love their social life, and tops on their lists are dancing and dressing up. Women should wear their killer heels (just watch the ballast stone streets), and men should show up decked out, too.

Dancing until dawn

Qué Pasa, the official visitor's guide, tries to keep abreast of San's Juan whirling club scene. Also, pick up a copy of the *San Juan Star, Quick City Guide,* or *Bienvenidos.* If your hotel has a concierge, he or she is usually a font of information about what's hot after dark.

Fridays and Saturdays are big nights in San Juan when clubs are their most crowded, and the only way you get into some of them without a reservation is if you're Ricky Martin or Jennifer Lopez. If you're staying at an upscale hotel, ask the concierge if he or she can reserve a good table at the most happening spots. The hottest action doesn't start until 10 p.m. or later.

Old San Juan's cobblestone streets are closed to auto traffic on Friday and Saturday nights, making the area perfect for a romantic stroll. If you're looking for more action, walk to **Calle San Sebastian,** lined with trendy bars and restaurants, where you'll see lines of people waiting to get through the doors. Outside of San Juan, nightlife is hard to come by beyond the resorts.

Some of the best clubs in San Juan are in hotels (which typically charge a minimum of $10 — and up to $20 — to get in), including **Babylon,** in El San Juan Hotel and Casino, 6063 Av. Isla Verde, Isla Verde (☎ **787-791-1000**).

In Old San Juan, there's **Rumba,** Calle San Sebastian 152 (☎ **787-725-4407**), for salsa dancing, and **Club Laser,** Calle del Cruz 251 (☎ **787-725-7581**), is a dance club sprawling across three floors of an antique building.

The most popular gay bar in San Juan is the open-air **Beach Bar** on the ground floor of the Atlantic Beach Hotel, Calle Vendig 1 (☎ **787-721-6900**), best on a Sunday afternoon. **Eros,** 1257 Ponce de Leon, Santurce (☎ **787-727-1390**), is another popular spot. Catering exclusively to lesbians, **Cups,** 1708 Calle San Mateo, Santurce (☎ **787-268-3570**), offers on occasion live music and cabaret.

Gambling the night away

Nearly all the large hotels in San Juan, Condado, and Isla Verde offer casinos; other large casinos are in some of the bigger resorts outside the metropolitan area. The atmosphere in the casinos is casual, but still you shouldn't show up in swimsuits or shorts. Most of the casinos open around noon, often closing at 2, 3, or 4 a.m. Patrons must be at least 18 years old to enter.

The casino generating all the excitement today is the 18,500-square-foot (1,718-sq.-m) casino at the **Ritz-Carlton,** 6961 State Rd., Isla Verde (☎ **787-253-1700**), the largest in Puerto Rico, clad in elegant 1940s décor. One of the splashiest of San Juan's casinos is at the **Sheraton Old San Juan Hotel and Casino,** Calle Brumbaugh 100 (☎ **787-721-5100**), where five-card stud competes with some 240 slot machines and roulette tables. You can also try your luck at the **El San Juan Hotel and Casino** (one of the most grand), 6063 Av. Isla Verde (☎ **787-791-1000**), or the **Wyndham Condado Plaza Hotel and Casino,** 999 Av. Ashford (☎ **787-721-1000**). And the best part is, you have no passports to flash or admissions to pay.

Fast Facts: Puerto Rico

Area Code

The area code is **787.**

ATMs

These machines are called ATH on Puerto Rico, but they operate the same as ATMs and are widely available on the island.

Babysitters

Expect to pay at least $8 and up per hour. Most Puerto Rican hotels can also arrange a babysitter for you, often a member of the staff.

Currency Exchange

The Yankee dollar is the coin of the realm.

Doctors

Puerto Rico has an excellent healthcare system. Ask your hotel for a referral if necessary.

Electricity

Puerto Rico uses a 110-volt AC (60-cycle) electrical system, the same as in the United States. European guests who have traveling appliances that use other systems can call ahead to confirm that their hotel has adapters and converters.

Emergencies

In an emergency, dial ☎ **911.** Or call the local police (☎ 787-343-2020), fire department (☎ 787-343-2330), ambulance (☎ 787-343-2550), or medical assistance (☎ 787-754-3535).

Hospitals

In a medical emergency, call ☎ **911.** Ashford Presbyterian Community Hospital, Av. Ashford 1451, San Juan (☎ 787-721-2160), maintains 24-hour emergency service. Service is also provided at Clinica Las Americas, 400 Franklin Delano Roosevelt Ave., Hato Rey (☎ 787-765-1919), and at Río Piedras Medical Center, Av. Americo Miranda, Río Piedras (☎ 787-777-3535).

Information

See the Appendix for helpful Web sites and locations of U.S.-based and local tourist offices.

Internet Access and Cybercafes

Public access to the Internet is available at some large-scale resorts; the staff often provides access from their own computers.

Newspapers and Magazines

Getting publications from all over the world is easy on this island. You'll find excellent newsstands at the airport. The *San Juan Star* comes out daily in English and Spanish.

Pharmacies

The most common and easily found pharmacies are Puerto Rico Drug Company, 157 Calle San Francisco, Old San Juan (☎ 787-725-2202), and Walgreens, 1130 Av. Ashford, Condado, San Juan (☎ 787-725-1510). Walgreens operates more than 30 pharmacies on the island. The one located in Condado is open 24/7.

Police

For police assistance with an emergency, call ☎ **911.** Otherwise, call ☎ 787-343-2020.

Post Office

Because the U.S. Postal Service is responsible for handling mail on Puerto Rico, the regulations and tariffs are the same as on the mainland United States. You can purchase stamps at any post office, all of which are open Monday through Friday from 8 a.m. to 5 p.m. and Saturday from 8 a.m. to noon. You can also purchase stamps at vending machines in airports, stores, and hotels. First-class letters to addresses within Puerto Rico, the United States, and its territories cost 39¢; postcards, 24¢. Letters and postcards to Canada both cost 60¢ for the first half-ounce. Letters and postcards to other countries cost 80¢ for the first half-ounce.

Major post office branches are located at 153 Calle Fortaleza in Old San Juan, 163 Av. Fernandez Juncos in San Juan, 60 Calle McKinley in Mayagüez serving western Puerto Rico, and 102 Calle Garrido Morales in Fajardo serving eastern Puerto Rico.

Restrooms

Restaurants, hotels, and casinos in Puerto Rico are required by law to admit nonresidents and nonplayers into their restrooms. As such, there's usually a stream of traffic from the sidewalk into the public facilities of the casinos, bars, and hotels along such crowded strips as the Condado in San Juan, or the beachfront *bodegas* of Rincón and Aguadilla on Puerto Rico's western edge. Many hotels and restaurants have restrooms located close to the main entrances.

Safety

At night, exercise extreme caution when walking along the back streets of San Juan, and don't venture onto the unguarded public stretches of the Condado and Isla Verde beaches. All these areas are favorite targets for muggings. Out on the island you're much safer, but you should always take the usual precautions: Don't leave any property unattended on a beach (in fact, stash your valuable in the hotel safe before venturing out), and don't put anything of value in your car or trunk.

Smoking

Smoking policies are left to the discretion of the individual establishments, and most restaurants have designated nonsmoking sections within their restaurants and bars. If you have a strong preference for a particular venue, ask a staff member.

Taxes

Many hotels and restaurants add a 10 to 15 percent service charge. Check to make sure that you don't end up tipping twice. In the little hotels, especially those in small beach towns or in the mountains, don't be surprised to see a surcharge for air-conditioning, often $5 a day, added to your tab. Puerto Rico taxes hotel rooms at the rate of 11 percent in casino hotels, 9 percent in standard hotels, and 7 percent in *paradores*.

Taxis

Some of the larger hotels send vans to pick up airport passengers and transport them to various properties along the beachfront. Find out if your hotel offers this service when you make a reservation. If your hotel doesn't have shuttle service between the airport and its precincts, you have to get there on your own steam — most likely by taxi. Dozens of taxis line up outside the airport to meet arriving flights, so you rarely have to wait. Fares can vary widely, depending on traffic conditions. Again depending on traffic, figure on about a 30-minute drive from the airport to your hotel along the Condado.

Technically, cabdrivers should turn on their meters, but more often than not they quote a flat rate before starting out, which usually works out fairly. The island's Tourist Transportation Division (☎ 787-999-2100)

establishes flat rates between the Luís Muñoz Marín International Airport and major tourist zones. Tip between 10 and 15 percent of that fare.

Weather Updates

Log on to the Caribbean Weather Man at www.caribwx.com/cyclone.html or listen to Radio WOSO (1030 AM), an English-speaking station.

Chapter 15

St. Lucia

In This Chapter

▶ Knowing what to expect when you arrive
▶ Getting around the island
▶ Deciding where you want to stay
▶ Sampling the local cuisine at the best restaurants
▶ Scoping out good beaches and diving into water sports
▶ Satisfying the landlubber: Shopping and nightlife
▶ Branching out: Other places to visit

*A*vocado-shaped St. Lucia (pronounced *loo*-shuh) is one of the beauty spots of the Caribbean, with some of the region's greatest resorts, most of them all-inclusive. Except for a heavy concentration of hotels in the northwest, most of the island is a nature lover's paradise, containing — among other wonders — the world's only drive-through volcano on Mount Soufrière, a 7,689-hectare (19,000-acre) rain-forest reserve with prehistoric-looking giant ferns and wild orchids. Other attractions include a waterfall that tumbles in six stages through sulfur springs, and some of the Caribbean's most beautiful natural harbors such as Marigot, a former hide-out for the most bloodthirsty pirates in the West Indies in days of yore.

In spite of all this natural grandeur, its capital, Castries, ravaged by fires in 1948 and 1951, is one of the dullest in the Caribbean — but that's not why you come to St. Lucia.

The mountainous island lies between French Martinique and St. Vincent, and consists of some 623 sq. km (243 sq. miles), with an estimated 120,000 inhabitants. Just 32km (20 miles) from Martinique, St. Lucia spent a good part of its history bouncing back and forth between France and Britain.

The picture postcard of St. Lucia is most often its twin peaks of the Pitons, soaring 0.8km (a half-mile) out into the Caribbean Sea. These are actually volcanic cones, with Petit Piton to the west and Gros Piton to the immediate east. Actually, the highest point on the island is Mount Gimie at 958m (3,145 ft.), rising out of the center of the southern part of the island, with Soufrière and the Pitons to its immediate west.

Arriving at the Airport

St. Lucia has two airports. The modern **Hewanorra International Airport** (☎ 758-454-6355), which lies in the South, is located 72km (45 miles) from the capital of Castries. If you're flying in from most international destinations, such as the United States, chances are you'll land at this well-run and up-to-date airport with modern facilities. Here you'll find ATMs, clean restrooms, a branch of the tourist office (☎ 758-454-6644), and available transportation waiting outside.

The other, more-antiquated airport, **George F.L. Charles** (☎ 758-452-1156), is also called Vigie Airport. It receives smaller craft and lies in the Northeast just outside Castries. It, too, has ATMs, restrooms, and a small tourist office (☎ 758-452-2596).

Navigating your way through passport control and Customs

Unless you look like a very suspicious character — read that, potential drug dealer — you should breeze through Customs relatively easily. Today, St. Lucia is virtually dependent on tourism, and the government instructs Customs officials to ease your entry onto the island with a minimum of difficulty. Officials check to see that you have an ongoing or return ticket, which you should have ready — along with a valid passport — as you wait in line. U.S. citizens can prove citizenship by presenting a birth certificate with a raised seal or else a government-issued photo ID. Even so, you should carry a passport which you'll need to produce upon your return to the United States. Chances are your luggage won't be inspected, but you can never be sure about that.

Getting from the airport to your hotel

Most likely, you'll land at Hewanorra Airport, lying at Vieux Fort at the southern tip of the island and a good distance from your resort, which will probably be on the Northwest Coast unless you're staying at **Anse Chastanet** (see our recommendation later in this chapter).

Chances are you'll have to spend about an hour and a half going along the potholed East Coast Highway to reach your final destination. Between Hewanorra and the resorts north of Castries, the average taxi fare ranges from $70 to $75 per carload. If you're booked at a resort along the Southwest Coast, including Soufrière, the average fare ranges from $55 to $60 per carload. The ride to a resort around Soufrière takes about an hour. Some resorts will send a shuttle bus to pick you up from the airport; ask about this option when you make your reservation.

Always ask the taxi driver to quote the fare before you get in. Make sure you determine which dollars he or she is quoting — U.S. or the Eastern Caribbean dollar, which is worth about 37¢ in American currency.

Although you may be tired after a long plane ride, you're at least rewarded with a panoramic coastline as you make your way from the southern tip of the island to the north end. Your taxi will traverse lush rain forests and oceanviews before you arrive at the hotel of your choice.

The commute is much easier from George F.L. Charles Airport (Vigie). Depending on your resort, you may be no more than 12 to 25 minutes away if you're lodging in and around Castries. From Vigie, it takes about half an hour to go to a resort at Marigot but a full 1¼ hours to reach Soufrière in the South. Expect to spend $20 per taxi ride for a resort on the periphery of Castries but $75 if you're booked around Soufrière, including Anse Chastanet.

Choosing Your Location

Where you stay in St. Lucia largely determines the quality of your vacation, because getting from one point to another on this mountainous island with its bad roads isn't easy.

Northwest Coast

All the beaches along the Northwest Coast are good for swimming, which is why most resort hotels have located here. The heaviest concentration of hotels is between Castries and Cap Estate in the North. The major attraction on the coast is **Vigie Beach,** a strip of white sand that stretches for 3km (2 miles). This beach begins near Vigie Airport and extends itself to **Choc Beach** and **Reduit Beach** before circling around Rodney Bay to **Pigeon Point,** the latter a small beach with a National Historic Park. Although the beaches are great, patrons of North Coast resorts are also removed from the great scenic wonders that lie in the Southwest.

If your main desire, other than lying on a beach, is to see some of the most spectacular natural wonders in the southern Caribbean, you'd do better to book a room at a resort in the southern city of Soufrière. A northwest location, however, affords you a better opportunity to travel into the capital for shopping (not sightseeing).

Getting around the Northwest, either by car or taxi, is easy because the roads here are flat and straight. If you're serious about boating, **Rodney Bay,** one of the premier yachting centers of the southern Caribbean and the goal of the Atlantic Rally for Cruisers (a transatlantic yacht crossing staged every Dec), is just a 15-minute drive north of Castries.

Marigot Bay

Marigot Bay gets our vote for the most beautiful natural harbor in the Caribbean. On the Western Coast of St. Lucia, a 13km (8-mile) drive south of Castries, Marigot Bay is known by the yachting crowd around the world who come here for its spectacular anchorage along a palm-fringed shoreline.

This harbor isn't a hotel district like the Northwest Coast or Soufrière, but you can find lodgings here if you deliberately seek seclusion and don't demand to be at the scene of the action. The calm waters and good swimming attract visitors to Marigot Beach. But if you're a true beach buff, you may seek more-expansive sands along the Northwest Coast.

However, if you'll happily settle for swimming, snorkeling, and hobnobbing with the yachties at the local bars, Marigot Bay is one of the snuggest and most romantic nests in the Caribbean. You have to drive or take a taxi for shopping at Castries or for seeing the wonders of nature at Soufrière.

Soufrière

For the sheer drama of nature, we always prefer to anchor in or around the little fishing port of **Soufrière** along the Southwest Coast. Dominated by Gros Piton and Petit Piton (the picture-postcard twin volcanic peaks), Soufrière is the second-largest town in St. Lucia outside of Castries. You'll find beaches here, and good ones, but the real reason to lodge here is to enjoy the French colonial–style town of Soufrière itself (which is a lot more interesting than Castries) and to experience the drive-in volcano, the rain forest, working banana plantations, and botanical gardens that evoke the South Pacific. **Anse Chastanet** (see our recommendation later in this chapter) is also the premier dive resort of St. Lucia. The **Jalousie Plantation** and **Ladera Resort** are the island's pockets of posh if you want to live in supreme luxury. These resorts are far more appealing to us than all those Sandals bedroom factories that dominate St. Lucia today.

Getting Around St. Lucia

Because of its mountainous terrain, St. Lucia is often hard to navigate. But locals have set up a fairly elaborate (at least for the Caribbean) system of hauling you about.

By taxi

By far, your local cabbie is the most popular and convenient means of transport, and prices are fairly reasonable except for the long hauls from one end of the island to the other (say, from the airport to your resort).

Taxis greet arriving planes at both airports, and these cabs also await prospective passengers outside all the major resorts. Taxis aren't metered, but the government regulates fares. Some typical fares are as follows: from Castries to Marigot Bay in the South, $25 to $30; from Castries to Rodney Bay in the North, $18 to $20; from Castries to Soufrière in the South — a long haul, $70.

Before getting in a cab, agree on the fare with the driver and, as we advise earlier in this chapter, determine if the quotation is in Eastern Caribbean or U.S. dollars. Because both currencies are in common use on the island, the taxi drivers will easily convert the rate for you.

Because most cabs are independently owned and operated, they don't have a central number for you to call. Your hotel can call a cabbie for you, though.

You can also arrange day tours of the island with a taxi driver, costing $135 per carload. Usually four passengers are recommended for maximum comfort. Most often, you coordinate these tours through the reception desk at your hotel. Your other option is to call **Toucan Travel,** The Marina (☎ **758-452-9963**), in Castries.

By car

All car-rental companies require drivers to be at least 25 years old and have a valid credit card. If you're a timid driver, use public transportation instead, because the winding, potholed roads are difficult for the faint of heart.

The most spectacular drive is from Castries in the North to Soufrière in the South, but the road is winding and difficult. You have to keep your eyes glued to the highway so much that you won't be able to appreciate the panoramic scenery passing in review.

Local policemen seem adept at giving out tickets, especially for those not obeying island speed limits. For example, in Castries you have to creep along at 48kmph (30mph). That's the bad news. The good news is that there aren't many policemen.

Several U.S. agencies such as Budget, Hertz, and Avis have franchises on the island; Avis and Hertz each have kiosks at both airports. They generally offer an unlimited mileage deal. Arrange car rentals at these U.S. agencies (or any local agency) before leaving home — you'll get a better rate and a guarantee of a car, which may be in limited supply during the winter season. Prices, of course, depend on your vehicle selection but range from $55 to $85 a day, or $250 to $400 per week.

If you arrive on the island without a reservation and decide to be adventurous and explore on your own, you can also call one of the local car-rental agencies, whose rates are competitive with the U.S. giants.

Here's how to contact the agencies:

- ✓ **Avis** (☎ **800-331-1212**, 758-452-2046; www.avis.com) has the most outlets — at both airports, at Vide Bouteille in Castries, and at Rodney Bay.
- ✓ **Hertz** (☎ **800-654-3131**, 758-454-9636; www.hertz.com) is also located at both airports and in Castries.

- ✔ **Budget** (☎ 758-452-0233; www.budget.com) has a desk at the Hewanorra Airport and in Castries.

- ✔ **C.T.I. Rent-a-Car,** Grosilet Highway, Rodney Bay Marina (☎ 758-452-0732), is a good bet if you're staying at one of the resorts north of Castries.

- ✔ **Cool Breeze Car Rental,** New Development, Soufrière (☎ 758-459-7729), is a good choice if you're staying in the South and want a local car-rental firm.

The government requires that you obtain a local driver's license, which costs $21. You can purchase a license either at the airport when you arrive or when you go to pick up your rental car.

Remember to drive on the left, and try to avoid some of the island's more gaping potholes. In St. Lucia, drive more carefully and be more alert than you usually are because of the difficult terrain, and honk your horn every time you go around a blind hairpin turn in the road.

By ferry

Rodney Bay Ferry (☎ 758-452-8816) is a useful way of getting around for visitors to the Northeast Coast. The ferry makes hourly trips daily from 9 a.m. to 4 p.m., costing $6 per person round-trip for sails between the Rodney Bay Marina and the shopping complex at Port Castries. The same company also operates a ferry service from Rodney Bay to Pigeon Island, costing $50 round-trip, including entrance to this national park. You can also rent equipment for a snorkeling jaunt, which costs $12.

By island shuttle

The island system of bus transport is a series of privately operated mini-vans and jitneys painted with such colorful names as "Heartbreaker" and "Amour Lucian Style." These shuttles link Castries in the North with such southern outposts as Soufrière or Vieux Fort. Fares are very cheap — $2.60 from Castries to Soufrière, for example — but the shuttles are uncomfortable and overcrowded, often filled with passengers carrying produce to the market. The minivans are used mainly by low-income islanders as their only mode of transport for getting around St. Lucia; only the most adventurous foreign visitors ride them.

If you're going on the long haul between Castries and Vieux Fort at the southern tip of the island, the trip takes at least two hours. You can hail these jitneys along the road, or else you can wait for one at a marked bus stop. In Castries, the main point of departure is at the corner of Bridge and Micoud streets.

By helicopter

The fastest mode of transport on this island is via helicopter, preferred by such visitors as Harrison Ford. **St. Lucia Helicopters** (☎ 758-453-6950;

www.stluciahelicopters.com) is the quickest way to go between Castries and the Hewanorra airport or Soufrière, costing $100 per person one-way. You can also arrange flights to The **Jalousie Plantation** (see our recommendation later in this chapter), which has its own helicopter pad. Or, you can fly over St. Lucia on scenic tours (see "Guided tours," later in this chapter).

Staying in Style

St. Lucia has even better and far more dramatically located all-inclusive resorts than Jamaica, its major competitor in the field. Regrettably, these "everything-included" resorts are a bit pricey (for details on how to save on accommodations, refer to Chapter 6).

Nearly all the hotels and resorts in St. Lucia, even the smaller inns, lie on the western side of the island, which is the more-tranquil Caribbean Sea as opposed to the Atlantic Coast in the East. Most of the resorts lie between Castries (the capital) and Cap Estate in the North. Others are found around Marigot Bay a few miles south of Castries, and a select few are at Soufriére on the Southwestern Coast. Nearly all the accommodations open onto St. Lucia's unspoiled beaches. Because the West Coast resorts are so spread out, you're likely to feel rather isolated when you reach your destination. For many visitors, this seclusion is exactly what they've come to find.

The Top Resorts

The rack rates listed in this section are in U.S. dollars and are for a standard double room during high season (mid-Dec to mid-Apr) unless otherwise noted. Lower rates are available during spring, summer, and autumn.

Anse Chastanet
$$$$–$$$$$ Soufrière

This isolated 73-room inn is the premier scuba-diving resort of St. Lucia. It lies 29km (18 miles) north of Hewanorra Airport (a 50-minute taxi ride) and 3km (2 miles) north of the town of Soufrière. Perched on a landscaped hill site, the inn is a 103-step climb above the idyllic and palm-fringed **Anse Chastanet Beach.** Architect Nick Troubetzkoy created a lush garden on this 242-hectare (600-acre) site, which also contains a second beach, Anse Mamim, reached by the resort's water taxi. All this is set against the dramatic backdrop of the Pitons.

If you want to be right at the water's edge, ask for one of the dozen or so beach-level units. The original rooms are perched on the hill, some in an octagonal-shaped gazebo in a white-washed cottage. Views from the rooms are of the gardens, the sea, or the Pitons. The rooms, under beamed or

St. Lucia Accommodations

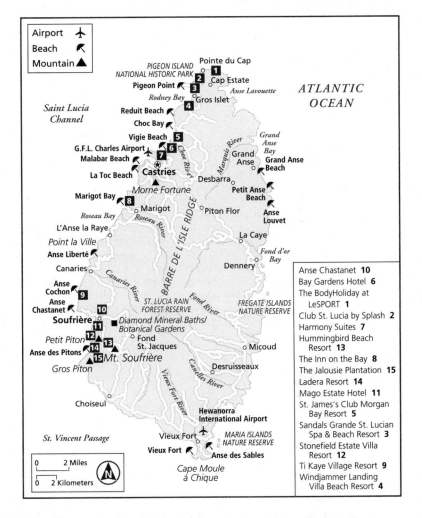

Airport ✈
Beach ⚓
Mountain ▲

PIGEON ISLAND
NATIONAL HISTORIC PARK
Pointe du Cap
Cap Estate
Pigeon Point
Anse Lavouette
Rodney Bay
Gros Islet

*ATLANTIC
OCEAN*

*Saint Lucia
Channel*

Reduit Beach
Choc Bay
Vigie Beach
G.F.L. Charles Airport
Malabar Beach
La Toc Beach
Castries
Morne Fortune
Marigot Bay
Marigot
Roseau River
Roseau Bay
L'Anse la Raye
Point la Ville
Anse Liberté
Canaries
Anse
Cochon
Anse
Chastanet
Soufrière
Diamond Mineral Baths/
Botanical Gardens
Petit Piton
Fond
St. Jacques
Anse des Pitons
Mt. Soufrière
Gros Piton
Choiseul

Choc River
Marquis River
Grand
Anse
Bay
Grand
Anse
Grand Anse
Beach
Desbarra
Petit Anse
Beach
Piton Flor
Anse
Louvet
La Caye
*Fond d'or
Bay*
Dennery
Canaries River
ST. LUCIA RAIN
FOREST RESERVE
BARRE DE L'ISLE RIDGE
Fond River
FREGATE ISLANDS
NATURE RESERVE
Micoud
Desruisseaux
Vieux Fort River
Canelles River
Hewanorra
International Airport

St. Vincent Passage
Vieux Fort
Vieux Fort
MARIA ISLANDS
NATURE RESERVE
Anse des Sables
*Cape Moule
à Chique*

0   2 Miles
0   2 Kilometers

Anse Chastanet **10**
Bay Gardens Hotel **6**
The BodyHoliday at
    LeSPORT **1**
Club St. Lucia by Splash **2**
Harmony Suites **7**
Hummingbird Beach
    Resort **13**
The Inn on the Bay **8**
The Jalousie Plantation **15**
Ladera Resort **14**
Mago Estate Hotel **11**
St. James's Club Morgan
    Bay Resort **5**
Sandals Grande St. Lucian
    Spa & Beach Resort **3**
Stonefield Estate Villa
    Resort **12**
Ti Kaye Village Resort **9**
Windjammer Landing
    Villa Beach Resort **4**

frescoed ceilings, are cooled by ceiling fans or sea trade winds; furnishings throughout the resort are made from local woods. The suites are spacious, each with one wall absent and opening onto a private pool. In 2005 the resort opened two dozen exclusive "infinity suites," which are called a resort within a resort, with their own reception, concierge, and the Jade Mountain Club restaurant. The food in the resort's two restaurants is among the best on the island, and the chefs use local ingredients whenever possible. The beachside restaurant, **Trou au Diable,** attracts nonguests with its grill and West Indian cuisine, plus its twice-weekly Creole dinner buffet.

The water-sports center here is the island's finest, attracting divers from around the world. Other facilities include tennis courts, a small spa and gym, and sailboat rentals.

See map p. 383. Anse Chastanet Beach, Soufrière. ☎ *800-223-1108, 758-459-7000. Fax: 758-459-7700.* www.ansechastanet.com. *Rack rates: $495–$795 double; from $845 suite. AE, MC, V.*

Bay Gardens Hotel
$$ **Rodney Bay**

Lying 4.5km (2¾ miles) north of Castries and Vigie Airport, Bay Gardens opens onto one of the most popular yachting harbors in the Caribbean. The 79-room hotel lies a five-minute walk (or a two-minute shuttle ride) away from **Reduit Beach,** one of the island's best. The property looks fresh and new and is well maintained; standard doubles, a few studios, and some more-luxurious suites are spread out in four different wings. Families may want to consider one of the eight apartments, each a self-contained unit with a kitchenette. Accommodations open onto a private terrace or balcony, and each room is furnished in a breezy tropical style. Although it can't compete with the facilities of the megaresorts, the hotel offers a restaurant with two bars, two freshwater pools (and a children's pool), a wade pool, twice-weekly entertainment, and an array of Caribbean buffets, barbecues, and rum-punch parties. Kids adore the on-site ice-cream shop.

See map p. 383. Rodney Bay. ☎ *877-620-3200, 758-452-8060. Fax: 758-052-8059.* www.baygardenshotel.com. *Rack rates: $120–$140 standard double; $170 suites and apartments. AE, MC, V.*

The BodyHoliday at LeSPORT
$$$$$ **Cariblue Beach**

A blond beach waits outside your door, but this 154-room resort offers much more than inviting sand, promoting a concept for the revitalization of both body and soul. *Condé Nast Traveler* recently named it the number-one destination spa in the world and one of the 100 "Best of the Best" resorts in *Travel + Leisure.* This luxury spa and resort lies at the northernmost tip of St. Lucia, a 13km (8-mile) drive from Castries. Everything you do, see, enjoy, drink, eat, and feel (yes, even *feel*) is included in the all-inclusive price. Guests are pampered in a setting of 6 hectares (15 acres), with fountains and luxuriant tropical planting. Steel bands and fire-eaters frequently entertain. During the day, the activity calendar is overloaded, with massages, seaweed wraps, mineral baths, aromatherapy, tai chi, yoga, stress management, and even dance classes and lessons to improve your golf game at a nearby course. A full water-sports program includes scuba diving and water-skiing. Other facilities include two bars, a tennis court, three pools, and a health club and spa. The well-furnished, first-class rooms are located in a four-story, Mediterranean-style building on a hillside looking down on the long, palm-lined beachfront. You'll also find sliding glass doors opening onto spacious balconies and a view. Meals, served in a choice of three restaurants, are as plush as the accommodations, and the cuisine is arguably the best of all offered by the St. Lucian all-inclusives.

Children age 12 and over are welcome from June 27 to September 25; otherwise, the minimum age is 16 years.

See map p. 383. Cariblue Beach. ☎ *800-544-2883, 758-457-7800. Fax: 758-450-0368.* www.thebodyholiday.com. *Rack rates: $600–$780 double; $1,000 suite for two. Rates are all-inclusive. AE, DISC, MC, V.*

Club St. Lucia by Splash
$$$$ **Cap Estate**

Lying at the very northern tip of St. Lucia (about 80km/50 miles north of Hewanorra International Airport — arrange for a shuttle pickup before you arrive), immediately east of **Pigeon Island National Park,** this all-inclusive, 369-room resort stands on a 26-hectare (64-acre) site, with two good sandy beaches at its doorstep. Very sports- and entertainment-oriented, the resort's recent $6-million renovation has considerably improved it. It sounds corny, but the hotel consists of five fantasy villages, each with a different theme. Perhaps you'll bed down at "Magic Parrot," or "Banana Liming." Accommodations are wide-ranging here, including Romance Rooms in the adults-only Hummingbird Village, with such features as self-service bars, Jacuzzis, and four-poster beds. You might also book into a family suite with a spacious master bedroom and separate sleeping quarters, suitable for two adults and three children. We prefer the deluxe oceanview accommodations with king-size four-poster beds. The food is good and varied in the five restaurants, where recipes range from Asian to Italian. Caribbean grills and buffets are also featured oceanside. Guests receive a discount if they dine at **Great House,** one of the island's premier restaurants (see the listing later in this chapter). The resort offers planned activities in three different kids clubs for various age groups. Other facilities include four bars, a dance club, five pools, nine tennis courts, a fitness center, and a water-sports program.

See map p. 383. Cap Estate. ☎ *877-92-SPLASH, 758-450-0551. Fax: 758-450-0281.* www.clubstluciabysplash.com. *Rack rates: $270–$350 double. Rates are all-inclusive. AE, DC, MC, V.*

Harmony Suites
$$–$$$ **Rodney Bay Lagoon**

Facing the marina at **Rodney Bay,** beloved by yachties, this 30-room inn lies only 183m (600 ft.) from one of the island's best beaches at Reduit. Alluring a youthful clientele, including families, the complex of two-story buildings offers suites that are well furnished in rattan and wicker and open onto views of a saltwater lagoon. Tiled floors, floral prints, small but well-organized bathrooms, wet bars, refrigerators, and safes make the units especially comfortable, along with the well-equipped kitchenettes that please families. For romantics, eight honeymoon suites open onto the lagoon, furnished with four-poster queen-size beds and whirlpool tubs. All the suites open onto balconies or patios facing the pool or tropical gardens. On-site is a respectable restaurant serving good Caribbean fare and a pool. The hotel also has a dive site.

See map p. 383. Rodney Bay Lagoon. ☎ *758-452-8756.* Fax: 758-452-8677. www. harmonysuites.com. *Rack rates: $120–$155 double. AE, MC, V.*

Hummingbird Beach Resort
$ Soufrière

Built on the site of a colonial-style mansion, the property is the personal statement of Joan Alexander Stowe (her guests quickly learn to call her Joyce), who started out as a waitress and gradually built her dream resort. The inn's charming ten bedrooms are furnished in part with antique four-poster beds and come with balconies and African wood sculptures for decoration. The better units have peaked ceilings, and mosquito netting is draped over elaborately carved bedsteads. In addition to the standard units, a country cottage, comfortable for two to four guests, is a favorite with families or two couples traveling together. Guests take a dip in the freshwater pool and often dine at the Hummingbird on-site, preferring a table on the veranda to sample Creole-style conch, local lobster, and other West Indian dishes, with some French specialties.

See map p. 383. Soufrière. ☎ *800-795-7261,* 758-459-7232. Fax: 758-459-7033. www. nvo.com/pitonresort. *Rack rates: $80 double; $170 suite. AE, DISC, MC, V.*

The Inn on the Bay
$$ Marigot Bay

One of the smallest inns in St. Lucia — housing only five bedrooms — is also one of the best and scenically located, lying 90m (300 ft.) above the waters of the Caribbean's most beautiful bay. Proprietors Normand Viau and Louise Boucher designed the hotel themselves. Each of the bedrooms is completely private and spacious, with well-kept bathrooms, a queen-size bed, fridge, ceiling fan, and security doors. Honeymooners and romantics are attracted to this nest. Children under 18 aren't accepted. Breakfast with homemade bread is served on a veranda overlooking the bay. Wait until you try the chocolate croissants. On-site is a small pool, and the golden sand at Marigot Beach is a shuttle-hop away. Restaurants and entertainment are down the hill at Marigot Bay; the hotel will shuttle you back and forth free of charge.

See map p. 383. Seaview Avenue, Marigot Bay. ☎ *758-451-4260.* Fax 928-438-3828. www.saint-lucia.com. *Rack rates: $155 double. Rates include breakfast. MC, V.*

The Jalousie Plantation
$$$$–$$$$$ Soufrière

This opulent complex sprawls across 130 hectares (325 acres) at one of the most beautiful and lushest tropical oases in the Caribbean. It faces an idyllic palm-fringed beach at the foot of two jagged lava peaks. Offering greater luxury than Anse Chastanet, The Jalousie Plantation lies 8km (5 miles) south of Soufrière and 40 winding kilometers (25 miles) north of the international airport. Well-heeled guests book the ten-minute helicopter ride from the airport to the hotel's own landing pad. At the core of the complex are two restored sugar mills, where you can lodge in a dozen guest rooms. Much more elegant living is available in the spacious series of 65 mountain-view villas and suites, and 35 oceanview villas and suites, each with a private plunge pool. Shuttles transport visitors around this hillside property. Interiors are ripped from the pages of *Architectural Digest*, with cathedral-like ceilings, rattan and mahogany furnishings, *Casablanca*-style ceiling fans, white tile floors, and French doors opening onto the palm-fringed beach. Clad in marble, the bathrooms are luxurious with deep tubs, robes, and scales. The cuisine is one of the reasons to stay here. Guests have a choice of four restaurants, our favorite being the elegant **Plantation Restaurant,** serving international and Continental cuisine. You can enjoy fresh seafood and Creole specialties at the waterside **Pier Restaurant.** Other facilities include an outdoor pool, a par-three executive golf course, four Laykold tennis courts, a health club and spa, children's activities, a business center, a dive shop, and a nightclub. As this book went to press, the Jalousie's new management team was in the process of renovating all the villas, some of which will not be open until after the winter 2007 season.

See map p. 383. Bay Street, Soufrière. ☎ *800-544-2883. Fax: 758-459-7667.* www.the jalousieplantation.com. *Rack rates: $450 double; $545 villa; $695–$795 villa suite. Breakfast and dinner $75 extra per person per day. AE, DISC, MC, V.*

Ladera Resort
$$$$$ Soufrière

Ladera looks as if it sprouted from the hilltop, its 6 villas and 19 suites each with an open-wall view to the west, taking in that stunning view. Even with an exposed wall, the architectural layout of the complex is such that privacy is maintained. We totally agree with the *Caribbean Travel and Life* assessment of this posh resort as one of the ten most romantic spots in the West Indies. A special feature is a free-form pool that scenically extends toward the cliff. Tropical hardwoods, stone, and tile, along with 19th-century French antiques or reproductions, fill the bedrooms, and all accommodations come with their own private plunge pools. The resort provides free shuttle service to a good beach at Anse de Pitons. The on-site **Dasheene Restaurant** (reviewed later in this chapter), is one of the finest in St. Lucia. The staff can arrange an array of activities, ranging from rain-forest walks to sailing excursions to the Grenadines.

See map p. 383. Soufrière. ☎ *800-738-4752,* 758-459-7323. Fax: 758-459-5156. www. ladera-stlucia.com. *Rack rates: $450–$640 one- or two-bedroom suite; $890 villa. Breakfast and dinner $75 extra per person per day. Three-night minimum stay. AE, MC, V.*

Mago Estate Hotel
$$–$$$ Soufrière

Opening onto one of the Caribbean's most panoramic backdrops, the Pitons, this lush estate lies directly north of the fishing village of Soufrière. Its German-born owner, Peter Gloser, named his ten-room inn "Mago," meaning mango in patois. Not only mango trees, but mahogany, papaya, banana, and *maracuya* (passion fruit) trees envelop the property. The staff will take you to nearby beaches in a free shuttle. Each room opens onto a view of the Pitons and is decorated with hand-carved furniture and antiques. Rooms are divided among the "Eden" units — luxury accommodations with panoramic sea views, a terrace, and plunge pool — and the six varieties of "Shangrila" rooms, each decorated in different styles. Four large bedrooms are the most recently built units, each with teakwood furnishings and handcrafted antiques along with plunge pools and hammocks for the lazy life. The food, a quality blend of Creole and French specialties, is carefully prepared, based on fresh ingredients, and served at communal tables with carved African chairs.

See map p. 383. Palm Mist, Soufrière. ☎ *758-459-5880. Fax: 758-459-7352.* www.mago hotel.com. *Rack rates: $200–$500 double. Rates include breakfast. MC, V.*

St. James's Club Morgan Bay Resort
$$$$ Choc Bay, Gros Islet

Catering mainly to Europeans, this all-inclusive resort stands on 8.9 hectares (22 acres) of landscaped grounds a ten-minute drive north of Castries. The hotel opens onto a palm-fringed beachfront of white sand. Unlike some all-inclusives on the island, this 240-room pile welcomes children. The club emphasizes day-and-night activities that range from theme buffets to scuba diving and deep-sea fishing. The food is good and bountiful, and you can work off the extra carbs in the health club or by swimming in one of two outdoor pools, playing tennis on four courts, or participating in water sports. If all else fails, you have the sauna and steam room. Rooms come in a variety of categories and are spread across a half-dozen different outbuildings. The most standard units, each midsize, offer private verandas, rattan and wicker furnishings, fridges, and queen-size or twin beds. Superior rooms are on the second floor, offering better views, and the deluxe units are oceanfront. Bathrooms are well maintained and trimmed in marble. Children are especially catered to with special programs. Local musicians, steel bands, and calypso singers keep you entertained in the evening.

See map p. 383. Choc Bay, Gros Islet. ☎ *800-858-4618, 758-450-2511. Fax: 758-450-1050.* www.eliteislandvacations.com. *Rack rates: $390–$450 double; $580 suite for two. Rates are all-inclusive. Children ages 13–18 in parent's room $100; ages 3–12, $60; ages 2 and under free. MC, V.*

Sandals Grande St. Lucian Spa & Beach Resort
$$$$–$$$$$ Gros Islet

Sandals operates three all-inclusive, couples-only (that's male/female couples only) resorts in St. Lucia, and this one is the best. We much prefer the laid-back elegance of Ladera or Anse Chastanet, but if you're a Sandals fan, this is as good as it gets on the island. The resort lies at the causeway on the northern tip of the island linking the main island with **Pigeon Island.** Originally, this was a Hyatt, standing 10km (6 miles) northwest of Castries at **Rodney Bay.** The sea surrounds the resort on both sides, and rooms open onto panoramic vistas. The 284 rooms are tastefully and rather luxuriously furnished, each with a private veranda along with designer bathrooms. Our favorites are the two dozen lagoon pool rooms where you can swim right up to your own patio. Service is a feature in the concierge rooms and suites with a staff at your beck and call 24 hours a day. The setting is on a 1-hectare (2½-acre) lagoon, with a private beach of golden sand, although many guests prefer the lavish lagoon-like swimming pool. All the rooms, even the standard ones, are quite large and furnished with plantation-style antique reproductions. The better views are on the fourth floor. Inquire about the "Stay at One, Play at Three" exchange program where you stay at one Sandals resort and use the facilities at all three — a nice way to avoid the "resort-bound" blues. Even on-site, you hardly dine in the same place every night — the resort has six specialty restaurants. Facilities include three bars, five outdoor pools, four tennis courts, a health club and spa, plus a dive shop. Golf is available at the nearby Sandals Regency, and water sports, such as snorkeling and windsurfing, can be arranged.

See map p. 383. Pigeon Island Causeway, Gros Islet. ☎ *888-SANDALS (888-726-3257), 758-455-2000. Fax: 758-455-2001.* www.sandals.com. *Rack rates: $385–$555 double; from $645 suite for two. Rates are per person and all-inclusive. AE, DISC, MC, V.*

Stonefield Estate Villa Resort
$$–$$$$ Soufrière

At the base of **Petit Piton,** this 16-room resort lies in the Southwest, covering a lush 10-hectare (26-acre) site complete with views at every turn and nature trails. The complex consists of a plantation house and a series of cottages with one, two, or three bedrooms each. The location is 2km (1¼ miles) south of Soufrière and 38km (23 miles) northwest of the Hewanorra airport. Guests who anchor at this secluded tropical oasis use the beach at The Jalousie Plantation (see the listing earlier in this chapter), a five-minute shuttle ride away. All the rentals are furnished with antiques and come with high ceilings, verandas, full bathrooms with intimate outdoor garden showers, and fully furnished kitchens. Mosquito netting covers the beds. The on-site Mango Tree Restaurant serves first-rate meals, using locally caught fish and fresh fruits and vegetables. Guests gather to toast the sunset at the Bamboo Bar, having swum earlier that day in a pool whose flagstone deck juts out over the edge of a cliff.

See map p. 383. Stonefield Villas, Soufrière. ☎ *758-459-7037.* Fax: 758-459-5550. www. stonefieldvillas.com. *Rack rates: $190–$350 one-bedroom villa; $260–$500 two-bedroom villa; $600–$700 three-bedroom villa. MC, V.*

Ti Kaye Village Resort
$$$ Anse Cochon

Ti Kaye Village Resort is a rare find and a retreat for escapists, built on a cliff overlooking the sea and standing on 6.4 hectares (16 acres) of lush grounds on the island's West Coast, about halfway between Castries and Soufrière. *Ti Kaye* means "small house" in local patois, and this charming little hideaway consists of 33 handsomely furnished and comfortable cottages opening onto panoramic views. Some of the units are in individual cottages, the rest in duplex villas. Furnishings are of local white cedar, and the design is traditional West Indian, each cottage with a large veranda featuring a hammock for two plus a king-size four-poster bed and a private open-air garden shower. You must take a steep stairwell of 166 steps to get down to a cove of silver sand and an excellent dive shop. An international chef serves scrumptious meals, often using local produce and freshly caught fish. Of course, you can dine elsewhere, but we highly recommended you eat here at night. Other facilities include a sunset bar, fitness center, and an outdoor pool.

See map p. 383. Anse Cochon. ☎ *758-456-8101.* Fax: 758-456-8105. www.tikaye. com. *Rack rates: $200–$380 double. Rates include full breakfast. AE, DC, MC, V.*

Windjammer Landing Villa Beach Resort
$$–$$$$ Labrelotte Bay

This unique St. Lucian resort is built like a village, with brick paths cut through 22 hectares (55 acres) of tropical landscaping directly north of **Reduit Beach** and a 20-minute drive north of Castries, but a long hour-and-a-half haul from the Hewanorra airport. The complex of Mediterranean-style villas opens onto the sea and a stretch of cream-colored sand. Windjammer Landing is an all-suite and villa resort, with the larger units containing their own private plunge pools. Although honeymooners come here, it's a family favorite, with a teen program, a children's club, nanny services, and two children's pools in addition to two regular pools. All the décor is light, breezy, and tropical, and each unit comes with a terrace or patio facing the garden or the ocean, plus a fully equipped kitchen and a spacious combination bathroom, along with a sun deck. Dining is in one of five restaurants that range from a barbecue grill on the beach to the Asian-influenced **Dragonfly.** For an extra change of culinary pace, **Papa Don's** serves pizza and pasta, and **The Upper Deck** features seafood delicacies. Other facilities include three bars, two tennis courts, a fitness center, and a dive shop plus other water sports.

See map p. 383. Labrelotte Bay. ☎ *800-958-7376,* 758-456-9000. Fax: 758-452-9454. www.windjammer-landing.com. *Rack rates: $290–$420 double; $135–$185 per person in two-, three-, four-bedroom villas. AE, DISC, MC, V.*

Dining Out

With the arrival of the all-inclusives, independent restaurants are being choked out of visitors' cash. Some excellent restaurants have closed because thousands of visitors prefer to stay at their hotels at night. Not only are the roads bad and poorly lit after dark, but also many guests have already paid for their dinner as part of their overall package.

Even though many guests are resort-bound at night, the picture isn't entirely dismal. Some resorts have several restaurants, and for the most part the fare is first-rate, a selection of American, Asian, and Continental dishes, with the inevitable Caribbean buffets for extra spice.

 Reservations in winter are important at the top-ranked restaurants even if you're staying at an all-inclusive. Guests at a hotel learn what the best specialty restaurants are and quickly book up all the seats at the choice dining spots, some patrons preferring to make their reservations even before they fly to St. Lucia.

Our advice is to make dinner reservations when booking your room. Otherwise, you're likely to be dining at a resort's less-appealing restaurant, even though you paid the same price as the guy enjoying the best table in — say, the Japanese specialty restaurant.

For an island with the tourist flow of St. Lucia, you'd expect a lot more top-quality specialty restaurants. What you get isn't bad, but the choice seems a bit small. Consider for the moment that some resorts in St. Lucia have six restaurants and ten bars.

Although islanders will deny it, St. Lucia has no distinctive cuisine like Cuba, Jamaica, or Puerto Rico. Its specialties, which are truly excellent, follow along with West Indian culinary traditions. We're talking banana bread, fried plantain, fried flying fish, stuffed crab backs, callaloo soup, stuffed breadfruit, and baked lobster.

The Best Restaurants

Camilla's Restaurant & Bar
$$–$$$ **Soufrière CREOLE**

A block inland from the waterfront at a little fishing harbor, this typically West Indian second-floor restaurant serves local fare that's among the best in the area — and the prices are right. Local matriarch Camilla Alcindor shops the local markets, seeking the best of island produce and stopping off at the fish market to see what the catch of the day brought in. Back in her little kitchen, she prepares her specialties, including an island fish Creole and fresh lobster, which she'll prepare thermidor style if you want. She doesn't even attempt to compete with the megaresorts but turns out a straightforward and unpretentious cuisine, of which her mother might approve. Chicken curry is an island favorite, and at lunch the restaurant offers the usual array of sandwiches, fresh salads, omelets, and the inevitable burgers. Try for a table on the balcony overlooking street life below.

See map p. 393. 7 Bridge St. ☎ *758-459-5379. Main courses: $11–$17. AE, DISC, MC, V. Open: Tues–Sun 8 a.m.–midnight.*

Capone's
$$$ Reduit Beach, Rodney Bay   ITALIAN/CARIBBEAN

Capone's take on the gangster days of Chicago in the speak-easy 1920s is a bit much — as if the place were a screen backdrop for that old Marilyn Monroe classic *Some Like It Hot* — but the food is good and the joint works, even if it's a bit gimmicky. Near the lagoon, the location is just north of **Reduit Beach,** where you'll probably spend most of your day. Naturally, in a dive calling itself Capone's, you expect "Little Caesar salad" to lead off the menu. Ingredients are fresh and well chosen, and the chefs are good, especially when they're grilling the fresh local catch of the day to perfection or throwing the island's best steaks on another grill. Next door is **La Piazza,** where typical American fare such as burgers, well-stuffed sandwiches, and savory pizzas are served noon to midnight Tuesday to Sunday.

See map p. 393. Reduit Beach, Rodney Bay. ☎ *758-452-0284. Reservations recommended. Main courses: $18–$33. AE, MC, V. Open: Tues–Sun 3 p.m.–midnight.*

The Charthouse
$$$ Reduit Beach, Rodney Bay   AMERICAN/CREOLE

The setting of The Charthouse is a Caribbean cliché — an open-air dining room overlooking a yacht harbor. Favored by yachties, this restaurant is one of the oldest and most frequented on the island, in a spacious sky-lit building with a mahogany bar. Outside in the water rest some of the most expensive yachts sailing the West Indies. This place is one of the best in St. Lucia to sample dishes with real island flavor. Our favorites are pumpkin soup, stuffed crab backs, and baby-back ribs along with fresh local lobster. The char-grilled steaks are also a delight, but the chef's specialty is the best roast prime rib of beef on the island.

See map p. 393. Reduit Beach, Rodney Bay. ☎ *758-452-8115. Reservations required. Main courses: $20–$39. AE, MC, V. Open: Daily 6–10:30 p.m.*

Dasheene Restaurant & Bar
$$$$ Soufrière   CARIBBEAN/INTERNATIONAL

Dasheene, in the previously recommended pocket of posh, **Ladera Resort,** is one of the most celebrated restaurants on the island — and with good reason. This stellar dining room enjoys a grand setting, opening onto views of the towering and forested Pitons set against the backdrop of the Caribbean Sea. Out on the terrace, with lights twinkling in the distance, the restaurant provides one of the most memorable romantic settings. The

St. Lucia Dining

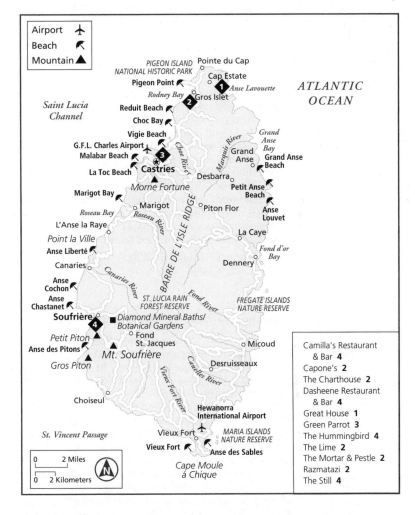

imaginative menu spotlights the finest of Caribbean cuisine, with a nouvelle touch, but also offers an array of international dishes. Launch your repast with such offerings as a garden salad of local greens or *christophene* (a squash-like vegetable) and coconut soup. The chef has a special flair for his pasta studded with "fruits of the sea," and his marinated sirloin steak is cooked to perfection. His roast chicken is also stuffed with a savory mixture of sweet red peppers, onions, and seasoned bread crumbs. We always opt for the catch of the day, often red snapper grilled to perfection or else baked kingfish. To make the night yours, order the chocolate soufflé flambé.

See map p. 393. At the Ladera Resort, between Gros and Petit Piton. ☎ *758-459-7323. Reservations recommended. Main courses: $22–$32. AE, MC, V. Open: Daily 7:30– 10 a.m., noon to 2:30 p.m., and 6:30–9:30 p.m.*

Great House
$$$$ Cap Estate   FRENCH/CREOLE/INTERNATIONAL

At the far northern tip of St. Lucia, the island's most acclaimed restaurant lies on the original foundation stones of a plantation Great House — hence, its name. You can find no more-elegant or more-romantic setting on the island than this dining room, which evokes the heyday of the rich planters whose wealth regrettably was based on slave labor. The refined service is St. Lucia's finest and most hospitable. Because the menu changes nightly, you never know what you're going to get. The chefs always adjust the menu to take advantage of the freshest and best ingredients in any season. You're likely to have your choice from such delectable fare as a starter of shrimp and scallops in a cheese sauce, followed by duck breast in a honey and balsamic vinegar sauce, or even a pork pepper pot. Desserts are luscious here, including a recently sampled passion-fruit cheesecake.

See map p. 393. Cap Estate. ☎ *758-450-0450. Reservations required. Main courses: $19–$37. AE, DC, DISC, MC, V. Open: Tues–Sun 6:30–10 p.m.*

Green Parrot
$$$ Morne Fortune, Castries   CONTINENTAL/CARIBBEAN

Chef Harry, who trained at the prestigious Claridges in London, is the island's most celebrated chef. His domain lies 2km (1½ miles) east of the center of Castries overlooking the attractively lit harbor at night. If you're walking it, count on 12 minutes — at a hearty pace. Guests come here for the entire evening, preferring to arrive early for an aperitif in the Victorian-inspired bar. The bartender's special is a Grass Parrot, made from coconut cream, crème de menthe, bananas, and white rum. The formal dining room is inspired by the British colonial era, and free entertainment on Wednesday and Saturday nights most definitely includes a limbo contest and a fire-eater. Whenever possible, Harry features St. Lucian specialties, using produce grown on the island and the fresh catch of the day. Beef-eaters go for the tender steak or mixed grill, perhaps beginning with the Creole soup prepared with callaloo (a spinach-like vegetable) and fresh pumpkin. Usually, five different curry dishes are available. Harry also rents inexpensively priced but comfortably furnished bedrooms with air-conditioning and phones, doubles costing only $100 a night, including breakfast.

See map p. 393. Chef Harry Drive, Morne Fortune. ☎ *758-452-3399. Reservations recommended. Lunch main courses: $17–$26. Prix-fixe dinner: $33–$41. AE, MC, V. Open: Daily 7 a.m.–midnight.*

The Hummingbird
$$$ Soufrière   CARIBBEAN/INTERNATIONAL

As you dine at this West Indian spot, you can enjoy the gardens and the local cuisine. Those gardens are likely to be fluttering with the namesake of this restaurant at this previously recommended island inn. Most visitors stop off here for lunch, when you can see the panoramic view of the Pitons, but dinner is magical as well. The freshwater crayfish in garlic or lime butter is our favorite meal, although you can also order Creole-style conch, freshly caught lobster, and filets of both snapper and grouper, each grilled to perfection. Of course, during the day you may settle happily for such American staples as a BLT or a juicy burger.

See map p. 393. At the Hummingbird Beach Resort, Soufrière. ☎ *758-459-7232. Reservations recommended. Main courses: $20–$40. AE, DISC, MC, V. Open: Daily 6:30 a.m.–11 p.m.*

The Lime
$$ Rodney Bay   AMERICAN/CREOLE

North of Reduit Beach, this old island favorite stands in an area increasingly known as "restaurant row" in St. Lucia. With its namesake lime-green curtains, The Lime is one of the most typical of all the bistros on the island. From seafood to steaks and chops, the fare is familiar, but the food is good and prepared with quality ingredients. In an open-air setting, you can begin with the bartender's special lime drink while perusing the menu. Fresh lobster frequently appears, as does the catch of the day. We recently enjoyed a zesty red snapper with island spices. The steaks emerge as you like them from a sizzling charcoal grill, and lamb and pork chops are always on hand. A specialty is roti, like a Caribbean burrito. Lighter fare, including well-made sandwiches, is available at lunch.

See map p. 393. Rodney Bay. ☎ *758-452-0761. Reservations recommended for dinner. Main courses: $10–$28. MC, V. Open: Wed–Mon 8 a.m.–1 a.m.*

The Mortar & Pestle
$$$ Rodney Bay Lagoon   CARIBBEAN/INTERNATIONAL

At this waterfront restaurant, with its view of the lagoon, you get a choice of dining alfresco or indoors. For inspiration, the chefs roam the world, not just the southern Caribbean. The rich menu is likely to reflect recipes from Africa, England, France, Spain, Portugal, the Netherlands, India, and China, and even some Amerindian dishes. You'll fill up on such rib-sticking fare as Bajan flying fish, Grenadian stuffed jack fish, Jamaican salt fish, or Guyana pepper pot. The stuffed crab backs are worth the trip, as is the rich and creamy conch chowder. Sometimes a steel band entertains at night.

See map p. 393. At the Harmony Suites, Rodney Bay Lagoon. ☎ *758-452-8756. Reservations recommended. Main courses: $17–$32. DISC, MC, V. Open: Daily 7 a.m.–5 p.m. and 6:30–10 p.m.*

Razmatazi
$ Reduit Beach Marina   INDIAN

Guests staying at one of the resorts along **Reduit Beach,** including the Royal St. Lucian, often flock to this eatery for a change of pace. Razmatazi brings the cookery of the subcontinent to St. Lucia, especially those tantalizing tandoori dishes. In a building painted a medley of colors with lots of gingerbread, the restaurant lies only a two-minute walk from the beach. We could fill up on the delectable appetizers alone, including fresh local fish marinated in a spicy yogurt and cooked in the tandoor or the mulligatawny soup made with lentils, herbs, and spices. Save your appetite for the tandoori dishes made with shrimp, fresh fish (especially red snapper), or chicken. Vegetarians will be happy with the best on-island assortment of tasty vegetable dishes. Live music entertains guests on weekends.

See map p. 393. Reduit Beach Marina. ☎ *758-452-9800. Reservations recommended. Main courses: $10–$22. MC, V. Open: Fri–Wed 4–11 p.m.*

The Still
$$$$ Soufrière   CREOLE

Right on the beach, this small inn lies less than a mile from **Soufrière** on the grounds of a plantation that grows citrus, cocoa, and copra. A pool landscaped into the lush tropical scene adds to the allure, and walks are possible in almost any direction. The site opens onto views of the towering Pitons in the distance. One of the most atmospheric and authentic island places, The Still is an ideal luncheon stopover in your tour of the southern tier of St. Lucia. In the more-formal and spacious dining room, you can feast on excellently prepared St. Lucian specialties, depending on what is fresh at the market that day. Try to avoid the place when it's overrun with cruise-ship passengers or tour groups.

See map p. 393. Soufrière. ☎ *758-459-7224. Reservations recommended. Main courses: $8–$22. AE, DC, DISC, MC, V. Open: Daily 8 a.m.–4 p.m.*

Enjoying the Sand and Surf

Rivaling the British Virgin Islands and the Grenadines (owned by St. Vincent), the fame of St. Lucia as a yachties' haven is growing, mainly because of its Marigot and Rodney bays along with Castries Harbour. The world's largest transatlantic sailing rally takes place here between November and the end of December.

The coral reefs surrounding the island are beautiful to explore. In addition, beautiful white sandy beaches edge the tranquil leeward side of St. Lucia — and are the best beaches for swimming. The waters on the windward or Atlantic side are more rugged with a rough surf, and swimming often isn't safe here.

Combing the beaches

All beaches in St. Lucia are open to the public, even those sands in front of the megaresorts. Most of the major resorts are built right on the sands so you can be out of your bedroom and into the water in minutes. Because St. Lucia offers some of the most dramatic views in the Caribbean, other resorts prefer to locate on hillsides but with easy access to the beach, either by stairs or a shuttle that will whisk you there in two to five minutes.

One of the best beaches in St. Lucia — and therefore the most popular — is **Reduit Beach,** stretching for 2km (1 mile) of soft beige sand along clear waters at Rodney Bay. This site hosts many resorts and also boasts the largest concentration of water-sports kiosks, especially along the strips bordering Royal St. Lucien Hotel. Many bars and restaurants are located here. Of course, if you come onto hotel grounds and patronize any of the facilities, you have to pay extra. Otherwise, the beaches are free.

Directly north of Reduit Beach is **Pigeon Point Beach,** lying off the northern shoreline and a part of the Pigeon Island National Historic Park (see "Exploring on Dry Land," later in the chapter). Pigeon Island is joined to the mainland of St. Lucia by a causeway. The beach here is one of the best in St. Lucia, filled with white sand, but it's small. Before coming over to Pigeon Island, many visitors secure the makings for a picnic lunch.

 Another good beach is **Choc Bay,** lying immediately south of Rodney Bay and Reduit Beach. Convenient to Castries and many of the mega-resorts, Choc Bay is a long stretch of golden sands against a backdrop of palm trees. Waters here are usually so tranquil that the locale has become a favorite with families, especially those with small children. The beach is easily accessible from the main road.

As you head down the coast, moving closer to Castries, you encounter more beaches, coming first upon **Vigie Beach,** which stretches for 3km (2 miles) of white sand. At one point, this beach runs parallel to the runway at Vigie Airport (also called George F.L. Charles Airport). Vigie Beach offers fine beige sand that slopes gently into the gin-clear waters. A final beach in the vicinity of Castries is **La Toc Beach,** which lies just south of the capital, opening onto a crescent-shaped bay and filled with golden sand.

Leaving the area around Castries and continuing in a southerly direction, you reach the calm waters of **Marigot Bay Beach** — a favorite of the yachting crowd. One of the most beautiful coves in the Caribbean, Marigot Bay is our favorite, and it's framed on three sides by steep forested hills, the beach itself set against a grove of palms. The beaches along this bay are small but choice. You can lie on them and take in a view of some of the most expensive yachts sailing in the West Indies. Several restaurants around the bay are open for lunch.

Between Marigot Bay and the fishing village of Soufrière are some other good beaches, notably **Anse Cochon,** lying directly north of Soufrière. If you like your sand white, however, stay away. Although the waters here are crystal clear, the sands, which feel like those of a perfect white-sand beach, are black volcanic. The shallow reefs are excellent for snorkeling, and the beach offers picture-postcard Caribbean charm — which makes it favored for romantic trysts. Anse Cochon is reachable only by boat and offers no facilities.

One of the most idyllic beaches of St. Lucia is found at **Anse Chastanet,** to the immediate north of Soufrière. Towering palms provide shade from the noonday sun, and the lush hills form a backdrop for this dark sandy strip. Scuba divers go exploring off the coast.

After passing through Soufrière and continuing south, you come to the next good beach, **Anse des Pitons,** lying between the twin peaks and opening onto Jalousie Bay, a crescent-shaped body of water. The owners of **The Jalousie Plantation** have transformed this natural black-sand beach into a white-sand beach by importing the sand. Divers and snorkelers alike are attracted to this popular beach, along with patrons of the resort.

Finally, at the very southern tip of St. Lucia are two small beaches. At **Vieux Fort,** coral reefs protect the tranquil waters, making them ideal for swimming. At the southern end on the windward side of St. Lucia, **Anse des Sables** opens onto a shallow bay swept by trade winds, which make it more ideal for windsurfing than for swimming.

Playing in the surf

In recent years, water sports as an activity have become more and more developed, as new outfitters have opened up kiosks on the beaches. Anse Chastanet, near the Pitons on the Southwest Coast, is a dive experience that attracts scuba divers from the States in large numbers. The diving here doesn't compare to Grand Cayman, but it's a thrilling experience to explore underwater reefs with stunning coral walls; you can rent snorkeling equipment from your hotel or from any number of scuba-diving outfitters. Kayaking has become big business in St. Lucia, which offers adventurers a combination of both ocean and river kayaking. Finally, windsurfing is also establishing a foothold on the island, with most resorts offering the sport.

Scuba diving

Most of the waters off the coast of St. Lucia are crystal clear, often with a visibility of 30 to 46m (100–150 ft.). The island is surrounded by coral reefs, and most scuba activity consists of reef diving. Lately, the government has been creating artificial reefs by sinking old boats, and wreck diving is growing in popularity. You can reach many of the most dramatic dive sites after only a 20-minute boat ride from shore.

At **Anse Cochon,** both north and south reefs, beach dives with coral and boulders start in 1.5m (5 ft.) of water. The north reef descends to 12m (40 ft.), but the south reef remains shallow to a depth of 9.1m (30 ft.). A 50m (165-ft.) freighter was sunk off the coast in 18m (60 ft.) of water to create an artificial reef teeming with damselfish, wrasse, grunts, yellow snapper, spotted drums, and both parrot and goat fish. A Japanese dredger was sunk at the south end of Anse Cochon and almost immediately became a favorite abode of eels and barracudas.

Another site rich in coral and rainbow-hued marine life is **Anse La Raye Wall,** midway up the West Coast. Such fish as spotted drums, Bermuda chubs, and jacks live in these waters, as do purple vase sponges and soft coral.

One of our favorite scuba-diving outfitters in St. Lucia is **Dive Fair Helen** (☎ **888-855-2206,** 758-451-7716). A one-day package (two dives) costs $84, with a two-day (four dives) package going for $155.

In the Anse Chastanet Hotel in Soufrière, **Scuba St. Lucia** (☎ **758-459-7000;** www.scubastlucia.com) offers one of the world's top dive locations at a five-star PADI dive center. At the southern end of Anse Chastanet's 0.4km-long (quarter-mile), secluded beach, it features premier diving and comprehensive facilities for divers of all levels. Some of the most spectacular coral reefs of St. Lucia, many only 3 to 6m (10–20 ft.) below the surface, lie a short distance from the beach. However, the underwater reef drops off from 7.6m (25 ft.) to some 41m (135 ft.) in a panoramic, multicolored coral wall.

Many professional PADI instructors offer five dive programs a day. Photographic equipment is available for rent (they can process film on the premises), and picture-taking instruction is available. Experienced divers can rent any equipment they need. PADI certification courses are available for $495. A two- to three-hour introductory lesson costs $85 and includes a short theory session, equipment familiarization, development of skills in shallow water, a tour of the reef, and all equipment. Single dives cost $35, including equipment rental. Hours are from 8 a.m. to 6 p.m. daily.

Another full-service scuba center, on St. Lucia's Southwest Coast, is at **The Jalousie Plantation,** Soufrière (☎ **758-456-8000**). The PADI center offers dives in St. Lucia's National Marine Park, where numerous shallow reefs lie near the shore. The diver certification program is available to hotel guests and other visitors ages 12 and up. Prices range from $70 for a single dive to $580 for a certification course. A daily resort course for noncertified divers includes a supervised dive from the beach and costs $83. A ten-dive package is $347; a six-dive package is $238. All prices include equipment, tax, and service charges.

Snorkeling

Most dive boats welcome snorkelers, charging them about $25 per person, including equipment, to go along on a trip. In the southern Caribbean, St. Lucia is one of the finest islands for snorkelers, because of its caverns, walls, coral reefs, and trenches teeming with rainbow-hued fish. Many of these sites lie right off West Coast beaches and within the marine reserves. **Dive Fair Helen** (☎ 758-451-7716; www.divefair helen.com) is the best outfitter for snorkelers, showing a *Discover the Underwater World* video and providing a *Snorkeler's Field Guide,* which offers previews of the sights and fish you may see. Its resort course for snorkelers costs $50, including taxi and boat transfers plus equipment.

Ocean and river kayaking

Dive Fair Helen hooks you up with the best kayaking in the area, offering both river kayaking and coastal kayaking. A two-hour river kayaking tour, costing $60 per person, starts from Marigot Bay and runs along the West Coast of the island on the River Roseau. The estuary is the feeding ground for many tropical birds. A three-hour coastal kayaking tour, costing $80 per person, starts from Anse Cochon and runs along the tranquil West Coast, passing fishing villages. Guests disembark at one point and take a short hike inland for lunch.

Windsurfing

Chances are, if you're staying at one of the big resorts along the West Coast, your hotel will offer windsurfing. As mentioned, the areas around **Vieux Fort** and **Anse de Sables** on the southern tip of the island are best for windsurfers. On the Northeast Coast, opening onto the rugged Atlantic, the best spot is **Cas-en-Bas.**

Island windsurfers tell us that August, September, and October are the worst months for windsurfing, because the winds seem to die down at this time.

The best place to hook up with windsurfing is at **St. Lucian Watersports** at the Rex St. Lucian Hotel (☎ 758-452-8351) at Reduit Beach opening onto Rodney Bay. Windsurfers are available for $17 per half-hour or $45 an hour.

Climbing aboard

Sunlink Tours, Reduit Beach Avenue, Rodney Bay (☎ 800-SUN-LINK or 800-786-5465, 758-456-9100; www.sunlinktours.com), offers the widest array of tours, many of them specially organized and on the water. The most extensive tour, *Tout Bagay* (meaning "a little bit of everything" in Creole dialect), costs $90 for adults and sails down the coastline in a catamaran to visit the drive-in volcano and an 18th-century working plantation where cocoa is produced. The price includes a buffet lunch. Kids love the tour aboard St. Lucia's famed "pirate ship," the *Brig Unicorn,* which is 42m (138 ft.) long and 7.6m (25 ft.) wide. The *Unicorn* is a replica of a mid-19th century, two-masted, fully square-rigged brig featured in the TV film *Roots*. For $95 for adults and $50 for children 2 to 11, you embark on a full-day sail around Rodney Bay, going on to Soufrière and the twin peaks of the Pitons; breakfast and lunch are included. Other tours include dolphin- and whale-watching jaunts, costing $70 for adults or children; half-day deep-sea-fishing charters at $105 per passenger; or an around-the-island scenic tour, costing $60 for adults and $35 for children 2 to 11. Many other tours, including rain-forest jaunts, are available; ask about the company's entire repertoire.

The island also offers several charter-boat operations for half-day or whole-day deep-sea-fishing jaunts. Most hotels can arrange fishing expeditions. Otherwise, you can call **Mako Watersports** (☎ 758-452-0412), which offers half-day fishing trips for $450 (four people) or full-day trips for $750. **Captain Mike's** (☎ 758-452-7044) also conducts fishing trips, renting boats for four to six people for $450 to $550 per half-day or $750 to $900 for a whole day. Seasonal catches include regular mackerel and king mackerel along with kingfish, sailfish, white marlin, tuna, and the fierce barracuda.

Exploring on Dry Land

Lovely little towns, beautiful beaches and secluded bays, mineral baths, banana plantations — St. Lucia has all this and more. You can even visit a volcano. This island is a much more lush and tropical destination than other "Saints" in this guide, including St. Croix, St. Thomas, and Sint Maarten/St. Martin.

Castries

Most tours of St. Lucia begin in its capital city of **Castries.** The capital city has grown up around its harbor, which occupies the crater of an extinct volcano. Charter captains and the yachting set drift in here, and large cruise-ship wharves welcome vessels from around the world. Because several devastating fires destroyed almost all the old buildings, the town today looks new, with glass-and-concrete (or steel) buildings rather than the French colonial or Victorian look typical of many West Indian capitals.

Castries may be architecturally dull, but its **public market** is one of the most fascinating in the West Indies, and our favorite people-watching site on the island. It goes full blast every day of the week except Sunday and is most active on Friday and Saturday mornings. The market stalls are a block from Columbus Square along Peynier Street, running down toward the water. The countrywomen dress traditionally, with cotton headdresses; the number of knotted points on top reveals their marital status (ask one of the locals to explain it to you). The luscious fruits and vegetables of St. Lucia may be new to you; the array of color alone is astonishing. Sample one of the numerous varieties of bananas: In St. Lucia, they're allowed to ripen on the tree and taste completely different from those picked green and sold at supermarkets in the United States. You can also pick up St. Lucian handicrafts such as baskets and unglazed pottery here.

To the south of Castries looms **Morne Fortune,** the inappropriately named "Hill of Good Luck." In the 18th century, some of the most savage battles between the French and the British took place here. You can visit the military cemetery, a small museum, the old powder magazine, and the "Four Apostles Battery" (a quartet of grim muzzle-loading cannons). Government House, now the official residence of the governor-general of St. Lucia, is one of the few examples of Victorian architecture that escaped destruction by fire. The private gardens are beautifully planted, aflame with scarlet and purple bougainvillea. Morne Fortune also offers what many consider the most scenic lookout perch in the Caribbean. The view of the harbor of Castries is panoramic: You can see north to Pigeon Island or south to the Pitons; on a clear day, you may even spot Martinique. To reach Morne Fortune, head east on Bridge Street.

Pigeon Island National Historic Park

St. Lucia's first national park, **Pigeon Island National Historic Park,** is joined to the mainland by a causeway. On its West Coast are two white-sand beaches (see "Combing the beaches," earlier in this chapter) and a restaurant, Jambe de Bois, named for a wooden-legged pirate who once used the island as a hide-out.

Pigeon Island offers an **Interpretation Centre,** equipped with artifacts and a multimedia display on local history, ranging from the Amerindian occupation of A.D. 1000 to the Battle of the Saints, when Admiral Rodney's fleet set out from Pigeon Island and defeated Admiral De Grasse in 1782. The Captain's Cellar Olde English Pub lies under the center and is evocative of an 18th-century English bar.

Pigeon Island, only 18 hectares (44 acres), got its name from the redneck pigeon, or ramier, that once colonized this island in huge numbers. Now the site of a Sandals Hotel and interconnected to the St. Lucian mainland, the island offers pleasant panoramas but no longer the sense of isolated privacy that reigned here prior to its development. Parts of it, those far from the hotel on-premises, seem appropriate for nature walks. For more information, call the exhibition center at ☎ **758-452-2231.**

Rodney Bay

The scenic **Rodney Bay** is a 15-minute drive north of Castries. Set on a man-made lagoon, it has become a chic center for nightlife, hotels, and restaurants — in fact, it's the most active place on the island after dark. Its marina is one of the top water-sports centers in the Caribbean and a destination every December for the Atlantic Rally for Cruisers, when yachties cross the Atlantic to meet and compare stories.

Marigot Bay

Movie crews, including those for Sophia Loren's *Fire Power,* have used **Marigot Bay,** one of the most beautiful in the Caribbean, for background shots. Thirteen kilometers (8 miles) south of Castries, it's narrow yet navigable by yachts of any size. Here, Admiral Rodney camouflaged his ships with palm leaves while lying in wait for French frigates. The shore, lined with palm trees, remains relatively unspoiled, although some building sites have been sold. It's a delightful spot for a picnic. A 24-hour ferry connects the bay's two sides.

Soufrière

The little fishing port of Soufrière, St. Lucia's second-largest settlement, is dominated by two pointed hills called **Petit Piton** and **Gros Piton.** The Pitons, two volcanic cones rising to over 738m (2,460 ft.), have become the very symbol of St. Lucia. Formed of lava and rock, and once actively volcanic, they're now covered in green vegetation. Their sheer rise from the sea makes them a landmark visible for miles around, and waves crash at their bases. It's recommended that you attempt to climb only Gros Piton, but doing so requires the permission of the **Forest and Lands Department** (☎ **758-450-2231;** 758-450-2375, ext. 316 or 317) and the company of a knowledgeable guide.

Near Soufrière lies the famous drive-in volcano, **Mount Soufrière,** a rocky lunar landscape of bubbling mud and craters seething with sulfur. You literally drive your car into a millions-of-years-old crater and then get out and walk between the sulfur springs and pools of hissing steam. Entrance costs $2.80 per person and includes the services of your guide, who will point out the blackened waters, among the few of their kind in the Caribbean. Hours are daily from 9 a.m. to 5 p.m. Call the Soufrière Development Foundation (☎ **758-459-7200**) for more information.

Nearby are the **Diamond Mineral Baths** (☎ **758-452-4759**) in the **Diamond Botanical Gardens.** Deep in the lush tropical gardens is the Diamond Waterfall, one of the geological attractions of the island. Created from water bubbling up from sulfur springs, the waterfall changes colors (from yellow to black to green to gray) several times a day. The baths were constructed in 1784 on the orders of Louis XVI, whose doctors told him these waters were similar in mineral content to the waters at Aix-les-Bains; they were intended to provide recuperative effects for French soldiers fighting in the West Indies. The baths have an average temperature of 41°C (106°F). For a cost between $4 and $5.55, depending on the degree of privacy, you can bathe and try out the recuperative effects for yourself.

From Soufrière in the Southwest, the road winds toward **Fond St-Jacques,** where you'll have a good view of mountains and villages as you cut through St. Lucia's **Cape Moule-Chique** tropical rain forest. You'll also see the **Barre de l'Isle Trail,** a 1.6km-long (1-mile) trail that divides the eastern and western parts of St. Lucia. It offers four lookout points that provide panoramic views of the finest reserve that envelops it; you can see the Atlantic on one side and the Caribbean Sea on the other.

Guided tours

St. Lucia is difficult terrain to traverse on your own. Guided tours not only make it easy for you, but take you to the most spectacular sights, which you may not locate as easily on your own.

Helicopter tours

St. Lucia Helicopters (☎ **758-453-6950;** www.stluciahelicopters. com) offers the island's most dramatic sightseeing. The ten-minute North Trip, costing $60 per person, flies you over Castries, the major resort hotels, the elegant Cap Estate homes, Pigeon Point, Rodney Bay, and the more turbulent Atlantic Coast. The longer, 20-minute South Tour, costing $100 per passenger, flies over Castries, the banana plantations, beautiful Marigot Bay, fishing villages, the lush rain forest, the Pitons, the Soufrière volcano, and even remote waterfalls, rivers, and lush valleys.

Nature tours

St. Lucia Heritage Tours (☎ **758-451-6220;** www.stluciaheritage. com) tailors trips to personal requirements and keeps its groups small. No other outfitter puts you as close to nature as Heritage. Tours, costing from $65 per person, take you to remote parts of the island that the average vacationer misses, including a waterfall on private lands. The emphasis is on off-the-beaten track discoveries such as a plantation house from the 1800s. Call for reservations.

Bike tours

Bike St. Lucia, Anse Chastanet, Soufrière (☎ **758-457-1400;** www.bike stlucia.com), is a trailblazing outfitter that penetrates deep into the lushness of the island along 19km (12 miles) of bike trails that date from the plantation era's beginnings in the 1700s. These unique tours accommodate both the first-time biker and the experienced rider. The most challenging ride, Tinker's Trail, was designed with the help of world champion biker Tinker Juarez. Along the way, bikers pass numerous French colonial ruins and luxuriant fruit trees, including mango, guava, cocoa, and breadfruit, plus plenty of wild orchids. Highlights of the bike trips, costing from $40 to $90 per person, include a picnic lunch and a swim in a river or at the beach. About a quarter of the trips (4.8km/3 miles) are by bike, the rest in your trusty hiking boots. The outfitter provides all gear.

Keeping Active

St. Lucia's chief adventure for the active vacationer is in hiking through its lush rain forests on so-called jungle tours. The island also offers some first-rate golf, even though it can't really compete with the courses on such islands as Puerto Rico or Barbados.

Hiking through lush forests

A tropical rain forest covers a large area in the southern half of St. Lucia, and the **St. Lucia Forest and Lands Department** (☎ 758-450-2231; 758-450-2375, ext. 316 or 317) manages it wisely. This forest reserve divides the western and eastern halves of the island. The most popular of the several trails available is the **Barre de l'Isle Trail,** located almost in the center of St. Lucia, southeast of Marigot Bay; the trail is fairly easy, and even children can handle it. Four panoramic lookout points offer dramatic views of the sea where the Atlantic and the Caribbean meet. It takes about an hour to walk this 2km-long (1-mile) trail, which lies about a 30-minute ride from Castries. You can usually arrange guided hikes through the major hotels or through the Forest and Lands Department.

For rain-forest hikes, **Jungle Tours,** Cas-en-Bas/Gros Islet (☎ 758-450-0434), is the best outfitter, offering both an easy tour (a short walk) and a trail of intermediate challenge, lasting 1½ hours both ways. On the latter tour, participants imitate Tarzan by climbing down a rope. Many other tours, including a private beach tour along the wild Atlantic Coast, are available. Costs range from $30 to $80 per person, the latter including a buffet lunch.

Teeing off in St. Lucia

The only public golf course on the island lies in the northern district within Cap Estate. Part of **St. Lucia's Golf and Country Club** (☎ 758-450-9905), it offers an 18-hole, 6,202m (6,815-yard), par-72 championship course that's a challenge to both serious and recreational golfers. The course is the design of John Ponko, who trained with the fabled golf architect Robert Trent Jones, Sr. On-site is a clubhouse and a pro shop, where club rentals are available for $20. Greens fees are $95 for 18 holes or $70 for 9 holes. The course offers no caddies — carts only. Reservations are necessary, and hours are from 7 a.m. to 6 p.m. daily.

Horsing around in St. Lucia

St. Lucia offers a variety of trail rides, from inland scenic rides through the countryside to beach picnics at Cas-en-Bas. **Trim's National Riding Stable,** north of Castries in Cas-en-Bas, Gros Islet (☎ 758-450-8139), is St. Lucia's oldest riding establishment. Its activities range from trail rides to beach tours to horse-drawn carriage tours of **Pigeon Island.** Rides begin at $45 for an hour, rising to $50 for two hours, or $70 for a three-hour beach ride with a picnic.

Having a ball with tennis

The best place for tennis on the island is the **St. Lucia Racquet Club,** adjacent to Club St. Lucia (☎ 758-450-0551) on the very northern tip of the island. This club is one of the finest tennis facilities in the Lesser

Antilles. Seven illuminated courts are maintained in state-of-the-art condition. You must reserve 24 hours in advance. Guests of the hotel play for free; nonguests pay $20 for a full-day pass. A good pro shop is on-site, where tennis racquets rent for $7.75 per hour.

The Jalousie Plantation, at Soufrière (☎ 758-459-7666), has a good program. Vernon Lewis, the top-ranked player in St. Lucia, is the pro. You'll find four brand-new Laykold tennis courts (three lit for night play). Hotel guests play for free (though they pay for lessons). Nonguests can play for $20 per hour. Because the hotel has just four courts, reserving in advance is best.

Shopping the Local Stores

Most of the shopping is in **Castries,** where the principal streets are William Peter Boulevard and Bridge Street. Many stores will sell you goods at duty-free prices (providing you don't take the merchandise with you but have it delivered to the airport or cruise dock). You can find good (but not remarkable) deals when buying bone china, jewelry, perfume, watches, liquor, and crystal.

Built for the cruise-ship passenger, **Pointe Seraphine,** in Castries, has the best collection of shops on the island, along with offices for car rentals, organized taxi service (for sightseeing), a bureau de change, a philatelic bureau, an information center, and international phones. Cruise ships dock right at the shopping center. Under red roofs in a Spanish-style setting, the complex requires that you present a cruise pass or an airline ticket to the shopkeeper when purchasing goods. Visitors can take away their purchases, except liquor and tobacco, which stores deliver to the airport. The center is open in winter, Monday to Friday from 8 a.m. to 5 p.m. and Saturday from 8 a.m. to 2 p.m.; off season, Monday to Saturday from 9 a.m. to 4 p.m. The shopping center is also open when cruise ships are in port. The following shops may strike your fancy:

- ✔ **Colombian Emeralds** (☎ 758-453-7721), although it can't compete with the inventory at Little Switzerland, has a more diverse selection of watches, gemstones, and gold chains. Of special value are the watches, which sometimes sell for up to 40 percent less than equivalent retail prices in North America.

- ✔ **Studio Images** (☎ 758-452-6883) offers designer fragrances, including some exotic locally made concoctions, often 20 to 40 percent lower than U.S. prices. The store also carries the latest Sony electronics, leather accessories from Ted Lapidus, Samsonite luggage, and a wide collection of souvenirs.

At **Noah's Arkade,** Jeremie Street (☎ 758-457-7501), many of the Caribbean handicrafts and gifts are routine tourist items, but you'll often find something interesting if you browse around: local straw place mats, baskets, rugs, wall hangings, maracas, shell necklaces, locally made bowls, dolls dressed in banana leaves, and warri boards (from an old game played by slaves, akin to checkers). Additional branches are at Hewanorra International Airport and the Pointe Seraphine duty-free shopping malls.

On Gros Islet Highway, 3km (2 miles) north of Castries, **Gablewoods Mall** contains three restaurants and one of the island's densest concentrations of shops. At **Sunshine Bookshop** (☎ 758-452-3222), you can buy works by Caribbean authors, especially the books of the poet Derek Walcott, St. Lucia's Nobel Laureate.

Bagshaws, La Toc Road, just outside Castries (☎ 758-451-9249), is the leading island hand-printer of silk-screen designs. They incorporate the birds (look for the St. Lucia parrot), butterflies, and flowers of St. Lucia into their original designs. The highlights are an extensive line of vibrant prints on linen, clothing, and beachwear for both men and women, and the best T-shirt collection on St. Lucia. At **La Toc Studios** (same number as above), you can view the printing process Tuesday to Friday, 8:30 a.m. to 4 p.m.

Caribelle Batik, Howelton House, 37 Old Victoria Rd., Morne Fortune (☎ 758-452-3785), a five-minute drive from Castries, is where you can watch St. Lucian artists creating intricate patterns and colors through the ancient art of batik. You can also purchase batik in cotton, rayon, and silk, made up in casual and beach clothing, plus wall hangings and other gift items. In the renovated Victorian-era building, the Dyehouse Bar and Terrace serves drinks.

Vincent Joseph Eudovic is a master artist and woodcarver whose sculptures have gained increasing fame. You can view and purchase his work at **Eudovic Art Studio,** Goodlands, Morne Fortune (☎ 758-452-2747). He usually carves his imaginative, free-form sculptures from local tree roots, such as teak, mahogany, and red cedar. Ask to be taken to his private studio, where you'll see his remarkable creations.

Living It Up After Dark

St. Lucia doesn't have much of a nightlife besides the entertainment you find in hotels. In the winter, at least one hotel has a steel band or calypso music every night of the week. Otherwise, check to see what's happening at **Capone's** (☎ 758-452-0284) or the **Green Parrot** (☎ 758-452-3399), both in Castries.

Indies, at Rodney Bay (☎ 758-452-0727), is a split-floor, soundproof dance club with a large wooden dancing area and stage and a trio of bars. The DJs keep the joint jumping with both West Indian and international sounds, often American. The action gets going Wednesday, Friday, and Saturday from 11 p.m. to 4 a.m.; the cover charge is $7.40. Indies has a sort of rock and sports bar around the side of the building called the **Back Door.** Featuring alternative music and reggae, it serves snacks until 3 a.m.

One of the island's most action-packed dance clubs is **Folley,** Rodney Bay (☎ 758-450-0022), adjoining La Creole Restaurant. Patrons age 21 and up can enjoy an array of music from reggae to rock. Entrance is $7.40.

If you want to go barhopping, begin at **Shamrocks Pub,** Rodney Bay (☎ 758-452-8725). This Irish-style pub is especially popular among boaters and gets really lively on weekends.

Among the dance clubs, islanders and visitors favor **Late Lime,** Reduit Beach (☎ 758-452-0761). A DJ plays dance music on Saturday. **The Chalet,** Rodney Bay (☎ 758-450-0022), near La Creole Restaurant, lies at Rodney Bay Marina, luring dancing feet to its wild disco nights. You'll hear some of the best zouk and salsa here.

At Marigot Bay, where the filming of the 1967 version of *Doctor Doolittle* starring Rex Harrison took place, the memory is perpetuated at **Doolittle's,** part of the Marigot Beach Club Hotel (☎ 758-451-4974), lying 15km (9 miles) south of Castries. The Marigot Bay ferry takes you to the palm-studded peninsula of the resort; tickets cost $1.85. On Saturday nights, a lavish seafood and barbecue buffet and a steel band make Doolittle's the best place to be on the island. You can come here for drinks (try the Singapore Slings) or dishes like chunky pumpkin soup, jerk chicken, or lobster and coconut shrimp Creole.

In the center of Rodney Bay is **Charlie's** (☎ 758-458-0565), which opened in 2004. It has an imported Italian chef and brings in piano players from both Britain and the States to entertain the crowd.

Fast Facts: St. Lucia

Area Code

The area code is **758.**

ATMs

ATMs are located at all bank branches, transportation centers, and shopping malls. Two of the most central banks are in Castries: the Bank of Nova Scotia, William Peter Boulevard (☎ 758-452-2100), and the National Commercial Bank of St. Lucia, Bridge Street (☎ 758-456-6000).

Babysitters

Your hotel probably can arrange this service for you at the cost of $8 to $10 an hour.

Currency Exchange

St. Lucia's official monetary unit is the Eastern Caribbean dollar (EC$), which is pegged at EC $2.70 per U.S. dollar. Because the Yankee coin is widely accepted, most visitors don't find it necessary to exchange U.S. dollars for EC dollars.

Doctors

Check with your hotel for a referral.

Embassies and Consulates

St. Lucia has no American embassy or consulate. The British High Commission is located at N.I.S. Building, Waterfront, Castries (☎ 758-452-2482).

Emergencies

Call the police at ☎ **999**. For an ambulance or in case of fire, call ☎ **911**.

Hospitals

Both St. Jude's Hospital, Vieux Fort (☎ 758-454-6041), and Victoria Hospital, Hospital Road, Castries (☎ 758-452-2421), have 24-hour emergency rooms.

Information

See the Appendix for helpful Web sites and locations of local tourist offices.

Internet Access

Use the services available at your hotel.

Newspapers and Magazines

Major U.S. newspapers such as the *New York Times* and the *Miami Herald* are flown in. On island, you can pick up a copy of the *St. Lucia Mirror* to find out what's going on.

Pharmacies

The best is M&C Drugstore, Bridge Street, in Castries (☎ 758-458-8146), open Monday through Friday from 8 a.m. to 5 p.m. and Saturday from 8 a.m. to 1 p.m.

Police

Call ☎ **999**.

Post Office

The general post office, on Bridge Street in Castries, is open Monday to Friday from 8:30 a.m. to 4:30 p.m.

Restrooms

In Castries, you'll find public restrooms with running water adjacent to the cruise-ship terminals on Place Carenage, and also adjacent to the public markets on Jeremie Street. But other than that, you'll have to duck into one of the island's many bars, hotels, and restaurants, each of which is required, by St. Lucian law, to admit members of the general public (who may or may not be a patron of their establishment) into their restrooms. Recognizing the way passersby have, to some degree, adopted the restrooms of many bars and restaurants, many owners position their restrooms conveniently close to the main entrance.

Safety

St. Lucia has its share of crime, like every other place these days. Use common sense and protect yourself and your valuables. If you've got it, don't flaunt it! Don't pick up hitchhikers if you're driving around the island. Narcotic drugs are illegal, and possessing or selling them could lead to stiff fines or jail.

Smoking

Smoking policies are left to the discretion of the individual establishments, and most restaurants have designated nonsmoking sections within their restaurants and bars. With so many open-air establishments, the natural ventilation of the trade winds helps resolve conflicts.

Taxes

The government imposes an 8 percent occupancy tax on hotel rooms, and you have to pay a $21 departure tax (included in your airfare) at either airport. Children under 12 are exempt from the departure tax.

Taxis

Taxis are readily available at airports, where the harbor cruise ships arrive, and in front of major hotels. No central number exists; however, your hotel desk keeps a list of the private numbers of cabbies to call if one isn't waiting outside. Although taxis aren't metered, most island cabbies are members of a taxi cooperative that agrees to charge standard rates: Castries to Marigot Bay in the South, $25 to $30; Castries to Soufrière, $70; or Castries to Rodney Bay, $18 to $20.

Weather Updates

Check www.weather.com for updates.

Chapter 16

Sint Maarten/St. Martin

● ●

In This Chapter

▶ Knowing what to expect when you arrive
▶ Getting around the island
▶ Deciding where you want to stay
▶ Sampling the local cuisine at the best restaurants
▶ Scoping out good beaches and diving into water sports
▶ Satisfying the landlubber: Shopping and nightlife

● ●

*E*ven though it's tiny, the split-personality island of Sint Maarten/
St. Martin is jointly owned by two European nations, the Netherlands
in the southern half and France in the northern half. Frankly, the French
government controls the better half. Both islands are overly developed,
but you can find more-tranquil places on the French side than the Dutch.
No international border formalities exist between the two countries, and
as you drive about, particularly if you're a first-time visitor, you often
don't know which nation you're in. Road markers indicate international
borders, however.

Though small, the island maintains two distinct personalities. The Dutch
half, about 44 sq. km (17 sq. miles) in area, is the smaller of the two but
has the largest airport, Princess Juliana Airport. Philipsburg, the capital
of Dutch Sint Maarten, is also the area's main arrival point for cruise
ships. Go to the Dutch side for large resorts, casino action, and the most
duty-free shopping possibilities. Nothing is particularly Dutch about Sint
Maarten, however.

In contrast, St. Martin exudes a definite French aura. Slightly larger than
its Dutch counterpart, at about 53 sq. km (20 sq. miles) in area, it maintains a small airport and contains some of the best restaurants in the
Caribbean. Except for some pockets of posh, French St. Martin is more
affordable than other French-held islands in the Caribbean, including
Guadeloupe and Martinique, and especially tony St. Barts.

Northernmost of the Netherlands Antilles, Sint Maarten/St. Martin lies
123km (144 miles) southeast of Puerto Rico. It is a lush land where bays
and good beaches rim the land. Both sides are blessed with magnificent
sands and a year-round temperature of 26°C (79°F).

Arriving at the Airport

Most foreign visitors arrive on the Dutch side at **Princess Juliana Airport** (☎ 599-54-54211), the second-busiest airport in the Caribbean, topped only by San Juan. The airport is completely modern and up-to-date; you can find ATMs here as well as limited tourist info. For more on ATMs and tourist information, see "Fast Facts: Sint Maarten/St. Martin," later in this chapter.

The airport caters to both international and interisland flights, lying 10km (6 miles) from the French capital of Marigot and 7km (5 miles) from the Dutch capital of Philipsburg.

On the French side, **L'Espérance Airport** (☎ 590-590-87-10-36), at Grand Case, is 7km (5 miles) from Marigot and 16km (10 miles) from Philipsburg. It has fewer facilities and is used mainly for smaller planes on island-hopping jaunts.

Although you should always guard your luggage, you don't face the danger of theft at either airport on Sint Maarten/St. Martin the way you do in such other Caribbean destinations as Jamaica.

Navigating your way through passport control and Customs

Both Dutch and French Customs officials smooth your way on the island and don't seem to unduly hassle arriving visitors, unless they have a suspicion of drugs or smuggling.

After you've cleared Customs at one airport — say, the Dutch side, you don't have to go through Customs control again until you leave, either from the French or Dutch side. For departures from Princess Juliana Airport on the Dutch side, the tax is $30 or only $10 if you're flying or boating to St. Eustatius or Saba. You don't have to pay a departure tax on the French side.

Getting from the airport to your hotel

Unless your hotel sends a van for you, all passengers arriving on the island must hire a taxi for transport to their hotels because an island-wide law prohibits anyone from picking up a car at an airport. You can, however, rent a car at the major airport, Juliana, which the agency will later deliver to your hotel.

As far as taxi fares are concerned, the government regulates them. For example, a trip from Princess Juliana Airport to Grand Case on the French side costs $20 and up for two passengers and up to two bags per person (more if you have an excess of luggage). From the same airport to Marigot costs $15. On the French side, the fare from the airport at Grand Case to Marigot is also $15.

Choosing Your Location

If you don't like depending on public transportation and prefer to walk where you're going, consider staying in the Dutch capital at **Philipsburg.** Those who are born to shop like to stay here because it has the largest concentration of duty-free shopping outside of St. Thomas. For white sands, Great Bay Beach runs behind Front Street in Philipsburg. Regrettably, the water here isn't always as clean as it is at the other beaches.

Philipsburg is the best embarkation point if you want to take one of several boat excursions, perhaps to a neighboring island. However, the capital is also the most congested part of both sides of the island, especially when cruise ships are in port. The downside of Philipsburg is that it could be virtually anywhere — it has little romance and island flavor.

Several resorts are located at **Simpson Bay** and **Maho Bay,** to the immediate west of Philipsburg. The sands are quite wonderful here, and the only drawback is the location near the Juliana airport, where you're subject to jet blasts throughout the day.

For more charm, you could consider staying north in the French capital, **Marigot,** which is less crowded and a long distance from the cruise-ship hordes — but the closest place on the French side for trips into Philipsburg. Its bustling harbor has more of the sounds, sights, and colors of the West Indies, as peddlers hawk everything from West Indian spices to French croissants; old Antillean buildings give it architectural charm. You'll find limited shopping here, but the city and its vicinity boast a concentration of good French restaurants.

Immediately west of the town are the golden sands of **Nettlé Beach** lying between Baie Nettlé and Marigot Bay. Much farther afield, but still preferred by many visitors, is the town of **Grand Case,** immediately west of Esperance Airport. This restaurant-glutted little town opens onto the Baie de Grand Case, which has a fine but thin beach with a lot of water sports. The French resorts in general are more intimate than those on the Dutch side.

If you rent a car to get about, you may prefer one of the more-remote and tranquil resorts on the island. These hotels are more for people who want to anchor into a place, perhaps venturing forth for such expeditions as dining in Grand Case or shopping in Philipsburg before retreating back to the sands of their resort of choice.

Among the more idyllic locations for a resort is **Oyster Pond,** which lies northeast of Philipsburg at the French-Dutch border. Two of the island's best beaches, Dawn Beach and Oyster Pond Beach, are here. Hills on one side and a lagoon and sea on the other make this spot a delightful and less-trampled one.

On the French side, **Baie Orientale** is another choice place for secluded resorts. It lies directly north of Oyster Pond and to the immediate east of Grand Case and Esperance Airport. Orient Bay, as it's called in English, boasts the island's finest white sandy beach with crystal clear waters. The backdrop of the bay is dotted with a widely varied assortment of little tropical restaurants and beach bar dives. Water sports are strong here, and many on-the-beach kiosks rent equipment. The southern section of this bay attracts a lot of nudists.

Getting Around Sint Maarten/St. Martin

Public transportation, except for taxis, is woefully inadequate. You have a choice to make. Rent a car if you're adventurous and want to go to a different beach every day and sample the quality restaurants and shopping on both sides of the island. If you plan to anchor mainly at your resort, venturing out infrequently for shopping trips and dining adventures, then consider relying on a taxi either on the French or Dutch side.

By taxi

Most visitors use taxis to get around. Because they're unmetered on both sides of the island, always agree on the rate before getting into a cab.

Rates are slightly different on the two sides of the island:

- ✔ **Sint Maarten** taxis have minimum fares for two passengers, and each additional passenger pays $4 extra. From Princess Juliana Airport you can expect to pay $15 to get to Marigot or Philipsburg and $6 to get to the Maho Beach Hotel.

  Fares are 25 percent higher between 10 p.m. and midnight, and 50 percent higher between midnight and 6 a.m. One piece of luggage per person is allowed free; each additional piece is $1 extra.

- ✔ **St. Martin** taxi fares are also for two passengers. From Princess Juliana Airport to either Marigot or La Samanna, expect to pay $15. From Marigot to Grand Case, the fare is about $6, and from Maho Beach to Philipsburg, $15.

  These fares are in effect from 7 a.m. to 10 p.m.; after that, they go up by 25 percent until midnight, rising by 50 percent after midnight. Plan to add about $1 for each suitcase or carry-on bag.

For late-night cab service on either side of the island, call ☎ 599-54-54317. The **Taxi Service & Information Center** operates at the port of Marigot (☎ 590-590-87-56-54) on the island's French side.

By car

If you want to experience both the Dutch and the French sides of the island, you may want to rent a car. Because a law prohibits anyone from picking up a car at the airport, every rental agency delivers cars directly to your hotel, where an employee completes the paperwork. If you prefer to rent a car on arrival, head for one of the tiny rental kiosks across the road from the Juliana airport, but beware of long lines. Several car-rental options are available:

- ✔ **Avis** (☎ **800-331-1212** in the U.S., 599-54-52847 on the Dutch side, 590-590-87-50-60 on the French side; www.avis.com) maintains offices on both sides of the island.

- ✔ **Budget** (☎ **800-472-3325** in the U.S., 599-54-54030 on either side of the island; www.budget.com) maintains offices on both sides of the island.

- ✔ **Hertz** (☎ **800-654-3131** in the U.S., 599-54-54541 or 599-54-54314 on the Dutch side; www.hertz.com) offices are located on both sides of the island.

- ✔ **National** (☎ **800-328-4567** in the U.S., 599-54-55552 on the Dutch side; www.nationalcar.com) has offices only on the Dutch side.

All four car-rental companies roughly charge equivalent prices ranging between $35 and $55 a day. They all require that renters be at least 25 years old. Your credit card issuer may provide insurance coverage, so check before your trip; otherwise, it may be wise to buy the fairly cheap **collision damage waiver** (CDW) when you rent.

The central roads along the coast are paved and generally in fair condition. When you venture farther afield, however, routes can be very narrow and potholed, with even hazardous conditions in some places, especially after a storm.

Drive on the right-hand side on both the French and Dutch sides of the island, and expect traffic jams near the major towns. The island uses international road signs, and you'll be able to cross the international borders without a problem.

By island shuttle

Minibus is a reasonable means of transport on Sint Maarten/St. Martin if you don't mind some inconvenience and overcrowding. Buses run daily from 6 a.m. to midnight and serve most of the major locations on both sides of the island. The most popular run is from Philipsburg on the Dutch side to Marigot on the French side. Privately owned and operated, minibuses tend to follow specific routes, with fares ranging from $1 to $1.50, depending on how far you travel.

Staying in Style

Most of the resorts on the Dutch side open onto one of the sandy beaches along **Maho Bay.** This location is most convenient to both the

Dutch side's international airport and its best shops and restaurants. Other resorts open onto **Simpson Bay** lying southeast of the airport, although traffic is more congested in this area.

For those who want to stay in Philipsburg, you can also find beaches here. This location is best for those who've come to shop, gamble, and spend the night bar-hopping. Some of Sint Maarten's best restaurants are also in Philipsburg, in case you want to try a new joint every night.

Alternatively, you can stay at one of the French resorts in the northern part of the island. The two major resorts here are the beachfronts along Baie Nettlé or Baie Orientale. For those who want to walk to most places and who want to be near most of the island's shopping, nightlife, and dining, seek out a hotel either in Grand Case or Marigot, the two largest settlements on the French side. In general, the French resorts are smaller and more intimate than the larger hotels on the Dutch side (many of which are timeshare properties).

The Top Resorts

The rack rates listed are in U.S. dollars and are for a standard double room during high season, running from mid-December through mid-April. Over the Christmas holidays, hotels tend to charge more and may even require a minimum booking. Lower tariffs are available in spring, summer, and fall. See Chapter 3 for more information on travel seasons.

Beach Plaza
$$$ Baie de Marigot

This is our favorite hotel within a reasonable distance of Marigot's commercial center. A three-story, 144-room building that centers on a soaring atrium festooned with live banana trees and climbing vines, it's within a cluster of buildings mostly composed of condominiums. Built in 1996, and painted in shades of blue and white, it's set midway between the open sea and the lagoon, giving all rooms water views. Inside, the décor is pure white, accented with varnished, dark-tinted woods and an inviting tropical motif. Each room contains a balcony, tile floors, native art, and simple hardwood furniture, including a writing desk and comfortable beds. Bathrooms have tub/shower combinations and generous shelf space. The hotel's restaurant, Le Corsaire, serves French food except for the all-you-can-eat buffets on Tuesday and Friday nights, which feature Creole and seafood, respectively.

See map p. 417. Baie de Marigot, 97150 St. Martin, F.W.I. ☎ *590-590-87-87-00. Fax 590-590-87-18-87.* www.hotelbeachplazasxm.com. *Rack rates: $253–$354 double; from $579 suite. Rates include buffet breakfast. AE, MC, V.*

Sint Maarten/St. Martin Accommodations

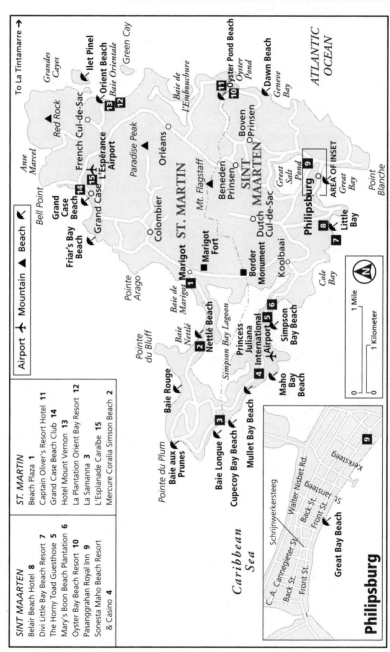

| Airport ✈ | Mountain ▲ | Beach 🏖 |

SINT MAARTEN
Belair Beach Hotel **8**
Divi Little Bay Beach Resort **7**
The Horny Toad Guesthose **5**
Mary's Boon Beach Plantation **6**
Oyster Bay Beach Resort **10**
Pasanggrahan Royal Inn **9**
Sonesta Maho Beach Resort
& Casino **4**

ST. MARTIN
Beach Plaza **1**
Captain Oliver's Resort Hotel **11**
Grand Case Beach Club **14**
Hotel Mount Vernon **13**
La Plantation Orient Bay Resort **12**
La Samanna **3**
L'Esplanade Caraïbe **15**
Mercure Coralia Simson Beach **2**

Belair Beach Hotel
$$$ Belair, Philipsburg

On the beach at Little Bay, this Dutch-side hotel is a ten-minute drive from the Sint Maarten airport. It attracts the family trade, who don't mind the self-catering at this 72-room timeshare condo. The 1980s architecture of this four-story building is cookie-cutter, with one- and two-bedroom condos for rent. Families like the fully equipped kitchens, the coin-operated laundries, and the fact that kids 17 and under stay for free in their parent's room. Each one-bedroom accommodations contains a master bedroom, a living room, and a spacious oceanfront terrace. The two-bedroom units have, in addition, a second small bedroom with a twin trundle bed that converts to a double, plus a sofa bed in the living room. The accommodations are well furnished and reasonably maintained, though some of the public areas could do with a spruce up. Facilities include an on-site restaurant (Sugar Bird Café) and bar, with an outdoor pool and tennis courts on the grounds. You can arrange water sports and car rentals through the hotel.

See map p. 417. Belair, Philipsburg. ☎ *800-480-8555, 599-54-23362. Fax: 599-54-25295.* www.belairbeach.com. *Rack rates: $299–$389 one-bedroom suite; $349–$419 two-bedroom suite. AE, DC, DISC, MC, V.*

Captain Oliver's Resort Hotel
$$–$$$ Oyster Pond

This 50-room marina resort lies on the more-tranquil eastern side, close to the Dutch border and a private taxi ride to that honey called **Dawn Beach.** At night you face a choice of dining in France or going nearby for dinner in the Netherlands. Oyster Pond itself is a government-protected lagoon enveloped by hills. In lieu of a beach location, an alluring swimming pool with walls made of glass makes do — it's called a people aquarium, with the deck extending over the lagoon for panoramic seascapes. Pink bungalows, trimmed in gingerbread, greet you and stand on a hill, opening onto beautiful views. Accommodations are three units to a bungalow and are furnished in white rattan and adorned with local artwork and marble-clad bathrooms. Each junior suite has two double beds and a sofa bed, which makes the resort suitable for families. Try for an oceanview room with a harborview balcony if possible. The resort buzzes around a 100-slip marina filled with charter boats and vagabond yachties. The open-air Captain Oliver's Restaurant, overlooking the marina, is reason enough to stay here. The chef prepares fresh seafood both French and Creole style, and you can select lobster from a tank.

See map p. 417. Oyster Pond. ☎ *590-590-87-40-26. Fax: 590-590-87-40-84.* www.captainolivers.com. *Rack rates: $190–$300 junior suite. Rates include buffet breakfast. AE, MC, V.*

Divi Little Bay Beach Resort
$$–$$$ Little Bay, Philipsburg

Opening onto a private beach of gravelly sand, this 235-room resort stands on a peninsula that's a ten-minute drive from the international airport of Sint Maarten. The property, transformed beyond all previous recognition, originated in 1955 as a guesthouse for Princess Juliana of the Netherlands when she arrived for vacation. After severe hurricane damage in 1997, the owners reconstructed it as the flagship of the Divi chain. The architect conceived the resort as a European seaside village with Dutch colonial touches. In its upper reaches are the ruins of Fort Amsterdam, formerly Sint Maarten's most prized military fortress, but today a mere historical site — and not much of one at that. The resort stands on landscaped grounds, and accommodations have a light tropical feeling, often with private patios that behold views of the bay. You're offered an array of choices for living, ranging from beachfront guest rooms to one-bedroom luxury suites — and even studios or *casitas,* the latter tucked into the hillside. Facilities include three restaurants with a varied cuisine, a tropical bar, three outdoor pools, a tennis court, and a gym, along with a well-operated dive shop; water sports are a big draw here. The suites are ideal for families, and kids' poolside activities are offered during the week.

See map p. 417. Little Bay, Philipsburg. ☎ *800-367-3484, 599-54-22333. Fax: 599-54-24336.* www.divilittlebay.com. *Rack rates: $263–$300 double; $286–$328 one-bedroom apartment; $475 two-bedroom apartment. Breakfast and dinner $42 per adult, $25 per child per day. Children under 15 stay free in parent's room. AE, DC, MC, V.*

Grand Case Beach Club
$$$–$$$$ Grand Case

On the Northwest Coast of the French side, this 69-condo complex opens onto the noble sands of **Grand Case Beach** looking out toward the neighboring island of Anguilla. Don't let the name "club" fool you. The resort is open to all. Along the crescent-shaped sands, the club rebuilt five white-trimmed motel-like buildings after the devastating hurricanes of the mid-1990s. Most of the midsize and well-furnished bedrooms open onto views of the sea. Guest rooms come with double or king-size beds along with a full bathroom clad in white tiles. The suites contain sofa beds in their living rooms for additional guests. You can dine in the restaurant on-site, but why bother? The village of **Grand Case,** the cuisine capital of the Caribbean, is just down the beach. Although the resort has a swimming pool, most guests opt for the beach, which is dotted with umbrellas for shade. Other facilities include an artificial grass tennis court and a water-sports center, offering scuba trips and snorkeling.

See map p. 417. 21 rue du Petit-Plage, Grand Case. ☎ *800-344-3016, 590-590-87-51-87. Fax: 590-590-87-59-93.* www.gcbc.com. *Rack rates: $275–$385 double; $360–$415 one-bedroom suite; $485–$515 two-bedroom suite. Rates include continental breakfast. AE, MC, V.*

The Horny Toad Guesthouse
$$ Simpson Bay

Overlooking the white sandy beach of Simpson Bay, this eight-room guest-house is the domain of Maine-born Betty Vaughan, who's been pampering guests for years at this amusingly named B&B. The property dates from the 1950s, when it was the private residence of a former governor. The complex was constructed near the runway of the Sint Maarten airport, and jet blasts periodically interrupt sojourns. Other than that, a stay here can be both idyllic and comfortable when you get over the concrete bunker architecture. Bedrooms are immaculately maintained and well furnished, ranging from midsize to large, and each comes with a kitchenette and a small bathroom with a shower. Guests meet fellow guests around the gas-fired barbecues outside. No pool or restaurant is on the premises, and the rooms lack TVs. Our preferred unit is Room 8, which is in a round house in the rear, the other units facing the beach. Children 7 and under aren't allowed.

See map p. 417. 2 Vlaun Dr., Simpson Bay. ☎ *800-417-9361, 599-54-54323. Fax: 599-54-53316.* www.thehornytoadguesthouse.com. *Rack rates: $198 double. MC, V.*

Hotel Mount Vernon
$$$$–$$$$$ Cul de Sac, Baie Orientale

Sitting on a 28-hectare (70-acre) French bluff overlooking Baie Orientale, this sprawling, 390-room resort opens onto the white sands of **Orient Beach,** stretching for 2.4km (1½ miles). Attracting many repeat clients, Mount Vernon boasts one of the largest freshwater swimming pools on either side of the island. All the midsize-to-spacious bedrooms are furnished in a breezy tropical style, each housing a maximum of four guests. Management allows three adults or two adults and two children per unit. Bedrooms open onto sea-view balconies. The architecture is Creole inspired, and sometimes package-tour groups from France dominate the clientele. Both a French- and Creole-inspired cuisine is available nightly in the resort's two restaurants, guests often gathering for premeal drinks in the two airy bars. During the day, water sports are big here, with guests frolicking in the outdoor pool and working off the extra carbs in the fitness center. Snorkeling, kayaking, windsurfing, and volleyball fill up the calendar, and in the morning and late afternoon the two tennis courts are busy. At night, free shuttles take guests to the casinos and nightlife in Philipsburg. Families appreciate the children's programs for tots ages 5 to 12.

See map p. 417. Cul de Sac, Baie Orientale. ☎ *590-590-87-62-00. Fax: 590-590-87-37-27. Rack rates: $350–$390 one to four persons. AE, DISC, MC, V.*

La Plantation Orient Bay Resort
$$ Baie Orientale

On the North Atlantic Coast on the French side, this 52-room resort lies within a five-minute walk from the beautiful sands of **Orient Beach.** It sits on a landscaped hillside on 3 hectares (7½ acres) of tropical grounds.

Scattered about the property are French colonial–style villas, rather spacious and stylish, and decorated in a theme that combines elements of both Polynesia and the West Indies. All the units open onto large ocean-view terraces, and each is a fully equipped villa, either a studio or suite. Studios contain kitchenettes and queen-size or twin beds, whereas suites have separate bedrooms with king-size beds, large living rooms, and full kitchens. Each comes with a tiled bathroom with tub and shower. Guests enjoy both a French and Creole cuisine in the two restaurants, preferring the beach bar and grill for lunch. Two tennis courts for day or night play are on the grounds, and an activities desk provides info about excursions. Facilities include an outdoor pool, a health club, and such water sports as diving and windsurfing.

See map p. 417. Parc de la Baie Orientale, Baie Orientale. ☎ *590-590-29-58-00. Fax: 590-590-29-58-08.* www.la-plantation.com. *Rack rates: $235–$325 studio; $340 suite. Rates include breakfast. DISC, MC, V. Closed Sept to mid-Oct.*

La Samanna
$$$$$ Marigot

This luxurious, Sybaritic, superpricey Mediterranean-style retreat lies on a 2km (1½-mile) stretch of one of the island's finest white sandy beaches, lying on 22 hectares (55 acres) of landscaped grounds. With its white-washed buildings, the 81-room resort evokes a village somewhere on North Africa's Mediterranean Coast. The location is 8km (5 miles) west of Marigot, and the operators are Orient-Express Hotels who pamper you with elegance, taste, and supreme comfort. Standard doubles, one- or two-bedroom suites, and even three-bedroom villas, each boasting an ocean-view, are available. Furnished with West Indian wicker, bamboo, and hardwood, they feature private terraces or patios opening onto those white sands. Some accommodations boast rooftop terraces as well. Art objects from Thailand and Morocco give an exotic aura to this plush resort. The on-site restaurant, with a candlelight terrace overlooking **Baie Longue,** serves a superb French cuisine alfresco. At the poolside grill, waiters serve food Riviera style on the beach. Amenities include a pool, three tennis courts, and a fitness center; you can arrange water sports such as sailing, windsurfing, and snorkeling.

See map p. 417. Baie Longue. ☎ *800-237-1236, 590-590-87-64-00. Fax: 590-590-87-87-86.* www.orient-expresshotels.com. *Rack rates: $875 double; from $1,330 suite or villa. Rates include breakfast. AE, MC, V. Closed late Aug–late Oct.*

L'Esplanade Caraïbe
$$$$ Grand-Case

This elegant collection of 24 suites lies on a steeply sloping hillside above the road leading into the village of Grand-Case from Marigot. Covered with cascades of bougainvillea, and accented with a vaguely Hispanic overlay of white walls, hand-painted tiles, and light-blue-colored roofs, the resort's various elements are connected by a network of concrete steps that add to the layout's drama. There's a pool, a series of gorgeous terraced gardens, and access to a beach via a six-minute walk on a winding, stair-dotted pathway. There's no restaurant (only a bar that's open in midwinter), but the village of Grand-Case is known for its restaurants. All views from the guest rooms and their terraces angle out toward the sea and the sunset. Each unit contains a kitchen with a large fridge, up-to-date cookware, mahogany and wicker furniture, and very comfortable queen-size or king-size beds. Bathrooms are beautifully equipped right down to elegant toiletries baskets, and showers. The loft suites on the upper floors are worth the extra charge, as they include a sofa bed that can sleep extra guests, an upstairs master bedroom with a king-size bed, and a partial bathroom downstairs.

See map p. 417. Grand-Case (B.P. 5007). ☎ *866-596-8365, 590-590-87-06-55. Fax 590-590-87-29-15.* www.lesplanade.com. *Rack rates: $320–$370 double studio; $370–$470 suite. Extra person winter $70. AE, MC, V.*

Mary's Boon Beach Plantation
$$–$$$ **Simpson Bay**

Opening onto a 4.8km (3-mile) stretch of white sand, this 28-room inn is one of the most atmospheric and charming on the island. The location at Juliana Beach is close to the airport and subject to occasional noise; otherwise, the property is relatively secluded. The latest addition is a series of beachfront bedrooms. All the accommodations come with private patios or terraces. Some open directly onto the sea, have high ceilings, and are comfortably unpretentious. Yet other rooms are set within the garden and are quite stylish, decorated in jewel tones and containing four-poster cherrywood beds and Balinese woodcarvings. The on-site restaurant is family style and serves an admirable cuisine. Other facilities include a tropical bar, a fitness center, and an outdoor pool.

See map p. 417. 117 Simpson Bay Rd. ☎ *599-54-57000. Fax: 599-54-53403.* www.marysboon.com. *Rack rates: $175–$250 double. AE, MC, V.*

Mercure Coralia Simson Beach
$$–$$$ **Baie Nettlé**

Five low-rise buildings constructed in the Creole style lie between a saltwater lagoon and the ocean, close to some of the French side's best beaches. The location is 8km (5 miles) west of Princess Juliana Airport and 5km (3 miles) west of Marigot. The immediate beach at the property, however, is a bit narrow, and the sea is rocky right off the coast. Nonetheless, the 168 units of this complex are desirable because of the affordable prices and comfort. In three-story Antillean-style buildings, the bedrooms are filled with ocean-inspired pastels, durable wicker furniture, kitchenettes, and ceiling fans (air-conditioning, too). The most desirable accommodations on the third, or top, floor contain sloping ceilings sheltering sleeping lofts and two bathrooms. Water sports get a heavy focus here, with a dive shop, snorkeling, windsurfing, and other possibilities. Guests make much use of the outdoor pool and tennis court. You can dine at two open-air restaurants, and the bar is built out over the lagoon with a flagstone terrace hosting steel bands.

See map p. 417. Baie Nettlé. ☎ *800-221-4542, 590-590-87-54-54.* www.mercure. com. *Rack rates: $281 studio; $310–$348 duplex. Rates include buffet breakfast. AE, DC, MC, V.*

Oyster Bay Beach Resort
$$$ Oyster Pond

Escapists from such megaresorts as Maho Beach Hotel often anchor here at this 173-room resort hotel, which rests at the end of a scenic but curving road. The location is only a one-minute walk from **Dawn Beach,** a beautiful strip of white sand with good snorkeling, and 13km (8 miles) from Philipsburg on the eastern shore near the French border. This condo resort is completely modern and up-to-date, having grown from an intimate inn into the present pile, which has Moorish arches and stone-built turrets. The resort sprawls over 14 hectares (35 acres). A great deal of this place's energy focuses on hawking timeshares. We prefer the 40 rooms in the original building, which have far more character and atmosphere than the newer units. All of them, however, are comfortably furnished. Size varies from studios to one- or two-bedroom suites, each opening onto a view of the **Oyster Pond Marina.** The suites contain either kitchenettes or fully equipped kitchens. You're a bit isolated here at night, but that's hardly a problem as the resort has an excellent on-site restaurant and bar (The Jade Restaurant). Other facilities include a fitness center and an outdoor pool.

See map p. 417. 10 Emerald Merit Rd., Oyster Pond. ☎ *866-978-0212, 599-54-36040. Fax: 599-54-36695.* www.oysterbaybeachresort.com. *Rack rates: $200–$290 double; $310–$600 suite. Chldren under 12 stay free in parent's room. AE, DISC, MC, V.*

Pasanggrahan Royal Inn
$$ Philipsburg

For inquiring minds who want to know, *Pasanggrahan* means "guesthouse" in Indonesian. In the center of town but opening onto a white sandy beach, this 31-room inn is built in the colonial style and was once the governor's home. It has hosted Queen Wilhelmina. If Bogie and Ingrid Bergman, stars of *Casablanca,* were alive today, you'd find them remembering Paris in the Sidney Greenstreet Bar. Peacock bamboo chairs, Indian spool tables, and four-poster beds with mosquito netting add to its romantic allure. The renovated bedrooms are small to midsize; some take up residence in the main building, and others in an adjoining but sterile annex. Set among the wild jungle of palms and shrubbery is a very good on-site restaurant. Catch-of-the-day specials are the nighttime feature, and the chef prepares excellent breakfasts and affordable lunches. If you want a hideaway, don't book here. But if you want to be able to enjoy a beach and be close to the attractions and shops of Philipsburg, this is an option, especially if you're a nostalgia buff.

See map p. 417. 19 Front St., Philipsburg. ☎ *599-54-23588. Fax: 599-54-22885.* www. pasanhotel.com. *Rack rates: $148–$178 double. DISC, MC, V. Closed Sept.*

Sonesta Maho Beach Resort & Casino
$$$–$$$$ **Maho Bay**

The island's largest resort, with 600 rooms, lies on the Dutch side opening onto crescent-shaped **Maho Beach.** The resort is close enough to the airport that you may hear jet blasts from your bedroom. Frequented by conventioneers and tour groups, the megaresort, which has benefited nicely from a multimillion-dollar rejuvenation program, stands on a 4-hectare (10-acre) site that straddles the constant traffic of the coast road. Because of its sheer size, however, nothing seems to operate at 100 percent efficiency at all times. Bedrooms come with wicker furniture, Italian tiles, and well-maintained bathrooms with tub/shower combinations and bidets. No hotel offers such varied dining; the megaresort hosts nine restaurants in all, some operated independently. During the day, guests frequent a trio of outdoor pools, play at four tennis courts, or avail themselves of the health spa and fitness center. Water sports are also offered here. At night, this resort is the most active one on the island, with its Las Vegas–style casino, four bars, and a dance club.

See map p. 417. Maho Bay. ☎ *800-223-0757, 599-54-52115. Fax: 599-54-53180.* www.sonesta.com/stmaarten. *Rack rates: $190–$385 double; $330–$475 suite; from $845 two-bedroom unit. AE, DC, MC, V.*

Dining Out

You won't find authentic Sint Maarten/St. Martin cuisine on this island — it doesn't exist. Like the island itself, its food is based on the inspirations of many foreign chefs, notably French, although a few Dutch dishes surface on menus as well. But it's the French cuisine — both the classics such as escargot as well as modern nouvelle touches — that predominate on menus across the island.

In spite of their varied cuisines, nearly all the restaurants have something in common: high prices. Even the cheaper dining choices might be called "upper moderate" on less-expensive islands such as Puerto Rico.

On the upside, however, you get a wealth of dining options on either side of the island. In addition to the Continental dishes, many entrees reflect Creole origins, such as curried conch or a savory fish stew called *blaff,* and most definitely *crabes farcis* (stuffed crabs). But if you want an old-fashioned 1950s-style banana split, bagels and lox New York–style, or a Texas steak, you can find them as well.

The Best Restaurants

Antoine's
$$$ **Philipsburg** **FRENCH/CREOLE/ITALIAN**

A romantic restaurant, set on the waterfront next to the pier, Antoine's is celebrated for making the island's best lobster Thermidor. The restaurant

Sint Maarten/St. Martin Dining

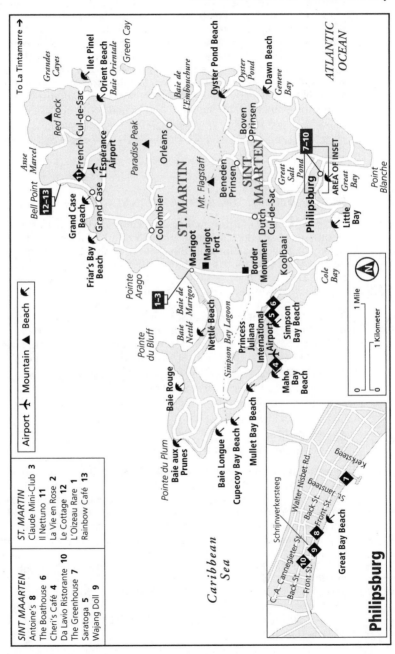

SINT MAARTEN
Antoine's **8**
The Boathouse **6**
Cheri's Café **4**
Da Lavio Ristorante **10**
The Greenhouse **7**
Saratoga **5**
Wajang Doll **9**

ST. MARTIN
Claude Mini-Club **3**
Il Nettuno **11**
La Vie en Rose **2**
Le Cottage **12**
L'Oizeau Rare **1**
Rainbow Café **13**

Airport ✈ Mountain ▲ Beach ⚓

overlooks **Great Bay** on the Dutch side, and tables at night are all aglow with candlelight. The owner, Jean-Pierre, has won a loyal following with many repeat visitors. The restaurant is popular with local business lunchers, drawing a more-international crowd of visitors at night to its first-rate cuisine composed of quality ingredients. Gallic specialties with Creole overtones are on the menu, including one of the island's best fish soups or a homemade pâté. Baked red snapper appears with white wine, lemon, and shallots, and Italian-inspired concoctions include veal scaloppini with a smooth and perfectly balanced sauce of mustard and fresh cream. If you so desire, you can enjoy lunch in a thatched roof hut right on the sand.

See map p. 425. 119 Front St., Philipsburg. ☎ **599-54-22964.** *Reservations recommended in winter. Main courses: Lunch $9–$17, dinner $16–$37. AE, DISC, MC, V. Open: Daily 11 a.m.–10 p.m.*

The Boathouse
$$ Simpson Bay   AMERICAN/INTERNATIONAL

Located just east of Princess Juliana Airport, on the Dutch side, this much-frequented bar and restaurant offers a nautical theme under heavy timbers, opening onto **Simpson Bay Beach.** Both islanders and in-the-know visitors flock here for the good food, affordable prices, and friendly atmosphere. Lunch is a busy time, with the cooks turning out some of the island's best sandwiches, pastas, and freshly made salads. At night the menu grows more ambitious, as does the polished service. Although not exactly flawless in their cuisine, the chefs continue year after year to turn out a time-tested menu that includes pepper steak, filet mignon, surf and turf, and char-grilled red snapper. You can also order the snapper or other catch of the day stuffed and served with a white-wine cream sauce.

See map p. 425. 74 Airport Rd., Simpson Bay. ☎ **599-54-45409.** *Reservations recommended for dinner. Main courses: Lunch $5–$18, dinner $13–$20. DISC, MC, V. Open: Lunch Mon–Sat 11:30 a.m.–3 p.m.; dinner daily 5:30–10:30 p.m.*

Cheri's Café
$$ Maho Beach   AMERICAN

Cheri's Café is the favorite expatriate hangout on the island — and with good reason. Cheri Baston's island hot spot is friendly, affordable, and offers both good food and a good time. This open-air cafe at the Cinnamon Grove Shopping Centre in Sint Maarten can seat as many as 400 revelers in an evening. Basically, the cafe is a roof without walls. Underneath that roof, patrons order more drinks than at any other bar on the island, including the bartender's special, a frozen Straw Hat with vodka, tequila, coconut, strawberry liqueur, and both pineapple and orange juice. Live music entertains nightly from 8 p.m. to about 10 p.m. Oh, yes, the food. It hardly wins any prizes but is substantial and good, including the most often ordered item — a juicy hamburger from the grill. The 18-ounce steaks please visiting Texas cowboys, and beach bums gravitate to the grilled fresh fish platters.

See map p. 425. 45 Cinnamon Grove Shopping Centre, Maho Beach. ☎ 599-54-53361. Reservations recommended. Main courses: $10–$30. DISC, MC, V. Open: Wed–Mon 11 a.m.–midnight. Closed Sept.

Claude Mini-Club
$$ Marigot CREOLE/FRENCH

An island favorite for more than three decades, Claude Mini-Club is prized by discerning visitors as much as die-hard locals. The setting is amusing as it takes up the second floor of a building whose centerpiece is an old tree. Against a backdrop of a Haitian-inspired décor, the restaurant opens onto a big terrace with views of the sea. A burst of yellow and orange, it's a dining delight. For authentic Creole flavor, dig into the stuffed crab with Creole sauce or conch stew in a zesty tomato sauce with hot spices. The grilled crayfish is succulent and tender, and more-classical fare includes a filet of beef, cooked to tender perfection and served with a green peppercorn sauce. Wednesday and Saturday are the most popular nights when the chefs present St. Martin's most tantalizing buffet, complete with roast suckling pig and Caribbean lobster.

See map p. 425. Boulevard de la Mer, Marigot. ☎ 590-590-87-50-69. Reservations required. Main courses: $19–$36. Prix-fixe menu $24. Buffets $48. AE, MC, V. Open: Mon–Sat 11 a.m.–3 p.m. and 6–10 p.m. Closed Sept.

Da Lavio Ristorante
$$$ Philipsburg ITALIAN

For dining Italian style on the Dutch side, Da Lavio Ristorante is as good as it gets. However, Il Nettuno on the French side has a more cutting edge (see our recommendation later in this chapter). While in Philipsburg, put yourself into the gracious hands of Venice-born Bergamasco Livio. He prepares dishes at his Front Street restaurant with ingredients imported from his homeland. The restaurant, rather romantic at night, opens onto a scenic vista of **Great Bay.** As background music plays softly, you can make your selections. The chefs keep faith with the regional traditions of Italy, turning out such classics as a homemade manicotti della casa filled with ricotta, spinach, and a zesty tomato sauce. A specialty is the tender and juicy veal chop with sage-flavored butter. Desserts, such as the *torta de ricottae pinoli* (ricotta cheesecake and pine nuts), the *semifreddo al cioccolato* (Grand Marnier chocolate mousse), or the fresh apple tart are luscious as well.

See map p. 425. 189 Front St., Philipsburg. ☎ 599-54-22690. Reservations recommended for dinner. Main courses: $18–$39. MC, V. Open: Lunch Mon–Fri noon to 2 p.m.; dinner Mon–Sat 6–10 p.m.

The Greenhouse
$$ Philipsburg AMERICAN

Located at Bobby's Marina off Front Street, this plant-filled restaurant provides dining in an open-air atmosphere with a view of the harbor. Well-prepared food at affordable prices keeps guests coming back. For all-around cuisine prepared as it is many places Stateside, The Greenhouse is your best bet in the bustling Dutch capital. This place is also an entertainment center, beginning at happy hour every day from 4:30 to 7 p.m., when it features two-for-one drinks and half-price appetizers. Pool tables and video games keep patrons occupied until the early hours. The food is standard and familiar, but still quite good — especially some of the island's best steaks, each cut certified Angus beef, including New York strip, T-bone, porterhouse, or filet mignon. The lobster Thermidor is a winner, as is the Jamaican jerk pork. Burgers, pizzas, and freshly made salads are other wise choices throughout the day. Sometimes exotic flavors appear that evoke the Caribbean, as in our recently sampled mango chicken.

See map p. 425. Bobby's Marina, Philipsburg. ☎ *599-54-22941. Reservations not required. Main courses: $10–$28. AE, MC, V. Open: Wed-Mon 11 a.m.–midnight; Tues 11 a.m.–2 a.m.*

Il Nettuno
$$$$ Grand Case   ITALIAN

You'll find the island's finest Italian dining along "restaurant row" here on the French side. Raymond Losito ran an acclaimed French restaurant in Washington, D.C., before packing up his kitchen utensils and heading south. Here he took over a building with a wooden veranda and attractively refurbished it, outfitting it in the colors of the Italian flag but retaining his loyalty, as banners indicate, to Washington's Redskins. Most everything in the chef's repertoire has to be imported on this island, but somehow it all tastes fresh. Try the blackened tuna, filet of seawolf cooked in parchment, or the house specialty, sea bass baked in rock salt. He harmoniously blends filet of grouper with prosciutto, and we'd walk a mile (at least) for the lobster risotto. Pastas, too, benefit from the kitchen's magic touch.

See map p. 425. 70 Blvd. de Grand Case, Grand Case. ☎ *590-590-87-77-38. Reservations recommended. Main courses: $22–$33. AE, DISC, MC, V. Open: Daily noon to 2:30 p.m. and 6–10:30 p.m. Closed for lunch Apr–Oct and closed completely in Sept to mid-Oct.*

La Vie en Rose
$$$ Marigot   FRENCH

This enduring St. Martin favorite has long been acclaimed as the grandest classic French restaurant on the island. The earlier you arrive, the better your chance of getting one of the sought-after balcony tables overlooking the harborfront. Menus change daily depending on the availability of ingredients. Ceiling fans, candlelight, and the décor evoke Paris in the 1920s. Dishes are marked by intense, well-defined flavors. Your meal may begin with sautéed fresh foie gras, followed by such main course delights as grilled filet of red snapper in puff pastry with a fresh basil sauce or breast of duck with an orange and walnut sauce. Other harmoniously blended dishes include medallions of smoked lobster with freshly made pasta and herbs and boneless breast of duck with raspberry sauce and fried bananas for a little Caribbean flavor.

See map p. 425. Boulevard de France at rue de la République, Marigot. ☎ *590-590-87-54-42. Reservations required. Main courses: Lunch $10–$22, dinner $24–$42. AE, DISC, MC, V. Open: Lunch Mon–Sat noon to 3 p.m.; dinner daily 6:30–10 p.m.*

Le Cottage
$$$$ Grand Case   FRENCH/CREOLE

In a little town of marvelous restaurants, Le Cottage stands out. It looks like a private house and stands on the inland side of the main road running through this beachfront community. All the region's gourmets, along with a constant stream of visitors, flock here to enjoy the elegant service and the changing array of classic and modern dishes that reflect the razor-sharp techniques of the kitchen staff. Among the selection of tasty dishes is a casserole of crayfish and avocado with a citrus sauce, or some of the best foie gras on the French side of the island. For a main dish specialty, we recommend the roasted rack of lamb with a fresh rosemary sauce or such Creole-inspired dishes as filet of local dorado served with essence of crayfish, a reduction sauce.

See map p. 425. 97 Blvd. de Grand Case, Grand Case. ☎ *590-590-29-03-30. Reservations recommended. Main courses: $27–$59. AE, DC, MC, V. Open: Daily 6–11 p.m.*

L'Oizeau Rare
$$$ Marigot   FRENCH/INTERNATIONAL

Justifiably well regarded, with a certain elegance and formality, this upmarket St. Martin restaurant might be found somewhere in the vicinity of St-Tropez on the French Riviera. Painted in cream and sea blue, the restaurant is housed in an antique building that offers tables with a view of a trio of waterfalls in the well-manicured garden. If you drop in for lunch, you'll dine on a covered terrace. Seasoned gourmets often request the fresh fish of the day such as red snapper or mahi-mahi. For real Caribbean flavor, the latter is sometimes available with a lemon-flavored coconut sauce. You can order a French classic such as filet of lamb with Provençal herbs, or perhaps something more exotic, such as ostrich steak or even duck with mango or raspberries. Firmly grounded in French cuisine, the chef also specializes in bouillabaisse.

See map p. 425. Boulevard de France, Marigot. ☎ *590-590-87-56-38. Reservations recommended. Main courses: Lunch $12–$24, dinner $18–$36. AE, DISC, MC, V. Open: Mon–Sat noon to 2:30 p.m. and 6–10 p.m. Closed in June.*

Rainbow Café
$$$$ Grand Case   FRENCH/INTERNATIONAL

Romantic nights dining at this charmer will be a memory to take back home. One of our favorite dining spots lies on the northeastern end of Grand Case's "restaurant row" in St. Martin, offering casually elegant dining right on the beach, with a view of the little island of Anguilla in the distance. The dining room is on two levels and painted a striking cobalt blue and white. Such a pleasant atmosphere emanates from this rustic abode that you'll want to linger long after dinner over a mellow Cognac. The chefs prepare an appetizing array of dishes that include such delights as chopped lamb with mashed potatoes and an onion-and-garlic marmalade, or red snapper in a Parmesan-onion flaked crust with a tomato-flavored vinaigrette. The menu is closely linked to the seasons, as represented by such unusual taste sensations as a fricassee of scallops and shrimp served with pineapple chutney. Also memorable is chicken breast marinated in lemon grass and ginger and served with grilled balsamic-glazed vegetables.

See map p. 425. 176 Blvd. de Grand Case, Grand Case. ☎ **590-590-87-55-80.** *Reservations recommended. Main courses: $24–$43. MC, V. Open: Mon–Sat 6:30–10:30 p.m.*

Saratoga
$$$ Simpson Bay   INTERNATIONAL

An innovative menu showcases local seafood at this cutting-edge restaurant on the island's Dutch side, enjoying a lovely setting that evokes a Spanish colonial building. You can sit inside or on a veranda overlooking the yacht club marina. Many diners arrive early for one of the bartender's fabled vodka martinis or one of the tangy margaritas. Every two days the chefs change the menu, but they always import quality ingredients, which they fashion into a series of delectable offerings. Inventiveness and a solid technique appear in such rewarding dishes as onion-crusted salmon on a compote of lentils and sweet corn. The menu lives up to its international billing with such dishes as yellowfin tuna grilled and served with basmati rice or wasabi-flavored butter and daikon leaves. Another dish to try is the crispy fried black sea bass with an Asian-style sauce of fermented black beans and scallions. Rack of venison with port-wine sauce is often a feature as well.

See map p. 425. Simpson Bay Yacht Club, Airport Road. ☎ **599-54-42421.** *Reservations recommended. Main courses: $24–$37. AE, MC, V. Open: Mon–Sat 6:30–10:30 p.m. Closed Aug to mid-Oct.*

Wajang Doll
$$$ Philipsburg   INDONESIAN

Dutch settlers brought this authentic cuisine back from the East Indies, and the tradition lives on here in a cement-built West Indian home on Sint Maarten's main street. Even Indonesians agree that Wajang Doll is the best showcase for their cuisine in the Caribbean. Large windows overlook the water in the bay, and the place is especially popular among Dutch expatriates. The chef's justified pride and joy is his 19-dish dinner, known as a *rijsttafel* or rice table in which rice is served with a medley of small, spicy, and tasty dishes. The chef crushes his spices daily for maximum pungency.

Specialties include fried red snapper with ginger, chili, onions, garlic, and lemon grass. Other favorites are Sumatran-style beef with white rice, a spicy seafood tofu, tempura made from soybeans, and zesty Javanese chicken dishes.

See map p. 425. 167 Front St., Philipsburg. ☎ 599-54-22687. Reservations required. Prix-fixe 14-dish rijsttafel dinner $22, 19-dish rijsttafel dinner $28. AE, MC, V. Open: Mon–Sat noon to 2 p.m. and 6:45–10 p.m. Closed Sept.

Enjoying the Sand and Surf

Regardless of where you stay, you're never far from the water. Both the Dutch and French sides of the island offer a full range of water sports from diving to deep-sea fishing. Snorkeling and scuba gear are available at most of the larger resorts.

If you're staying at a small inn, you'll also find a number of independent outfitters who'll link you with your sport of choice. Windsurfers and small sailing craft are easy to come by. At some of the beaches, little kiosks will also hook you up with parasailing or Jet Skiing.

Combing the beaches

The island of Sint Maarten/St. Martin offers 37 lovely white sandy beaches. Chances are your hotel will open onto one of these strips of sand. If not, you can likely find a good beach within a five- to ten-minute walk from your hotel.

 Away from the cruise-ship and vacationing hordes, many beaches on both the Dutch and French sides are relatively unexplored. However, if a beach is too secluded, be careful. Carrying valuables to the beach is unwise — robberies are commonplace on some of the more-remote strips.

 If you're a beach sampler, you can often use the changing facilities at some of the bigger resorts for a small fee. Nudists should head for the French side of the island, although the Dutch side is getting more liberal about such things.

Going Dutch

Popular **Cupecoy Bay Beach** is very close to the Dutch-French border, on the western side of the island. It's a string of three white-sand beaches set against a backdrop of caves, beautiful rock formations, and cliffs that provide morning shade. You don't find any restaurants, bars, or other facilities here, but locals come around with coolers of cold beer and soda for sale. The beach has two parking lots, one near Cupecoy and Sapphire beach clubs, the other a short distance to the west. Parking costs $2. You must descend stone-carved steps to reach the sands. Cupecoy is also the island's major gay beach.

Also on the west side of the island, west of the airport, white-sand **Mullet Bay Beach** is shaded by palm trees. At one time it was the most crowded beach on the island, but Sint Maarten's largest resort, Mullet Bay, remained closed at press time, so the crowds aren't so bad anymore. Weekdays are best, as many locals flock here on weekends. A kiosk here rents water-sports equipment.

Another lovely spot near the airport, **Maho Bay Beach,** at the Maho Beach Hotel and Casino, is shaded by palms and is ideal in many ways, if you don't mind the planes taking off and landing nearby. This beach is one of the busiest on the island, buzzing with windsurfers. Food and drinks are available for purchase at the hotel.

Stretching the length of Simpson Bay Village are the 2km-long (1-mile) white sands of crescent-shaped **Simpson Bay Beach,** west of Philipsburg before you reach the airport. This beach is popular with windsurfers, and it's an ideal place for a stroll or a swim. You can rent water-sports equipment here, but no other facilities are available.

Great Bay Beach is best if you're staying along Front Street in Philipsburg. This 2km-long (1-mile) beach is sandy, but because it borders the busy capital, it may not be as clean as some of the more-remote choices. On a clear day, you'll have a view of Saba. Immediately to the west, at the foot of Fort Amsterdam, is picturesque **Little Bay Beach,** but it, too, can be overrun with visitors. When you tire of the sands here, you can climb up to the site of Fort Amsterdam itself. Built in 1631, it was the first Dutch military outpost in the Caribbean. The Spanish captured it two years later, making it their most important bastion east of Puerto Rico. Only a few of the fort's walls remain, but the view is panoramic.

Heading for the border

On the east side of the island, **Dawn Beach** is noted for its underwater life, with some of the island's most beautiful reefs immediately offshore. Visitors talk ecstatically of its incredible sunrises. Dawn is suitable for swimming and offers year-round activities such as sand castle–building contests and crab races. Plenty of wave action draws both surfers and windsurfers. The road to this beach is bumpy, but worth the effort. Nearby are the pearly white sands of **Oyster Pond Beach,** near the Oyster Bay Beach Resort. Bodysurfers like the rolling waves here.

Parlez-vous français?

Top rating on French St. Martin goes to **Baie Longue** on the west side of the island, a beautiful beach that's rarely overcrowded. Chic, expensive La Samanna opens onto this beachfront. Its reef-protected waters are ideal for snorkeling, but be watchful of the strong undertow. Baie Longue is to the north of **Cupecoy Bay Beach,** reachable via the Lowlands Road.

In spite of its beauty, you can't let your guard down completely while enjoying Baie Longue. Don't leave any valuables in your car, as many break-ins have been reported along this occasionally dangerous stretch of highway.

If you continue north along the highway, you'll reach another long and popular stretch of sand and jagged coral, **Baie Rouge.** Swimming is excellent here, and snorkelers are drawn to the rock formations at both ends of the beach. This intimate little spot is especially lovely in the morning. The beach doesn't have any changing facilities; a local kiosk sells cold drinks.

 Isolated **Friar's Bay Beach** lies at the end of a winding country road; its clearly signposted entrance intersects with the main highway between Grand Case and Marigot. Although you certainly won't be alone here, this is a less-visited beach with ample parking and the occasional top-less sunbathers.

 White-sand **Grand Case Beach** is right in the middle of Grand Case and is likely to be crowded, especially on weekends. The waters are very calm, so swimming is excellent, and this beach is a good choice for kids. A small but select beach, it has its own charm, with none of the carnival-like atmosphere found elsewhere.

On the eastern side of the island, **Orient Beach** is the island's only offi-cial nudist beach. Bouncy Caribbean bands, refreshments of all kinds, water sports, and clothing, crafts, and jewelry vendors keep the action going all day on its stretch of velvety white sands. The coral reef off the beach teems with marine life, making for great snorkeling. Club Orient, the nude resort, is at the end of the beach; voyeurs from cruise ships are always present. This is also a haven for windsurfers.

 Finally, for the most isolated and secluded beach of all, you have to leave St. Martin. **Ilet Pinel,** off the coast at Cul de Sac, is reached by a boat ride off the Northeast Coast (you can hire a local boatman to take you from Cul de Sac for about $5 one-way). The island has no residents (except wild goats), phones, or electricity. You'll find fine white-sand beaches, idyllic reefs with great snorkeling (although you can't rent equipment on the island), and waters great for bodysurfing. Two beach bars rent lounge chairs and serve dishes such as lobster, ribs, and grilled chicken.

Playing in the surf

For great scuba diving, many sportsmen fly to Saba (or take a boat), Sint Maarten's neighboring island, which is also Dutch affiliated. However, Sint Maarten also has fine diving all on its own. Offshore visibility is usu-ally excellent averaging some 30m (100 ft.). Snorkeling is also excellent, particularly around the rocks below Fort Amsterdam off Little Bay Beach and around Dawn Beach and Oyster Pond.

Diving right in

Scuba diving is excellent around St. Martin, with reef, wreck, night, cave, and drift diving; the depth of dives is 6 to 21m (20–70 ft.). Off the Northeastern Coast on the French side, dive sites include **Ilet Pinel,** for shallow diving; **Green Key,** a barrier reef; and **Tintamarre,** for sheltered coves and geologic faults. To the north, **Anse Marcel** and neighboring **Anguilla** are good choices. Most hotels arrange scuba excursions on request.

The island's premier dive operation is **Scuba Fun,** whose offices are immediately adjacent to the West Indies Mall on the French side, Chemin du Port, Marigot (☎ **590-590-87-36-13**). Operated by Englishman Philip Baumann, it offers morning and afternoon dives in deep and shallow water, wreck dives, and reef dives, at a cost of $40 per dive. A resort course for first-time divers with reasonable swimming skills costs $75 and includes 60 to 90 minutes of instruction in a swimming pool and a one-tank dive above a coral reef. Full PADI certification, an experience that requires five days and includes classroom training sessions with a scuba tank in the safety of a swimming pool and three open-water dives, costs $350.

Sint Maarten's crystal-clear bays and countless coves make for good scuba diving as well as snorkeling. Underwater visibility runs from 23 to 38m (75–125 ft.). The biggest attraction for divers is the 1801 British man-of-war, **HMS *Proselyte,*** which came to a watery grave on a reef 2km (1 mile) off the coast. Most of the big resorts have facilities for scuba diving and can provide information about underwater tours, photography, and night diving.

Snorkeling adventures

The calm waters ringing the shallow reefs and tiny coves found throughout make the island a snorkeler's heaven. The waters off the northeastern shores of French St. Martin are classified as a regional underwater nature reserve, **Réserve Sous-Marine Régionale,** which protects the area around Flat Island (also known as Tintamarre), Ilet Pinel, Green Key, Proselyte, and Petite Clef. You can rent equipment at almost any hotel, and most beaches have water-sports kiosks.

One of St. Martin's best sources for snorkeling and other beach diversions is **Carib Watersports** (☎ **590-590-87-51-87**), a clothing store, art gallery, and water-sports kiosk on the beachfront of the Grand Case Beach Club. Its French and U.S. staff provides information on island activities and rents kayaks for $20 an hour, paddle boats for $25 an hour, and snorkeling equipment for $10 a day. The main allure, however, is the guided snorkeling trips to St. Martin's teeming offshore reefs, including **Creole Rock,** an offshore clump of reef-ringed boulders rich in underwater fauna. The 1½-hour trips depart daily at 10 a.m., noon, and 2 p.m., and cost $30, with all equipment included. Reservations are recommended.

The dive outfitter **Scuba Fun** (see the preceding section) also arranges snorkeling trips, which cost $30 for a half-day plus $10 for equipment rental.

The best scuba-diving outfitters on the Dutch side are **Dive Safaris,** Bobby's Marina, Philipsburg (☎ 599-54-29001), and **The Scuba Shop,** La Palapa Marina, Simpson Bay (☎ 599-54-53213).

Water-skiing and parasailing

Most of French St. Martin's large beachfront hotels maintain facilities for water-skiing and parasailing, often from kiosks that operate on the beach.

Two independent operators on Baie Orientale, close to the cluster of hotels near the Esmeralda Hotel, include **Kon Tiki Watersports** (☎ 590-590-87-46-89) and **Bikini Beach Watersports** (☎ 590-590-87-43-25). They both rent Jet Skis for around $40 to $45 per half-hour; parasailing costs $50 for ten minutes, or $80 if two go together.

Jet-Skiing and water-skiing are also especially popular in Dutch Sint Maarten. The unruffled waters of **Simpson Bay Lagoon,** the largest lagoon in the West Indies, are ideal for these sports, and outfitters have facilities right on the sands.

Boarding the surf

Most windsurfers gravitate to the eastern part of the island, most notably **Coconut Grove Beach, Orient Beach,** and to a lesser extent, **Dawn Beach.** The best of the several outfitters here is **Tropical Wave,** Coconut Grove, Le Galion Beach, Baie de l'Embouchure (☎ 590-590-87-37-25). Set midway between Orient Beach and Oyster Pond, the beach here has an ideal combination of wind and calm waters. Tropical Wave is the island's leading sales agent for Mistral Windsurfers. They rent for $24 per hour, with instruction available for $36 per hour.

In Sint Maarten, visitors usually head to **Simpson Bay Lagoon** for windsurfing, where plenty of outfitters have taken up shop right on the sand.

Reeling in the big one

Sailfish, wahoo, tuna, dolphin fish (mahi-mahi), and marlin are all around for the catching in offshore waters. Most outfitters can tailor their trips to cater to the needs of their on-board fishermen, whether experienced anglers or novices.

Pelican Watersports, on the Dutch side, at the Pelican Resort and Casino, Simpson Bay (☎ 599-54-42640), is part of one of the island's most comprehensive resorts. Their 12m (40-ft.) *Kratuna* is available for deep-sea fishing expeditions priced at $125 for a half-day excursion (7:30–11 a.m.) or $250 for a full day (7:30 a.m.–3 p.m.). Another well-recommended fishing charter is **Rudy's Deep Sea Fishing,** 14 Airport

Rd., Simpson Bay (☎ 599-54-52177), one of the best in the business. Half-day (8 a.m. to noon) excursions cost $450, with full-day (8 a.m.–4 p.m.) jaunts going for $750.

Climbing aboard

Sint Maarten/St. Martin offers more sailing excursions than almost any other island in the Caribbean. The waters enveloping the island are idyllic for sailing. Speedboats, Jet Skis, sailboats, motorboats, and other craft are available for rent at a number of locations.

Seaworld Explorer, Boulevard de Grand Case at Grand Case (☎ 599-54-24078), is a semisubmersible submarine, featuring daytrips from Grand Case to Creole Rock. Large windows allow you to view the multicolored marine life and the stunning coral reefs. A highlight of the trip is when a diver feeds the fish and eels. This trip costs $30 for adults and $20 for children.

Random Wind (☎ 599-55-75742) is a 16m (54-ft.) schooner, carrying 18 passengers on half-day and full-day sailing charters around Sint Maarten to secluded coves. The charter features snorkeling (and provides the gear), beaches, coastal sightseeing, and an open bar. The cost is $85 per passenger per full day or $50 for children under 12.

Exploring on Dry Land

You come to Sint Maarten/St. Martin for its natural sights, its beaches, and its sea excursions — not for man-made attractions. But for those who want a goal to their sightseeing, a few diversions are worth your time.

Chasing butterflies

Far from the crowds, you may want to seek a bucolic part of St. Martin — the little village of **Orléans** (also called the French Quarter), which is the island's oldest French settlement. Its houses (called *cases*) are set in meadows that blossom with hibiscus, bougainvillea, and wisteria. On the road to Bayside and Galion is the charming **Butterfly Farm,** Route de Le Galion (☎ 590-590-87-31-21), run by two Englishmen who created this Eden-like setting. Visitors receive a rare insight into the amazing transformations between an egg and a butterfly. You learn all about these delicate creatures and meet such beauties as the Brazilian blue morpho and the Cambodian wood nymph. Hours are daily from 9 a.m. to 3 p.m., and admission is $12.

Spending a day at a nudist beach

Many cruise-ship passengers, in St. Martin only for two or three hours, head immediately to the wild and wacky beach at **Baie Orientale,** especially if they have a voyeuristic streak. This is the best-known clothing-optional beach in the Caribbean, and most of the bodies on display are at the naturalist resort Club Orient, at the middle of the beach.

In the center are several local hangouts, often with bars and restaurants featuring live bands throughout the day. Our favorite spot is the open-air bar/restaurant **Kontiki** (☎ **590-590-87-43-27**), where most patrons are clothed; the nudie area for the less-inhibited drinker is a short stroll away. You can stick around for lunch, ordering reasonably good sushi or fresh lobster from saltwater holding tanks. After lunch you can rent a Jet Ski, go parasailing, join in a Hobie Cat race (a type of boat race), or try some snorkeling.

People-watching in Philipsburg

At **Wathey Square** (pronounced *waht*-ee), in the center of Sint Maarten's Dutch capital, you can sit and watch the world go by. This square is the heartbeat of the thriving little town, with its duty-free shops. It's filled with tourists and cruise-ship passengers, trinket peddlers, vendors, and all sorts of shops. The building across the street from the square, with its white cupola, dates from 1793 and has been everything from a jail to a fire station, but today it's the town hall and courthouse.

Directly off the square is the town's largest collection of shops, restaurants, and cafes, most of them on **Front Street.** Running parallel to Front Street is the so-called Back Street, which also has a cluster of shops, cafes, and restaurants. Branching off from here are little narrow alleyways called *steegjes.* Take any one of them for an adventure. You'll pass through arcades with flower-filled courtyards, more little shops, and plenty of eateries. The town is filled with West Indian cottages decorated with gingerbread trim.

Boating to remote Ilet Pinel

At the north end of Baie Orientale on the Atlantic Coast, **Etang de la Parrière** is the island's most beautiful cove, its sand banks filled with hundreds of ancient shells. Offshore to the north is the remote Ilet Pinel, with fine white-sand beaches and reefs idyllic for snorkeling. Sometimes schools of rainbow-hued fish surround this island. The only inhabitants, other than visitors for the day, are wild goats feeding on the cacti and scrub brush. In an hour you can traverse the entire island. At Cul de Sac, the settlement on the French side, you can take a shuttle boat to this little bit of Eden ($5 round-trip).

Meandering through Marigot

The capital of French St. Martin is a colorful place for wandering, taking in its lovely waterfront, West Indian vendors, chic French boutiques, and open-air cafes and restaurants. The best streets for wandering, especially if you're a shopper, are **rue de la Liberté** and **rue de la République,** bordering the bay.

The best photo op is at the **Marina Royale** shopping complex at the harborfront. On Thursday nights, the shops remain open until 10 p.m., and live bands perform. To crown your visit, you can climb up to **Fort Louis**, which towers over the town. French soldiers built this fort in 1789. From its lofty precincts, one of the most panoramic views on the island unfolds.

Climbing the highest peak

From Friar's Bay Beach on the French side, near the settlement of Orléans, you take a rough, tree-canopied road, **Route de Pic du Paradis,** to the highest point on the island — the top of **Pic du Paradis** (Paradise Peak), at 455m (1,492 ft.). If you manage to get here, the views are the most panoramic on the island.

After your look, you can head for **Loterie Farm** at the foot of this mountain. This 61-hectare (150-acre) farm stands on the grounds of a former sugar plantation. Opened to the public in 1999, the farm is the domain of B. J. Welch, an American expatriate, and is the only private nature reserve on the island. The site affords a rare look at a West Indian rain forest, with aged mango trees, guavaberry trees, and dozens of other rare tropical plants and trees. Mr. Welch offers a number of activities here, including eco-tours, horseback riding, mountain biking, and hiking. You can also stop in for lunch at the Hidden Forest Café. The farm stands at Route de Pic du Paradis (☎ **590-590-87-86-16**) and is open daily from sunrise to sunset. A 1½-hour tour costs $25, and a 4-hour tour is $35.

Keeping Active

Golf on either side of the island doesn't compare with the courses on, say, Puerto Rico, but if golf is an integral part of your vacation, Sint Maarten has a course to suit your needs. Horseback riding along the sandy beaches is one of the island's best activities, and all the big resorts have tennis courts.

Linking up with a round of golf

The **Mullet Bay Resort** (☎ **599-54-53069**), on the Dutch side, has the island's only golf course. It's a slightly battered, slightly dusty 18-hole Joseph Lee–designed course, whose fate has hung in the balance, based on some ongoing court battles, for years. Although the resort itself is closed, the golf course is still operational. Mullet Pond and Simpson Bay Lagoon provide both beauty and hazards. Greens fees are $60 for 9 holes or $88 for 18 holes for players who opt to walk instead of ride. Renting an electric cart, serviceable for up to two players at a time, costs an additional $8 to $18, depending on how many holes you play. Club rentals cost $21 for 9 holes or $26 for 18 holes.

Horseback riding

One of the most memorable experiences on the island is to ride a horse along one of the white sandy beaches. Stables on both sides of the island charge about $60 per person for two hours of riding. Our favorite outfitter is **Bayside Riding Club,** Route Galion Beach, Baie Orientale (☎ 590-590-87-36-64). Another good stable, on the Dutch side, is called **Lucky Stables,** Traybay Drive, Cay Bay (☎ 599-54-45255), which features not only beach rides, but trailblazing into the hills as well. Romantics might ask about their champagne night ride.

Playing tennis

You can try the courts at most of the large resorts, but you must call first for a reservation. Preference, of course, goes to hotel guests.

On the Dutch side, **The Pelican,** Simpson Bay (☎ 599-54-42503), **Divi Little Bay Beach Resort,** Little Bay Road (☎ 599-54-22333), and **Maho Beach Hotel,** Maho Bay (☎ 599-54-52115), each have three courts that are lit for night play. You must be staying at the Pelican or Divi Little Bay to play those courts.

On the French side, the **Privilège Resort & Spa,** Anse Marcel (☎ 590-590-87-46-15), offers four lit tennis courts and two squash courts; and the **Hotel Mont Vernon,** Baie Orientale (☎ 590-590-87-62-00), has two courts.

Taking a Guided Tour

Two companies offering bus tours of the island's Dutch side are **Dutch Tours,** Cougar Road, 8 Unit One (☎ 599-54-23316) and **Sint Maarten Sightseeing Tours** (☎ 599-54-53921), whose buses can accommodate anywhere from 22 to 56 passengers. Tour prices vary depending on how many people booked on any given tour and what bus you're assigned. Always clarify which bus you want when calling for a reserved seat.

On the French side, you can book tours through **R&J Tours,** north of Marigot at Colombier (☎ 590-590-87-56-20), now only a car renting agency.

Shopping the Local Stores

The arrival of some 500 cruise ships a year at the port of Philipsburg on the Dutch side has turned Front Street and the capital town itself into one giant shopping bazaar. The variety of duty-free shops, selling merchandise at 30 to 50 percent below stateside (or Canadian) levels, make Sint Maarten a rival of St. Thomas in the U.S. Virgin Islands.

The best buys are likely to be in Irish linen, Scandinavian crystal, leather, designer fashions, Swiss watches, French perfumes, and jewelry. Although shopping isn't heavily developed in French St. Martin, the little boutiques here often carry exquisite merchandise shipped in from Paris, along with the French perfumes and fashion.

On Dutch Sint Maarten

Not only is Sint Maarten a free port, but also it has no local sales tax. Prices are sometimes lower here than anywhere else in the Caribbean, except possibly St. Thomas. On some items (fine liqueurs, cigarettes, Irish linen, German cameras, French perfumes), we've found prices 30 to 50 percent lower than in the U.S. or Canada.

Except for the boutiques at resort hotels, the main shopping area is in the center of **Philipsburg.** Most of the shops line **Front Street** (called Voorstraat in Dutch), which stretches for about 2km (1 mile). More shops sit along the little lanes, known as *steegjes,* that connect Front Street with **Back Street** (Achterstraat), another shoppers' haven.

In general, the prices marked on the merchandise are firm, though at some small, very personally run shops where the owner is on-site, bargaining may be in order.

If you're just starting out your trip and realize you've forgotten your camera, you may want to hit the **Caribbean Camera Centre,** 79 Front St. (☎ 599-54-25259). This shop has a wide range of merchandise, but knowing the prices charged back home before making a major purchase is always wise. Cameras here may be among the cheapest on Sint Maarten; however, we've discovered better deals on St. Thomas.

Bringing home a taste of Sint Maarten

Guavaberry Company, 8–10 Front St. (☎ 599-54-22965), sells the rare "island folk liqueur" of Sint Maarten, which for centuries locals made only in their private homes. This rum-based liqueur is flavored with rare guavaberries, usually grown in the hills in the center of the island. (Don't confuse guavaberries with guavas — they're very different.) The liqueur has a fruity, woody, almost bittersweet flavor. You can blend it with coconut for a guavaberry colada or pour a splash into a glass of icy champagne. Gift items and various hot sauces are also for sale.

Antillean Liquors, Princess Juliana Airport (☎ 599-54-54267), has a complete assortment of liquor and liqueurs (including the guavaberry island liqueur), cigarettes, and cigars. Prices are generally lower here than in other stores on the island, and the selection is larger.

Belgian Chocolate Shop, 109 Old St. (☎ 599-54-28863), is the best of its kind on the island. Contrary to popular rumor, only *some* of the velvety chocolates sold in this upscale shop are pornographic.

Decorating yourself or your home

Del Sol Sint Maarten, 23 Front St. (☎ 599-54-28784), sells men's and women's sportswear. Embedded into the mostly black-and-white designs are organic crystals that react to ultraviolet light, which transforms the fabric into a rainbow of colors. Step back into the shadows, and the colors disappear.

Colombian Emeralds International, Old Street Shopping Center (☎ 599-54-23933), sells unmounted emeralds from Colombia, as well as emerald, gold, diamond, ruby, and sapphire jewelry. Prices are approximately the same as in other outlets of this famous Caribbean chain.

Some huckster vendors around the island pawn fakes to unsuspecting tourists; if you're seriously shopping for emeralds, Colombian Emeralds International is the place.

Little Switzerland, 52 Front St. (☎ 599-54-22523), is part of a chain of stores spread throughout the Caribbean. These fine-quality European imports are made even more attractive by the prices, often 25 percent (or more) lower than stateside. Elegant famous-name watches, china, crystal, and jewelry are for sale, plus perfume and accessories. Little Switzerland has the best overall selection of these items of any shop on the Dutch side.

Prices at the upscale **Little Europe,** 80 Front St. (☎ 599-54-24371), are inexpensive compared to North American boutiques. Inventory includes porcelain figurines by Hummel; jewelry; and watches by Concorde, Piaget, Corum, and Movado.

Decking the walls

Greenwich Galleries, 20 Front St. (☎ 599-54-23842), is the most sophisticated art gallery on the island, with Bajan pottery in tones of sea greens and blues, replicas of Taíno artifacts from the Dominican Republic, enameled metal cutouts that are both quirky and perplexing, and an international array of paintings and lithographs.

On French St. Martin

Many day-trippers come over to Marigot from the Dutch side of the island just to visit the French-inspired boutiques and shopping arcades. Because St. Martin is also a duty-free port, you'll find some of the best shopping in the Caribbean here as well, with a wide selection of European merchandise, much of it luxury items such as crystal, fashions, fine liqueurs, and cigars, sometimes at 25 percent to 50 percent less than in the United States and Canada. Whether you're seeking jewelry, perfume, or St-Tropez bikinis, you'll find what you're looking for in one of the boutiques along **rue de la République** and **rue de la Liberté** in Marigot. Look especially for French luxury items, such as Lalique crystal, Vuitton bags, and Chanel perfume.

Prices are often quoted in U.S. dollars, and salespeople frequently speak English. Vendors generally accept credit cards and traveler's checks. When cruise ships are in port on Sundays and holidays, some of the larger shops stay open.

At harborside in Marigot, a lively **morning market** features vendors selling spices, fruit, shells, and handicrafts. Shops here tend to be rather upscale, catering to passengers of the small but choice cruise ships that dock offshore.

At bustling **Port La Royale,** mornings are even more active: Schooners unload produce from the neighboring islands, boats board guests for picnics on deserted beaches, a brigantine sets out on a sightseeing sail, and a dozen different little restaurants are readying for the lunch crowd. The largest shopping arcade on St. Martin, Port La Royale has lots of boutiques.

Walking out in style

Havane Boutique, 50 Marina Port La Royale (☎ 590-590-87-70-39), is a hyperstylish menswear store, more couture than ready-to-wear. **Serge Blanco "15" Boutique,** Marina Port La Royale (☎ 590-590-29-65-49), is a relatively unknown name in North America, but in France, Blanco is revered as one of the most successful rugby players of all time. His menswear is sporty, fun, and elegant.

The **Galerie Périgourdine** complex, facing the post office, also has a cluster of boutiques. Here you might pick up designer wear for both men and women, including items from the collection of Ted Lapidus.

Act III, 3 rue du Général-de-Gaulle (☎ 590-590-29-28-43), is the most glamorous women's boutique on St. Martin. It prides itself on its evening gowns and chic cocktail dresses. The bilingual staff is accommodating, tactful, and charming.

La Romana, 12 rue de la République (☎ 590-590-87-88-16), specializes in chic women's clothing, swimwear, handbags, and perfumes, and its selection is a bit less pretentious and more fun and lighthearted than Act III's. The emphasis is on Italian rather than French designers. A small collection of menswear is also available.

Adorning your home or office

Gingerbread & Mahogany Gallery, 4–14 Marina Royale (☎ 590-590-87-73-21), featuring Haitian art, is among the finest galleries on the island, though not the easiest to find (on a narrow alleyway at the marina). Both fine art and charming, inexpensive crafts are for sale.

Roland Richardson Paintings and Prints, 6 rue de la République (☎ 590-590-87-84-08), is a beautiful gallery. A native of St. Martin, Mr. Richardson is one of the Caribbean's premier artists, working in oil, watercolors, pastels, and charcoal. Called a "modern-day Gauguin," he is known for his landscapes, portraits, and still lifes.

Considering a little bit of everything

Maneks, 24 rue de la République (☎ 590-590-87-54-91), has a little bit of everything: video cameras, electronics, liquors, gifts, souvenirs, beach accessories, film, watches, T-shirts, sunglasses — even Cuban cigars (no, you can't bring them home).

Living It Up After Dark

After-dark activities begin early here, as guests start off with a sundowner, perhaps on the garden patio of **Pasanggrahan Royal Inn.** The most popular bar on the island is **Cheri's Café.** (See our recommendations for both hot spots earlier in this chapter.)

Many hotels sponsor **beachside barbecues** (particularly in season) with steel bands, native music, and folk dancing. Outsiders are welcome at most of these events, but call ahead to see if it's a private affair.

Checking out the bar scene

Sunset Beach Bar, 2 Beacon Hill Rd., Airport Beach (☎ 599-54-53998), is directly on the sands of the Dutch side's Airport Beach and resembles an oversize gazebo. This place is mobbed most afternoons and evenings with office workers, off-duty airline pilots, beach people, and occasional celebs like Sandra Bullock. No one seems to mind the whine of airplane engines overhead, or the fumes that filter down from aircraft, which seem to fly at precarious altitudes just a few dozen feet overhead. Drinks are cheap, and you can order burgers, sandwiches, steaks, fish, chicken, and hot dogs from an outdoor charcoal grill. Many local residents time their arrival here for sundown (usually beginning around 6:30 p.m.), when shooters of the day cost only $1 each.

At the previously recommended **The Boathouse,** 74 Airport Rd., Sint Maarten (☎ 599-54-45409), you get not only good food and drinks but entertainment as well.

On the French side in Grand Case, **Calmos Café,** Blvd. du Grand Case no. 4, St. Martin (☎ 590-590-29-01-85), is funky and low-key. This beachfront shack draws a young, hip crowd, with an occasional pop icon like Linda Evangelista dropping in. In winter, the cafe sometimes has live music after 9:30 p.m. Good, affordable food is available, if you like. Jazz and lounge music accompany your meal. The house special drink is a Ti Punch, a local variation on an old-fashioned rum punch. Open daily from 10 a.m. to 1 a.m.

From the Orient Beach parking lot, **Kon Tiki** (☎ 590-87-43-27) is the most distant of the several bars that flank the sands of Orient Bay.

Inside, you'll find everything you'll need to amuse yourself for a day at the beach. Facilities include two bars, a water-sports facility, volleyball courts, and a bandstand where there's often live music. On Sunday there is a beach party. Chaise longues with mattresses rent for $6 for a full day's use, and there's a staff member who'll bring you drinks like Sex on the Beach ($5). If you opt to spend part of a day here, you won't be alone. Sundays are particularly animated, thanks to a live band that plays between 3 and 8 p.m. and around midnight, and a mousse machine that spits out dozens of gallons of foam onto the party goers gathered on the outdoor deck. The party goes until 4 a.m. Sunday, year-round.

Rolling 'em high and low

Casino Royale, at the Sonesta Maho Beach Resort & Casino on Maho Bay, Sint Maarten (☎ 599-54-52590), has the usual casino fare (blackjack, roulette, craps, stud poker, slot machines), but raises the stakes with baccarat and minibaccarat. It's open daily from 2 p.m. to 4 a.m. The **Showroom Royale** is the largest and most technologically sophisticated theater on either side of Sint Maarten/St. Martin; its glittery shows change according to whatever act is booked. Within the same building is the island's loudest disco, the **Q-Club.** Containing wraparound catwalks that look down on the dance floor, multiple bars, and colored lights, the Q-Club is open nightly from around 10 p.m., attracting dancers from both sides of the island. Sometimes, depending on the season and the night of the week, the club imposes a cover charge between $5 and $10.

One of the island's most visited casinos, the **Oasis** is at The Caravanserai on Sint Maarten's Beacon Hill Road (☎ 599-54-54000). Gamblers start pouring in here at 3 p.m. daily, some staying until 4 the next morning. **Pelican Resort Club,** Simpson Bay, Sint Maarten (☎ 599-54-44463), has a popular Vegas-style casino with a panoramic view of the bay. The Pelican also features horse-racing, bingo, and sports nights with events broadcast via satellite, plus nightly dancing on the Pelican Reef Terrace and island shows featuring Caribbean bands. Open daily from 2 p.m. to 4 a.m.

Right in the heart of the Dutch Philipsburg's shopping-crazed Front Street, **Rouge et Noir** (☎ 599-54-22952) has a futuristic design. It offers slot machines, a Sigma Derby horse machine, video Keno, and video poker. The joint opens Monday to Saturday at 9 a.m. and Sunday at 11 a.m. to snag cruise-ship passengers.

Fast Facts: Sint Maarten/St. Martin

Area Code

The area code for Dutch Sint Maarten is **599**; for French St. Martin, **590.** When dialing French St. Martin, each phone number also begins with 590, so you must dial 590 twice.

ATMs

All island banks have ATMs. On the Dutch side, the most central one is RBTT, Emnaplein in Philipsburg (☎ 599-54-23344); on the French side, Banque des Antilles

Françaises, rue de la République, Marigot (☎ 590-590-29-13-30).

Babysitters

Most hotels can arrange this service for you at a cost of $8 to $10 per hour.

Emergencies

On the Dutch side, call the police at ☎ 599-54-22222 or an ambulance at ☎ 599-54-22111, or report a fire at ☎ 911 or ☎ 120.

On the French side, you can reach the police by dialing ☎ 17 or 590-590-87-88-33. In case of fire, dial ☎ 18.

Hospitals

On the Dutch side, go to the Medical Center, Welegen Road, Cay Hill (☎ 599-54-31111). On the French side, the local hospital is Hôpital Concordia Mont Accords (☎ 590-590-52-25-25).

Information

See the Appendix for helpful Web sites and locations of local tourist offices.

Internet Access

Chances are you can avail yourself of this service at your hotel.

Newspapers and Magazines

The *New York Times* and the *Miami Herald* are flown in daily, and *Time* and *Newsweek* are available at local stands. An English-language newspaper, the *Daily Herald,* is widely distributed on the Dutch side of the island and contains information about local events.

Pharmacies

The most central drugstore on the Dutch side is Central Drug Store, Camille Richardson St., Philipsburg (☎ 599-54-22321). On the French side, try Pharmacie

du Port, rue de la Liberté, Marigot (☎ 590-590-87-50-79).

Police

In Dutch Sint Maarten, call the police at ☎ 599-54-22222; on the French side, dial ☎ 17.

Post Office

On the Dutch side, the main post office is at Walter Nisbeth Road in Philipsburg; on the French side, on rue de la Liberté in Marigot.

Restrooms

In downtown Philipsburg, you'll find public restrooms with running water adjacent to the marketplace, midway between Front Street and Back Street. In downtown Marigot, on the French side, you'll find public restrooms with running water at the Marketplace adjacent to the harborfront. But other than that, you have to duck into one of many bars, hotels, and restaurants, each of which is required by local ordinance to allow nonpatrons to use their facilities. A few of the local bars may resist, and a very few of them may display signs announcing that they charge $1 for nonpatrons, but in reality, these charges are rarely collected. If you're really desperate and faced with such a sign, we advise buying a cold drink at the bar before or after using the facilities.

Safety

If possible, avoid night driving — it's particularly unwise to drive on remote, unlit, back roads at night. Also, let that deserted, isolated beach remain so. You're safer in a crowd, although under no circumstances should you ever leave anything unguarded on the beach.

Smoking

Smoking policies are left to the discretion of the individual establishments, and most restaurants have designated nonsmoking sections within their restaurants and bars. With so many open-air establishments, the natural ventilation of the trade winds helps resolve conflicts.

Taxes

Departures from Esperance Airport on the French side cost 3€ ($3.60). For departures from Princess Juliana Airport on the Dutch side, the departure tax is $30 ($10 if you're leaving the island for St. Eustatius or Saba).

On the Dutch side, a government tax of between 5 and 8 percent, depending on the category of hotel you stay in, is added to hotel bills. On the French side, hotels must levy a *taxe de séjour* (hotel tax); this differs from hotel to hotel, depending on its classification, but is often 5 percent a day. In addition to these taxes, most hotels add a mandatory service charge of around 10 to 15 percent to your bill.

Taxis

In Dutch Sint Maarten, call ☎ 599-54-54317; in French St. Martin, ☎ 590-590-87-56-54.

Weather Updates

Go to www.weather.com for updates.

Chapter 17

The U.S. Virgin Islands

*L*ying 1,609km (1,000 miles) from the southern tip of Florida, the trio of U.S. Virgin Islands — St. Thomas, St. Croix, and St. John — is billed as the "American Paradise." That is a gross exaggeration, of course. American Caribbean would be more apt. Yet the islands are populated with a blend of American expatriates and native-born islanders who do live more or less in harmony.

St. Thomas is the most visited of the islands in the U.S. archipelago, thanks to a combination of cruise-ship passengers and other vacationers. Its panoramically scenic harbor at Charlotte Amalie is rivaled only by San Juan as the most active cruise port in the Caribbean. The island is also the shopping mecca of the West Indies, and many cruise-ship passengers arrive to shop — a more important activity to some than hitting the beaches.

Our favorite of the island trio, tiny St. John, lies only a short ferry ride from St. Thomas. Two-thirds of St. John is a national park, and the island possesses a laid-back, casual feel that attracts far more artists than any other island in the Caribbean.

The largest of the U.S. Virgin Islands, St. Croix is often overlooked, yet its atmosphere is unique. It boasts plenty of beaches for exploration, and it has two towns known for their colonial architecture, the capital at Christiansted and the second city, Frederiksted, where cruise ships arrive.

White-sand beaches or golden sands trace all these islands, but each of the three is remarkably different from the rest. If you visit one island, you haven't seen the others. The lucky visitor is the one who plans a trip long enough to sample all three. Even if you're visiting only St. Thomas, in just a day or even a half-day if you're rushed, you can take the ferry over to St. John for a tour in a safari bus.

Arriving at the Airport

Except for San Juan, **Charlotte Amalie,** capital of St. Thomas, is easier to reach by air or sea from the U.S. mainland than any other destination in the Caribbean. From St. Thomas, you can make easy connections by air to St. Croix or by ferryboat to St. John.

All the U.S. Virgins, especially St. Thomas, are major stopovers for cruise ships as well. St. Thomas can also serve as your gateway to the British Virgin Islands (see Chapter 11) because the BVIs aren't serviced by direct flights from the U.S. mainland.

You land on narrow St. Thomas (19km/12 miles long and 4.8km/3 miles wide) at its western edge, right outside the capital of Charlotte Amalie. **Cyril E. King Airport** (☎ 340-774-5100) is modest but handles a lot of traffic, including continuing flights to St. Croix as well as the British Virgin Islands.

If you live in an East Coast city such as Miami or New York, you can fly out in the morning and within three to four hours be resting on the beach on St. Thomas. As a U.S. citizen, you avoid the long lines at U.S. Customs. You walk right into the airport and head for ground transportation.

Before leaving the airport, pick up free copies of *What to Do: St. Thomas & St. John* and *This Week in St. Croix* — you'll find stacks of them around the airport (as well as in hotels, restaurants, and shops on the islands). These helpful little magazines are kept up-to-date with news on island happenings. They also contain coupons for discounts to use later for restaurants, tours, sightseeing, and whatever.

In addition, you'll find ATMs and a branch of the tourist office dispensing information.

Getting from the Airport to Your Hotel

Because most visitors to the USVIs arrive on St. Thomas, this section guides you either directly to your hotel or to means for making your way to your next destination.

If you're staying on **St. Thomas:**

> ✔ **By taxi:** Unlike Jamaica, most resorts on St. Thomas won't have a hotel van waiting to take you for free to your hotel. Regulated by the Virgin Island Taxi Commission, taxi vans meet all incoming flights. A ride into the capital, Charlotte Amalie, takes 20 minutes

unless you run into morning or late-afternoon rush-hour traffic. The commission sets fees: The typical fare for two or more sharing a taxi is $12 to **Frenchman's Reef & Morning Star Marriott Beach Resort.** You're charged $2 to $4 extra for each piece of luggage. Most of the resorts are in the island's East End, which you can reach in 30 minutes, unless you encounter heavy traffic (then count on 45 minutes or more). For 24-hour radio taxi dispatch service, call ☎ 340-774-7457.

✔ **By car:** The major car-rental firms from the U.S. are ready and waiting for you at the airport. Giving them serious competition are a number of island-based, smaller car-rental outfitters where you can sometimes make a good deal. These independents on St. Thomas are more reliable than any of the similar firms throughout the Caribbean. Even before you go, you can often make a good deal with one of the four national biggies (Avis, Budget, Hertz, and National), especially in the off season. (For contact information for both local and national agencies, see the section "Getting Around the USVIs," later in this chapter.) A midsize vehicle costs from $320 per week. Nearly all cars come with air-conditioning and automatic transmission. In summer, many hotel packages include a rental car, at least for a day or two, and many private villas also include the price of your auto.

If you're uncertain of your home car-insurance policy and feel you need extra **collision damage insurance,** the daily costs range from $14 to $18 in most cases. Check local policies carefully. Even with this extra insurance you could still get hit with a huge deductible. This policy varies from rental company to rental company — from $250 to $500 per contract, depending on the fine print.

Even though St. Thomas is part of the U.S. territories, driving is still on the left, dating from the days of the Danish occupation. In town, the speed limit is 32kmph (20 mph), rising to only 56kmph (35 mph) out on the island. When you see the local roads, you won't want to speed anyway. Nighttime driving is hazardous because of poorly lit, narrow, curvy roads — and that left-handed driving.

If you're staying on **St. Croix:**

✔ **By air:** Traveling between St. Thomas and St. Croix is now easier than ever before. **American Airlines** (☎ 800-433-7300 in the U.S.) has five flights a day. In addition, **Seaborne Airlines** (☎ 340-773-6442) offers 20 round-trip flights daily, costing $80 to $135 one-way. Flight time is 20 to 30 minutes.

✔ **By ferry:** Ferry service to St. Croix comes and goes. **Virgin Islands Fast Ferry** (☎ 340-719-0099) operates a seasonal ferry from mid-December to April between St. Thomas and St. Croix, taking 1 hour and 15 minutes each way. Vessels leave from the port of Charlotte Amalie on St. Thomas, going to the port of Christiansted on St. Croix. One-way fares are $35 for adults and $30 for children under 12 Monday to Friday, going up to $40 for adults and $35 for children on weekends.

If you're staying on **St. John:**

✔ **By ferry:** The easiest and most common way to get to St. John is by ferry (☎ **340-776-6282**), which leaves from the Red Hook landing pier on St. Thomas's eastern tip; the trip takes about 20 minutes each way. Beginning at 6:30 a.m., boats depart more or less every hour. The last ferry back to Red Hook departs from St. John's Cruz Bay at 11 p.m. The service is frequent and efficient enough that even cruise-ship passengers temporarily anchored in Charlotte Amalie can visit St. John for a quickie island tour. The one-way fare is $3 for adults and $1 for children age 12 and under. Schedules can change without notice, so call in advance.

To reach the ferry, take the Vitran bus from a point near Market Square (in Charlotte Amalie) directly to Red Hook. The cost is $1 per person each way. In addition, privately owned taxis will negotiate a price to carry you from virtually anywhere to the docks at Red Hook.

If you land on St. Thomas and want to go straight to the ferry dock, your best bet is to take a cab from the airport (Vitran buses run from Charlotte Amalie but don't serve the airport area). After disembarking from the ferry on St. John, you'll have to get another cab to your hotel. Depending on the traffic, the cab ride on St. Thomas is about 30 to 45 minutes and costs about $20 to $22.

In addition, a ferry service between Charlotte Amalie on St. Thomas and Fajardo, Puerto Rico, with a stop in Cruz Bay, St. John, is available every other Friday and Sunday (sometimes more often in high season). The trip takes about two hours, costing $70 one-way or $105 round-trip, including ground transportation to the San Juan airport or Condado. For more information, call ☎ **340-776-6282**.

✔ **By boat:** You can also board a boat for St. John directly at the Charlotte Amalie waterfront for a cost of $7 each way. The ride takes 45 minutes. The boats depart from Charlotte Amalie at 9 a.m. and continue at intervals of between one and two hours, until the last boat departs around 5:30 p.m. (The last boat to leave St. John's Cruz Bay for Charlotte Amalie departs at 3:45 p.m.) Call ☎ **340-776-6282** for more information.

Traveling Inland from the Docks

From Carnival lines to Princess cruises, all the major ships call at Charlotte Amalie on St. Thomas. Some lines feature stopovers at the satellite island of St. John, and a few ships also call on St. Croix, anchoring at the pier at Frederiksted. You usually book an island tour with a ship staff member before you disembark. If you do, your designated van will be waiting. In case you prefer to negotiate your own independent island tour, taking a breather from your fellow cruise-ship passengers, taxis meet every arriving ship along St. Thomas's Havensight and Crown Bay docks.

Air-conditioned vans and open-air safari buses will take you to Charlotte Amalie for shopping or hitting the beach. The cab fare from Havensight to **Charlotte Amalie** is $6 per person; you can, however, walk the 2.4km (1½ miles) along the waterfront to town in about 30 minutes. From Crown Bay to town, the taxi fare is $4 per person; it's a 1.6km (1-mile) walk, but the route passes along a busy highway. A taxi from Havensight to **Magens Bay** for swimming is $8.50 per person ($6 per person if you share a ride).

On St. Croix, taxis greet arriving cruise ships at the Frederiksted pier. All the shops are just a short walk away, and you can swim off the beach in **Frederiksted,** where snorkeling is good. From the airport, expect to pay about $14 to $26 to Christiansted and about $12 to $24 to Frederiksted. Cabs are unmetered so agree on the rate before you get in.

Some cruise ships stop at St. John to let passengers disembark for a day. The main town of **Cruz Bay** is near the ship terminal. If you want to swim, the famous **Trunk Bay** is an $8 taxi ride (for two) from town.

Choosing Your Location

The widest choice of accommodations are east and north of **Charlotte Amalie,** the capital of St. Thomas. To the east, you'll find the megaresorts, including two Marriott properties. Most of these large-scale resorts open directly onto the beach.

If having direct access to a beach isn't your top priority, and if money is tight, consider staying at one of the smaller inns in Charlotte Amalie itself. You're only about a ten-minute ride from a good beach at any of these properties, and you can walk to shops, nightlife, and the little dives of adjoining Frenchtown.

Neighboring St. John has few large hotels, the biggest being the **Westin St. John Resort.** If you're not renting a car, staying at **Cruz Bay,** where the ferryboat docks, is most convenient. That way, you can walk to shops and restaurants. Otherwise, most of the campsites and villas lie above **Cinnamon Bay.**

On St. Croix, the largest cluster of hotels and inns is located near the waterfront in the historic capital of **Christiansted,** where you can take a ferry across the water to a good beach. Most of the finest accommodations lie outside Christiansted, in some cases in the second city of St. Croix, **Frederiksted.** Some of the best and largest hotels are scattered along the coastline opening directly onto golden sandy beaches.

Not all our hotel picks are on a beach, but all have access to some of the best beaches in the Caribbean.

Getting Around the USVIs

Roads on St. Croix are easy to navigate because the island is flat. Narrow routes going through hillsides and far too much traffic make driving on St. Thomas less than a pleasure. Except for a few main arteries, roads on St. John are very difficult — blind curves; narrow, hilly terrain; and some potholed dirt roads that even a motorist with a four-wheel-drive vehicle will find all but impossible. Businesses and residents are accustomed to handling visitors, so if you're confused, just ask for directions or other information.

By ferry

Hopping aboard a ferry is a great way to see the islands. Not only do you get to where you're going, but you can also enjoy a scenic boat ride — all for an affordable price. If you're staying on St. John, you can easily get to the resort of your choice via ferry after flying into Charlotte Amalie on St. Thomas. Ferry service from St. Thomas to St. Croix, however, has been discontinued.

The most frequented ferry routing in the Virgin Islands is from St. Thomas to Cruz Bay on St. John. You have a choice of taking a ferry from the Charlotte Amalie waterfront, lying west of the Coast Guard's dock, or from the funky little community of Red Hook in the East End, where you can arrive early and have a beer or soda in one of the raffish taverns and perhaps order a fish patty or two from one of the local vendors.

- ✔ **From the dock at Charlotte Amalie,** St. John–bound ferries sail daily at 9 and 11 a.m., and at 1, 3, 4, and 5:30 p.m. The ferry leaves Cruz Bay for returns to Charlotte Amalie at 7:15, 9:15, and 11:15 a.m. and at 1:15, 2:15, and 3:45 p.m. Trip time is 45 minutes, with one-way tickets costing $7 for adults and $3 for children 2 to 11. Call ☎ 340-776-6282 for more ferry-service information.

- ✔ **From the dock at Cruz Bay,** daily departures are at 6:30 and 7:30 a.m., and then from 8 a.m. hourly until midnight. On St. John, ferries heading back to Red Hook sail on the hour beginning at 6 a.m. The last one pulls out at 11 p.m. The Red Hook linkup takes from 15 to 20 minutes, costing $3 one-way for adults or $1 for children under 12. Call ☎ 340-776-6282 for more information.

Depending on weather conditions or mechanical failures, schedules can vary, so check with the ferry services themselves if you're trying to keep an appointment such as an airplane connection.

To get to the East End of St. Thomas from the Charlotte Amalie waterfront without the hassle, you can hop aboard the 26-passenger skiff known as *The Reef* (☎ 340-776-8500). The water taxi takes you to **Frenchman's Reef & Morning Star Marriott Beach Resort** (see the listing later in this chapter) every 30 minutes daily from 8:30 a.m. to 5 p.m. Returns from the East End are daily from 9 a.m. to 5:30 p.m., 19 times a day. Even if you're not staying at one of Marriott's resorts, this is the easiest way to reach the highly desirable **Morning Star Beach.** A one-way ticket costs $5 for adults and $3 for children. Trip time is 15 minutes.

Ferries also leave from St. Thomas plying the waters to the other Virgins, the British Virgin Islands. Two ferry services, **Smith's Ferry** (☎ **340-775-7292**) and **Native Son, Inc.** (☎ **340-774-8685**), link St. Thomas with Tortola. Ferries leave from both Charlotte Amalie and Red Hook on St. Thomas, landing at Road Town or West End on the island of Tortola. Call for schedules, because hours of departure can vary from day to day. The cost of a one-way ticket is $22, $40 round-trip. The trip from Charlotte Amalie to Tortola's West End takes anywhere from 45 minutes to an hour, and the trip to Road Town takes 1½ hours. The Red Hook to Road Town run is only 30 minutes.

Smith's Ferry also provides service to Virgin Gorda, the second main island of the BVIs. The journey from Charlotte Amalie to Virgin Gorda sails only two times a week, costing $25 one-way or $40 round-trip.

From the island of St. John, you can ferry to Tortola's West End on the *Sundance* (Inter Island Boat Services; ☎ **340-776-6597**); the 30-minute trip costs $21 one-way and $35 round-trip.

To enter the British Virgin Islands, you need proof of citizenship. A valid passport is always best, although a birth certificate or voter's registration card with photo ID usually does the trick.

By plane

If your final destination isn't St. Thomas, three other carriers fly to other nearby islands. **American Airlines** (☎ **800-433-7300;** www.aa.com) offers frequent flights daily from St. Thomas to St. Croix's Henry E. Rohlsen Airport. **Cape Air** (☎ **800-352-0714;** www.flycapeair.com) offers hourly air service to St. Croix and Tortola. **Seaborne Airlines** (☎ **340-773-6442;** www.seaborneairlines.com), which you catch from a terminal on the waterfront across from Charlotte Amalie's main drag, also flies between St. Thomas and St. Croix 20 times daily, as well as to Tortola.

Make reservations for the seaplane and check your luggage early, noting the strict weight limit of 18kg (40 lbs.) of luggage per passenger. Your baggage may be on the next flight if you don't check in early. The 20-minute flight to St. Croix is scenic, and it lands right at the dock, a five-minute walk from Christiansted. If you do get caught waiting for your luggage, you can wander around and look at the little shops or grab a bite at one of the waterfront restaurants there.

By taxi

Taxis are the most convenient way to travel on all three islands, and fares are generally lower than in mainland U.S. cities. Taxis aren't metered, but tariffs are set by the government. Rates are posted at the airport and in hotel lobbies. A cabdriver is required by law to show you the published rates if you request them. Rates are also printed in the widely distributed *St. Thomas This Week, St. Croix This Week,* and *St. John This Week* booklets.

Even though the rates are government controlled, settling on the charge before getting in the cab is still wise. Rates are per person. Cabbies often take more than one passenger, charging you a lower fee than if you book the taxi just for yourself.

On St. Thomas, you can request a taxi by phone. Try one of the following: **East End Taxi** (☎ 340-775-6974), **Islander Taxi** (☎ 340-774-4077), or the **VI Taxi Association** (☎ 340-774-4550).

Taxis are plentiful on St. Croix and St. Thomas, less so on St. John. As in most places, you can hail cabs on the street. They're especially plentiful along the waterfront in Charlotte Amalie. Stands lie across from Emancipation Garden. On St. Croix, taxis cluster at the airport and at the Frederiksted pier when cruise ships arrive; you also can easily find them in the center of Christiansted. To request a taxi by phone, try the **St. Croix Taxi Association** (☎ 340-778-1088), located at the airport. In Christiansted, call either **Antilles Taxi Service** (☎ 340-773-5020) or **Cruxan Taxi and Tours** (☎ 340-773-6388).

Taxis on St. John are not only a convenient way to get about, but they're also a lot of fun, because most are in open-air safari buses. Taxis meet ferries arriving at the Cruz Bay ferry dock coming either from Charlotte Amalie or Red Hook. They're also available at the two major island hotels, and you can flag one down whenever you see one. Just because other people are in the cab doesn't mean they won't stop for you if they have room; shared taxis are commonplace. Cabbies on St. John don't respond to calls as efficiently as drivers on St. Thomas and St. Croix. On St. John they may show up — then again, they may not. It's more laid-back here.

On foot

The most interesting towns for walks are **Charlotte Amalie** on St. Thomas and both **Frederiksted** and **Christiansted** on St. Croix. A good self-guided tour of Charlotte Amalie's central district is included in the freely distributed *St. Thomas–St. John Vacation Handbook,* available at the airports and around town. The St. Thomas Historical Trust also issues a self-guided tour of the historic sector (this one available for $1.95 in bookstores).

By public transportation

The public bus service on St. Thomas is better than on most Caribbean islands but woefully inadequate for those coming from metropolitan centers in the United States. Vitran buses, charging 75¢ for runs in Charlotte Amalie or $1 to outlying places on the island, run about every half-hour from town to the East End. Buses also run to western St. Thomas, with more-limited service to northern outposts.

On neighboring St. John, Vitran buses offer more-limited service, making the run from the Cruz Bay ferry dock to Coral Bay and to the eastern end of the little island at Salt Pond. Some locals use this bus, which makes endless stops — so it isn't a convenient way to get anywhere fast. Vitran fares are $1.

On St. Croix, buses cross the island frequently, mostly going along Route 70 between the capital of Christiansted to Frederiksted. A one-way fare is $1.50.

By car

Driving is on the left side of the road, although the steering wheel is on the left as well. Seat belts are mandatory, and the roads are narrow and hilly on St. Thomas and even worse on St. John. St. Croix is relatively flat and therefore somewhat easy to navigate. A valid U.S. driver's license is good for a 90-day stay. The minimum age is 18 years. Even so, many car-rental firms don't rent to anyone under 25.

In-depth explorations of St. Thomas and St. Croix require a private vehicle. On St. John, you can usually get around without a car unless you're staying at a private villa far from Cruz Bay. Then you're rather isolated and a car will come in handy.

Because of winding, narrow roads, the government wisely limits the speed to 32 to 56kmph (20–35 mph). If you have a breakdown, call the car-rental outfitter. All three islands have garages that tow in broken-down vehicles.

Driving on St. Thomas

Try to avoid driving in and out of Charlotte Amalie Monday through Saturday from 7 to 9 a.m. and from 4:30 to 6:30 p.m. Traffic is bumper to bumper, and no one seems to be moving. Drivers' patience wears thin, but you'll find little of the road rage that you'd find in California.

You can rent a car on St. Thomas from the following companies: **Avis** (☎ **888-864-8894,** 340-778-9355), **Budget** (☎ **800-472-3325**), **Cowpet Rent-a-Car** (☎ **340-775-7376**), **Dependable Car Rental** (☎ **800-522-3076,** 340-774-2253), **Discount** (☎ **340-776-4858**), or **Sun Island Car Rental** (☎ **340-774-3333**).

Driving on St. Croix

Because the island is mainly flat, the roads on St. Croix are better than on hilly St. Thomas or St. John. Speed limits are higher too, especially at 88km/h (55 mph) along the four-lane Melvin H. Evans route linking Christiansted with Frederiksted. Elsewhere on the island, speed limits are 48 to 64km/h (35–40 mph).

Occasionally, all the rental companies run out of cars at once, especially in winter. To avoid disappointment, make your reservations early. Call one of the following: **Avis** (☎ **800-331-1084,** 340-778-1468), **Budget** (☎ **888-227-3359,** 340-778-9636), **Olympic** (☎ **888-878-4227,** 340-773-2300), or **Thrifty** (☎ **888-400-8877,** 340-773-7200).

Driving on St. John

St. John has the most beautiful landscape of the USVIs, but it's the most difficult to navigate by car. If you're going into the interior, especially the national park, you need a four-wheel-drive vehicle. The very-limited major routes are paved and passable. When you veer from them, however, expect dirt roads that are potholed and sometimes impassable after heavy rainfalls.

If you're traveling at the height of the winter season, reserve a car well in advance to ensure that you get the vehicle of your choice. In 2004, **Hertz** opened an office on St. John (☎ **800-654-3131,** 340-693-7580). Otherwise, call one of the following: **Cool Breeze** (☎ **340-776-6588**), **Delbert Hill Taxi Rental Service** (☎ **340-776-6637**), **Denzil Clyne** (☎ **340-776-6715**), **Spencer's Jeep** (☎ **888-776-6628,** 340-693-8784), or **St. John Car Rental** (☎ **340-776-6103**).

By helicopter

Flying high in a helicopter is the most expensive way — yet also the most dramatic — to see the U.S. Virgins. You get the best deal with **Air Center Helicopters** (☎ **340-775-7335**) from its base at the Charlotte Amalie waterfront. A one-hour tour for four passengers costs $804, or $1,208 for six passengers, the cost divided among the group. You can also arrange longer flights to the BVIs.

Staying in Style

The U.S. Virgin Islands, especially the most visited St. Thomas, offer one of the densest concentrations of hotels in the Caribbean. Island promoters like to boast that whatever your requirements — Grand Palazzo living or B&B — a bed is waiting for you. Supplementing the regular hotels and inns is a vast array of timeshares, condos, and private villas.

Familiar chains such as Ritz-Carlton, Marriott, and Westin show their shining faces in the USVIs, but simpler West Indian inns are available for the frugal traveler. The good news for the eco-sensitive traveler is that little St. John offers more award-winning campgrounds than anywhere else in the Caribbean and is also a safe destination. (Except for the British Virgin Islands and St. John, we consider safety a problem while camping in much of the Caribbean, especially in Jamaica.) If you're traveling in winter, be sure to reserve St. John's campgrounds as early as possible. (See Chapter 6 for more on booking accommodations.)

The Top Resorts

The rack rates listed in this section are in U.S. dollars and are for a standard double room during high season (mid-Dec through mid-Apr), unless otherwise noted. Lower rates are available during the off season and shoulder season; see Chapter 3 for information on travel seasons.

On St. Thomas

Bluebeard's Castle Hotel
$$–$$$$ Charlotte Amalie

The days when Bluebeard's was the island's number-one hotel have long since passed, but the 160-unit resort still remains the best choice for those who want to be close to Charlotte Amalie and not in one of the East End resorts. Bluebeard's isn't on a beach but operates a free hotel shuttle to **Magens Bay.** If you feel you were born to shop, this place is also your best bet because you can walk to the leading shops of St. Thomas or at least take a taxi if the hill climb is too steep. The view is panoramic here, and bedrooms are priced according to their vista. All units come with terraces. Standards are the less-attractive rooms without a view. Deluxe gives you a panoramic sweep of the harbor. A small pool, two tennis courts, and three restaurants add to the allure.

See map p. 459. Bluebeard's Hill (P.O. Box 7480), St. Thomas. ☎ *800-438-6493, 340-774-1600. Fax: 340-714-1320. Rack rates: $175–$375 double. Additional person $25 extra per night. AE, DISC, MC, V.*

Bolongo Bay Beach Club and Villas
$$$ South Shore

A 15-minute drive from Charlotte Amalie, this beachfront resort is casual and fun, because it's heavy on activities. Its white-sand beach, set against a backdrop of palm trees, is one of its biggest assets. Over the years, this resort, operated by the Doumeng family, has offered decent value and the widest array of choices for lodging on the island. The majority of rooms are in three-floor wings opening onto the beach and graced with a small terrace or upper balcony. Efficiency kitchens come with many of the accommodations. For families, some two-bedroom units are an option. Bolongo Bay presents a rather confusing array of both living arrangements and package deals, so you need to talk directly to the hotel or with a good travel agent to select the best option for your vacation needs. If you're a very frugal traveler, the cheapest deal is a room at the Bayside Inn across the street. Amenities include two restaurants and bars, three pools, two tennis courts, a large health club, and a dive shop; Bolongo's water-sports program ranks among the island's best. Kids age 12 and under stay free year-round and eat free during the summer.

See map p. 459. 7150 Bolongo, St. Thomas. ☎ *800-524-4746, 340-775-1800. Fax: 340-775-3208.* www.bolongobay.com. *Rack rates: $255–$285 double with continental breakfast; $499–$529 all-inclusive double. AE, MC, V.*

Frenchman's Reef & Morning Star Marriott Beach Resort
$$$–$$$$$ **South Shore**

About 5km (3 miles) east of Charlotte Amalie, two of the grandest resorts on St. Thomas are really a pair of twins. Of the two, Morning Star is more luxurious, tranquil, and intimate. A glass-enclosed elevator takes guests down to a white-sand beach. As this book went to press, the Morning Star was preparing to reopen its rooms after extensive renovation. On a bluff overlooking both the harbor and the sea, Frenchman's Reef offers a total of 408 units — it's been called a "human zoo" here in winter — and Morning Star boasts only 96 units housed in five cottage buildings containing between 16 and 24 units each. The Frenchman offers the most facilities — five restaurants and nine bars — but guests at Morning Star are free to walk next door and use them, along with the tennis courts, pools, and the finest and most state-of-the-art spa of any hotel on the island. The twins also have a children's program, and they boast the best hotel entertainment on the island.

See map p. 459. Estate Bakkeroe, Flamboyant Point (P.O. Box 7100), St. Thomas. ☎ *800-524-2000, 340-776-8500. Fax: 340-715-6193.* www.marriott.com. *Rack rates: $210–$499 Morning Star double; $320–$700 Frenchman double. Wedding packages available. AE, DC, DISC, MC, V.*

Hotel 1829
$$ **Charlotte Amalie**

Having far more atmosphere and charm than Bluebeard's Castle, this 15-room inn is yet another option for those who want to stay close to Charlotte Amalie and its bevy of shops. You're not at a beach, the hotel pool is much too small, and you've got a steep climb from town back to the hotel, but those are minor drawbacks for travelers seeking an old-fashioned inn. Registered as a National Historic Site, the hotel was a former home, said to have been built by a French sea captain for his new bride. You get what you pay for here. If you'll settle for a "cozy" bedroom (that means small) and one that doesn't get much sunlight, you can live like a frugal traveler. Costing more, the accommodations in the main house are spacious and often filled with antiques such as four-poster beds evoking the colonial era. Try to get a room with a balcony overlooking the harbor, one of the grandest panoramas in the West Indies. Be warned: You'll climb a lot of steps here to reach the various levels (the hotel has no elevator). **Magens Bay Beach** lies a 15-minute drive or taxi ride away.

This hotel isn't a good pick if you have children or are physically challenged in any way.

See map p. 459. Kongens Gade (P.O. Box 1567), St. Thomas. ☎ *800-524-2002, 340-776-1829. Fax: 340-776-4313.* www.hotel1829.com. *Rack rates: $105–$180 double; from $220 suite. Rates include continental breakfast. AE, DISC, MC, V.*

St. Thomas Accommodations

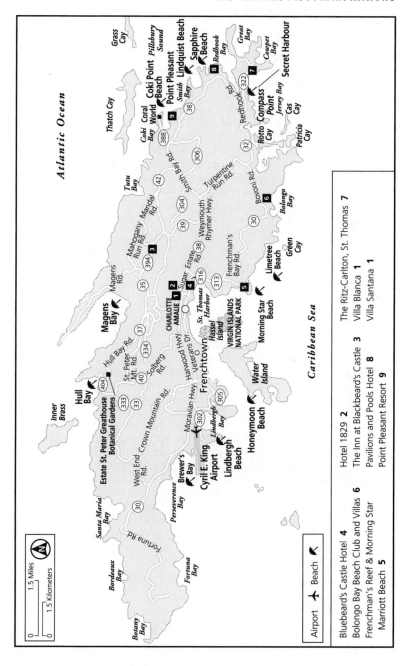

Atlantic Ocean

Caribbean Sea

Airport ✈   Beach 🏖

Bluebeard's Castle Hotel **4**
Bolongo Bay Beach Club and Villas **6**
Frenchman's Reef & Morning Star
Marriott Beach **5**

Hotel 1829 **2**
The Inn at Blackbeard's Castle **3**
Pavilions and Pools Hotel **8**
Point Pleasant Resort **9**

The Ritz-Carlton, St. Thomas **7**
Villa Blanca **1**
Villa Santana **1**

The Inn at Blackbeard's Castle
$$ Charlotte Amalie

Not to be confused with Bluebeard's Castle (see the listing earlier in this chapter), Blackbeard's is far more intimate and private, more like a restored home, whereas Bluebeard's is a full-service resort. Because of its charm and friendliness, we infinitely prefer our beards black. On a hillside overlooking the harbor of Charlotte Amalie, the so-called castle grew up on the site of a 1679 tower erected by the Danish governor of the island. Blackbeard himself may have used the site as a lookout post for unfriendly ships. The nearest good beach is a ten-minute shuttle ride away. We rank the gay-friendly Blackbeard's as the most atmospheric of all the small inns on St. Thomas, offering a total of 11 handsomely furnished bedrooms. The least expensive are the garden units, which are small and have no balconies. The larger rooms, actually junior suites, are more spacious and open onto balconies; many contain four-poster beds.

See map p. 459. Blackbeard's Hill, P.O. Box 6227, Charlotte Amalie, St. Thomas. ☎ *800-344-5771, 340-776-1234. Fax: 340-776-4321.* www.blackbeardscastle. com. *Rack rates: $110–$195. AE, DISC, MC, V.*

Pavilions and Pools Hotel
$$$ Estate Smith Bay

Ideal for a honeymoon, this 25-room resort, 11km (7 miles) east of Charlotte Amalie, comprises a string of tastefully rebuilt and furnished condominium units. It resides near **Sapphire Bay,** which boasts one of the island's best beaches and water-sports concessions, although the well-known hotel that stands there is in decline and in need of renovation. At P&P, you get your own villa, with floor-to-ceiling glass doors opening directly onto your own private swimming pool. After checking in, you don't have to see another soul until you leave. The fence and gate are high, and your space opens onto greenery. Around your own pool is an encircling deck. Inside, a high room divider screens a kitchen, and each bedroom offers ample closet space behind louvered doors. The little pavilion has a garden shower where you can bathe Adam and Eve–style surrounded by greenery, while being screened from Peeping Toms. A small bar and barbecue area sit against a wall on the reception terrace, where the hotel hosts rum parties and cookouts. Informal, simple meals are served nightly, and occasionally a musician or singer entertains. Free snorkeling gear is available, as are honeymoon packages.

See map p. 459. 6400 Estate Smith Bay, St. Thomas. ☎ *800-524-2001, 340-775-6110.* www.pavilionsandpools.com. *Rack rates: $250–$275 double. Rates include continental breakfast. AE, MC, V.*

Point Pleasant Resort
$$$$ Water Bay

This private, unique resort sits on **Water Bay,** on the northeastern tip of St. Thomas, just a five-minute walk from Stouffer's Beach but far removed from the bustle of Charlotte Amalie. The resort rents out its 95 villa-style suites when their owners aren't in residence. From your living room gallery, you look out on the islands of Tortola, St. John, and Jost Van Dyke. The complex sits on a 6-hectare (15-acre) nature preserve lush with flowering shrubbery, century plants, and frangipani trees. Waiting for your discovery are secluded nature trails, old rock formations, and lookout points. Some of the villas have kitchens, and the furnishings are light and airy, mostly with rattan and floral fabrics. The restaurant, **Agavé Terrace,** one of the finest on the island, offers three meals a day. The cuisine, featuring seafood, is a blend of nouvelle American dishes with Caribbean specialties. Locals entertain several nights a week. Three freshwater swimming pools, a lit tennis court, snorkeling equipment, Sunfish sailboats, and a daily shuttle to shopping and dining round out the offerings.

See map p. 459. 6600 Estate Smith Bay #4, St. Thomas. ☎ *800-524-2300, 340-775-7200. Fax: 340-776-5694.* www.pointpleasantresort.com. *Rack rates: $255–$275 junior or superior suite; $355 deluxe suite; $525 two-bedroom suite; $525 two-bedroom villa. Packages available for families, honeymoons, and anniversaries. AE, DC, DISC, MC, V.*

The Ritz-Carlton, St. Thomas
$$$$$ Charlotte Amalie

If money is no object, and you want to live in the grandest style the USVIs have to offer, make it the 152-room Ritz-Carlton. Opening onto white-sand beaches, this hotel is luxury set on a 6-hectare (15-acre) oceanfront estate at the eastern end of St. Thomas, 7.2km (4½ miles) southeast of Charlotte Amalie. In landscaped gardens, it evokes a grand Italian *palazzo,* with its array of fountains, courtyards, and columns. At the heart of the resort is a 38m (125-ft.) lagoon (actually a pool). You'll need to check in to a European hotel to find appointments like these handcarved furnishings, elegant linens, and tasteful fabrics along with spacious marble-clad bathrooms. The most affordable rooms are on the ground floor with a tiny peek of an oceanview. The magnificent and spacious oceanview rooms open onto views of St. Thomas's neighboring island of St. John. As this book went to press, the Ritz-Carlton was preparing to reopen after a $40-million renovation and enhancement that includes a new Club Lounge with 55 guest rooms, 16 executive suites, and 4 presidential suites

See map p. 459. 6900 Great Bay Estate, St. Thomas. ☎ *800-241-3333, 340-775-3333. Fax: 340-775-4444.* www.ritzcarlton.com. *Rack rates: $489–$995 double; $1,250 suite. Honeymoon packages available. AE, DC, DISC, MC, V.*

Villa Blanca
$$ Charlotte Amalie

Inn hunters (as opposed to resort hoppers) often seek out this cozy, 14-room charmer lying immediately to the east of St. Thomas's capital, Charlotte Amalie. It occupies a hilltop site on 1.2 landscaped hectares (3 acres) with a panoramic view of one of the most scenic harbors in the

Caribbean, most often filled with cruise ships. Guests take up residence in either two rooms in the house's main core (these larger units are preferable) or in one of the rooms in the annex opening onto the garden. Units range from small to midsize and come with a small kitchenette and a balcony or patio. On-site is a freshwater pool, but the nearest beach is **Morning Star Bay,** a distance of 6.4km (4 miles) by car or taxi.

See map p. 459. Raphune Hill, Route 38, Charlotte Amalie. ☎ *800-231-0034, 340-776-0749. Fax: 340-779-2661.* www.villablancahotel.com. *Rack rates: $125–$145. Rates include continental breakfast. AE, DISC, MC, V.*

Villa Santana
$$ **Charlotte Amalie**

More luxurious than its major competitor, Villa Blanca (see the previous listing), Villa Santana dates from the 1850s, when it was constructed by a Mexican general. Beautifully restored, it lies a 5-minute walk from Charlotte Amalie but a 15-minute drive from the nearest good beach at **Magens Bay.** Long an island favorite for those clients who prefer inns, the property opens onto one of the grand vistas of the ship-clogged harbor. Guest rooms are installed in a wide range of places from the general's former library to what used to be a wine cellar. The owners have even fit a bedroom into a lookout tower, La Torre, which was the old pump house. Accommodations are handsomely and comfortably furnished with kitchenettes. Much of the décor, in honor of the place's founder, is Mexican inspired, including the clay tiles. On-site is a pool.

See map p. 459. Denmark Hill, Charlotte Amalie, St. Thomas. ☎ *and fax 340-776-1311.* www.villasantana.com. *Rack rates: $125–$195 suite for two. AE, MC, V.*

On St. Croix

The Buccaneer
$$$–$$$$$ **East End**

Lying 3.2km (2 miles) east of Christiansted, this family-owned resort is the island's traditional luxury choice, with a trio of white-sand beaches and the best sports program on St. Croix. On the 138-hectare (340-acre) site of a cattle ranch and a sugar plantation, the property has roots back in the 17th century. Both honeymooners and up-market families find it ideal. After taking a palm tree-lined private road to a pink hilltop colonial building, the hosts take you to a spacious bedroom with a Mediterranean and West Indian motif, four-poster beds, tile floors, and marble bathrooms. Families book the cottages, honeymooners preferring one of the suites with private terraces overlooking the water. The Buccaneer's eight tennis courts are the best on the island, as is its children's program. The resort is also the choice for golfers because of its first-rate, 18-hole course.

Many couples marry at this elegant property. The Doubloon rooms, with whirlpool tubs, are the best and are right on the water.

St. Croix Accommodations

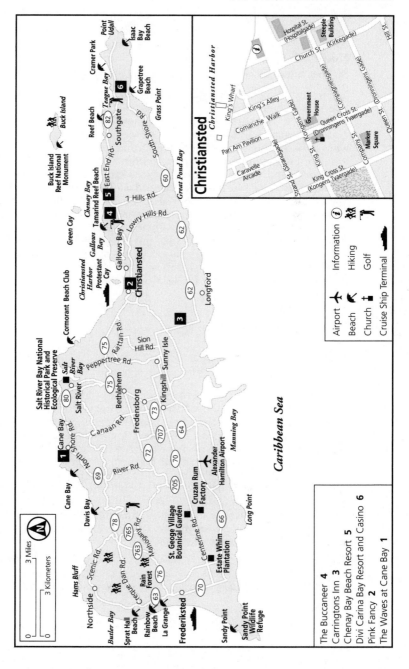

Christiansted

Christiansted Harbor

Hospital St. (Hospitalsgade)
Steeple Building
Church St. (Kirkegade)
King's Wharf
King's Alley
Government House
Comanche Walk
Queen Cross St. (Dronningens Tvaergade)
King St. (Kongens Gade)
Pan Am Pavilion
Caravelle Arcade
King Cross St. (Kongens Tvaergade)
Market Square
Strand St. (Strandgade)
Company St. (Compagniesgade)
King St. (Dronningens Gade)
Queen St. (Dronningens Gade)
Hill St.

Point Udall
Isaac Bay Beach
Cramer Park
Grapetree Beach
Grass Point
Teague Bay **6**
Reef Beach
Southgate
82
South Shore Rd.
Buck Island
Buck Island Reef National Monument
Great Pond Bay
60
Chenay Bay
Tamarind Reef Beach **5**
East End Rd.
Green Cay
Gallows Bay **4**
7 Hills Rd.
Lowry Hills Rd.
62
Christiansted Harbor
Protestant Cay
Gallows Bay
Christiansted **2**
62
Longford
Cormorant Beach Club
3
Rattan Rd.
Sion Hill Rd.
Sunny Isle
Salt River Bay National Historical Park and Ecological Preserve
Salt River Bay
75
Peppertree Rd.
Kingshill
Manning Bay
Salt River
80
Shore Rd.
Salt River
75
Bethlehem
Fredensborg
73
707
64
Canaan Rd.
Cane Bay **1**
North
72
70
705
Alexander Hamilton Airport
Shore Rd.
69
River Rd.
Cruzan Rum Factory
Davis Bay
78
Long Point
Hams Bluff
765
St. Geoge Village Botanical Garden
66
Northside
763
Estate Whim Plantation
Scenic Rd.
Mahogany Rd.
Centerline Rd.
Caribbean Sea
Creque Dam Rd.
Rain Forest
76
70
Sprat Hall Beach
Butler Bay
Rainbow Beach
63
La Grange
Frederiksted
Sandy Point
Sandy Point Wildlife Refuge

N
0   3 Miles
0   3 Kilometers

Information *i*
Hiking
Golf
Airport ✈
Beach
Church ✝
Cruise Ship Terminal

The Buccaneer **4**
Carringtons Inn **3**
Chenay Bay Beach Resort **5**
Divi Carina Bay Resort and Casino **6**
Pink Fancy **2**
The Waves at Cane Bay **1**

See map p. 463. Route 82 (P.O. Box 25200), Gallows Bay, St. Croix. ☎ *800-255-3881,* *340-712-2100. Fax: 340-712-2104.* www.thebuccaneer.com. *Rack rates: $295–$590 double; $550–$840 suite. Rates include full breakfast. AE, DISC, MC, V.*

Carringtons Inn
$$ Hermon Hill

If you've read all those magazine stories about celebrities such as screen legend Maureen O'Hara who own villas on St. Croix, and you wonder what life is like in them, here's your chance to experience one firsthand. This grandly elegant B&B was formerly the home of a wealthy family who spent winters here. Much evidence of their former lifestyle remains. This is an intimate B&B with personalized attention and five spacious and beautifully furnished guest rooms with first-class private bathrooms. Some rooms have a king-size canopy bed, and wicker furnishings are in tasteful abundance. When guests gather around the pool, a house-party atmosphere prevails. You can even enjoy your breakfast of such delights as rum-flavored French toast poolside. The staff delivers thoughtful touches such as full concierge service, bathrobes, and even freshly baked cookies in the evening. You'll need transportation to get to the nearest good beach, Tamarind Reef Beach, as the location of the hotel is 8km (5 miles) east of the airport but only 1.6km (1 mile) west of Christiansted.

See map p. 463. 4001 Estate Hermon Hill, St. Croix. ☎ *877-658-0508, 340-713-0508. Fax: 340-719-0841.* www.carringtonsinn.com. *Rack rates: $120–$150 double. Rates include breakfast. AE, DC, MC, V.*

Chenay Bay Beach Resort
$$$–$$$$ East End

On a wildlife preserve 6.4km (4 miles) east of Christiansted, Chenay Bay Beach Resort is the most desirable cottage colony on St. Croix. Fifty cottages are scattered over the site of a former sugar plantation. The beachfront is one of the best on the island for swimming, snorkeling, and windsurfing. The resort is also our favorite for families. Not only are the spacious accommodations suitable for families, but Chenay Bay boasts a good children's program and free tennis and water sports, including snorkeling and kayaking. You take a gravel path to the sea where you find a big pool, picnic tables, and an informal restaurant. The kitchen will prepare picnic baskets for two, or for families. An extensive menu for children is available at night, and during the day they can order traditional kiddie fare such as burgers, hot dogs, and fries.

See map p. 463. Route 82 (P.O. Box 24600), Christiansted, St. Croix. ☎ *800-548-4457, 340-773-2918. Fax: 340-773-6665.* www.chenaybay.com. *Rack rates: $299–$357 cottage for one or two. Wedding and honeymoon packages available. AE, MC, V.*

Divi Carina Bay Resort and Casino
$$–$$$ Christiansted

Divi Carina is where the high rollers stay. Over many objections, this 146-room resort introduced casino gambling to the USVIs. As a resort, it's a fine choice even if you don't go to the tables at night. The hotel opens onto 305m (1,000 ft.) of white-sand beach and, to make it more alluring, Divi operates **The Spa,** the finest such facility on the island. If you don't want to go to the beach, you can take advantage of one of the five pools on-site. The most desirable accommodations are the oceanfront rooms and villa suites. All the rooms here, however, are good-size and completely modern, with excellent bathrooms and such grace notes as balconies. You're faced with three restaurants for your dining options, and such facilities as a water-sports center and a children's program.

See map p. 463. 25 Estate Turner Hole, St. Croix. ☎ *888-823-9352, 340-773-9700. Fax: 340-773-6802.* www.diviresorts.com. *Rack rates: $279–$345 double; $519 suite. AE, DC, MC, V.*

Pink Fancy
$–$$ Christiansted

Those seeking an evocative West Indian inn, as opposed to a resort, will take a fancy to this pink complex. Its core is a historic 1780 Danish-style town house from the colonial era. But it wasn't until the 1950s that it gained a lot of publicity as a hangout for writers and artists, attracting playwright and actor Noel Coward among other celebrities. The famous and fabled have long checked out, but the 12-unit complex is as good as ever. This little hotel is the most atmospheric one in town, filled with antiques, comfortable furnishings, and tropical motifs such as rattan. In the best and larger rooms are canopied or iron beds in the plantation style. For the beach, guests have to take a three-minute launch to the **Sands on the Cay,** an islet that lies in the harbor of Christiansted.

See map p. 463. 27 Prince St., Christiansted, St. Croix. ☎ *800-524-2045, 340-773-8460. Fax: 340-773-6448.* www.pinkfancy.com. *Rack rates: $95–$150. AE, DC, MC, V.*

The Waves at Cane Bay
$$ East End

One of the best-run condo properties — rented to visitors when the owners aren't in residence — is between Christiansted and Frederiksted on the ocean at **Cane Bay Beach.** The beach itself is rock-strewn and at high tide seems to drop out of sight, although the scuba diving and snorkeling here are good, with a dive shop on the grounds. The resort lies a 20-minute drive west of Christiansted and a 5-minute drive east of the golf course at the Sunterra Resort. Mostly, the resort attracts divers. The rooms, in two-story buildings with verandas overlooking the water, are spacious and come with kitchens, tile floors, and neat little bathrooms with showers.

Families often check in here, preparing light meals and sometimes hardly leaving the premises during their vacation. You need a car if you stay at this remote North Coast location.

See map p. 463. Route 80 (P.O. Box 1749), Kingsbill, St. Croix. ☎ *800-545-0603, 340-778-1805.* www.canebaystcroix.com. *Rack rates: $140–$155 double. AE, DC, DISC, MC, V.*

On St. John

Cinnamon Bay Campground
$–$$ **Cinnamon Bay**

Enveloped by tropical vegetation and opening onto **Cinnamon Bay Beach,** this campsite is the most complete one you'll find in the Caribbean. In winter, getting a booking is difficult unless you reserve well ahead of time. The campgrounds are popular because they're well kept and contain far more facilities than similar properties in the Caribbean except for Maho Bay Camps (see the listing later in this chapter), which is equally fine. The cheapest rental is a bare site; for that, you must bring in your own tent and equipment. A more-comfortable way to stay here is to rent a tent (3 × 4m/10 × 14 ft. with a floor), including such extras as linens and cooking equipment. The most luxurious offering is one of the cottages, consisting of a 4.5-×-4.5m (15-×-15-ft.) room with two concrete walls and two screen walls. Cottages come with kitchen facilities and four twin beds. In an outbuilding are the toilets and the cool-water showers.

See map p. 467. Route 20 (P.O. Box 720), Cruz Bay, St. John, USVI 00831. ☎ *800-539-9998, 340-776-6330. Fax: 340-776-6458.* www.cinnamonbay.com. *Rack rates: $27 bare site; $80 tent; $110–$140 cottage. AE, MC, V.*

Estate Concordia Studios/Concordia Eco-Tents
$$ **Coral Bay**

Developer Stanley Selengut is known as the most eco-sensitive man on St. John. On some 20 sea-bordering hectares (50 acres) at Salt Pond Bay, a 45-minute drive from St. John's capital, Cruz Bay, he has created a series of 20 studios and 11 tent-cottages (eco-tents), which provide an alternative choice for those who find Maho Bay and Cinnamon Bay camps fully booked in winter. The studios are solar- and wind-powered, each opening onto a panoramic view. Cooled by trade winds, they can sleep two in comfort, and each unit comes with a kitchen. The eco-tents are also a comfortable way to camp, because each one comes with a kitchen and a small private shower along with a composting toilet. Tents can hold up to six campers.

See map p. 467. 20–27 Estate Concordia, Coral Bay, St. John. ☎ *800-392-9004, 212-472-9453, 340-776-6226.* www.maho.org. *Rack rates: $135–$210 studio for two. Additional person $25 extra per night (studio); $15–$25 per night (tent-cottage). MC, V.*

St. John Accommodations

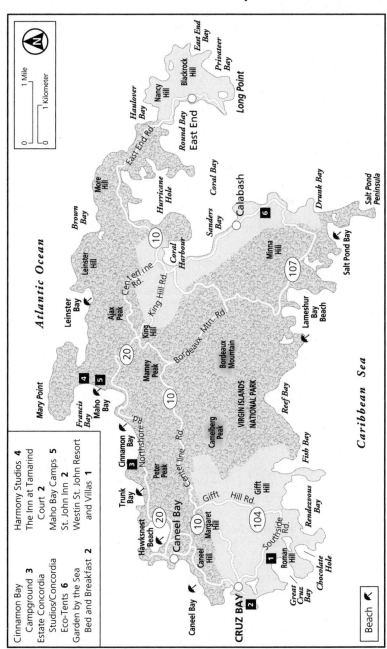

Cinnamon Bay Campground **3**
Estate Concordia Studios/Concordia Eco-Tents **6**
Garden by the Sea Bed and Breakfast **2**
Harmony Studios **4**
The Inn at Tamarind Court **2**
Maho Bay Camps **5**
St. John Inn **2**
Westin St. John Resort and Villas **1**

Garden by the Sea Bed and Breakfast
$$$ Cruz Bay

A ten-minute walk south from the port at **Cruz Bay** where the ferry docks, Garden by the Sea is the best B&B on the island. The place is ideally located as well, lying within easy reach of some of the best beaches between Turner and Frank bays and only a minute's walk along a little trail by Audubon Pond, which takes you to the white sands of **Frank Bay Beach.** The house with three bedrooms to rent was built in the 1970s with West Indian gingerbread trim and high ceilings. Bedrooms are a bit exotic, decorated with objects from all over the globe, such as fountains from Tokyo or elephant bamboo canopied beds from Thailand. Served on the terrace, the breakfast equals that of the finest B&Bs in America.

See map p. 467. P.O. Box 1469, Cruz Bay, St. John, USVI 00831. ☎ *340-779-4731.* www.gardenbythesea.com. *Rack rates: $225–$240 double. No credit cards; prepayment okay with check or money order.*

Harmony Studios
$$–$$$ Maho Bay

Stanley Selengut, St. John's most eco-sensitive developer (see the Estate Concordia Studios/Concordia Eco-Tents listing, earlier in this section), does it again at this hillside site above Maho Bay Camps. He created a dozen first-rate studios in six two-story houses, with some of the island's most panoramic views. The entire resort operates on solar and wind power. Not only that, even the building materials were created from recycled discards — old tires, scrap lumber, yesterday's newspaper. Glass bottles and plastic were reconstituted to make inviting, livable materials, perhaps a sign of the future. The recycling was carried out beautifully. To see these materials at Harmony, you'd never know they had a previous incarnation. A computer monitors energy consumption in each studio, which comes with a bathroom with shower, a kitchenette, and an outdoor terrace. Guests are allowed to use the water-sports facilities at Maho Bay Camps (see the listing later in this section). The closest beach is near Maho Bay Camps as well.

See map p. 467. Maho Bay (P.O. Box 310), Cruz Bay, St. John. ☎ *800-392-9004, 340-776-6226. Fax: 340-776-6504.* www.maho.org. *Rack rates: $200–$225 studio for two. Additional person $25 extra per night. MC, V.*

The Inn at Tamarind Court
$$ Cruz Bay

If you're traveling light, you can walk to this inn right from the ferryboat dock. Long a fan of the budget traveler, this 20-room West Indian hostelry enjoys a repeat clientele who know they get a good value here. The bedrooms are small but reasonably comfortable and well maintained, 16 of them coming with a tiny bathroom with a shower. Four units share a bathroom, but the hall plumbing is adequate. The patio bar is an island favorite and a good place to meet locals; the on-site restaurant is also reasonably priced. From the hotel, you can walk to shuttles that take you to the beaches. No rooms have phones.

See map p. 467. P.O. Box 350, South Shore Road, Cruz Bay, St. John. ☎ *800-221-1637, 340-776-6378. Fax: 340-776-6722.* www.tamarindcourt.com. *Rack rates: $148 double; $240 suite; $240 apartment. Rates include continental breakfast. AE, DISC, MC, V.*

Maho Bay Camps
$$ **Maho Bay**

Surrounded by the **Virgin Islands National Park,** Maho Bay Camps is the most luxurious camping site in the Caribbean, slightly better than the also highly rated Cinnamon Bay Campground. This campsite is part of the string of eco-sensitive resorts on St. John, including the Harmony. From its site, a 13km (8-mile) drive northeast of Maho Bay, it lies above a good sandy beach within walking distance. At the beach you can arrange kayaking, sailing, and windsurfing, and the waters have good visibility and quite a bit of marine life, attracting the snorkeler in you. The tents are linked by steps, walkways, and ramps. Covered with screens and canvas, the tent-cottages can sleep as many as four campers, who quickly learn to use the electric lamps and propane stoves. Linen, an ice chest, and cooking and eating utensils come with the tent.

See map p. 467. Maho Bay (P.O. Box 310), Cruz Bay, St. John. ☎ *800-392-9004 or 340-715-0501. Fax: 340-776-6504.* www.maho.org. *Rack rates: $125 tent-cottage (minimum stay of seven nights). AE, MC, V.*

St. John Inn
$$ **Cruz Bay**

For years this was a closely guarded address among frugal travelers to St. John. This 13-room inn overlooking Enighed Pond was formerly known as Cruz Inn. Now rechristened as St. John Inn and much rejuvenated, the place is better than ever, even though its rates have gone up. The place has more flair now, and in some ways it evokes one of the small inns you'll find in Northern California. Some bedrooms are tiny, but others are of generous size. An occasional antique or a wrought-iron bed adds a decorative touch. For the highest rate, you get a junior suite with a kitchenette and a sitting area. The inn has a 13m (43-ft.) motor yacht, *Hollywood Waltz,* available to rent for daily excursions to private snorkeling spots along the coast and private beaches on uninhabited islands.

See map p. 467. P.O. Box 37, Cruz Bay, St. John. ☎ *800-666-7688, 340-693-8688. Fax: 340-693-9900.* www.stjohninn.com. *Rack rates: $155–$275 double. AE, MC, V.*

Westin St. John Resort and Villas
$$$$–$$$$$ **Great Cruz Bay**

This posh retreat is set on 14 oceanfront hectares (34 acres) in the southwest of St. John. The lushly planted property lies a ten-minute drive south of Cruz Bay. St. John is noted for its small inns and villas; this sprawling mass of a megaresort is anything but. The resort is just what many visitors like: a flashy, architecturally appealing property with the largest array of facilities on the island, including four restaurants, three bars, a fitness center, a dive shop, and six tennis courts. The pool is the largest in the Virgin Islands, and when you tire of it you always have that 365m (1,200-ft.) white-sand beach. Spacious accommodations and good children's programs make it a family favorite as well.

See map p. 467. Route 104 (P.O. Box 8310), Great Cruz Bay, St. John. ☎ *800-808-5020, 340-693-8000. Fax: 340-779-4985.* www.westinresortstjohn.com. *Rack rates: $406–$679; $939–$1,589 suite. AE, DC, DISC, MC, V.*

Dining Out

From the most elegant, refined cuisine of France to casual deli food, the USVIs have it all, with much emphasis on international fare such as Mexican, Chinese, and Italian — though it doesn't come cheap. In many places, such as little taverns and shanties near the beach, you can also sample local island dishes. As one old-time Virgin Island cook told us, "We like to show some of you visitors how to escape from hamburger hell from time to time."

The large resorts of the USVIs have long recognized that good food is an integral part of your vacation experience. They've hired some of the best chefs from both the United States and Europe to tempt you to stay on their premises at night and not venture out on badly lit, narrow roads heading for some distant independent restaurant. The larger resorts offer a widely varied cuisine on their grounds, giving you several choices for dining, ranging from simple fare to more-elaborate menus with generally excellent wine lists.

Those high prices become easier to tolerate when you consider that you'll take most of your meals at a table where you'll have a panoramic view of the sea and a tropical atmosphere. Hopefully, a cool, soothing trade wind will be blowing when the waiter presents your check.

 For those on the tightest of vacation budgets, we also include many little taverns where you can't dine on haute cuisine, but you can eat reasonably well at an affordable price.

You'll find the most varied cuisine on St. Thomas, which has a wider selection of restaurants and better-trained kitchen staffs than all the other islands. You can find almost anything you want on the island.

St. Croix has had many invaders, with a total of seven flags of different nationalities having flown over the island. That varied heritage remains in its cuisine today. The food ranges from Danish to American, with a lot of fusion recipes in between, plus a strong focus on French and Italian.

Some smaller places serve West Indian dishes. Although they feed you well, St. Croix restaurants don't have the scope of those on St. Thomas.

As the smallest of the islands, St. John has the least number of restaurants, but, even so, the range is varied from shacks to the most formal and elegant dining rooms at the two major hotels. St. John is said to have more artists than all the other islands combined, and that creative diversity is also reflected in the imaginative cuisine served here. For such a small, laid-back island, you'll find a surprisingly sophisticated dining scene.

Each year, dining in the USVIs seems to grow more and more laid-back and informal as top restaurant owners have long ago abandoned their demand that men wear jackets and ties. Many visitors, at least at the dives, eat in their shorts and tank tops.

At the top-rated restaurants, men should show up in slacks and a button-up shirt, whereas women will feel comfortable in the evenings in a tailored pants suit or a stylish sundress. After all, you don't want the maitre d' to take one look at what you're wearing and seat you in a dark corner, a potted palm hiding you from view.

Enjoying a Taste of the USVIs

Most of the foodstuff is imported from the U.S. mainland, and the added cost of shipment is reflected in the prices. If you're a fish fancier, your best bet is locally caught fish, which ranges from yellowtail to grouper and red snapper to mahi-mahi and wahoo. Virgin Islanders often serve it grilled with a hot lime sauce, and we view this as the tastiest of island specialties.

Way back when, locals gave colorful names to the various fish brought home for dinner, everything from "ole wife" to "doctors," both of which are whitefish. "Porgies and grunts," along with yellowtail, kingfish, and bonito, also show up on many dinner tables. Chefs usually boil the fish in a lime-flavored brew seasoned with hot peppers and herbs and commonly serve it with a Creole sauce of peppers, tomatoes, and onions, among other ingredients. Salt fish and rice is an excellent low-cost dish, the fish flavored with onion, tomatoes, shortening, garlic, and green pepper.

Conch Creole is a savory brew, seasoned with onions, garlic, spices, hot peppers, and salt pork. Another local favorite is chicken and rice, usually made with Spanish peppers. More-adventurous diners may try curried goat, the longtime classic Virgin Island dinner prepared with herbs, cardamom pods, and onions.

If you want a light meal of local food, order a johnnycake (an unleavened cornbread/flour treat), a pâté (a small pastry filled with meat or fish), or a thick slice of *dumb bread* (a round loaf cut into pieces and stuffed with cheese) from any of the mobile food vans you see around the islands.

For a *belonger* experience (as locals call themselves), stop at a local restaurant for goat stew, leg of lamb with guava, curry chicken, or fried pork chops. Local cooks pile on the sides, so dining is akin to eating at a "meat-'n'-three" in the southern U.S. Nearly all locals eat peas and rice with their main dishes. Pigeon peas, the most common Virgin Island vegetable, are called *gunga* or congo peas. They're often flavored with ham, salted meat, onions, tomatoes, fresh herbs, and even an occasional slice of pumpkin.

The Best Restaurants

On St. Thomas

Agavé Terrace
$$$–$$$$ **East End   SEAFOOD/CARIBBEAN**

Perched high above a steep and heavily forested hillside on the eastern tip of St. Thomas, this outstanding restaurant offers a sweeping panorama of St. John and the BVIs at night. Although diners come here mainly for such dishes as rich and creamy lobster bisque, mahi-mahi and crab cake, or simply fresh fish prepared to your liking, meat eaters will also be pleased with such offerings as tenderloin of steak with béarnaise sauce. The side dishes here are especially appealing, including cheesy Alfredo pasta salad and spicy beans and rice. The fare has gleaned six gold medals in Caribbean cooking competitions. At the Lookout Lounge, you can order the house drink, Desmond Delight, a combination of rum, pineapple juice, and a secret ingredient. The extensive wine list won a *Wine Spectator* award. A live steel-drum band draws listeners Tuesday and Thursday nights.

See map p. 473. Point Pleasant Resort, 6600 Estate Smith Bay. ☎ *340-775-4142. Reservations recommended. Main courses: $24–$48. AE, DC, MC, V. Open: Daily 6–10 p.m.*

Banana Tree Grille
$$$ **Charlotte Amalie   INTERNATIONAL/CARIBBEAN**

The choice dining spot at the recommended **Bluebeard's Castle Hotel** (see the listing earlier in this chapter) is this smoothly run restaurant overlooking romantic-at-night panoramic views of the Charlotte Amalie harbor. When making a reservation, try for a table at the edge of the multi-tiered restaurant. The Grille offers a real aura of the tropics, with lights winking at you in palm trees, a hip wait staff in Hawaiian shirts, bartenders blending tropical drinks, and flickering candlelight. Start with the bacon-wrapped horseradish shrimp, going on to such main events as lobster tail tempura with an orange sambal sauce or mustard-glazed salmon. Meat aficionados gravitate to a shank of lamb slowly braised in Chianti and served

St. Thomas Dining

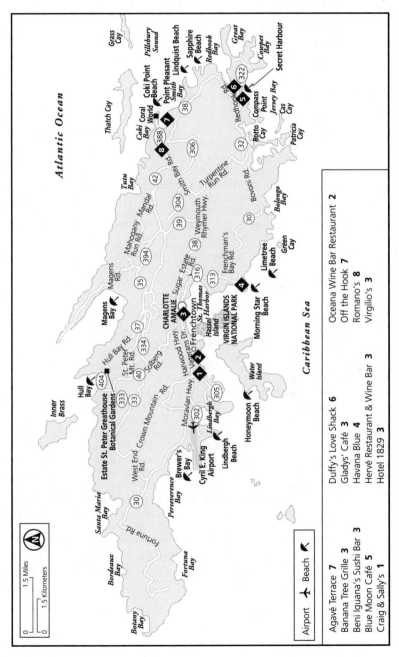

Airport ✈ Beach ☚

Agavé Terrace **7**
Banana Tree Grille **3**
Beni Iguana's Sushi Bar **3**
Blue Moon Café **5**
Craig & Sally's **1**

Duffy's Love Shack **6**
Gladys' Café **3**
Havana Blue **4**
Hervé Restaurant & Wine Bar **3**
Hotel 1829 **3**

Oceana Wine Bar Restaurant **2**
Off the Hook **7**
Romano's **8**
Virgilio's **3**

with an aioli sauce over white beans and garlic mashed potatoes. Desserts are justifiably called "decadent."

See map p. 473. At Bluebeard's Castle, Bluebeard's Hill, Charlotte Amalie. ☎ *340-776-4050. Reservations required. Main courses: $18–$39. AE, MC, V. Open: Tues–Sun 6–9:30 p.m.*

Beni Iguana's Sushi Bar
$-$$ **Charlotte Amalie ASIAN/JAPANESE**

Across from Emancipation Park, Beni Iguana's Sushi Bar is the restaurant that brought the cuisine from Japan to St. Thomas. The bar and restaurant are installed in a former cistern with an open-air courtyard. The old Danish colonial doors are still in place, and the interior is coated with red-and-black Chinese lacquer. Sushi comes in familiar packaging here, and the tuna or salmon sashimi is a delight. If you're uncertain of menu terms, all you have to do is look at the pictures of the various dishes. If you like a little of everything and are traveling with friends or family, you can order combo plates for four to five diners. The savory green-lipped mussels come from Australia.

See map p. 473. At Grand Hotel Court, at Norre Gade and Tolbod Gade. ☎ *340-777-8744. Reservations recommended. Main courses: $8–$17; sushi: $4–$18 per portion (two pieces); combo plates for four to five diners: $26–$36 each. AE, DC, MC, V. Open: Mon–Sat 11:30 a.m.–3 p.m. and 5–9:30 p.m.*

Blue Moon Café
$$ **Nazareth Bay CREATIVE AMERICAN**

For romantic dining in an open-air setting under the Caribbean moon, this beachfront restaurant claims, with some degree of accuracy, one of the most memorable settings for panoramic sunset views. *The Wine Spectator* acclaimed the restaurant for having the most romantic setting on St. Thomas. In winter, the setting is accompanied by piano bar music on Wednesday night with a steel drum band on Friday. The menu, based on market-fresh ingredients, changes twice a season and is designed to appeal to a wide range of palates, beginning with such tropical starters as coconut honey shrimp with a guava dipping sauce or a portobello mushroom and goat cheese tart with field onions. The chef handles the best ingredients with imagination, fashioning them into zestful combinations such as mahi-mahi with pecans, bananas, and a coconut rum sauce, or grilled scallops with a tomato-basil risotto with fresh asparagus. For lunch, you may want to confine yourself to burgers, wraps, salads, and sandwiches.

See map p. 473. At the Secret Harbour Beach Resort, 6280 Estate Nazareth Bay. ☎ *340-779-2262. Reservations required. Main courses: $14–$30. AE, DC, DISC, MC, V. Open: Daily 8 a.m.–3 p.m. and 6–10 p.m.*

Craig & Sally's
$$-$$$ Frenchtown INTERNATIONAL

Islanders, often with kids in tow, as well as savvy visitors make their way to this St. Thomas favorite to sample the culinary skills of Chef Sally Darash, the best female chef on the island. Sally runs the place with her husband, Craig, who's in charge of the wine cellar. Always inventive, the fusion chef borrows from Asia, the West Indies, and the Mediterranean, but gives all the dishes her special touch, as evoked by such starters as an eggplant "cheesecake" with a pine-nut-and-garlic-breaded crust. For main dishes, we go for her sautéed Chilean sea bass with a tangy mango barbecue glaze and a fresh mango couscous. Or you may opt for her baked halibut in a Mexican mole sauce with rice and a jalapeño black-bean quesadilla. Nothing is finer for dessert than Sally's white chocolate cheesecake.

See map p. 473. 3525 Honduras. ☎ *340-777-9949. Reservations recommended. Main courses: $18–$45. MC, V. Open: Lunch Wed–Fri 11:30 a.m.–3 p.m.; dinner Wed–Sun 5:30–10 p.m.*

Duffy's Love Shack
$–$$$ East End ECLECTIC

Duffy's Love Shack is a funky local dive that's somewhat of an island legend. Near the Red Hook ferry dock, Duffy's became known when the Mamas and the Papas came over from St. John to entertain. They proved such an island favorite that the group went on to glory in the States. Theme parties on Thursday nights still keep the entertainment memory alive at this open-air shack, with lots of bamboo and a thatched roof over the bar. The bar is more popular than the dining room, because the bartenders here are known for their lethal rum drinks, including a 50-ounce flaming extravaganza. The chef combines a standard American cuisine with recipes that have West Indian flair, including everything from "cowboy steak" to "junkanoo" chicken in a coconut and pineapple sauce. Habitués praise the chef's blackened shark if that's your idea of good eating. If not, we recommend the jerk tenderloin. After 10 p.m., a more-limited menu appears, mainly sandwiches.

See map p. 473. 6501 Red Hook Plaza. ☎ *340-779-2080. Main courses: $8–$16. No credit cards. Open: Daily 11:30 a.m.–2 a.m.*

Gladys' Café
$ Charlotte Amalie WEST INDIAN/AMERICAN

When Gladys Isles arrived here from her native Antigua, she brought her local island recipes with her, and today she concocts some of the best West Indian fare in Charlotte Amalie. Her breakfast is the biggest in town (think omelets, bacon and eggs, thick French toast, and freshly baked breads), served with unlimited coffee. If you come back for lunch (you can't get dinner here), you can dig into her hearty fare, including pan-fried whitefish, a savory conch in a lemon butter sauce, and various *rotis* (like stuffed crepes). She also makes such old island favorites as salt fish 'n dumplings or a robust red bean soup. As you're leaving, you can buy her special bottles of hot sauce for $5 to $10 (depending on size).

See map p. 473. Royal Dane Mall. ☎ 340-774-6604. Main courses: $9–$10 at breakfast, $9–$19 at lunch. AE, DC, MC, V. Open: Mon–Sat 7 a.m.–6 p.m. (breakfast until 11 a.m.)

Havana Blue
$$$$ Charlotte Amalie   CUBA/PACIFIC RIM/FUSION

This chic venue at a resort hotel enjoys a beachfront ambience and a sophisticated menu that is the island's most inspired. An inventive crew is in the kitchen, running wild in their culinary imagination. Cool cigars, hip drinks (mango mojitos), and a chic décor draw serious foodies to this cutting-edge restaurant, where chef Omar Sanchez often intoxicates with his aromas and flavors. After launching yourself with the black-bean hummus or the tuna tartare with a soy lime vinaigrette, it's on to such delights as breaded chicken breast stuffed with manchego cheese and diced jalapeños or a miso-crusted sea bass. What about ancho chili-rubbed beef filet with espresso sauce. Desserts are worth crossing the island for if it means Cuban chocolate cake with coconut ice cream or a warm banana and macadamia spring rolls with a strawberry balsamic purée.

See map p. 473. In the Frenchman's Reef & Morning Star Marriott Beach Resort, 5 Estate Bakkeroe. ☎ 340-715-2583. Reservations required. Main courses: $30–$42. AE, DC, MC, V. Daily 5–10 p.m.

Hervé Restaurant & Wine Bar
$$$–$$$$ Charlotte Amalie   AMERICAN/CARIBBEAN/FRENCH

Hervé Chassin is arguably the island's best chef, operating next to (and surpassing) the viands served at that classic landmark, Hotel 1829 (see our recommendation that follows). Opening onto a panoramic view of yacht-clogged Charlotte Amalie, Chassin attracts with an innovative menu of top-quality ingredients and a romantic atmosphere with flickering candles and beautifully served tables. You can dine on a large open-air terrace or in the intimate wine room. Start with the pistachio-encrusted brie, shrimp in a stuffed crab shell, or conch fritters with mango chutney. From here, you can let your taste buds march boldly forward with red snapper poached with white wine, or a delectable black-sesame-crusted tuna with a ginger-raspberry sauce. The chef features well-prepared nightly specials of game, fish, and pasta. Desserts here are equally divine — you'll rarely taste a creamier crème caramel or a lighter, fluffier mango or raspberry cheesecake.

See map p. 473. Government Hill. ☎ 340-777-9703. Reservations required. Main courses: $7–$18 at lunch, $19–$34 at dinner. AE, MC, V. Open: Daily lunch 11:30 a.m.–3 p.m., dinner 6–10 p.m.

Hotel 1829
$$$$$ **Charlotte Amalie** **CONTINENTAL/CARIBBEAN**

We suggest that you make an evening of it here by arriving early for a sun-downer in the darkly atmospheric bar tavern still haunted by the ghosts of yesteryear, when it was a celebrity favorite and you never knew who you were likely to encounter, perhaps Edna St. Vincent Millay. The celebs are long gone, but the romantic aura lingers. Hotel 1829 has long ceased to be the finest restaurant on the island — the competition today is too fierce for that — but it does offer the most elaborate prix-fixe menu on St. Thomas, backed up by an award-winning wine list, the island's finest. The menu changes nightly and the chefs adjust it seasonally; the cooking is first-rate, with solid technique. The menu has a distinctively European twist, with many of the dishes prepared and served from trolleys beside your table. The chefs are long known for their delectable and feathery light soufflés (order when you place your dinner order): chocolate, Grand Marnier, coconut, and a marvelous raspberry one.

See map p. 473. Kongens Gade (at the east end of Main Street). ☎ *340-776-1234. Reservations essential but not accepted more than one day in advance. Prix-fixe dinner $40–$70. AE, MC, V. Open: Mon–Sat 5:30–9:30 p.m. Closed June 1–Dec 1.*

Oceana Wine Bar Restaurant
$$$$ **Frenchtown** **STEAKS/SEAFOOD**

This upscale restaurant is known for serving the finest cut of prime rib on the island. But it also features grilled seafood, which on occasion is even better. The stripped-down 19th-century villa that contains the Chart House was the Russian consulate during the island's Danish administration. It lies a short distance beyond the most densely populated area of Frenchtown village. The dining gallery is a spacious open terrace fronting the sea. Cocktails start daily at 5 p.m., when the bartender breaks out the ingredients for his special Bailey's banana colada. Calamari, pasta dishes, coconut shrimp, and Hawaiian chicken are part of the expanded menu. For dessert, order the famous mud pie.

See map p. 473. Oceana, Frenchtown. ☎ *340-774-4262. Reservations recommended. Main courses: $20–$40. AE, DISC, MC, V. Open: Mon–Sat 5–10 p.m.*

Off the Hook
$$$–$$$$ **East End** **ASIAN/CARIBBEAN**

Diners at Off the Hook enjoy an eclectic medley of specialties inspired by Asia, although the chefs concoct dishes with some of the freshest and finest ingredients of the West Indies. In an open-air dining room near the **American Yacht Harbor,** close to the departure point for the ferry to St. John, the fresh catch of the day — hauled off the little fishing boats just pulling in — is delivered to the kitchen, where the chef grills it to perfection. The yellowfin tuna keeps us coming back. The chef is also adept at preparing a tuna and salmon sushi platter, and the black Angus steak is always a pure delight. The décor is rustic, with outdoor dining and wooden tables.

See map p. 473. 6300 Estate Smith Bay. ☎ *340-775-6350. Reservations required. Main courses: $18–$26. AE, MC, V. Open: Daily 6–10 p.m. Closed Sept 15–Oct 15.*

Romano's
$$$–$$$$ East End   NORTHERN ITALIAN

In a setting near Coral World, a New Jersey–born chef, Tony Romano, brings the savory cuisine of Northern Italy to St. Thomas. Romano's has been an island tradition since it opened in 1988. The dishes he creates would even please the late Frank Sinatra, who was known to toss a plate of spaghetti across the room if it wasn't cooked to his specifications. Tony's dishes are full of flavor and beautifully spiced with lots of herbs. We delight in his linguine with pesto and find his lasagna, made with four different kinds of cheese, velvety and creamy. You can have fish if you want it, perhaps a perfectly broiled salmon, although we suggest his classic Italian meat dishes, especially *osso buco* and scaloppini flavored with Marsala.

See map p. 473. 97 Smith Bay Rd. ☎ *340-775-0045. Reservations recommended. Main courses: $20–$40; pastas $19–$23. MC, V. Open: Mon–Sat 6–10:30 p.m. Closed Sept and one week in Apr for Carnival.*

Virgilio's
$$$–$$$$ Charlotte Amalie   NORTHERN ITALIAN

For Northern Italian cuisine even better than Romano's (see the preceding listing), you can stay right in Charlotte Amalie and head for the domain of Virgilio del Mare. Under heavy ceiling beams and brick vaulting, you can dine in a soothing atmosphere under crystal chandeliers with soft Italian background music. Virgilio has taught his chefs well, and they invariably feature fresh-tasting ingredients that they handle with razor-sharp technique. The *cinco peche* (clams, mussels, scallops, oysters, and crayfish simmered in a saffron broth) is a delectable house special, while the fettuccine Alfredo here is the best on the island. Classic dishes have a distinctive flair — the rack of lamb, for example, is filled with a porcini mushroom stuffing and glazed with a roasted garlic aioli. The marinated grilled duck comes chilled. You can even order an individual margherita pizza.

See map p. 473. 18 Dronningens Gade (entrance on a narrow alleyway running between Main Street and Backstreet). ☎ *340-776-4920. Reservations recommended. Main courses: $14–$30 lunch, $21–$40 dinner. AE, MC, V. Open: Mon–Sat 11:30 a.m.–10:30 p.m.*

On St. Croix

Bacchus
$$$ Christiansted   STEAKHOUSE/CONTINENTAL

In a restaurant dedicated to the god of wine, the wine *carte* receives as much attention as the regular menu. Both *Wine Spectator* and *Food & Wine*

St. Croix Dining

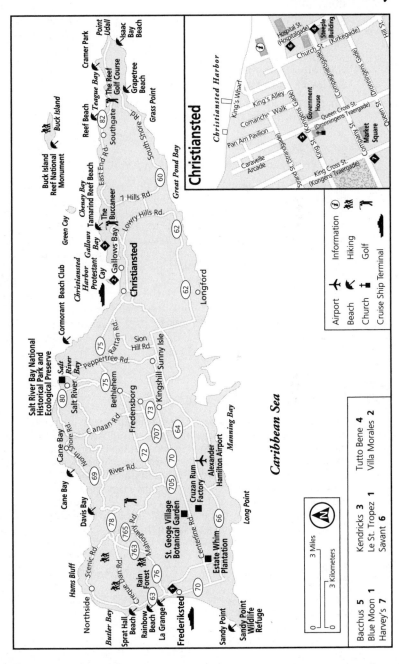

Christiansted

Christiansted Harbor

Hospital St. (Hospitalgade)
Church St. (Kirkegade)
Steeple Building
King's Wharf
King's Alley
Comanche Walk
Government House
Pan Am Pavilion
Queen Cross St. (Dronningens Tvaergade)
Caravelle Arcade
Market Square
King Cross St. (Kongens Tvaergade)

Information ℹ
Hiking
Golf
Airport ✈
Beach
Church ✝
Cruise Ship Terminal

Point Udall
Isaac Bay Beach
Cramer Park
Reef Beach
The Reef Golf Course
Grapetree Beach
Grass Point
Buck Island
Buck Island Reef National Monument
Teague Bay
Southgate
South Shore Rd.
Great Pond Bay
7 Hills Rd.
Chenay Bay
Tamarind Reef Beach
The Buccaneer
Green Cay
Gallows Bay
Lowry Hills Rd.
Cormorant Beach Club
Christiansted Harbor
Protestant Cay
Christiansted
Longford
Salt River Bay National Historical Park and Ecological Preserve
Sion Hill Rd.
Peppertree Rd.
Rattan Rd.
Salt River Bay
Salt River
Sunny Isle
Kingshill
Bethlehem
Fredensborg
Canaan Rd.
Manning Bay
Caribbean Sea
Cane Bay
North Shore Rd.
River Rd.
Davis Bay
Alexander Hamilton Airport
Cruzan Rum Factory
St. George Village Botanical Garden
Long Point
Hams Bluff
Scenic Rd.
Rain Forest
Mahogany Rd.
Estate Whim Plantation
Centerline Rd.
Northside
Butler Bay
Sprat Hall Beach
Rainbow Beach
La Grange
Frederiksted
Sandy Point
Sandy Point Wildlife Refuge

3 Miles
3 Kilometers
0
0

N

Bacchus **5**
Blue Moon **1**
Harvey's **7**
Kendricks **3**
Le St. Tropez **1**
Savant **6**
Tutto Bene **4**
Villa Morales **2**

have praised Bacchus's cellar. The décor, fine service, and dish presentation make for a fine evening out. The kitchen uses first-class ingredients, many imported, to craft a number of dishes that combine flavor and finesse. You're sure to delight in the lobster Bacchus or the rib-eye steak Florentine, a local favorite. One tantalizing dish is the apple-smoked bacon wrapped around a filet mignon. To finish, it doesn't get any better than the rum-infused sourdough bread pudding. Most dishes, except lobster, are at the lower end of the price scale.

See map p. 479. Queen Cross Street, off King Street. ☎ *340-692-9922. Reservations recommended. Main courses: $16–$28. AE, MC, V. Open: Tues–Sun 6–10 p.m.*

Blue Moon
$$$ Frederiksted   INTERNATIONAL/CAJUN

Your best bet for dining in St. Croix's Frederiksted is this waterfront bistro that draws big crowds on Friday night for its live jazz. In a two-century-old stone house, it's a bit funky with its homemade art, including a trash-can lid advertising its name. In an informal, laid-back atmosphere, you can begin with the *lunar pie,* which is feta, cream cheese, onions, mushrooms, and celery in phyllo pastry, or the artichoke-and-spinach dip. Main courses include the catch of the day and, on occasion, Maine lobster. The clams served in garlic sauce are also from Maine. Vegetarians opt for the spinach fettuccine. The menu also offers the usual array of steak and chicken dishes. Save room for the yummy apple spice pie.

See map p. 479. 17 Strand St. ☎ *340-772-2222. Reservations recommended. Main courses: $18–$25. AE, DISC, MC, V. Open: Lunch Tues–Fri 11:30 a.m.–2 p.m. and Sun 11 a.m.–2 p.m.; dinner Tues–Sat 6–9:30 p.m.*

Harvey's
$ Christiansted   WEST INDIAN

Sarah Harvey is mistress of those pots and pans at this friendly, casual eatery. Locals and an occasional visitor quickly fill up the dozen tables, partaking of the island-inspired cuisine based on recipes handed down through the generations. No one bothers to print a menu, and daily specials are listed on the blackboard. The ambience is of the 1950s with plastic and flowery tablecloths. Try one of Sarah's homemade soups, especially the callaloo (similar to spinach) or the chicken. For an appetizer, we go for the conch in butter sauce. For a main dish, it's hard to beat the broiled kingfish or red snapper, although you can opt for the savory barbecue spareribs. Sarah is also known for making the best curried goat stew in town. Main dishes come with seasoned rice and beans, local sweet potatoes, fried plantain, and fungi. To end on a sweet note, Sarah makes her pies with guava, pineapple, or coconut.

See map p. 479. 11B Company St. ☎ *340-773-3433. Reservations not required. Main courses: $8–$14. No credit cards. Open: Mon–Sat 11:30 a.m.–5 p.m.*

Kendricks
$$$$ Gallows Bay FRENCH/CONTINENTAL

The staff of *Bon Appétit* has discovered the succulent, finely honed cuisine available at the historic Quin House complex at Company and King Cross streets in the center of Gallows Bay (about a mile east of Christiansted), with dining rooms both upstairs (more formal, better view) and down. To learn of the culinary prowess of the chefs, we recently enjoyed some of the house specialties, including pan-seared Thai shrimp with cucumber relish and a coconut-infused rice. The signature appetizer that night was seared scallops and artichoke hearts in a lemon-cream sauce. We discovered no finer dish than the pecan-crusted roast loin of pork with a ginger-laced mayonnaise.

See map p. 479. 2132 Company St. ☎ *340-773-9199. Reservations recommended. Main courses: $22–$33. AE, MC, V. Open: Mon–Sat 6–9:30 p.m. Closed Mon June–Oct.*

Le St. Tropez
$$ Frederiksted FRENCH MEDITERRANEAN

Le St. Tropez is the most popular bistro in Frederiksted. The place is small, so call ahead for a table. If you're visiting for the day, make this bright little cafe your lunch stop and enjoy crepes, quiches, soups, or salads in the sunlit courtyard. At night, the atmosphere glows with candlelight and becomes more festive. Try the pâté de champagne and escargots Provençal or one of the freshly made soups. Main dishes are likely to include rack of lamb with mushrooms, the fish of the day, or a magret of duck. Ingredients are always fresh and well prepared.

See map p. 479. Limetree Court, 227 King St. ☎ *340-772-3000. Reservations recommended. Main courses: $17–$36. AE, MC, V. Open: Mon–Fri 11:30 a.m.–2:30 p.m.; Mon–Sat 6–10 p.m.*

Savant
$$$ Christiansted CARIBBEAN/THAI/MEXICAN

The spicy fusion cuisine here provides a marvelous burst of palate-awakening flavors. The bistro atmosphere is stylish, yet fun and laid-back. Black-and-white photos and other original artwork line the walls of the restaurant. Fresh fish is deftly handled. We gravitate to the tantalizing Thai curries, most of which are mildly spiced. You can ask the chef to "go nuclear" if you prefer hotter food. The red-coconut-curry sauce is one of the best we've ever had on the island. If you're craving an enchilada, try the one stuffed with seafood. The maple-teriyaki pork tenderloin, one of the chef's specialties, is terrific, as are the steak choices. Savant has only 20 candlelit tables, so call for a reservation as far in advance as you can.

See map p. 479. 4C Hospital St. ☎ *340-713-8666. Reservations required. Main courses: $14–$30. AE, MC, V. Mon–Sat 6–10 p.m.*

Tutto Bene
$$$ Christiansted   ITALIAN

In the center of Christiansted, this trattoria is the domain of Smokey Odom and Kelly Williams, who are known for their robust and hearty Italian recipes. "We feed you well here," Williams accurately told us. Nothing is fancy, and service is on wooden tables covered with painted tablecloths. The place attracts an equal number of visitors and locals who feast on the succulent pastas and the perfectly grilled fish. A signature dish is the chef's special, *tutto di mare,* with mussels, clams, and shrimp in a white-wine and pesto sauce spread over linguine. We also recommend the juicy veal chop with sun-dried tomatoes.

See map p. 479. 2 Company St. ☎ *340-773-5229. Reservations accepted only for parties of five or more. Main courses: $18–$30. AE, MC, V. Open: Daily 5–10 p.m.*

Villa Morales
$ Frederiksted   PUERTO RICAN

At a location 3.2km (2 miles) from Frederiksted, you can select a table either indoors or outdoors to enjoy some real island cookery. If you come early you can mix with the locals in the cozy bar. Those with a taste for Hispanic cuisine will be richly rewarded here with all those favorite dishes your Puerto Rican mama (assuming you had one) prepared for you. Savory examples include fried snapper with white rice and beans, stewed conch, roasted or stewed goat, and stewed beef. Meal platters are garnished with beans and rice. Most of the dishes are at the lower end of the price scale. About once a month, the owners transform the place into a dance hall, bringing in live salsa and merengue bands (the cover ranges from $5–$15).

See map p. 479. Plot 82C (off Route 70), Estate Whim. ☎ *340-772-0556. Reservations recommended. Main courses: $8–$15 at lunch, $8–$35 at dinner. MC, V. Open: Thurs–Sat 10 a.m.–10 p.m.*

On St. John

Asolare
$$$$$ Cruz Bay   ASIAN/FRENCH

At night, our favorite retreat on the island is this refined restaurant, where you can linger at a table on a balcony perch overlooking **Cruz Bay** with a panorama of the moonlit water. Asolare is one of the best places on St. John at which to arrive early for a sundowner, perhaps waiting for the moment when the sun sinks to see the legendary green flash that Hemingway wrote about. The chef roams the world for inspiration and cooks with flavor and flair, using some of the best and freshest ingredients available on the island. To begin, try the grilled Asian barbecued shrimp and scallion wonton or the marinated vegetable spring rolls. For a main course, you may be tempted by crispy Peking duckling with sesame glaze or the peppercorn-dusted filet of beef. Two truly excellent dishes are the

St. John Dining

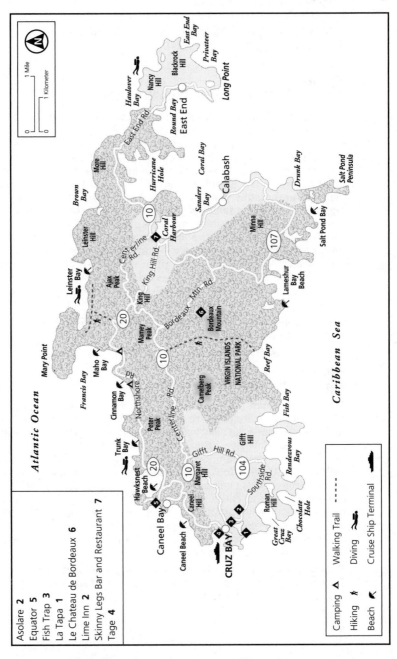

Asolare **2**
Equator **5**
Fish Trap **3**
La Tapa **1**
Le Chateau de Bordeaux **6**
Lime Inn **2**
Skinny Legs Bar and Restaurant **7**
Tage **4**

Camping ▲ Walking Trail -----
Hiking 🚶 Diving 🤿
Beach 🏄 Cruise Ship Terminal

lime-sautéed chicken with yellow curry sauce and sashimi tuna on a sizzling plate with plum passion-fruit sake vinaigrette. For dessert, try the frozen mango guava soufflé or chocolate pyramid cake.

See map p. 483. Caneel Hill. ☎ *340-779-4747. Reservations required. Main courses: $30–$50. AE, MC, V. Open: Daily 5:30–9 p.m.*

Equator
$$$$–$$$$$ Caneel Bay   CARIBBEAN/FUSION

On the grounds of the deluxe Caneel Bay Resort, the retreat of the wintering wealthy, you can dine near the remains of an 18th-century sugar mill. Take stairs to a circular dining room with a wraparound porch. In its center, the restaurant grows a giant poinciana-like Asian tree of the *Albizia lebbeck* species. Islanders call it "woman's tongue tree." The cuisine is the most daring on the island, and for the most part, the chefs pull off their transcultural dishes. A spicy and tantalizing opener is lemon-grass-and-ginger-cured salmon salad (get *Gourmet* magazine on the phone). A classic Caribbean callaloo (something like spinach) soup is available, and the salads use fresh ingredients such as tomatoes and endive. The menu offers daily Caribbean selections, or you can opt for such fine dishes as seared Caribbean mahi-mahi with a lentil or pumpkin mélange or penne pasta with shiitake mushrooms and roasted tomatoes in an herb garlic cream sauce. Dry, aged Angus steak or a grilled veal chop satisfy the more-traditional palates.

See map p. 483. At the Caneel Bay Resort. ☎ *340-776-6111. Reservations required. Main courses: $22–$42. AE, MC, V. Open: Tues–Sun 6:30–9:30 p.m.*

Fish Trap
$$$ Cruz Bay   SEAFOOD

This aptly named place serves St. John's best seafood. Fish Trap has a casual, laid-back atmosphere with tables placed on a covered patio open to the trade winds, an easy walk up from the ferry dock. Chef Aaron Willis is the island's favorite, bringing his New York culinary training with him but showing a total familiarity with West Indian seasonings and flavors. Nobody on St. John does conch fritters better than this skilled cook, and national magazines such as *Vogue* and *Gourmet* have voiced their praise. Depending on the catch of the day, he features six fresh fish specials nightly, most likely wahoo, shark, mahi-mahi, or snapper. The grilled tuna, for example, comes in a wasabi sauce, and the swordfish is made more appetizing by the use of lemon grass. An array of steaks, tasty pastas, chicken cutlets, and burgers are always on hand.

See map p. 483. In Town Center, next to Our Lady of Mount Carmel Church. ☎ *340-693-9994. Reservations accepted only for parties of six or more. Main courses: $8–$25. AE, DISC, MC, V. Open: Tues–Sun 4–9:30 p.m.*

La Tapa
$$$–$$$$ **Cruz Bay**   **TAPAS/INTERNATIONAL**

An equal mixture of local habitués and visitors flock here at night to sample tapas, Spanish-inspired bite-size morsels of fish, meat, or marinated vegetables, accompanied by pitchers of sangria. The restaurant has a tiny bar with no more than five stools, a two-tiered dining room, and lots of original paintings (the establishment doubles as an art gallery for emerging local artists). Menu items are thoughtful and well conceived, and include fast-seared tuna with a Basque-inspired relish of onions, peppers, garlic, and herbs; a steak soaked with rum, and served with a cracked pepper sauce and mashed potatoes; and linguine with shrimp, red peppers, and leeks in peanut sauce.

See map p. 483. Centerline Road. ☎ *340-693-7755. Reservations recommended. Main courses: $22–$36. AE, MC, V. Open: Wed–Mon 5:30–10 p.m.*

Le Chateau de Bordeaux
$$$$–$$$$$ **Bordeaux Mountain**   **CONTINENTAL/CARIBBEAN**

Patrons are always comparing the romantic setting of Le Chateau de Bordeaux at night to dining in a treehouse. Close to the geographical center of the island and considered the loftiest restaurant on St. John, the château lies 8km (5 miles) east of Cruz Bay. If you sit at one of its terrace tables, you get a panoramic view in every direction. Chefs have a talent for making sauces and combining flavors, and they heavily feature their namesake, Bordeaux reds, on the wine *carte*. A lunch grill on the patio serves burgers and drinks daily from 10 a.m. to 4:30 p.m. In the evening, amid the Victorian décor and lace tablecloths, you can begin with a house-smoked chicken spring roll or velvety carrot soup. After that, move on to one of the saffron-flavored pastas or savory West Indian seafood chowder. Smoked salmon and filet mignon are a bow to the international crowd, and the wild-game specials are more unusual. The well-flavored Dijon-mustard and pecan-crusted roast rack of lamb with shallot port reduction is also a good choice. For dessert, a changing array of cheesecakes complements other options.

See map p. 483. Junction 10, Centerline Road. ☎ *340-776-6611. Reservations recommended. Main courses: $28–$34. AE, MC, V. Open: Daily 6–9 p.m. Closed Sun–Mon in summer.*

Lime Inn
$$ **Cruz Bay**   **SEAFOOD/AMERICAN**

This eatery enjoys a devoted local following thanks to its fresh fish and seafood dishes prepared in many ways. Most diners are pleased with the affordable fish dinners, especially the Wednesday-night feast with all the shrimp you can eat. In a tropical garden setting in the heart of **Cruz Bay,** steaks, Caribbean lobster, juicy burgers, and charcoal-grilled fish emerge beautifully cooked from the outdoor grill. Backing up these dishes is an array of homemade soups and fresh salads.

See map p. 483. Lemon Tree Mall, Kongens Gade. ☎ 340-776-6425. Reservations not necessary. Main courses: Lunch $6–$15, dinner $18–$28. AE, MC, V. Open: Lunch Mon–Fri 12.–3 p.m.; dinner Mon–Sat 5:30–10 p.m. Closed July 1–Aug 5.

Skinny Legs Bar and Restaurant
$ Coral Bay   AMERICAN

This funky eatery serves good food and shows you a good time while you're enjoying its convivial atmosphere. It is said, and we concur, that Skinny attracts the largest number of Willie Nelson look-alikes in the West Indies. The dive is also known as the best restaurant and bar for meeting locals. The place is really a shack, known for cooking the best burgers on the island, which many people down with St. John's own home-brew, Blackbeard Ale. A lot of the fare is pub grub, such as sandwiches, salads, grilled chicken, and daily specials — perhaps pot roast.

See map p. 483. Route 107 (near the Coral Bay dinghy dock). ☎ 340-779-4982. Reservations not necessary. Main courses: $6–$8. AE, MC, V. Open: Daily 11 a.m.–10 p.m.

Tage
$$$ Cruz Bay   AMERICAN/INTERNATIONAL

The island's best chef, a devotee of the "Alice Waters Northern California" approach to cuisine, walks the beach every morning with his dogs, dreaming up the night's five or six food specials that he plans to offer. Perhaps it will be ahi and carambola with a mango Key lime salsa, or a maple bourbon-glazed smoked tenderloin panini with a roasted tomato aioli. He recently won the hearts of our dinner party with such dishes as pan-seared, fennel-pollen-dusted, yellowfin tuna with a champagne truffle vinaigrette. Locally grown organic produce is used whenever possible. His menu is elegant, as is the ambience of his restaurant, but Robinson claims he likes to "keep it simple" (he doesn't even own a pair of shoes). Other highlights of his ever-changing menu include shiitake-filled porcini ravioli with arugula oil or pan-roasted duck breast with roasted sweet potato, prosciutto, smoked almonds, and a binding rum vinaigrette. There's no doubt about it: Tage is the "hot" dining ticket on St. John.

See map p. 483. Cruz Bay. ☎ 340-715-4270. Reservations required. Main courses: $10–$30. AE, DC, MC, V. Mon–Sat 6–9:30 p.m.

Enjoying the Sand and Surf

No rule says you have to confine yourself to a beach chair within arm's length of the bar while visiting the U.S. Virgin Islands (though there's no rule against it, either). You'll have endless opportunities to sit by the surf sipping rum drinks, but remember that opportunities abound to actively explore the islands. Coral reefs and stunning beaches provide breathtaking backdrops for a variety of water sports, from snorkeling to kayaking.

Combing the beaches

"We're from Canada, and we came here for the beaches," a husband-and-wife team told us one February. That couple came to the right place. Some Caribbean beaches are made of black volcanic sand. Not those in the USVIs — they rank near the top of all the beaches in the Caribbean.

On St. Thomas

Depending on who's counting, St. Thomas boasts nearly 50 beaches, and all of them are open to the public, even those in front of the megaresorts. Sometimes you have to walk across a hotel's grounds to reach a beach. Although the sands belong to everyone, you have to pay extra if you use any of the resort's equipment such as chaise longues. The major St. Thomas beach is **Magens Bay,** known for its heart-shaped shoreline and crystal-clear waters ideal for snorkeling around the rocks. It lies 4.8km (3 miles) north of Charlotte Amalie at Route 35 and 42; the beach charges a $3 entrance fee and is open daily from 5 a.m. to 6 p.m. Lined with lush green palms and equipped with showers and changing rooms, this beach is a good place to spend a whole day.

Magens Bay gets very crowded when a lot of cruise ships are in port. The beach is especially busy on Saturday and Sunday and on all holidays. Bathhouses are located here, along with snack bars and rum bars. Traditionally, at some point visitors to Magens drop in for a drink at the little **Udder Delight (☎ 340-777-6050),** a stand serving tasty milkshakes laced with Cruzan rums, Amaretto, Kahlúa, and crème de menthe. The stand sits on a hillside close to the entrance of Magens Bay Beach. Your kids can enjoy one of the fruit-infused shakes, such as soursop.

Coki Point Beach, in the Northeast near Coral World, is good but often very crowded. Noted for its warm, crystal-clear water, the bay is ideal for swimming and snorkeling (you'll see thousands of rainbow-hued fish swimming among the beautiful corals). Locals even sell small bags of fish food so you can feed the sea creatures while you're snorkeling. From the beach, you get a panoramic view of offshore Thatch Cay. Concessions can arrange everything from water-skiing to parasailing. An East End bus runs to Smith Bay and lets you off at the gate to Coral World and Coki. Watch out for pickpockets.

 Sapphire Beach, popular with windsurfers, is set against the backdrop of the Sapphire Beach Resort and Marina, where you can have lunch or order drinks. From here you get good views of offshore cays and St. John; a large reef is close to the shore. You can rent snorkeling gear and lounge chairs from the resort/marina. To get to the beach, take the East End bus from Charlotte Amalie, going via Red Hook. Ask to be let off at the entrance to Sapphire Bay; you don't have to walk far to reach the water.

Small and special, **Secret Harbour** is near a collection of condos. With its white sand and coconut palms, this beach is the epitome of Caribbean charm. The snorkeling near the rocks is some of the best on the island.

No public transportation stops here, but you can take an easy taxi ride east of Charlotte Amalie heading toward Red Hook.

Morning Star Beach (also known as Frenchman's Bay Beach) is near the **Frenchman's Reef & Morning Star Marriott Beach Resort,** about 3.2km (2 miles) east of Charlotte Amalie. Here, among the often-young crowds (many of whom are gay), you can don your skimpiest bikini. Sailboats, snorkeling equipment, and lounge chairs are available for rent. You can easily reach the beach via a cliff-front elevator at Frenchman's Reef.

On St. Croix

The most celebrated beach is offshore **Buck Island,** part of the U.S. National Park Service network. After a snorkeling trip here in the early '60s, President Kennedy declared it a government-protected marine park. Buck Island is actually a volcanic islet surrounded by some of the most stunning underwater coral gardens in the Caribbean. The white-sand beaches on the Southwest and West Coasts are beautiful, but the snorkeling is even better. The islet's interior is filled with such plants as cactus, wild frangipani, and pigeonwood. Picnic areas are good for those who want to make a day of it. Boat departures are from Kings Wharf in Christiansted; the ride takes half an hour.

Your best choice for a beach in Christiansted is the one at the **Hotel on the Cay.** This white-sand strip is on a palm-shaded island. To get here, take the ferry from the fort at Christiansted; it runs daily from 7 a.m. to midnight. The four-minute trip costs $3; it's free for guests of the Hotel on the Cay. Eight kilometers (5 miles) west of Christiansted is the **Cormorant Beach Club,** where some 366m (1,200 ft.) of white sand shaded by palm trees attracts a gay crowd. Because a reef lies just off the shore, snorkeling conditions are ideal.

We highly recommend **Davis Bay** and **Cane Bay,** with swaying palms, white sand, and good swimming and snorkeling. Because they're on the North Shore, these beaches are often windy and their waters aren't always tranquil. The snorkeling at Cane Bay is spectacular; you'll see elkhorn and brain corals, all lying some 229m (750 ft.) off the Cane Bay Wall. Cane Bay adjoins Route 80 on the North Shore. Davis Bay, located near the Carambola Beach Resort, doesn't have a reef; it's more popular among bodysurfers than snorkelers.

On Route 63, a short ride north of Frederiksted, lies **Rainbow Beach,** which offers white sand and ideal snorkeling conditions. Nearby, also on Route 63, about five minutes north of Frederiksted, is another good beach, **La Grange.** You can rent lounge chairs here, and a bar is nearby.

Sandy Point, directly south of Frederiksted, is the largest beach on the U.S. Virgin Islands. Its waters are shallow and calm, perfect for swimming. Try to concentrate on the sands and not the unattractive zigzagging fences that line the beach. To reach this beach, take the Melvin H. Evans Highway (Route 66) west from the Alexander Hamilton Airport.

On St. John

Most visitors to St. John flock to the North Shore bordering the 4,678-hectare (11,560-acre) national park. Like all USVI beaches, these sandy strips are the most crowded during cruise-ship arrivals and on Saturday, Sunday, and holidays. If you're seeking more-secluded beaches, head for the East and South Coasts.

The best beach, hands down, is **Trunk Bay,** the biggest attraction on St. John. To miss its picture-perfect shoreline of white sand is like touring Paris and skipping the Eiffel Tower. One of the loveliest beaches in the Caribbean, it offers ideal conditions for diving, snorkeling, swimming, and sailing. The only drawback is the crowds (watch for pickpockets). Beginning snorkelers in particular are attracted to the underwater trail near the shore; you can rent snorkeling gear on the beach. Lifeguards are on duty. Trunk Beach is the best-equipped beach on St. John, with the best facilities such as changing rooms and lockers. Its facilities and calm waters make it idyllic for families. Admission is $4 per person for those over age 16. If you're coming from St. Thomas, both taxis and safari buses to Trunk Bay meet the ferry from Red Hook when it docks at Cruz Bay.

Caneel Bay, the stamping ground of the rich and famous, has seven beautiful beaches on its 69 hectares (170 acres) — all are open to the public, but getting to them can be difficult. **Caneel Bay Beach** is the only beach accessible by foot; it is easy to reach from the main entrance of the Caneel Bay Resort. A staff member at the gatehouse will provide directions. **Hawksnest Beach** is one of the most beautiful beaches near the Caneel Bay properties. It's not a wide beach, but it is choice. Because it lies near Cruz Bay, where the ferry docks, it is the most overpopulated, especially when cruise-ship passengers come over from St. Thomas. Safari buses and taxis from Cruz Bay will take you along Northshore Road to the beach.

The campgrounds of **Cinnamon Bay** have their own beach, where forest rangers sometimes have to remind visitors to put their swim trunks back on. This beach is our particular favorite, a beautiful strip of white sand with hiking trails, great windsurfing, ruins, and wild donkeys (don't feed or pet them). Changing rooms and showers are available, and you can rent water-sports equipment. Snorkeling is especially popular; you'll often see big schools of purple triggerfish. This beach is best in the morning and at midday, because afternoons are likely to be windy. A marked nature trail, with signs identifying the flora, loops through a tropical forest on even turf before leading straight up to Centerline Road.

Maho Bay Beach, immediately to the east of Cinnamon Bay, and bordering campgrounds, is also a popular beach, often with the campers themselves. As you lie on the sand here, you can take in a whole hillside of pitched tents.

Playing in the surf

The islands of St. Croix, St. John, and St. Thomas are the premier places to snorkel in the Caribbean, outdistancing Puerto Rico and the other islands. Diving is still best in the Cayman Islands, but Buck Island off St. Croix is one of the major diving meccas in the West Indies, with an underwater visibility of 30m (100 ft.). All three islands have enough labyrinths and grottoes for the most experienced divers, plus massive gardens of fiery coral inhabited by black sea urchins, barracudas, stingrays, and other creatures of the deep. And in the past quarter of a century, more than 20 sports fishing records have been set in the U.S. Virgins, whose waters are filled with bonito, tuna, wahoo, sailfish, and skipjack, among other species.

On St. Thomas

With its 30 spectacular reefs, St. Thomas, says *Skin Diver* magazine, is one of the best waterworlds in the Caribbean for both snorkeling and scuba diving. The best scuba-diving site off St. Thomas, especially for novices, is **Cow and Calf Rocks,** off the Southeast End (45 minutes from Charlotte Amalie by boat); here you'll discover a network of coral tunnels riddled with caves, reefs, and ancient boulders encrusted with coral. The *Cartanser Sr.,* a sunken World War II cargo ship that lies in about 11m (35 ft.) of water, is beautifully encrusted with coral and home to myriad colorful resident fish. Another popular wreck dive is the *Maj. General Rogers,* the stripped-down hull of a former Coast Guard cutter.

One of the island's best outfitters is **Aqua Action** (☎ 340-775-6285), a full-service, PADI, five-star dive shop at Secret Harbour Beach Resort. Owner Carl Moore, a certified instructor for the Handicap Scuba Association, teaches scuba to visitors with disabilities. This scuba organization is the only one on St. Thomas that's qualified to conduct scuba tours for those with limited mobility.

Chris Sawyer Diving Center, 6100 Red Hook Quarters, Building E1-1 (☎ 340-775-7320), at Compass Point Marina, operates from a base adjacent to the American Yacht Harbour at Red Hook. Designated as a PADI five-star dive center, it operates tours that depart for interesting dive sites in the USVIs Monday to Friday (and sometimes Sat) to sites in the British Virgin Islands, including the underwater wreck of the legendary *RMS Rhône,* the evocative underwater ruins of a site that is featured in several Hollywood films. (Don't forget your passport or your scuba certification papers if you opt for this trip.)

For an aerial view of the reefs even if you're not a particularly good swimmer, check out **Caribbean Parasail and Watersports,** 6501 Red Hook Plaza (☎ 340-775-9360). With an armada of five speedboats, each equipped with the kinds of harnesses and parasails you need for a parasail flight, they've captured an estimated 85 percent of the parasailing business of both St. Thomas and St. John. You sit in a harness that's linked to a specially designed aerodynamic parachute and you soar high in the air, from a seat directly on the dock, pulled behind a speedboat. If this sport appeals to you, one of their craft will come directly to the docks of pretty much any hotel you specify on the island, including the cruise-ship docks in Charlotte Amalie, any day of the week between 9 a.m. and 5 p.m. A ten-minute flight costs $65 for a single flyer, and $120 for a pair of tandem flyers linked together. Most of the hotels on both St. Thomas and St. John funnel interested parasailers to this outfitter.

Local residents who happen to love windsurfing sometimes devote part of their weekends to the sport, often heading out to the island's West Coast, where the constant and usually gentle winds seem to favor the sport. One of the best outfitters is **West Indies Windsurfing,** Vessup Beach, No. 9 Nazareth (☎ **340-775-6530**), which charges about $60 for a one-hour lesson, and around $15 per hour for rental of a windsurfer. Regular hours are Saturday and Sunday only from 9 a.m. to 5 p.m., but if you're in a group and are hankering to windsurf on a weekday, they'll happily make special arrangements.

Nineteen world records — eight for blue marlin — have been chalked up in recent years. Fishermen (and -women) have nabbed the legendary catches such as 454kg (1,000-lb.) blue marlins at the **North Drop,** lying some 32km (20 miles) off the island's North Coast. Big catches of mahi-mahi, wahoo, tuna, skipjack, and sailfish also turn up.

To book a boat, contact the **Charter Boat Center,** 6300 Red Hook Plaza (☎ **800-866-5714,** 340-775-7990) or **Sapphire Beach Marina,** Sapphire Bay (☎ **340-775-6100**). Or, to find the trip that will best suit you, walk down the docks at either American Yacht Harbor or Sapphire Beach Marina and chat with the captains.

On St. Croix

Sponge life, black coral (the finest in the West Indies), and steep drop-offs into water near the shoreline make St. Croix a snorkeling and diving paradise. The island is home to the largest living reef in the Caribbean, including the fabled North-Shore wall that begins in 7.6 to 9.1m (25–30 ft.) of water and drops to 4,023m (13,200 ft.), sometimes straight down.

Buck Island, about 2.4km (1½ miles) off the Northeastern Coast of St. Croix, is a major scuba-diving site, with a visibility of some 30m (100 ft.). It also has an underwater snorkeling trail.

Other favorite dive sites include the historic **Salt River Canyon** (northwest of Christiansted at Salt River Bay), which is for advanced divers. Submerged canyons' walls are covered with purple tube sponges, deep-water gorgonians, and black coral saplings. You'll see schools of yellowtail snapper, turtles, and spotted eagle rays. We also like the gorgeous coral gardens of **Scotch Banks** (north of Christiansted) and **Eagle Ray** (also north of Christiansted), the latter so named because of the rays that cruise along the wall there. **Cane Bay** is known for its coral canyons.

Davis Bay is the site of the 3,658m-deep (12,000-ft.) Puerto Rico Trench. **Northstar Reef,** at the east end of Davis Bay, is a spectacular wall dive, recommended for intermediate or experienced divers only. The wall is covered with stunning brain corals and staghorn thickets. At some 15m (50 ft.) down, a sandy shelf leads to a cave where giant green moray eels hang out.

Because of the wide variety of dive sites ringing the island, St. Croix has attracted some of the best dive outfitters on the U.S. Virgin Islands. (Local experts cite its offshore waters as one of the few places in the world where a scuba enthusiast can arrange a pier dive, a wall dive, a wreck dive, and a reef dive all in one day.) One of the best respected of the island's outfitters, reorganized in 2003, is **S.C.U.B.A.** (Saint Croix Ultimate Blue Water Adventures). Headquartered at 14 Caravelle Arcade, Christiansted (☎ **877-773-5994,** 340-773-5994; www.stcroixscuba.com), S.C.U.B.A. is a PADI-certified, five-star dive outfitter that's well rehearsed in taking divers to dozens of interesting dive sites, at least 20 of which lie at varying depths along the sheer wall that flanks the island's North Coast.

A well-qualified competitor, also affiliated with PADI, offering almost the same number and variety of underwater tours is **Anchor Five Center,** which is headquartered at the Salt River Marina, Route 801 (☎ **800-532-3483,** 340-778-1522).

Blue marlin has made its way into record catches in the waters off St. Croix, with the best sport fishing at **Lang Bank** off the North Coast. Bonito, sailfish, wahoo, and tuna turn up in large catches.

The best outfitter that can arrange fishing trips in its 12m (38-ft.) power-boat, *Fantasy,* is **Mile Mark Watersports,** based at Gallows Bay (☎ **340-773-2628**).

On St. John

The best beaches on St. John for good snorkeling are **Watermelon Cay** at Leinster Bay and **Haulover Bay,** the latter a favorite among local divers. **Cinnamon Bay** is another much-favored spot among divers. To escape the hordes such as those that flock to **Trunk Bay** on the North Shore, you need a boat to reach the best dive places and the greatest snorkeling spots. All the water-sports outfitters that we recommend will take you to the little places of enchantment, including

 ✔ **Johnson Reef** on the North Coast

 ✔ **Fishbowl** and **Steven Cay** at Cruz Bay

 ✔ **South Drop** and **Horseshoe** on the Southern Tier

 Along the sandy coves of Caneel Bay at its **Honeymoon Beach,** you can see the rare spotted eagle ray — called the "flying saucer of the deep blue sea." Other good locations include the ledges at **Congo Cay,** the wreck of the *General Rogers,* and the tunnels at **Thatch Cay.**

The largest outfitter — and the best — is **Cruz Bay Watersports** (☎ 340-776-6234), a PADI five-star diving center, charging $65 for a one-tank dive or $90 for a two-tank dive, including equipment and an underwater tour; snorkeling tours are $65 for a half-day. **Low Key Watersports** at Wharfside Village (☎ 340-693-8999) is known for its wreck dives, and the outfitter can also hook you up with snorkeling ($50 for a half-day) and an array of water sports including parasailing and kayak tours. Prices vary.

Windsurfers head for the **Cinnamon Bay Campground,** Route 20 (☎ 340-776-6330), with rentals costing from $20 to $40 per hour. A one-hour introductory lesson goes for $60 to $80.

The famous North Drop (which we mention in the St. Thomas part of this section) is also reachable by way of a fishing charter sailing out of St. John. Deep-sea fishing, however, is illegal in the waters of the island's national park. What they do allow is rod-and-reel fishing from St. John's beaches. **American Yacht Harbor** (☎ 340-775-6454) offers sport-fishing trips, and though it's based in Red Hook on St. Thomas, the operator will pick you up on St. John. On St. John itself, the best local outfitter catering to visiting fishermen is **St. John World Class Anglers** (☎ 340-513-9454), which lives up to its name in its series of half- and full-day fishing trips to offshore cays. For a powerboat containing all necessary angling gear and equipment, with room for up to four participants, rates are $450 for a half-day and $750 for a full-day fishing expedition.

Climbing aboard

Frankly, we prefer to go sailing in the neighboring islands of the British Virgins, but the USVIs also offer many thrilling opportunities for sailing the seas. Boating outfitters are actually more plentiful on St. Thomas than in the BVIs. Fishing and sailing charters are readily available, and if you're not a sailor and need to depend on a captain, an array of boating tours is available.

On St. Thomas

 With more than 100 vessels to choose from, St. Thomas is the charter-boat mecca of the USVIs. You can go through a broker to book a private sailing vessel with a crew, or you can contact a charter company directly.

Island Yachts, 6100 Red Hook Quarter, 18B (☎ 800-524-2019, 340-775-6666), is a charter-boat company in Red Hook. **Nauti Nymph,** 6501 Red Hook Plaza, Suite 201 (☎ 800-734-7345, 340-775-5066), has a large selection of powerboats for rent. Rates range from $345 to $420 a day and include snorkel gear.

Virgin Islands Eco-Tours, 2 Estate Nadir (☎ 340-779-2155), offers one of the most interesting eco-tours available, which they conduct mostly from the seats of two-passenger sea kayaks. Positioned beside Route 32 East, 2.4km (1½ miles) west of Red Hook, the site of ferryboat departures for St. John, it features three-hour tours that depart every day, pending reservations, at 9 a.m. and 2 p.m. for $50 per person. Tours depart from the outfit's eco-marina at the above-noted address and include 45 minutes of kayak paddling, about 20 minutes of orientation and safety lectures, about an hour of snorkeling in a reef-sheltered lagoon, with lots of time to appreciate a trained ecologist's ongoing commentaries about the rich ecosystems of the mangrove swamps. Advance reservations are strongly advised.

On St. Croix

The big sailing adventure on St. Croix is over to **Buck Island Reef National Monument,** a 121-hectare (300-acre) volcanic islet surrounded by 223 hectares (550 acres) of underwater coral gardens. Most charterboat outfitters operate out of the Green Cay Marina along the waterfront in Christiansted. All captains sailing over to the island will drop anchor and allow you ample time for hiking, swimming, or snorkeling. Most visitors also plan to have a picnic lunch here.

One of the most reliable operators is **Mile Mark Watersports** in the King Christian Hotel, 59 King's Wharf, Christiansted (☎ **340-773-2628**), which conducts two different types of tours. The first option is a half-day tour aboard a glass-bottom boat departing from the King Christian Hotel daily from 9:30 a.m. to 1 p.m. and 1:30 to 5 p.m.; it costs $45 per person. The second is a full-day tour, offered daily from 10 a.m. to 4 p.m. on a 12m (40-ft.) trimaran for $85. Included in this excursion is a small picnic on Buck Island's beach.

Captain Heinz (☎ **340-773-3161,** 340-773-4041) is an Austrian-born skipper with more than 25 years of sailing experience. His trimaran, *Teroro II,* leaves Green Cay Marina "H" Dock at 9 a.m. and 2 p.m., never filled with more than 23 passengers. This five-hour snorkeling trip costs $50 for adults and $30 for children age ten and under. The captain is not only a skilled sailor but also a considerate host. He'll even take you around the outer reef, which the other guides don't, for an unforgettable underwater experience.

On St. John

With most operators located at **Cruz Bay** on St. John, sailing opportunities are plentiful, especially to secluded beaches or offshore islets, and on even longer jaunts to the British Virgin Islands, where you need a passport. Cruises allow time for snorkeling and swimming.

St. John is legendary for the size and, in some cases, glamour, of the yachts it berths. One of the best outfits for matching a party of up to six persons with large-scale yachts (full-day or half-day sails only) is **Proper Yachts,** P.O. Box 1570, St. John (☎ **340-776-6256**), which operates out of the posh Caneel Bay Resort. It specializes in relatively large sailing craft (their average length is a whopping 16m/51 ft.), whose crews also happen to be either the owners or the designated agents of the owners. The outfit charges $120 per person per day for a full-day sail and $50 per person for either a half-day sail or a sunset sail. Drinks, but not lunch or snorkeling gear, are included in the price. The advantage of a full-day sail with this outfit is that you can visit relatively remote destinations, often in the BVIs, upon request. A worthy competitor, which usually operates slightly smaller sailing craft (for example, from 9–12m/30–40 ft. in length) at somewhat more-reasonable prices, is **Connections** (☎ **340-693-8809**), working from a storefront in Cruz Bay.

For half-day or full-day rentals of open-deck Mako powerboats, sized from 6 to 8.8m (20–28 ft.) long with either one or two (usually outboard) engines and outfitted only with a canvas canopy to protect its occupants from the elements, contact **Ocean Runner** (☎ **340-693-8809**). Depending on size, each rents for between $245 and $295 for a half-day and comes with a guide and driver (optional), the presence of which eliminates all responsibility on the part of the renters for damage to the boat. Know in advance that full-day rentals of these motorboats cost a supplement of only $50 extra, making it very tempting to book these rentals for the whole shebang.

Sea kayaking is as popular on St. John as it is on St. Thomas. On this island, **Arawak Expeditions** (☎ **800-238-8687,** 340-693-8312) will guide you along coastal waters and across secluded bays, charging $50 per passenger for a half-day jaunt.

Exploring on Dry Land

Unlike their neighbors, the BVIs, St. Thomas and St. Croix actually have historical cities to explore. St. Thomas is known for the architecture and museums of its old port city of Charlotte Amalie, built by the Danes. The Danes also built under two historic cities on St. Croix: Christiansted, the capital, and Fredericksted, its "second city." Much Danish architecture remains to be enjoyed in both ports. As for St. John, the wonders of its national park compensate for its lack of historical treasures, although it does have a plantation ruin or two.

On St. Thomas

Most visitors begin their sightseeing in **Charlotte Amalie,** which has all the color and charm of an authentic Caribbean waterfront town. In days of yore, seafarers from all over the globe flocked here, as did pirates and members of the Confederacy, who used the port during the American Civil War. (Sadly, St. Thomas was the biggest slave market in the world.)

The old warehouses formerly used for storing pirate goods still stand, and today, many of them house shops. In fact, the main streets are now a virtual shopping mall and are usually packed. Sandwiched among these shops are a few historic buildings, most of which you can cover on foot in a couple of hours:

✔ **Government House,** Government Hill (☎ **340-774-0001**): This building is the administrative headquarters for the U.S. Virgin Islands. It's been the center of political life on the islands since it was built around the time of the American Civil War. Visitors are allowed on the first two floors. Some paintings by former resident Camille Pissarro are on display, as are works by other St. Thomas artists. Admission is free. Open Monday to Friday from 9 a.m. to 5 p.m.

✔ **Synagogue of Beracha Veshalom Vegmiluth Hasidim,** 16 Crystal Gade (☎ **340-774-4312**): This synagogue is the oldest one in continuous use under the American flag and the second-oldest in the Western Hemisphere. Sephardic Jews erected it in 1833, and it still maintains the tradition of having sand on the floor, commemorating the exodus from Egypt. The structure is made of local stone, along with ballast brick from Denmark and mortar made of molasses and sand. To the rear of the synagogue, the Weibel Museum showcases Jewish history on the island. Open weekdays from 9 a.m. to 4 p.m.

Outside of Charlotte Amalie, check out the following:

✔ **Coral World Ocean Park,** Coki Point (☎ **340-775-1555;** www.coralworldvi.com): This marine park is the best on the islands. The only thing close to it is the Seaquarium on Curaçao, but we give this one the edge because of Coral World's multilevel offshore underwater observatory. The Predator Tank here is one of the world's largest coral reef tanks. An aquarium with two dozen portholes offers views of marine life in the West Indies. Activities include daily fish and shark feedings and exotic bird shows. Admission is $18 for adults and $9 for children 3 to 12. Open daily from 9 a.m. to 5 p.m. Expect to spend at least three hours here, especially if you have kids. To reach the park, turn north off Route 38 at the sign approximately 20 minutes from Charlotte Amalie.

✔ **Frenchtown:** Route 30 (Veterans Drive) takes you west of Charlotte Amalie to this colorful little settlement. Early French-speaking settlers arrived on St. Thomas from St. Barts after the Swedes uprooted them. Many island residents today are the direct descendants of those long-ago immigrants who were known for speaking a distinctive French patois. This village contains a number of restaurants and taverns. Because Charlotte Amalie has become somewhat dangerous at night, Frenchtown has picked up its after-dark business and is the best spot for dancing and other local entertainment.

✔ **Mountain Top:** For the most panoramic view of St. Thomas, both its land- and seascape, head here and stand on its observation deck at a point 457m (1,500 ft.) above sea level. Ordering a banana daiquiri at the bar is customary. A number of shops are here as well, but they're very touristy. To reach it, drive north (or take a taxi) along Route 33, following the signposts.

✔ **Paradise Point Tramway,** Route 30 at Havensight (☎ **340-774-9809**): This contraption affords visitors a dramatic view of Charlotte Amalie harbor, with a ride to a 212m (697-ft.) peak. The tramway, similar to those at ski resorts, operates four cars, each with an eight-person capacity, for the seven-minute one-way ride. It transports customers from the Havensight area to Paradise Point, where they can disembark to visit shops and the popular restaurant and bar. Admission is $15 round-trip, $7.50 for ages 6 to 12, and free for children age 5 and under. Open daily from 9 a.m. to 5:30 p.m. In summer (roughly between May and Oct), it operates more erratically, usually only during periods when cruise ships are moored temporarily in the harbor.

On St. Croix

Of particular interest on St. Croix for the history buff are **Fort Christiansvaern**, one of the best preserved of its type in the West Indies, and **Fort Frederick,** completed in 1760 (see the recommendations later in this section). The streets of both Christiansted and Fredericksted are worth exploring, with many shops today installed in the former Danish buildings. St. Croix is also blessed with the best botanical gardens in all the Virgins, U.S. or British.

The capital: Christiansted

One of the most historic and well-preserved towns in the Caribbean, **Christiansted** is an old, handsomely restored (or at least in the process of being restored) Danish port. On the Northeastern Shore of the island, on a coral-bound bay, the town is filled with Danish buildings erected by prosperous merchants in the booming 18th century. These red-roofed structures are often washed in pink, ocher, or yellow. Arcades over the sidewalks provide shade for shoppers. The whole area around the harbor front is designated a historic site, which the U.S. National Park Service looks after.

For information on Christiansted or the island itself, stop in at the **Visitor's Center** at 53A Company St. (☎ 340-773-0495), which is open Monday to Friday from 8 a.m. to 5 p.m., dispensing guidance, maps, and brochures.

These sites in Christiansted may interest you:

   ✔ **Fort Christiansvaern,** on the waterfront between King and Queen streets (☎ 340-773-1460): This fortress overlooking the harbor is the best-preserved colonial fortification in the Virgin Islands. The U.S. National Park Service maintains it as a historic monument. Its original four-pronged, star-shaped design was in accordance with the most advanced military planning of its era. The fort is now the site of the St. Croix Police Museum, which has exhibits about police work on the island from the late 1800s to the present. Admission is $3, which includes admission to the Steeple Building (see the following bullet). Open Monday to Friday 8 a.m. to 5 p.m., Sunday 9 a.m. to 5 p.m.

✔ **Steeple Building,** on the waterfront off Hospital Street (☎ 340-773-1460): This building's full name is the Church of Lord God of Sabaoth. Built in 1753, it first served as St. Croix's first Lutheran church, and it was deconsecrated in 1831; the building subsequently served at various times as a bakery, a hospital, and a school. Today, it houses exhibits relating to island history and culture. Admission is $3 (including admission to Fort Christiansvaern). Open Monday through Friday from 8 a.m. to 4:45 p.m.

The "second city": Frederiksted

Known by locals as the "second city" of St. Croix and sitting at the western end of the island, about 27km (17 miles) from Christiansted, **Frederiksted** is a former Danish settlement, now a sleepy port town that comes to life only when a cruise ship docks at its shoreline. Frederiksted was destroyed by a fire in 1879. Its citizens subsequently rebuilt it with wood frames and clapboards on top of the old Danish stone and yellow-brick foundations.

Most visitors begin their tour at russet-colored **Fort Frederik,** at the northern end of Frederiksted next to the cruise-ship pier (☎ 340-772-2021). This fort, completed in 1760, is said to have been the first to salute the flag of the new United States. When a U.S. brigantine anchored at port in Frederiksted hoisted a homemade Old Glory, the fort returned the salute with cannon fire, violating the rules of neutrality. Also, it was here on July 3, 1848, that Governor-General Peter von Scholten emancipated the slaves in the Danish West Indies, in response to a slave uprising led by a young man named Moses "Buddhoe" Gottlieb. The fort has been restored to its 1840 appearance and is today a national historic landmark. You can explore the courtyard and stables, and a local history museum fills what was once the Garrison Room. Admission is free. The fort is open Monday through Friday from 8:30 a.m. to 4:30 p.m. To the south of the fort is the **Visitors' Bureau,** at Strand Street (☎ 340-772-0357), where you can pick up a free map of the town.

Other sites near Frederiksted worth a visit are

✔ **Estate Whim Plantation Museum,** Route 70, Centerline Road, 3.2km (2 miles) east of Frederiksted (☎ 340-772-0598): This restored Great House is unique among those of the many sugar plantations whose ruins dot the island. The house has only three rooms. With 0.9m-thick (3-ft.) walls made of stone, coral, and molasses, the house resembles a luxurious European château. A division of Baker Furniture Company used the Whim Plantation's collection of models for one of its most successful reproductions, the "Whim Museum–West Indies Collection." A showroom here sells the reproductions, plus others from the Caribbean, including pineapple-motif four-poster beds, cane-bottomed planters' chairs with built-in leg rests, and Caribbean adaptations of Empire-era chairs with cane-bottomed seats. Admission is $8 for adults and $4 for children. Open Monday to Saturday 10 a.m. to 4 p.m.

✔ **St. Croix Leap,** Mahogany Road, Route 76 (☎ 340-772-0421): If you're on western St. Croix, near Frederiksted, visit St. Croix Leap for an offbeat adventure. In this open-air shop, you can see artisans fashioning stacks of rare and beautiful wood into tasteful objects — a St. Croix Life and Environmental Arts Project, dedicated to manual work, environmental conservation, and self-development. The end result is a fine collection of local mahogany serving boards, tables, wall hangings, and clocks. Sections of unusual pieces are crafted into functional, artistic objects. St. Croix Leap is 24km (15 miles) from Christiansted, 3.2km (2 miles) up Mahogany Road from the beach north of Frederiksted. Large mahogany signs and sculptures flank the driveway. Visitors should bear to the right to reach the woodworking area and gift shop. The site is open daily from 9 a.m. to 5 p.m.

✔ **St. George Village Botanical Gardens,** 127 Estate St., just north of Centerline Road, 6.4km (4 miles) east of Frederiksted, Kingshill (☎ 340-692-2874): Here you'll find a 6.4-hectare (16-acre) Eden of tropical trees, shrubs, vines, and flowers. The garden is a feast for the eye and the camera, from the entrance drive bordered by royal palms and bougainvillea to the towering kapok and tamarind trees. It was built around the ruins of a 19th-century sugar-cane-workers' village. Self-guided walking-tour maps are available at the entrance to the garden's great hall. Facilities include restrooms and a gift shop. Admission is $6 for adults and $1 for children 12 and under. Open daily from 9 a.m. to 5 p.m.; closed holidays.

The connection: In between the two major cities

For a more-comprehensive view of the island, **St. Croix Heritage Trail,** launched at the millennium, helps visitors relive St. Croix's Danish colonial past. All you need are a brochure and map, available at the tourist office in Christiansted (53A Company St.; ☎ 340-773-0495), and you can set out on this 115km (72-mile) road, which is teeming with historical and cultural sights. The route, among the trail's other historic sites, connects the two major towns of Christiansted and Frederiksted, going past the sites of former sugar plantations. The trail traverses the entire 45km (28-mile) length of St. Croix, passing cattle farms, suburban communities, and even industrial complexes and resorts. So, it's not all manicured and pretty. But much of it is scenic and worth the drive. Allow at least a day for this trail, with stops along the way.

Nearly everyone gets out of the car at **Point Udall,** the easternmost point under the U.S. flag. You'll pass an eclectic mix of churches and even a prison. The route consists mainly of existing roadways, and that pamphlet you pick up identifies everything you're seeing. The highlight of the trail is the **Estate Mount Washington,** a strikingly well-preserved sugar plantation. Another highlight is **Estate Whim Plantation,** one of the best of the restored Great Houses with a museum and gift shop (see the description in the preceding section). Another stop along the way is along **Salt River Bay,** which cuts into the Northern Shore. This is the site of Columbus's landfall in 1493.

On St. John

The government inaugurated route numbers in the '90s, but no one seems to bother with them or remember them. Therefore, you'll need a good map if you get lost (and you probably will). Carry a swimsuit because you'll be passing along a shoreline of some of the loveliest beaches in the USVIs. Expect narrow, steep, winding, potholed roads, which means you should allow plenty of time to get to your destination. See our recommendations earlier in this chapter for some of the best luncheon stopovers along the way. Gathering the makings for a picnic at **Cruz Bay** before heading out is even more fun. If you really want to see the island in any depth, you need to rent a car. If you're uneasy about driving on bad roads, you can generally hook up with a safari bus at Cruz Bay with a load of passengers trailblazing it around the island. Here are some favorite spots to visit:

- **Annaberg Plantation,** Leinster Bay Road (☎ 340-776-6201): Constructed in 1780, this plantation — now in ruins — used to be the most important in that century when the smell of boiling molasses permeated the air for miles around. Partially restored, Annaberg is the best-preserved plantation on the island. The other Great Houses were burned during slave uprisings. Plaques that the National Park Service placed here identify and describe the ruins of each building and its former functions. You just wander about, because the place has no set visiting hours. Seek out the **St. John National Park Service Visitor's Center,** 1300 Cruz Bay Creek, near the Ferry dock (☎ 340-776-6201). Park Service tours cost $4.

- **Bordeaux Mountain,** Route 10: For a panoramic view of the island, the best lookout point is on this mountain, which we like to visit for dining (see our recommendation of **Le Chateau de Bordeaux,** earlier in this chapter). Centerline Road runs almost to the pinnacle at 389m (1,277 ft.), the loftiest point on St. John. You can view the most panoramic scenery at the aptly named **Picture Point.** The Park Service Visitor's Center (see the preceding bullet) distributes free maps.

- **Catherineberg Ruins,** Route 70: A scenic drive along Centerline Road leads to what remains of the Catherineberg Sugar Mill. The decaying remains of a windmill here evoke this plantation's heyday in the 18th century, when it was the nerve center for a thriving sugar plantation. A slave revolt in 1733 brought an end to this prosperity.

Keeping Active

The USVIs provide many opportunities for golfing, horseback riding, playing tennis, hiking, or whatever. Golf isn't as extensive as in Puerto Rico, but the islands offer limited courses. The best island for hiking is St. John, while the best island for horseback riding is St. Croix.

Hitting the links

If a holiday on the golf course is the way you want to spend your vacation, you'll find far greater courses in Montego Bay, Jamaica (see Chapter 13) or on the island of Puerto Rico (see Chapter 14). St. Thomas has only one course, St. Croix three, and St. John none.

On St. Thomas

Mahogany Run, on the North Shore at Mahogany Run Road (☎ 800-253-7103), is an 18-hole, par-70 course. This beautiful course rises and drops like a roller coaster on its journey to the sea; cliffs and crashing sea waves are the ultimate hazards at the 13th and 14th holes. Former President Clinton pronounced this course very challenging. Greens fees are $140 to $160 for 18 holes, reduced to $100 to $125 in the late afternoon. Carts are included, and club rental costs $40.

On St. Croix

St. Croix has the best golf in the USVIs. Guests staying on St. John and St. Thomas often fly over for a day's round on one of the island's three courses. The **Carambola Golf Course,** on the northeast side of St. Croix (☎ 340-778-5638), was created by Robert Trent Jones, Sr., who called it "the loveliest course I ever designed." It's been likened to a botanical garden. The par-3 holes here are known to golfing authorities as the best in the tropics. The greens fee of $54 in winter, or $34 summer, allows you to play as many holes as you want and includes a cart.

The Buccaneer, Gallows Bay (☎ 340-773-2100, ext. 738), 3.2km (2 miles) east of Christiansted, has a challenging 5,198m (5,685-yard), 18-hole course with panoramic vistas. Nonguests of this deluxe resort pay $86 in winter or $61 off-season, including the use of a cart. **The Reef,** on the East End of the island at Teague Bay (☎ 340-773-8844), is a 2,834m (3,100-yard), 9-hole course, charging greens fees of $30 including carts. The longest hole here is a 529m (579-yard) par-5.

Having a ball with tennis

Because the noonday sun is fierce, tennis buffs like to play before 10 a.m. or after 5 p.m. Most courts are lit for night matches, and nonguests who call and reserve space are welcome at the various resorts.

On St. Thomas

Several tennis facilities are available on St. Thomas. To make a reservation, try one of the following: **Grand Beach Palace,** Smith Bay Road (☎ 340-775-1510), **Mahogany Run Tennis Club,** Route 42 (☎ 340-777-6006), **Frenchman's Reef & Morning Star Marriott Beach Resort Tennis Courts,** Estate Bakkeroe (☎ 340-776-8500), **Ritz-Carlton, St. Thomas,** 6900 Great Bay Estate (☎ 340-775-3333), or **Sapphire Beach Resort,** Sapphire Bay (☎ 340-775-6100). The government of St. Thomas offers two public courts at the Sub Base, adjacent to the Water and

Power Commission; it's a five-minute ride from the center of Charlotte Amalie at Estate Contant (off Route 306). Courts are open daily until 8 p.m. You can't reserve space; you just have to show up and wait your turn.

On St. Croix

Tennis buffs will be tempted to tuck into **The Buccaneer,** Route 82 (☎ **340-773-2100**), with its eight courts (two lighted), plus a pro and a full tennis pro shop. You'll also find three courts (one lighted) at **Club St. Croix,** Route 752 (☎ **340-773-4800**), and five courts (two lighted) at the **Carambola Golf and Country Club,** Route 80 (☎ **340-778-5638**).

On St. John

The **Westin St. John Resort,** 8310 Great Cruz Bay, St. John (☎ **340-693-8000**), offers six lighted courts; nonguests who call in advance can play on them for $10 per hour. In **Cruz Bay,** the local government maintains some public courts adjacent to the St. John Fire Department. Courts are lit until 9 p.m., and you don't need reservations. Just show up and wait your turn.

Horseback riding

St. Thomas is too built up for serious trail-riding on a horse. However, St. John has an outfitter that will take you along scenic trails in the national park. But for the best horseback-riding outfitter in the Caribbean, head for St. Croix.

On St. Croix

The largest stables are **Paul and Jill's Equestrian Stables,** Route 58 (☎ **340-772-2880**), at Sprat Hall, the island's oldest plantation Great House, lying near Frederiksted. The operator, Jill Hurd, is an island character from one of St. Croix's best-known families. For $60, she offers two-hour rides through the rain forest and along the shore. She also conducts moonlit rides. Reserve at least a day in advance.

On St. John

For $75 for a 90-minute ride, the staff at **Carolina Corral,** 13 Estate Carolina (☎ **340-693-5778**), will take you horseback riding along St. John's most scenic trails. You can mount a donkey if you prefer. Riding lessons are also available.

Hiking

Get a ground-level view of all the flora, fauna, and other attractions by strapping on your most comfortable shoes and setting out to explore. (St. Thomas doesn't rate high scores for cool hiking sites.)

On St. Croix

The island's western district contains a 6-hectare (15-acre) **"Rain Forest"** with a network of footpaths offering some of the best nature walks in the USVIs. The nonprofit **St. Croix Environmental Association,** Arawak Building, Suite 3, at Gallows Bay (☎ 340-773-1989), at a cost of $30 per hiker, takes you through this treasure emerging at Salt River, where Columbus first sighted land here. They conduct three- to five-hour hikes year-round and clearly define in advance the level of exertion each hike requires. For more information, go to www.stxenvironmental.org.

On St. John

St. John has the most rewarding hiking in the Virgin Islands. The terrain ranges from arid and dry (in the East) to moist and semitropical (in the Northwest). The island boasts more than 800 species of plants, 160 species of birds, and more than 20 trails maintained in fine form by the island's crew of park rangers. Much of the land is designated as **Virgin Islands National Park** (☎ 340-776-6201). Visitors are encouraged to stop by the **Cruz Bay Visitor Center** to pick up the park brochure, which includes a map of the park and the *Virgin Islands National Park News,* providing the latest information on park activities. Be sure to carry a lot of water, and wear sunscreen and insect repellent when you hike.

St. John is laced with a wide choice of clearly marked walking paths. At least 20 of these originate from Northshore Road (Route 20) or from the island's main east-west artery, Centerline Road (Route 10). Each is marked at its starting point with a preplanned itinerary; the walks can last anywhere from ten minutes to two hours.

One of our favorite hikes, the **Annaberg Historic Trail** (identified by the U.S. National Park Service as Trail 10), requires only a 0.8km (about a half-mile) stroll. It departs from a clearly marked point along the island's North Coast, near the junction of routes 10 and 20. This self-guided tour passes the partially restored ruins of a manor house built during the 1700s. Signs along the way give historical and botanical data. Visiting the ruins costs $4 per person for those over age 16.

One of the most informative and popular hiking tours on St. John is the guided 4km (2½ mile) **Reef Bay Hike,** a two- to three-hour experience conducted every Monday, Thursday, and Friday at 9 a.m. by the wardens inside the Virgin Islands National Park (☎ 340-776-6201 for advance reservations and last-minute schedule changes). Included is a stop at the only known petroglyphs on the island, a tour of the ruins of an 18th-century sugar mill, and a running commentary on the botany, zoology, and ecology of the Caribbean. The tour itself is free, but participants are encouraged (but not required) to take a taxi, for a cost of $5, from the park's Visitor's Center to the beginning of the hiking trail, and to take a prearranged boat ride, for a cost of $15 per person, at the conclusion of the tour back to the Visitor's Center. Advance reservations, by phone, are encouraged.

Shopping the Local Stores

Duty-free shopping has made St. Thomas the shopping bazaar of the West Indies. Even if you're going only to St. Croix and skipping St. Thomas, you'll still find a huge array of similar shops, but not as many. St. John, on the other hand, is the home of little specialty shops, often featuring handcrafted items.

You can find well-known brand names on these islands at savings of up to 60 percent off mainland U.S. prices. But be warned: Savings aren't always so good. Before you leave home, check prices in your local stores if you think you may want to make a major purchase, so you can be sure that you are, in fact, getting a good deal.

The best buys include china, crystal, perfume, jewelry (especially emeralds), Haitian art, fashion, watches, and items made of wood. Cameras and electronic items, based on our experience, aren't the good buys they're reputed to be. St. Thomas is also the best place in the Caribbean for discounts on porcelain, but remember that you often can purchase U.S. brands on the mainland for 25 percent off the retail price. Look for the imported patterns for the biggest savings.

Most shops, some of which occupy former pirate warehouses, are open Monday through Saturday from 9 a.m. to 5 p.m. Some stores open Sunday and holidays if a cruise ship is in port. *Tip:* Friday is the biggest cruise-ship day in Charlotte Amalie (we once counted eight ships in port), so try to avoid shopping then. It's a zoo.

Shoppers with U.S. passports can take advantage of a generous $1,200-per-person duty-free allowance. Remember to save your receipts. A final bit of good news: no sales tax in the USVIs.

Living It Up After Dark

Among the USVIs, St. Thomas offers the most varied nightlife. St. Croix offers the only gambling casino in the USVIs. On St. John, the idea of a fun night is to head to one of the raffish saloons for some heavy drinking.

On St. Thomas

Charlotte Amalie is no longer the swinging town it used to be. Many of the streets are dangerous after dark, so visitors have mostly abandoned the town except for a few places. Much of the action has shifted to **Frenchtown,** which has some good restaurants and bars. However, just as in Charlotte Amalie, some of these little hot spots are along dark, badly lit roads. The big hotels, such as **Frenchman's Reef & Morning Star Marriott Beach Resort** and **Bluebeard's,** have the most lively after-dark scene. Others places to stop in include

- **Agave Terrace,** Point Pleasant Resort, 4 Smith Bay (☎ 340-775-4142): This restaurant is especially pleasant, set on a breezy veranda and specializing in upscale Caribbean food and seafood. Many local residents visit this place every Tuesday and Thursday night, when live West Indian–style bands perform beginning at 6:30 p.m.

- **Greenhouse,** Veterans Drive (☎ 340-774-7998): This restaurant/bar is the most popular spot after dark in Charlotte Amalie, not the safest place to wander around at night. You may want to take a taxi here. It lies directly on the waterfront and offers entertainment ranging from live reggae to recorded dance music. During live reggae on Tuesday and Friday nights, starting at 10 p.m., they charge a $4 to $8 cover.

- **Iggies,** at Bolongo Bay Beach Resort, 50 Estate Bolongo (☎ 340-775-1800): Named after one of the resident iguanas that used to sun on the nearby rocks, Iggies is a convivial and active singles bar/sports bar with access to pool tables, nighttime volleyball games, and karaoke. The bar opens daily at 11:30 a.m. and closes around midnight.

- **Turtle's Rock Bar,** at Wyndham Sugar Bay Beach Club, 6500 Estate Smith Bay (☎ 340-777-7100): This popular bar presents live music, steel bands, and karaoke. There's space to dance, but most folks just sway and listen to the steel pan bands that play daily from 1 p.m. to 2 a.m. Sunday night is karaoke. Burgers, salads, steaks, and grilled fish are available at the Iguana Grill a few steps away. There's no cover.

On St. Croix

Christiansted has a lively and casual club scene near the waterfront. Here's what the island has to offer:

- **Cormorant,** 4126 La Grande Princesse (☎ 340-778-8920): On Thursday night during the winter season, this gay-friendly club dishes up a West Indian cuisine with a small local band.

- **Divi Carina Bay Casino,** Divi Carina Bay Resort, 25 Estate Turner Hole (☎ 340-773-9700): The big nightlife news of St. Croix is the opening of this casino, the first on St. Croix, at the **Divi Carina Bay Resort.** The casino boasts 20 gaming tables and 300 slot machines.

- **Hotel on the Cay,** Protestant Cay (☎ 340-773-2035): If you're in Christiansted on a Tuesday night, the place to be isn't there but on a ferryboat taking you across the harbor to this hotel with its Tuesday-night West Indian buffet and native folkloric show.

- **2 Plus 2 Disco,** 17 La Grande Princesse (☎ 340-773-3710): This is a real Caribbean disco. It features the regional sounds of the islands, not only calypso and reggae, but also salsa and *soca* (a hybrid of calypso and reggae). Usually a DJ puts on the tunes, except on weekends when the joint brings in local bands. The place isn't fancy or large. Come here for *Saturday Night Fever.*

On St. John

Unless you count lots of drinking in the local taverns, St. John isn't a party island. Yet St. John is a pleasant place to be at night, especially when **Cruz Bay** is lit up. Locals listen to music, talk, drink, and often dance. Two local papers, *St. John Times* and *Tradewinds,* keep you tuned to anything that's happening, which often isn't very much.

- ✔ **Caneel Bay Bar,** Route 20, at the Caneel Bay Resort (☎ **340-776-6111**): This bar presents live music nightly from 8 to 11:30 p.m. The most popular drinks here include the Cool Caneel (local rum with sugar, lime, and anisette) and the trademark of the house, Plantation Punch (lime and orange juice with three different kinds of rum, bitters, and nutmeg).

- ✔ **Fred's,** Cruz Bay (☎ **340-776-6363**): Across from the Lime Inn, this little hole-in-the-wall bar is very popular with locals, especially when the owner brings in bands for dancing on Wednesday and Friday nights. Open 11:30 a.m. to about midnight daily.

- ✔ **Skinny Legs Bar and Restaurant,** Route 107 (☎ **340-779-4982**): The best sports bar on the island is a shack made of tin and wood. The yachting crowd likes to hang out here. The bar has a satellite dish, a dartboard, and horseshoe pits. Live music plays on Saturday nights. Open daily 11 a.m. to 9 p.m.

- ✔ **Woody's,** Cruz Bay (☎ **340-779-4625**): This bar is the local dive and hangout at Cruz Bay, 46m (150 feet) from the ferry dock. You can come here to eat or drink. The place is particularly popular during happy hour from 3 to 6 p.m. and is about the only place on the island where you can order food at 10 p.m.

Going Beyond the USVIs: Daytrips

To break the "monotony" of having to go to the beach every day, you can take a ferryboat ride from either St. John (for info, call **Inter-Island Boat Service** at ☎ **340-776-6597**) or St. Thomas (for info, call **Smith's Ferry Service** at ☎ **340-775-7292**). From their respective headquarters, both companies offer daily waterborne daytrips to both Tortola and Virgin Gorda in the BVIs as well as such distractions as horseback riding, historic tours, and car rentals after you get there. See Chapter 11 for more activity ideas in the BVIs.

Fast Facts: USVIs

Area Code

The area code is **340**.

ATMs

On St. Thomas, the branch of First Bank (☎ 340-776-9494) near Market Square, the

Banco Popular (☎ 340-693-2777), and First Bank of V.I. (☎ 340-775-7777) have ATMs. On St. Croix, contact Banco Popular (☎ 340-693-2777) or First Bank of V.I. (☎ 340-775-7777) for information on branch and ATM locations. First Bank of V.I. (☎ 340-775-7777) at Cruz Bay, St. John, has the island's only ATM.

Babysitters

You can usually find sitters easily through your hotel, but try to reserve 24 hours in advance. Expect to pay $8 or more per hour.

Doctors

On St. Croix, go to Sunny Isle Medical Center (☎ 340-778-0069). On St. Thomas, Doctors-on-Duty, Vitraco Park (☎ 340-776-7966), in Charlotte Amalie, is a reliable medical facility.

Emergencies

On all USVIs, call ☎ 911 for ambulance, fire, and police.

Hospitals

Roy Lester Schneider Hospital on St. Thomas (☎ 340-776-8311) has a decompression chamber. On St. Croix outside Christiansted, you'll find the Gov. Juan F. Luis Hospital and Medical Health Center, 6 Diamond Ruby, north of Sunny Isle Shopping Center on Route 79 (☎ 340-778-6311). You can also try the Myrah Keating Smith Community Hospital, Route 10, about seven minutes east of Cruz Bay (☎ 340-693-8900).

Information

See the Appendix for locations of U.S. and local tourist offices.

Internet Access

Check with your hotel for information about Internet access.

Newspapers and Magazines

Copies of U.S. mainland newspapers, such as the *New York Times, USA Today,* and the *Miami Herald,* arrive daily on St. Thomas and are available at hotels and newsstands, but the markup is high. The latest copies of *Time* and *Newsweek* are also for sale. *St. Thomas Daily News* covers local, national, and international events. Pick up *Virgin Islands Playground* and *St. Thomas This Week;* both are packed with visitor information and are distributed free all over the island.

Newspapers such as the *Miami Herald* are flown into St. Croix, which also has its own newspaper, *St. Croix Avis. Time* and *Newsweek* are widely sold as well. Your best source for local information is *St. Croix This Week,* which tourist offices distribute for free.

On St. John, copies of U.S. mainland newspapers arrive daily and are for sale at Mongoose Junction, Caneel Bay, and the Westin. The latest copies of *Time* and *Newsweek* are also for sale. Complimentary copies of *What to Do: St. Thomas & St. John* contain many helpful hints, although this publication is a commercial mouthpiece. It's the official guidebook of the St. Thomas and St. John Hotel Association and is available at the tourist office and at various hotels.

Pharmacies

On St. Thomas, Havensight Pharmacy (☎ 340-776-1235) in the Havensight Mall is open daily from 9 a.m. to 6 p.m. Kmart (☎ 340-777-3854) operates a pharmacy inside the Tutu Park Mall; it's open from 8 a.m. to 8 p.m.

On St. Croix, most drugstores are open daily from 8 a.m. to 8 p.m. Off-season hours may vary; call ahead to confirm times. Kmart (☎ 340-692-2622) operates a pharmacy at its Sunshine Mall store.

On St. John, the St. John Drug Center (☎ 340-776-6353) is in the Boulon shopping center, up Centerline Road in Cruz Bay. It's open Monday through Saturday from 9 a.m. to 5 p.m.

Police

Dial ☎ 911.

Post Office

Hours may vary slightly from branch to branch and island to island, but on week-days the post offices generally open between 7:30 and 8 a.m. and close between 4 and 5:30 p.m.; on Saturday, they generally open between 7:30 and 8 a.m. and close between noon and 2:30 p.m.

The main U.S. Post Office on St. Thomas is near the hospital, with branches in Charlotte Amalie, Frenchtown, Havensight, and Tutu Mall. You'll find a post office at Christiansted, Frederiksted, Gallows Bay, and Sunny Isle on St. Croix, and one at Cruz Bay on St. John.

Restrooms

The law requires bars, hotels, and restaurants in the USVIs to admit nonpatrons into their restrooms. As such, there's usually a stream of traffic from the sidewalk into the public facilities of the casinos, bars, and hotels within the crowded commercial neighborhoods of Charlotte Amalie. Many establishments have positioned their rest-rooms conveniently close to the main entrances. In addition, most public shopping malls, including the Havensight Mall, adja-cent to the cruise-ship terminals of Charlotte Amalie, maintain restrooms. Most public beaches have rows of portable toilets that the local Parks Department maintains.

Safety

St. Thomas, especially around its capital, Charlotte Amalie, has the highest crime rate in the U.S. Virgin Islands. You may want to avoid it at night. St. Croix has less crime than St. Thomas but caution is advised, especially if you plan night visits to the dives of Frederiksted or Christiansted, where muggings may occur. St. John is relatively safe, even at night.

Smoking

Smoking policies are left to the discretion of the individual establishments, and most restaurants have designated nonsmoking sections within their restaurants and bars. With so many open-air establishments, the natural ventilation of the trade winds helps resolve conflicts. If you have a strong pref-erence, ask a staff member.

Taxes

The U.S. Virgin Islands have no departure tax and no sales tax. Hotels add on an 8 percent tax (always ask if the original price you're quoted includes tax).

Taxis

For 24-hour radio dispatch taxi service, call ☎ 340-774-7457 on St. Thomas, ☎ 340-778-1088 on St. Croix, and ☎ 340-693-7530 on St. John. If you want to hire a taxi and a driver (who just may be an ideal tour guide) for a day, expect to pay about $20 per person for two hours of sightseeing in a shared car, or $50 for two people.

Weather Updates

You can hear radio weather reports at 8:30 a.m. and 7:30 p.m. on 99.5 FM, or check it online at www.weather.com.

Part IV
The Part of Tens

The 5th Wave   By Rich Tennant

"You and your big idea to vacation at one of the lesser known Caribbean islands! Whoever heard of St. Bronx anyway?"

In this part . . .

*W*e appeal to the shopper in you by listing our ten favorite souvenirs to bring home from the Caribbean. We also reveal the ten (or so) dishes that we crave the most whenever we're away from the islands for too long. The short chapters in this part will whet your appetite (and your wallet) and get you ready to hop on the next Caribbean-bound plane.

Chapter 18

Ten Favorite Caribbean Souvenirs

. . . .

In This Chapter

▶ Taking home unique stuff

▶ Finding the best products and deals

. . . .

*W*hen it comes to souvenirs, we'll never understand why so many visitors' good taste evaporates as quickly as their cares in the Caribbean. How else can we explain the voluminous number of items with the name of the island emblazoned, stitched, or painted on virtually every hunk of cloth, wood, or plastic you can imagine? And another thing: Why must people buy only duty-free items made elsewhere in the world when they're in the Caribbean? These folks are so busy snapping up Irish linens and French perfume that they ignore some of the nifty island items. In the pages that follow, we highlight some of those unique island offerings.

If you're shopping for locally produced art and crafts, know that you're almost guaranteed a better buy in the markets than in the gift shops or from authorized vendors at resorts and airports. But remember: In the market, you're expected to haggle; in shops with marked prices, you're generally not. In the markets, expect to pick up items for about 30 percent less than the first offer you hear or see. Bring lots of small bills.

Aloe Products

The aloe plant grows extensively on Aruba, and you can find soothing skin-care products and soaps manufactured from this natural plant. Aloe is also the key ingredient in several soothing sunburn remedies.

Coffee Beans

You can learn a lot about coffee production by visiting a Blue Mountain coffee plantation. One important tip: If you can smell the coffee through the bag, it's losing freshness. We discovered that much like wine producers, different coffee plantations produce different-tasting beans. Blue

Mountain coffee is expensive, unless you're in Jamaica. The coffee is one of the few items sold at the airport at about the same price you can get it for on the island.

Puerto Rico's plantations produce a strong, aromatic coffee that they used to import from the Dominican Republic. Look for the brand names Café Crema, Café Rico, Rioja, and Yaucono.

Gouda Cheese and Dutch Chocolates

The direct connection to the Netherlands that Aruba enjoys makes its buys on Gouda cheeses and luscious Dutch chocolates too good to pass up. Enjoy the duty-free prospects.

Island Art

Serious art collectors head to Puerto Rico and Jamaica for fine selections. Old San Juan, Puerto Rico, is ground zero for a vibrant art scene, which highlights internationally known sculptors and painters. In Old San Juan, **Galeria Botello,** 314 F.D. Roosevelt Ave. (☎ **787-754-7430**), features the beautiful but terribly pricey works of Angel Botello Barros. At **Round Hill Hotel & Villas,** Route A1, Montego Bay, Jamaica (☎ **876-956-7050**), you'll find a small but excellent gallery that features both Jamaican and Haitian artists.

Pottery

The quintessential Barbados handicrafts are black-coral jewelry and clay pottery. The latter originates at **Highland Pottery, Inc.** (☎ **246-422-9818**), which is worth a visit. Potters turn out different products, some based on designs that are centuries old. The potteries (which are signposted) are on the East Coast, in St. Joseph Parish near Barclay's Park. In shops across the island, you'll also find a selection of locally made vases, pots, pottery mugs, glazed plates, and ornaments.

In Negril, Jamaica, some craftspeople from the Rastafarian communes in the hinterlands come into the center of town, hawking their well-made and rather handsome clay pots — definitely worth a look.

Rum

Several islands produce their own rums, including Barbados, St. Croix, Jamaica, and Puerto Rico; of course, each island claims that it has the best rum. If you visit a distillery, you'll often find a rum-tasting counter in the gift shop, much like a wine tasting if you were visiting a vineyard. You can sample a few and make your own selection.

Santos

Art historians view the carving of *santos* (religious figures) as Puerto Rico's greatest contribution to the *plastic arts* (3-D artworks, such as sculpture or ceramics). Producing these figures on the island since the 1500s, craftspeople often used handmade tools to carve the *santos* from clay, gold, stone, or cedar wood. You can identify the saints that *santos* represent by their accompanying symbols; for example, Saint Anthony is usually depicted with the infant Jesus and a book.

Art experts claim that *santos*-making approached its zenith at the turn of the 20th century, although hundreds of *santeros* still practice their craft throughout the island. Serious collectors view the former craftsmen of old as the true artists in the field. The best collection of *santos* resides at **Puerto Rican Arts & Crafts,** Calle Fortaleza 204, Old San Juan (☎ 787-725-5596).

Spices

You can't bring home the fresh fruits or vegetables from your vacation, but you can liven up your meals with fresh spices from the islands. At the open-air market in Road Town on Tortola (BVIs), ladies sell tidy little baskets packed with carefully labeled spices. Just walking through the place is a heady experience.

Straw Hats

Hats are inexpensive, and you can actually use them at home when you're gardening or lounging by the pool reflecting on your Caribbean adventure. You can find decent woven hats at most of the markets — you'll notice a variation of techniques from island to island. Or if you want to spend more and get a good-quality hat, spring for a spiffy Panama straw hat in Puerto Rico's Old San Juan.

Woodcarvings

We've seen highly skilled works, mostly by self-taught artists, in Jamaica and on St. Croix. In Jamaica, we prefer shopping in the craft markets in Negril, or if you're near Ocho Rios, about a hundred craftspeople live and work in **Fern Gully.** In the middle of St. Croix near Frederiksted, an open-air shop, **St. Croix Life and Environmental Arts Project (LEAP)** on Mahogany Road (☎ 340-772-0421), features furniture and decorative objects fashioned from naturally fallen island wood. Before you buy any woodcarving, though, inspect it carefully for problems with worms or bugs.

Chapter 19

Ten (Or So) Favorite Caribbean Dishes

In This Chapter

▶ Finding local taste treats
▶ Revisiting recipes back home

*F*ood can be a big expense in the Caribbean, especially if you stick with familiar dishes that you recognize from home (because much of what you eat has to be imported). To us, one of the great pleasures of traveling is experimenting by trying locally produced foodstuff. One great advantage of sampling local cuisine is that it's almost always the cheapest choice. Another is that your sense of adventure will be rewarded by delicious food and drink.

Although you aren't allowed to bring fresh fruit and vegetables from the islands through Customs, you can bring spices and alcoholic beverages used in many recipes. Islanders are warm and generous people, so if you love a particular recipe, the chef generally will be quite flattered and glad to pass on the secrets if you ask.

 If you fall in love with a particular type of cooking, pick up a recipe book while you're on the island. Of the Caribbean cookbooks we surveyed, we especially like *Caribbean Cookbook,* edited by Rita Springer (published by Ian Randle Publishers), and *Culinaria: The Caribbean,* edited by Rosemary Parkinson (published by Konemann).

Ackee and Salt Fish (Jamaica)

The first time you see ackee and salt fish, the national dish of Jamaica and a Jamaican favorite for breakfast, you may mistake it for scrambled eggs. Ackee is actually a fruit, but Jamaicans tend to use it like a vegetable. When prepared, it resembles scrambled eggs and tastes a lot like them, too, with a hint of nuttiness. It's not commonly shipped to other parts of the world, because the fruit must be eaten when it turns ripe. If you eat ackee at the wrong time, its seeds are poisonous.

Salt fish is cod cured in salt and it gives the dish just the right flavor. Air Jamaica occasionally serves ackee and salt fish on its flights. The best salt fish and ackee that we've sampled was prepared by a Jamaican chef at **Jake's** (see Chapter 13). You'll sometimes see this dish on the morning buffet at all-inclusive resorts, but you may need to request it a day ahead. Restaurants on Grand Cayman also serve it fairly regularly.

Callaloo and Fungi (U.S. Virgin Islands)

In the South, we'd call this down-home cooking "greens and grits," but the names are certainly more fun in the U.S. Virgin Islands (see Chapter 17). Callaloo will remind you of spinach, but island cooks add crabs and hot pepper sauce to spice up the popular dish. Fungi (far from mushrooms) is a cornmeal concoction that falls somewhere in between the consistency of cornbread and grits. It's one of those things you just have to try — you'll either love it or hate it.

Caribbean Lobster (Anegada, British Virgin Islands)

The small coral atoll of Anegada is known for the spiny Caribbean lobsters caught in its waters. You'll find lobster on every menu of every restaurant on the island. Our favorite place to sup on lobster on Anegada is the **Cow Wreck Beach Bar and Grill** (see Chapter 11). If you want to try a Caribbean cholesterol jamboree diet with lobster and butter at every meal, the British Virgin Islands are the place to do it.

Conch Fritters (Grand Cayman)

Pronounced *conk,* this edible mollusk resides in a beautiful shell with a pink interior that lines the yards of many houses on Grand Cayman. Chefs either pound out the meat to tenderize it, or they often serve it chopped up, made into tasty fritters. Conch has become so popular that it suffers from overcollection. Therefore, on some islands, conch fritters and chowder, along with marinated and stewed conch, are no longer as common.

Flying Fish (Barbados)

These small, silvery fish, which look like they have wings when they leap out of the sea, are the national fish of Barbados and the main ingredient in several Bajan specialties. For a change of pace, try flying fish for breakfast.

Grouper Sandwich (Anywhere in the Caribbean)

You'll see grouper listed on almost every Caribbean menu that carries a catch-of-the-day selection. Grouper inhabit shallow-to-midrange reefs. The meat is a white, sweet, mild-tasting fish. Fried in a proper batter, this fish is the main ingredient of many a lunch sandwich in the Caribbean.

Jerk Chicken (Jamaica)

Spicy jerk chicken is, perhaps, the most widely known Caribbean dish. It originated in Jamaica and is a method of barbecuing by using well-seasoned meat. It originated with the Maroons, escaped slaves who lived in the mountains. They would roast pork seasoned with scotch bonnet pepper, pimento seeds, thyme, and nutmeg over sizzling hot coals covered with the branches of pimento or allspice wood. Although pork was the meat the originators used, chicken has become more popular.

Besides jerk pork, grill men operating pits around Jamaica have added chicken, sausage, and fish to their repertoire. Port Antonio's Boston Beach is best known, but we'd skip it. Only a few pits remain open, and the quality has suffered for lack of competition. Instead, get a good taste at the **Pork Pit** in Montego Bay, the **Ocho Rios Village Jerk Centre,** or the stalls by the beach in **Negril** (see Chapter 13).

Keshi Yena (Aruba)

The Dutch treat of Keshi Yena tastes better than it sounds. You take a wheel of Gouda cheese, pack the hollowed-out center with a spicy meat mixture of either chicken or beef, and then bake the whole concoction. This dish is especially popular at Christmastime. You can find it at restaurants that serve traditional Aruban fare, including **Brisas del Mar** (see Chapter 9).

Rice and Beans/Peas (Puerto Rico and Jamaica)

The Spanish influence on Puerto Rico is evident in the simple local fare. You can get a steamy plate of rice with either black or red beans for a few dollars. We like to order it with a side of sweet plantains, which are a cousin to the banana, but you can't eat them raw. (Try plantains baked or fried with a little brown sugar.)

In Jamaica, you'll often find a variation of this cheap but good dish. There, chefs cook rice and peas (red kidney beans) with coconut milk, a ham bone or bacon, and spices. Rice and peas come as a side dish to almost every traditional Jamaican meal.

Appendix

Quick Concierge

Toll-Free Numbers and Web Sites

Airlines

Air Canada
☎ 888-247-2262
www.aircanada.ca

Air Jamaica
☎ 800-523-5585 in U.S.
☎ 888-359-2475 in Jamaica
www.airjamaica.com

Air St. Thomas
www.airstthomas.com

Air Sunshine
☎ 800-327-8900
www.airsunshine.com

American Airlines
☎ 800-433-7300
www.aa.com

American Eagle
☎ 800-433-7300 in U.S.
www.aa.com

British Airways
☎ 800-247-9297
☎ 0870-850-9850 in Britain
www.british-airways.com

BWIA
☎ 800-538-2492
www.bwee.com

Cape Air
☎ 800-352-0714
www.flycapeair.com

Cayman Airways
☎ 800-GCAYMAN
www.caymanairways.com

Continental Airlines
☎ 800-525-0280
www.continental.com

Copa
☎ 800-344-3333
www.copaair.com

Delta Air Lines
☎ 800-221-1212
www.delta.com

Dutch Caribbean Airlines
☎ 800-327-7230
www.flydca.net

Iberia
☎ 800-772-4642 in U.S.
www.iberia.com

JetBlue Airways
☎ 800-538-2583
www.jetblue.com

LIAT
☎ 800-744-5428 in U.S.
www.liatairline.com

Northwest Airlines
☎ 800-225-2525
www.nwa.com

Seaborne Airlines
☎ 888-359-8687
www.seaborneairlines.com

Spirit Airlines
☎ 800-772-7117
www.spiritair.com

United
☎ 800-241-6522
www.united.com

US Airways
☎ 800-428-4322
www.usairways.com

Major hotel and motel chains

Allegro by Occidental
☎ 800-858-2258
www.occidental-hoteles.com

Best Western International
☎ 800-780-7234
www.bestwestern.com

Couples
☎ 800-268-7537
www.couples.com

Divi Resorts
☎ 800-367-3484
www.diviresorts.com

Hedonism
☎ 877-467-8737
www.superclubs.com

Hilton
☎ 800-445-8667
www.hilton.com

Holiday Inn
☎ 800-424-4343
www.holiday-inn.com

Hyatt
☎ 888-591-1234
www.hyatt.com

Le Meridien
☎ 866-559-3821
www.lemeridien.com

Marriott
☎ 888-236-2427
www.marriott.com

Mercure
☎ 800-221-4542
www.mercure.com

Radisson Hotels & Resorts
☎ 888-201-1718
www.radisson.com

Renaissance Hotels & Resorts
☎ 800-228-9290
www.renaissancehotels.com

Ritz-Carlton
☎ 800-241-3333
www.ritzcarlton.com

Sandals
☎ 888-726-3257
www.sandals.com

Splash Resorts
☎ 877-92-SPLASH
www.splashresorts.com

Westin Hotels & Resorts
☎ 800-937-8461
www.westin.com

Wyndham Hotels & Resorts
☎ 877-999-3223
www.wyndham.com

Major car-rental agencies

Avis
☎ 800-331-1212
www.avis.com

Budget
☎ 800-527-0700
www.budget.com

Dollar
☎ 800-800-3665
www.dollar.com

Hertz
☎ 800-645-3131
www.hertz.com

National
☎ 800-227-7638
www.nationalcar.com

Thrifty
☎ 800-847-4389
www.thrifty.com

Where to Get More Information

Aruba

In the United States: Aruba Tourism Authority, 1000 Harbor Blvd., Weehawken, NJ 07087 (☎ 800-TO-ARUBA, or 800-862-7822).

On Aruba: Call ☎ 297-582-3777 or visit www.aruba.com.

Barbados

In the United States: Barbados Tourism Authority, 800 Second Ave., 2nd Floor, New York, NY 10017 (☎ 888-BARBADOS, 800-221-9831, 212-986-6516; www.barbados.org).

In Barbados: Barbados Tourism Authority, Harbour Road, Bridgetown (☎ 246-427-2623; Fax: 246-426-4080; www.barbados.org). Hours are 8:30 a.m. to 4:30 p.m. Monday to Saturday. The Barbados Hotel and Tourism Association (☎ 246-426-5041; www.bhta.org) is also helpful.

British Virgin Islands

In the United States: Call ☎ 800-835-8530.

On Tortola: The British Virgin Islands Tourist Board office is above the FedEx office on the AKARA building's second floor, Wickham's Cay, Road Town (☎ 284-494-3134; www.bviwelcome.com).

Grand Cayman

On Grand Cayman: The main office of the Department of Tourism is in the Pavilion, Cricket Square and Elgin Avenue, P.O. Box 67 (☎ 345-949-0623; Fax: 345-949-4053; www.caymanislands.ky). You can find information booths at the airport (☎ 345-949-2635).

You can contact the Tourist Information and Activities Service (☎ 345-949-6598) day or night for complete tourist information and free assistance in booking island transportation, tours, charters, cruises, and other activities.

Jamaica

In the United States: Jamaican Tourist Board, 5201 Blue Lagoon Drive, Suite 607, Miami, FL 33126 (☎ 800-233-4582, 305-665-0557; Fax: 305-666-7239; www.visitjamaica.com).

In Jamaica: You'll find the Jamaican Tourist Board offices at the international airports and at 2 St. Lucia Ave., Kingston (☎ 876-929-9200); Cornwall Beach, St. James, Montego Bay (☎ 876-952-4425); in the Ocean Village Shopping Centre, Ocho Rios, St. Ann (☎ 876-974-2582); in City Centre Plaza, Port Antonio (☎ 876-993-3051).

Puerto Rico

In the United States: The Puerto Rico Tourism Company has branches located at 666 Fifth Ave., New York, NY 10013 (☎ 800-223-6530, 212-586-6262); 3575 W. Cahuenga Blvd., Suite 620, Los Angeles, CA 90068 (☎ 800-874-1230, 323-874-5991); and 901 Ponce de León Blvd., Suite 101, Coral Gables, FL 33134 (☎ 800-815-7391, 305-445-9112).

On Puerto Rico: Puerto Rico Tourism Company, P.O. Box 902-3960, La Princesa Bldg. #2, Paseo La Princesa, San Juan, PR 00902-3960 (☎ 787-721-2400; www.gotopuertorico.com).

St. Lucia

In St. Lucia: The main visitor information center is at the Sureline Building, Vive Boutielle, Castries (☎ 758-452-4094). St. Lucia information is on the Web at www.stlucia.org.

Sint Maarten/St. Martin

On Sint Maarten/St. Martin: On the Dutch side, the Tourist Information Bureau is at Vineyard Park, 33 W.G. Buncamper Rd., in Philipsburg (☎ 599-54-22337), open Monday to Friday from 8 a.m. to noon and 1 to 5 p.m. On the French side, check with the Office du Tourisme, Route de Sandy Ground in Marigot (☎ 590-590-87-57-21), open Monday to Friday 8:30 a.m. to 1 p.m. and 2:30 to 5:30 p.m., Saturday 8 a.m. to noon.

U.S. Virgin Islands

In the United States: USVI Division of Tourism, 1270 Avenue of the Americas, Suite 2108, New York, NY 10020 (☎ 800-372-8784; www.usvi.net).

On St. Thomas: You'll find a visitor center in downtown Charlotte Amalie and a cruise-ship welcome center at Havensight Mall. Call ☎ 800-372-8784 or 340-774-8784 for information. The National Park Service operates a visitor center across the harbor from the Red Hook ferry dock.

On St. Croix: The USVI Division of Tourism has offices at 53A Company St., Christiansted (☎ 340-773-0495) and on the pier at Strand Street, Frederiksted (☎ 340-772-0357).

On St. John: The USVI Division of Tourism (☎ 340-776-6450) has a branch in the compound between Sparky's and the U.S. Post Office in Cruz Bay. The National Park Service (☎ 340-776-6201) also has a visitor center at the Creek in Cruz Bay.

Index

• H •

• T •

Accommodations Index

SINESS, CAREERS & PERSONAL FINANCE

Also available:

- ✔Accounting For Dummies †
  0-7645-5314-3
- ✔Business Plans Kit For Dummies †
  0-7645-5365-8
- ✔Cover Letters For Dummies
  0-7645-5224-4
- ✔Frugal Living For Dummies
  0-7645-5403-4
- ✔Leadership For Dummies
  0-7645-5176-0
- ✔Managing For Dummies
  0-7645-1771-6

- ✔Marketing For Dummies
  0-7645-5600-2
- ✔Personal Finance For Dummies *
  0-7645-2590-5
- ✔Project Management
  For Dummies
  0-7645-5283-X
- ✔Resumes For Dummies †
  0-7645-5471-9
- ✔Selling For Dummies
  0-7645-5363-1
- ✔Small Business Kit For Dummies *†
  0-7645-5093-4

-7645-5307-0   0-7645-5331-3 *†

)ME & BUSINESS COMPUTER BASICS

Also available:

- ✔ACT! 6 For Dummies
  0-7645-2645-6
- ✔iLife '04 All-in-One Desk Reference
  For Dummies
  0-7645-7347-0
- ✔iPAQ For Dummies
  0-7645-6769-1
- ✔Mac OS X Panther Timesaving
  Techniques For Dummies
  0-7645-5812-9
- ✔Macs For Dummies
  0-7645-5656-8
- ✔Microsoft Money 2004 For Dummies
  0-7645-4195-1

- ✔Office 2003 All-in-One Desk
  Reference For Dummies
  0-7645-3883-7
- ✔Outlook 2003 For Dummies
  0-7645-3759-8
- ✔PCs For Dummies
  0-7645-4074-2
- ✔TiVo For Dummies
  0-7645-6923-6
- ✔Upgrading and Fixing PCs
  For Dummies
  0-7645-1665-5
- ✔Windows XP Timesaving
  Techniques For Dummies
  0-7645-3748-2

-7645-4074-2   0-7645-3758-X

)OD, HOME, GARDEN, HOBBIES, MUSIC & PETS

Also available:

- ✔Bass Guitar For Dummies
  0-7645-2487-9
- ✔Diabetes Cookbook For Dummies
  0-7645-5230-9
- ✔Gardening For Dummies *
  0-7645-5130-2
- ✔Guitar For Dummies
  0-7645-5106-X
- ✔Holiday Decorating For Dummies
  0-7645-2570-0
- ✔Home Improvement All-in-One
  For Dummies
  0-7645-5680-0

- ✔Knitting For Dummies
  0-7645-5395-X
- ✔Piano For Dummies
  0-7645-5105-1
- ✔Puppies For Dummies
  0-7645-5255-4
- ✔Scrapbooking For Dummies
  0-7645-7208-3
- ✔Senior Dogs For Dummies
  0-7645-5818-8
- ✔Singing For Dummies
  0-7645-2475-5
- ✔30-Minute Meals For Dummies
  0-7645-2589-1

-7645-5295-3   0-7645-5232-5

TERNET & DIGITAL MEDIA

Also available:

- ✔2005 Online Shopping Directory
  For Dummies
  0-7645-7495-7
- ✔CD & DVD Recording For Dummies
  0-7645-5956-7
- ✔eBay For Dummies
  0-7645-5654-1
- ✔Fighting Spam For Dummies
  0-7645-5965-6
- ✔Genealogy Online For Dummies
  0-7645-5964-8
- ✔Google For Dummies
  0-7645-4420-9

- ✔Home Recording For Musicians
  For Dummies
  0-7645-1634-5
- ✔The Internet For Dummies
  0-7645-4173-0
- ✔iPod & iTunes For Dummies
  0-7645-7772-7
- ✔Preventing Identity Theft
  For Dummies
  0-7645-7336-5
- ✔Pro Tools All-in-One Desk
  Reference For Dummies
  0-7645-5714-9
- ✔Roxio Easy Media Creator
  For Dummies
  0-7645-7131-1

-7645-1664-7   0-7645-6924-4

SPORTS, FITNESS, PARENTING, RELIGION & SPIRITUALITY

0-7645-5146-9   0-7645-5418-2

Also available:

✔Adoption For Dummies
0-7645-5488-3

✔Basketball For Dummies
0-7645-5248-1

✔The Bible For Dummies
0-7645-5296-1

✔Buddhism For Dummies
0-7645-5359-3

✔Catholicism For Dummies
0-7645-5391-7

✔Hockey For Dummies
0-7645-5228-7

✔Judaism For Dummies
0-7645-5299-6

✔Martial Arts For Dummies
0-7645-5358-5

✔Pilates For Dummies
0-7645-5397-6

✔Religion For Dummies
0-7645-5264-3

✔Teaching Kids to Read
For Dummies
0-7645-4043-2

✔Weight Training For Dummies
0-7645-5168-X

✔Yoga For Dummies
0-7645-5117-5

TRAVEL

0-7645-5438-7   0-7645-5453-0

Also available:

✔Alaska For Dummies
0-7645-1761-9

✔Arizona For Dummies
0-7645-6938-4

✔Cancún and the Yucatán
For Dummies
0-7645-2437-2

✔Cruise Vacations For Dummies
0-7645-6941-4

✔Europe For Dummies
0-7645-5456-5

✔Ireland For Dummies
0-7645-5455-7

✔Las Vegas For Dummies
0-7645-5448-4

✔London For Dummies
0-7645-4277-X

✔New York City For Dummies
0-7645-6945-7

✔Paris For Dummies
0-7645-5494-8

✔RV Vacations For Dummies
0-7645-5443-3

✔Walt Disney World & Orlando
For Dummies
0-7645-6943-0

GRAPHICS, DESIGN & WEB DEVELOPMENT

0-7645-4345-8   0-7645-5589-8

Also available:

✔Adobe Acrobat 6 PDF
For Dummies
0-7645-3760-1

✔Building a Web Site For Dummies
0-7645-7144-3

✔Dreamweaver MX 2004
For Dummies
0-7645-4342-3

✔FrontPage 2003 For Dummies
0-7645-3882-9

✔HTML 4 For Dummies
0-7645-1995-6

✔Illustrator CS For Dummies
0-7645-4084-X

✔Macromedia Flash MX 2004
For Dummies
0-7645-4358-X

✔Photoshop 7 All-in-One Desk
Reference For Dummies
0-7645-1667-1

✔Photoshop CS Timesaving
Techniques For Dummies
0-7645-6782-9

✔PHP 5 For Dummies
0-7645-4166-8

✔PowerPoint 2003 For Dummies
0-7645-3908-6

✔QuarkXPress 6 For Dummies
0-7645-2593-X

NETWORKING, SECURITY, PROGRAMMING & DATABASES

0-7645-6852-3   0-7645-5784-X

Also available:

✔A+ Certification For Dummies
0-7645-4187-0

✔Access 2003 All-in-One Desk
Reference For Dummies
0-7645-3988-4

✔Beginning Programming
For Dummies
0-7645-4997-9

✔C For Dummies
0-7645-7068-4

✔Firewalls For Dummies
0-7645-4048-3

✔Home Networking For Dummies
0-7645-42796

✔Network Security For Dummies
0-7645-1679-5

✔Networking For Dummies
0-7645-1677-9

✔TCP/IP For Dummies
0-7645-1760-0

✔VBA For Dummies
0-7645-3989-2

✔Wireless All In-One Desk Refere
For Dummies
0-7645-7496-5

✔Wireless Home Networking
For Dummies
0-7645-3910-8